CW00920598

EXPLORING PARLIAMENT

If anybody wants to explore Parliament, this is where I would recommend that they start: why not trust the experts? The line-up of over 50 contributors, an eclectic mixture of academics, commentators, and practitioners, and the breadth of subjects they cover constitute an enduring legacy of the work over the last few years of those engaged in our Parliamentary Studies modules, now taught in 20 universities all over the UK. This collection of essays and illustrative examples of real life in Parliament will give every student of Parliament a chance to see behind the clichés and engage in further exploration.

David Natzler, Clerk of the House of Commons

I am delighted to have the opportunity to welcome the publication of *Exploring Parliament*. The Parliamentary Studies module programme has been hugely successful in enabling students in an increasing number of universities to learn about Parliament from insiders. This book will make it possible for others to benefit from the work which has gone into that programme.

Collaboration between academics and parliamentary officials in writing about Parliament was pioneered as long ago as the 1960s by the Study of Parliament Group, of which both Cristina Leston-Bandeira and Louise Thompson are members, and of which I myself have been a member since 1978. Long ago, under the auspices of the Group, I co-edited *The House of Lords at Work: A Study based on the 1988–1989 Session*, also published by Oxford University Press, and co-authored by academics and officials. Much water has flowed under the bridge since then, and this new up-to-date study of both Houses will be essential reading for students wanting to learn about the United Kingdom Parliament as it is now.

As I write, I am about to retire as Clerk of the Parliaments. Over 42 years working in the House of Lords I have seen many changes, including—encouragingly for someone whose career has been spent in supporting the work of the House—a move away from debate on whether the House had any future to debate focusing on its reform, and nowadays mostly in relation to its composition rather than its functions. Apart from the removal of most of the hereditary peers in 1999, most recent changes have been incremental—for example, the introduction in 2014 of provision for members to retire—and the difficulty of achieving any sort of consensus in relation to reform leads me to think that, as far as the House of Lords is concerned, *Exploring Parliament* will have a long shelf life.

David Beamish, Clerk of the Parliaments

Exploring Parliament

EDITED BY

CRISTINA LESTON-BANDEIRA
AND LOUISE THOMPSON

UNIVERSITY PRESS

Great Clarendon Street, Oxford, OX2 6DP,
United Kingdom

Oxford University Press is a department of the University of Oxford.
It furthers the University's objective of excellence in research, scholarship,
and education by publishing worldwide. Oxford is a registered trade mark of
Oxford University Press in the UK and in certain other countries

© Oxford University Press 2018

The moral rights of the authors have been asserted

Impression: 3

All rights reserved. No part of this publication may be reproduced, stored in
a retrieval system, or transmitted, in any form or by any means, without the
prior permission in writing of Oxford University Press, or as expressly permitted
by law, by licence or under terms agreed with the appropriate reprographics
rights organization. Enquiries concerning reproduction outside the scope of the
above should be sent to the Rights Department, Oxford University Press, at the
address above

You must not circulate this work in any other form
and you must impose this same condition on any acquirer

Published in the United States of America by Oxford University Press
198 Madison Avenue, New York, NY 10016, United States of America

British Library Cataloguing in Publication Data
Data available

Library of Congress control number: 2017949322

ISBN 978-0-19-878843-0

Printed and bound in the UK
by CPI Group (UK) Ltd, Croydon, CR0 4YY

Links to third party websites are provided by Oxford in good faith and
for information only. Oxford disclaims any responsibility for the materials
contained in any third party website referenced in this work.

To past, present, and future students of Parliament

Foreword

Exploring Parliament is an invaluable companion, not just to those students undertaking the Parliamentary Studies module, but to all of those interested in understanding how our democratic institutions work.

As a passionate advocate for the Parliamentary Studies module right from its inception, I am delighted that so many eminent academics and House officials involved in its delivery have contributed to this work. Quite often, the understanding of what goes on in the Commons Chamber is viewed through the prism of the personalities of its participants, with little thought given to the processes, history, conventions, and rules that shape the debate and, ultimately, the legislation that arises as a result. The Module, and this book, seek to shed light on these neglected aspects of the work of Parliament; an endeavour that is important in its own right of course, but it is also valuable for our legislature and politicians. A public educated in, and engaged with, its democracy can better scrutinize its decisions, and better scrutiny produces better laws.

I frequently speak to students on the Parliamentary Studies module in my regular Outreach visits, and have always been struck by their enthusiasm and ability to ask probing and well thought-through questions. As a result, answering some of them is not always a comfortable experience, but it is absolutely necessary that they are asked. If Parliament is to continue to reform itself in order to more accurately represent the people that we serve, it is crucial that everyone has access to the tools and the knowledge required to press for those changes.

This book is an important contribution to the process of education, understanding, and reform.

Rt Hon John Bercow MP
Speaker of the House of Commons
July 2017

Preface

Cristina Leston-Bandeira and Louise Thompson

As academics who teach Parliament to undergraduate students, we are well acquainted with the institution and those who work there. Given that we spend most of our spare time researching that same institution, we are at times perhaps a little too familiar with it. We know that Parliament is central to our representative democracy, that its members and staff work long hours to keep it going, and that it can make a real difference to people's lives. We are fascinated by the daily comings and goings of MPs and ministers, by the quirks of procedure which can stall a bill or stop a government minister in their tracks. But we also know that we are by no means representative, and that to many these same procedures and activities may seem obscure at best; that what we—'Parliament nerds'—often take for granted needs to be unpicked and explained so that Parliament's central role in our representative democracy can be understood. This is the reason why we have put our collective energies into this textbook.

Indeed, as we write this preface, Stella Creasy MP has moved an amendment to the 2017 Queen's Speech prompting the government to make a significant concession so that all Northern Irish women will be able to access medical services (including abortions) in England without charge. Her success demonstrates quite succinctly many of the themes which run through this book, such as the role of formal and informal processes and pressure, as well as the importance of Parliament and individual MPs.

We first discussed the idea of putting together a textbook on Parliament in early 2014. For this we must credit Philip Cowley, who first suggested that we bring together a large group of experts to write short pieces on aspects of the institution which would help to bring it to life. The presence of a Parliamentary Studies module (a collaboration between the UK Parliament and universities), now taught at 20 universities, made this initial idea even more compelling. The module has demonstrated how successful partnerships between academics and parliamentary practitioners can be. It seemed that by bringing these two groups even closer together, to collaborate on a book for students and the general public, we could present an image of Parliament which only the combination of these two groups could achieve. Many of those who currently teach on the Parliamentary Studies module have therefore contributed to this book. But it goes further than that. As the then Co-Convenors of the Political Studies Association's Parliaments and Legislatures specialist group, we were able to bring in additional experts, contributing chapters on everything from parliamentary ritual to All-Party Parliamentary Groups.

Academia, just like parliamentary institutions, can be quite traditional and hierarchical. Wherever possible, we have tried to be inclusive in our approach and to cross traditional boundaries in terms of the authorship of our chapters. The textbook therefore includes contributions from PhD students through to professors, and junior as well as more senior parliamentary officials from both the House of Commons and the House of Lords. Many have been co-authored by an academic and an official and, as such, the book has also instigated new working relationships (and friendships) between members of these two, often very separate, communities. Coordinating this group of nearly 60 authors has been a challenge, and we hope that, despite our many emails and detailed editing notes, we too have forged some new friendships along the way.

In the time it has taken to produce this book, Parliament has seen enormous change; proof as ever that the institution does not stand still. It has accompanied us through two general elections, two prime ministers, and two referendums. We first put together our list of contributors at a time of coalition government. These contributors wrote their chapters and case studies during a period of majority government. And they delivered their final versions to us in the very beginnings of a minority government. Inevitably, with British politics and Parliament in a state of flux at the time of writing (July 2017), there are likely to be changes to the institution which we have not been able to record. This should not affect the contents of our chapters, as the book goes beyond current politics, capturing general trends alongside contemporary developments in the institution.

We thank all authors for their hard work and patience with our requests, and practitioners in particular for bearing with us and our seemingly pointless suggestions. We hope the published versions show there was some logic to it after all. In particular, we are very grateful to Paul Evans, Clerk of Committees, for his support and belief in this project, which was key to ensuring the book was owned by practitioners as much as academics. We are also very thankful to Martyn Atkins, Clerk of the Procedure Committee, for adding much precision to our Glossary. Philip Cowley provided sound advice and gave us a hint of the many challenges which lay ahead! Thanks also to Matthew Flinders for facilitating the initial contacts with Oxford University Press. We reserve a very special thank you for David Judge, who proved incredibly helpful with different parts of the book and was a continuing source of support (and the very model of efficiency!) throughout.

As is often the case, the publication of this book required the effort of many people who you will not find listed on our contents page. First of all we would like to thank Naomi Saint, the ever brilliant Manager of the Universities Programme in Parliament. Be it her enthusiasm, efficiency, or simply subtle but very wise advice, the fact that the book exists is in part thanks to her unwavering support. Sarah Iles and Emily Spicer, from Oxford University Press, were very accommodating of our many ideas throughout this process. We thank them for their patience in responding to our queries. Many others assisted and advised the individual authors of each chapter and we wish to record here our thanks to them all, on the authors' behalf.

Those who know us will know how important our little families are to us and we cannot end without giving them an extra special mention here. They put up with a lot, especially as we tried to meet the final deadline. For that we are really grateful. We will enjoy celebrating with them properly once we see this book in print.

How to use this Book

Chapters in this book are very short and focus on specific topics. Collectively they aim to cover a wide range of topics, but they do not pretend to be exhaustive of each topic. As such, each chapter is accompanied by four key features which will help readers to explore each topic further: Further Reading; Case Study; Primary Sources; Further Case Studies. The book is also complemented by a Glossary of Parliamentary Terms.

Further Reading

BRAND, J. (1992) *British Parliamentary Parties*, Oxfor

MINKIN, L. (2014) *The Blair Supremacy*, Mancheste chapter 13.

NORTON, P. (1979) 'The organisation of Parliament

Further Reading

As each chapter aims to introduce the key debates and trends on a very specific topic, the Further Reading feature aims to guide readers towards other sources of information where the chapter's topic can be explored in more depth.

Case Study 24: The government defeat c August 201

On 29 August 2013, following the recall of Parliament by 283 votes to 270 on the issue of whether Britain s Syria. The government lost by 13 votes. Although t

Case Study

The accompanying case studies aim to illustrate the topic covered in the main chapter. They focus on a very specific instance of a debate, a policy, or an activity, to illustrate in practice some of the points made in the main chapter.

For example, the Immigration Bill is used in Chapter 8 to illustrate how Parliament is able to influence legislation outcomes; and anonymized accounts of constituency casework are used in Chapter 25 to illustrate the type of issues MPs deal with on a regular basis.

Primary sources

- David Anderson QC (2015) *A Question of Trust: R* London: The Stationery Office. Online at: https://t gov.uk/wp-content/uploads/2015/06/IPR-Report-P
- Joint Committee on the Draft Investigatory Powers

Primary Sources

One of the key aims of this book is to encourage further research of Parliament and to initiate readers to the use of parliamentary primary sources. Interacting with the actual parliamentary record is a key component of learning about Parliament. It helps to develop a learner's understanding of the institution, as well as encouraging them to develop their own research skills. This is why each case study lists up to five relevant primary sources. These materials can be explored by learners in their own time. They could also be used to support revision or essay writing, or as the basis for a teaching activity.

For example, students may be encouraged to watch the video on the election of the Speaker, on 18 May 2015, listed as a primary source in Chapter 5, before discussing the role of rituals in class. Or indeed students could be encouraged to calculate the number of urgent questions submitted in 2015–16 by using the House of Commons Sessional Return listed in Chapter 17. Just as a seminar could be developed around the written record of a debate, such as the debate in January 2011 on anti-Semitism recommended in Chapter 11.

Further Case Studies

FURTHER CASE STUDIES

- 'After the duck house ... where MPs' expenses w https://www.theguardian.com/politics/2016/ma parliament-ltd
- 'MPs spend £250,000 of public money on vanity

This feature aims to give lecturers and students ideas for other interesting examples that could be investigated to explore the respective chapter's key ideas. This will help learners develop their understanding of the chapter's topic. Likewise, the Further Case Studies could be used also to support revision or essay writing, as a basis for a teaching activity, or indeed of an assignment.

For example, following one of Chapter 4's suggestions, students could role play in class the challenge of giving good, but impartial, advice when advising on amendments to legislation. And Chapter 21's instructions for further case studies could be used as the basis for an assignment through which students explore the differences in professional backgrounds in a specific cohort of MPs.

Glossary of Parliamentary Terms

SCRUTINY The detailed examination of government action, policy, proposals, and spending.

SECOND READING A debate on the general principles of a bill in which any MP or peer is eligible to speak. No amendments can be made at this stage. There is a vote at the end

Parliamentary language can often seem confusing or unclear. We have compiled a glossary of parliamentary terms, located at the end of the book, which gives short explanations of a wide range of terms—from 'division' to 'probing amendments', for instance. Please refer to the Glossary if unsure about a specific term. The Glossary also includes explanations for key bodies and roles such as the Appointments Commission or the Clerk of the Parliaments. Most chapters also recall some of these definitions, where most relevant, to ease understanding.

Further examples of teaching activities

More ideas for teaching activities can be found in the *Case Study Portfolio: Applying Parliamentary Resources in Teaching*. This portfolio lists ten different teaching activities, such as 'Hunt the Hansard' Treasure Trail, MP 'Speed Dating' Workshop, and a Select Committee Role Play. This is available online at: https://www.psa.ac.uk/sites/default/files/Case_Study_Portfolio_Applying_Parliamentary_Resources_in_Teaching.pdf

Online Resources

A collection of web links to a wealth of relevant videos, reports, records, and other primary sources enables you to extend your understanding of UK Parliament and discover further information online.

 www.oup.com/uk/leston-bandeira_thompson/

Acknowledgements

Oxford University Press and the editors would like to thank the academic reviewers who have given thorough and constructive feedback to help shape this book. Their assistance is greatly appreciated and their expertise invaluable. In alphabetical order, they are:

Dr Nicholas Allen, Royal Holloway

Dr Andrew Blick, King's College London

Prof. J. P. Bradbury, Swansea University

Prof. Paul Cairney, University of Stirling

Dr Philip Catney, Keele University

Dr Alan Convery, University of Edinburgh

Dr Andrew Crines, University of Liverpool

Dr Einion Daffyd, Cardiff University

Dr Sue Griffiths, Global Partners

Dr Martin Hansen, Brunel University London

Dr Maarja Luhiste, University of Newcastle

Dr Felicity Matthews, University of Sheffield

Dr Ben Seyd, University of Kent

Dr Mark Shanahan, University of Reading

Prof. Martin Smith, University of York

Prof. Dan Stevens, University of Exeter

Prof. Colin Talbot, University of Manchester and University of Cambridge

Prof. Colin Thain, University of Birmingham

Dr Richard Whitaker, University of Leicester

Contents

Part I Introducing *Exploring Parliament*

Part II The Organization of Parliament

Part III Law-making

Detailed Contents

Part VII Concluding Thoughts

List of Case Studies

The Contributors

Peter Allen is a Reader (Associate Professor) in Comparative Politics at the University of Bath. He works mainly on issues of political representation.

Margaret Arnott is Professor of Public Policy at the University of the West of Scotland. She has published widely on UK territorial politics and governance. In 2016 she was awarded a House of Commons Fellowship to research 'The future of Parliament and devolution'.

Martyn Atkins is Clerk of the House of Commons Procedure Committee. He has worked in the House of Commons for 20 years, previously as Clerk of the Political and Constitutional Reform Committee, a clerk in the Table Office, and as the Commons Clerk at the UK National Parliament Office in Brussels.

Stephen Bates is a Senior Lecturer in Political Science at the University of Birmingham. His research is concerned with parliamentary power, Prime Minister's Questions, and select committees.

Ed Beale is Clerk of the Communities and Local Government Committee in the House of Commons. He has worked in the House of Commons for 14 years, including in the Table Office and on several select committees. He has also been the UK National Parliament Representative in Brussels.

Mark Bennister is Reader in Politics at Canterbury Christ Church University. His main research expertise is on political leadership and prime ministerial power. He held a parliamentary academic fellowship (2016–18) researching the prime minister's appearances before the Liaison Committee.

Rosie Campbell is Professor of Politics at Birkbeck, University of London. Her research focuses on political behaviour, including representation and participation. She is the principal investigator of the Economic and Social Research Council-funded representative audit of Britain, a survey of all candidates who stood in the 2015 and 2017 general elections.

Thomas Caygill is a PhD student at Newcastle University researching post-legislative scrutiny in the UK Parliament. He has previously worked for the House of Commons Petitions Committee on a Political Studies Association/House of Commons Placement.

Sarah Childs is Professor of Politics and Gender at Birkbeck, University of London. She has published widely on gender and representation theory, and the feminization of UK politics. She is the author of *The Good Parliament* report (2016).

Philip Cowley is Professor of Politics at Queen Mary University of London, and has published widely on Parliament's composition and behaviour.

Emma Crewe is a Professorial Research Associate at the School of Oriental and African Studies, University of London. She researches parliaments, civil society, and the relationship between the two in the UK, Africa, and Asia.

Mark D'Arcy is the BBC's parliamentary correspondent.

Andrew Defty is Reader in Politics at the University of Lincoln. He has published widely on the policy influence of Parliament. His research has focused on parliamentary scrutiny of social policy and also on legislative oversight of the intelligence and security agencies.

Peter Dorey is Professor of British Politics at Cardiff University. He was co-author of *House of Lords Reform since 1911: Must the Lords Go?* (2011) with Alexandra Kelso, and has published several journal articles and book chapters on the contemporary House of Lords.

Paul Evans is the Clerk of Committees in the House of Commons, where he has worked since 1981, including as Clerk of the Journals. He has published extensively on parliamentary matters, including the *Handbook of House of Commons Procedure* (2012). He is an Associate of the Institute for Government, an Honorary Research Associate of UCL, a Fellow of the Academy of Social Sciences, and a Fellow of the Royal Society of Arts.

Matthew Flinders is Professor of Politics and Founding Director of the Sir Bernard Crick Centre for the Public Understanding of Politics. He was President of the Political Studies Association (2014–17) and is a board member of the Academy of Social Sciences. His research focuses on modes of depoliticization, governance and public policy, constitutional reform, and political disengagement.

Stacey Frier is Parliamentary Affairs Manager at Historic England. Past roles have included Senior Parliamentary Officer at the RSPCA and Senior Policy Advisor for the Department of Culture, Media and Sport where she also worked on the Cultural Property (Armed Conflicts) Bill team.

Oonagh Gay is the former Head of the House of Commons Parliament and Constitution Centre and worked in Parliament for thirty years. She is currently an associate of Global Partners Governance. Oonagh has published widely, particularly in the regulation of parliamentary behaviour.

Marc Geddes is Lecturer in British Politics at the University of Edinburgh. His research looks at everyday practices in parliaments, with a particular focus on accountability relationships between legislative actors.

Mark Goodwin is Lecturer in the Department of Political Science and International Studies at the University of Birmingham. His current research project is an evaluation of the select committee system of the UK House of Commons.

Cathy Gormley-Heenan is Pro-Vice-Chancellor (Research and Impact) and Professor of Politics at Ulster University. Her research focuses on governance, public policy, and devolution, as well as the politics of divided societies.

Daniel Gover is a researcher at Queen Mary University of London. His research has focused on the Westminster legislative process, including the English votes for English laws procedures.

Anne-Marie Griffiths is Clerk of the Petitions Committee in the House of Commons. She has worked in the House of Commons since 2008, and has been Clerk of the Petitions Committee since 2015.

Robert Hazell is Professor of Government and the Constitution at University College London. He has written extensively on Parliament and constitutional matters.

Tom Healey is Director of the Restoration and Renewal Programme. He has worked in Parliament for over 20 years, as Clerk of the Home Affairs Committee and as adviser to the Leader of the House of Commons.

Elizabeth Hunt is Deputy Head of the Journal Office. She has worked in the House of Commons for 21 years and has worked in a variety of roles, including periods as Clerk in the Private Bill Office, as Clerk of the Northern Ireland Affairs Committee, and as Joint Secretary of the Speaker's Conference on Parliamentary Representation.

David Judge is Emeritus Professor of Politics at the University of Strathclyde. His primary research focus is upon representative democracy and parliamentary institutions.

Richard Kelly is a Senior Researcher at the Parliament and Constitution Centre in the House of Commons Library.

Alexandra Kelso is a former Associate Professor of British Politics at the University of Southampton. She has written extensively on Parliament.

Peter Kerr is Senior Lecturer in Politics at the University of Birmingham. He is co-editor of the journal *British Politics*, and researches issues relating to UK party politics, political leadership, statecraft, and the politics of depoliticization.

Matt Korris is Clerk of the House of Lords Constitution Committee and has worked in the Lords for three years. He previously worked at the Hansard Society where he specialized in Parliament, the legislative process, and public engagement with politics.

Libby Kurien is a Clerk in the Table Office of the House of Commons. She has worked in the House of Commons since 2002, including for the European Scrutiny Committee. She was the Permanent Member of the COSAC (Conference of Parliamentary Committees for Union Affairs of Parliaments of the European Union) Secretariat 2012–14.

Phil Larkin is Adjunct Professor of Public Policy at the University of Canberra. He has written on parliaments and legislatures, political parties, and British and Australian politics.

Liam Laurence Smyth has been a clerk at the House of Commons since 1977. He is now Clerk of Legislation.

Cristina Leston-Bandeira is Professor of Politics at the University of Leeds, where she co-leads the Centre for Democratic Engagement. Her research focuses on parliament and public engagement.

Leanne-Marie McCarthy-Cotter is a Post-Doctoral Research Associate at the Crick Centre, University of Sheffield. Her research interests focus upon institutional reform. She has recently been working on a Joseph Rowntree-funded project, 'Designing for Democracy', examining the restoration and renewal of the Palace of Westminster.

Glenn McKee OBE worked in Parliament for 15 years until his retirement in 2017. His previous posts include: Clerk of Private Members' Bills, Grand Committees, and several select committees. His research focuses on the operation and development of the Irish House of Commons in the early eighteenth century.

Tony McNulty is a PhD student at Queen Mary University of London, where he also teaches British politics. Tony was previously an MP for 13 years and a government minister for ten. He researches the role of ministers in government and Parliament, looking particularly at policing, counterterrorism, and immigration policy.

Patrick Milner is a clerk in the House of Lords and is currently the Private Secretary to the Lord Speaker. Prior to this he was the clerk to a number of committees, including the European Union Committee.

Jessica Mulley is Deputy Principal Clerk in the House of Commons. She has 25 years of experience and specific expertise in pre-legislative scrutiny, supporting members, and in harnessing technology for parliamentary scrutiny and legislation.

Philip Norton (Lord Norton of Louth) is Professor of Government at the University of Hull. His research focuses on the UK Parliament, comparative legislatures, the Conservative Party, and the British Constitution. Philip has been a member of the House of Lords since 1998, and was the first Chairman of the House of Lords Select Committee on the Constitution.

Rebecca Partos is a research analyst for the civil service. She has recently completed her PhD on British immigration policy. Rebecca has previously worked for two MPs as a parliamentary researcher and caseworker.

Sarah Petit is Secretary to the Executive Committee and the Board at the House of Commons, and responsible for the private offices supporting the Clerk and the Director General. She has worked in Parliament since 2007, primarily as a specialist or clerk to various select committees.

Matthew Purvis is Head of Research Services in the House of Lords. He has worked in the House of Lords for over a decade, firstly in the External Communications Office answering public enquiries, then as a research clerk in the Library. He has been Head of Research Services since 2015.

Fergus Reid is Clerk of the International Development Committee. During his 25-year career in Parliament, he has worked in all the core procedural offices of the House, for a number of select committees, and as a Director in Parliament's ICT department.

Meg Russell is Professor of British and Comparative Politics and Director of the Constitution Unit at University College London. She has written extensively on Parliament and parliamentary reform, and has held various roles inside Parliament itself, including specialist adviser to several select committees, and to the Leader of the House of Commons.

Eve Samson is Clerk of the Joint Committee of Human Rights. In over 30 years at the House of Commons she has worked for numerous select committees, including the European Scrutiny Committee, and has also served as Government Adviser on Parliamentary Procedure.

Mark Sandford is a senior research analyst at the House of Commons Library, specializing in local government and decentralization in England and further afield.

Ruxandra Serban is a PhD student and Research Assistant at the Constitution Unit, University College London. Her research focuses on the relationship between prime ministers and parliaments in parliamentary democracies.

Mark Shephard is Senior Lecturer in Politics at the University of Strathclyde. His current research focuses on behaviour, particularly behaviours that are less than optimal both in parliaments and on social media.

Jack Simson Caird is Senior Library Clerk in the House of Commons. Prior to joining the Commons he was a lecturer in public law at the University of Sussex. In the Commons, he covers a range of constitutional subjects, including judicial review, human rights, and inquiries.

Mark Stuart is Assistant Professor at the University of Nottingham. His research focuses on parliamentary rebellions and political biography.

Paul E. J. Thomas is a Social Sciences and Humanities Research Council (SSHRC) postdoctoral fellow in Political Science at Carleton University, Canada. His research focuses on the influence of backbench parliamentarians in Canada and the UK. He has previously worked in politics in both countries.

Louise Thompson is Lecturer in British Politics at the University of Surrey. Her research focuses on Parliament, political parties, and legislation.

Aileen Walker is an Associate at Global Partners Governance, working as a public engagement expert on parliamentary strengthening projects in countries around the world. She worked at the House of Commons for 34 years, latterly as Director of Public Engagement.

Hannah White is Director of Research at the Institute for Government. She worked as a clerk in the House of Commons for ten years, including running select and legislative committees. Her current research focuses on the impact of parliamentary committees on government effectiveness.

Ben Worthy is Lecturer in Politics at Birkbeck, University of London. His specialisms include political leadership, government transparency, and British politics. He is the author of *The Politics of Freedom of Information: How and Why Governments Pass Laws that Threaten their Power* (2017).

Ben Yong is Lecturer in Law at the University of Hull. His research focuses on actors within the legislature and executive, and the institutional norms and conditions under which they work.

PART I

Introducing *Exploring Parliament*

1

Introduction: Exploring the UK Parliament in the Twenty-first Century

*Paul Evans, Louise Thompson, and
Cristina Leston-Bandeira*

INTRODUCTION

Standing in the very heart of London, the Palace of Westminster is a building which is recognized the world over. Said to be the most photographed building in the world, it is a UNESCO World Heritage site which receives around one million visitors a year, making it one of the UK's top visitor attractions (Visit England 2015). But it is more than a prominent tourist attraction—it is the core of the UK's political system. The ceremonies of constitutional monarchy, the rhetoric of parliamentarians, the clash of political ideologies, and the exercise of government all come together within its two chambers, many committee rooms, lobbies, and places of informal gathering. It is the place where laws are debated, amended, and voted on—the arena in which the prime minister and wider government are held to account, and the venue for MPs to voice the concerns of constituents from every part of the UK. It is both a symbol of a stable state, and a theatre in which dissent and disagreement are played out.

This drama is enacted within a seemingly antiquated institution. Although much of the building we see today was rebuilt following a fire in 1834, Westminster Hall dates back to the eleventh century. To some observers it reflects a pre-democratic past, in contrast to the newer devolved assemblies in Edinburgh or Cardiff Bay. To others it is a symbol of the continuity and capacity for adaptation of the 'British Constitution'. At the time of writing, the Palace is also in urgent need of repair, with an extensive renewal project planned to restore it and ensure that it can continue to be a working parliamentary building. Many believe Parliament itself is also in need of repair and modernization; it is not just the architecture which seems old-fashioned. We can say the same for many of its rules, procedures, and customs, which can also appear dated and can make the day-to-day work of MPs and peers much more difficult to understand.

A vibrant twenty-first century Parliament, which has seen a great deal of change over the last 30 or 40 years, sits within these traditions and time-hallowed ways of working. In physical terms, the Parliamentary Estate now runs far beyond the Palace itself, resembling something like 'a small town' (Rogers and Walters 2015, 16). The functions which we typically ascribe to the institution—those of legislation and accountability—continue, but are more complex and multifaceted than ever before. Parliament has, in this century, increasingly seen its work and functions as stretching far beyond Westminster and Whitehall, incorporating constituency work, transactions with the electorate through e-petitions and social media, increased engagement by its select committees with the world outside Westminster, and a comprehensive public engagement programme.

The aim of this textbook is to shed light on these changes, and on the continuities. The following chapters will take us behind the walls of the Palace, to explore this incredibly diverse institution through the eyes of the academics who observe it and the officials who work within it.

The ever changing relationship between the monarch, Commons, and Lords

The Parliamentary Estate may be filled with the hustle and bustle of twenty-first century parliamentary work, but understanding Parliament's history and origins is crucial if we are fully to understand its position in the political system. It also enables us to appreciate its transformation into a modern-day legislature. We can divide Parliament into three distinct elements: the House of Commons, the House of Lords, and the monarch or sovereign (or, when all three are gathered together, the Queen-in-Parliament). The UK is a parliamentary democracy. But it is also a constitutional monarchy. As we shall see, the sovereign still plays a symbolic role in the legislative work of Parliament, though her powers are limited (almost to the point of non-existence) by law and by constitutional conventions. The history of the development of the British Constitution could be characterized as a slow but steady handing over of the prerogative and unaccountable powers of a single sovereign to the control of an accountable Parliament (the most recent of these shifts being the ending of the sovereign's right to dissolve Parliament by the Fixed-term Parliaments Act 2011). Alongside this has been the inexorable shift of power from the House of Lords to the House of Commons. It is the elected House of Commons which is now the most politically powerful component of the formal structure, though its strength in relation to the government (still formally known as 'the Crown') is contested. The largely appointed (or hereditary) House of Lords complements and mirrors the work of the Commons, but its powers are weaker, and have been shrinking since at least the seventeenth century. The Parliament Act of 1911 formally established it as the junior partner in Parliament. Indeed, Norton (2013, 16) describes it as the Commons' 'poor relation'. The role of the monarch is barely felt in the day-to-day work of both Houses, but the cabinet ('Her Majesty's Ministers') has inherited much of the sovereign's power and prerogatives.

Things were not always this way. The relationship between these three elements of Parliament has not remained constant; it has been evolving for over 1,000 years. This long history is why England is often known as the 'mother of parliaments' (a term coined by nineteenth-century MP John Bright), reflecting the fact that it has maintained a parliamentary body of some form for many centuries. The sovereign was not always the vestigial political presence it now is. If we look back to Anglo-Saxon times, the earliest conceptions of Parliament only came into being because the monarch of the day willed it. As a body of trusted noblemen (and church leaders), these early Parliaments would provide advice and counsel to the monarch; and at a local level, the ordinary clergy and representatives of villages and towns would meet with local nobility to discuss and resolve local issues. The former would eventually become the House of Lords, while the latter would evolve into a representative House of Commons. These early parliamentary bodies would facilitate the resolution of disputes and the implementation of the monarch's policies, as well as approving taxes to fund wars and other activities of the sovereign. When the powers of the monarch grew over the centuries, the importance of Parliament grew with it.

It is from the thirteenth century that we see the first shift in this relationship and the beginnings of parliamentary authority. The signing of the Magna Carta in 1215 established, for the first time, written legal boundaries on what the monarch could or could not do. Although only a handful of its clauses remain relevant today, it continues to be an important constitutional foundation for the contemporary parliamentary system, as it symbolizes the limits placed on monarchical power within the political system. By 1265, the House of Commons began to emerge as a separate entity in the Parliament convened by Simon de Montfort. By the sixteenth century it was quite distinct, and the King gave it permission to use St Stephen's Chapel in the former royal palace of Westminster as its meeting place. However, it was the seventeenth century that saw the greatest and most violent change in this relationship. Charles I's rejection of the constitutional role of Parliament, and his determination to assert his right to be the sole possessor of sovereignty (combined with a range of other factors, including religious conflict), eventually led to the two English civil wars, in quick succession, between 1642 and 1649. These wars were characterized then, as now, as between the King and Parliament. The parliamentary forces finally and conclusively prevailed, and in January 1649 Charles was tried for treason, sentenced to death, and executed, just a few hundred metres away from the Palace of Westminster. After the third civil war, against Charles I's heir, a Commonwealth was declared, and between 1650 and 1653 the nation was governed directly by the House of Commons (the House of Lords having been abolished). Between 1653 and 1660 the country was governed by a Lord Protector (Oliver Cromwell, succeeded briefly by his son Richard).

In 1660, Parliament made a treaty with Charles II and the monarchy (and the House of Lords) was restored. The truce between Parliament and the Crown broke down under Charles' successor James II, and in 1688 he was deposed and Parliament invited William of Orange and Charles' daughter Mary to take the throne jointly. The Bill of Rights, presented to William and Mary in 1688 and ratified by Parliament in 1689, was essentially a contract between Parliament and the Crown which stands to this day as the foundation of the British Constitution as a constitutional monarchy ruling with, and only with, the consent of Parliament. In effect, sovereignty had been transferred from the sovereign alone to the Crown-in-Parliament.

Although the concept of parliamentary sovereignty is a highly contested constitutional theory, it remains a talismanic assertion about the contemporary parliamentary system and the UK Constitution. It has given us the so-called 'Westminster system', where the executive (nowadays the cabinet, rather than the Crown) is composed of members of the legislature, in apparent contradiction to the principle of separation of powers. It is from this point onwards that the struggle for supremacy within the Crown-in-Parliament shifted to one between the Commons and the Lords.

Since the seventeenth century the relationship between these two parliamentary chambers has also shifted. By the end of the eighteenth century the supremacy of the Commons had been fairly clearly established, though the Lords continued to resist. The matter was not settled until the early twentieth century and the climax of the long-running conflict between the Liberal Governments and the Tory/Conservative-dominated House of Lords, mostly over the question of Home Rule for Ireland. At this time, the House of Lords shared equal legislating powers with the Commons and could use these to overturn the decisions of the Commons. This came to a head in 1909 when the upper Chamber rejected Lloyd George and the Liberal Government's People's Budget, breaching a centuries-old constitutional convention that the Lords had no say in matters of public finance. Following two general elections (and the death of Edward

VII) in 1910, during which questions of House of Lords reform were paramount, the 1911 Parliament Act neutered the power of the upper Chamber, removing its ability to reject legislation and introducing a delaying power of two years in its place (the so-called 'suspensory veto'). It lost its power over legislation dealing with taxing and public spending altogether.

In 1949, following a similar stalemate over Clement Attlee's post-war reform programme, an amendment to the Parliament Act reduced this delaying power to just one year. This alteration to the relative power and status of the two chambers remains in place today. All legislation dealing exclusively with taxing and spending starts in the Commons and must receive royal assent within a month once it reaches the Lords, where it cannot be amended. And while the override provisions of the Parliament Act to enable laws to be made without the consent of the House of Lords have been used formally only six times since 1911,[1] the existence of this power means it is generally pointless for the Lords to defy the Commons more than once or twice during the final stages of agreeing an Act of Parliament (the so-called 'ping-pong' stage—see Chapter 7). Although the Parliament Acts have circumscribed the powers of the Lords, they have not completely taken away its ability to frustrate the government or to force it to change its mind. As we shall see in Chapter 8, the relationship between Parliament and government is more complex than this. But what they have achieved is to emphasize the primacy of the elected House of Commons over the appointed House of Lords. The House of Commons remains the most powerful, and thus the most studied, element of the UK Parliament today.

Understanding the UK Parliament in the twenty-first century

Traditionally, observers of Parliament have focused overwhelmingly on the House of Commons and, in particular, its interactions with the government of the day. This is to be expected given that the parliamentary system brings a government which is drawn almost entirely from that House, usually with a clear parliamentary majority there. This also means that there is an overwhelming emphasis on Parliament's legislative or decision-making role. Students will usually be familiar with occasions where the government was defeated in the Commons, such as the Shops Bill of 1986 when the Thatcher Government was defeated by 14 votes at second reading. More recently we could point to the Commons rejection of Prime Minister David Cameron's proposal for air strikes in Syria by 285 votes to 272 in 2013 (although this was a motion and not a piece of legislation) or, in an echo of the 1986 defeat, when the extension of Sunday trading hours in England was rejected during the passage of the Enterprise Bill in March 2016. These occasions stand out because they seem to be exceptions to an otherwise very proven rule. The government's parliamentary majority brings with it huge control over the legislative agenda and, as such, it is very easy to see the relationship as one-sided; a match in which government always dominates.

This is because the emphasis is usually placed on the key divisions at the second and third reading of bills. But if we look beyond this, to other stages of the legislative process, we see that Parliament actually has much stronger powers of scrutiny and influence. This is because there are opportunities for the Commons and the Lords either to amend legislation themselves, or (as is more common) to persuade the government to make amendments to its own legislation. As Chapters 7, 8, and 9

[1] The Welsh Church Act 1914, the Government of Ireland Act 1914, the Parliament Act 1949, the War Crimes Act 1991, the European Parliamentary Elections Act 1999, the 'Hunting' Act 2004.

demonstrate, MPs and peers use formal tools to do this, such as pressing a minister in committee or in the Chamber. But they also work outside the formal legislative process using informal tools, such as individual meetings with ministers, to push for changes to be made. The Lords is a particularly good place to see these changes and, as Chapter 19 demonstrates, it is the arena for many government defeats. In recent years we can point, for example, to the Tax Credits debacle (see Case Study 19) or Lord Dubs' amendment to the 2016 Immigration Bill regarding asylum for unaccompanied child refugees (see Case Study 8).

Informed observers of Parliament, however, appreciate that its work goes far beyond the approval or amendment of pieces of legislation. They also focus on the less formal and visible aspects of the institution and, as a result, are able to capture a much stronger influence on government and on legislation than had previously been considered. But it is not just the nature of the study of Parliament that has shifted from sometimes abstract theories about procedural and constitutional mechanisms; the institution itself has undergone some significant internal parliamentary reform. Probably the most significant change of the last 50 years remains the establishment in 1979 of a select committee system which scrutinizes the whole waterfront of government activity in a sustained and continuous way. The Commons has, in many ways, become a committee-based legislature. The Lords have slowly followed suit, though that House is still far more concentrated on the making of legislation in the Chamber. The biggest change for the Lords has probably been the expulsion of all but 92 of the hereditary peers in 1999, along with (to a lesser extent) the loss of its judicial role with the establishment of the Supreme Court in 2009.

Select committees have been pivotal to further reforms in more recent times, with the Modernisation Committee (which existed from 1997 to 2010) and the Wright Committee (2009–10) putting forward a series of proposals about how the House of Commons should modernize and reform itself. As we will see in Chapter 15, changes made to the legislative committee system of the Commons in 2006 mean that bill committees can now take oral evidence from expert witnesses to aid the scrutiny of government bills. The introduction of the Liaison Committee's oral evidence sessions with the prime minister in 2002 enables him or her to be held to account in far more detail than at Prime Minister's Questions for government decisions, and to be pushed into explaining and defending the government's strategy. The election of select committee chairs from 2010, and the creation of the Backbench Business Committee in the same year, were all the result of reforms proposed by the Wright Committee, and have been key in empowering backbenchers and reducing the power of the government and the Whips over the behaviour of MPs and of the parliamentary agenda. We can also add here the reinvigoration of the urgent questions (UQ) procedure. Chapter 17 shows the significance of Parliamentary Questions as a fundamental mechanism through which to hold government to account. Speaker Bercow's recognition of this has brought about a huge increase in the number of urgent questions being granted, enabling the Commons to question ministers on the most pressing topics. UQs have become an important weapon in the arsenal of opposition and backbench MPs.

Procedures such as these are integral to the functioning of parliamentary democracy, but those outside the institution rarely observe them directly. When they do, they may be unclear what they are actually observing. Clear and concise reporting of Parliament's work is crucial for its scrutiny and accountability activities to be understood by the wider public; though the relationship between Parliament and the media has never been an easy one, as the 2009 expenses scandal demonstrated so forcefully. Chapter 20 provides us with a first-hand insight into the world of the parliamentary correspondent. The means through which the public receive their information about the institution may have changed, with a growing reliance on social media, but their appetite for this information has not diminished. As Case Study 20 demonstrates, new forms of media are as challenging as they are essential for showing and explaining the work of the institution.

Representation in the twenty-first century is also a very different affair to previous centuries. After the enfranchisement of most men, and women from the age of 30 (and their gaining of the right for the first time to sit as MPs), in 1918, full equality of voting rights had to wait until 1929. Only in 1948 did the final vestiges of the rotten boroughs disappear with the abolition of the university constituencies, and the electoral system become fully one-person-one-vote. In 1969, the vote was extended to 18-year-olds, and it may eventually be given to 16-year-olds, as it already has been in Scottish elections. The two-party system which had dominated the House from almost the first decades of franchise reform in the mid-nineteenth century (with Labour replacing the Liberals as the alternative to the Conservatives after the First World War) appears, in recent decades, to have begun to give way to a more complex arrangement of forces, though the 2017 general election indicated that the two party system may be returning. The House of Lords has also changed, almost beyond recognition: in 1958, life peerages were created (including, for the first time, women peers), and in 1999 the majority of hereditary peers were excluded. However, recent prime ministers have created peerages at an almost unprecedented rate, and the House is now bursting at the seams. As Chapter 23 shows, its much more diverse membership is generally agreed to have made it a more professional, but also a more assertively political Chamber.

Although we can identify tensions between constituencies and the House of Commons from the late nineteenth century, this seems particularly acute in the twenty-first century. The votes on the triggering of Article 50 in early 2017 illustrated this tension, with the press being very quick to highlight the group of MPs who voted against Brexit in the Commons, despite representing constituencies in which a majority of voters had chosen to 'leave' the European Union in the independence referendum of June 2016. As Part V of the book shows, constituency representation is a fundamental feature of any MP's activity; it entails some of the most emotionally rewarding parts of the job, through which MPs have direct contact with their constituents. Paradoxically, it also often constitutes the less well known part of MPs' activity. Chapters 25 and 26 outline the degree to which this constituency role has changed over the past 50 years. They also show how constituency work contributes towards their parliamentary activity, namely in terms of feeding into campaigns for specific policies. Constituency representation is undoubtedly one of the key multiple pressures on MPs when it comes to their voting pattern, as analysed in Chapter 24. But representation is also about understanding who parliamentarians are.

The 2017 Copeland by-election marked the first time the number of women ever elected to the UK Parliament surpassed the number of male MPs currently sitting as MPs, and the general election of that year brought us the House with the largest ever number of women MPs (208, or 32 per cent). As we approach another memorable date, a hundred years in 2018 since the first woman was elected to Parliament, Chapter 22 reminds us of the key changes in women's representation over the last century, while interrogating its significance for wider parliamentary practice. This follows Chapter 21, which reviews wider changes in MPs' socio-professional backgrounds, demonstrating a rise in the career politician while questioning commonly held beliefs of their overwhelming presence among MPs. The multifaceted nature of representation comes to life through the very interesting discussion in Chapter 23, which analyses the different dimensions of the House of Lords' representative role. The Lords' representativeness is particularly important for understanding the role it performs in the contemporary UK Parliament.

The final section of the book focuses on the challenges facing Parliament today; challenges which also stretch beyond the traditional legislative, scrutiny, and representative roles of the institution. These are indeed coming under pressure. The planned UK withdrawal from the European Union will push Parliament's capacity to scrutinize primary and delegated legislation to its limits. But we also demonstrate here the pressures brought to the institution as a result of the Freedom of Information Act, the devolution of power to Scotland and Wales, and the resumption of devolution in Northern Ireland. These challenges are set within a society which has rising expectations of its politicians and institutions, but one in which actual knowledge of what these actors and institutions do is often low, and perceptions of its role continue to be misunderstood. As Chapter 29 shows, the expansion of outward facing services has been a key area of development of the UK Parliament over the last decade. At one time a very small area of activity, public engagement is now a key role of the UK Parliament, and is illustrated by the rise of e-petitions, expanding tools for public consultation, and the creation of a new Education Centre in July 2015. There is still very little understanding of this activity and what it achieves, if anything, but it is an important part of understanding the twenty-first century UK Parliament.

The contemporary Parliament is a multifaceted institution, performing a wide range of roles within an increasingly complex environment where representative democracy itself seems to be increasingly challenged as our ruling paradigm. This is why it matters not only to understand what it does, but also how it is structured and organized, which is the main focus of Part II. Parliament and government, MPs and peers, all navigate an institution which is hundreds of years old, and one which has had to open up to external modern pressures of professionalization and the growth of civil society pressure groups, while dealing with increasing complexity of roles for the individual MP. As Chapter 5 shows, rituals, traditions, conventions, and unspoken rules are key to understand how Parliament is organized—they tell us of its history, but also crucially they depict power relationships, roles, and responsibilities. But they also operate in an external environment that more and more expects clear, transparent, sleek, and efficient processes. While Chapter 2 explains how political actors and groups, such as parties and government, are organized to sustain Parliament's key roles, other chapters show the increasing importance of the administrative structure to support the functioning of a representative democracy in an environment where parliamentarians have to rely increasingly on professional support to be able to deal with what are ever more complex and specialized tasks. And the radical and disruptive effects of the 2016 referendum on the UK's membership of the EU reminds us that representative democracy itself may not be securely anchored in popular consent, as we discuss in the book's Conclusion. Understanding the contemporary UK Parliament therefore necessitates an understanding of its multifaceted roles, beyond its most traditional ones such as legislation. But, crucially, it also requires us to consider how it combines and reconciles centuries of history with the volatile electorates and fast-paced politics of today.

The book's structure

This book delineates the contemporary work of the UK Parliament in its wide range of roles. It covers the informal work of the institution and its members, alongside the more formal ones, interrogating common notions about Parliament's relationship with the executive as a one-sided affair. It aims to offer a much more rounded view of the work of Parliament and its place in the wider political context. But it also serves as a useful companion for those wishing to understand where Parliament has come from, and to appreciate the importance of its historical development to its work today.

The book is composed of short chapters which cover a wide range of aspects of parliamentary activity. This enables us to cover more traditional areas, such as Parliament's legislative process, through a number of perspectives, but also to consider aspects of Parliament often neglected in similar books, such as the significance of design and space. Due to their concise nature, these chapters do not pretend to be exhaustive in their coverage. They aim primarily to raise and challenge common assumptions usually associated with discussions of Parliament, examine how, or if, these have changed recently, and provide an overview of their key constitutive ideas. All chapters list further reading, which aims to help readers develop further knowledge and understanding of each specific topic. Some chapters cover less well-known ground, such as the governance of the Parliament, where broad assumptions have not yet become common currency. The focus in these chapters is on explaining the nature of the topic and introducing key debates. Each chapter is accompanied by a contemporary case study to illustrate the ideas being discussed. The case studies aim to illustrate the key concepts, debates, or insights outlined in the chapters in order to bring the topic to life.

The book's chapters and case studies have been written by some of the most active academics researching Parliament today, including established scholars of the UK Parliament, together with key parliamentary practitioners, who walk the corridors of the Palace and observe its business on a daily basis—in some cases, for a number of decades. In many cases, the practitioners and the political scientists have worked together to bring theory and the lived texture of direct professional engagement together. The combination of academics and practitioners aims to provide solid scholarly contributions grounded in expert parliamentary practice. This is a central purpose of the book: it aims to bring the study of Parliament as a constitutional entity together with the study of Parliament as a multi-layered and complex actor which shapes, and is shaped by, the life of the nation. Reflecting the mix of authors, some of the contributions are more procedurally based, and some draw more heavily from ongoing research. Each chapter includes a selection of additional case study material, offering further examples which readers, whether students, lecturers, or interested observers may wish to explore further as a way of bringing the theory of Parliament into contact with its practice.

Parliamentary language is often seen as a barrier for people seeking to engage with Parliament; but it is also part and parcel of what makes Parliament. It reflects its history, practices, and norms. While the book is written for the reader who may know little about Parliament, and therefore attempts to avoid the more specialized parliamentary jargon, this is not always possible. This is why we also offer a Glossary of Parliamentary Terms to help guide a better understanding of Parliament. Where relevant, specific parliamentary terms are explained in chapters, but the Glossary compiles all entries.

It is in this spirit—to encourage engagement with the scholarship on Parliament and further understanding of its contemporary practice—that each chapter also lists primary sources for readers to explore in their own time. Primary sources include, among many others, Hansard verbatim records of parliamentary debates, select committee reports, written or oral evidence from outside experts, the increasingly comprehensive audio-visual archives of parliamentary proceedings, and news stories on Parliament. These are the things which make the stuff of politics and should ultimately be our point of departure in understanding an institution such as the UK Parliament. The listing of primary sources aims to help readers find original material, and therefore engage directly with the nuts and bolts of parliamentary politics, as well as helping lecturers guide their students to explore parliamentary material in their own way, and at their own pace.

Whether you are exploring Westminster for the first time, or are a seasoned parliamentary scholar, we hope that within these pages you find something of interest, something new, and something that challenges your perspective.

References

NORTON, P. (2013) *Parliament in British Politics*, 2nd edition, Basingstoke: Palgrave Macmillan.

ROGERS, R. and WALTERS, R. (2015) *How Parliament Works*, 7th edition, London: Routledge.

VISIT ENGLAND (2015) *Most Visited Paid Attractions—England 2015*. Online at: https://www.visitbritain.org/sites/default/files/vb-corporate/Documents-Library/documents/England-documents/most_visited_paid_attractions_national_2015.pdf [accessed 25 June 2017].

PART II

The Organization of Parliament

2

The Political Organization
of Parliament

Philip Norton

INTRODUCTION

Political parties are at the heart of the relationship between Parliament and government. Government is chosen through elections to the House of Commons. Political parties compete to win seats. A party gaining an absolute majority of seats is invited to form a government. Party determines not only who forms a government, but also its capacity to deliver on the promises it made in the election. Political organization in Parliament helps the governing party deliver its programme and enables other parties to challenge the government. It also enables Members of Parliament to make sure their voices are heard by party leaders.

Political organization is thus central to parliamentary life, and it matters because Parliament matters. Parliament is the body that has to give assent to measures of public policy that are to be binding. Acts of Parliament are the means through which public policy is enacted. There is no alternative authoritative conduit for achieving implementation of a programme of public policy. Parties compete with one another, thus rendering Parliament an inherently political body. A party majority enables the government to get its measures passed, but the existence in Parliament of other parties enables different views to be heard.

Each party has some degree of organization to ensure that its voice is heard effectively and to maximize its strength when votes are held. The government, in particular, needs to mobilize its supporters to get its measures passed. The House of Commons has traditionally been characterized as a Chamber dominated by two large parties who sit facing one another, engaged in adversarial conflict, and with MPs being loyal to their parties. Samuel H. Beer (1969) referred to the 'Prussian discipline' of MPs. The enforcers of this discipline in popular perception are the party whips.

In practice, the situation is not quite as stark as this picture conveys. Parties dominate Parliament, especially the House of Commons, but there is more to party activity than what goes on in the Chamber and more to political organization than the existence of the whips. Each party—the two largest in particular—has developed an infrastructure that fulfils a range of functions, not least enabling Members to engage in private deliberations and to convey their views to party leaders. Even whips are much more than enforcers of the party line. The relationships between parties—and between Parliament and government—are more complex than a simple picture of adversarial conflict (government versus opposition) would suggest, and the relationships have changed in recent years.

We look first at how parties themselves are structured. Each has some degree of internal organization. We then look at how parties shape the relationship between Parliament and the executive, and how these have changed over time.

Internal organization

The rules of both Houses are essentially premised on the existence of two principal parties facing one another. The party in government comprises ministers, forming Her Majesty's government, and backbenchers. Other parties are constituted as opposition parties, the largest being designated as the official opposition. As with the government party, the opposition comprises frontbench Members (shadow ministers) and back-benchers. Smaller parties may also designate some Members as 'frontbenchers' (official spokespeople for the party).

The frontbench of each party includes whips, headed in the larger parties by a chief whip. They make up a core and consistent element to party activity. Each party also has its own infrastructure. In the larger parties, this may be well developed, with party subject groups or committees in addition to regular meetings of the whole parliamentary party. The parties have their own officers (such as chairs and secretaries), distinct from the party leaders.

The whips

Whips are Members appointed to facilitate party cohesion (see Chapter 24). They act as communicators, informing their Members of business and the importance attached to that business. They also serve as managers, the government whips discussing business with the whips of other parties (forming what is known as the 'usual channels'), and work to ensure that they have sufficient Members present to fulfil the work of the House. For the purpose of contact with government business managers, even very small parties—with just two or three Members—designate one of their number as a whip. Government whips have to make sure they have enough Members present to form a majority in the event of a vote (division) taking place. Although the whips have traditionally had different tools at their disposal to induce cohesion—'carrots', such as putting Members on favoured committees, or 'sticks', such as limiting promotion prospects—their most powerful weapon has always been appeals to party loyalty (see Crowe 1986).

There are differences between the whips in the two chambers. In the House of Commons, the whips are seen but not heard. Other than formally moving certain motions, they do not speak. In the House of Lords, in effect the whips act as junior ministers. They speak at the despatch box as spokespersons for particular departments, given that not all departments have ministers in the House, or not enough to cover all the business. They lack the tools available to whips in the Commons to facilitate cohesion. There are no sanctions of any note that they can deploy against peers, given that peers serve for life unless they choose to retire or are expelled by the House. They cannot therefore be deselected and withdrawing the party whip from a peer would be symbolic, but have little practical effect.

The whips are, in essence, key to party organization in each House. They have a long history, existing—in both human and paper form—prior to the Reform Act of 1832 (Norton 1979, 10). They dominated party organization in Parliament throughout the nineteenth and early twentieth centuries. Indeed, they were the political organization. There were few meetings of a party's MPs, and when they were summoned it was by the party leaders. The form of organization was essentially top-down, from leaders to led.

Parliamentary parties

The parties in both Houses now have their own organization, separate from the leadership and whips, designed to facilitate communication between their leaders and backbenchers. The organization is especially well developed in the House of Commons and is a product of developments in the twentieth century (Norton 1979, 7–68). The two largest parties—Labour and Conservative—are sufficiently large not only to sustain weekly meetings of their MPs, but also to have subject groups.

 Parliamentary terms Parliamentary group

A group of MPs from the same political party.

The Parliamentary Labour Party (PLP) comprises all Labour MPs and has its origins in 1906, when Labour MPs were first elected. From its beginnings, it has met weekly and elected officers. In 1945, the parliamentary party set up a series of subject committees, creating some element of specialization and enabling Members interested in a particular subject to discuss it and communicate on it with the relevant minister. In 1970, the posts of leader and chairman of the parliamentary party, normally combined when in opposition, were separated.

The Conservative party also has its own structure. Some Conservative backbenchers first elected in 1922 got together to form a body to discuss matters of mutual concern. It elected officers and in time the body, styled the Conservative Private Members (1922) Committee—more commonly known as the 1922 Committee—was opened up to other Conservative MPs, not just those elected in 1922; eventually it came to comprise all Conservative private Members. It differs from the PLP in that it includes only private Members—that is, all MPs bar the leader when in opposition, and all bar the prime minister and ministers when in government—though whips attend as observers, and from 2010 ministers may also do so. The 1922 Committee has developed into an influential body, and although weekly meetings may sometimes be lightly attended, discussion of controversial policies or ministerial actions can produce packed meetings. Both the PLP and the 1922 Committee meet in Committee Room 14, the largest committee room in the Palace of Westminster. Both may be attended by the party's peers, though peers also meet weekly in their own party groups.

The meetings of the parliamentary parties are complemented by more specialized bodies. In government, the Labour Party has a Parliamentary Committee, comprising elected backbenchers, ministers, and some *ex officio* Members, to act as a liaison between the parliamentary party and government (Norton 1979, 24–5; Minkin 2014, 406). The PLP also has subject groups covering the main areas of public policy. Backbench committees covering different policy areas were formed on the Conservative benches in the 1920s. They reported to the 1922 Committee, even though from 1924 they were formal party groupings and the 1922 Committee was essentially an autonomous body formed by MPs. The party committees proved to be active bodies (Norton 1994, 113–25), but were discontinued after the 1997 general election when a much reduced parliamentary party and competing demands made them difficult to sustain. More recently, policy groups were formed and in the 2015 Parliament backbench committees were brought back into being, covering each government department, though they were somewhat slow in getting under way.

The smaller parties hold regular meetings of Members, and the third largest party—the Liberal Democrats until 2015 and the Scottish National Party since 2015—may also appoint 'frontbench' or shadow ministers. During the period that the Liberal Democrats were in coalition with the Conservatives, from 2010 to 2015, they appointed a series of committees, each co-chaired by an MP and a peer (see Case Study 2).

Organized parliamentary parties fulfil a number of purposes (Norton 2013, 59–74). They provide important channels of communication. They enable leaders to keep abreast of feelings among their supporters. Meetings can provide an important safety valve, allowing Members to let off steam in private (or supposedly in private—details often get leaked to the media) rather than in the Chamber. Members may signal opposition to a policy before it is formally introduced. It also enables leaders to communicate with their supporters, sometimes at short notice, and can be used to inform and raise support.

The parliamentary parties also serve to promote the interests of their Members, not just with leaders but also with parliamentary authorities, on such issues as MPs' pay and resources. At times of coalition (see Case Study 2), they may serve to maintain the distinct identity of the party. They provide a platform for Members to make a mark, both backbenchers—some of whom are more influential in party meetings than in the Chamber—and frontbenchers keen to bolster support. They may also serve as bodies to influence policy, either positively in terms of feeding into discussions on party policy, such as in preparation for an election manifesto, or negatively, in terms of signalling opposition to a particular policy proposal. They may sometimes serve to determine the fate of ministers. The 1922 Committee is responsible for organizing the election of the party leader, and Conservative MPs choose the two candidates to be placed before the party membership (until 2001, the MPs elected the leader; that was the case with Labour MPs until 1981). The 1922 Committee has played a notable role in prompting the resignation of ministers who have become embroiled in controversy, such as Chief Whip Andrew Mitchell over a clash with police officers in Downing Street in 2012. A minister cannot afford to lose the support of the party's MPs.

The role of party organization is varied and a key feature of parliamentary life. This is formally recognized in the fact that opposition parties receive public money to enable them to carry out their parliamentary work. The Leader of the Opposition, opposition chief whip, and two assistant whips are salaried posts, paid out of public funds. Opposition parties also receive what is known as 'Short money' (named after Edward Short, Leader of the House of Commons when the scheme was introduced), allocated through a formula based on the number of MPs and votes received at the last election. In the House of Lords, there is equivalent support in terms of 'Cranborne money'.

 Parliamentary terms Short money

Financial assistance allocated to opposition parties using a formula based on the number of MPs returned and votes received at the last election.

 Parliamentary terms Cranborne money

Similar to Short money in the Commons, Cranborne money is assistance given to the two largest opposition parties in the House of Lords, as well as to the Convenor of the cross-bench peers.

Legislative-executive relations

Political parties, then, have their own internal organization. They are not monolithic entities, but rather have developed a set of internal and institutionalized relationships over time. Each House of Parliament is made up of several parties with varying degrees of organization. The stance of each House in dealing with the executive is shaped by the differing relationships within and between the parties.

In a seminal article, Anthony King has argued that there are five modes of executive–legislative relations (King 1976, 11–34). The *opposition mode* is the most prominent in the UK, characterized by conflict between the party in government and the party or parties in opposition. Since the emergence of mass-membership political parties in the latter half of the nineteenth century, this mode has been the dominant, and certainly the most visible, mode of executive–legislative relations. The House of Commons has formed the arena for the clash between the two main parties, initially the Conservative and Liberal parties and then the Conservative and Labour parties. The opposition has ensured a consistent and structured means of questioning government.

The *inter-party mode* is not usually a feature of British politics, as it refers to conflict between parties in a coalition, although it was a notable feature of the 2010–15 Parliament with a coalition government formed by the Conservative and Liberal Democrat parties. We explore this mode in more detail in Case Study 2.

The *intra-party mode* has been more of a feature of UK politics in recent decades, denoting conflict within a party. Although the opposition mode is the most visible, and shapes behaviour on the Floor of the House, the intra-party mode is most significant in influencing the position taken by government (see Brand 1992). As long as ministers have the support of their backbenchers, they can see off challenges by the opposition. The opposition relies primarily on having an impact through voice rather than vote. MPs on the government benches can utilize both voice and vote. If voice expressed privately, through backbench group meetings or the whips, fails to have an impact, they may take to the Floor of the House and, if necessary, the division lobbies. The threat of voting against the party line by government MPs may be persuasive, potentially attracting unwanted publicity for the government, and if carried through may bring about an embarrassing result for ministers. The impact may move beyond the persuasive to the coercive if government backbenchers vote with the opposition on such a scale as to defeat the government.

Cohesion was a marked feature of parliamentary parties throughout the twentieth century. There were actually two parliamentary sessions in the mid-1950s when not a single MP on the government backbenches voted against the party. Behaviour changed, especially in the 1970s (see e.g. Norton 1980), with MPs becoming more willing than ever before to vote against their own party and on occasion to do so in some numbers, sometimes sufficient to result in a government defeat. The 1970s was a high point for defeats, but all subsequent governments, despite having overall majorities, suffered defeats. In 1986, for example, 72 Conservative MPs voted with the Labour opposition to defeat the second reading of the Shops Bill to deregulate Sunday trading. In 2013, Prime Minister David Cameron had to accept defeat when a combination of government and opposition MPs voted against military action in Syria.

The *cross-party mode* is when parties work together, or at least do not oppose one another. This is a characteristic of many continental legislatures, but it can be seen in Parliament in the UK: it is not unusual for government bills to be passed without the opposition voting against them on second reading (when the bill as a whole is debated and approved). This mode is not unusual, but it is sporadic, occurring when party views coincide. There is a mechanism for contact (the usual channels), but no formal institutional structure.

The *non-party mode* is distinctive because, as the name indicates, it does not involve any party engagement, but rather covers Members acting more as MPs than as party MPs. This has become more pronounced with the formation of investigative select committees in which MPs often act independently of their party (see Chapter 16) and with the phenomenal growth of all-party parliamentary groups where MPs come together to pursue an issue that is not contentious between the parties (see Chapter 11).

Party thus shapes relations between each House and the executive, but the nature of this relationship varies considerably. The opposition and non-party modes are important for ensuring that issues are raised. Government may be persuaded, but it is under no obligation to accept proposals put forward. The intra-party mode is most important for government, at least a majority government, in that it may be forced to act against its wishes if some of its own MPs vote with opposition parties to deny it a majority. In conditions of coalition, the government is vulnerable in terms both of the intra-party mode and the inter-party mode. Dissenting backbenchers may be a problem, as may one or more of the parties to the coalition. This was the problem faced by the Coalition government formed in 2010.

Conclusion

Parties are at the heart of the political organization of Parliament. The rules of each House, especially the House of Commons, are premised on the existence of a governing party facing an opposition party, and therefore Parliament's political organization emanates from this. Members sit in the Chamber on the basis of party. Party determines the relationship between Parliament and the executive. Neither House could operate without party. Party determines who forms the government and the outcomes of public policy. The government needs to mobilize its Members to carry its measures. It may face opposition not only from other parties—using the Chamber to give voice to their arguments—but also from some of its own Members. Party organization maximizes the capacity of each party to achieve its goals—the enactment of public policy in the case of the governing party and challenging government in the case of opposition parties. For opposition parties, the Chamber is a means of demonstrating that they have alternative policies to those of government, which merit voters' confidence at the next election. Parties are organized in Parliament not only in order to debate the measures before them, but also with a view to the next general election.

Political parties have existed throughout the era of modern British politics—indeed, they have largely shaped that era—but over time they have become more organized in Parliament. They provide the basis for differing relationships between the Houses and government. It is impossible to understand either House without reference to organized political parties.

Further Reading

Brand, J. (1992) *British Parliamentary Parties*, Oxford: Clarendon Press.

Minkin, L. (2014) *The Blair Supremacy*, Manchester: Manchester University Press, especially chapter 13.

Norton, P. (1979) 'The organisation of Parliamentary parties' in S. A. Walkland (ed.), *The House of Commons in the Twentieth Century*, Oxford: Clarendon Press, pp. 7–68.

Norton, P. (2013) *The Voice of the Backbenchers: The 1922 Committee: the first 90 years, 1923–2013*, London: Conservative History Group.

Norton, P. (2016) 'The House of Commons: Does the opposition still matter?', *Politics Review*, Vol. 25 (4), pp. 30–3.

Case Study 2: The effect of coalition government on the structure and organization of Parliament

The outcome of the 2010 general election resulted in a situation unprecedented in British politics: two parties negotiating an agreement in order to form a coalition government. The UK had not previously had a coalition government formed as a result of an indecisive general election outcome. The creation of a coalition also caused a difficult situation for the parliamentary parties—the Conservative and the Liberal Democrat—that became partners in government.

Each remained a distinct party, but the leaders of each came together to form a ministry, supported by the two parties in Parliament. This created two problems. One was finding ways of resolving disputes between the two parties. Although the parties took the same or similar positions on some policies, on others it was a case of compromising or making a concession. There was not always going to be a meeting of minds. For resolving issues on a day-to-day basis, a four-Member working group, known as the Quad, was formed, comprising the two senior Members of each party, to meet weekly or as required. Other issues were resolved bilaterally between the two party leaders, David Cameron and Nick Clegg.

The other problem was enabling the parties to maintain their individual integrity. One way of conveying the distinctiveness of the two partners was for the Members of the two parties, although sitting on the same side of the House, to sit separately. This applied in both Houses. The only intermingling of Conservatives and Liberal Democrats was on the government frontbench. Sitting separately was seen by the Liberal Democrats as necessary but not sufficient for the purpose of maintaining their particular identity. In the House of Lords, they wanted to maintain the practice of rotation between the different political groupings in the House when it came to Question Time. The Lords is a self-governing chamber and at Question Time peers jump to their feet to get in first with a supplementary question, but the House accepts that if a Labour peer gets in first, then the next supplementary should be from a Liberal Democrat, a cross-bencher, or a Conservative backbencher, with the order rotating between the four. Under the period of the Coalition government, various Labour peers challenged attempts by Liberal Democrats to retain their distinct identity, arguing instead that Conservative and Liberal Democrat peers formed one distinct grouping and therefore the rotation should be three-sided (Labour, cross-bench, Coalition) and not four-sided. The issue was never formally resolved and generated some ill will between the Labour and Liberal Democrat parties throughout the Parliament.

Sitting arrangements, however, were essentially symbolic. The more important means of achieving party distinctiveness was through the respective organization of the parliamentary parties. Weekly meetings of the Parliamentary Liberal Democrat party allowed MPs to discuss their position on the stance taken by the Coalition. To ensure that it had a distinctive voice, the parliamentary party also created backbench party committees, each co-chaired by an MP and a peer, with the chairs able to express a party view. Each committee shadowed a government department and met weekly, the meetings sometimes being attended by party officials. The press would sometimes treat the chairs as the equivalent of party spokespersons, enabling them to offer a view detached from that of the government.

On the Conservative side, the 1922 Committee served to maintain a distinct party voice. It remained detached from the party leader. When the leader, David Cameron, sought at the start of the Parliament to change the 1922 Committee so that ministers were members, and to influence the outcome of the election of the Chair, he was rebuffed. Ministers were invited to attend meetings, but only as observers, and the members elected Graham Brady, rather than Cameron's presumed choice, as Chair.

The 1922 Committee was important as a sounding board for Tory MPs' views, and sometimes disagreement, and was important in putting pressure on the leadership in 2011 to play a more prominent role in campaigning in the referendum against the introduction of the Alternative Vote for parliamentary elections (Norton 2013, 62). The executive of the 1922 Committee continued the practice, established in the previous Parliament, of meeting the party leader three times a year. The 1922 also established five policy groups (covering economic affairs, foreign affairs, home affairs, the environment, and public services), each with an elected chair, to discuss issues in particular policy sectors. The groups met at regular intervals, sometimes weekly, and at least one chair used the position for making public pronouncements.

The parliamentary parties provided an arena in which Members could express their candid views, wearing their party hats, and for sometimes frank exchanges with leading party figures, including the party leader. These could include making clear their dissatisfaction with Coalition policy or the stance taken by their coalition partner.

The Parliament, then, was distinctive for the significance of the inter-party and intra-party modes of executive–legislative relations, and the challenge for party leaders was balancing the relationship between the two. The early part of the Parliament was notable for intra-party dissension, the Coalition pushing for policies, such as House of Lords reform, that were not necessarily supported by the backbenchers in one or both of the parliamentary parties (Cowley 2015, 149–51).

As the Parliament progressed, and the parties in coalition looked to the next election— when they would be fighting one another for votes—tension increased between them. Conservative Prime Minister David Cameron sought to unite his own party and switched his stance on some issues to facilitate that aim, most notably on holding an in/out referendum on the UK's membership of the European Union (Norton 2015, 483–5). Seeking to respond to the demands of his own backbenchers entailed conflict with his coalition partner, and inter-party conflict became more pronounced as time went on. There was particularly bad blood between the two parliamentary parties as a result of the failure of a bill to reform the House of Lords—a key measure in Liberal Democrat eyes—which was undermined by active opposition from some Conservative MPs. In retaliation, Nick Clegg instructed Liberal Democrats to vote with Labour to reject motions to implement changes to parliamentary constituency boundaries, changes championed by the Conservatives. Each party accused the other of bad faith.

The Coalition survived the full five years of the Parliament, facilitated by each side having some outlet for expressing a distinctive party view. This case study shows the importance of the parliamentary parties as the means to facilitate such expression. They enabled each party to the coalition to maintain its integrity, without losing its identity as part of a coalition government.

Primary sources

- HM Government (2010) *The Coalition: Our Programme for Government*, London: Cabinet Office. Online at: https://www.gov.uk/government/uploads/system/uploads/attachment_data/file/78977/coalition_programme_for_government.pdf [accessed 28 July 2017].

- Jack, M., Hutton, M., Johnson, C., Miller, D., Patrick, S., and Sandall, A. (2011) *Erskine May: Parliamentary Practice*, 24th edition, London: Butterworths/Lexis Nexis.

→ FURTHER CASE STUDIES

- The removal of Iain Duncan Smith MP as Conservative Party leader (2003).
- Owen Smith MP's challenge to Jeremy Corbyn for the role of Labour Party leader (2016).
- The 1922 Committee.

References

BEER, S. (1969) *Modern British Politics*, London: Faber and Faber.

BRAND, J. (1992) *British Parliamentary Parties*, Oxford: Clarendon Press.

COWLEY, P. (2015) 'The coalition and Parliament' in A. Seldon and M. Finn (eds.), *The Coalition Effect 2010–2015*, Cambridge: Cambridge University Press, pp. 136–56.

CROWE, E. (1986) 'The Web of Authority: Party Loyalty and Social Control in the British House of Commons', *Legislative Studies Quarterly*, Vol. 11, pp. 161–85.

KING, A. (1976) 'Modes of Executive–Legislative Relations: Great Britain, France, and West Germany', *Legislative Studies Quarterly*, Vol. 1 (1), 11–34.

MINKIN, L. (2014) *The Blair Supremacy*, Manchester: Manchester University Press.

NORTON, P. (1979) 'The organisation of Parliamentary parties' in S. A. Walkland, (ed.), *The House of Commons in the Twentieth Century*, Oxford: Clarendon Press, pp. 7–68.

NORTON, P. (1980) *Dissension in the House of Commons 1974–1979*, Oxford: Clarendon Press.

NORTON, P. (1994) 'The Parliamentary Party and Party Committees' in A. Seldon and S. Ball (eds.), *Conservative Century*, Oxford: Oxford University Press, pp. 97–145.

NORTON, P. (2013) *The Voice of the Backbenchers: The 1922 Committee: the first 90 years, 1923–2013*, London: Conservative History Group.

NORTON, P. (2015) 'The coalition and the Conservatives' in A. Seldon and M. Finn (eds.), *The Coalition Effect 2010–2015*, Cambridge: Cambridge University Press, pp. 467–91.

3

The Administrative Organization and Governance of Parliament

Sarah Petit and Ben Yong

INTRODUCTION

This chapter is about *House governance*—the way in which the Houses of Parliament are each directed, managed, and led. It thus excludes all discussion of procedure, and instead concerns the administration (used synonymously in this chapter with governance) of services to parliamentarians, and how that is organized. It is not usually a subject which thrills. But how parliamentary resources and infrastructure are managed with a view to the short, medium, and long-term are vital: without efficient and effective administration, the two Houses of Parliament cannot act to meet their institutional and constitutional functions. House governance is therefore of fundamental importance to understanding 'how Parliament works'.

The peculiar nature of Parliament

We begin with a broad proposition: Parliament is a 'they, not an it' (Shepsle 1992, 239). It is shorthand for a bundle of sometimes overlapping institutions and functions. Parliament has five features which make governance and reform of governance difficult.

First, like all legislatures, Westminster faces serious problems of collective action: each House consists of politicians who are nominally equal—this makes it difficult for them to act collectively (Loewenberg 2011, 49). Moreover, in Parliament's intensely politicized environment, disagreement is inevitable (Leston-Bandeira 2014, 422): proposed changes to the administration of Parliament may be difficult to separate from political perspectives, and as such, difficult to get agreement on. Second, the government exercises a strong influence over decisions made in and about the legislature. This is particularly clear in the UK due to its specific form of parliamentary system, which implies a fusion between the executive and the legislature, and often results in situations where the executive commands a majority of the House of Commons (but not necessarily in the House of Lords). Third, Parliament's functions within the constitution are ambiguous—it is expected to scrutinize, but also authorize, the work of the executive. Due to this, and the previous feature, reforms which enhance the effectiveness of Parliament as a 'check' on the executive have been regarded with deep ambivalence. Fourth, Westminster is a bicameral legislature: each House is fiercely protective of its own interests and privileges. Hence, each House is wary of changes which might affect its own autonomy and status. Finally, Parliament is effectively self-regulating: neither House administration is subject to formal external scrutiny processes.

These features reflect the unique nature of Parliament: it is the most political of all institutions, and yet its administration must act in a non-political way in order to respect all political allegiances (Leston-Bandeira 2014, 421). Its governance structures reflect this; it lacks the singular leadership of public sector entities. The result of these features is that changes in governance arrangements in each House have tended to be abrupt in nature. While there have been some slow, almost invisible shifts to the governance arrangements over long periods of time, radical changes in governance were more often responses to 'external shocks' to the system—i.e. made in response to some exogenous event (such as the expenses scandal in 2009, or the controversy in 2014 over the appointment of a new Clerk of the Commons), rather than being internally initiated. Thus, governance reforms have tended to lack a long-term strategic vision for House administration. This means that Parliament finds it difficult to act in a coherent way and carry out its core constitutional functions in an efficient and effective manner.

House governance and administration

In each House there is a governing body—the statutory House of Commons Commission and the non-statutory House of Lords Commission—which have historically consisted of the leaders of the key parties or groups in each House. These governing bodies ostensibly set the strategic direction of the particular House they govern. The Commission is usually chaired by the respective House's presiding officer (e.g. the Commons Speaker); other members include the leaders of the major political parties, representative backbenchers, and very recently, non-executive members. The presiding officer may also chair Chamber debates, serve as the key political figurehead for the House as a whole (although this is not so in the Lords), and, along with the Clerk, is the key officer for the administration of each House.

 Parliamentary terms House of Commons Commission

The statutory body responsible for overseeing the administration of the House of Commons.

There is a Management Board (Lords) and an Executive Committee and Board (Commons), responsible for the day-to-day administration of each House, and implementation of the Commissions' strategies. These mostly consist of permanent staff: the legislature's own civil servants, expected to assist all legislators while maintaining political neutrality. In the Lords, the Management Board is chaired by the Clerk of the Parliaments, the most senior official in that House. The Clerk is both chief procedural adviser to the presiding officer and CEO to parliamentary staff as a whole. In the Commons, the role of the Clerk of the House is similar, but following the 2015–16 reforms many of their administrative responsibilities now lie with a Director General.

 Parliamentary terms Clerk of the Parliaments

The most senior official in the House of Lords.

 Parliamentary terms Clerk of the House

The most senior official in the House of Commons.

Finally, the governance of Parliament's administration is supported by a set of 'domestic com-mittees' (so-called because they deal with internal matters of House governance; by compari-son, select committees look 'outward' towards the work of the executive), such as the Finance Committee in each House—responsible for preparing and scrutinizing the House's budget and expenditure. These have traditionally been comprised entirely of parliamentarians. They are forums through which parliamentarians in each House are connected to the political and administrative leadership (i.e. the Commissions and senior House officials). They usually advise the respective Commission on finance, services, and administration, and in some cases domestic committee chairs also sit on the Commission.

Such is the basic structure of governance in both Houses (see UK Parliament 2017a, 2017b). But focusing on formal structure would tell us little about where power over gov-ernance resides, and how change takes place. The presiding officer in each House is not like a minister of a government department: they may speak for the House on a limited range of matters (such as public outreach), but they do not govern. They cannot set the strategic direction of the House single-handedly—that is the Commission's responsibil-ity. Their influence over administration usually stems from their day-to-day involvement with House staff. The Commissions, on the other hand, in practice are limited in action by the very different interests of their members and their necessarily limited involvement in administration. Moreover, the 'usual channels' (i.e. the leader and shadow leader of the Houses, the chief whips of the major parties) tend to prefer things to stay as they are. This is particularly so given it is assumed that the Houses are there, at least in part, to support the executive. Finally, the role of the domestic committees is explicitly advisory—they may provide 'voice' for the 'customers' of the Houses (i.e. parliamentarians), but their recom-mendations are not binding.

Thus, historically, it has been the Parliamentary officials who have managed each House on a day-to-day basis and who, by default, have engaged in incremental reform (usually of a non-controversial nature). There are around 2,500 House of Commons staff and about 500 House of Lords staff. In both Houses, staff are broadly organized into functional groups such as committees, research and information, and corporate services. As permanent staff (permanent in the sense that they do not leave following a general election), House staff are perhaps best placed to see where changes need to be made, and how to carry them out. But they too are limited in what they can do: being politically neutral, they must be careful not to be identified with any particular cause in such an intensely political arena. This means that broader, strategic direction and governance reforms cannot explicitly come from them.

Finally, it should be clear that the difficulties of governance are compounded when any joint action between the Houses is considered. That said, in recent years there has been growing pressure on both Houses to work together and share services, particularly in the wake of growing concerns about security, intense pressure on budgetary matters, and the impending Restoration and Renewal Programme of the Palace of Westminster (see Case Study 6). So, for instance, there is now a joint Parliamentary Digital Service supporting Members of both Houses.

Contemporary developments

House of Commons

The framework for the current administration was set by the House of Commons Administration Act 1978, which established the House of Commons Commission and gave the House formal responsibility for its staffing and expenditure. This followed the 1975 Bottomley Committee's Report, which found that existing governance arrangements (a group of Commissioners consisting primarily of ministers) were outdated. Between 1978 and 2010, piecemeal reforms focused on the management of resources and the professionalization of the House Service—for example, adding an element of external challenge (i.e. laypeople) to governance arrangements which previously exclusively involved Members. Of these reforms, the Ibbs Report (House of Commons Commission 1990) was perhaps the most important: it led to a more robust financial management system and the transfer of responsibility for maintaining the Parliamentary Estate from the Department of the Environment to Parliament.

However, recommendations for more significant modernization of the management of the House Service through the introduction of professional organizational machinery, processes, and systems foundered without internal or external impetus to drive them through. In 2007, the Tebbit Review cautioned that the House Service had been too slow to respond to previous reports because there was no strong impetus, in part because it had not faced the same level of external pressure experienced by government departments or commercial organizations.

This warning hit home when the *Daily Telegraph* published details of expenses claimed by MPs via the Additional Costs Allowance in 2009—including details of duck houses and moats—to huge public outcry. The expenses scandal, which cost the Commons Speaker Michael Martin his job, was widely regarded as a failure by both the political leadership of the House and the administration to challenge MPs who are not, after all, employees. It was also considered to be a result of the reluctance of successive prime ministers to raise the salary of MPs in line with independent recommendations.

It was the government which took action to address this. It put an end to self-regulation by transferring responsibility for MPs' pay and allowance to a new Independent Parliamentary Standards Authority (IPSA), established by statute in 2009. The implementation of the new arrangements was—and continues to be—unpopular with many MPs who find the new requirements placed on them excessively time-consuming and burdensome. But it was essential for the leaderships of all political parties facing election the following year to demonstrate their ability to take speedy action in response to public concern.

While its constitutional position means that Parliament has not been subject to the same austerity measures as most other public bodies, the House of Commons has, since 2010, imposed upon itself a measure of financial restraint: through an efficiencies programme carried out in the last Parliament, the House Service reduced its budget by 17.5 per cent over four years (House of Commons Commission 2014, 5). The Commons has avoided further significant criticism in relation to financial management and control (though trust in MPs' integrity remains low), but found itself embroiled in 2014 in a governance crisis of an entirely different nature, as we explore in Case Study 3. This crisis led to the House reviewing its governance arrangements for the first time in 40 years.

More recent events have tested where the limits of Parliamentary administration lie. Historically, the House Service has been funded to provide accommodation and services for Members of Parliament in Westminster, but not in their constituencies. The murder of Jo Cox MP in June 2016 has led to considerable pressure from MPs to extend the reach of the House Services to cover security measures in their constituencies (to supplement support from local police forces). This poses a wider question about what MPs need to be effective.

House of Lords

The governance of the Lords has been slower to change than that of the Commons. The non-elected and relatively subordinate nature of the House meant that there was little pressure, either internally or externally, to reform governance arrangements. For decades, House management and services were run in a mostly autonomous fashion, with limited control by House peers or external oversight. This only began to change at the beginning of the twenty-first century, following Labour's removal of most hereditary peers in 1999, shifting the composition of the Lords towards appointed peers. The House redefined itself more as a Chamber of scrutiny, and pressure began to build on resources. Below, we briefly focus on two governance reforms: the 2001 and 2016 rationalizations of administrative structures, and a 'non-reform', the creation of the Lord Speakership.

In 2001, the Select Committee on the House of Lords' Offices carried out a review of the Lords' governance structure, and found it severely wanting. In particular, there was a deep lack of clarity about who was responsible for what, and very little overall strategic direction. So, for instance, the then governing body of the Lords, the Offices Committee, consisted of an unwieldy 28 people—such a large body could not, in practice, provide leadership for governance and administration. The Tordoff Review (named after its Chair, Lord Tordoff) led to the establishment of a governance structure similar to that of the Commons: a much smaller House Committee, a Board of Management, and domestic committees which would act as user groups. A later 2007 review, however, hinted that although there had been improvement, there continued to be limited strategic direction from the House Committee, and domestic committees were not functioning in the way intended.

Tony Blair's decision in 2003 to abolish (later amended to 'reform') the post of Lord Chancellor was an opportunity for the Lords to create an office of Lord Speaker with greater autonomy, responsibility, and authority for administration. Historically, the key link between parliamentarians and the administration in the Lords has been the Chairman of Committees (now confusingly known as the Senior Deputy Speaker). This was due to their role as Chair of key domestic committees (including the House Committee, the equivalent of the Commons House Commission), and their office's physical proximity to that of the Clerk of the Parliaments. But office holders have always been appointed via the usual channels: thus, they have often been conservative.

The office that was finally created in 2005 was limited in scope. Most of the Lords' energy was devoted to ensuring the new office would not become a Commons-style Speaker (which would offend the Lords' view of all peers as equals in the Chamber). The Lord Speaker was to be elected, and become the public face of the Lords. They would now chair the House Committee, but had very little connection with the administrative staff of the House, except in matters of security. The Chairman of Committees remained the key link between peers and the administration. The result was that the Lords now had a triumvirate of officers: the Leader and Speaker sharing quasi-presiding officer status, the Lord Speaker being the public face of the Lords, and the Chairman of Committees being the administrative face.

The most recent governance reforms in 2016 reflect this chapter's general thesis that governance reform tends to be a response to 'external' pressures. Following a report and the House's agreement, certain domestic committees were merged and responsibilities clarified via explicit delegation. Moreover, external members were to be appointed to the (newly named) House of Lords Commission. The change came about because of concerns about transparency, but, more importantly, increasing daily attendance (brought about by appointments by successive prime ministers, which put pressure on scarce resources), and the impending Restoration and Renewal Programme of the Palace of Westminster. The new structure was intended to reflect the 2015–16 governance changes made in the Commons, and allow the two Houses to work together in a more coherent fashion.

Conclusion

Parliament's peculiar nature as a public institution consisting of two separate Houses of nominal equals and somewhat ambiguous goals, being subject to the strong influence of the executive and (for many years) limited internal or external oversight, has meant that its administrative and governance arrangements have rarely been subject to scrutiny. Change, where it has come, has mostly been of an incremental nature. It has usually taken external pressure or a crisis before reforms of a more serious nature have been considered.

Two future developments may introduce new elements to parliamentary governance and administration. The first is the restoration and renewal of the Palace of Westminster. If the Joint Committee's recommendations are accepted by Parliament, Members of both Houses will sit together on a Sponsor Board to oversee delivery of the programme by an arms-length Delivery Authority. The Commissions of the two Houses currently meet jointly only occasionally; increased interaction on the Board may lead to more joined-up working between the two political leaderships on other issues. At the same time, the establishment of a Delivery Authority will add a layer of complexity, but will also distance both Parliament and its government representatives from the (multimillion pound) decision-making process, perhaps circumventing the problems of collective action and executive interference in the work of the House that we have alluded to.

The second is the issue of shared parliamentary services. Since 2007, the two Houses have had a statutory power to create joint departments, a power they have exercised once in creating the Parliamentary Digital Service. One of the recommendations of the House of Commons Governance Committee, in 2014, was to 'begin the process of drawing up a phased medium-term programme towards a single bicameral services department' (House of Commons Governance Committee 2014, 73). A joint working programme was established to consider how the two Houses might share more services while safeguarding their constitutional independence from one another. This was driven by pressure from across the political spectrum on grounds of cost—influenced by recent governments' austerity agenda—and featured prominently in evidence to the Governance Committee. It has, however, now fallen off the political radar.

Further Reading

Cocks, B. (1977) *Mid-Victorian Masterpiece: The Story of an Institution Unable to Put its own House in Order*, London: Hutchinson.

Leston-Bandeira, C. (2014) 'The pursuit of legitimacy as a key driver for public engagement: the European Parliament case', *Parliamentary Affairs*, Vol. 67 (2), pp. 415–36.

Loewenberg, G. (2011) *On Legislatures: The Puzzle of Representation*, Boulder: Paradigm Publishers.

Winetrobe, B. (1998) 'The autonomy of Parliament' in Dawn Oliver and Gavin Drewry (eds.), *The Law and Parliament*, London: Butterworths, pp. 14–32.

Case Study 3: The House of Commons Governance Committee

INTRODUCTION

The Governance Committee was established in 2014 to determine a seemingly innocuous question—who would be the next Clerk of the House of Commons? In this case study we explore why this issue became headline news, why a select committee was required, and what it tells us about the governance of the House of Commons.

WHAT HAPPENED?

In April 2014, the Clerk of the House of Commons announced his retirement. As Clerk and Chief Executive, Sir Robert Rogers was both the primary source of procedural advice to the House, and ultimately responsible for the delivery of all the services provided by the House Service. The Clerk is formally appointed by the sovereign, but the selection process is chaired by the Speaker. For the first time, the post was open to candidates from outside Parliament, and Speaker Bercow announced the appointment of Carol Mills, an Australian parliamentary official. The suitability of Mills to fill the role was immediately challenged by some Members of Parliament on the grounds that she had no procedural experience; further Members and sections of the media hostile to Bercow also voiced their dissent. A 'pause' was then announced.

To resolve the resulting impasse, the House established a Governance Committee under the chairmanship of Jack Straw (a former Leader of the House and an MP well respected by both sides of the House) in 2014, tasked with considering 'the governance of the House of Commons, including the future allocation of the responsibilities for House services currently exercised by the Clerk of the House and Chief Executive' (HC Debates, 10 September 2014, c. 1014).

The Committee took oral and written evidence from a wide range of MPs, House staff, and external governance experts, and published its recommendations in December 2014—the vast majority of which were later implemented. The Committee recommended that the paused recruitment process be formally terminated; that the Clerk of the House should remain Head of the House Service, but should not also be titled Chief Executive; and that a new post of Director General should be created, reporting to the Clerk, but with clearly delineated autonomous responsibilities for the delivery of services. The Acting Clerk, David Natzler, was subsequently appointed Clerk of the House, and an outside appointment was made to the post of Director General.

The inquiry went much further than this specific issue and made a number of other recommendations regarding the role and membership of the House of Commons Commission, in order to deliver 'an organisational framework which will enable the House to operate more effectively and efficiently' (Governance Committee 2014, 3). It highlighted what members of the Committee saw as the key challenges facing the House of Commons over the coming years—political and constitutional change, engaging the public in its work, making efficient use of resources, and delivering the restoration and renewal of the Palace of Westminster—and made recommendations (such as encouraging shared services) aimed to deliver an organizational structure and culture to meet these challenges head on.

WHAT DOES THIS TELL US ABOUT THE GOVERNANCE OF PARLIAMENT?

This was the first time that Members of the House of Commons had considered how well it was run in 40 years (the last one being the 1975 Bottomley Report, although there had been three reviews run by external consultants between 1990 and 2007). The inquiry was, in effect, an accident, triggered by a political row which made it expedient for Members, as well as the media, to take a rare interest in this issue. Because of the government's customary majority in the Commons, and the way in which parliamentary business is decided, select committees can only be set up with executive support, and the internal processes of the House of Commons are rarely at the top of any government's agenda. At least initially, it was the opportunity to damage a Speaker who was seen to have increased the power of Parliament at the government's expense which moved the issue up the political agenda. Additionally, although the service MPs receive from the House administration is naturally of interest to them, House governance tends not to be of burning interest to MPs either, who are busy enough engaging with their constituents, their party, their careers, and the pressing issues of the day. Like the IPSA example cited earlier, it took a very particular, high-profile circumstance to force this level of engagement.

Secondly, the circumstances leading to the establishment of the Governance Committee demonstrated the challenge of collective decision-making for the House of Commons administration. Although partially driven by political expediency, the debate about the role of the Clerk, and the most suitable candidate to fill it, also reflected a genuine discrepancy of views between 'traditionalist' MPs who valued the status quo, and those frustrated by an organization they perceived as outdated and unprofessional. The former were not content to abide by a decision taken by a representative of the latter, despite the formal authority he possessed. The Committee was a means of mediating between these views and tackling the underlying issues exposed by the row. As the Committee's report noted, 'the Commons is run by its 650 Members, who have all been through the hard test of election and who are skilled at articulating concerns and making an argument. This places it in a different position not only from PLCs in the private sector, but from every other public institution' (Governance Committee 2014, 9). The fact that an official appointment could effectively be overturned by Members who were not involved in the formal selection process highlights the difficulty House governance bodies face every day in taking and—critically—implementing contentious decisions: from multimillion pound building projects, to compliance with cyber-security requirements, to the price of a cup of tea in the canteen.

Finally, the conclusions of the report itself highlighted the scale of the challenges facing Parliament as a whole over the coming years, and the growing complexity involved in running the organization. It made a compelling argument both for building capacity/professional expertise among the workforce who serve Parliament, and for strong leadership on the part of politicians to take the tough strategic and financial decisions that lie ahead.

In a sense, the Governance Committee is the exception that proves the rule in relation to the core argument outlined in our chapter. It was a rare example of where, in setting up the Committee, the government gave time to the administration of the House; where politicians were genuinely interested in discussing the governance of the House; where, in agreeing the report, politicians who began the process with divergent views came to a common agreement on the issues under discussion; and where subsequent decisions about the governance of the House had genuine legitimacy, and have become fixed. The unplanned nature of its establishment, and the lack of an established mechanism for resolving the original impasse and the wider questions it exposed, do however, demonstrate the unique challenges parliamentarians face in governing themselves.

Primary sources

- Governance Committee (2014) *House of Commons Governance: Report of Session 2014–15*, London: The Stationery Office, HC 692. Online at: https://www.publications.parliament.uk/pa/cm201415/cmselect/cmgovern/692/692.pdf [accessed 27 June 2017].

- Leader's Group on Governance (2016) *Governance of Domestic Committees in the House of Lords: Report of Session 2015–16*, House of Lords, HL 81. Online at: https://www.publications.parliament.uk/pa/ld201516/ldselect/ldleader/81/81.pdf [accessed 27 June 2017].

FURTHER CASE STUDIES

- The creation of the post of Lord Speaker in the House of Lords (2005).
- The Tebbit Review of the Management and Services of the House of Commons (2007).
- Parliament and the expenses scandal (2009).

References

GOVERNANCE COMMITTEE (2014) *House of Commons Governance: Report of Session 2014–15*, London: The Stationery Office, HC 692. Online at: https://www.publications.parliament.uk/pa/cm201415/cmselect/cmgovern/692/692.pdf [accessed 27 June 2017].

HOUSE OF COMMONS COMMISSION (1990) *House of Commons Services*, London: The Stationery Office, HC 38 (The Ibbs Report).

HOUSE OF COMMONS COMMISSION (2014) *Financial Year 2013/14: Thirty-sixth report of the Commission and annual report of the Administration Estimate Audit Committee*, London: The Stationery Office, HC 596. Online at: http://www.parliament.uk/documents/commons-commission/36-report-HC-596.pdf [accessed 27 June 2017].

LESTON-BANDEIRA, C. (2014) 'The pursuit of legitimacy as a key driver for public engagement: the European Parliament case', *Parliamentary Affairs*, Vol. 67 (2), pp. 415–36.

LOEWENBERG, G. (2011) *On Legislatures: The puzzle of representation*, Boulder: Paradigm Publishers.

SHEPSLE, K. (1992) 'Congress Is a "They," Not an "It": Legislative Intent as Oxymoron', *International Review of Law and Economics*, Vol. 12 (2), pp. 239–56.

UK PARLIAMENT (2017a) *The Governance Structure of the House of Commons Administration*. Online at: http://www.parliament.uk/documents/commons-governance-office/governance-structure-commons-administration.pdf [accessed 27 June 2017].

UK PARLIAMENT (2017b) *House of Lords Commission and Domestic Committees*. Online at: http://www.parliament.uk/business/lords/house-lords-administration/how-the-lords-is-run/lords-administration/domestic-select-committees/ [accessed 27 June 2017].

4

Supporting Members and Peers

Marc Geddes and Jessica Mulley

INTRODUCTION

Chapter 3 covered the way Parliament is administered and organized. In this chapter, we ask more directly what this means in terms of the support offered by Parliament as an institution to Members of Parliament and peers to fulfil their parliamentary, political, and policy functions. Though often overlooked, staff play a crucial role in Parliament through the invaluable and impartial support they offer in both Houses. There are around 2,500 members of staff in the House of Commons and 500 in the House of Lords, and further staff in the bicameral Parliamentary Digital Service. As well as providing support to run Parliament efficiently, they offer policy and procedural advice. They also offer an institutional memory and act as gatekeepers or guardians of knowledge, all of which indicate that staff are placed in an important position vis-à-vis parliamentarians.

In this chapter, we argue three things. First, MPs and peers have a range of sources of support in carrying out their role (not all of which come from parliamentary staff). Second, the resources available to parliamentarians have increased significantly over the past 20 years through a range of parliamentary reforms. Third, and perhaps most importantly, the way parliamentarians are supported is an inherently political decision because of the finite resources available to Parliament and the contested nature of delivering targeted support given the diversity of roles that MPs and peers perform.

Sources of support

Political

MPs and peers have a range of sources of parliamentary and policy support available to them. The party with which they are affiliated will provide support, especially around policy analysis. MPs' staffing allowances are provided from the public purse via the Independent Parliamentary Standards Authority (IPSA), but, within that, MPs have discretion to design their own staffing structures and many choose to appoint policy staff or research assistants, on whom they may rely to whatever extent they choose (Dale 2015). There is a mass of lobby organizations and single-issue interest groups able to provide information and policy analysis too, either proactively or reactively. For instance, all-party parliamentary groups (APPGs) bring together interested MPs and peers providing support and advice on specific issues, and often involve stakeholders from outside Parliament in their policy work and administration (see Chapter 11).

Non-political

The support provided to MPs and peers is distinctive in a number of ways. Typically, staff of either House are permanent appointees, serving in one capacity or another for decades or more. Parliamentary staff do not change at the time of a general election or with a mid-term change in the administration. This has long been the position in Parliament and is intended to frame and underline staff independence from the political machinery of party and government. So support is provided on an impartial basis, one which does not favour one party's position over another, and is available equally to all. This is crucial to ensure the effective functioning of legislative support: all parties need to be able to trust the support given to them by Parliament. The permanence and longevity of impartial support also means that staff can act as an institutional memory for parliamentary procedure.

Staff perform a number of distinctive roles (summarized in Table 4.1). In the House of Commons and House of Lords libraries, policy specialists will concentrate on providing impartial policy analysis on topical matters. Some of this is provided at a generic level through 'debate packs' in advance of debates, while some is provided confidentially through the libraries' inquiry services where only the requesting MP or peer will receive information. In parliamentary committees, officials are essential to the effective functioning of committee tasks. Importantly, this will include a clerk of the committee who, rather than being a policy specialist, will have expertise and experience in parliamentary processes. They are crucial to ensure that committees work in a fair manner and comply with the procedures set out by the House of Commons or House of Lords. A committee will have a broader team of policy specialists and administrative staff, as Case Study 4 demonstrates. Elsewhere, staff provide advice and support to MPs and peers on specific topics, for instance the Parliamentary Office of Science and Technology. Also known as POST, this offers scientific advice across the Houses of Parliament, and has seen a steady increase in both its funding and remit since it was introduced in 1989. For example, in 2013, in partnership with the Economic and Social Research Council (and with support from University College London), POST established a dedicated Social Sciences Section to integrate social science research. The expanding role of POST has been important in strengthening wide-ranging scientific notes, known as POSTnotes, which are available to parliamentarians and to the public.

It is important to note that the House of Commons and House of Lords services are delivered independently and tailored to the needs of Members in each House. As a result, there are differences between the services available from Parliament to MPs and peers, and it is they themselves who decide from whom to draw their support. There is no obligation to use services provided by Parliament if they are not required or if advice can be sought from elsewhere. This freedom ensures parliamentarians have primacy in deciding how to enact their role, but it also means that decisions on the targeting of finite resources are inherently political. Parliamentary staff could be involved in emphasizing certain aspects of an MP or peer's work, which could condition it one way or another.

This can be clearly ascertained by examining the different types of support available to MPs. They are not necessarily familiar with all the procedures and workings of the House of Commons, so staff in the Table Office or Journal Office can offer crucial support. This support is key for MPs' participation in parliamentary functions, such as debates in the main Chamber or Westminster Hall, submitting Early Day Motions (EDMs), etc. They may also require support in order to carry out their role in law-making. This may include assistance with understanding established processes, and procedural advice (answering questions along the lines of 'How do I …?'), which is largely drawn from specialist staff in the legislation offices in each House (e.g. Public and Private Bill Offices). Alternatively, MPs may want assistance with policy implications, which, at a general level, is drawn from policy specialists in the House of Commons Library (or Lords Library for peers).

Table 4.1 Selected parliamentary services available to MPs and peers

Service	Description
Public and Private Bill Offices	Administer all business relating to legislation and provide advice to MPs and others on public and private legislation. The House of Lords has equivalent offices.
Journal Office	Manages the procedural knowledge and knowledge of the law and privileges of the House, as well as providing the secretariat for the Standards, Procedure, Privileges and Petitions Committees and the Speaker's Committees on IPSA and the Electoral Commission. The House of Lords has an equivalent office.
Table Office	Assists MPs in tabling Parliamentary Questions (PQs) and Early Day Motions (EDMs). It also coordinates clerk support in the Chamber and Westminster Hall, and produces the House of Commons' order papers and associated business papers. It provides the secretariat for the Backbench Business Committee.
Vote Office	Supplies parliamentary and government documents (including EU documents) to MPs and others. The equivalent in the House of Lords is the Printed Paper Office.
Committee Office	Provides secretariat, advice, research, and administrative services for each of the House of Commons' departmental select committees and most other select committees. It also contains the Scrutiny Unit, and the Web and Publications Unit. The House of Lords has an equivalent for its committees.
The Official Report (Hansard)	Provides a record of the proceedings in the House of Commons and House of Lords. It is a verbatim report of proceedings in the Chamber, Westminster Hall, and public bill committees as well as written answers and written ministerial statements.
Library	Provides impartial information and research services for MPs, peers, and their staff in support of their parliamentary duties. Among other things, it produces briefing papers and debate packs. It also has an enquiry service for confidential research enquiries. The House of Lords also has an equivalent library.
POST	Parliament's in-house source of independent, balanced, and accessible analysis of public policy issues related to science and technology.

Note: This list excludes administrative and logistic support (e.g. parliamentary security, catering, estates, etc.)

An MP may also require direct support in order to fulfil Parliament's scrutiny and oversight function, holding the government to account. This may be drawn from the Library, for instance through one of their research briefings, or, if an MP is serving on a select committee, from the Committee Office staff team. Committee staff may also offer procedural advice to their committee members, especially where this is relevant to the work of their committee. Committee teams are tailored to their committee remits: the Treasury Committee, for example, has economic advisers among its staff, while the Justice Committee staff team often includes a lawyer. Staff in the Table Office may support MPs in tabling parliamentary questions (oral or written). Parliamentary officials may also offer indirect support for constituency work. MPs can make requests through the Library's inquiry service for bespoke research and analysis to assist with and inform their constituency work. For example, an MP may want to know the specific breakdown of poverty levels, or the number of students in their constituency.

Parliamentary terms Public Bill Office

Administers all business relating to legislation and provides advice to MPs and others on public legislation. The House of Lords has an equivalent office.

 Parliamentary terms Journal Office

The office responsible for the *House of Commons Journal*, the formal record of proceedings in the House, and for advice on Commons procedure and privilege. The House of Lords has an equivalent office.

 Parliamentary terms Table Office

The Commons office in which parliamentary questions, motions for the Order Paper, and EDMs may be tabled.

All of these services are available to MPs (with equivalents for peers) free of charge but they are limited by capacity. As already mentioned, there are only around 2,500 members of staff in the House of Commons Service, so there are finite resources regarding what staff can offer. This means that, across Parliament, services are largely reactive and provided at the request of MPs or peers. So, for example, libraries will produce debate packs shortly before debates in plenary session; other services are provided following direct requests from parliamentarians. A more proactive service could politicize Parliament's impartial service because it would play a role in deciding what resources to emphasize to parliamentarians.

Growing services

Support available to MPs and peers has increased significantly over the past 15 years. There were only 800 members of staff in the House of Commons Service in 1981 (Ryle 1981), which increased to approximately 1,300 in 2000–1 (House of Commons Commission 2001), reaching the figure of over 2,000 in 2015 (House of Commons Commission 2015). Meanwhile, the House of Lords currently employs approximately 500 members of staff (UK Parliament 2017). These increases have occurred for a number of reasons, predominantly due to a growth and increase in complexity of services, as well as the need to make those resources more flexible and responsive.

With respect to select committees, there has been a steady growth of support to the secretariat. This has often happened alongside reforms to increase the effectiveness of Parliament in scrutinizing the executive (e.g. directly electing chairs in 2010 has led to the introduction of further institutional support). In 2004, the Committee Office introduced a Scrutiny Unit to pool resources and offer specific support for financial and legal scrutiny across committees. More recently, a dedicated Media Service has been introduced, as well as a Web and Publications Unit in an attempt to improve the communication of committees and to produce reports. Increasingly, resources are shared in these units or co-located physically as part of a shift to offer more holistic support. Since 2016, for example, an experimental 'procedural hub' has been created—a one-stop shop for procedural advice, available to both MPs and their staff—which offers advice and guidance on parliamentary business in a more holistic manner. In the past, procedural advice was drawn almost exclusively from clerks working out of small groups of procedural offices (see Table 4.1). These reforms typify a more general trend in Parliament to provide services which are customer-driven, easier to access, and more tailored to the ways in which MPs and peers work. Co-location and sharing institutional support, for example, ensures that there exists a flexible pool of expertise that can be readily deployed to MPs and peers in a bespoke manner.

A number of these changes took place following wider reforms to the decision-making structures for the House of Commons. In 2014, the House of Commons Governance Committee recommended the appointment of a Director General. This saw changes to allow for a more customer-focused service. The changes are still being implemented, and are identified as only Phase One of much wider reforms to transform the way the House of Commons serves MPs (House of Commons Director General 2016). However, while these changes were sparked in response to a specific crisis over the role of Clerk of the Commons (see Case Study 3), the changes to the way Parliament offers its support to MPs and peers reflect wider changes in the role of Parliament in British politics. Importantly, the balance of power between the executive and the legislature has shifted (even if only incrementally) to strengthen the scrutiny capacity for Parliament. For example, the shift from appointing MPs to select committees in the House of Commons (often informally through the usual channels) to a system of elections (direct elections for chairs and indirect for members) has removed an informal power of the whips and given Parliament more control over scrutiny. Committee chairs have since increased their resources to reflect their growing role in the House of Commons. Academic research has consistently shown that Parliament is an influential actor in the policy process (for an overview, see Russell and Cowley 2016). Elsewhere, we have seen the growing independence of the role of MP (Cowley and Stuart 2014), indicating a need for greater resources for MPs, not reliant on their political parties. So while resources for Parliament have grown, they have done so alongside wider changes to Parliament's role.

Key issues and debates

This discussion, and the developments over the past 15 years, raise a number of further questions. We cannot provide answers here, but pose these questions for further study by parliamentary scholars, students, and practitioners. First, there is a question of quantity versus quality of support available. While we have given an indication of the changing way the Service is organized, we give no indication of whether these changes have been effective. There is also an underlying question about the reasons for the growth of resources. While we imply a link between growing scrutiny capacities and resources, this broader institutional account can be supplemented by a more actor-centred analysis. In other words, has the change of resources come about because parliamentarians are dissatisfied with their service or because parliamentary staff believe that politicians need to have further institutional support—e.g. were the reforms MP-driven or staff-driven? This question aims to problematize the notion that support is delivered to MPs and peers in a neutral manner. Choices over where resources are emphasized (e.g. increasing support for directly elected select committee chairs rather than the House of Lords Library) and who makes those decisions reveals the broader priorities of, and power relationships between, parliamentarians in how they undertake their functions.

Third, and more fundamentally, there is an issue over who staff exist to serve: is it to support the institution of Parliament or to support parliamentarians? This issue is brought out in the following interview with a Member of Parliament, quoted in Tinkler and Mehta (2016, 16): 'MPs want services that will help them carry out their duties more effectively but don't know if these services exist; the House Service provides services but does not understand the work of MPs.' This question brings us back once again to our belief that the support offered to staff is an inherently political issue. This chapter has predominantly concentrated on the needs of MPs and peers, but if you look at it from the perspective of staff, then you come to understand the complexities of the role they must fulfil (see Case Study 4). Even though parliamentary staff are assumed to be politically neutral, this does not quite capture the reality of the difficult choices they have to make in offering support for their political masters. Choices over resources have a direct impact on the ability of parliamentarians to carry out their functions. Ultimately, this means that questions about support to MPs and peers are issues about power and politics.

Conclusion

Press headlines—especially from tabloid newspapers—do not shy away from pointing out the money spent on Parliament. Too often, they also imply erroneously that all expenditure on Parliament is directed at MPs and not also used to sustain a sizeable institution which provides services for others as well. In addition to intense questioning over MPs employing relatives as paid members of staff (e.g. Herbert 2013; Woodhouse 2016), the resultant perceptions around parliamentary support available to MPs and peers is rarely seen in a positive light, especially in the context of the MPs' expenses scandal (Kelso 2009). However, this negative portrayal is often associated with MPs' personal staffing arrangements and less to do with institutional support, and so less is known about the role of permanent parliamentary staff. This is not only confined to the press. Institutional support has received little attention from academic researchers. There are possibly two reasons for this. First, academic research has traditionally focused on institutional relationships, and especially the activities of politicians as part of those institutions, rather than the operational or institutional support available to politicians. This is arguably because parliamentarians are seen as the most direct and explicit political actors. Consequently, the role of staff has not been regarded as an important explanatory factor in UK legislative studies. It may also be that the staffing and administration of Parliament, albeit existing almost exclusively to sustain MPs and peers, appears dull in contrast to the vivacity of politicians. The second reason is one of access. Parliamentary staff rely on being trusted by parliamentarians to offer impartial, confidential, and equitable services to all MPs and peers. To achieve and maintain a high level of trust, the organization and its staff have arguably been reluctant to become subjects of political science.

This chapter has sought to open a debate on the role of staff, which is part of a broader trend in which Parliament is modernizing as an institution, becoming more reflective and open. The 2014 television series *Inside the Commons* typified this change with its focus on the administration and functioning of the House and the work of its Members rather than on a specific policy issue. Moreover, academic priorities have begun to shift focus, in part driven by contemporary developments in how support for MPs and peers is organized. We welcome this change of priorities and the increasing interest in parliamentary staff. As we have sought to demonstrate in this chapter, parliamentary staff offer a crucial level of support to ensure the effective functioning of Parliament. Furthermore, this is often political. So, understanding how staff shape the institution will significantly help us to understand Parliament as a whole.

Further Reading

Governance Committee (2014) *House of Commons Governance: Report of Session 2014–15*, London: The Stationery Office, HC 692. Online at: https://www.publications.parliament.uk/pa/cm201415/cmselect/cmgovern/692/692.pdf [accessed 27 June 2017].

House of Commons Director General (2016) *Director General's Review*, London: The Stationery Office. Online at: https://www.parliament.uk/documents/commons-governance-office/Director-General's-Review-Report.pdf [accessed 27 June 2017].

Ryle, M. (1981) 'The Legislative Staff of the British House of Commons', *Legislative Studies Quarterly*, Vol. 6 (4), pp. 497–519.

Case Study 4: Clerks in Parliament

INTRODUCTION

In this case study, we summarize the roles of clerks in general, and the committee clerks in particular. We demonstrate the range of support that clerks must offer and how they navigate the complex role of offering loyalty to the institution of Parliament as a whole while simultaneously offering advice and support to specific groups of MPs and peers. In this way, the case study highlights the reactive nature of the support offered by Parliament.

CONTEXT: CLERKS OF THE PARLIAMENTS

The House of Commons and House of Lords both have a leading clerk. In the House of Lords, the lead clerk is the Clerk of the Parliaments. The position has existed since at least 1315, where records are available to show that Edward II in Lincoln refers to a clerk being nominated by the King to act as a special deputy. However, the position didn't become permanent until the reign of Henry VII. Meanwhile, the formal title of the leading clerk of the House of Commons is the Under Clerk of the Parliaments. The use of the plural in both titles denotes that their appointments are for life and not just a particular Parliament. This has significant symbolic value because it highlights their independence from the monarchy, the government of the day, individual MPs and peers, or political parties, which remains crucial to this day. Staff are non-partisan servants of their House. As Chapter 4 has shown, the independence and permanence of staff is crucial to ensure they are able to offer equitable service across Parliament and across political divides.

The duties of the clerks in both the House of Lords and the House of Commons are similar. Traditionally, they include preparing minutes of proceedings, advising on proper parliamentary procedure, and announcing royal assent. The range of tasks falling to the Clerk and Under Clerk of the Parliaments has expanded greatly over the centuries and now many are fulfilled by deputies in both Houses. This brings us to the many clerks that now populate Parliament; we focus on one type in particular: the committee clerk.

COMMITTEE CLERKS IN THE HOUSE OF COMMONS

For most MPs, scrutiny is a key part of their role. Many choose to do this by serving in one of the Commons' many select committees, which have been charged with holding the government to account. To ensure that committees carry out their functions effectively, they are supported by a small secretariat. As Chapter 4 explained, this support is growing as a result of the expanding role and reputation of committees in Parliament and beyond (see also Chapter 16). At present, each committee is supported by around six permanent members of staff, including a clerk of the committee, responsible for the committee overall; a second clerk, who will lead on some inquiries and provide support to the clerk of the committee; one or two committee specialists, who are usually subject-specific experts; one or two committee assistants to provide predominantly administrative support; and finally a media officer, usually shared between committees. This is a typical structure, and at its head is the clerk.

The key function of the clerk is to support the committee to ensure that its proceedings are conducted within the rules of the House, including the compilation of proper minutes and records of the committee's formal proceedings. In practice, though, this may take only a small proportion of their time and effort. A committee clerk will also take the lead on: advising their committee on policy and other matters within its remit; planning and delivering the committee's programme of work; advising their committee's chair and other members on policy and practical matters; liaising with other committees, stakeholders, and external organizations on the committee's behalf; drafting reports against instructions either from the chair or the committee (or both) and advising members on how to submit amendments to draft reports; and overseeing the work of the secretariat as a whole (e.g. if the committee plans a visit outside Westminster, the clerk will oversee logistical arrangements). The range of roles is therefore diverse, and a committee clerk's role is often defined by the pattern of work that their chair and committee adopt. Moreover, the clerk often faces difficult choices over what support to emphasize, given that all MPs on the committee must be treated equally (e.g. if two MPs ask to take a committee in very different directions, a clerk must know how to serve them both equally).

However, that is not all. Clerks are also a key lynchpin between the work of the committee and that of the Chamber. For instance, they may assist in securing a debate on one of the committee's reports in the Chamber, or highlight where the committee's findings and recommendations have specific relevance to other parliamentary business. So, the clerk must be aware of parliamentary business at all times. Furthermore, a clerk must advise on the committee's relationship with the media too, so they must be aware of political developments outside Parliament.

WHAT DOES THIS TELL US ABOUT SUPPORT IN PARLIAMENT?

This demonstrates the diversity of a clerk's job and the extent to which a clerk must be flexible to meet the needs of parliamentarians. In Chapter 4 we have argued that parliamentary service, on an institutional level, is reactive to the needs of MPs and peers. This case study demonstrates how this plays out in the minutiae of a clerk's everyday life: the balancing of roles is unending. A committee clerk is partly a confidential procedural adviser, partly a team leader, partly a policy adviser, and partly a political manager.

Finally, a clerk must be reactive to the specific needs and wishes of each committee and its membership. This indicates that the role of staff is inherently political because it involves choices over the extent and type of support that clerks offer, and how they choose to enact this role. Clerks are often guided by the traditions and conventions of the House, which makes this job slightly more secure. However, as with politics generally, there are lots of unpredictable events and situations, and very often the clerks play a hidden but considerable role in influencing the direction of their committee.

Primary sources

- Marsden, P. (1979) *Officers of the House of Commons, 1363–1978*, London: The Stationery Office.
- Governance Committee (2014) *House of Commons Governance: Report of Session 2014–15*, London: The Stationery Office, HC 692. Online at: https://www.publications.parliament.uk/pa/cm201415/cmselect/cmgovern/692/692.pdf [accessed 27 June 2017].

- House of Commons Commission (2015) *Thirty-seventh Report of the Commission, and Annual Report of the Administration Estimate Audit Committee: Financial Year 2014/15*, London: The Stationery Office, HC 341. Online at: https://www.parliament.uk/documents/commons-commission/HoCCommission-Annual-Report-2014-15-HC341.pdf [accessed 27 June 2017].

 ## FURTHER CASE STUDIES

- The role of the House of Commons and House of Lords Libraries in giving support and advice to MPs and peers.
- Changes in the House of Commons Service following on from the report of the Governance Committee on House of Commons Governance, published in December 2014.
- The challenges faced by the Public Bill Office in giving impartial yet effective advice to MPs in making amendments to bills.

References

COWLEY, P. and STUART, M. (2014) 'In the Brown Stuff?: Labour Backbench Dissent Under Gordon Brown, 2007–10', *Contemporary British History*, Vol. 28 (1), pp. 1–23.

DALE, R. (2015) *How to be a Parliamentary Researcher*, London: Biteback Publishing.

GOVERNANCE COMMITTEE (2014) *House of Commons Governance: Report of Session 2014–15*, London: The Stationery Office, HC 692. Online at: https://www.publications.parliament.uk/pa/cm201415/cmselect/cmgovern/692/692.pdf [accessed 22 June 2017].

HERBERT, D. (2013) 'Four years after the expenses scandal 145 MPs are STILL employing family members', *Daily Mirror*, 25 August. Online at: http://www.mirror.co.uk/news/uk-news/four-years-after-expenses-scandal-2218024 [accessed 9 May 2017].

HOUSE OF COMMONS COMMISSION (2001) *Financial Year 2000–01: Twenty-third Annual Report*, London: The Stationery Office.

HOUSE OF COMMONS COMMISSION (2015) *Financial Year 2014/15: Thirty-seventh report of the Commission, and annual report of the Administration Estimate Audit Committee*, London: The Stationery Office, HC 341. Online at: https://www.parliament.uk/documents/commons-commission/HoCCommission-Annual-Report-2014-15-HC341.pdf [accessed 27 June 2017].

HOUSE OF COMMONS DIRECTOR GENERAL (2016) *Director General's Review*, London: The Stationery Office. Online at: https://www.parliament.uk/documents/commons-governance-office/Director-General's-Review-Report.pdf [accessed 9 May 2017].

KELSO, A. (2009) 'Parliament on Its Knees: MPs' Expenses and the Crisis of Transparency at Westminster', *The Political Quarterly*, Vol. 80 (3), pp. 329–38.

RUSSELL, M. and COWLEY, P. (2016) 'The Policy Power of the Westminster Parliament: The "parliamentary state" and the empirical evidence', *Governance*, Vol. 29 (1), pp. 121–37.

RYLE, M. (1981) 'The Legislative Staff of the British House of Commons', *Legislative Studies Quarterly*, Vol. 6 (4), pp. 497–519.

TINKLER, J. and MEHTA, N. (2016) *Report to the House of Commons Administration Committee on the Findings of the Interview Study with Members on Leaving Parliament*, London: The Stationery Office.

UK PARLIAMENT (2017) *House of Lords, Frequently Asked Questions*. Online at: http://www.parliament.uk/mps-lords-and-offices/offices/lords/lordshro/faqs/ [accessed 9 May 2017].

WOODHOUSE, C. (2016) 'Keeping it in the family: MPs pay spouses and kids £5.6k more on average than other staff', *The Sun*, 11 May. Online at: https://www.thesun.co.uk/archives/politics/1170407/keeping-it-in-the-family-mps-pay-spouses-and-kids-5–6k-more-on-average-than-other-staff/ [accessed 9 May 2017].

5

The Significance of Rituals in Parliament

Emma Crewe and Paul Evans

INTRODUCTION

Rituals are traditionally associated with religion and royalty, but can be found operating widely across society in sport, the military, politics, and even in the private sphere. Rituals and symbols, and the power relationships that they relate to, are important in all political institutions including Parliament. Describing all Parliament's formal and informal rituals, and the rules and symbols within them, could consume volumes, so our chapter merely highlights some to reveal their political and social significance. We explain the centrality of rules in rituals, how parliamentary debates are ritualized for various reasons (to reconcile differences or emphasize hierarchies), and how ceremonies order relationships between different groups in our political world.

The purpose of rituals

In democratic systems of government, elections are the rituals that aim to allow leaders, and their parties of government and opposition, to emerge without violence. They are moral dramas in which voters express their belonging to a particular group or faction, but also, in a general election, to a whole democratic nation. For voters, appearing at the polling station and marking their choice on a ballot in secret is their key participation in a ritual of both division and reconciliation. In contrast, the appointment of Members of the House of Lords entails various private meetings between party leaders, whips, or the Appointments Commission for non-party peers, which have neither the ritual nor the perceived legitimacy of elections.

Rituals are not merely a means to an end, though they are sometimes imbued with a perceived magical quality that enables them to confirm the reality of a political act. Political processes and institutions are largely grounded in a context created by symbolic means, whether through rituals, objects with symbolic meaning (flags, logos, uniforms), or words (Kertzer 1988). They can be imposed from above or appear to grow spontaneously and are always charged with symbolic meaning, regulated by written and unwritten rules. They often reinforce or challenge a hierarchy. So to understand a particular ritual, the symbols, rules, and hierarchies of an institution have to be fathomed first, as well as any contradictions or tensions that the ritual may be designed to reconcile.

Some rituals are quite old—State Opening is one example. Rituals are often assumed to be traditional but they are not necessarily relics of the past; just as often they are invented, reinvented, or remain important in the present (Hobsbawn and Ranger 1983).

An example of a new ritual in the Commons is the Tuesday afternoon 'Dragons' Den' event held by the Backbench Business Committee (see Case Study 18) where MPs pitch their subjects for debate during the time controlled by the Committee. The process is not ordained by any rule and could be done differently, but it is now an established path to winning precious debating time.

The experience of the Palace of Westminster affects how people judge the rituals. To some the House of Lords is seductive, to others absurd. Ex-public schoolboys, Oxbridge graduates, members of the Inns of Court (that is, barristers), and people who frequent London clubs near Pall Mall tend to feel at home in the House of Lords. The past is everywhere: soaring arches, the luxuriance of sculpted dead kings sprouting from mouldings, and painted histor-ical tableaux on the walls. For others the elaborate architecture and historical associations jar on the nerves (see Chapter 6).

The House of Commons, with its green carpets and benches to contrast with the red colour of the Lords, is more intimate and less ornate, but provokes equally strong and polar-ized opinion. That the same symbol may be understood differently by different people can be useful for building solidarity in the absence of shared beliefs, although for some it can also act to suppress dissent and demand conformity to a set of values to which they are opposed. In fact, the fluidity of meaning in symbols can be the source of their strength. The shape-shifting meanings in the State Opening may be one of the reasons that this ritual endures and attracts a huge global audience (see Crewe 2015 and Case Study 5).

Rules in parliamentary rituals

The rituals in institutions within which power is fought over, whether parliaments or courts of law, are highly regulated. The more that is at stake in a political, social, or cultural event, the more likely it is that it will tend to become ritualized. Power brings with it the potential for conflict; so ritual is vital for ensuring that power is legitimized.

While a meeting of MPs and interested parties may be run informally with few rigid rules and minimal sense of hierarchy—for example, an all-party parliamentary group (APPG)—a political event at which power is directly exercised, such as turning a bill into an Act, is replete with strict rules, symbols of power, and ritualized assertions of status and hierarchy. So the more power that is at stake, the more rigidly rule-bound the ritual will tend to be. Such rituals happen every day that Parliament sits.

Business is punctuated at the beginning and end of each day's sitting, of each annual session, and of a whole Parliament, by elaborate ceremonial rituals that may be difficult for outsiders to decipher. Whether the Commons Speaker's daily processions or annual State Openings, these ceremonies allow no room for spontaneity and seem designed to remind us who is in charge of what.

The proceedings of select committees fall somewhere between the highly ritualized con-tests of the Chambers and the largely informal proceedings of, say, an APPG. By and large, select committees do not make decisions of direct effect, so their private proceedings are informal, consensual (for the most part), and need scant attention to rules. When a select committee is meeting in public, perhaps to 'cross-examine' a minister, then the arrangement of the room and the language of strained politeness become part of the symbolic assertion of Parliament's supremacy over the executive. But when, during a committee inquiry, MPs fire questions at members of the public giving evidence rather than gently inviting them to share their views and experience, the ritualized element of the contest can be intimidating.

The value attached to the way Parliament ritualizes its interaction is strongly contested between MPs themselves, as well as by outside commentators inclined to characterize one House or the other as 'out of touch'. This affects how much and how often the rules are changed. This inclusion/exclusion dilemma means that the same ritual may be loathed by some and loved by others, have different meanings for different participants, and have differing purposes according to where you stand in the pecking order. For example, the opening of each day's sitting is marked by prayers led by the Speaker's Chaplain—a ritual that is loved by some and disdained by others for its unambiguously Christian nature and its invocations of the monarchy. But it has so far survived the winds of modernization, even though some ask why it is felt necessary for this ritual to frame the tone and temper of what is to follow—more often than not an hour of aggressive questioning of ministers. The rules of the rituals change only when the meaning symbolized becomes offensive or unconvincing to those with enough influence to bring about reforms.

 Parliamentary terms Standing Orders

Rules, made by either House, which set out the way certain aspects of House procedures operate. They establish procedures for important matters such as the election of the Speaker and Lord Speaker, the operation of programming on bills, and nominations to select committees.

Explicit rules tend to seek to be transparent and unambiguous. The 'rules' of the House of Commons are called its 'Standing Orders'. There were only eight Standing Orders in 1832. Up to this time the nature of those representing the nation in the Commons was highly restricted and the ideological clashes engendered by universal franchise and the growth of national parties had yet to emerge. Since then rules have been invented mostly to clarify who wins and who loses in circumstances where attempts at consensus have failed to contain the heat of politics— as the Commons became the theatre where a much wider range of interests were in play, as the franchise gradually extended over the century after 1832. Now there are over 200 Standing Orders printed in an A5 volume running to 250 pages or so. The Lords, in contrast, survive with far fewer rules and less rigid ritual in the way their debates are conducted—perhaps because less is at stake there. The Lord Speaker announces the next item of business but may not intervene or choose participants in debate because peers are 'self-regulated'. The will of the House is expressed by the peers calling the name of the speaker they wish to hear from or growling 'order, order' with displeasure at rule-breaking.

But even in the House of Commons the Standing Orders regulate only a fraction of what goes on there. There is another thick book, written and guarded by the clerks, known as 'Erskine May', which runs to over a thousand pages of close text. Where the rules seem not to answer a particular case, or are ambiguous, Erskine May sets out what the House did in the past and invites MPs to 'follow precedent'. To emphasize its ritual significance, Erskine May is invariably referred to as the 'Bible of parliamentary procedure'. It sits on the 'Table' of the House as the Bible sits on the lectern in a church—a powerful presence, whether being consulted or merely acting as a reminder of the solemnity of the rules and the dangers of breaking them.

The ultimate judge of what happens in the Commons is the Speaker: the high priest whose presence is essential to validate its rituals. As a presiding officer, the Speaker is generally acknowledged to be an outlier in international comparisons in the degree of discretion and authority they have in interpreting the unwritten—and indeed the written— rules of the House, choosing who speaks (within the conventional ritual), what is debated (within the limits of other agenda-setters), and what is in or out of order (that is, what is permitted). That is in part why so much ritual surrounds the office of the Speaker, from the ceremony surrounding their election at the beginning of a Parliament, their role in State Openings, the way in which MPs are required to bow to them whenever they enter or leave the Chamber, to the sometimes insincere politeness with which they are addressed by MPs in the heat of debate. MPs recognize the need to venerate the office of the Speaker, however much they may love or loathe the individual who holds it, because that position is a lynchpin on which the business of the House hangs.

Rituals as paths for conflict and conciliation

The 'business' of the two Houses is ritualized in ways that resemble a theatre. Each season has a new programme with different actors, and each day of the week has scenes with different moods, rules, and participants. The business usually begins with the ritual of Question Time—when ministers are interrogated by backbenchers and frontbench spokespersons to defend their achievements and explain their mistakes (see Chapter 17). Prime Minister's Questions—occurring at noon every Wednesday in the Commons—show the ritualized aggression of the occupants of the terraced green benches at its most unabated. For some participants, the experience is cathartic—the ritualized show of loyalty to their own party and antagonism to opponents, for the benefit of colleagues but also the public. For others the aggression is alienating, an enemy of rational debate, and infects the atmosphere of the Chamber more generally by legitimizing behaviour that would not be acceptable in most other contexts. Observers of Question Time are similarly divided: it has outlived its relevance to the way they want their politics to be done, or it reminds us that politics is a matter of life and death, not a polite debate over details.

Debates on legislation have different rituals depending on the stage a bill has reached (see Chapter 7), and while controversial bills can attract a huge crowd of MPs, press, and spectators, others might only have a handful of participants. These debates can seem theatrical; although they are verbal collisions between different moral and ideological outlooks, their ritualized nature enables differences to be expressed and resolved without a descent into violence. The language of these occasions is riddled with largely incomprehensible jargon which may deflect passion; they form periods of intense debate punctuated by mini-rituals conducted between the Speaker, the clerks, and the whips clustered around the Table of the House, where huge stretches of law are agreed in seconds. At other less fraught times the rules and rituals are less important, but by the same token the theatricality is lessened and the spectator's attention is likely to flag.

When disagreements cannot be reconciled they are resolved by votes, called 'divisions', where MPs signal their opinion by walking through one of two lobbies (the 'ayes' or the 'noes') signifying assent or dissent. Divisions in the Commons, where the result in 99 per cent of cases is a foregone conclusion, may appear to serve no practical purpose—these are the rituals where the House appears to be at its most theatrical. The Speaker's calls of 'clear the lobby' and 'lock the doors', and MPs' tumultuous arrival in the Chamber within the prescribed eight minutes emphasize the drama of two sides expressing their polarized positions, thereby both allowing opposition to government and forging solidarity within political parties.

For a bill to become law, the two Houses must agree a single text. When one House has finished with a bill, it is endorsed in Norman French by the Clerk of that House and ceremonially 'walked' by another clerk to the 'Bar' of the other House, where a copy of the bill, tied up like a Christmas present in red or green ribbon, is ceremonially handed over. This procedure is symbolic—in the background, the public bill offices of the two Houses have already exchanged electronic copies of the relevant material. When the two Houses disagree about a bill, the legislation passes between them in a 'ping-pong' until agreement is reached. At each exchange, the endorsing of the bill in Norman French and the ceremonial promenade of the clerks between the two Houses symbolize a process in physical form in the eyes of the public: emphasizing the independence of the two Houses from each other, the negotiation of a single text, and that the text faithfully represents what has been agreed. Norman French and the clerks' court dress (worn until it was recently abolished) act as a reminder of parliamentary and regal history, which brings gravitas to the event, conferring legitimacy on the process of law-making for those in awe of history.

Fifty years ago the ritual that transformed a bill into an Act of Parliament involved the House of Commons trooping up to the House of Lords, where the bill was anointed in front of a special commission appointed by the monarch. Since 1967, the act of royal assent has been done privately and is simply announced to each House. But the ritual survives in an attenuated form at the end of each annual session, in a ceremony known as 'prorogation', which is conducted in fancy dress and in a dead language, and which could be seen as a back-to-front version of State Opening. When the Clerk of the Parliaments announces 'La Reine le Veult' (the Queen wishes it), the historical reference is designed to remind the audience of the solemnity of the creation of law.

Rituals as markers of power, hierarchy, and identity

Once Members of Parliament win an election, their entry into the House of Commons is marked by the taking of the oath of allegiance to the monarch (or a non-religious affirmation). This ritual has formed a kind of shibboleth historically, deliberately deployed in the past to exclude Catholics, dissenters, Jews, and atheists. Although the House has largely removed such cultural and religious tests of loyalty, the ceremony still demands that some MPs do a deal with their conscience in order to gain access to power—as indicated by the refusal of MPs elected on the Sinn Féin ticket in Northern Ireland to take an oath of loyalty to a monarch whose legitimacy they do not recognize. The Ceremony of Introduction for peers dates back to 1621 and is more elaborate. Newly appointed peers are escorted into the Chamber by the Gentleman Usher of the Black Rod, the monarch's representative in the House of Lords, and Garter Principal King of Arms, the monarch's chief adviser on matters of ceremony and heraldry, to underline the new peer's proximity to the Queen at the top of the UK's social pyramid—a sort of compensation for the absence of perceived democratic legitimacy.

 Parliamentary terms Black Rod

The official responsible for order and security in the House of Lords.

Rituals mask power in the Lords, but in the Commons they often mask consensus. In practice, most decisions about policy are made outside the theatre of the Commons Chamber, and it is the government's aim to minimize controversy there, especially with its most dangerous opponents, the dissenting backbenchers on the government's own side. Debates are organized in ways that ensure the dominance of the 'frontbenchers', especially those on the government side in the Commons. The time allocated to these power-brokers is far greater. The whips in each political party (the 'usual channels') encourage their members to support their side in debate, votes, and public communications, although in practice they cut deals with each other to focus on the symbolic areas of disagreement between the parties, and often deliberately conspire to squeeze out dissenters on the back benches on both sides.

Votes ('divisions') are also often orchestrated by the usual channels. The performance is more important than the result (which is usually entirely predictable)—it is more important to the party managers that they are seen to oppose than that they win an argument. The whips issue instructions on how to vote in a document—the whip—which indicates the party line to be supported. These instructions are underlined once, twice, or three times to indicate the insistence with which a visible display of loyalty is demanded, and the phrase 'a three-line whip' has acquired a mythic status beyond the confines of Westminster. Obedience or resistance by backbenchers to the rules and norms that are policed by the whips are more significant when the governing party has a small majority (see Chapter 24), but whatever the circumstances, the choice to 'defy' a three-line whip has immense symbolic significance for every MP who has to choose between party loyalty and pleasing others or their own conscience.

The rules and rituals of the Chamber may thus reveal the dynamic of power struggles not only between, but also within, political parties. The symbols in parliamentary rituals like the three-line whip emphasize the constancy of power hierarchies, while rituals like State Opening also recall historic shifts in the negotiation and distribution of power (see Case Study 5). The mace is the symbol of royal authority, for example, and is carried before the Speaker in his daily procession to start a sitting; when placed on its stand on the Table of the House of Commons it indicates that the House is in session. The monarch is never present in person in the Commons and the mace stands in for her, but when she takes her place in the House of Lords during State Opening the mace is absent. The continuing power of the mace as symbol of an idealized constitutional settlement is underlined by the shock caused by four incidents during the last century where MPs picked up the mace and brandished it during debate.

 Parliamentary terms Mace

Symbolizes the authority of the monarch and is placed in the Commons and Lords Chambers whenever they meet.

Bestowing respect on key figures in rituals is achieved by marking their special roles through a mixture of performance, rules, positioning, and symbols. They are also mini-dramas of inclusion and exclusion—who exercises the power over whom, and who is subject to it or struggling for it. It is this function that can cause the deepest offence to the symbolically excluded. Backbenchers are infuriated by how private members' bills are nearly always defeated in a weekly ritual (see Chapter 12).

When the Commons Speaker processes slowly through Central Lobby each day, the police inspector on duty removes their helmet and shouts, 'Hats Off, Strangers', to indicate that visitors should show respect to the Speaker—and also to show that they are not members of either House but are present on sufferance. Of course, very few people are actually wearing hats nowadays.

The manners of debate in the two Houses are linked to the difference in their powers. The less powerful House of Lords prizes a more discursive and deliberative style. The House of Commons is competitive and often more combative, not only between parties but also within them. The style of address reveals different roles between Commons and Lords. MPs are addressed as 'the honourable Member for Middlemarch' to draw attention to their status as representative of a constituency, while peers are referred to by their title, representing only themselves.

The language of debate in both Houses is still highly stylized and ritualized: even in the Commons, which sees itself as more modern, MPs 'have the floor' and 'give way' to others; 'address their remarks through the Chair', not to each other; address those in the same party as 'My honourable friend'; 'beg to move', 'seek leave', and do things 'with permission' which they have not actually sought. They 'object' and express approbation by muttering 'hear, hear', and they shout 'aye' or 'no' to indicate their opinion. These might emphasize who has power, define how MPs relate to each other—who is taking sides with whom—or avoid disorder: the specific meaning of each convention can only be discerned in context.

Conclusion

One way of depicting the work of MPs is as a series of rituals in Westminster or in constituencies requiring them to adjust to different rules, audiences, and purposes; even MPs' constituency surgeries involve an everyday ritualized process. Even more than peers, MPs' work requires extraordinary skills at shape-shifting between the needs of these various rituals.

Parliamentary rituals remind us where protagonists are supposed to be in formal hierarchies, even if the practice of politics entails endless power struggles over these hierarchies. They are also the processes by which moral values, ideas, and relations between people can be performed and contested in ways that avoid violence. But rituals designed to demonstrate solidarity, unity, or common values inevitably carry with them a risk of excluding rather than including—indeed that must be an inevitable part of their purpose. Rituals designed to cement authority carry the risk of appearing to deny dissent.

For parliaments, which are intended to 'represent' a political unit (usually a nation) at all kinds of levels, this can only be a difficult dilemma to negotiate. Parliaments must continually update themselves, so as to reflect more faithfully those they represent; but they also have to express the continuity of a constitutional settlement through time. Parliaments are equally threatened by an excess and a deficit of authority. Simultaneously they must defend individual freedom and enact a collective and shared identity. It is no surprise that the rituals of Westminster are both hallowed and highly contested, traditional but constantly reinvented.

Further Reading

Abélès, M. (2000) *Un ethnologue à l'Assembleé*, Paris: Odile Jacob.

Crewe, E. (2005) *The House of Lords, Manners, Rituals and Politics*, Manchester: Manchester University Press.

Crewe, E. and Muller, M. G., eds. (2006) *Ritual in Parliament*, Frankfurt am Main: Peter Lang.

Rai, S. M., ed. (2010) 'Special Issue: Ceremony and Ritual in Parliament', *The Journal of Legislative Studies*, Vol. 16 (3).

Rai, S. M. and Johnson, R., eds. (2014) *Democracy in Practice: Ceremony and Ritual in Parliament*, Basingstoke and New York: Palgrave Macmillan.

Case Study 5: The State Opening of Parliament

The period between two general elections is known as a 'Parliament'. Each Parliament is divided into annual 'sessions' which, since the passing of the Fixed-term Parliaments Act 2010, generally run for one year from May/June. The beginning of each session is marked by a ceremony involving all three elements of the sovereign Parliament: the monarch, the House of Lords, and the House of Commons. It is the only regular occasion on which all three gather in the same space, in the Palace of Westminster.

The whole panoply of State Opening, and much of the mid-Victorian architecture and layout of the Palace of Westminster, is designed to tell a story about a unitary state governed by an indivisible Trinitarian structure of monarch, Lords, and Commons, even though the actual power hierarchy is nowadays reversed and the monarch is a synecdoche for the government. At the same time, the perspective of each throws a different significance on different elements of State Opening.

The first part of the day is about the enduring stability and majesty of the monarch. State Opening begins with the Yeoman Usher marching down to the basement of the Palace to make sure that no explosives have been placed there, a reminder of Guy Fawkes' foiled plot to assassinate King James I.

The Queen comes in procession from Buckingham Palace to Westminster, preceded by her crown travelling separately. She is accompanied by a troop of her own personal lifeguards, dressed in full ceremonial uniforms. When she arrives at Westminster, the Queen's carriage enters through a gate exclusively reserved for this occasion. All these symbols represent her status as the embodiment of the state, not as an individual.

The corridors and lobbies linking the two Houses, and the Royal Gallery linking the Lords to the Robing Room, form the processional route at the heart of the ceremony. A throne, empty but present for 364 days of the year, stands in the Chamber of the House of Lords, and the Queen takes her place in it, accompanied by much ceremony. The Lords Chamber is thronged by peers in their ermine robes (the only day on which they wear these). Also present are the two archbishops and 24 bishops of the Church of England, who sit in the House of Lords as of right (the 'Lords Spiritual'). Although there are no longer law lords, on the wool-sacks, in the middle of the Chamber in front of the Lord Speaker's woolsack, sit senior judges from the High Court and Supreme Court.

The Queen then sends her messenger, the Gentleman Usher of the Black Rod, to fetch the Commons. No monarch has entered the House of Commons in person since Charles I attempted to arrest five MPs in January 1642. Black Rod makes the long journey through the Palace corridors and lobbies, and as he approaches the Chamber of the House of Commons the door is ritually slammed in his face, signifying the Commons' right to deny the Queen's messenger entry. Black Rod knocks three times on the door, and the Serjeant-at-Arms, having received the permission of the Speaker, lets him in.

Black Rod then, with great ceremony, invites the Commons to come up to the Lords. In what has become its own modern ritual, he is insulted by Dennis Skinner, a republican-inclined Labour MP seeking to puncture the perceived pomposity of the occasion. While a few republican sympathizers remain ostentatiously seated in the Commons Chamber, most of the House make their way to the Lords in a rather shambolic procession led by the Speaker. Cabinet and shadow cabinet members walk side by side to demonstrate the need sometimes to set aside personal animosity and assert the unity of the House, making clear that though the monarch may summon them with pomp, they obey only voluntarily and in their own time and manner.

The MPs stand in a huddle at the 'Bar' of the House of Lords (that is, not formally inside the Chamber) and listen to the Queen reading out the speech written for her by the prime minister. The Queen's Speech has a serious political purpose: it announces her government's programme for that session, but often in the most general of terms. For MPs, the rituals of State Opening emphasize their political power over the second Chamber, but the Queen surrounded by her ermine-clad counsellors are also asserting the ancient social power of the monarch and aristocracy from their viewpoint.

After the speech, the Commons returns to its chamber without further discussion. When the Commons reassembles later in the day, the Speaker reports that the Queen has made her speech. Before the House begins debating its contents, it gives a ritual first reading to the Clandestine Outlawries Bill, symbolizing its assertion of the right of the House to legislate on any matter, whether or not the Queen has asked it in her speech to do so. The Lords does the same with its Select Vestries Bill.

The two Houses then go on to debate, over several days, a very polite motion of thanks to the Queen for 'her gracious speech' (more formally known as the Loyal Address), during which the opposition parties explain with some vigour why the speech represents a complete political failure of the imagination. They move and vote on amendments that 'regret' that the gracious speech fails to include this or the other provision. Although the motion is bland, and although the amendments (because notionally addressed to the Sovereign) are very polite, the political importance of these final votes is immense, and to be defeated on one of these amendments would spell disaster for the government. In January 1924 the defeat of the Conservative government on an amendment to its King's Speech heralded the arrival of the first ever Labour government. The next time an amendment was agreed was in 2016, when David Cameron allowed his final Queen's Speech to be amended without a vote, because the Eurosceptic backbenchers in his own party had indicated that they would vote against the government. Although the amendment was only about the Transatlantic Trade and Investment Partnership, the prime minister's retreat nonetheless carried great ritual significance. Within less than a month he lost the referendum on the EU that he had called, and resigned as prime minister. Votes on Queen's Speeches may seem an empty ritual, but they dramatize a fundamental rule of the British Constitution—a government that cannot command a majority in the House of Commons will not survive.

Rather than finding one meaning for the State Opening of Parliament, this complex series of rituals endures because it evokes different meanings according to the perspective of the observer. You might see the stability of our longest-serving monarch through the visible presence of history and pomp, the social significance of peers (bearing in mind that the key event takes place in their House), or the power and independence of the Commons when they slam the door in Black Rod's face or start their proceedings with a bill the Queen has not requested. As Bourdieu has stated, to possess things from the past is to master time, and this mastery is a form of social power (Bourdieu 1984, 71), but it is MPs in the House of Commons that aspire to use their political power to mould the future. It is by communicating both achievements and aspirations that the State Opening of Parliament retains its significance for many.

Primary sources

- Queen's speeches. Online at: http://www.parliament.uk/about/how/occasions/stateopening/queensspeeches/ [accessed 27 June 2017].
- Election of the Speaker (House of Commons) on 18 May 2015. Online at: http://www.parliamentlive.tv/Event/Index/7527f1cc-a1e3-44c7-b1b8-02baaceeb073 [accessed 27 June 2017].
- Prorogation (House of Lords) on 12 May 2016. Online at: http://parliamentlive.tv/event/index/1f135982-1844-499e-bd86-6a014b3c6fcb?in=13:11:16 [accessed 27 June 2017].
- Members taking the Oath (House of Commons) on 1 March 2017. Online at: http://parliamentlive.tv/event/index/c2227266-7ad0-43a8-9eb1-0ff0fe962685?in=09:38:18 [accessed 27 June 2017].
- Introduction of new peer to the House of Lords on 22 January 2015. Online at: http://www.parliamentlive.tv/Event/Index/6cd8b2a6-17cc-4ade-a6a9-25f37920b2a5 [accessed 27 June 2017].

 FURTHER CASE STUDIES

- The introduction ceremonies of peers and MPs.
- The ritualization of Prime Minister's Questions.
- Royal assent.

References

BOURDIEU, P. (1984) *Distinction: A Social Critique of the Judgement of Taste*, Cambridge, MA, Harvard University Press.

CREWE, E. (2005) *Lords of Parliament*, Manchester, Manchester University Press.

CREWE, E. (2015) *The House of Commons: An Anthropology of MPs at Work*, Bloomsbury, London.

HOBSBAWN, E. and RANGER, T. (1983) *The Invention of Tradition*, Cambridge: Cambridge University Press.

KERTZER, D. (1988) *Ritual, Politics and Power*, Yale: Yale University Press.

6

Design and Space in Parliament

Leanne-Marie McCarthy-Cotter, Matthew Flinders,
and Tom Healey

INTRODUCTION

This chapter highlights the importance and role that design and space play within the Palace of Westminster. We start by assessing 'how' and 'why' design and space matters. We then provide a brief overview of the history of design and space in the Palace of Westminster, before emphasizing three core insights. Firstly, we highlight that the Palace of Westminster was never intended to be the space of a democratic institution. Secondly, that there is an historical relationship between crises and change in relation to issues of UK Parliament's architecture and design. Thirdly, that there has been a reluctance to embrace change in terms of the design and architecture of Parliament. The chapter ends by highlighting the issue of whether we can accurately assess the impact of space and design. The contemporary relevance of this chapter and its arguments could not be greater given the planned multibillion pound Restoration and Renewal Programme for the Palace of Westminster (see Case Study 6).

Why does design and space matter?

Parliaments are symbolic buildings which embody and communicate myths about national power and identity (Vale 2008, 3). The architecture and design of parliamentary buildings and chambers are fundamental to the construction of political culture. As Goodsell stated, 'they perpetuate the past, they manifest the present and they condition the future' (1988, 288). Lawrence Vale describes parliaments and other government buildings as having innate cultural value, representing 'metonymous reinforcement for an idealized and stable democratic government, worthy of our tacit trust' (2008, 72). Thus, the architecture of parliaments is critical to conveying reassurance in the democratic process.

Goodsell's simple argument was that the physical architecture of parliaments is—or should be—of interest to political scientists, not just architects, planners, or officials, due to the manner it embeds, reflects, and perpetuates a specific political culture. National parliaments, in particular, are among the most prominent symbols of politics in any country—self-consciously built theatres with stages within them for (*inter alia*) the performance of political rituals, the representation of specific communities, and the brokering of compromises.

Parliaments, government offices, and other public buildings are aesthetically reflective of the values held by a society at the time they were designed and constructed. Goodsell highlights the role of architecture and design across three dimensions. The first dimension looks at 'preservation'. Preservation relates to the mobilization, conservation, and maintenance of cultural values over long periods of time, and would therefore be captured in the concept of 'path dependency'. Path dependency is the idea that decisions we are faced with today will depend on past decisions made, and thus we are limited in our degree of choice. The structural composition of buildings in materials—wood, glass, stone, metal—ensures that they have an enduring quality in terms of the expression of dominant ideas. Both explicitly and implicitly, public buildings embody deeply rooted cultural concepts that will cast a shadow over future generations. In relation to parliamentary buildings, this manifestation of cultural identity frequently focuses on the relationship between individuals and the state, and the territorial boundaries or political 'reach' of a country.

The second dimension is 'articulation'. The design and architecture of a building reflect the values and ideas extant in political life at the time of the building's construction or remodelling; they constitute a form of non-verbal language stating features of the political culture. This is particularly true in relation to interior design where surfaces, objects, and layout arguably act as an index to expected behaviour. While we suggest that there is a relationship between space and behaviour, and that buildings are a manifestation of the values and ideas of the time of their creation, we are not claiming that this transports the individual back in time and prevents the advancement of ideas and values. Those individuals who come to work within, or visit, the Palace of Westminster are not suddenly robbed of any capacity for rejecting or amending the dominant institutional culture. Pre-existing cultures and traditions can, and will, absorb new values, demands, and expectations.

The third dimension is 'formation'. This focuses on how architecture and design influences behaviour in both a direct and indirect manner: directly, in the sense of defining a space and setting conditions on usage, flow, light, and the costs of future changes to the built environment; indirectly, in the sense of influencing the thoughts and actions of individuals in subtle and complex ways. The challenge, however, for designers and academics lies in understanding exactly how these informal and institutionally embedded cues operate. 'Formation' can also be viewed in a further sense.

If 'preservation' relates to the past and 'articulation' to the present, then 'formation' relates to the future in the sense that the sunk costs and path dependency surrounding existing parliamentary buildings, especially when they are viewed as having iconic status or specific heritage significance, cast a long shadow over debates concerning change. That is not to say that significant change cannot occur, but it is to recognize the existence of institutional embeddedness and how the physical environment can exert a degree of 'bounded rationality', in the sense that decision makers work within limitations which reduce the scale of what are deemed 'legitimate' reform proposals.

Crises, wars, and catastrophes can open 'windows of opportunity' into which radical reform agendas can be proposed and taken forward. This is something that Churchill understood in his argument for retaining a small chamber in the House of Commons. He understood the link between space, culture, and behaviour. At 45 × 68 feet (3,060 square feet), the House of Commons is one of the smallest parliamentary spaces in the world; to put this in perspective a full tennis court is 78 × 36 feet—i.e. 252 square feet smaller. Its benches—not desks or chairs—can accommodate 437 MPs, not the 650 who actually 'sit' in the House. But if the House was big enough to accommodate all of its Members, Churchill argued 'nine-tenths of its debates will be conducted in the depressing atmosphere of an almost empty or half-empty chamber' (HC Debates, 28 October 1943, cc. 403–73). The US Senate is also small and known for a sense of intimacy (84 × 51 feet—4,284 square feet), but the German Bundestag is large at 115 × 112 feet (12,880 square feet). Churchill recognized the link between space and behaviour: for him, a cramped Chamber with limited space and seating, and a confrontation-inducing layout, was a virtue. The space was fit for lively and intense confrontation, not calm and consensual discussion.

Another effective way to understand the role and influence of design is to think of it like a constitution. Constitutions reflect an attempt to impose, through institutional mechanisms, the realization and protection of a set of principles. Different constitutions emphasize different sets of values, embedding and entrenching those values in order to create stability. In many ways the 'physical' institutions of politics, public buildings such as town halls, ministerial departments, supreme courts, and legislatures are another key element of the constitutional configuration's emphasis on stability.

Framing it in this manner enables us to understand the design and architecture of the Palace of Westminster in three elements. Firstly, the external projection of the building— the image it seeks to present to the world within which it exists. Secondly, the internal structure and the manner in which it defines and dictates the use of space—the resources available to staff and visitors. Thirdly, the manner in which the internal structures affect user-interactions in more subtle ways, such as inspiring deference, augmenting partisanship, dividing groups, or perpetuating and preventing forms of democratic inequality. Rai and Johnson (2014) uncover this understanding through the analysis of the importance of ceremony and ritual as an institutional frame which mediates the circulation of meanings (see also Chapter 5). More specifically, this scholarship assesses the values ascribed to particular forms of institutional power rather than others—to understand why certain behaviours, rituals, and ceremonies are normalized and others deemed deviant.

Above we highlighted how architecture and design could embed political principles or values. However, the relationship between the two is not linear. We also need to note the role and importance of the 'unspoken politics' of design and architecture in a manner that points to the role of individuals, such as politicians, officials, and special advisers. Individuals can also *influence* structures in a manner that may perpetuate certain embedded assumptions. The 'hard' institutions of politics therefore prefigure a range of 'soft' institutional characteristics such as language, standard operating procedures, definitions of appropriate behaviour, customs, traditions, and rules that can be too easily overlooked or dismissed.

Yet, as the intellectual shift from 'old institutionalism' to 'new institutionalism' demonstrated with great precision, it is often these 'soft' institutional characteristics that define and perpetuate a specific distribution of power within an institution. Goodsell (1988, 287) highlighted this argument superbly when he stated: 'The physical architecture of parliaments is—or should be—of interest to political scientists [because] they are themselves artefacts of political culture.'

Design and space within the Palace of Westminster

The grandeur and Gothic magnificence of the Palace exemplifies the once imperial UK state and the combined strength of its constituent nations. Its imposing limestone structure, topped with spires and turrets, abruptly defines the space within which great political business is transacted. The exterior is spectacular, and anyone admitted inside the building is immediately awed by the architecture and confused by the parliamentary warren that comprises more than a thousand rooms. Its physical features contribute toward a certain way of doing politics. In the following text, we show how behaviours, rituals, language, and procedures are shaped by physical features, space, and architecture.

 Parliamentary terms Bar (of the House)

The point beyond which guests and visitors are not allowed when the House of Commons is sitting. This takes the form of a (retractable) bar and a white line in the carpet across the entrance to the House of Commons Chamber, and a railing in the House of Lords Chamber.

The Bar of the House, while being a physical feature, also plays an important symbolic role. In the House of Commons it is represented by a white line on the floor across the Chamber's width; in the House of Lords it is marked by a railing. The Bar marks the boundary beyond which visitors may not pass when either House is at work. It also has a procedural role: MPs are called to the Bar of the House of Lords at the Opening of Parliament and to hear the royal assent to Acts of Parliament.

 Parliamentary terms Table (of the House)

The table or desk in the House of Commons Chamber between the two front benches and in front of the Speaker's Chair. House of Commons clerks sit here when the House is sitting. There is a similar table in the Lords.

Other examples include: 'to table', 'backbenchers' and 'frontbenchers' and 'crossing the Floor'. 'To table' is to begin consideration of a proposal. This originates from the act of physically laying legislation on the Table in Parliament. Once an item has been laid on the Table it formally becomes the subject for debate. The terms 'backbenchers' and 'frontbenchers' also derive from the layout of the Chamber. Backbenchers sit on the back benches in the Chamber and are Members who hold no official position in government or the party. The first bench on either side of the House of Commons is reserved for ministers and leaders of the principal political parties (frontbenchers). The phrase 'crossing the Floor' means to change sides—to leave one political party and join another. The expression comes from the Chamber's seating arrangements where the ruling party sits to the right of the Speaker, and the opposition to the left. To change party allegiance means physically crossing the Floor of the House from one side of the Chamber to the other. Furthermore, the House of Commons Chamber, with its adversarial layout whereby government and opposition parties face each other on opposing benches, both configure and reinforce an adversarial political culture. By contrast, a circular chamber, like in the German Bundestag or the Danish Folketing, encourage and facilitate consensus.

The design of the building also embeds a deep-rooted cultural concept. The totemic despatch boxes imbue the frontbenchers who stand before them with a gladiatorial prowess, symbolically legitimated by the ceremonial mace sitting between them. The public, cordoned off from the political action in what was known until very recently as the Strangers' Gallery (above the Chamber), are segregated as mere spectators who are largely ignored by the political actors below. Dovey claimed that the layout of Westminster incorporates a regulated distance between different classes of people, akin to the observances of court society (1999, 93). Puwar goes on to highlight that the building's architectural split is pivoted upon an axis that runs along its centre, in which the throne in the House of Lords is positioned opposite to the Speaker's Chair in the House of Commons, with the elected Chamber leading off to one side of the central lobby and the Lords to the other (2010, 304). Puwar claims that this is 'one of the most obvious practical markings of class divisions, as are the spaces made available for the separate rooms and entrance for royalty' (2010, 304). Puwar also claims that hereditary hierarchical asymmetry is present in the decor of the chambers, such as the decoration of the Lords Chamber in regal red and gold (2010, 304).

The building and rebuilding of the Palace of Westminster

The old Palace of Westminster, in which Parliament met until the fire of 1834, was never intended or designed to operate as a functioning legislature. It was, and to some extent remains, a royal palace. The site in and around the present day Houses of Parliament has been a location for ecclesiastical buildings, kingship, and power since at least the Middle Ages, as the Palace of Westminster expanded from an eighth-century church to the ceremonial centre of the kingdom. Its architectural development is intertwined with the transfer of power from the monarch to Parliament, and the emergence of 'the parliamentary state'. The Palace only became the permanent home of Parliament after 1512, when Henry VIII moved to the nearby Palace of Whitehall following a fire. But even after the departure of the royal family, the site remained a royal palace with the official title of the Palace of Westminster. This might explain the common 'Hogwarts-on-Thames' description of the building, but it also reflects deeper issues—that the home of the British Parliament was forged in a pre-democratic era. As such, its architecture and design arguably and understandably reflected the elite nature of politics at the time.

The present-day Palace of Westminster was built after the great fire of 1834. Both Houses of Parliament were destroyed, along with most other buildings on the site. In June 1835, the Royal Commission charged with leading the rebuilding of the Palace declared that Parliament should be rebuilt in either a Gothic or Elizabethan style. The neo-classical style popular at the time, as seen in United States of America's White House, was dismissed, as it was associated with revolution and republicanism. Instead, it was felt that the Gothic style would embody conservative values. As Cannadine states, the Gothic style was chosen precisely in order to 'articulate a hierarchical image of the political and social order' in which authority and subordination structured public life (2000, 15).

In February 1836, after considering 97 applications, Charles Barry, with the help of Augustus Pugin, was chosen as the architect tasked with redesigning and rebuilding Parliament. Barry's winning proposal was a neo-Gothic design that preserved the embedded conservative aspects of the status quo. Barry's plans, alongside Pugin's interior designs, 'projected a backward-looking, conservative, and exclusive image of the British constitution' (Cannadine 2002, 4). At a broader level, the 'New' Palace of Westminster articulated a 'hierarchical image of the social and political order, stressing venerable authority, presidential subordination and true conservative principles' (Cannadine 2000, 15). The foundation stone was laid on 27 April 1840, the House of Lords completed in 1847, and the House of Commons in 1852, with the whole Palace only complete in 1870.

The next major restoration of the Palace of Westminster came as a result of the Second World War. On 10 and 11 of May 1941, the Luftwaffe dropped two incendiary bombs onto the Palace of Westminster, causing significant damage and destroying the Commons Chamber. A bomb also landed on the House of Lords, but failed to explode. As a consequence, from 13 May, both Houses moved to Church House. Once again, Parliament was presented with the task of rebuilding the Palace of Westminster. And just as after the 1834 fire, it was presented with the opportunity to redesign Parliament, and in turn to reshape institutions and procedures. The context was, however, very different.

While the post-1834 new Palace marked continuity, and indeed can be seen as a missed opportunity to revitalize the institution, initial conversations immediately in the wake of the fire were ambitious and bold. However, the debate in the wake of the 1941 bombing was significantly restrained and subdued. As Goodsell explains, it was decided that the 'Gothic design be reproduced almost without change. Winston Churchill himself insisted on the meticulous replication of the old Commons, arguing that its dimensions and appointments are inseparable from the British political tradition' (Goodsell 1988, 291). All furniture and ceremonial objects were perfectly reconstructed, and agreement was made to retain Parliament's adversarial rectangular pattern, instead of introducing a semicircular design favoured by some legislative assemblies. Churchill insisted that the shape of the old Chamber was responsible for the two-party system that is the essence of British parliamentary democracy (HC

Debates, 28 October 1943, cc. 403–73). Churchill's views dominated, and as a result continuity prevailed. The new House of Commons Chamber, designed by Giles Gilbert Scott, was completed in 1950.

> **Parliamentary terms**   Parliamentary Estate
>
> The group of buildings which houses MPs, peers, and parliamentary staff.

By the 1950s and 1960s, the changing role of politicians and modern politics meant that it could no longer be contained inside the Palace of Westminster. Instead, what had evolved was a much larger Parliamentary Estate, with the Palace of Westminster as its iconic core, where the chambers of both Houses of Parliament are located. Increasing demand for space has meant the Parliamentary Estate now extends well beyond the Palace. Eventually this led to the acquisition of 6–7 Old Palace Yard in 1994, leasing part of Millbank House in 2000, the construction of Portcullis House in 2001, the acquisition of Fielden House in 2001, the eventual acquisition of the whole of Millbank in 2005, and the expansion to 14 Tothill Street in 2011. The Palace of Westminster has evolved, slowly responding to the needs of a changing politics. These changes can be described as ad hoc, incremental, piecemeal, disconnected, and born from necessity rather than desire.

Attempts to change the design and architecture of Parliament

Historical institutionalism underlines the importance of path dependency and institutional 'stickiness' (Hall 1986; Thelen 1999; Sanders 2006). Institutions tend to be incredibly resilient and often unresponsive when faced with external demands for change. As a result, institutions evolve through a process of incremental change that can often seem frustrating to observers who fail to appreciate how the weight of history is embedded in a building's design features. Path dependency and institutional 'stickiness' are clearly patent when analysing the history of the Palace of Westminster.

The Palace of Westminster's two large-scale restoration and renewal projects represented two major 'windows of opportunity' for change. Yet, on each occasion, continuity triumphed over change. The first opportunity, in 1834, could have heralded significant architectural changes, yet it resulted in an embedding of the existing system being favoured over taking the opportunity to update the space and design of Parliament. That is not to say that change did not occur, but the extent of those changes was confined physically and constitutionally within the bounds of the pre-existing Westminster model of governing.

The second window of opportunity was opened as a consequence of the Second World War bombing. But then again, reform proposals were dismissed by the government of the day in favour of stability. This 'lock-in' function of design is best captured in Winston Churchill's (1943) phrase that 'We shape our buildings, and afterwards our buildings shape us.'

The Houses of Parliament has evolved *without conscious design* in a classically British '*muddling through*' manner. This is Bryant's argument: 'evidence for an intelligent plan behind the development of parliament is extremely thin. Rather, this has been a great improvised experiment in which caprice has played every bit as important a role as any consciously pursued constitutional ideology. So the history of parliament is not the tracing out of some hidden, intelligent design, but a story of the vagaries of chance' (2014, 4–5). However, denying the existence of design principles within the history of the Palace of Westminster risks overlooking that deeper and generally implicit *politics of design*. An alternative argument is that design has always played a critical component in British constitutional history. The reluctance for change in favour of ad hoc organic evolution was, in itself, a design principle that 'locked-in' an adversarial model of politics. A resistance to change, and the desire to maintain tradition, rituals, and ceremonies, is itself a chosen design. A third 'window of opportunity' opened in 2015, with the Restoration and Renewal project (which forms Case Study 6), but it is not yet clear what role design will play.

The difficulties of assessing design and space

The role of design and space is incredibly hard to specify, measure, or interrogate for the simple reason that their impact is often hard to discern. It is of course possible to measure and observe how any building is used by those who work within or visit it, but it is far more difficult to understand how factors such as shape, light, height, and layout actually affect behaviour. Indeed, a vast literature highlights the relevance and critical importance of design and architecture, yet the evidence-base for exactly *why* or *how* specific features matter is remarkably thin.

It is naïve and over-simplistic to assume that altering a parliament's design or architecture will automatically lead to the birth of a new form of politics. Glass walls, and the ability to look down upon elected representatives, as in the German Bundestag, may reflect a commitment to increasing transparency and a new relationship between the governors and the governed, but whether that commitment is delivered in practice will depend on a range of factors. Moving to a new building, changing the seating plan, introducing electronic voting, or replacing bricks with glass will not automatically change the political culture. Modification to design and space may achieve some elements of cultural change, and may create a new hybrid of political cultures; but the existing culture will often find ways of subverting and circumnavigating the ambitions of the 'new' building. To fully appreciate *how* and *why* design and space matters, we need to develop a subtler, more sophisticated, and empirical understanding of this phenomenon.

Conclusion

This chapter argues that the architecture and design of Parliament matter, because they embed a specific set of political values or assumptions in a very solid and tangible form. The argument is not that those individuals who work within or visit an institution have no power to shape or challenge the political culture that architecture and design seek to embed. Individuals retain some sense of agency (i.e. they are not robots). But as we demonstrated, the physical structure of Parliament can influence the language of politics and procedure. Design and space play a significant role within the Palace of Westminster and are deeply rooted in cultural concepts that have, and may continue to, cast a shadow over future generations of how we 'do politics', and how we 'perceive politics' in Parliament.

Further Reading

CANNADINE, D. (2000) 'The Palace of Westminster as Palace of Varieties' in C. Riding and J. Riding (eds.), *The Houses of Parliament: History, Art, Architecture*, London: Merrell, pp. 11–29.

COCKS, B. (1977) *Mid-Victorian Masterpiece: The Story of an Institution Unable to Put Its Own House in Order*, London: Hutchinson.

Dovey, K. (1999) *Framing Places, Mediating Power in Built Form*, New York: Routledge.

Puwar, N. (2010) 'The Archi-texture of Parliament: Flaneur as Method in Westminster', *Journal of Legislative Studies*, Vol. 16 (3), pp. 298–312.

Shenton, C. (2012) *The Day Parliament Burned Down*, Oxford: Oxford University Press.

Case Study 6: The Palace of Westminster Restoration and Renewal Programme

THE ONGOING RESTORATION AND RENEWAL PROGRAMME

The Palace of Westminster is facing a serious and growing threat of failure. With no major restoration or renewal having taken place since 1950, a half-century of neglect has left the building's mechanical and electrical systems in a state of severe disrepair, directly affecting the power, heating, water, drainage, ventilation, security systems, data and communications networks that make the building work. The Grade 1 listed building (part of a UNESCO World Heritage Site) faces a looming crisis. Crumbling masonry, leaks, damp, electrical failures, fire risks, and asbestos reveal the scale of the challenge. And yet the scale of the problems may be far greater than currently anticipated.

As the official pre-feasibility report was forced to concede, 'the state of dilapidation and therefore of risk is largely uncharted' (UK Parliament 2012, 6). It concluded that without urgent and significant intervention, a major failure of existing service infrastructure is inevitable. In June 2015, a subsequent Independent Options Appraisal (IOA), commissioned by both Houses of Parliament, was published, setting out the ways in which the essential repairs could be achieved. These proposals—ranging from a full decant of Parliament to a rolling programme of repairs—have been estimated to cost between £3 billion and £6 billion. The IOA bolstered the argument that significant work needed to be carried out by stating that there was 'risk of catastrophic failure'. It stated: 'business continuity risk has continued to steadily rise and while the Members and users do not always see the full effects, building services issues are ever present and the risk of catastrophic failure is increasing. Examples include a burst water pipe flooding the Committee Room corridor and a component of the ceiling in the Lords Chamber falling into the benches below' (Deloitte 2014, 34).

In response to the IOA report, a Joint Select Committee on the Palace of Westminster was formed in July 2015. After a year-long inquiry, the Committee published its report on 8 September 2016, with a recommended text of a motion on which its report should be debated and agreed. If agreed, it would trigger the next stages in the process of the Restoration and Renewal Programme, including the establishment of a Sponsor Board and Delivery Authority by legislation, and authorize the development of a fully costed business case for a full decant of the Palace of Westminster, subject to approval by both Houses (Joint Committee on the Palace of Westminster 2016).

On 25 January 2017, a Westminster Hall debate on the restoration and renewal of the Palace of Westminster took place, initiated by Chris Bryant MP, joint spokesman for the Committee. This was followed in March by a report published by the Public Accounts Committee supporting the recommendations that Parliament should leave the Palace while major works to the building are carried out (Public Accounts Committee 2017). On 17 March, the Treasury Committee also published their preliminary report on the restoration and renewal of the Palace of Westminster. This report declared: '[the Treasury Committee] will attempt to assist the House by challenging and testing the work and the conclusions of Deloitte and the Joint Committee. Because of the extensive investigations already carried out, our inquiry is likely to be relatively short and specific. Until this work has been carried out, it is our view that it would be imprudent for the House to commit to a specific option or timetable' (Treasury Committee 2017). However, by the end of the 2015–17 Parliament, both Houses were yet to make a decision regarding how to carry forward the Restoration and Renewal Programme.

THE OPPORTUNITY TO REDESIGN THE PARLIAMENT

Therefore a window of opportunity is currently open. We are presented with a chance to design a parliament that is not only fit for purpose, but also one that speaks to the views and attitudes of a modern society. It is a chance to update the fabric of Parliament, to remove outdated attitudes and values and embed a progressive set of principles that the public recognize, while acknowledging and preserving the building's magnificent Victorian heritage.

However, as the March 2015 Designing Democracy report by the Design Commission illustrated, the issues of design and architecture are not forming the core elements of the debate regarding the rebuilding of Parliament (Design Commission 2015). Discussions about restoration and renewal have not explored the impact of design, space, and architecture on how we 'do politics'. While the needed restoration and renewal of Parliament presents an opportunity to think more explicitly about the role of space and design, and to create a building that reflects a more modern form of politics, this appears to be absent from the current debate. This links to our idea of the 'implicit' politics of design, as discussed in our chapter, a reluctance, or failure, to fully explore the options for change and discuss the role of space, can be seen itself as a design principle that 'locks-in' the existing model of politics. A resistance to change, and the desire to maintain tradition, rituals, and ceremonies, is itself a chosen design.

There has been little public discussion of what a restored or rebuilt Palace of Westminster should look like, or how—with an increasing problem of 'anti-politics'—this could be an opportunity to design a Parliament that revitalizes democracy. There has been limited public engagement to develop an understanding of what the public wants from its parliamentary building. Public and media debates have largely centred on Parliament leaving the Palace of Westminster and moving to a new purpose-built building, with some calling to use this as an opportunity to move Parliament out of London. There has been no attempt to understand public expectations about the space in which politics is conducted, and how they perceive the design and space of Parliament. But as Kate Jones from the Design Council states: 'Design plays a critical role in the relationship between people and politics … Design could help the renovation programme to deliver a Parliamentary Estate that functions better for its purpose today … Design can also help adapt and create new systems in and around Westminster following the shift in the way people in the UK engage with democracy' (Design Commission 2015, 20).

Therefore, the current Restoration and Renewal Programme is an opportunity to create a space that reflects and enables twenty-first century politics. However, the decision to remain within the current Palace of Westminster has cast a shadow over the Programme's capacity for change, as the fabric of the building and its layout are subject to tight heritage safeguards. The tension will therefore be delivering a legislature fit for the twenty-first century within a building that has never been designed for such a purpose, and is permeated by a very specific political culture that an increasing number of people seem to reject or find problematic (Childs 2016).

Primary sources

- UK Parliament (2012) *Restoration and Renewal of the Palace of Westminster: Pre-Feasibility Study and Preliminary Strategic Business Case*, October 2012. Online at: http://www.parliament.uk/documents/commons-commission/PED-Modernisation-Report-Oct12.pdf [accessed 4 August 2017].

- Deloitte (2014) *Palace of Westminster Restoration and Renewal Programme: Independent Options Appraisal*, London: Deloitte. Online at: http://www.parliament.uk/documents/lords-information-office/2015/Independent-Options-Appraisal-final-report-A3.pdf [accessed 22 June 2017].

- Joint Committee on the Palace of Westminster (2016) *Restoration and Renewal of the Palace of Westminster: First Report of Session 2016–17*, London: The Stationery Office, HC 659. Online at: http://www.publications.parliament.uk/pa/jt201617/jtselect/jtpow/41/41.pdf [accessed 22 June 2017].

 FURTHER CASE STUDIES

- The rebuilding of the Palace of Westminster after the fire of 1834, and again after the damage caused by bombing during the Second World War.
- The design and building of Portcullis House (1992–2001).
- The design and building of the Senedd—the Welsh Assembly.

References

BRYANT, C. (2014) *Parliament: The Biography* [Vols. 1 and 2], London: Doubleday.

CANNADINE, D. (2000) 'The Palace of Westminster as Palace of Varieties' in C. Riding and J. Riding (eds.), *The Houses of Parliament: History, Art, Architecture*, London: Merrell, pp. 11–29.

CANNADINE, D. (2002) *In Churchill's Shadow*, London: Penguin.

CHILDS, S. (2016) *The Good Parliament*, Bristol: University of Bristol. Online at: http://www. bristol.ac.uk/media-library/sites/news/2016/july/20%20Jul%20Prof%20Sarah%20Childs%20 The%20Good%20Parliament%20report.pdf [accessed 22 June 2017].

COCKS, B. (1977) *Mid-Victorian Masterpiece: The Story of an Institution Unable to Put Its Own House in Order*, London: Hutchinson.

DELOITTE (2014) *Palace of Westminster Restoration and Renewal Programme: Independent Options Appraisal*, London: Deloitte. Online at: http://www.parliament.uk/documents/lords-information-office/2015/Independent-Options-Appraisal-final-report-A3.pdf [accessed 22 June 2017].

DESIGN COMMISSION (2015) *Designing Democracy: How designers are changing democratic spaces and processes*, London: Design Commission. Online at: http://www.policyconnect.org.uk/ apdig/sites/site_apdig/files/report/497/fieldreportdownload/designingdemocracyinquiry.pdf [accessed 22 June 2017].

DOVEY, K. (1999) *Framing Places, Mediating Power in Built Form*, New York: Routledge.

GOODSELL, C. T. (1988) 'The Architecture of Parliaments: Legislature Houses and Political Culture', *British Journal of Political Science*, Vol. 18 (3), pp. 287–302.

HALL, P. (1986) *Governing the Economy*, New York: Oxford University Press.

JOINT COMMITTEE ON THE PALACE OF WESTMINSTER (2016) *Restoration and Renewal of the Palace of Westminster: First Report of Session 2016–17*, London: The Stationery Office, HC 659. Online at: http://www.publications.parliament.uk/pa/jt201617/jtselect/jtpow/41/41.pdf [accessed 22 June 2017].

PUBLIC ACCOUNTS COMMITTEE (2017) *Delivering Restoration and Renewal: Forty-fifth Report of Session 2016–17*, London: Stationery Office, HC 1005. Online at: https://publications.parliament. uk/pa/cm201617/cmselect/cmpubacc/1005/1005.pdf [accessed 23 August 2017].

PUWAR, N. (2010) 'The Archi-texture of Parliament: Flaneur as Method in Westminster', *Journal of Legislative Studies*, Vol. 16 (3), pp. 298–312.

RAI, S. and JOHNSON, R. (2014) *Democracy in Practice: Ceremony and Ritual in Parliament*, Basingstoke: Palgrave.

RIDING, C. and RIDING, J. (2000) *The Houses of Parliament: History, art, architecture*, London: Merrell.

SANDERS, E. (2006) 'Historical Institutionalism' in R. A. W. Rhodes, S. A. Binder, and B. A. Rockman (eds.), *The Oxford Handbook of Political Institutions*, Oxford: Oxford University Press, pp. 39–55.

THELEN, K. (1999) 'Historical Institutionalism in Comparative Politics', *Annual Review of Political Science*, Vol. 2, pp. 369–404.

TREASURY COMMITTEE (2017) *Restoration and Renewal of the Palace of Westminster: Preliminary Report: Thirteenth Report of Session 2016–17*, London: The Stationery Office, HC 1097. Online at: https://www.publications.parliament.uk/pa/cm201617/cmselect/cmtreasy/1097/1097.pdf [accessed 22 June 2017].

UK PARLIAMENT (2012) *Restoration and Renewal of the Palace of Westminster: Pre-feasibility Study and Preliminary Strategic Business Case, October 2012*. Online at: http://www.parliament.uk/documents/commons-commission/PED-Modernisation-Report-Oct12.pdf [accessed 4 August 2017].

VALE, L. (2008) *Architecture, Power, and National identity*, New York: Routledge.

PART III

Law-making

7

The Legislative Cycle

Liam Laurence Smyth, Glenn McKee, and Matt Korris

INTRODUCTION

This chapter examines the legislative cycle, focusing on its operation within the annual parliamentary session (typically June to May), discussing the main processes and terminology. The focus is on government bills, which take up most available time. In 2015–16, a fairly typical annual session, 30 per cent of the time taken up in the Chamber of the House of Commons was on legislative business (360 hours out of 1,215 hours in total) with a further 255 hours spent on bills in public bill committees. In the same session, the House of Lords spent 527 hours in the Chamber on legislative business, slightly over half its total time overall (52 per cent of the total), with a further 52 hours spent on legislative business in the Grand Committee. This isn't the only legislative work which Parliament carries out. We can supplement these totals with, for example, the work of committees examining draft bills and secondary legislation. Regardless of the format of the business, it is clear that Parliament spends a great deal of time considering legislation. We explain here the typical means by which it does so and discuss the planning and organization of business, which is often less visible to the outside observer.

Setting out the legislative programme

The session begins with the ceremonial State Opening of Parliament which centres on the Queen's Speech announcing the main items in the government's forthcoming legislative programme. There is no requirement for government bills to be pre-announced in the Queen's Speech, and nor are all the bills mentioned necessarily brought forward by the government. In 2015, the Queen's Speech mentioned bills on buses, extremism, and Wales which did not materialize in that session.

 Parliamentary terms Legislative programme

The bills which the government wishes to introduce (and pass) in a given parliamentary session. Most of these will be listed in the Queen's Speech at the start of the session.

Legislative drafting

While the Queen's Speech provides the public fanfare announcing the legislative cycle, much work will have been done beforehand. Legislative drafting is a particular skill, exemplified by the highly trained lawyers in the Office of Parliamentary Counsel, part of the Cabinet Office. Access to Parliamentary Counsel is controlled by the Cabinet Committee on Parliamentary Business and Legislation (PBL), chaired by the Leader of the House of Commons. The Committee's systems for scrutinizing bids for legislation balance the interests of departments with those of the government as a whole, within the constraints of parliamentary capacity and difficulty of passage. They involve setting the government's priorities for what the programme should deliver, and rigorous scrutiny of preparedness and progress (Cabinet Office 2017).

 Parliamentary terms Parliamentary Counsel

A group of experienced legislative drafters who are familiar with the technical and legal wording of legislation, and who draft bills for ministers.

The web of cabinet committees, including PBL, is the hidden hand in the legislative cycle. Policy is agreed through these committees, and once a bill is under way they have to agree any changes and concessions. This process ensures comprehensive agreement across Whitehall departments (and during the 2010–15 Coalition government, agreement by both parties), but it can take time and may block changes to a bill.

Pre-legislative scrutiny

A small number of bills are sent by government for pre-legislative parliamentary scrutiny, where a select committee will examine and publish a report on the draft bill. It will often be a joint committee of the Houses of Commons and Lords—in the case of the Investigatory Powers Bill this consisted of seven Members of each House (see Case Study 7). In addition, and unusually, this draft bill was reviewed by the House of Commons Science and Technology Committee (2016) and the Intelligence and Security Committee (2016). Such a degree of scrutiny is exceptional, but there is appetite among parliamentarians for pre-legislative scrutiny on significant legislation, and it can be of real value.

Pre-legislative scrutiny has, however, fallen out of regular use. From a high point of 15 draft bills published in 2012–13, it fell back to just four in 2014–15 (Kelly 2015a). This may be because there has been uncertainty about the best route for pre-legislative scrutiny—existing departmental select committees or joint committees—and because scrutiny needs to be completed to a tight deadline to publish the finalized bill. Moreover, the introduction of oral evidence sessions to the committee stages of some bills may have eased the need for pre-legislative scrutiny. Without a clear objective for scrutiny, the process risks becoming indistinct from scrutiny of the actual bill, with a focus on policy to the exclusion of, for example, technical operation.

Parliamentary procedure and bills

When a bill is ready for introduction, Parliamentary Counsel consult the Clerks of Legislation in the Public Bill Offices in each House on technical issues engaging parliamentary procedure: titles, scope, and (for the Commons) money. All bills need to have a 'short' and a 'long' title. The short title is the ordinary name of the bill, such as the Transport Bill. They should be self-explanatory and must not be political slogans, though some arguably loaded terms have been used, such as the Protection of Freedoms Bill. The long title of a bill sets out its main purposes succinctly: for example, the long title of the Investigatory Powers Bill said that its purpose was:

> to make provision about the interception of communications, equipment interference and the acquisition and retention of communications data, bulk personal datasets and other information; to make provision about the treatment of material held as a result of such inter-ception, equipment interference or acquisition or retention; to establish the Investigatory Powers Commissioner and other Judicial Commissioners and make provision about them and other oversight arrangements; to make further provision about investigatory powers and national security; to amend sections 3 and 5 of the Intelligence Services Act 1994; and for connected purposes.

The long title of a bill does not determine its limits or 'scope', as it may itself be amended in the course of the bill's passage. The notion of 'scope' in the Commons, or 'relevance' in the House of Lords, is an important discipline in maintaining focus on the bill's subject matter and whether a proposed amendment is in order. A bill's scope comprises the reasonable lim-its of its collective purposes as defined by its existing clauses and schedules. Amendments must fall within the scope of a bill in order to be selected for debate in the Commons.

The Commons' control of money—public spending and taxation—was one of the levers by which Parliament in the seventeenth century gained control over the executive and is fundamental to the Constitution. Since the early eighteenth century, this power has been balanced by a requirement for ministerial agreement to new taxes and significant additional public expenditure; the original purpose was to prevent MPs adding expenditure favouring their own interests or constituencies to bills. The result is that many bills require incidental 'ways and means' cover to allow for the imposition of levies, charges, or taxes to enable their implementation; or, more commonly, a money resolution to authorize the spending of public money to achieve a bill's intention. Only ministers may move these motions or resolutions. Without these, a bill requiring money cover cannot progress beyond second reading.

Managing the consideration of a bill

Bills, like all parliamentary business, require management. This relates most obviously to when and where they begin their scrutiny. For the government, good management will mean that the bill progresses with little or no delay. Some of this is transparent, but some is opaque. The content of a bill itself may be part of the strategy. A bill may be drafted with overly ambitious targets in full recognition that some will be reduced as concessions, to ease its passage through the parliamentary process (see Chapter 8). The session in which a bill is brought forward may also have a bearing. Most Parliaments since the 1980s have run for four or five annual sessions, though the 2015 Parliament was an exception. Incoming governments prioritize legislation which implements their key electoral promises. Complex, controversial, or unpopular measures will typically dominate the middle years of a Parliament. With a general election on the horizon, the last session of a Parliament may be devoted to less controversial measures, or to legislation which is expected to build electoral support.

 Parliamentary terms Carry-over

A procedure which allows a bill to move from one parliamentary session to the next if its scrutiny has not been completed. This procedure stops a bill from failing if it has not been approved by Parliament at the end of a session.

Consideration also has to be given to which House a bill should start in. The two Houses have broadly parallel legislative competence. Owing to the important constitutional distinction where money (taxation and public spending) is concerned, Finance Bills (dealing with taxation) and Supply and Appropriation Bills (dealing with public spending) must begin in the Commons.

After a bill is introduced, the government whips office works closely with the opposition whips to reach common agreement, where possible, on a programme motion. Programme motions provide a timetable to consider bills, establishing the time allowed for debate in each of the legislative stages. This usually includes an 'outdate' (i.e. deadline) for bills to be reported from public bill committees, or fixed times for proceedings. As a result of the routine use of programme motions (made permanent in 2004), seeking to delay progress is now rarely an effective way of opposing government bills.

 Parliamentary terms Programme motion

A proposed timetable for the progress of a bill's scrutiny. The programme motion sets out the date and/or time by which each stage of scrutiny should be completed, or the schedule for scrutiny of certain parts of the bill. The programme motion is typically agreed following the second reading vote on the bill.

The legislative stages of a bill

First reading

As Figure 7.1 demonstrates, bills must pass a series of stages in both Houses. Regardless of the Chamber in which a bill begins, it will receive a first reading. This is mainly a formal stage performed by the clerk at the Table, who simply reads its short title out loud, following which a date is given for its second reading. The first reading is accompanied by the publication of the bill online and in hard copy. Government bills will also have explanatory notes, offering a jargon-free explanation of the contents.

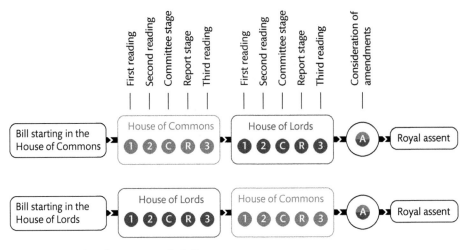

Figure 7.1 The legislative stages of a bill
Source: www.parliament.uk/about/how/laws/passage-bill/

Second reading

The first point at which a bill can be debated is second reading. This is usually conducted as a one-day debate. Second readings in the Lords are normally not the subject of a vote. In the Commons however, a division on party lines is the norm. Debate focuses on the principles and purpose of the bill, and often provides indications of areas of discussion and disagreement for later stages.

A Commons second reading is usually followed immediately by a programme motion, which commits the bill to either a Committee of the whole House or to a public bill committee. Programme motions are infrequently voted on, and failure to agree a programme motion after second reading may be fatal to a bill: such a failure led to the withdrawal of the Coalition government's House of Lords Reform Bill in September 2012.

Committee stage

The bill then moves to committee (see Chapter 9). This is the first point at which it is possible to change its wording. If a bill is particularly urgent, of great constitutional importance, or completely non-controversial, it will be considered in a Committee of the whole House, where all MPs sit in the Chamber. It is rare for programme motions to allocate more than a handful of days in Committee of the whole House, even for constitutional bills, as this displaces other business in the Chamber. Most bills in the Commons are sent to a public bill committee. It is up to the committee to set its own timetable, as long as it meets the outdate set by the programme motion. Some committees are very short (as little as one hour), but some are much longer. The Investigatory Powers Bill public bill committee spent over 38 hours carrying out scrutiny, across 16 sittings (see Case Study 7).

The pace in committee is normally set by the opposition frontbench, in whose name dozens of amendments may be tabled. In contrast to government amendments, these are often drafted by House of Commons staff for Members. Many are designed to probe the bill, and the government may also table amendments of its own to improve or correct the bill's drafting, to add new material within the bill's scope, to respond to criticisms made, or to anticipate or forestall likely defeats.

Report stage

When a bill leaves a Commons committee, it moves to its 'report stage', where it may again be amended. This takes place in the Commons Chamber, and all MPs may participate, though consideration is constrained by programming. Time to discuss amendments is therefore very limited, as the report stage of the whole bill may only last a few hours. As a result, the opposition parties typically press only a few of their amendments to a vote. In the Lords, which does not have programming, time is not limited. All amendments can be debated and voted on if peers choose to test the opinion of the House.

Third reading

At the conclusion of report stage, a bill will receive a 'third reading'. Third reading debates are usually short (less than one hour in the Commons). A speech is made by the government minister responsible for the bill, the main opposition spokespeople, and a handful of other MPs, who usually reflect on the scrutiny of the bill and the changes which have been made. There is also a final vote where MPs may again display their opposition to the bill. In the Lords, third reading provides a further opportunity to make amendments to the bill.

'English votes for English laws' procedures

In October 2015, the House of Commons adopted the 'English votes for English laws' (EVEL) Standing Orders. Third reading may now sometimes be preceded by a perfunctory Legislative Grand Committee stage where Members sitting for constituencies in England (or in England and Wales) agree to any provisions of the bill certified by the Speaker as relating exclusively to England (or to England and Wales). EVEL, which applies only in the Commons, has added considerably to the complexity of the legislative process (as Figure 7.2 illustrates), though it appears to have satisfied the government's political objective of allowing Members for English (and Welsh) constituencies to have the opportunity of a veto (see also Kelly 2015b).

Lords bills

Legislation is dealt with by the two Houses in series, rather than in parallel. A bill is considered by one chamber before moving to the other. In the Lords, committees are rarely appointed to consider bills because its composition does not lend itself to replication in miniature, owing to the disparate character of cross-benchers with no party affiliation. As an alternative to Committee of the whole House, some bills may be taken in a Grand Committee, sitting in the Moses Room as a kind of parallel chamber. All peers may take part in these proceedings.

There are a number of differences with Commons procedure. Programming would be profoundly inimical to the nature of Lords proceedings, where bills are fully and

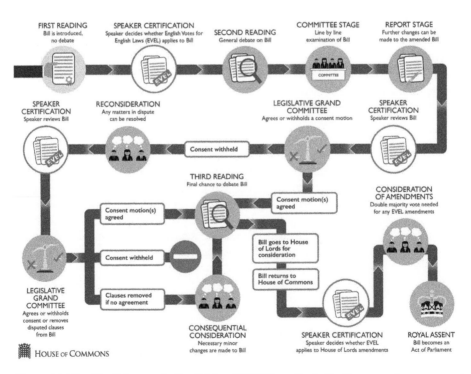

Figure 7.2 How 'English votes for English laws' (EVEL) applies in the Commons to government bills

Source: https://www.parliament.uk/about/how/laws/bills/public/english-votes-for-english-laws/

7 THE LEGISLATIVE CYCLE **73**

comprehensively debated, taking as long as needed. There is no provision for written or oral evidence to be taken; nor is there any provision to give money cover to bills. Bills starting in the Lords will often have a 'privilege amendment' inserted, recognizing the financial primacy of the Commons. This procedural fig leaf is removed by the Commons before the bill returns to the Lords, and the government will table any necessary money or ways and means motions.

To-and-fro, or 'ping-pong'

When a bill has completed its passage through its second House, it returns to the House where it began. If no amendments were made in the second House, it is ready for royal assent.

Any amendments which have been made since leaving the first House need to be considered by that House. When a bill that started in the Commons, for example, is received back, the Commons considers only the Lords amendments and does not reopen debate on unchanged parts of the bill. The process requires passing the bill back and forth with amendments, until it is agreed to by both Houses in identical form. If one House insists on the same amendment twice—known as double-insistence—the process becomes deadlocked, and the legislation is lost. This is avoided by ensuring the exchange of alternative amendments until a compromise is reached, or one House backs down (see Russell 2013, 131–4).

If any Lords amendments have financial implications (spending or taxation), money or ways and means cover will be required (see Russell and Gover 2014). Here, the government can table the necessary motion before the Lords amendments are considered. Similarly, EVEL may apply in the Commons when considering Lords amendments.

There is an 'override' mechanism that applies to bills, rather than amendments. The Parliament Act 1911 allows the Commons alone to present a bill for royal assent if it is not passed by the Lords, but only if the Commons passes the same bill in successive sessions, and provided that a year and a month have elapsed since the bill's original second reading in the Commons. The Act was last used in respect of the Hunting Act 2004. It also provides for a bill certified as a Money Bill to be presented for royal assent after a month has elapsed since it was passed by the Commons.

 Parliamentary terms Money Bill

A bill which focuses on changes to taxation, or involves public money or loans. If a bill is certified as such by the Speaker of the House of Commons under the Parliament Act 1911, and has not been passed unamended by the Lords within one month of passing the Commons, it may become law, regardless of whether the House of Lords has agreed to it.

Time taken to pass a bill

It is hard to generalize on how long it takes for a bill to successfully navigate these stages and receive royal assent. Table 7.1 shows the length of time taken for a selection of bills introduced in the 2015–16 session. The length of time taken for these bills to pass varied considerably.

Emergency legislation can be passed within a couple of days if the House accelerates its normal procedures. An example was the Northern Ireland (Welfare Reform) Act 2015.

Table 7.1 Time taken to scrutinize government bills, 2015–16

Act	Elapsed days from introduction to royal assent	Time under scrutiny (Hours)			Total (hours)
		Commons Chamber*	Commons Committee	Lords	
Childcare Act 2016	289	7.0	6.1	12.8	26
Driving Instructors (Registration) Act 2016	106	0.3	0.3	0.5	1
Immigration Act 2016	238	15.5	30.2	52.1	98
Investigatory Powers Act 2016	265	22.4	38.1	41.8	102
NHS (Charitable Trusts Etc.) Act 2016	273	4.5	3.3	1.3	9
Northern Ireland (Welfare Reform) Act 2015	6	3.1	1.0**	1.0	5
Northern Ireland (Stormont Agreement and Implementation Plan) Act 2016	84	5.9	3.0**	4.4	13
Trade Union Act 2016	294	15.6	21.8	36.9	74
Welfare Reform and Work Act 2016	251	16.2	25.3	68.2	110

Notes: *excludes Committee of the whole House (CwH); **CwH, with allocation of time motion
Source: House of Commons Public Office

Following extensive negotiations, an agreement was reached which included an under-taking for the UK government to legislate for welfare reform in Northern Ireland, and a bill was published on 19 November. The bill came before the Commons on 23 November, which approved an allocation of time motion, setting out deadlines for the Commons stages of the bill. Significantly, the official opposition did not oppose the motion or legislation, though opposition came from Northern Ireland parties. The bill completed its second reading, Committee of the whole House, and third reading that day, and the Lords disposed of its proceedings on the following day, with royal assent given on 25 November. Instead of taking several months to complete its passage through both Houses, this Bill completed its entire passage in six days.

Parliamentary terms Statute book

A term used to describe all of the bills which have successfully passed through Parliament and are currently in force. Once a bill has received royal assent it is considered to be 'on the statute book' until repealed.

Money and Finance Bills

Distinct arrangements govern legislation authorizing taxes and public expenditure. Each year the Commons passes two Supply and Appropriation Bills to give legislative authority for government spending out of the Consolidated Fund, into which most taxes are paid. These bills follow an archaic procedure requiring them to be brought in as resolutions rather than presented simply as bills. They receive virtually no legislative scrutiny. Once presented in the Commons, there cannot be any debate (and normally there is not even a vote) on either second or third reading. There is no possibility of amendment, and third reading follows immediately on second reading, bypassing any committee stage.

Finance Bills receive much more substantial legislative scrutiny. The Chancellor of the Exchequer delivers an annual Budget Statement which covers the national finances, planned public spending, and borrowing and taxation. At the conclusion of the statement, and after motions are passed without debate to allow provisionally the implementation of tax changes before the legislation is passed, debate begins on a number of ways and means motions authorizing taxes for the following financial year. When the debate concludes several days later, all these are put to the vote, and the Finance Bill is brought in. A few weeks later, the Finance Bill receives a full day's debate on second reading, after which the bill's most important provisions are committed to a Committee of the whole House, with the remainder sent to a public bill committee. The bill, as a whole, is later considered at report stage, followed by third reading.

Conclusion

While some parliamentary processes are essential, and the sessional pattern is ingrained, the legislative cycle is the product of several centuries of development producing anomalies and exceptions, such as those for Finance Bills. Much of the management of the cycle is shielded from view within Whitehall machinery, or affords only a restricted view, even to parliamentarians, as their whips' offices make arrangements for the scheduling and conduct of parliamentary business.

As each House sets its own rules—known as exclusive cognizance—it can develop and alter its procedures as circumstances require. The Commons has developed timetabling—through programming—and the incorporation of oral evidence sessions into some committee stages. While Members may push against the constraints of timetabling, and the whips' arrangements may from time to time break down, the structure operates with a degree of cooperation in the management of the time available for scrutiny and allows opposition parties to press key issues to a division in the Chamber itself. We will see, in Chapter 8, the ways in which MPs and peers use these scrutiny processes to try to amend legislation.

Further Reading

CABINET OFFICE (2017) *Guide to Making Legislation*, London: Cabinet Office. Online at: https://www.gov.uk/government/uploads/system/uploads/attachment_data/file/608496/guide_to_making_legislation.pdf [accessed 22 June 2017].

UK PARLIAMENT (n.d.) *Standing Orders of the House of Commons—public business*. Online at: http://www.parliament.uk/business/publications/commons/standing-orders-public11/ [accessed 22 August 2017].

UK PARLIAMENT (n.d.) *Sessional Returns of the House of Commons*. Online at: https://www.parliament.uk/business/publications/commons/sessional-returns/ [accessed 22 June 2017].

UK PARLIAMENT (n.d.) *Bills before Parliament*. Online at: http://services.parliament.uk/bills/ [accessed 22 August 2017].

Case Study 7: Investigatory Powers Act

The Investigatory Powers Act 2016 is a good example of the whole legislative cycle in a complex and highly contested policy area. The bill sought to consolidate and extend the powers of law enforcement and the security services to intercept and monitor communications and related data. Investigatory powers such as these go to the heart of the debate about the individual right to privacy versus the requirement for the state to provide security and effective law enforcement—a debate that cuts across traditional party lines. The issue also poses considerable practical challenges for government to keep pace with the rapidly growing volume and changing patterns of communications facilitated by the internet. Despite these challenges, the bill passed relatively smoothly through Parliament. This was due to the combination of detailed independent reviews of the issues, pre-legislative scrutiny of a draft bill, and the willingness of the government to engage with, and accommodate, the concerns of the opposition.

BEFORE THE BILL

The powers for law enforcement to access communications and related data were primarily granted by the Regulation of Investigatory Powers Act 2000, in combination with the EU Data Retention Directive 2006. A successful legal challenge to the Directive led to the rapid approval by Parliament of the Data Retention and Investigatory Powers Act 2014 to ensure those powers were retained. As part of the political negotiations to secure passage of that legislation at short notice, a sunset clause was included which meant that the Act expired at the end of 2016. This required the government bringing forward new legislation to replace it if they wanted to keep the powers.

A review of investigatory powers undertaken by David Anderson QC (the government's independent reviewer of terrorism legislation) in June 2015 called for an entirely new legislative framework to replace the existing laws on investigatory powers, both for law enforcement and the security and intelligence agencies. The review was complemented by separate reports from Parliament's Intelligence and Security Committee and the Royal United Services Institute, which also called for a significant overhaul.

The government responded with the publication of the Draft Investigatory Powers Bill in October 2015, which sought to restate and update the law on the investigatory powers for law enforcement and the security and intelligence agencies. The draft bill was subjected to pre-legislative scrutiny by a joint committee of both Houses, which reported in February 2016 (Joint Committee on the Draft Investigatory Powers Bill 2016).

The Committee did not fundamentally object to any of the proposed powers, but it raised a number of concerns about their details and practicality. The Committee's report made 86 recommendations: some of these were changes to the bill, but many others called on the government to provide further explanation and justification of the proposals. The scrutiny of the joint committee was complemented by reports by the Intelligence and Security Committee (2016) and the Science and Technology Committee (2016), which considered specific aspects of the draft bill.

THE PASSAGE OF THE INVESTIGATORY POWERS BILL THROUGH PARLIAMENT

Following its pre-legislative scrutiny, the government published the Investigatory Powers Bill in March 2016. The draft bill had been amended, and it was accompanied by more explanatory materials about the powers, but its proposals were still politically controversial. While the power to intercept telephone calls was long established and not contested, requirements for communication service providers to retain user data and powers to conduct equipment interference (accessing computer equipment, mobile phones, etc.) were questioned and opposed. In particular, the 'bulk powers' for the security and intelligence agencies to undertake such interception and interference activities on a large scale were resisted by politicians and campaign groups. The power for the security and intelligence agencies to retain large data sets containing information about people who were not under investigation was also challenged.

However, despite the controversial nature of the powers, the bill's passage through Parliament was relatively smooth. This was achieved in large part by close communication between the government and the Labour Party throughout the stages in both Houses. Ministers demonstrated willingness to listen and make changes in response to points raised by opposition parties, and provided much of the additional information and assurance sought.

At report stage in the Commons, the government made amendments to insert new privacy principles and protections into the bill, to strengthen the safeguards on journalistic material and medical records, and to change the procedures for modifying the warrants to use the powers (see HC Debates, 6 and 7 June 2016). The government also agreed to a further review of the operational case for the bulk powers, to be undertaken by David Anderson QC in time for consideration of the bill in the House of Lords, and accepted amendments proposed by the Chair of the Intelligence and Security Committee to improve the privacy safeguards for warrants and to strengthen the oversight arrangements.

The responsive attitude of the government was sufficient for the Labour Party to abstain on the bill throughout its passage through Parliament, and therefore, while it was opposed by the Scottish National Party and the Liberal Democrats, there was little prospect of it being defeated. One sticking point came in the Lords, where cross-bench peer Baroness Hollins successfully pressed an amendment that would introduce a civil liability for unlawful interceptions of public telecommunications systems, such that any future victims of 'phone hacking' by journalists or others would be able to seek damages. The amendment was rejected twice by the House of Commons during 'ping-pong', and the Lords chose not to press it a third time, so it did not become part of the Act.

Less than a month after the bill received royal assent, the European Court of Justice ruled that EU member states may not impose a general obligation to retain data on providers of electronic communications services. At the time of writing, it is not clear whether the Investigatory Powers Act will need to be amended to comply with this judgment, although the prospect of Britain leaving the EU may make it irrelevant. The Investigatory Powers Act includes a provision requiring the government to produce a report for Parliament on the operation of the Act after five years. The legislative cycle for investigatory powers might well then begin again.

WHAT DOES THIS TELL US ABOUT THE LEGISLATIVE CYCLE?

The Investigatory Powers Act is an example of the repeating cycle of policy review and legislation, with changes in society, judgments from the courts, and the expiring of existing legislation prompting the cycle to begin again.

The Act demonstrates the value of pre-legislative scrutiny to Parliament, with three reports providing views and raising questions about the draft bill. In particular, the Joint Committee's report identified and examined most of the key issues that would occupy Members of both Houses throughout scrutiny of the bill. Pre-legislative scrutiny allows government to address problems in legislation prior to its introduction, and provides opposition politicians with a valuable starting point for their scrutiny and challenge of the bill.

The Investigatory Powers Act also shows how even a very controversial political issue can be taken through Parliament relatively smoothly. The independent reviews, the pre-legislative scrutiny, and the parliamentary handling, with concessions and agreements between the two main parties, all combined to assist its passage.

The Act also highlights the challenges Parliament faces when scrutinizing the powers of the security and intelligence agencies, as there were limits to the explanations that government could provide while protecting the agencies' trade secrets. In these circumstances, parliamentarians must interpret the findings of independent reviews and rely on the judgement of the Intelligence and Security Committee, which has privileged access to classified materials, in order to make their decisions on such matters.

Primary sources

- David Anderson QC (2015) *A Question of Trust: Report of the Investigatory Powers Review*, London: The Stationery Office. Online at: https://terrorismlegislationreviewer.independent. gov.uk/wp-content/uploads/2015/06/IPR-Report-Print-Version.pdf [accessed 22 June 2017].

- Joint Committee on the Draft Investigatory Powers Bill (2016) *Draft Investigatory Powers Bill*, London: The Stationery Office, HL Paper 93, HC 651. Online at: http://www.publications.parliament.uk/pa/jt201516/jtselect/jtinvpowers/93/93.pdf [accessed 22 June 2017].

- Investigatory Powers Bill (2014–15 and 2015–16). Online at: http://services.parliament.uk/bills/2015-16/investigatorypowers.html [accessed 22 June 2017].

- Korris, M. (2016) *Investigatory Powers Bill*, House of Lords Library Note LLN 2016/032. Online at: http://researchbriefings.files.parliament.uk/documents/LLN-2016-0032/LLN-2016-0032.pdf [accessed 22 June 2017].

 FURTHER CASE STUDIES

Recent Acts that have received pre-legislative scrutiny

- Charities (Protection and Social Investment) Act 2016.
- Modern Slavery Act 2015.

Recent Acts in areas of policy that are regularly legislated upon

- Housing and Planning Act 2016.
- Serious Crime Act 2015.

References

CABINET OFFICE (2017) *Guide to Making Legislation*, London: Cabinet Office. Online at: https://www.gov.uk/government/uploads/system/uploads/attachment_data/file/608496/guide_to_making_legislation.pdf [accessed 22 June 2017].

INTELLIGENCE AND SECURITY COMMITTEE (2016) *Report on the draft Investigatory Powers Bill*, London: The Stationery Office, HC 795. Online at: http://isc.independent.gov.uk/files/20160209_ISC_Rpt_IPBill(web).pdf [accessed 22 June 2017].

JOINT COMMITTEE ON THE DRAFT INVESTIGATORY POWERS BILL (2016) *Draft Investigatory Powers Bill: Report*, London: The Stationery Office, HL Paper 93, HC 651. Online at: https://www.publications.parliament.uk/pa/jt201516/jtselect/jtinvpowers/93/93.pdf [accessed 22 June 2017].

KELLY, R. (2015a) *Pre-Legislative Scrutiny under the Coalition Government*, House of Commons Library Briefing Paper Number 05859, 13 August. Online at: http://researchbriefings.parliament.uk/ResearchBriefing/Summary/SN05859#fullreport [accessed 22 June 2017].

KELLY, R. (2015b) *English Votes for English Laws*, House of Commons Briefing Paper Number 7339, 20 June. Online at: http://researchbriefings.files.parliament.uk/documents/CBP-7339/CBP-7339.pdf [accessed 22 June 2017].

RUSSELL, M. (2013) *The Contemporary House of Lords: Westminster Bicameralism Revived*, Oxford: Oxford University Press.

RUSSELL, M. and GOVER, D. (2014) *Demystifying Financial Privilege: Does the Commons' Claim of Financial Primacy on Lords Amendments Need Reform?*, London: Constitution Unit.

SCIENCE AND TECHNOLOGY COMMITTEE (2016) *Investigatory Powers Bill: Technology Issues: Third Report of Session 2015–16*, London: The Stationery Office, HC 573. Online at: https://www.publications.parliament.uk/pa/cm201516/cmselect/cmsctech/573/573.pdf [accessed 22 June 2017].

8

Parliamentary Scrutiny and Influence on Government Bills

Meg Russell and Daniel Gover

INTRODUCTION

'Legislating' is a central function of 'legislatures'—whose consent is required before bills become law. At Westminster, the treatment of legislation is one of the most time-consuming activities on the Floor of both chambers, and the great majority of that time is spent scrutinizing government bills. In addition to plenary time, hundreds more hours are spent considering such bills 'off the Floor' in Commons public bill committees, and in grand committees in the Lords. Yet despite the centrality of this activity, and the time expended on it—by MPs and peers, parliamentary staff, ministers, and civil servants, and also by various outside groups—sceptics often question the extent to which it actually matters. That is, whether Parliament really plays much role in shaping what reaches the statute book.

Rather than describing the mechanics of the legislative process (for which see Chapter 7), this chapter focuses on the political dynamics of legislative scrutiny, paying particular attention to how parliamentary policy influence works. We start with common assumptions, central among them being the idea that government dominates the process, with Parliament acting as little more than a 'rubber stamp'. We then go on to question these various assumptions. Fundamentally, we suggest that Parliament is far more influential on government legislation than is commonly assumed, once the full complexity of the process, and different forms of influence, are taken into account.

Common assumptions about the Westminster legislative process

The great majority of bills passed at Westminster originate with the government. As Chapter 12 shows, a small number of private members' bills are agreed, but most of these are on very narrow issues. In the 2015–16 session, for example, 23 of the 29 bills reaching the statute book were government-sponsored. This means that they were drafted by government lawyers, and debate in both chambers was led by ministers; the role of other parliamentarians was to respond to the proposals made. Unlike in some other parliaments, Westminster has no formal mechanism for specialist committees (such as select committees) to propose bills on a cross-party basis; nor do opposition parties propose their own bills. Hence Philip Norton (2013, 77) describes the formulation of legislation as 'overwhelmingly a government-centred activity'.

The appearance of government dominance continues during the parliamentary scrutiny of bills. While numerous amendments are proposed every session, the great majority of those that are agreed are proposed by ministers themselves. For example, in the 2008–9 session the Lords agreed 1,806 amendments, but 1,732 of these (i.e. 96 per cent) were sponsored or co-sponsored by a minister (Russell 2013, 169). In the Lords there is no government majority, so the Chamber sometimes inflicts defeats on hostile amendments (some of which subsequently go on to reach the statute book, while others are overturned). In the Commons the number of amendments agreed is broadly similar, but in a typical year the number of these without government backing is nil. While thousands of amendments are proposed to bills each year by non-government parliamentarians (including opposition Members, government backbenchers, and non-party peers in the Lords), almost all fail to be agreed.

 Parliamentary terms Amendment

A proposed addition, removal, or change to a motion or to the wording of a clause or schedule in a bill.

These features can readily create an impression that Parliament, despite its formal power in the legislative process, is in practice peripheral to the agreement of policy. Illustrating the common view, a leading British politics textbook suggests that 'it may be questioned whether Parliament effectively makes the law' (Leach, Coxall, and Robins 2011, 236), while another describes the House of Commons as 'misunderstood if viewed as a legislator' (Moran 2015, 111). Media criticisms of Parliament's toothlessness are often even sharper and more dismissive.

In summarizing the dynamics of legislative scrutiny at Westminster, the following sections question various common assumptions. They all explore whether criticisms of parliamentary powerlessness are really justified, concluding that Westminster plays a much bigger role in the formulation of government policy than is often understood. Part of the difficulty is that much parliamentary influence is not readily captured by the public record. Another is that the boundaries are often not as straightforward as they appear. Parliamentary approval of legislation is ostensibly a discrete and well-defined process—comprising the first, second, and third readings, committee stage, and report stage—but in fact many other parliamentary activities contribute in less direct and obvious ways. The formal legislative process is meanwhile used by non-government parliamentarians partly for purposes beyond influencing the bill at hand. Crucially, Parliament can play a major role in influencing legislation before it is introduced. All of this means that a focus only on on-the-record proceedings during the formal legislative stages can be misleading.

Non-government amendments may 'fail' but can nonetheless be influential

Different groups in Parliament each bring their own perspective and style to the legislative process, and each uses it to further their own goals. Government backbenchers often largely want to support and defend government bills, where these changes are in line with agreed party policy. Opposition frontbenchers may in contrast seek to embarrass the government and use the process to broadcast the merits of their own alternative policies. One objective that most parliamentarians share is to improve the quality of government legislative proposals. As already indicated, the great majority of amendments proposed during the Westminster legislative process come from non-government parliamentarians, and very few of these are agreed. But non-government amendments are not all designed to be accepted; many serve other purposes.

One of the quirks of the Westminster legislative process is that it remains very much structured around amendments, and to trigger debate Members table numerous 'probing' amendments. Most of these come from the opposition, but some also come from government backbenchers and non-party peers. Their primary purpose is not to change the bill, but instead to get the minister to explain its content. So a Member might propose deleting a clause, in order that the minister will explain why the clause is necessary, or might propose changing words so that the minister will specify why the current wording was chosen. After receiving an explanation, the Member proposing the amendment will often withdraw it, declaring themselves satisfied by what the minister has said.

 Parliamentary terms Probing amendment

An amendment to a bill put forward by an MP or peer to provoke debate or seek clarification about a proposal. The proposers of these amendments typically do not intend them to be approved: once the required information has been received in debate, they will withdraw them from consideration rather than pressing them to a vote.

Despite relatively few non-government amendments resulting in changes to bills, this process can be very testing for ministers. Because bills will be subjected to close scrutiny in both Chambers—with often quite hostile questioning from opposition Members in the Commons, and potentially intervention by established subject experts in the Lords—preparation in Whitehall must be thorough. Civil servants provide briefings on every amendment for ministers, whose arguments must withstand public scrutiny in Parliament. An unconvincing ministerial response could cause negative headlines, reputational damage, and serious parliamentary pressure to change the bill. Those in Whitehall know that opposition frontbenchers, government backbenchers, and non-party peers, all frequently working closely with specialist outside groups, will subject bills to careful scrutiny—and this has an important indirect effect. In the words of one civil servant we interviewed, 'you know that Parliament is going to give you a tough time, and therefore you prepare really well'. A huge amount of government time goes into getting ready for legislative debates, both in terms of briefing and (as discussed later) thinking through policy carefully at the drafting stage.

 Parliamentary terms Withdrawing an amendment

To remove an amendment from further consideration, usually following a reply from a government minister.

Other amendments enable parliamentarians to raise new issues. As indicated in Chapter 7, amendments proposed to a bill must be considered 'in scope' in order to be debated—that is, they must cover issues of clear relevance to the bill. Nonetheless, the legislative process provides opportunities for Members to propose amendments on loosely connected topics (e.g. the 'Dubs amendment' in Case Study 8). This ensures that these issues receive attention in Whitehall—from both ministers and civil servants—and clear on-the-record responses in Parliament. Hence the legislative process can serve as an agenda-setting device for non-government Members, in a similar way to parliamentary questions, private members' bills, and backbench or opposition debates. But the stakes for government are higher, because an amendment attracting widespread support could potentially be voted into the bill. Nonetheless, like probing amendments, if such proposals are not immediately accepted this does not mean that they have failed in their purpose.

Government amendments don't necessarily imply government dominance

The fact that most agreed amendments originate with government initially appears to tell a simple story. But the true dynamics of this are also far more complex. Academic studies from the 1970s onwards, at Westminster and elsewhere, have shown that government amendments often respond to concerns raised earlier in the process by non-government parliamentarians (Griffith 1974; Shephard and Cairney 2005; Thompson 2013, 2015). Indeed the government's own guide to the legislative process now makes this clear (Cabinet Office 2017). As described in Chapter 9, many opposition or government backbench amendments during the House of Commons committee stage are followed by government 'concessionary' amendments at report stage. Where bills begin in the Commons (as the majority do), points raised by non-government MPs may likewise subsequently be responded to by government amendments in the Lords. The same pattern continues during the Lords stages, with committee stage amendments attracting government concessions at report or third reading. When a minister accepts a proposal in principle, government expert lawyers are almost invariably asked to redraft it, rather than simply allowing a non-government amendment to stand.

The most recent study of the legislative process, based on 12 government bills passing through both Chambers over the period 2005–12, illustrates this very clearly (Russell and Gover 2017; Russell, Gover, and Wollter 2016). It shows that of 728 government amendments agreed to these bills, 297 (41 per cent) responded to proposals from non-government parliamentarians. Among government amendments with the greatest policy substance (i.e. excluding those merely 'tidying up' or clarifying legislative drafting), 60 per cent responded to Parliament.

There are various reasons why ministers propose concessionary amendments. Sometimes MPs or peers bring new matters to government's attention, which ministers feel could genuinely improve a bill. For example, government backbenchers might propose changes based on contact with constituents or party members, on issues which civil servants preparing the bill had not considered and which ministers are sympathetic towards. At other times if the opposition draws attention to weaknesses in a bill, ministers may wish to avoid potential public embarrassment. Generally, whatever their source, ministers will be most concerned about those amendments which trigger concerns among government backbench MPs, on whose support they rely. Ultimately, many concessions are aimed at avoiding the prospect of defeat in one or other Chamber.

Hence, parliamentarians can make a visible impact on the bill which is nonetheless not immediately obvious, because the changes are implemented through government amendments.

The two Chambers often operate in cooperation, not competition

It might be assumed that the Lords and Commons operate relatively separately, and have a largely adversarial relationship. This is often how the popular media presents Parliament. But scrutiny in the two Chambers is in fact quite closely connected, and often quite cooperative.

Because a bill passes through one Chamber after the other, similar issues are often raised through amendments in both. Most bills start in the Commons, allowing peers to monitor the issues raised by MPs and respond to them. Although Commons defeats are rare, often it is clear—from debates, rebellious votes, or informal private conversations—that government backbenchers have concerns about a bill. Peers pursue their own agendas, often based on expertise, but they also pay particular attention to issues on which there is disquiet in the Commons.

Proposals put on the agenda by the Commons opposition frontbench frequently continue to be pursued in the Lords. Ministers are under greater pressure to respond in that Chamber, given the government's lack of majority and hence its greater risk of defeat. Government concessions are therefore often 'held back' for the Lords, which can create an impression that peers have greater influence. But ministers can readily overturn Lords defeats with the support of their backbench MPs—it is where that support is lacking that they become most vulnerable (see Case Study 8). Peers essentially send bills back to the Commons asking MPs 'are you sure?', which empowers government backbenchers in particular. Many of the biggest changes achieved in Parliament hence involve a combination of Commons and Lords pressure.

Most government bills do get amended to some extent in Parliament, often through government concessions. Some changes are relatively modest, while on more major changes Lords defeats often play a role. In our study of 12 government bills during 2005–12, examples of major changes included delay to the introduction of Labour's identity card scheme (allowing the 2010 Coalition to drop the scheme before it had been introduced), the extension of the new offence of corporate manslaughter to deaths in police and prison custody, and substantial reworking of the Coalition's Public Bodies Bill (2010–12) which sought to abolish and merge numerous 'quangos'. In the last of these cases major concessions were given to avoid Lords defeats, with government climbdowns on issues such as the proposed privatization of public forests. On Labour's Health Bill (2005–6), significant changes were made to the provisions banning smoking in public places, this time to head off likely defeat in the Commons.

Parliamentary influence occurs throughout the policy process

This same study also shows how a focus on the formal legislative stages, and on amendments, overlooks important parliamentary influence. Such influence can be successfully exerted before government legislation has been introduced, and also after it has been passed. Scholars of public policy often present the policy process as a series of stages, beginning with 'agenda setting', then 'policy formulation', followed by 'decision-making', and ultimately 'implementation and evaluation' (John 2012). While Parliament's role might most obviously be at the decision-making stage, it actually affects outcomes throughout.

Hence the smoking ban for example, and corporate manslaughter legislation, had both been publicly demanded by backbench Labour parliamentarians for years before their introduction. This illustrates Parliament's role in setting the policy agenda. During the policy formulation stage, as already indicated, ministers and civil servants are keenly aware of the need to make bills 'Parliament-ready'. For this purpose the cabinet subcommittee responsible for approving all government bills requires departments to prepare a written 'parliamentary handling strategy'—to demonstrate that possible objections have been thought through, and that the bill will withstand public scrutiny (see Cabinet Office 2017). After the bill has been passed, parliamentarians continue to play an important role (for example, through question times and select committees) in holding government to account for its implementation. Some proposals made during this process may go on, in turn, to influence future bills.

The legislative process is less separate from other processes than it might appear

Westminster's legislative process is ostensibly self-contained, comprising a set of debates on the Floor of both Chambers and in committee. But the political dynamics of parliamentary policy influence are actually far less bounded than this suggests.

Importantly, both pre- and post-introduction of a bill, numerous private discussions take place between those in government and those in Parliament—involving all the main parties and groups, particularly in the Lords. Major bills will be discussed from an early stage within the parliamentary group of the governing party (e.g. the Parliamentary Labour Party or Conservative 1922 Committee) and in smaller meetings between ministers and concerned government backbenchers. Civil servants and ministers often hold open meetings for parliamentarians once a bill is published, and meet privately with Members who wish to amend the bill. For obvious reasons, such interactions are particularly intense in the Lords and on issues where there is government backbench concern.

Informal and hidden mechanisms are thus very important to parliamentary influence on legislation. But other formal and visible mechanisms can also play a part. One example is parliamentary question times, the most high-profile of which is the weekly Prime Minister's Questions (PMQs) (see Chapter 17). Members can use these to draw media and public attention to any deficiencies in a bill. Other forums in the Commons include various types of debate. For example, Labour frontbenchers used both PMQs and a Commons opposition day debate to pressurize the Coalition on the forestry proposals in the Public Bodies Bill—contributing to these being dropped.

Similar patterns are particularly visible at earlier stages of the policy process. For example, when pushing the issues of corporate manslaughter and smoking in public places up the political agenda, backbenchers used private members' bills and Early Day Motions. While such mechanisms might appear relatively toothless, they succeeded in mobilizing parliamentary opinion and encouraging government to legislate. Likewise, select committees—despite having no formal role in amending legislation—frequently make suggestions that get taken up in government bills. Post-introduction, their recommendations also often inspire non-government amendments. Our study found several examples of 'agenda setting' by select committees, plus numerous amendments made that reflected select committee recommendations.

Conclusion

All in all, a close analysis of Parliament's involvement in the making of government bills shows a complex picture. While some parliamentary influence is visible and on the record, much is relatively hidden and behind the scenes. The influence of different groups in Parliament, and of the two Chambers, is difficult to tease apart. It takes various forms, starting before bills are introduced, and continuing during their formal passage through Parliament. Sometimes such influence even continues after bills have passed, for example, by monitoring their implementation or pushing for changes through future legislation.

Those who dismiss Parliament's power over legislation tend to base this on the lack of visible conflict between government and Parliament, and the limited number of government policy defeats—particularly in the Commons. But the nature of the relationship between the executive and the legislature is very subtle. Because the government depends on the confidence of Parliament (unlike in systems such as the US) conflict is risky, and ministers operate within the constraints of what parliamentarians (and ultimately their own backbenchers) will accept. Hence our study noted six interconnected forms of parliamentary power exerted through the process. The first is the obvious one of amending government legislation (which in practice usually occurs through concessionary government amendments). The second is 'anticipated reactions', whereby government consciously thinks through what Parliament will accept and devises its proposals accordingly. The third is more subtle, whereby those in government subconsciously limit their ambitions in line with the parliamentary mood—and particularly that inside the governing party. Fourth, Parliament has significant agenda-setting power, and can 'politicize' issues once bills have been introduced. Fifth, as a very public forum, it has a power of 'exposure', where the requirement for ministers to explain policy on the record has a clear deterrent effect. Finally, Parliament may of course exert its power not by challenging government policy, but by supporting it.

In a parliamentary system such as Britain's, the last of these outcomes will be the norm—but this does not mean Parliament is subservient to government. Ministers are drawn from Parliament, depend on Parliament's confidence, and must work hard to minimize conflict and retain parliamentary support. Bills introduced already reflect what ministers think will be acceptable to Parliament, and often what parliamentarians themselves have called for. The content of bills is tested quite hard through parliamentary scrutiny, and where they are found wanting they are often amended in line with Parliament's demands.

Further Reading

CABINET OFFICE (2017) *Guide to Making Legislation*, London: Cabinet Office. Online at: https://www.gov.uk/government/uploads/system/uploads/attachment_data/file/616341/Guide_to_Making_Legislation_Apr_2017_v2.0_final_May_update.pdf [accessed 22 June 2017].

RUSSELL, M. (2013) *The Contemporary House of Lords: Westminster Bicameralism Revived*, Oxford: Oxford University Press.

RUSSELL, M. and GOVER, D. (2017) *Legislation at Westminster: Parliamentary Actors and Influence in the Making of British Law*, Oxford: Oxford University Press.

RUSSELL, M., GOVER, D., and WOLLTER, K. (2016) 'Does the Executive Dominate the Westminster Legislative Process?: Six Reasons for Doubt', *Parliamentary Affairs*, Vol. 69 (2), pp. 286–308.

THOMPSON, L. (2015) *Making British Law: Committees in Action*, Basingstoke: Palgrave.

Case Study 8: Immigration Bill

While no single bill can fully capture the Westminster legislative process, the Conservative government's Immigration Bill, scrutinized between September 2015 and May 2016, was in many respects fairly typical. This relatively wide-ranging piece of legislation included provisions on labour market exploitation and illegal working, illegal migrants' rights, immigration appeals, and border security. It was introduced shortly after the 2015 general election and implemented several of the Conservatives' manifesto commitments. Despite being largely supported on the Conservative side, the bill demonstrated examples of both consensual and adversarial parliamentary influence during its passage. This included one high-profile issue, that of unaccompanied refugee children, which was still being debated long after it was passed.

At first sight, the government's bill appears to have been agreed with little traceable parliamentary influence. During its initial passage through both chambers, MPs and peers proposed around 950 amendments on a wide range of topics. Almost 400 were agreed to, three-quarters of them in the Lords. But 99 per cent of agreed amendments were sponsored by the government, with only five non-government amendments being passed. Opposition MPs forced around 40 separate divisions on the bill—including 35 at Commons committee stage alone—but each time the government's majority ensured ministers' victory. The bill's parliamentary opponents fared better in the Lords, defeating the government in five out of nine divisions during its initial passage—leading to the five agreed non-government amendments. Two of these were subsequently overturned in the Commons, while the remaining three (explained below) survived in modified form.

Yet, beneath the surface, Parliament shaped the legislation in various other hidden ways. Some government amendments responded to earlier non-government ones. The bill created a new offence of illegally working in the UK, and at Commons committee stage the Labour opposition frontbench proposed an amendment to add a legal defence where the person had a 'reasonable excuse', for example, where they believed they were entitled to work. This was rejected when MPs voted on it. Labour subsequently proposed similar amendments at the Commons report and Lords committee stages, neither of which were agreed. But the minister committed to reflect carefully on points raised in the debate. At the next stage, Lords report, the government tabled a package of five amendments, to provide that the offence would only apply where someone had 'reasonable cause to believe' they were not entitled to work. The minister explained that these resulted from the 'compelling case' made during the earlier debate (see HL Debates, 9 March 2016, c. 1311 onwards). Similar patterns occurred elsewhere on the bill, for instance regarding the offences of driving when illegally in the UK, or leasing properties to those disqualified by their immigration status. On some more technical matters, government amendments responded to the recommendations of a Lords select committee.

These examples were all negotiated consensually, but in other cases pressure was more adversarial. Around the time that the bill was being considered by Parliament, the Syrian refugee crisis began to attract significant public and political attention, sparking an external campaign which urged the UK government to accept 3,000 unaccompanied refugee children. Though slightly tangential to the original topic of the bill, its passage provided an opportunity for MPs and peers to push for progress on this matter. In the Lords, Labour peer Alf Dubs—who had himself arrived in the UK as a child refugee from Czechoslovakia in 1939—tabled an amendment requiring the government to relocate and support 3,000 such children. This was formally co-sponsored by a cross-bencher, a Liberal Democrat, and a bishop—underlining its cross-party appeal—and when pressed to a division the government was heavily defeated by 306 votes to 204. Dubs' amendment was initially rejected by the Commons, but when the bill returned to the Lords he reintroduced his proposal in weaker form, removing reference to the number of children to be accepted, and peers backed it a second time.

This was a policy on which there was known disquiet among government backbenchers. So if ministers had asked their MPs to overturn the Lords amendment again, this might have undermined backbench goodwill, and even risked being defeated. In advance of the previous Commons vote on Dubs' amendment, one backbencher had initiated a Westminster Hall debate on the topic, while press reports suggested that at least 12 were considering defying the whip (Helm 2016); five ultimately did so. The possible vote on Dubs' revised amendment sparked rumours of an even larger Commons rebellion. Opposition parties raised the issue at Prime Minister's Questions, pressurizing the government in the full glare of the media. Ultimately, ministers chose to accept the revised amendment, and the first children arrived later that year—clearly demonstrating Parliament's capacity to force change. Compromises were similarly reached on two other Lords defeats (covering time limits for immigration detention and detention of pregnant women). Nonetheless the 'watering down' of the Dubs amendment, to omit the number of children from the commitment, allowed the government to announce nine months later that far fewer than 3,000 would be accepted. This triggered fresh parliamentary pressure—including a Commons urgent question, e-petitions, a report by the Home Affairs Select Committee (2017), and an amendment proposed to a subsequent bill (see Elgot 2017).

This bill illustrates several things about how parliamentary influence works. Its main principles were clearly supported by government backbenchers, and hence were never under threat. It passed with little appearance of change wrought by Parliament, but in fact there were some clear concessions on points of detail, not easily visible from the public record because they were extracted relatively consensually through government amendments. Other compromises were, in contrast, achieved through more visible conflict. In each case, pressure in the formal legislative stages was supplemented by other parliamentary mechanisms—including select committee reports, Westminster Hall debates, and PMQs. The case study also shows how influence on bills typically involves both Chambers acting together, with points raised in one House followed up in the other. Crucially, while adversarial pressure may involve government defeats in the Lords, where the government lacks a majority, these achieve influence primarily by asking MPs to 'think again'. In particular they empower government backbench MPs, the key pivotal group in that Chamber. In the Commons, it is often a mistake to look for visible conflict at all: on key matters the government chooses to concede rather than to risk the embarrassment of possible defeat.

Primary sources

- Immigration Bill (Bill 74), as introduced in the Commons, 17 September 2015. Online at: https://publications.parliament.uk/pa/bills/cbill/2015-2016/0074/cbill_2015-20160074_en_1.htm [accessed 27 June 2017].

- Immigration Bill, Report stage, HL Debates, 21 March 2016, cc. 2091–114. Online at: https://hansard.parliament.uk/lords/2016-03-21/debates/AAE552DF-70A7-4220-8B67-D59EAA007FF4/ImmigrationBill [accessed 27 June 2017].

- Brown, L. (2016) 'Thirty Tory MPs set to rebel on child refugees: Ministers forced to reconsider letting youngsters in', *Daily Mail*, 30 April. Online at: http://www.dailymail.co.uk/news/article-3566684/Thirty-Tory-MPs-set-rebel-child-refugees.html [accessed 27 June 2017].

  FURTHER CASE STUDIES

- Public Bodies Bill (2010–12 session).

- Health Bill (2005–6 session).

- Budget Responsibility and National Audit Bill (2010–12 session).

References

CABINET OFFICE (2017) *Guide to Making Legislation*, London: Cabinet Office. Online at: https://www.gov.uk/government/uploads/system/uploads/attachment_data/file/616341/Guide_to_Making_Legislation_Apr_2017_v2.0_final_May_update.pdf [accessed 22 June 2017].

ELGOT, J. (2017) 'Government defeats attempt to restart Dubs scheme', *The Guardian*, 7 March. Online at: https://www.theguardian.com/uk-news/2017/mar/07/government-defeats-attempt-to-restart-dubs-scheme [accessed 4 August 2017].

GRIFFITH, J. A. G. (1974) *Parliamentary Scrutiny of Government Bills*, London: Allen and Unwin.

HELM, T. (2016) 'David Cameron faces knife-edge vote on child refugee policy', *The Observer*, 23 April. Online at: https://www.theguardian.com/world/2016/apr/23/david-cameron-defeat-child-refugees [accessed 22 June 2017].

HOME AFFAIRS SELECT COMMITTEE (2017) *Unaccompanied Child Migrants: Thirteenth Report of Session 2016-17*, London: Stationery Office, HC 1026.

JOHN, P. (2012) *Analysing Public Policy*, London: Routledge.

LEACH, R., COXALL, B., and ROBINS, L. (2011) *British Politics*, Basingstoke: Palgrave.

MORAN, M. (2015) *Politics and Governance in the UK*, London: Palgrave.

NORTON, P. (2013) *Parliament in British Politics*, Basingstoke: Palgrave.

RUSSELL, M. (2013) *The Contemporary House of Lords: Westminster Bicameralism Revived*, Oxford: Oxford University Press.

RUSSELL, M. and GOVER, D. (2017) *Legislation at Westminster: Parliamentary Actors and Influence in the Making of British Law*, Oxford: Oxford University Press.

RUSSELL, M., GOVER, D., and WOLLTER, K. (2016) 'Does the Executive Dominate the Westminster Legislative Process?: Six Reasons for Doubt', *Parliamentary Affairs*, Vol. 69 (2), pp. 286–308.

SHEPHARD, M. and CAIRNEY, P. (2005) 'The Impact of the Scottish Parliament in Amending Executive Legislation', *Political Studies*, Vol. 53 (2), pp. 303–19.

THOMPSON, L. (2013) 'More of the Same or a Period of Change? The Impact of Bill Committees in the Twenty-First Century House of Commons', *Parliamentary Affairs*, Vol. 66 (3), pp. 459–79.

THOMPSON, L. (2015) *Making British Law: Committees in Action*, Basingstoke: Palgrave.

9

Committee Scrutiny of Legislation

Louise Thompson and Tony McNulty

INTRODUCTION

Legislation which follows the normal passage of a bill in the UK Parliament will at some point have a committee stage, where MPs or peers can examine the text of the bill in detail. It is a very time-consuming aspect of Parliament's work, accounting for more parliamentary time than any other legislative stage. In 2015–16, for example, the Commons saw 18 bill committees sitting for over 250 hours. Yet committee scrutiny is afforded little attention by outside observers. This chapter discusses the common perceptions of committee stage and highlights its role in bringing about changes to government legislation.

 Parliamentary terms Sitting

Used to describe a parliamentary day: i.e. the period between prayers at the opening of the sitting and the time when the House adjourns for the day.

There are several types of committee stage. In the Commons, high-profile bills, and constitutional bills such as the European Union Referendum Bill (2015–16), have some or all of their committee stage in the main Chamber. This is referred to as a Committee of the whole House. Occasionally, bills are considered by a select committee. More commonly, though, bills receive their committee stage in the upper corridors of the Palace of Westminster, in a public bill committee (PBC). In the Lords, the diversity of political groups means that there is no equivalent to a PBC. Instead, committee stage is taken in a Committee of the whole House or in a Grand Committee away from the Chamber. Any peer can participate, regardless of the format. While much of what is written here can apply also to committees taken on the Floor of either House, we focus mainly on PBCs.

 Parliamentary terms Public bill committee

A group of MPs, typically numbering between 16 and 50, who consider a bill in detail on a 'line by line' basis following its second reading in the Commons. Although any MP can table an amendment to the bill, only members of the committee are able to speak in committee or formally move amendments.

Planning for the committee stage

By the time a bill committee meets, a number of decisions will already have been made by government (typically the government whips' office, in discussion with the relevant department and ministers), which set the parameters for scrutiny. Of particular importance is the decision as to whether the bill should start in the Commons or the Lords. This sounds relatively simple but can be of huge importance, especially if the bill is contentious. The government has greater control of bills that start in the Commons, but the government whips need to ensure that the broader programme of legislation is balanced between the two chambers. In recent times, anything from 20 to 40 bills have been passed in each parliamentary session. Both the government and opposition need to organize for the parliamentary year (Institute for Government 2017). Agreement will usually be sought through the 'usual channels'—that is, the whips' offices of all parties.

Public bill committees vary in size, ranging from around 16 to 50 MPs. They are ad hoc bodies established after the second reading of a bill in the Commons, and are known by the name of the bill they will be scrutinizing (e.g. Housing and Planning Bill Committee). Membership is decided by the Committee of Selection; a group of (mainly) party whips who meet weekly. Committees usually contain MPs from the three main parties in proportion to their strength in the House. The government therefore usually has a majority on each committee. MPs can request to serve on a committee but it is the party whips who decide. It used to be that MPs had to participate at the second reading of a bill to be considered for committee, but this is less so now. The size of the committee will depend on factors such as the size of the bill, the number of ministers required, and its territorial reach. If it has a Scottish, Irish, or Welsh dimension, the smaller parties from those countries are usually included, leading to a larger committee to maintain party proportionality. The regional dimension has been further complicated by the recent dominance of the Scottish National Party and the introduction of EVEL—English votes for English laws (see Chapter 7).

The party whips control the amount of time set aside to scrutinize the bill. PBCs usually meet in the mornings and afternoons on Tuesdays and Thursdays—each meeting is called a sitting. The whips' offices discuss how many sittings and oral evidence sessions are required and when the bill's committee stage should complete. All these points are presented in a 'programme motion' which is then proposed and agreed by the committee.

Oral evidence sessions can take place at the start of the committee's proceedings and are a recent innovation, becoming standard practice from 2007. Committees typically hold between one and four evidence sessions, where MPs can question government ministers, departmental officials, lobby group representatives, and other stakeholders. This is followed by sittings where MPs undergo detailed line-by-line scrutiny, which is more time-consuming. The Digital Economy Bill of 2016–17 held three oral evidence sessions, followed by eight scrutiny sessions.

 Parliamentary terms Line-by-line scrutiny

MPs or peers go through a bill in great detail, with the ability to discuss any line or clause of the bill.

For the government whips' office, the most important thing is the date by which the bill's committee stage is complete and reported back to the House of Commons. This is called the 'outdate'. As Chapter 7 explains, with an outdate secured, the government business managers can plan for the bill's further stages. Generally, the time in committee is viewed as the opposition's time—and the government whips are normally quite relaxed about proceedings. If necessary they can control the pace of scrutiny and make sure that particular items of the bill are discussed.

Beyond this, it is up to the opposition how they proceed. Spending a lot of time discussing one clause may be to the detriment of scrutiny of other clauses. If the bill is contentious, it may be that the government seeks to have as much debate as possible at the committee stage, to forestall claims of railroading contentious material through the Commons. Although committee scrutiny of a bill may seem rather dry and dreary, those for and against the bill in both Houses will look with great interest on how the bill was dealt with in committee and whether or not sufficient time was spent on particular issues. A lot of work and detail is therefore determined before the committee even meets—much of which is summarized in the first order of business—agreeing the programme motion.

The term 'line-by-line' scrutiny means that the committee works through the bill in order, debating each clause in turn. MPs may move amendments that will try to add, amend, or remove words, phrases, clauses, or schedules of the bill in question. They are also able to probe (question) the relevant government minister about the wording of the bill. To do any of these things they must submit written amendments in advance before speaking on them in committee. The officials supporting the Chair of the committee determine whether or not amendments are relevant and 'in order', publishing the list of amendments to be considered on each sitting day of the committee. Many of these amendments are used to tease out more information on the government's thinking behind a particular clause or policy issue—and are called 'probing amendments'. Often they are then withdrawn, perhaps to be explored further at report stage or in the other House—depending on where the greatest political impact will be and the scope for success of the amendment. As formal bodies, committees follow the same traditions and procedures as the main House of Commons Chamber. MPs sit in an adversarial fashion, with government MPs directly opposite opposition MPs, who typically sit with colleagues from the same party, as in the main Chamber. They follow the same rules of debate as in the Commons Chamber too. An amendment may therefore be withdrawn by the MP who moved it, accepted with or without a vote, or defeated. Withdrawal is by far the most common outcome.

Legislative, procedural, and political contexts

Bill committees have a difficult and demanding role. To understand this, we must think carefully about the different contexts in which they work. Firstly, there is the legislative context. Legislation is written by expert legislative draftsmen from a government office known as Parliamentary Counsel and is designed to allow the bill to be interpreted and implemented correctly. But this can make it very complex; it is not always easy for MPs and their researchers to understand. Support for ministers in PBCs can resemble an American football team, with key experts (civil servants) coming 'on and off the pitch' at will depending on the clauses being discussed. By contrast, the lead shadow ministers for the opposition will have, at best, a researcher or two to assist them, perhaps with some support from outside bodies with an interest in the bill—such as lobbyists, pressure groups, and charities.

The procedural context adds a further constraint. The fact a bill has already been debated and voted on by MPs at second reading means that its core principles have been formally agreed to. MPs in committee are bound by this decision and cannot make changes which go beyond the scope of the bill. Amendments which try to do this will not be selected for debate—so the grounds for scrutiny are narrowly defined. At the end of committee stage, a bill is reported back to the Floor of the House, but here the rules are quite strict on what can be debated. As Chapter 7 explains, committee stage may be the first point at which MPs can try to amend a bill, but it is the first of several stages, which always interact and relate to each other. For instance, when the Lords debates a bill that started in the Commons, it considers the amount of time spent on issues in committee and report in order to determine its scrutiny.

Finally, and most importantly, committee stage takes place within a highly political context. Government bills may come directly from an election manifesto. As such, the government can claim a mandate to make the changes which the bill seeks to introduce. Legislation not outlined in the government's manifesto will often be treated with less parliamentary respect. Government wishes to see all of its legislation passed. Defeat at any stage brings political as well as legislative consequences, and there is considerable pressure on government ministers not to concede any ground. MPs of all parties must therefore navigate the complexities of these legislative, procedural, and political contexts as they scrutinize bills—and this has an enormous impact on their capacity to carry out that scrutiny.

Traditional assumptions about committee scrutiny

Bill committee scrutiny has often gone under the radar of those studying and reporting on the UK Parliament. Although a famous study (Griffith 1974) described their work in painstaking detail as part of a wider analysis of the legislative process, the role of PBCs was not studied comprehensively until the twenty-first century. The introduction of oral evidence sessions in 2007 made them slightly more newsworthy, but it is still rare to find bill committee work being discussed outside Parliament.

This lack of attention is matched by the very poor reputation PBCs have long held in the corridors of Westminster. The long hours involved, often not visible to outsiders, means that appointment to a bill committee is typically seen as a punishment inflicted on backbenchers by the party whips or a laborious but necessary duty for new MPs. A series of assumptions about committee work therefore prevailed over the latter half of the twentieth century and the early twenty-first century:

i) *MPs appointed to committee are generalists not specialists:* The Standing Orders require Members' qualifications to be taken into account alongside the party composition of the Chamber, but observers have often cast doubt on whether this actually happens in practice. Conservative MP Sarah Wollaston hit the headlines in 2011 when she felt she had been deliberately excluded from serving on the Health and Social Care Bill Committee despite being a GP until her election the previous year, in favour of MPs with little experience of healthcare. Labour MP Diane Abbott stated in the same year that 'anyone who knows or cares about the legislation does not get on the committee in the first place' (Abbott 2011). Although this is not always the case (former Labour MP Neil Gerrard was an avowed expert in immigration and sat on many PBCs in this area in the 2001 and 2005 Parliaments), it is generalists and not specialists who tend to examine legislation in detail.

ii) *Behaviour is partisan and ritualistic:* The appointments process and the design of the committee rooms makes the behaviour of MPs very similar to that in the main Chamber. In fact, they are often described as the House of Commons 'in miniature' (see Rush 2000, 110). Debates and divisions are held on partisan lines. Government backbenchers are commanded to be quiet and to not delay proceedings. The much-quoted stories of backbenchers using committees to get on with paperwork or sign their Christmas cards are not altogether untrue. Procedural tactics are often used, with opposition MPs encouraged to table amendments, to prolong debates, and to push amendments to a vote when their whips tell them to. There can be real debate and discussion in committee, but critics concentrate on the broader caricature of partisan inertia.

iii) *Committees make no changes to bills:* Given what has just been said, it is no surprise that committees are considered to be ineffective. Literature suggests that they make no changes to legislation (Modernisation Committee 2006, 23; Brazier 2004, 14). This is often supported by statistics citing the number of successful opposition or backbench amendments made at committee stage (see Thompson 2015, 42). In the Commons this is less than 0.5 per cent and even these are mostly very minor changes, including correcting spelling mistakes in the bill. By contrast, amendments proposed by the government have a success rate of over 99.9 per cent (ibid., 54). Committee scrutiny thus seems futile. Government amendments rejected by committees are usually the result of whipping errors (including MPs arriving late to committees or simply getting confused and voting the wrong way).

Together, these assumptions cast doubt on the utility of the committee stage as a feature of the legislative process. They also contribute to the image of the House of Commons as an executive-dominated legislature which lacks the capacity to make the government reconsider legislation. However, contemporary analysis of committee work challenges this view somewhat.

Contemporary developments

Over the last decade academic attention has shifted towards the analysis of the effectiveness of parliamentary scrutiny of legislation. This stems partly from the commitment of successive governments to pre-legislative scrutiny or the publication of a bill well in advance of the committee stage (see Kelly 2015). It also stems from the Modernisation Committee's (2006) proposals to reform the legislative process whereby, as part of a package of recommendations, standing committees were renamed public bill committees and were given the opportunity to take oral evidence at the start of proceedings. A further factor is the increasing attention being given to the informal work of Parliament—the activity and behaviours that take place behind the scenes, as outlined in Chapter 8. This means resisting committees being seen as a discrete stage of the legislative process and instead considering how the scrutiny that begins in PBCs continues after the formal sittings have ended. It also means going beyond the usual quantitative indicators of successful versus unsuccessful amendments and investigating more informal indicators of scrutiny. Contemporary understandings of committees include a much stronger understanding of the political role of legislation and a much broader interpretation of the function of the committee stage as a whole.

The benefits of evidence-taking

The introduction of oral evidence has enhanced the information available to the MPs on committees. Information from experts helps MPs become better informed and puts them on a more level playing field. It also enhances the quality of the scrutiny undertaken, highlighting flaws which may otherwise have gone unnoticed. MPs put forward amendments to rectify such flaws, citing the oral evidence and putting the government under greater pressure to concede. It is a key weapon for backbench MPs, particularly the opposition. The efficacy of the oral evidence sessions is very dependent, however, on how the evidence providers are chosen and how much pressure the government has put on these choices.

Ministerial behaviour in committees

This depends in part on whether the bill has been scrutinized in draft and how contentious the subject matter is. Committee scrutiny is about more than government ministers simply accepting or rejecting amendments. It can also include: making changes to the way a bill is to be implemented (e.g. changes to codes of practice); promises to consider an issue at a later date or to take an amendment away for discussion with colleagues (usually called an agreement to 'reconsider'); or ministerial promises to redraft amendments and table them again at report stage on the Floor of either House, where they will be approved. This behaviour is crucial to the way the committee system works. But these ministerial undertakings are not formally recorded on the face of the bill when it leaves committee and so are missed by those who focus only on the text of the bill at the end of committee stage. Combined, around five times as many changes are made to legislation through these informal means (see Thompson 2015).

The impact of committees later on in the legislative process

Legislative scrutiny does not end following its committee stage. A bill originating in the House of Commons will be discussed by MPs in the Chamber at report stage and will then move to the House of Lords to be scrutinized at length by peers. The Commons report stage is particularly important as committee members often lobby the government minister between committee stage and report, in order to try to move forward some of their amendments. MPs often move similar amendments again at report. Ongoing discussions with ministers mean that they have a greater chance of being accepted. In total, around 8 per cent of all of the amendments proposed in bill committees are accepted by ministers at a later stage of the process (Thompson 2013, 475).

The wider function of committee stage

Alongside their role in scrutinizing legislation, committees are a forum for the exchange of ideas between parties. Discussions can be longer and far more detailed than would be possible elsewhere. The Investigatory Powers Bill, for instance, was debated for over 34 hours during its committee stage, compared to a second reading debate of just five hours in the Commons Chamber. There is greater scope for backbenchers to develop their arguments and an opportunity to question ministers at close range. Committees also play a crucial role in the process of parliamentary socialization. Most new MPs are appointed to a PBC in their first year and this can help them to learn the procedures and speaking customs of Westminster, along with the more technical details of legislation. They are equally important for those seeking advancement in government. Junior departmental ministers are usually responsible for taking bills through committee and there is much pressure on them to perform well. This means avoiding making concessions, but it also means having the composure, technical knowledge, and political nous to defend their department's bill for many hours at a time. Thus committees constitute an important parliamentary and ministerial training ground.

Conclusion

The primary role of the committee stage is undoubtedly to scrutinize bills in detail. Contextualizing the work of committees in Parliament by identifying the different legislative, procedural, and political contexts in which they work brings a stronger appreciation of the challenges of committee work. Adopting a broader view of committee scrutiny, one which focuses on its impact at later stages of the legislative process and which appreciates the alternative functions of committees, provides a very different perspective and helps to challenge long-standing assumptions about the purpose and effectiveness of committees. Contemporary studies have highlighted that committee stage is a crucial component of legislative scrutiny and of parliamentary life.

Further Reading

GRIFFITH, J. A. G. (1974) *Parliamentary Scrutiny of Government Bills*, London: Allen & Unwin.

LEVY, J. (2010) 'Public Bill Committees: An Assessment. Scrutiny Sought: Scrutiny Gained', *Parliamentary Affairs*, Vol. 63 (3), pp. 534–44.

MODERNISATION COMMITTEE (2006) *The Legislative Process: First Report of Session 2005–06*, London: The Stationery Office, HC 1097. Online at: https://www.publications.parliament.uk/pa/cm200506/cmselect/cmmodern/1097/1097.pdf [accessed 22 June 2017].

THOMPSON, L. (2015) *Making British Law: Committees in Action*, London: Palgrave.

THOMPSON, L. (2016) 'Debunking the Myths of Bill Committees in the British House of Commons', *Politics*, Vol. 36 (1), pp. 36–48.

Case Study 9: The Children and Families Bill 2013

The Children and Families Bill is a good illustration of the challenges of committee scrutiny. Parliament's scrutiny of the bill was extensive, and many changes made to the bill can be traced back to the public bill committee. This bill demonstrates the ability of the Commons and the Lords to force the government to make changes to legislation.

LEGISLATIVE CONTEXT

The bill's title suggests that it set out to improve services for children and their families. But it was very wide-ranging, with nine distinct parts, 110 clauses, and seven schedules. It covered changes to adoption processes, family justice, support for children with special educational needs, and flexible working rights, among others. The bill began in the House of Commons on 4 February 2013. Pre-legislative scrutiny of draft clauses had been carried out by four parliamentary select committees in autumn 2012. The bill's second reading took place on 25 February 2013, after which it was sent to a PBC.

The Children and Families Bill Committee met for 19 sessions in March and April 2013. Four of these were oral evidence sessions, in which 35 individuals gave evidence. These included government ministers (Edward Timpson, Liz Truss, and Jo Swinson) as well as representatives from charities including Every Disabled Child Matters and Diabetes UK. The Committee also accepted 137 submissions of written evidence. Its members included two government ministers plus one government whip, nine backbench MPs from the governing Coalition parties (seven Conservative MPs and two Liberal Democrats), eight MPs from the official opposition (Labour Party), and one from a small party (Democratic Unionist Party).

AMENDMENTS MADE IN COMMITTEE

At the end of the Committee's final sitting, the Children and Families Bill was reported 'as amended'. This means that the text of the bill which went into the PBC was different to that which came out of it. Amendments had been made over the course of the committee stage. As

Table 9.1 Amendments to the Children and Families Bill

	Number of amendments*	Successful amendments*	
		N	%
Government backbench	62	0	0
Government	64	64	100
Opposition backbench	56	0	0
Opposition frontbench	166	0	0
Total	*348*	*64*	*18.4*

* Includes new clauses and schedules

Table 9.1 shows, 348 amendments were discussed in committee. Of these, 64 were passed formally (a success rate of 18 per cent). Most of these were minor technical amendments, making clarifications about the words used in the bill, including the replacement of the phrase 'special educational needs' with 'learning difficulties and disabilities' (amendment 58 to clause 26). But all of the amendments passed were government amendments. None of the 284 non-government amendments was accepted.

This demonstrates the control the executive holds over the bill committee system. The government whip (Anne Milton MP) performed her role well. Five opposition amendments were pushed to a vote but were defeated. The government maintained its majority on the Committee throughout the sittings and thus won all divisions comfortably.

EVIDENCE OF SIGNIFICANT COMMITTEE INFLUENCE

The evidence presented so far suggests that the scrutiny of the bill was very linear. Amendments were put before the committee, which decided either to accept or reject them. But in practice committee scrutiny is much more multifaceted. If we delve deeper into the less visible elements of committee stage and consider the broader legislative process, we find evidence that MPs were actually laying the foundations for substantial changes to the bill.

Over the course of the committee, ministers gave 17 undertakings to take further action. These related to 54 amendments (19 per cent of all of the non-government amendments). This number of undertakings is high, and probably the result of the bill having received pre-legislative scrutiny. The government may have been already aware of the issues which would be raised and may have identified areas where compromise was possible. Ministerial undertakings included commitments to reconsider amendments on issues such as increasing the age at which information on special educational needs progress and targets are published, from 19 to 25 years. A commitment was also made to amend the guidance issued by the government to employers regarding time off for antenatal appointments. Government ministers agreed to meet with Liberal Democrat MP Annette Brooke to discuss mental health provisions for looked after children following her New Clauses 12, 27, and 28. They also agreed to commission research on kinship carers and special guardians in response to a series of amendments tabled by Labour MP Lucy Powell.

Four of the government amendments introduced at the bill's report stage were a direct response to issues raised in committee. These included changes to enable education, health, and care plans to move between local authorities. A further example of this could be seen in the Lords, where an amendment was made to include children with disabilities in the legislation. This picked up on amendments which had first been tabled in committee by Labour MP Sharon Hodgson and Conservative backbencher Robert Buckland.

Perhaps the most significant change, however, was the result of a long campaign by Labour backbencher Steve Reed MP on the issue of smoking in cars when children are present. He tabled an amendment in the nineteenth sitting of the bill committee. At the time, the minister gave a commitment to examine the issue further. It was debated again at report stage, before finally being made by the government through an amendment at the bill's third reading in the House of Lords.

This bill's committee stage therefore demonstrates the importance of viewing committee scrutiny in broader terms. Although the only changes made in the committee room itself were minor government amendments, committee scrutiny played a pivotal role in MPs' campaigns on issues of passive smoking, employment rights, and children with disabilities, helping opposition and backbench MPs to set the agenda and forcing government to make changes to its own legislation.

Primary sources

- Second reading, Children and Families Bill (HC Debates, 25 February 2013, cc. 45–134). Online at: https://hansard.parliament.uk/commons/2013-02-25/debates/13022511000001/ChildrenAndFamiliesBill [accessed 22 June 2017].

- Children and Families Bill, as amended in public bill committee, 29 April 2013. Online at: https://www.publications.parliament.uk/pa/bills/cbill/2012-2013/0168/2013168.pdf [accessed 22 June 2017].

- Report stage and third reading, Children and Families Bill (HC Debates, 11 June 2013, cc. 175–294). Online at: https://hansard.parliament.uk/commons/2013-06-11/debates/13061171000001/ChildrenAndFamiliesBill [accessed 22 June 2017].

- Third reading, Children and Families Bill (HL Debates, 5 February 2014, cc. 204–56). Online at: https://hansard.parliament.uk/lords/2014-02-05/debates/14020581000654/ChildrenAndFamiliesBill [accessed 22 June 2017].

   FURTHER CASE STUDIES

- Scotland Bill (2015–16): Committee of the whole House.
- Digital Economy Bill Committee (2016–17).
- European Union (Notification of Withdrawal) Bill (2016–17): Committee of the whole House.

References

ABBOTT, D. (2011) 'The Dead Hand of the Whips', *The Guardian*, 15 February.

BRAZIER, A. (2004) 'Standing Committees' in A. Brazier (ed.), *Parliament, Politics and Law Making: Issues and Developments in the Legislative Process*, London: Hansard Society, pp. 14–21.

GRIFFITH, J. A. G. (1974) *Parliamentary Scrutiny of Government Bills*, London: Allen & Unwin.

INSTITUTE FOR GOVERNMENT (2017) *Passing Legislation*, Whitehall Monitor. Online at: https://www.instituteforgovernment.org.uk/publication/whitehall-monitor-2017/passing-legislation [accessed 22 June 2017].

KELLY, R. (2015) *Pre-Legislative Scrutiny under the Coalition Government 2010–2015*, House of Commons Library Briefing Paper Number 05859, 13 August.

MODERNISATION COMMITTEE (2006) *The Legislative Process: First Report of Session 2005–06*, HC 1097, London: House of Commons. Online at: https://www.publications.parliament.uk/pa/cm200506/cmselect/cmmodern/1097/1097.pdf [accessed 22 June 2017].

RUSH, M. (2000) 'Parliamentary Scrutiny' in R. Pyper and L. Robins (eds.), *United Kingdom Governance*, London: Macmillan, pp. 107–37.

THOMPSON, L. (2013) 'More of the Same or a Period of Change? Bill Committees in the Twenty First Century House of Commons', *Parliamentary Affairs*, Vol. 66 (3), pp 459–79.

THOMPSON, L. (2015) *Making British Law: Committees in Action*, Basingstoke: Palgrave Macmillan.

10

EU Legislation

Ed Beale, Libby Kurien, and Eve Samson

INTRODUCTION

EU law is made by negotiations in and between European institutions. Although this law takes precedence over national law, national parliaments have limited direct influence over the EU legislative process and must largely work through their governments. As the 2016 EU referendum result has demonstrated, the UK holds the principle of parliamentary sovereignty close to its heart. This could simply be construed as resistance to the supranational nature of EU law, but it may also demonstrate the UK's unease with governance systems in which positions have to be negotiated between parties or institutions, and transparency about legislative change can be limited.

Until recently, the progress of negotiations on European matters were not a focus for UK political debate, and the Parliament's scrutiny systems were of little interest. While the UK system is seen as less effective a check on government mandating models of scrutiny—favoured by countries such as Denmark—where ministers must get a mandate from the Parliament on its position in advance of Council meetings, it is not ineffective. This chapter focuses on the ways in which each House formally constrains the government and engages with EU institutions. The Lords and Commons both have processes to ensure that legislation proposed at the EU level has been properly examined before it takes effect in UK law. The 'scrutiny reserve' which stipulates that ministers should not agree to proposals under scrutiny, provides a tool for eliciting information about the government's negotiating position. The Lords EU Committee and its subcommittees look at individual policies in depth, while the Commons concentrates on subjecting every document to committee oversight. Parliament also has a role in examining EU legislation and direct access to European institutions through its own office in Brussels.

Overview of the EU legislative process

UK parliamentary scrutiny can only be understood by reference to the EU structures and legislative process. There are three principal EU institutions:

- member states, meeting together in the Council of the EU (composed of ministers from each of the 28 EU member states);
- European Parliament (EP), directly elected representatives from each country;
- European Commission, the EU Executive and civil service.

Most legislation is proposed by the Commission, and must then be agreed by both the Council and the EP. This is a process which requires negotiation and amendment. Member states negotiate to agree the Council position, often on the basis of unpublished documents. The EP also comes to its own view. While there is a structure of stages to refine and agree legislation between the Council and the EP, informal discussions can take place at any stage between the Council and the EP with the support of the Commission (known as a trilogue), aimed at forming a consensus on a final text for the next formal legislative stage. Trilogues are held in private, and there is limited information about the negotiations until they conclude.

Formal role of national parliaments in the EU legislative process

The role of national parliaments in EU decision-making is a source of contention. The EP sees itself as the directly elected, democratic institution for the Union, recognized in the treaties, while national parliaments, and arguably the UK Parliament in particular, affirm the importance of their role representing their national electorates. Turnout in EP elections averages 42.61 per cent across the EU, and 35.6 per cent in the UK (European Parliament 2014). This can be contrasted with the higher turnout in national elections, such as the 66.4 per cent in the UK in 2015 (Electoral Commission 2015).

 Parliamentary terms Subsidiarity

A principle intended to indicate the respective responsibilities of legislatures at EU, national, and subnational level. Its aim is to ensure that decisions are taken as closely to the citizen as possible. Under this principle, EU legislation should only refer to matters that cannot be dealt with at national level. If one or both chambers of a national parliament considers that draft legislation at EU level breaches this principle, they may object to it.

The Lisbon Treaty gave national parliaments a role in the formal legislative process, through policing the principle of subsidiarity. National parliaments can object when they believe that the EU is trying to introduce proposals for which the objectives could be sufficiently achieved by the member states individually. Draft legislation must contain a statement attesting to its compliance with the principle of subsidiarity, and each chamber must judge whether it thinks this principle has been breached. If enough national parliaments (usually around a third) submit such an objection (a 'Reasoned Opinion') the 'yellow card' mechanism is triggered. The Commission must then review the proposal for compliance with the principle and decide whether to maintain, amend, or withdraw it. But this power depends on enough national parliaments raising concerns. The yellow card mechanism has only been triggered three times. First in 2012, on a proposal related to the rights of workers to take collective action ('Monti II'); second in 2013, on a proposal to establish a European Public Prosecutors Office; and third in 2016, on a directive related to posted workers.

 Parliamentary terms Reasoned opinion

An objection expressed by a national parliament in relation to EU draft legislation that seems to breach the principle of subsidiarity (e.g. proposals for which the objectives could be sufficiently achieved by the member states individually).

The short (eight-week) window during which a Reasoned Opinion can be adopted, and the high thresholds and limited teeth—the Commission can ultimately choose to continue with a proposal regardless of the mechanism being triggered—of the yellow card mechanism have been cited as discouraging factors in its use and effectiveness. Moreover, as Case Study 10 shows, many controversial proposals do not breach the principle. To be effective, parliamentary scrutiny has to focus on national governments.

The UK Parliament's scrutiny of the EU legislation and its effectiveness

Even though select committees may be more explicitly focused on UK government policy, this does not mean that they have no interest in EU policy and legislation affecting their subject area; on the contrary. The UK government approach to EU negotiations is constrained by the scrutiny system which is relatively open, reflecting the expectations of ministerial accountability to Parliament, and the accountability of the government to the electorate. Much is common to both Houses. All EU legislative proposals, and all policy documents of any significance, will be deposited in each House. Within ten days of deposit, the government submits (and publishes online) an Explanatory Memorandum setting out its position, including its analysis of the principle of subsidiarity, the political implications for the UK, and the legal base under which the proposal has been brought forward by the EU institution concerned (usually the Commission).

 Parliamentary terms Explanatory memorandum

A government document sent to Parliament setting out its position in relation to a specific EU legislative proposal, outlining its main financial, legal, and policy implications.

The 'scrutiny reserve' is the most important factor in parliamentary scrutiny: resolutions of each House specify that ministers shall not agree to a proposal in the Council while it is still under scrutiny. If there are special circumstances requiring an override of the reserve, ministers must report the override and explain as quickly as possible why it occurred. The business of scrutiny is then largely delegated to committees—the EU Committee in the Lords, and the European Scrutiny Committee (ESC) in the Commons.

House of Commons

The ESC has the task of identifying documents of political and/or legal importance and reporting on them to the House. Its role is to ensure that the attention of the House is drawn to important issues before the government agrees to them at EU level; it assesses importance rather than merits (although the two cannot always be clearly separated). The ESC can alert other committees to proposals on matters within their remit, but it is not expected to run extensive inquiries into the merits of individual EU proposals—though the ESC can, and does, conduct free-standing inquiries, which have addressed matters such as Council transparency or the scrutiny system itself.

EU documents are cleared from scrutiny by the ESC itself lifting the scrutiny reserve or, for particularly important documents, by the House as a whole agreeing to a motion endorsing the government's position. ESC itself decides whether or not to recommend debates, and whether debates should be in a European committee or on the Floor of the House. Debates in the House last for 90 minutes, while proceedings in committee can last for up to two and a half hours and include opportunities to question the responsible minister. Despite the shorter time, the assumption is that really important proposals will be recommended for high-profile Chamber debates. While the Committee can recommend debates, the government business managers are responsible for scheduling them, and debates have been delayed for years or demoted to committee.

The Committee publishes report chapters or reports on important documents summarizing the document and the questions it has raised (which may be substantive, or may simply be a request to be kept informed over future negotiations). For example, in its recent scrutiny of a proposal to require non-EU travellers to the Schengen area to file advance travel notifications, the Committee asked whether post-Brexit UK citizens will require visas, and what steps are being taken to ensure the system is as light touch as possible. The Committee frequently raises legal issues, often about the division of powers between the EU and the respective member states.

There is transparency about what has been cleared and what remains under scrutiny. The near weekly Committee reports contain both these substantive chapters on legally and politically important proposals, and a list of documents cleared without a full report. A single recent report included coverage of all of the following: reform of EU decision-making process, mutual recognition of legal penalties, the digital single market (including consumer rights and wholesale roaming charges), organ donation, and aviation emissions (European Scrutiny Committee 2017c). Correspondence with ministers about less important documents is published online.

The ESC is large by comparison with most other Commons committees (16 members) and briefed by an expert staff. Its most important role is the way in which it exercises cross-party political control of the judgement as to whether matters are of legal and political importance. The entire Committee is briefed on every EU document (numbers used to average 1,000 a year, but have now dropped to about 700). As the Committee itself noted in its 2015–16 report (European Scrutiny Committee 2016a), although its members were divided between Leavers and Remainers, it rarely disagreed about the significance of a particular document.

Since the scrutiny reserve on an important document is rarely lifted until near the close of negotiations, which may take years, there will be repeated chapters on the same document, reporting progress and setting out the government's answers to questions.

House of Lords

The Lords adopts a different approach. Rather than all Members seeing information on all documents, the Chair of the Lords EU Committee carries out a 'sift' of the documents laid by the government resulting in around 30–40 per cent of them being retained for scrutiny.

Moreover, while the Commons EU Committee does not use its power to appoint subcommittees, in the Lords six subcommittees each scrutinize a specific policy area: Financial Affairs, Internal Market, External Affairs, Energy and Environment, Justice, and Home Affairs. All in all, 72 peers are involved in the Lords scrutiny. The Lords EU Committee and its subcommittees include former MEPs, former Permanent Representatives of the UK to the EU, academics, and lawyers.

Documents which merit scrutiny are referred to the relevant subject subcommittee with possible outcomes of scrutiny, including: clearing the document from scrutiny, allowing the government to proceed to agreement in Council (usually after correspondence with ministers on proposals); holding the document under scrutiny while engaging the government in correspondence on the matter; holding evidence sessions or seminars with stakeholders; or carrying out an in-depth inquiry on the matter resulting in a committee report.

In sharp contrast to the Commons ESC, the bulk of the time for scrutiny in the Lords EU committees has been on inquiries into EU policy areas. The Committee and subcommittees' reports on subjects such as youth unemployment, Common Fisheries Policy reform, the Financial Transaction Tax, and future trade between the UK and the EU are well read by officials, academics, and even EU staff and others in Brussels. Influencing upstream policymaking is one of the main objectives of their work. Reports are aimed at informing the debate, as well as shaping the actions of the government, the Commission, and other stakeholders.

How else does the UK Parliament engage with and scrutinize the EU?

The UK Parliament has a direct relationship with the EU. It has had a National Parliament Office in Brussels since 1999. The officials in this office gather intelligence for UK committees and provide information to the EU institutions about the UK Parliament's activities. The Brussels-based network of national parliament officials has grown steadily, and the EP now hosts a representative from most EU national parliaments. The regular Monday morning meeting of officials of national parliaments allows the network to exchange information and to work together to represent the views and causes of national parliaments 'on-the-ground' in Brussels and Strasbourg.

Many of these officials are also involved in the biannual Conference of Parliamentary Committees for European Union Affairs—COSAC—which is the only treaty-recognized inter-parliamentary meeting, and brings together parliamentarians from the UK Parliament, other national parliaments, and the EP to discuss subjects of common interest and to agree contributions (addressed to the EU institutions). These contributions have been used by COSAC to lobby the EU institutions, in particular the Commission, to change its behaviour towards national parliaments.

While Commons and Lords committees play an active part in inter-parliamentary forums, there is here, too, a potential tension between the way in which the EU works and common UK constitutional assumptions. It is rare for UK Parliament committees to have direct powers to make policy or take decisions; such matters usually revert to each House. In the EU, committees play an active and independent role in agreeing the contributions of parliamentary meetings, without reference back to their parent House.

Effectiveness

There is a tension between ensuring detailed scrutiny of every proposal emanating from Brussels and wider EU policy scrutiny. Taking the UK Parliament as a whole, the approaches adopted by the two Houses provide both types of scrutiny. The breadth and detail of the Commons European scrutiny system may be seen as its primary advantage. The exhaustive approach to reporting should mean that MPs and committees (and the wider public) have access to information about all important proposals. However, the sheer volume of material dealt with by the Committee means that it can be hard for the outsider to follow particular policies, even though committee reports contain details of previous reports on particular subjects.

Some have also argued that the Commons system lacks detailed scrutiny of EU policy both upstream and upon implementation. Although both potentially fall within the remit of departmental select committees, and are considered, committees have until recently taken a UK focus, seeking to hold UK ministers to account and influence their policy. Given that the government is responsible for negotiations at EU level, this is not illogical. In contrast, the Lords EU scrutiny system is aimed at influencing EU policy development and regularly reports on particular EU policies, as well as conducting scrutiny of individual documents. In both Houses, documents are published regularly, but this information is overwhelming to all but the expert.

Scrutiny after the UK vote to exit the EU

Since the referendum, most Explanatory Memoranda have included text indicating that: 'Until exit negotiations are concluded, the UK remains a full member of the EU … During this period the Government will continue to negotiate, implement and apply EU legislation. The outcome of … negotiations will determine what arrangements apply in relation to EU legislation in future once the UK has left the EU.' Scrutiny is arguably more important than ever in the run up to Brexit. The EU will remain a major trading partner and close neighbour, even after the UK has left it. Furthermore, a large part of UK law reflects EU law, which continues to develop.

The Commons committee structure was quickly altered to reflect changes in the machinery of government following the referendum result, with new Committees for Exiting the EU and for International Trade. The former was notable for its large membership, divided equally between Leavers and Remainers. Despite this division, only one of its reports really split the Committee (Exiting the European Union Committee 2017, see 114–17). Besides this, the majority of departmental committees have now undertaken Brexit-related inquiries. The fact that the Lords does not have departmental committees means that the EU Committee and its subcommittees have undertaken a series of Brexit-related inquiries into particular policy areas, highlighting key issues in each. The EU Committee has recommended a change in the Committee's Standing Order to reflect its wider post-Brexit role.

The ESC's (2017a) report considered that the scrutiny system in the Commons remained vital, and that it was essential to ensure that negotiations on EU law currently under development were given proper priority to ensure changes did not disadvantage the UK post-Brexit. It demanded clearer information about post-Brexit implications of each proposal. For example, the Committee has asked how much importance the government places on continued involvement with Europol, and what legal mechanisms might be required to allow such involvement. It has also said it will share the expertise of its staff with other committees.

The government has refused to give a 'running commentary' on its negotiating position, but has indicated that the UK Parliament will be given at least as much information as the EP. It is not yet clear what that will mean. The ESC regularly presses for more information on Brexit-related issues. If Brexit was, as the PM suggested in her speech on the government's negotiating objectives for exiting the EU (May 2017), at least partly provoked by a mismatch between a system based on negotiation at the supranational level and the structures of parliamentary sovereignty and government accountability, it is perhaps ironic that it is clear the government's willingness to give information is likely to be a key political issue in the months to come.

Conclusion

National parliaments are challenged in their scrutiny of EU matters by the sheer volume of EU documents produced, the opacity of the EU legislative process, and the limitations of their formal role. The Commons and Lords have a complex system which ensures that everything coming out of Brussels is scrutinized. Ministers may ultimately override the scrutiny reserve; the only sanction is political pressure. Nonetheless, the reserve provides a weapon for eliciting information and, in the Commons, if a matter has been referred for debate, overriding it is a serious matter. The UK Parliament's system has evolved to ensure wider scrutiny through the exploitation of new powers provided to national parliaments in the Lisbon Treaty, the production of detailed policy reports by the ESC, departmental select committees and the Lord's EU committees, the presence of UK parliamentary representatives based in Brussels, and the attendance by UK parliamentarians at inter-parliamentary forums. Changes can be, and are made, to scrutiny structures in both Houses, but the referendum result has resulted in a rapid increase of parliamentary interest in EU issues, and this can only be expected to continue in the new Parliament. While individual committees and Members may have different views on the desirability of any given government position, it is clear that there will be pressure from all sides for the government to provide information, or, if it considers that such information would jeopardize negotiations, to explain the reasons for that belief.

Further Reading

COOPER, I. (2015) 'A Yellow Card for the Striker: national parliaments and the defeat of EU legislation on the right to strike', *Journal of European Public Policy*, Vol. 22 (10), pp. 1406–25.

EUROPEAN SCRUTINY COMMITTEE (2016) *Report of the Committee on Session 2015–16: Fifth Report of Session 2016–17*, London: Stationery Office, HC 177. Online at: https://www.publications. parliament.uk/pa/cm201617/cmselect/cmeuleg/177/177.pdf [accessed 22 June 2017].

EUROPEAN SCRUTINY COMMITTEE (2017) *Brexit and the European Scrutiny System in the House of Commons: Thirty-Eighth Report of Session 2016–17*, London: Stationery Office, HC1124. On-line at: https://www.publications.parliament.uk/pa/cm201617/cmselect/cmeuleg/1124/1124. pdf [accessed 22 June 2017].

EXITING THE EUROPEAN UNION COMMITTEE (2017) *The Process for Exiting the European Union and the Government's Negotiating Objectives: First Report of Session 2016–17*, London: The Stationery Office, HC 815. Online at: https://www.publications.parliament.uk/pa/cm201617/ cmselect/cmexeu/815/815.pdf [accessed 22 June 2017].

HUFF, A. (2013) *Problems and Patterns in Parliamentary Scrutiny of the CFSP and CSDP*, OPAL Online Paper Series 14/2013, Maastricht: Observatory of Parliaments after the Lisbon Treaty. Online at: http://www.pademia.eu/wp-content/uploads/2014/02/14.pdf [accessed 22 June 2017].

Case Study 10: The Ports Regulation 2013–17

This case study demonstrates the complexity and length of EU negotiation on contested pro-posal, the difficulties the ESC had in forcing debate on the government's approach to negoti-ations, and the way in which the ESC used the scrutiny system to ensure that the government provided regular updates, and exerted consistent political pressure for several years. In add-ition to the formal scrutiny process described, there was a great deal of informal interaction between Parliament and various European players. The ESC discussed progress with the Italian presidency, since the presidency is responsible for deciding which proposals should get priority. Also, unusually, the minister and his shadow went to Brussels to lobby some of the most influential MEPs on this dossier.

THE STORY

The European Commission proposed a regulation on market access to ports services in May 2013; it was finally agreed in January 2017.

The UK differs from almost all other European countries in that most of its ports are pro-vided and run by private companies, rather than being state enterprises. The government consistently said it believed that problems were best addressed at national level. UK ports and unions were also opposed. The ESC quickly identified this as a politically important proposal, which needed debate, but said the debate would be recommended when negotiations had progressed. Note that it did not consider subsidiarity concerns merited a Reasoned Opinion; this was, in essence, about the merits of the proposal.

It was not until mid-2014 that negotiations had progressed to the point where Council was expected to agree its approach; the Committee then recommended a debate on the Floor of the House before the Council meeting on 8 October 2014. Although a European Committee debate was scheduled, it broke up in disorder, as the documents which formed the basis for the motion endorsing the government's position were out of date. The most up-to-date documents were limité—an EU privacy marking which prevented the documents being publicly referred to—indeed, the ESC had pressured the government into providing it. The Committee kept the House up to date through a succession of report chapters. When the Council met, the UK government abstained in the vote agreeing the General Position, on the grounds the scrutiny reserve applied, even though it had secured most of its negotiating aims.

There was then a hiatus of nearly two years, as the European Parliament agreed its negotiating position (elections led to lengthy delays). Once it was clear the EP was soon to make progress, the Committee recommended a debate (again on the Floor of the House) before trilogues negotiations commenced. A Committee debate was scheduled, but cancelled. On 20 July 2016, the ESC reported that trilogues had resulted in an agreed draft regulation. It had been over two years since the Committee first recommended a debate which would have lifted the scrutiny reserve. Despite repeated attempts, it had not happened.

In strict terms, the scrutiny reserve had not been breached, as the reserve prevents ministers agreeing to proposals in Council, but the Committee noted that the Committee of Permanent Representatives (COREPER), which includes the UK representative to the EU, had agreed to the deal, so negotiation was effectively over. The Committee was outraged and considered the episode 'illustrates a remarkable refusal by the Government to pay even lip service to accountability to Parliament' (European Scrutiny Committee 2017a, para 1.7).

When no debate was forthcoming, the Minister of State, John Hayes, was called to give evidence to the Committee on 14 December 2016. He was devastatingly frank about the UK's negotiating tactics:

> The original advice ... was to try to do three things: to delay it, to dilute it and to get Britain out of it. My officials went about trying to do all those three things and, to some degree, succeeded ... by changing the regulation, removing some of the things from its original incarnation, including pilotage, dredging and other such matters, and by suggesting and getting agreed the competitive-market exemption ... It is absolutely clear now that there is no point continuing down that road. We will vote against it, because it is not right for Britain. (European Scrutiny Committee 2016b, Q3)

The UK did indeed vote against the Regulation when the agreed text returned to Council on 23 January 2017—and the scrutiny reserve, which prevents ministers *agreeing* to a matter under scrutiny, was not breached.

WHAT THIS TELLS US ABOUT THE SCRUTINY SYSTEM

This episode suggests several tensions in the scrutiny process. First, the difficulty of marrying a UK system based on legislative transparency and clear time limits on legislation with a system which, naturally, requires lengthy negotiations. The Committee needed the government to say when negotiations were likely to progress, and, in the late stages, supplemented this information with reports back from the national parliamentary office. The Committee was particularly concerned that EU-level documents underpinning the legislative process were not publicly available, saying that: 'As a legislature in a democratic society the Council should operate transparently, in particular abandoning the constant resort to Limité markings, and should be very vigorously urged to do so by any UK Government' (European Scrutiny Committee 2014).

Second is the degree of committee control of the location of debate. The government has argued that committee debates are longer, and allow questions to be put to the minister, and that there is limited time for debates on the Floor, particularly since MPs now value predictability in sitting hours. There are several other reasons why the government might prefer to have debates in committee: there is limited time in plenary; committee debates attract less attention; fewer MPs need be involved. It is possible that whipping is made easier because the vote on the resolution agreeing the government's negotiating position is separated from the debate. The ESC was always clear the ports regulation should go to the Floor; members of the aborted European Committee urged a Floor debate, but the government was never willing to concede one.

Third, it is difficult for the government to give a clear view at the early stages of negotiations. In most cases, the support of other member states is required to scrub a blocking majority. Signalling outright opposition might prejudice the chance of getting desirable changes or making alliances. So while it was clear that the government did not like the regulation, it either could not or would not say it would vote against it until the very end.

WAS THE SYSTEM EFFECTIVE?

It is clear the Commons scrutiny process did not produce a timely debate on the ports regulation. Nor could it ensure that any debate took place on the Floor of the House. But it did stop a debate taking place on the basis of out-of-date documents: this is important, as proposals are cleared from scrutiny once they have been debated.

Moreover, in addition to the regular updates which both committees received, the ESC:

- provided regular reports from the Committee to the House (and the public), promptly summarizing developments: ten reports were published over the three-year negotiating period;
- put information about the progress of the negotiations into the public domain, which would not otherwise have been available;
- gave stakeholders an opportunity to engage with the Committee by inviting evidence from them;
- required the minister to explain the government's position in a public evidence session.

The scrutiny reserve was not breached, and government opposition to the regulation may have been strengthened by the sustained political pressure from the ESC. Indeed, it is possible, though unprovable, that the final vote against the regulation was prompted by the danger of breaching the scrutiny reserve on such a significant and contested proposal, which the ESC was monitoring closely.

Primary sources

- European Scrutiny Committee: Inquiry pages on EU Port Regulation (2016). Online at: http://www.parliament.uk/business/committees/committees-a-z/commons-select/european-scrutiny-committee/inquiries/parliament-2015/ports1/ [accessed 22 June 2017].
- European Scrutiny Committee (2016) *Twenty-sixth Report of Session 2016–17: Documents Considered by the Committee on 18 January 2017*, London: The Stationery Office, HC71-xxiv

(see especially chapter 1). Online at: http://www.publications.parliament.uk/pa/cm201617/cmselect/cmeuleg/71-vi/7104.htm [accessed 22 June 2017].

- House of Commons European Committee (2014) Debate on Ports, 3 September. Online at: https://www.publications.parliament.uk/pa/cm201415/cmgeneral/euro/140903/140903s01.htm [accessed 22 June 2017].

- Department for Transport's Explanatory Memorandum (access to port services). Online at: http://europeanmemoranda.cabinetoffice.gov.uk/memorandum/proposal-for-regulation-of-the-european-parliament-of-the-council-establishing-framework-on-the-market [accessed 22 June 2017].

➡ FURTHER CASE STUDIES

- Compare European scrutiny between the House of Lords European Union Committee and the House of Commons European Scrutiny Committee report on Operation Sophia.

- The European Scrutiny Committee's consideration on the establishment of a European travel information and authorization system.

- Scrutiny of the Brexit process and negotiations (we advise you choose just one area of legislation or time period).

References

ELECTORAL COMMISSION (2015) *The May 2015 UK Elections: Report on the Administration of the 7 May 2015 Elections, Including the UK Parliamentary General Election*, London: Electoral Commission. Online at: http://www.electoralcommission.org.uk/__data/assets/pdf_file/0006/190959/UKPGE-report-May-2015-1.pdf [accessed 22 June 2017].

EUROPEAN PARLIAMENT (2014) *Results of the 2014 European Elections*. Online at: http://www.europarl.europa.eu/elections2014-results/en/turnout.html [accessed 22 June 2017].

EUROPEAN SCRUTINY COMMITTEE (2014) *Ports: Fourteenth Report from the European Scrutiny Committee of Session 2014–15*, London: The Stationery Office, HC 219-xiv. Online at: https://www.publications.parliament.uk/pa/cm201415/cmselect/cmeuleg/219-xiv/21903.htm [accessed 22 June 2017].

EUROPEAN SCRUTINY COMMITTEE (2016a) *Report of the Committee on Session 2015–16: Fifth Report of Session 2016–17*, HC 177. Online at: https://www.publications.parliament.uk/pa/cm201617/cmselect/cmeuleg/177/177.pdf [accessed 22 June 2017].

EUROPEAN SCRUTINY COMMITTEE (2016b) *Oral Evidence: Ports*, London: House of Commons, HC 884.

EUROPEAN SCRUTINY COMMITTEE (2017a) *Brexit and the European Scrutiny System in the House of Commons: Thirty-eighth Report of Session 2016–17*, London: Stationery Office, HC1124. Online at: https://www.publications.parliament.uk/pa/cm201617/cmselect/cmeuleg/1124/1124.pdf [accessed 22 June 2017].

EUROPEAN SCRUTINY COMMITTEE (2017b) *Twenty-sixth Report of Session 2016–17: Documents considered by the Committee on 18 January 2017*, London: Stationery Office, HC 71-xxiv. Online at: https://www.publications.parliament.uk/pa/cm201617/cmselect/cmeuleg/71-xxiv/71-xxiv.pdf [accessed 22 June 2017].

EUROPEAN SCRUTINY COMMITTEE (2017c) *Fortieth Report of Session 2016–17: Documents Considered by the Committee on 25 April 2017*, London: The Stationery Office, HC 71-xxxvii. Online at: https://www.publications.parliament.uk/pa/cm201617/cmselect/cmeuleg/71-xxxvii/71-xxxvii.pdf [accessed 22 June 2017].

EUROPEAN UNION COMMITTEE (2016) *Operation Sophia, the EU's naval mission in the Mediterranean: an impossible challenge: 14th Report of Session 2015–16*, London: Stationery Office, HL Paper 144. Online at: https://www.publications.parliament.uk/pa/ld201516/ldselect/ldeucom/144/144.pdf [accessed 22 June 2017].

EXITING THE EUROPEAN UNION COMMITTEE (2017) *The Government's Negotiating Objectives: The White Paper: Third Report of Session 2016–17*, HC 1125. Online at: https://www.publications.parliament.uk/pa/cm201617/cmselect/cmexeu/1125/1125.pdf [accessed 22 June 2017].

MAY, T. (2017) *The Government's Negotiating Objectives for Exiting the EU: PM Speech*, 17 January. Online at: https://www.gov.uk/government/speeches/the-governments-negotiating-objectives-for-exiting-the-eu-pm-speech [accessed 4 June 2017].

11

Campaigning to Change Law and Policy

Paul E. J. Thomas and Stacey Frier

INTRODUCTION

This chapter examines the ways in which backbench MPs and peers seek to change laws and government policies. Although some may work alone, in most cases policy and legislative campaigning is conducted by groups of MPs and peers who work together across party lines. Such groupings are typically supported by external pressure groups, who help to keep the parliamentarians informed on the issue, and who can also provide resources to support campaigning activities.

Advocacy by MPs, peers, and their external partners is unlikely to focus on any single tool. Instead, most will employ a range of approaches, including both formal tools rooted in parliamentary procedure and informal methods. In many instances, MPs and peers will also coordinate their parliamentary activities with lobbying by their pressure group partners.

As this chapter will show, MPs and peers who campaign to change laws or policies face a challenge: the more far-reaching or controversial the measures proposed, the more likely they are to be rejected by ministers, their fellow parliamentarians, and the general public. Campaigning to change laws or policies can therefore be a long and convoluted process, with parliamentarians and pressure groups regularly toiling for years with little to show for their efforts. However, this seemingly unsuccessful campaigning is often what builds the support and awareness needed for later victories. Reflecting this reality, policy and legislative advocacy by backbench parliamentarians is increasingly being conducted through sophisticated, long-term campaigns that combine the production of policy reports with more traditional advocacy tools.

Traditional assumptions about influencing government

It is often assumed that those seeking to change laws or government policies should focus their efforts on ministers or senior public servants. Backbench MPs and peers are seen at best as reactive, reviewing proposed legislation and suggesting amendments, but rarely changing bills.

In reality, parliamentarians have more influence than this traditional understanding suggests. Ministers are themselves parliamentarians, and generally seek to develop initiatives that respond to the concerns of their colleagues. Indeed, governments that ignore the views of backbenchers can find their agendas stymied, with MPs and peers working to delay the passage of bills. A prime example is the 2011 *Health and Social Care Bill*, which had its progress through Parliament paused for a 'listening exercise' after many MPs and peers opposed the initial draft (Ramesh 2012).

Yet while ministers typically develop policies and legislation that backbenchers will support, limits to both the government funds and parliamentary time available mean that ministers must prioritize some initiatives over others. Consequently, parliamentarians regularly employ a range of parliamentary tools and advocacy tactics to lobby and pressure ministers in the hope of moving projects up the priority list. In other cases, MPs and peers may pressure ministers to adopt policies that the government actively opposes. While such campaigns use the same tools and tactics, they typically require much more time and energy than those on issues the government already supports.

Actors

Although the media often focuses on instances of partisan conflict, MPs and peers regularly work together across party lines to change the law. Such collaboration reflects the fact that many policy issues cut across partisan divides, and that backbenchers will not always agree with their party leadership. Cooperation is also a practical strategy: backbenchers are more likely to succeed in changing the law if their proposals have cross-party support.

Every MP has paid staff, but their time is largely consumed with constituency service and supporting MPs' regular parliamentary duties. The situation is worse for peers, who typically have no staff at all. Consequently, parliamentarians seeking policy or legislative change often work in coalition with external pressure groups that provide them with information, resources, and publicity.

The term 'pressure group' encompasses a wide range of organizations. The two largest types are business associations, which advocate corporate interests, and civil society coalitions, which work on behalf of not-for-profit organizations and charities. An example of the former is the British Beer and Pub Association, which represents the major breweries and pub companies, while an example of the latter is the Smokefree Action Coalition, which brings together charities and public health bodies seeking to reduce tobacco use. Backbenchers working to change the law may reach out to pressure groups for assistance, and pressure groups may also seek out parliamentarians who support the groups' policy goals.

Coalitions between parliamentarians and pressure groups are often structured into cross-party all-party parliamentary groups (APPGs), which bring together MPs and peers with shared interests in a topic. The number of APPGs has jumped in recent years, rising from 242 in 1996, to 631 in 2017. Of those, one-fifth focused on relations with other countries, such as Azerbaijan, France, or Zambia. The remainder dealt with virtually every conceivable policy issue, from the steel industry and cancer to mountaineering and classical music. APPGs greatly vary in their level of activity. Some meet just a few times per year to mark symbolic days, such as St George's Day or the national holidays of foreign countries. Others hold regular events to exchange information with external stakeholders or government officials. A long-running example is the APPG on Health's monthly sessions with leading health experts.

 Parliamentary terms   APPGs (all-party parliamentary groups)

Cross-party and non-partisan groups of MPs and peers who seek to further the interests of a particular policy concern, country, or region.

APPGs receive no parliamentary funding, and so rely on financial and administrative support from pressure groups, or from individual charities or corporations. For instance, the Animal Welfare APPG receives funding from over 80 animal welfare organizations, and secretariat support from the RSPCA (APGAW 2017). Such reliance on external support has long led to concerns that APPGs could be used for inappropriate lobbying, which in turn has prompted the creation of rules requiring groups to disclose the external support they receive.

Tools

Backbench MPs and peers who campaign for policy or legislative change can employ a variety of tools, including both formal parliamentary tools as well as informal activities like meetings with ministers. However, no one activity is likely to succeed independently. Instead, each action is focused more on raising awareness of the need for change among ministers, parliamentarians, and the general public in the hope of building pressure on government.

Parliamentary tools

There tends to be an inverse relationship between the ease with which MPs and peers can utilize a parliamentary tool and its overall impact on policy or legislative outcomes. The most accessible tool for backbench MPs is Early Day Motions (EDMs), which are officially motions for parliamentary debates, but have evolved into a kind of petition system for MPs. Once MPs introduce a motion, others can sign on as well, allowing them to indicate support for the initiative. For instance, 138 MPs signed an EDM introduced by MP Julian Huppert, Chair of the APPG on Cycling, which endorsed the findings of the group's *Get Britain Cycling* report and called for the government to produce a national cycling plan (Huppert 2012–13).

 Parliamentary terms EDMs (Early Day Motions)

A mechanism in the Commons whereby MPs may add their names to a motion in order to show their support for, or draw attention to, an issue or concern.

However, the ease with which EDMs can be introduced has led to large numbers—typically over 1,000—being tabled each year. Many focus on narrow or local issues, and the sheer volume makes it challenging for anyone to stand out. Many MPs and lobbyists now question their utility, with some MPs refusing to sign them (see BBC News 2013). For example, Dr Sarah Wollaston, Chair of the Health Select Committee since 2014, will no longer sign EDMs because they cannot directly change the law and have been largely succeeded by e-petitions, making them, in her opinion, a waste of money to administer (Wollaston 2016). Nonetheless, a 2013 inquiry into EDMs concluded that they remain a valuable tool for MPs (Procedure Committee 2013). Those Members who supported EDMs said they enabled backbenchers to raise local issues and to gauge their colleagues' support for campaigns. A small portion of the motions are also used to make allegations of wrongdoing under the protection of parliamentary privilege, or to make 'prayers' against statutory instruments. While there are much more impactful tools available to backbenchers, no other formal or informal method delivers the same quantity of opportunity to MPs.

A more effective way for backbenchers to pursue policy and legislative change is through parliamentary debates. For MPs, most of these debates take place in Westminster Hall, which serves as a parallel debating chamber to the main Commons Chamber. Backbench peers can secure 'general' or 'short' debates within the Lords Chamber itself. Westminster Hall debates, and those in the Lords, are limited to general discussions, with no votes held. However, a minister must attend and respond to the proceedings. As such, the debates allow for awareness raising, providing an opportunity to outline a problem and present solutions to a captive ministerial audience. For example, a 2010 Westminster Hall debate on metal theft proposed by MP Tom Watson (HC Debates, 1 December 2010, c. 309WH) was the first step in a campaign that included the formation of an APPG, a petition, and ultimately a successful private members' bill to regulate scrap metal dealers. Lords debates are generally allocated by a ballot of proposals submitted to the Lord Speaker by backbench peers. The Commons uses a similar procedure to select Westminster Hall debates on Tuesday afternoons and Wednesdays, while the Backbench Business Committee (see Case Study 18) controls those on Tuesday mornings and Thursdays.

 Parliamentary terms   Ten-minute rule bill

A form of private members' bill which can be introduced by backbenchers in the Commons. An MP is allocated ten minutes to make a speech about a proposed new bill and why it should be introduced. If the bill is introduced and granted a first reading, it is printed and published.

Beyond Westminster Hall, the Backbench Business Committee also controls a portion of the debating time in the main Commons Chamber. However, unlike those in Westminster Hall, backbench debates in the Commons Chamber can be devoted to votable motions. While not binding on the government, successful backbench business motions can provide symbolic victories to campaigners. For example, in 2013 and again in 2014, members of the APPG on Cycling secured Backbench Business debates in the Commons Chamber on motions that endorsed the group's *Get Britain Cycling* report, and called for the government to develop a Cycling Action Plan and to increase funding for cycling (HC Debates, 2 September 2013, c. 66; HC Debates, 16 October 2014, c. 487). The second was planned after the Cycling Delivery Plan that the government had promised following the first debate failed to materialize. Worried about potential criticism, the government hastily released a draft of the plan just before the second debate took place (Department for Transport 2014). Nevertheless, MPs still expressed their frustration for the delay when the debate occurred. As MP Richard Burden remarked, 'We were told by Ministers more than a year ago … that there would be a cycling delivery plan … It has been a bit like waiting for Godot, but, amazingly, one backbench debate and suddenly, hey presto, the delivery plan appears' (HC Debates, 16 October 2014, c. 519).

Campaigns to secure policy and legislative change can also be strengthened by petitions and e-petitions. While any citizen can launch a petition, many are organized by external pressure groups and their parliamentary partners. For instance, in 2008 Cancer Research UK presented MP David Taylor, Chair of the APPG on Smoking and Health, with a petition signed by over 50,000 supporters that called for a ban on the display of tobacco products (Cancer Research UK 2008). The measure was eventually included in the 2009 Health Act. The requirement for e-petitions receiving over 100,000 signatures to be considered for parliamentary debates has increased their value to campaigners by linking public support to parliamentary proceedings (see Chapter 30). A case in point was the 2011 e-petition, submitted then through the old government e-petitions system, which called for compulsory financial education in the school curriculum. The petition was launched just as the APPG on Financial Education for Young People issued a report making the same recommendation. It received over 100,000 signatures, leading to a backbench debate in the Commons Chamber that was led by the APPG's Chair, MP Justin Tomlinson (HC Debates, 15 December 2011, c. 979). The curriculum was revised in 2013.

A seemingly more direct way for backbenchers to change the law is through private members' bills (see Chapter 12). However, most bills have little chance of passing, meaning that in practice they serve as another opportunity for awareness raising. In some cases, though, MPs and peers can build off past campaigning and actually change the law, as was the case with the metal theft bill noted above. Defeated private members' bills may also become catalysts for subsequent government legislation. For example, MP Ian Cawsey's failed Animal Sanctuaries (Licensing) Bill in 2002 helped to prompt the consultations that led to the government's Animal Welfare Act 2006.

MPs and peers can also attempt to change the law by proposing amendments to government legislation. Such efforts are unlikely to succeed without government support. However, if ministers think they may lose a vote on an amendment or genuinely believe that a proposal would improve a bill, then they may promise to come back with their own version drafted by Parliamentary Counsel (see Chapters 8 and 9). Moreover, even failed amendments can raise awareness on an issue. Indeed, many proposed amendments are not serious attempts to change the law, but 'probing' initiatives to extract information from the government.

Informal tools

Despite the formal tools available, parliamentarians may also seek to meet privately with ministers to express their concerns with particular policies or bills. The rhetoric of parliamentary debates can be dispatched in behind-the-scenes meetings, and backbenchers and ministers can be more frank when there are no cameras rolling. While securing formal meetings with ministers is challenging, they still must vote on House business, allowing backbenchers to catch them in the division lobbies. A quick word in the right person's ear can have a profound effect on the direction of a policy. The parliamentarians who lead APPGs will often arrange to meet with ministers to voice the views of group members and their external partners.

Ministers may also reach out to MPs and peers when developing new initiatives, especially when complex issues are involved. Meetings with their parliamentary private secretaries, senior backbenchers, or chairs of the relevant APPGs will let ministers know how new policies or legislation may be received. They can then attempt to iron out any issues before the matter is debated. In such cases, ministers may prefer to meet parliamentarians away from Westminster so they can discuss the matters with the support of their officials.

Parliamentarians also frequently host pressure groups on the Parliamentary Estate for receptions or briefing sessions to raise awareness about an issue among their colleagues. These sessions are often held by APPGs, such as the APPG on Health's monthly meetings with health experts (noted earlier), or may be sponsored by individual members.

Contemporary developments

Over the past decade, policy and legislative campaigning by MPs, peers, and their external partners has been increasingly conducted through coordinated, long-term initiatives that employ a series of actions over time to slowly build the case for policy and legislative change. This style of campaigning requires more resources than shorter-term initiatives, but has achieved significant changes in some policy areas.

One of the most notable parts of these longer-term campaigns is the trend for APPGs to hold inquiries and issue reports that resemble those from select committees. Many of these inquiries address issues that may be too narrow for select committees to consider, like financial education or body image among young people. Others, however, tackle major issues like the need for high-speed rail. In some cases, APPGs also issue follow-up reports to track the uptake of their recommendations.

The inquiry and report approach offers several advantages to backbench MPs and peers campaigning for policy or legislative change. First, the inquiry process itself can help to attract media attention and raise awareness around an issue, especially if parliamentarians hear from witnesses or travel to gather evidence. The reports produced (which are often slick documents produced by professional designers) then provide further opportunities for activism, such as parliamentary receptions to launch the publications, EDMs and petitions to endorse their findings, parliamentary debates on the need for policy change, and private members' bills to implement the recommendations. Furthermore, the inquiry process gives the findings more legitimacy than if they were put forward by pressure groups or backbenchers directly.

This longer-term strategy can be seen in the work of the APPG on Hunger and Food Poverty. In April 2014, the group launched an inquiry into rising use of food banks in Britain, using a letter in *The Guardian* to publicize its call for evidence (Field and Thornton 2014). The final report was released in December 2014 at a press conference with the Archbishop of Canterbury, whose foundation had sponsored the inquiry (APPG on Hunger and Food Poverty 2014). The report, which partially blamed rising food bank use on the government's changes to the benefits system, attracted extensive media attention, and was regularly cited in subsequent parliamentary debates. The group then issued follow-up reports at three, six, and twelve months after the initial study to track the implementation of the recommendations, with each attracting further media coverage (APPG on Hunger and Food Poverty 2015a, 2015b, 2015c). In December 2015, the group's co-chair, MP Frank Field, then introduced a private members' bill that would implement one of its key recommendations by requiring local authorities to automatically enrol all eligible children in free school meal programmes. The bill did not pass due to a shortage of parliamentary time, but set a record for cross-party support with 125 MP co-sponsors, further increasing the pressure on the government (Field 2015). The APPG then issued a further progress report in April 2016, and a report on child hunger during school holidays in April 2017, both of which were widely covered in the press (APPG on Hunger and Food Poverty 2016, 2017; Pells 2016; Butler 2017).

The APPG on Hunger and Food Poverty illustrates both the long-term approach and reliance on inquiries and reports that is increasingly evident among MPs and peers who seek to change policy and legislation. Moreover, it demonstrates that a cross-party approach can help backbenchers to directly challenge government policies. However, its efforts also underline the substantial external resources that such advocacy requires, a reality that can make it challenging to know where the views of parliamentarians stop and those of pressure groups begin. While few would doubt the objectives of the APPG on Hunger or its main donor, the Archbishop of Canterbury's Charitable Trust, other groups are less transparent. For instance, in May 2017 the Parliamentary Commissioner for Standards found that the APPG on Fixed Odds Betting Terminals had failed to fully disclose the external support that it received for an inquiry that recommended tougher restrictions on the industry. Notably, this included assistance from other gambling firms that could benefit from the measures proposed (Davies 2017; Moore 2017).

Conclusion

Backbench MPs and peers are often presented as bickering bystanders who do little more than argue with each other while the government pursues its policy and legislative agenda. In reality, backbench parliamentarians can use a range of formal and informal tools to slowly build support for change. Most often, these campaigns are conducted hand-in-glove with pressure groups, which provide backbenchers with the information and resources they need to make such campaigns successful. Such collaboration can blur lines of accountability and raise concerns over lobbying, but is often essential to campaign success.

In recent years, MPs, peers, and their partners have begun to undertake longer-term campaigns, many of which include the holding of inquiries and preparation of policy reports. Such initiatives are, in turn, used to attract media attention, provide opportunities for parliamentary activism, and also increase campaigners' legitimacy in the eyes of the government and the public. As a result, such longer-term, report-driven campaigns are well suited to instances where parliamentarians pursue policy initiatives opposed by the government.

Further Reading

FLYNN, P. (2012) *How to be an MP*, London: Biteback Publishing.

GRANT, W. (2000) *Pressure Groups and British Politics*, New York: St Martin's Press.

PARVIN, P. (2007) *Friend or Foe? Lobbying in British Democracy*, London: Hansard Society.

RUSH, M. (1990) *Parliament and Pressure Groups*, Oxford: Oxford University Press.

Case Study 11: All-Party Parliamentary Group Against Antisemitism

Many backbench MPs and peers claim to have influenced government policy or legislation. Most often such influence is indirect, with parliamentarians being just one of several actors advocating for change. However, in some cases it is possible to trace developments directly to backbenchers. One group of parliamentarians that has exerted significant influence on the government is the APPG Against Antisemitism (APPGAA). The group's original Inquiry on Antisemitism published in 2006 resulted in multiple policy changes, making it a model for subsequent APPG inquiries at Westminster and the catalyst for the launching of similar groups in parliaments worldwide.

The APPGAA was established in 2005 as the successor to the All-Party Inter-Parliamentary Council Against Antisemitism. While most APPGs are supported by financing or in-kind assistance from external pressure groups, the APPGAA sought to increase its independence by establishing a dedicated charity, the Parliamentary Committee Against Antisemitism Foundation (PCAA), to receive donations on its behalf, putting MPs and peers at arm's length from contributors.

In 2005, the APPGAA commissioned an inquiry into antisemitism in the UK and potential measures to confront it. To ensure objectivity, the inquiry was not conducted by the group's officers, but by a separate panel of 14 MPs, which included senior parliamentarians such as former Conservative leader Iain Duncan Smith MP and Labour MP Bruce George. The inquiry operated like a select committee, holding four evidence sessions and receiving over 100 written submissions. Despite having no official powers to call witnesses, several leading public figures, including the Home Secretary, agreed to be questioned. The costs were covered by donations channelled through the PCAA, the providers of which were made public. The final report, with 35 recommendations, was published in September 2006 (APPGAA 2006).

While not the first study undertaken by an APPG,[1] the inquiry set new benchmarks for the quality of the inquiry process and the 'unprecedented' policy influence that it achieved (APPGAA 2015a). In particular, the government took the unusual step of responding to the report through an official command paper—something typically reserved for select committee reports (HM Government 2007). Even more surprisingly, it also produced additional command papers one year and three years later to detail the progress made (HM Government 2008, 2010). A final progress report was then released by the Department of Communities and Local Government (DCLG) in 2014. This engagement went far beyond the typical response to select committee inquiries, showing the issue's importance to successive governments. What's more, it actually resulted in tangible policy changes.

The policy changes sparked by the inquiry are too numerous to list in full, but included:

- the establishment of the Inter-Departmental Working Group on Antisemitism, which brings together government departments, the APPGAA, and Jewish community leaders;
- £2m over three years for school-linking programmes;
- funding for security at Jewish schools;
- support for research on antisemitism and for Holocaust education;
- improved data collection on antisemitic incidents by police; and
- the publishing of guidance on hate crimes and intolerance at universities (HM Government 2008, 2010; DCLG 2014).

Moreover, the government provided £20,000 to help establish an international network of parliamentary groups against antisemitism, with similar all-party groups formed in the national legislatures of Canada, Germany, Italy, and the United States (HC Debates, 21 November 2007, c. 871W; APPGAA 2015a). In 2009, it also supported the inaugural conference of the Inter-parliamentary Coalition for Combating Antisemitism, which was held in London.

However, this continued commitment from the government did not come without considerable effort by the APPGAA. Rather than resting after the original report into antisemitism, the group continued to investigate different facets of the issue. In 2008, it published a report on antisemitism in football, and in 2013 it held an inquiry into discrimination during elections (Mann and Cohen 2008; APPGAA 2013). Following an upswing in hate crimes in 2014, it also carried out a second general inquiry into antisemitism in the UK, publishing a report in 2015 (APPGAA 2015b).

APPGAA members have also used the full range of tools available to bring the issue to the attention of their colleagues, government, and the public. Since 2005, group members have put forward dozens of parliamentary questions, introduced over 20 EDMs, and secured five Westminster Hall debates. Outside of Parliament, Members have been vocal in raising the issue through both traditional and social media, and the group holds numerous events to engage with community groups, academics, and other stakeholders.

---

[1] For instance, the Associate Parliamentary Group for Animal Welfare undertook a similar inquiry into the use of wild animals in circuses in 1997, albeit on a smaller scale.

Much of the APPGAA's success is attributable to its cross-party nature. As of early 2017, its membership included 140 MPs and peers from eight parties. Moreover, the group's inquiries have all been conducted by cross-party panels that included not only Members of the three largest parties, but at least one Member from the smaller parties as well. Given the political sensitivities around antisemitism and discussions of Israel, this deliberate cross-party approach has helped to prevent accusations that the group's findings are biased towards one agenda or another.

LESSONS FOR CAMPAIGNING TO CHANGE THE LAW

Together, the APPGAA's combination of non-partisanship and expertise has allowed the group to develop a close, almost symbiotic, relationship with successive ministers in the DCLG. While the group needs ministers to act on its suggestions, ministers have leaned heavily on the group for policy ideas. This reality can be seen in the Best Practice Guide for Combating Antisemitism that was jointly published by the APPGAA and the DCLG in 2016 (APPGAA and DCLG 2016).

However, the APPGAA has also benefitted from extensive external funding. Charity Commission documents show that between 2011 and 2015, the PCAA had average annual expenditures of £255,000 (Charity Commission 2016). These resources allowed the APPGAA to operate in a more systematic way than is possible for backbenchers campaigning on other issues. In particular, the group has a dedicated full-time staff person and can cover the sizeable costs of transcription and travel for group inquiries.

Overall, the APPGAA demonstrates the potential influence that campaigning by backbench MPs and peers can have on government decisions. Such influence is not easy to achieve. It takes time, resources, dedication, and a commitment to collaboration both with those from other parties and with external partners. However, those backbench MPs and peers willing to invest the effort can have a meaningful impact on policy and legislative outcomes.

Primary sources

- All-Party Parliamentary Group Against Antisemitism (2006) Report of the All-Party Parliamentary Inquiry into Antisemitism, London: APPGAA. Online at: https://web.archive.org/web/20170603030402/http://www.antisemitism.org.uk/wp-content/uploads/All-Party-Parliamentary-Inquiry-into-Antisemitism-REPORT.pdf [accessed 22 June 2017].

- Anti-Semitism adjournment debate (HC Debates, 20 January 2011, cc. 327–66WH). Online at: https://www.publications.parliament.uk/pa/cm201011/cmhansrd/cm110120/halltext/110120h0001.htm#11012058000001 [accessed 22 June 2017].

- Department of Communities and Local Government (2014) Government Action on Antisemitism, London: The Stationery Office. Online at: https://www.gov.uk/government/uploads/system/uploads/attachment_data/file/390904/Government_Action_on_Antisemitism_final_24_Dec.pdf [accessed 22 June 2017].

 FURTHER CASE STUDIES

- APPG on Cancer.
- APPG for Excellence in the Built Environment.
- Independent Parliamentary Inquiry into Stalking Law Reform.

References

APPG Against Antisemitism (2006) *Report of the All-Party Parliamentary Inquiry into Antisemitism*, London: APPGAA. Online at: https://web.archive.org/web/20170603030402/http://www.antisemitism.org.uk/wp-content/uploads/All-Party-Parliamentary-Inquiry-into-Antisemitism-REPORT.pdf [accessed 29 October 2015].

APPG Against Antisemitism (2013) *All-Party Parliamentary Inquiry into Electoral Conduct*, London: APPGAA. Online at: https://web.archive.org/web/20170221223128/http://antisemitism.org.uk/wp-content/uploads/3767_APPG_Electoral_-Parliamentary_Report_emailable.pdf [accessed 29 October 2015].

APPG Against Antisemitism (2015a) *The All-Party Parliamentary Group Against Antisemitism: A Decade in Review*, London: APPGAA. Online at: https://web.archive.org/web/20160712152317/http://antisemitism.org.uk/wp-content/uploads/2009/12/PCAA_Year-in-Review_2015_06_combined_V4_SPREADS.pdf [accessed 14 June 2017].

APPG Against Antisemitism (2015b) *Report of the All-Party Parliamentary Inquiry into Antisemitism*, London: APPGAA. Online at: https://web.archive.org/web/20161224154502/http://www.antisemitism.org.uk/wp-content/themes/PCAA/images/Report-of-the-All-Party-Parliamentary-Inquiry-into%20Antisemitism-1.pdf [Accessed 29 October 2015].

APPG Against Antisemitism and Department for Communities and Local Government (2016) *Combating Antisemitism: A British Best Practice Guide*, London: APPGAA and DCLG. Online at: https://web.archive.org/web/20160712192149/http://antisemitism.org.uk/wp-content/uploads/2009/12/Combating-Antisemitism.pdf [accessed 14 June 2017].

APPG for Animal Welfare (APPGAW) (2017) *Membership Directory*. Online at: https://web.archive.org/web/20170207203703/http://www.apgaw.org/membership-directory [accessed 14 June 2017].

APPG on Hunger and Food Poverty (2014) *Feeding Britain: A strategy for zero hunger in England, Wales, Scotland and Northern Ireland*. Online at: https://foodpovertyinquiry.files.wordpress.com/2014/12/food-poverty-feeding-britain-final.pdf [accessed 29 October 2015].

APPG on Hunger and Food Poverty (2015a) *Feeding Britain: Six Months On*. Online at: https://feedingbritain.files.wordpress.com/2015/06/feeding-britain-six-months-on.pdf [accessed 18 January 2016].

APPG on Hunger and Food Poverty (2015b) *Feeding Britain: The first 100 days*. Online at: http://www.frankfield.co.uk/upload/docs/Feeding%20Britain%20100%20Days.pdf [accessed 18 January 2016].

APPG on Hunger and Food Poverty (2015c) *A Route Map to Ending Hunger as we Know it in the United Kingdom: Feeding Britain in 2015–16*. Online at: https://feedingbritain.files.wordpress.com/2017/01/437487_a-route-map-to-ending-hunger-as-we-know-it-in-the-united-kingdom_full.pdf [accessed 18 January 2016].

APPG on Hunger and Food Poverty (2016) *Britain's Not-so-hidden Hunger: A progress report from the All-Party Parliamentary Group on Hunger*. Online at: https://feedingbritain.files.wordpress.com/2017/01/437488_tso_britains-not-so-hidden-hunger.pdf [accessed 14 June 2017].

APPG on Hunger and Food Poverty (2017) *Hungry Holidays: A report on hunger amongst children during school holidays*. Online at: https://feedingbritain.files.wordpress.com/2015/02/hungry-holidays.pdf [accessed 14 June 2017].

BBC News (2013) 'Call to reform "narcissistic" Early Day Motions tabled by MPs', *BBC News*, 24 April. Online at: http://www.bbc.co.uk/news/uk-politics-22284669 [accessed 9 June 2017].

Butler, P. (2017) 'School holidays leave 3 million children at risk of hunger, report says', *The Guardian*, 24 April. Online at: https://www.theguardian.com/society/2017/apr/24/school-holidays-leave-3-million-children-at-risk-of-hunger-report-says [accessed 14 June 2017].

CANCER RESEARCH UK (2008) 'Keep tobacco out of sight of children, say Cancer Research UK', Cancer Research UK press release, 19 November. Online at: http://www.cancerresearchuk.org/about-us/cancer-news/press-release/2008-11-19-keep-tobacco-out-of-sight-of-children-say-cancer-research-uk [accessed 6 June 2017].

CHARITY COMMISSION (2016) *Antisemitism Policy Trust: Accounts Received for 31 December 2015*. Online at: http://apps.charitycommission.gov.uk/Showcharity/RegisterOfCharities/CharityWithoutPartB.aspx?RegisteredCharityNumber=1089736&SubsidiaryNumber=0 [accessed 9 June 2017].

DAVIES, ROB (2017) 'MPs' report on FOBTs found to breach parliamentary standards', *The Guardian*, 3 May. Online at: https://www.theguardian.com/uk-news/2017/may/03/mp-report-fobts-betting-gambling-breach-uk-parliamentary-standards [accessed 10 May 2017].

DEPARTMENT FOR TRANSPORT (2014) *Cycling Delivery Plan*, London: Department for Transport. Online at: https://www.gov.uk/government/uploads/system/uploads/attachment_data/file/364791/141015_Cycling_Delivery_Plan.pdf [accessed 17 November 2015].

DEPARTMENT OF COMMUNITIES AND LOCAL GOVERNMENT (DCLG) (2014) *Government Action on Antisemitism*, London: The Stationery Office.

FIELD, F. (2015) 'My proposed bill could give 160,000 hungry children a hot dinner each day', *The Guardian*, 15 December. Online at: http://www.theguardian.com/society/2015/dec/15/frank-field-bill-hungry-children-hot-dinner [accessed 18 January 2016].

FIELD, F. and THORNTON, T. (2014) 'Gaining the full picture on food poverty', *The Guardian*, 24 April. Online at: http://www.theguardian.com/society/2014/apr/24/gaining-full-picture-food-poverty [accessed 2 November 2015].

HM GOVERNMENT (2007) *Report of the All-Party Parliamentary Inquiry into Antisemitism: Government Response*, London: The Stationery Office.

HM GOVERNMENT (2008) *Report of the All-Party Parliamentary Inquiry into Antisemitism: Government Response—One year on progress report*, London: The Stationery Office.

HM GOVERNMENT (2010) *All-Party Parliamentary Inquiry into Antisemitism: Government Response—Three years on progress report*, London: The Stationery Office.

HUPPERT, J. (2012–13) *Get Britain Cycling*, EDM 697. Online at: http://www.parliament.uk/edm/2012-13/679 [accessed 22 June 2017].

MANN, J. and COHEN, J. (2008) *Antisemitism in European Football: A scar on the Beautiful Game*. Online at: https://web.archive.org/web/20160712160948/http://antisemitism.org.uk/wp-content/uploads/2009/12/Football_Booklet.pdf [accessed 14 June 2017].

MOORE, J. (2017) 'The murky battleground over Fixed Odds Betting Terminals is of MPs' making', *The Independent*, 31 January. Online at: http://www.independent.co.uk/news/business/comment/bookies-blast-mps-fobt-report-over-funding-by-rival-gambling-outfits-a7554921.html [accessed 10 May 2017].

PELLS, R. (2016) 'Thousands of children start school hungry, MPs warn', *The Independent*, 15 April. Online at: http://www.independent.co.uk/news/uk/home-news/thousands-children-starting-school-hungry-malnourished-underweight-mps-warn-a6985321.html [accessed 14 June 2017].

PROCEDURE COMMITTEE (2013) *Early Day Motions: First Report of Session 2013–14*, London: Stationery Office, HC 189. Online at: https://publications.parliament.uk/pa/cm201314/cmselect/cmproced/189/18902.htm [accessed 23 August 2017].

RAMESH, R. (2012) 'NHS reform bill—timeline', *The Guardian*, 18 January. Online at: https://www.theguardian.com/politics/2012/jan/18/nhs-reform-bill-timeline [accessed 22 June 2017].

WOLLASTON, S. (2016) *EDMs*. Online at: http://www.drsarah.org.uk/campaigns/edms [accessed 24 October 2016].

12

Private Members' Bills

Robert Hazell and Fergus Reid

INTRODUCTION

This chapter explores the ways backbenchers in both Houses exploit their right to introduce legislation—known as private members' bills (PMBs). The PMB process has been heavily criticized as being opaque, misleading, and virtually discredited inside and outside Parliament. Yet, each session, over 450 backbenchers enter the Commons PMB ballot for a priority slot and over 100 more introduce a PMB subsequently through other routes. In the Lords, between 40 and 50 peers pursue a PMB each session. This chapter, and the associated Case Study 12, seek to explain why, despite flaws and frustrations, many Members of both Houses see PMBs as a useful tool for advancing their agendas and campaigns—and, occasionally, for changing the law of the land.

What's in a name?

Parliamentary jargon can be confusing. Members of either House who are not Ministers of the Crown, and so not part of the government (no matter which party they belong to), are known as 'private' Members. This is an awkward phrase but perhaps better than 'Unofficial Members' which was in vogue for the first half of the last century. To complicate matters further, the 'p' word is also used in distinguishing between bills which affect everybody by proposing changes to the general law ('public bills') and bills which affect only the rights or interests of identifiable individuals or organizations ('private bills')—and there are rare bills which do both, of which HS2 is an example ('hybrid bills'). Confusingly, *private* Members can only bring forward *public* bills, as the time available for PMBs would not fit with the additional procedures that private and hybrid bills need to follow. One can see why the term 'backbench bill' has been recommended as an alternative to simplify matters. To reduce confusion, *in this chapter*, the term 'PMB' will be used for a non-government public bill in either House.

 Parliamentary terms Hybrid bill

A government bill which affects the general public but which may also have a significant impact for specific individuals or groups. The procedure for considering these bills is complex, as individuals and companies specifically affected are able to submit petitions which are considered by committees in either House.

Parliamentary terms Private bill

A bill put forward by those outside Parliament, typically companies or local authorities. These types of bills affect only a specific group of people or a particular area, e.g. Faversham Oyster Fishery Company Act 2017. Procedures for scrutinizing private bills are different from those for public bills.

 Parliamentary terms Public bill

General bills which affect the whole population. They comprise the majority of primary legislation considered by Parliament in each session. They can be government bills or private members' bills.

The existence of different types of PMBs often causes confusion. There are three *routes* for a backbencher to get their PMB in front of the House—the 'ballot', 'presentation', and the 'ten-minute rule' (the process and implications of each are explained in detail in the section 'The three routes to a PMB in the Commons')—but once introduced all PMBs are substantively the same *type*: short, public bills seeking to add to or amend the UK statute book.

How do PMBs differ from government bills?

PMBs are invariably public bills (i.e. aimed at changing the law as it applies to everybody). The majority of government bills are also public bills. The key differences between a government bill and a PMB arise out of a mix of practical, political, and procedural considerations, and they create an environment in which the passage of PMBs is much more challenging.

Government has a national mandate, specialist resources for legislative drafting, a Commons majority (usually), and means with which to marshal support for its proposals. The government also controls the public finances with sole discretion for the initiation of spending and taxation measures. This last point means that the House must separately agree an authorizing motion for any PMB whose implementation would incur more than incidental increases in public spending or changes in taxation. Such a motion can only be proposed by ministers, giving the government a further 'brake pedal' over the progress of some PMBs (see our suggested further case studies). Also, in the Commons, the rules complement a government's majority with some heavy-duty procedural advantages in making progress with its legislation. First, government business has priority most of the time. Secondly, the government can set dates and times for the conclusion of stages of their bills after second reading through 'programming' (see Chapter 7).

Private Members have none of these comforts. Due to limited time for debate, constrained resources, and restrictions on spending and tax measures, a typical PMB is likely to: be short, with a narrow scope and limited main purpose(s); have only indirect public expenditure implications at most; and be drafted in a relatively simple style. Due to PMBs' vulnerability to opposition, sponsoring Members effectively have a binary decision to make about their bill. They will either choose: a ground-breaking, partisan, or otherwise controversial proposal that is unlikely to make progress but will attract attention to the issue and achieve 'a day in the sun'; or a government-drafted or otherwise uncontroversial, non-partisan matter, which will attract no opposition from government, opposition, or those backbenchers who take a particular interest in PMBs, and will therefore be likely to progress.

The importance of time when considering PMBs

The time allocated to PMBs varies between the two Houses. In the Lords, there is no formal concept of government or private Members' time, nor are there any specific periods when government bills or PMBs are taken. Stages of PMBs are often taken as 'dinner break' business, Monday to Thursday, and on sitting Fridays.

In the Commons, only 13 Fridays are allocated for PMBs in each session and these are scheduled by the government. For MPs this presents difficulties. Fridays have become days for constituency business, creating a dilemma for PMB supporters and opponents alike, as well as inequity in terms of juggling competing commitments which may be far away from Westminster. Proposals for reforming the PMB process often include allocating midweek, 'prime', time for their consideration. From a government whip's perspective, one can understand the attraction of quarantining less favourable PMBs to their own special days.

The first seven Commons PMB Fridays are effectively reserved for second readings. On the last six Fridays, priority is given to bills that have made the most progress. For example, a bill returning to the Floor of the House from committee will be considered ahead of a bill waiting for its second reading. The bill's place in the queue (i.e. the list of Future Business) is thus an important factor in its chances of being debated.

The three routes to a PMB in the Commons

The most well-known route to a PMB is through the private members' bill ballot in the Commons, 'an event' enjoyed by many MPs. The vast majority of eligible backbenchers put their names in, variously *inspired* by the opportunity to sponsor a bill and change the law and *encouraged* by their whips (to reduce the chances of the other parties dominating the outcome).

The ballot winners introduce their bills on the fifth Wednesday of the session. Conventionally, the first seven winners each take number one spot on one of the first seven Fridays—they cannot be usurped as first item of business, and thus are virtually guaranteed a full day's debate. They will have about four weeks to settle on the subject matter of their PMB (described and circumscribed by short and long titles). Table 12.1 shows results of these ballots broken down by party. After these slots have been taken, ballot winners 8–20 have various tactical choices to make. They may gamble on going first on a later Friday (hoping not to be trumped by a bill coming out of committee or derailed by running out of days to make further progress). They may take a chance on going down as a second or third item of business on an earlier Friday (looking for *some* airtime after the first bill or hoping to get a second reading without any debate, i.e. 'on the nod').

The second and third routes to a PMB can be used by MPs who were unsuccessful in the ballot. On the day *after* ballot winners have introduced their bills, other backbenchers are allowed to start giving notice of PMBs. Members may give notice, on a sitting day, of their intention to introduce one or more PMBs on any future sitting day (it is rare for a Member to introduce more than one at a time). These are known as presentation bills. They are

Table 12.1 PMB ballot dividends (1997/98–2015/16)

Position in ballot	Conservative	Labour	Other parties
1st place	6	9	3
2nd to 7th place	55	58	13
8th to 20th place	161	150	49

much more low-key; the bill titles simply appear on the published Order Paper on the day and the short title is read out in the Chamber by the clerk.

Another option available to MPs at this time is the 'ten-minute rule' mechanism. Each sitting Tuesday and Wednesday after the PMB ballot, one MP can make a ten-minute speech asking the permission of the House to introduce a PMB. This can be opposed by another MP for a further ten minutes. Sometimes there is a vote, though this is relatively infrequent. For MPs selecting this route, the ten-minute speech, rather than the bill, is often their primary objective. In such cases a substantive bill is rarely even drafted.

Competition to be successful in the PMB ballot, or to get the first ten-minute rule slot, is fierce. MPs have often queued overnight to be the first in the PMB 'queue' after the 20 ballot winners and/or to get the first ten-minute rule slot. The practice appears to be lapsing, but very early morning attendance outside the relevant clerk's office is commonplace. After the initial excitement, the ten-minute rule slots are allocated according to an informal rota based on the composition of the House. All the conceivable opportunities for debate of a PMB on any of the 13 available Fridays will invariably be filled up very quickly.

Deals and arrangements on which PMBs get taken on which days will have been sought between MPs of the same party, between backbenchers and whips on all sides, and with relevant departmental ministers. This wheeler-dealing process continues throughout the session, getting more and more complicated as PMBs at different stages of progress begin to pile up on the later Fridays. Deals may be commonplace, but they aren't always effective.

A typical Commons second reading Friday

On the first seven PMB Fridays there may be any number of PMBs on the Order Paper, but typically only the first two bills are 'in play' until 2.30 p.m. when the time for debate runs out. One common event is that straight after the initial daily prayers (around 9.35 a.m.), before any business is started, a *supporter* of the first bill moves a procedural motion 'That the House sit in private'. A vote like this is the only way to test whether the House has enough MPs present (a quorum), but this motion can only be used once per sitting. This premature calling of a vote thus prevents an *opposer* of the bill doing so once consideration of the bill has started, and potentially stopping its further consideration.

Debate on the first bill would be expected to last for all, or the vast majority, of the available time (9.35 a.m. until 2.30 p.m.). In the absence of rules or any other provision to bring matters to a close, debate on a question in the Commons will continue until there is nobody left wishing to speak or the available time runs out. If time runs out, and an MP is still speaking, the debate is adjourned until the existing business, on whatever future day the sponsoring Member picks, is finished. This effectively means that the bill is dead as all the future PMB Fridays will be crowded.

Another possibility is that the sponsoring MP of the first bill will seek to conclude the debate and get a decision, using a motion called the 'Closure': 'That the question be now put.' However, there are hurdles to such a proposal: enough debating time must have passed for the Chair to allow the Closure to be moved at all (and about four hours is the minimum); 100 or more MPs must vote in its favour (if it is opposed); *and*, of course, the MP must win the vote. If all those conditions are met, then the question on second reading is immediately put and the bill would move successfully to its next stage. The House would then move on to consider a second bill.

At 2.30 p.m., any debate in progress is adjourned and the titles of the remaining bills down for that day will be read out. If one of these PMBs is uncontroversial, popular, and nobody objects to it 'on principle', then it may go through 'on the nod'. The vast majority of PMBs, however, are objected to at this stage and will have to be moved to the bottom of the queue on a future day named by their sponsoring MP. Another tactic used by MPs is to try to extend the debate of the first bill of the day, in order to prevent a later objectionable bill ever getting started. If a PMB passes its second reading and moves to committee stage, opposers of the bill can table large numbers of amendments in committee or during its report stage to try to delay proceedings further.

Lords PMB ballot

The PMB ballot in the Lords serves a very different purpose. The Lords ballot is for prioritizing all those who enter it to determine the order in which all the relevant PMBs will be introduced (and, in practice, the order of second readings). It does not make a *selection* from those entries. The qualification for the Lords version of the PMB ballot is also different from that of the Commons ballot, in which MPs need only submit their names. After the ballot, other private Lords Members may give notice of bills but they will only be introduced after the original Lords ballot bills. Again, unlike in the Commons, a fully drafted text of the bill must have been written.

Counting by numbers?

The presence of several different routes for PMBs means that the number put forward is large. Success rates, however, are low. The headline figure for the last 19 years was that 108 out of 2,138 PMBs became law, a success rate of about 5 per cent. Performance has varied from no success in 2000–1, to 13 successful PMBs in 2002–3 (Priddy 2016, 5). However, drawing meaningful conclusions from the proportion of PMBs passing into law is bedevilled by a number of factors. Firstly, not all 'PMBs' are actually bills. A substantial proportion of PMBs are never developed beyond their short and long titles, acting as little more than 'legislative press releases'. Secondly, not all PMBs are actually designed and written by private Members. Some originate in the government. These 'hand-out' bills are typically modest departmental bills that did not make it into the government's legislative programme. Although government departments are but one voice among many suitors for the attention of an MP who has a good chance of having a PMB debated—including constituency organizations, charities, businesses, industry and professional federations, trade unions, and campaign groups of all sorts—they are an important one. Unsurprisingly government-side MPs do better, achieving nearly 70 per cent of successful PMBs.

There can also be added complexities. For instance, in 2015–16, an unprinted PMB was negotiated into effect via a government amendment to one of its own bills. This meant that the Events and Festivals (Control of Flares, Fireworks and Smoke Bombs Etc.) PMB became section 134 of the Policing and Crime Act 2017 without ever actually being printed. Any successful privately drafted PMB is also likely to have been heavily amended during its committee stage, sometimes almost entirely rewritten, by the government. Such changes, agreed with the sponsoring MP, must be made to ensure that any measure heading for the statute book is technically effective. Some hand-out bills may have been asked for, inspired by, or tailored to suit sponsoring MPs and, finally, by no means do all government-drafted PMBs succeed.

Reforming PMB procedures

The Commons Procedure Committee, responsible for monitoring the effectiveness of Commons rules, has had a running battle with government over reform of the PMB process since 2013 (see Procedure Committee 2013, 2014, 2016a, 2016b). The Committee has recommended substantial changes aimed, it argues, at retaining (perhaps regaining) the engagement of Members and making the system easier to understand outside Parliament. The Committee wanted, in particular, an end to filibustering and a far clearer distinction between PMBs introduced simply to highlight an issue and PMBs genuinely seeking a specific legislative change (e.g. Procedure Committee 2016, 20). The Committee's reforms seemed to be aimed at a stronger focus on fewer, better developed, and more widely supported proposals on which the Commons in particular would be enabled to have genuine debate and a guaranteed vote.

From the government's perspective, one can imagine how unattractive would be propositions designed to require ministers to make more explicit formal decisions to support, or not, a range of potentially popular or populist measures that may be regarded as unbudgeted for, in conflict with other policies, or technically unworkable. Whatever the reasons, the government has yet to schedule debate and decisions on any of the various evolutions of the Committee's recommendations. This run of reports, and the relevant government replies (see Procedure Committee 2014, 2016b), is an excellent exposition of the process, its strengths and weaknesses.

Conclusion

On the face of it, the list of socio-politically significant changes with their roots in a private members' bill is startling: the abolition of slavery, abolition of capital punishment, de-criminalization of homosexuality, the availability of abortion on certain grounds, same-sex marriage. On further consideration, it is far less surprising that such matters would be first put forward by individual campaigners, then reflected, assayed, or brokered via these procedures. After all, Parliament is the forum where such debates focus and the crucible where they are tested—sometimes for many years before society as a whole is 'ready for change' and an effective legislative vehicle is found or developed for technically viable implementation.

Much of the discussion and guidance around PMBs refers to the complicated parliamentary procedures that come with them. To the extent that parliamentary procedure—in calibrating and balancing the rights of the majority to make progress, and of the minority to make trouble—is always going to look complicated to the uninitiated, there is some truth in this. However, with regard specifically to PMBs, the procedures could be said to remain in their historically simplest and purest form (no guillotines, no programming, no EVEL) and, of necessity, bills are shorter and far less complicated. Second readings, amendments at all stages, and third readings simply require the exhaustion of debate, the acquiescence of the House or committee, or a majority of Members voting in support. The complexities arise out of the behaviours of supporters and opposers, as the clock counts down the limited time available and more business is on the agenda than could ever be accommodated. Complexity and confusion then arises from two factors: the efforts made, and deals sought, by the few with some expectations of seeing their bills making progress; and the exploitation of the opportunities for exposure and airtime by the many whose bills have no realistic chance.

Further Reading

BOWLER, S. (2010) 'Private Members' Bills in the UK Parliament: Is there an "Electoral Connection"?', *Journal of Legislative Studies*, Vol. 16 (4), pp. 476–94.

BRAZIER, A. and FOX, R. (2011) *Enhancing the Role of Backbench MPs: Proposals for Reform of Private Members' Bills*, London: The Hansard Society. Online at: https://assets.contentful.com/u1rlvvbs33ri/VbMtf24V66WAYUAyM02IM/64e33886657c6c24e90239d67ecfd944/Publication__Enhancing-the-role-of-Backbench-MPs-Proposals-for-reform-of-Private-Members-Bills-2011.pdf [accessed 25 June 2017].

KELLY, R. (2016) *Private Members' Bills*, House of Commons Library Briefing Paper Number 7554, 11 April. Online at: http://researchbriefings.parliament.uk/ResearchBriefing/Summary/CBP-7554#fullreport [accessed 25 June 2017].

MARSH, H. and MARSH, D. (2002) 'Tories in the Killing Fields? The Fate of Private Members' Bills in the 1997 Parliament', *Journal of Legislative Studies*, Vol. 8 (1), pp. 91–112.

SCOTT, E. (2016) *Private Member's Bills in the House of Lords*, House of Lords Library Note 28, 24 May. Online at: http://researchbriefings.parliament.uk/ResearchBriefing/Summary/LLN-2016-0028 [accessed 25 June 2017].

Case Study 12: The Assisted Dying (No. 2) Bill of Session 2015–16

In 2015, Rob Marris, Labour MP for Wolverhampton South West, introduced a PMB to clarify and liberalize the law around helping someone with a painful terminal illness to end their own life. The bill became a rare example of a PMB debated on its merits and subject to a clear decision of the House in being rejected at second reading on a vote.

BACKGROUND

Under the Suicide Act 1961 it is a criminal offence deliberately to perform 'an act capable of encouraging or assisting the suicide or attempted suicide of another person'. The law is strict: if A assists B to take B's own life, then A may face prosecution. English law bans helping someone who wishes to end their life but cannot do so unaided because of the crippling effects of their illness. This blanket ban is regularly challenged in court and in Parliament.

Previous attempts to change the law on assisted suicide had failed due to procedural obstacles in the Lords. In 2003, Lord Joffe's Patient (Assisted Dying) Bill ran out of time after its second reading in the Lords. Another attempt in 2006 failed after a motion was passed to defer consideration of the bill for six months. In 2015, Lord Falconer introduced a similar bill and it passed second reading. However, Parliament was then prorogued for the 2015 general election. The progress of Lord Falconer's bill indicated that the Lords might favour legislative change. Against this background, Rob Marris MP, winner of the Commons PMB ballot for 2015–16, introduced his Assisted Dying (No. 2) Bill.

The Bill sought to allow those of sound mind with a medical prognosis of less than six months to be given aid to take their own lives following approval by two doctors and a High Court judge. It had the hallmarks of the larger ethical 'society-shaping' PMBs of the past—on slavery, capital punishment, the banning of abortion, and the criminality of homosexual behaviour—that started debates leading to substantial change.

THE DEBATE ON THE BILL

In the lead-up to the debate there was considerable public campaigning on both sides. MPs' inboxes and postbags ballooned and some MPs ran specific constituency polls. The second reading debate lasted for nearly five hours and 76 MPs contributed out of an unprecedented 85 who had applied to do so. This is more than double the average number of participants on equivalent previous occasions.

Unlike previous occasions on which this type of bill had been considered in the Commons, there was no filibustering, nor any other procedural tricks. Natascha Engel, the Deputy Speaker, had made huge efforts during the week beforehand to gain a picture of those broadly in favour or against to ensure that her calling of MPs would be fair. And the debate—as with a mainstream government bill—was allowed to draw to a close in time to hold a division. This was effected by an unopposed Closure motion ('That the Question be now put'), which enabled the House to express and record an unequivocal decision that the public could see and inspect (overall and in the case of each MP attending); 448 out of a possible 638 MPs voted. This is in contrast to the fate of so many PMBs, which are simply 'talked out' and thereby halted without a specific and accountable decision. In a free vote, 118 MPs voted in favour, and 330 against, so the bill was defeated by three to one.

Rob Marris told us that 'opinion polls consistently show that about 75 per cent of the public support this type of legislation, whereas about 75 per cent of current MPs oppose it. In a mature democracy, this imbalance cannot continue indefinitely. Either the public changes its view, or the MPs do. I know which my money is on' (Marris 2016). It might be hard to see the law shifting any time soon. But in the world of PMBs no debate is ever settled, and in June 2016 Lord Hayward introduced a new Assisted Dying Bill into the Lords.

By way of contrast, it is worth considering a PMB from the other end of the scale. On 27 January 2016, Sir David Amess MP received the leave of the House, after a short explanatory speech under Standing Order No. 23 (*the ten-minute rule*), to introduce a bill 'to make provision about the registration of driving instructors'. The background is that there was no simple way of leaving nor rejoining the list of approved instructors to reflect life circumstances such as caring responsibilities or a long-term illness. Sir David's bill proposed—in seven clauses and less than 2,000 words—an uncontroversial solution which the government supported and nobody objected to. The bill received a second reading without debate on 5 February; was examined in committee on 1 March and not amended; received its third reading on 4 March; and went through its Lords stages between 7 March and 5 May without being amended; it received royal assent on 12 May 2016. In total, this bill received 60 minutes of substantive parliamentary attention and became law.

CONCLUSION

This case study and the latter example illustrate two classic uses of PMBs. On the one hand, providing the opportunity for debate of a substantial issue concerning what kind of society we want to be; on the other hand, effecting small, uncontroversial legislative tweaks. What was unusual about Rob Marris' bill was the consensus that emerged—likely to be the result of the depth and breadth of public campaigning—that here was an issue to be debated and decided rather than just obstructed or exhausted by procedural means.

Primary sources

- Assisted Dying (No. 2) Bill, Session 2015–16, Bill No. 7. Online at: https://www.publications. parliament.uk/pa/bills/cbill/2015-2016/0007/16007.pdf [accessed 27 June 2017].

- Barber, S., Lipscombe, S., and Dawson, J. (2015) *The Assisted Dying (No. 2) Bill 2015*, House of Commons Library Briefing Paper No. 7292, 4 September. Online at: http://researchbriefings. parliament.uk/ResearchBriefing/Summary/CBP-7292 [accessed 27 June 2017].

- Second reading of the Assisted Dying (No. 2) Bill (HC Debates, 11 September 2015, cc. 656–725). Online at: https://www.publications.parliament.uk/pa/cm201516/cmhansrd/cm150911/debtext/150911-0001.htm [accessed 27 June 2017].

 FURTHER CASE STUDIES

- Homelessness Reduction Act 2017.
- The failed Parliamentary Constituencies (Amendment Bill) (2016–17).
- Access to Medical Treatments (Innovation) Act 2016.

References

MARRIS, R. (2016) Email correspondence with the author.

PRIDDY, S. (2016) *Successful Private Members' Bills Since 1983*, House of Commons Library Paper Number 04568, 5 July. Online at: http://researchbriefings.files.parliament.uk/documents/SN04568/SN04568.pdf [accessed 5 August 2017].

PROCEDURE COMMITTEE (2013) *Private Members' bills: Second Report of Session 2013–14*, London: The Stationery Office, HC 188-1. Online at: https://www.publications.parliament.uk/pa/cm201314/cmselect/cmproced/188/188.pdf [accessed 5 August 2017].

PROCEDURE COMMITTEE (2014) *Private Members' bills: Government response and revised proposals: Fifth Report of Session 2013–14*, HC 1171. Online at: https://www.publications.parliament.uk/pa/cm201314/cmselect/cmproced/1171/1171.pdf [accessed 24 June 2017].

PROCEDURE COMMITTEE (2016a) *Private Members' bills: Third Report of Session 2015–16*, London: The Stationery Office, HC 684. Online at: https://www.publications.parliament.uk/pa/cm201516/cmselect/cmproced/684/684.pdf [accessed 24 June 2017].

PROCEDURE COMMITTEE (2016b) *Private Members' bills: Observations on the Government response to the Committee's Third Report of Session 2015–16 HC 684: Second Report of Session 2016–17*, HC 701. Online at: https://publications.parliament.uk/pa/cm201617/cmselect/cmproced/701/701.pdf [accessed 24 June 2017].

13

Small Parties and Law-making

Margaret Arnott and Richard Kelly

INTRODUCTION

This chapter explores the role of smaller parties in Parliament. UK general elections are conducted with an electoral system which militates against the representation of smaller political parties, particularly those with no strong regional support. In consequence, Westminster is perceived as a dichotomous institution with government and opposition involving only two parties, and any smaller parties present are something of a side show. However, events at Westminster over the last decade have increased the prominence of smaller parties in the operation of parliamentary business: for instance, the participation of the Liberal Democrats in the Coalition government of 2010, the assumption of the role of third party in the Commons by the SNP following the 2015 general election, and in 2017 the 'confidence and supply' agreement between the DUP and the minority Conservative administration. In this chapter we consider how the political and electoral context of Parliament, especially in the twenty-first century, has affected smaller party representation and how reforms to parliamentary procedure since the 1980s have enhanced the role of the second opposition party. We also inquire whether reforms in this area have potentially offered smaller parties new routes to influence policy. Finally, we explore smaller parties' influence in Parliament in the more fluid political environments of recent years.

Electoral performance

The decline in support for Britain's two traditional parties from 85–90 per cent at elections from the 1930s to the 1970s to around two-thirds of the vote in 2005, 2010, and 2015 is well documented (Denver 2014, 122). Some revival of the two-party system in the UK may be noted in the results of the 2017 general election, where the Conservative Party and Labour Party together secured just over 82 per cent of the vote and 89 per cent of the seats in the Commons. The UK Independence Party (UKIP) lost votes and failed to secure any seats, the Liberal Democrats made only modest gains from 2015, and the Green Party retained their one seat. But a total of eight political parties still gained representation in the House of Commons.

The UK's single-Member constituency-based electoral system is not proportional. As a result, an increase in votes for a party does not necessarily translate into a corresponding increase in the number of seats, as only one Member is elected in each constituency contest. At the 2015 general election UKIP received 3.9 million votes (12.6 per cent) across the UK but won only one seat; the Scottish National Party (SNP) received 1.5 million votes (4.7 per cent) across the UK but only contested the 59 seats in Scotland, where it received 50 per cent of the vote, and won 56 seats (i.e. 95 per cent of the seats in Scotland) (Hawkins, Keen, and Nakatudde 2015, 11).

Constitutional changes to the governance of the UK have brought opportunities for the country's smaller political parties. We see this clearly from 1999 with the introduction of legislative devolution in Scotland and Northern Ireland and executive devolution in Wales. It presented a new context for party representation in Westminster (Arnott 2015; Hazell and Rawling 2015). As a consequence, there has been significant reform of Parliament in terms of its processes, procedures, and scrutiny over the past 16 years. Constitutional reforms have also brought challenges. Most obviously, Parliament faced a number of questions in relation to the suitability and effectiveness of its law-making and scrutiny roles following the 2016 EU referendum, and again following the 2016 Scotland Act and the 2014 and 2017 Wales Acts. Arrangements between a minority Conservative UK administration and one of the smaller parties in the Commons, the DUP, following the 2017 general election brought the potential for a small party to have considerable influence over government legislation. It also increased the significance of other small parties in opposition, such as the SNP and Plaid Cymru, whose MPs could potentially bring about the success or failure of government bills.

Parliament and the role of smaller parties

Where elections lead to single-party governments with a large majority, such as the Labour government of 1997–2001, smaller parties have found their role in Parliament to be more marginal. Their votes are unlikely to make a difference to decisions made in the Commons. But the changed party composition in Parliament following the 2010 UK general election, together with the election in 2009 of a new Speaker pledged to further parliamentary reform, initiated a new phase of parliamentary politics with potential consequences for smaller party participation.

Electoral events would have a greater impact on the role of small parties from 2010 onwards, particularly in the House of Commons. Following the 2010 general election, the third largest party—the Liberal Democrats—entered into a formal coalition arrangement with the largest party, the Conservatives. Adopting government status, the Liberal Democrats would no longer receive Short money. Hazell and Yong comment that the Liberal Democrats had to adjust to being a party of *coalition government* in terms of their contribution to debates from the government side compared to their contributions to debates from the opposition benches as the third largest party (Hazell and Yong 2012). Liberal Democrats occupying a ministerial role experienced new tensions in the dynamic between their involvement in government and their relationship with backbench Liberal Democrat MPs. Tensions within Parliament became apparent on some key policy issues, particularly university tuition fees and the Welfare Reform Bill in the 2010–12 parliamentary session, where the Coalition government's plans seemed to contradict the Liberal Democrats' 2010 election manifesto. The reputational effects for the Liberal Democrats contributed to their poor electoral performance in 2015 (Russell and Cowley 2016). As a smaller party, the decision to enter a formal coalition government not only changed their operation in the Parliament but also their status, as for the first time they entered the 2015 UK general election as a party of government rather than as an opposition party.

The return to single-party government following the 2015 general election arguably produced a different parliamentary environment for the operation and influence of smaller political parties once again, but this was especially true for the Liberal Democrats and the SNP. The Liberal Democrats were reduced from 57 seats to just eight, while in Scotland the SNP secured 56 of the 59 Scottish seats. With three MPs, Plaid Cymru's representation remained unchanged. The Green Party and UKIP each secured one seat. Northern Ireland parties competing for election also returned similar representation in Westminster, with the Democratic Unionist Party securing an additional seat (bringing their total to eight MPs) and the Ulster Unionist Party winning two seats.

Many of the practices and conventions of Parliament were developed before the advent of recognizable party politics, and this means that parties are hardly mentioned in the Standing Orders of the House. They developed at a time when parliamentary politics was dominated by two opposing groups of representatives. This has two implications. Firstly, it means that government dominates the parliamentary and legislative agenda, with little formal means of involving non-government parties. Secondly, it means that when opposition parties in Parliament do receive some privileges and recognition in parliamentary activities, they are overwhelmingly directed at the 'official opposition' party. In the 2017 Parliament this means that the Labour Party is well placed in terms of committee appointments, speaking time, and the right to select opposition day debates in the Commons. The Leader of the Opposition, for example, has six guaranteed questions at Prime Minister's Questions (PMQs) each week and the party receives 17 days to debate topics of its choosing in the Chamber (House of Commons 2016, SO 14). The SNP, as the second opposition party, receives some privileges. Since May 1985, the leader of the second largest opposition party has been able to choose the subject of debate on three opposition days (House of Commons 2016, SO 14) and they receive two guaranteed questions at PMQs, but this is much less than the official opposition.

 Parliamentary terms Opposition days

In the Commons, 20 days in each session during which the topic of debate is selected by one of the two largest opposition parties; smaller opposition parties can only get an opposition day debate through negotiation with the government or with larger parties.

But there is little recognition of the other parties in the Commons. The three smaller parties with elected representatives in the 2017 Parliament (Liberal Democrats, Plaid Cymru, Greens)[1] receive very few privileges. Their party leaders, for example, cannot expect to be called each week at PMQs. In the 2015–16 session, there were 33 PMQs, but Nigel Dodds, Leader of the DUP group at Westminster, was called on only eight occasions. These parties are only able to determine the subject of Commons debates if the government provides them with time or if the two larger opposition parties give away some of the time set aside for their opposition day debates. As such, these parties rely on being viewed favourably by the Speaker and Deputy Speakers, as it is they who have the power to call them to speak during debates in the Chamber. Informal consultations held between the government chief whip and the opposition chief whip (the 'usual channels') can be held with these parties too regarding business arrangements, but these cannot be guaranteed (McKay et al. 2004, 250). There is thus little formal recognition of small parties in Commons procedures.

Parliament has considered extending greater rights to small parties on several occasions, but this has brought only partial change. For example, the Jopling Committee on Sittings of the House recommended that when time limits were imposed on speeches by the Commons Speaker, one Member from the second largest opposition party should not be subjected to any time limits (Rogers and Walters 2015, 263). This was trialled in 1995 and made permanent later in the same year (HC Debates, 2 November 1995, cc. 449–50). However, as with opposition day debates, this recognition was not matched by proposals to enhance the recognition of any of the smaller parties in the Chamber.

---

[1] This figure excludes the seven Sinn Féin MPs elected in the 2017 general election, as these MPs do not take their seats at Westminster.

Parliamentary terms Time limits in debates

Some speeches by backbench MPs in the Commons are governed by time limits, imposed by the Speaker or Deputy Speaker, to allow all MPs who wish to speak to do so. Often an announced time limit will decrease as a debate progresses.

The scale of the SNP's electoral victory in Scotland in 2015 would later raise questions about procedures and practices in Parliament. SNP MPs in 2015 adopted an approach intended to highlight the divergence between the policy intentions of the devolved SNP-led minority government in Scotland and the UK Conservative-led government, but, as Case Study 13 shows, they would find themselves frustrated by procedural hurdles. The SNP sought to present itself as a united parliamentary party and opposition in Westminster, in open contrast to the dissension in the Parliamentary Labour Party (PLP) following the election of Jeremy Corbyn as party leader. As the second largest opposition party, the SNP could make more contributions in the Chamber via opposition day debates and Prime Minister's Questions, and had the right to chair two select committees. The party therefore had to juggle its parliamentary concerns in Westminster with its political strategy following the Scottish independence referendum, all within a parliament which does not readily facilitate smaller party involvement.

The role of small parties in committees and legislation

The Standing Orders relating to the nomination of general committees, grand committees, and European committees stipulate that the Committee of Selection 'shall have regard to the qualifications of those Members nominated and to the composition of the House' (House of Commons 2016, SOs 86, 92, 117, and 119). Whereas the Standing Orders relating to select committees do not specify an equivalent requirement, it has been the practice of the Committee of Selection to apply this principle also to the nomination of select committees. The principle is often seen to apply not simply to each committee in isolation, but across the full range of select committees. This makes it easier to allocate a 'reasonable' number of seats to smaller parties. The enhanced legitimacy of chairs following the introduction of elections in 2010 potentially offers smaller parties more influence on parliamentary business. In the aftermath of their landslide victory in Scotland in 2015, the SNP chaired two select committees—Scottish Affairs, and Energy and Climate Change. Smaller parties did receive representation on select committees in the 2015 Parliament, but only as committee members. Green MP Caroline Lucas, for example, was a member of the Environmental Audit Committee, and DUP MP Gavin Robinson was a member of the Defence Committee. There were no committee chairs from the smaller parties.

When it comes to the scrutiny of legislation, the role for smaller parties is also much more about informal arrangements rather than formal rights. All MPs are eligible to speak during the second reading debates on legislation, but—from a party perspective—the larger parties are more likely to see their MPs make contributions. This is because the Speaker needs to take party balance into account when calling MPs to speak. Smaller parties receive no guaranteed slots (unlike the spokespeople from the three largest parties) and this can mean waiting in the Chamber for a long time. MPs are usually expected to be present at the start of a debate and for the winding up speeches. For example, during the second reading of the EU (Notification of Withdrawal) Bill the Speaker noted that 99 backbenchers were seeking to make a speech (HC Debates, 31 January 2017, c. 818). The debate started at 12.50 p.m., but the first MP from a small party (Sammy Wilson, DUP) was not called to speak until 3.18 p.m. (see c. 858). MPs from these parties tend to make interventions early in the debates to ensure that their concerns are placed on the record. Liberal Democrat Tom Brake and SDLP MP Alasdair McDonnell, for instance, intervened to ask a question during the speech by Secretary of State David Davis at the very start of the debate (cc. 822–3).

The committee stage of bills brings the opportunity to scrutinize legislation in detail (see Chapter 9). But it is just as challenging to appoint MPs from small parties to bill committees as it is to appoint them to select committees. Bill committees would need to be much larger to ensure that Members of more than one of the smaller parties were selected. Having said that, in the 2010 Parliament, most public bill committees included at least one representative of parties other than the three largest. And they can have an effect. Caroline Lucas, the sole Green Party MP, for example, commented on her struggles to get appointed to a bill committee. She notes, though, that when she was appointed, she felt that she could make a difference to the bill in question:

> In my first year, after a protracted tussle, I won a place on the Energy Bill Committee and could work with other backbench MPs and with campaigners and experts outside Parliament, and argue the case for a range of improvements. You can't usually change the overall shape of the legislation—the Energy Act still had many flaws and failings—but I think we helped to avoid it being an awful lot worse: and in Parliament that often counts as a victory. (Lucas 2015, 130)

In its 2009 report on *Rebuilding The House*, the House of Commons Reform Committee noted that the report stage of a bill, which is taken in the Chamber, 'in many cases will be the only opportunity for Members from the smaller parties to participate in legislative activity' (2009, para 110). As Chapter 7 outlined, there are no restrictions on who can attend the report stage debate, and it brings opportunities for small parties to introduce amendments. For instance, during the report stage of the Digital Economy Bill (2015–16 session) Plaid Cymru MP Hywel Williams was able to table and speak to a new clause in which he sought to place an obligation on the government minister to issue a code of practice to improve the performance of social media platforms in tackling online abuse (see HC Debates, 28 November 2016, c. 1303). Although the pressure of time at report stage meant that he had only a couple of minutes in which to speak, he was able to get his suggestions across and express a wish that the points he made 'will be taken up in another place' (i.e. the House of Lords). Where small parties have representatives in both Chambers, they are able to work closely together to try to push for changes to bills. It can also be effective for small parties to work together. When Plaid Cymru tabled an amendment to stop the EU (Notification of Withdrawal) Bill from proceeding past its second reading, they were supported by the Greens, SDLP, and SNP in the Commons (Plaid Cymru 2017; HC Debates, 1 February 2017, Division 134).

Backbench debates

The Wright Committee reforms implemented in the 2010 Parliament (see Chapter 28) brought opportunities to enhance the activity and influence of small parties and their MPs in the Commons. One of these reforms was the creation of the Backbench Business Committee. The Committee itself is dominated by MPs from the two main parties. In the 2015 Parliament it comprised five Conservative, two Labour, and one SNP MP. Smaller parties also found themselves ineligible for consideration for the position of committee chair as the Standing Orders specified that nomination required the support of ten party colleagues (see Martin and Kelly 2015, 7). During the course of the 2010 Parliament, proposals came forward to ensure that smaller parties were represented on the Committee. Since 2012, the Committee has had the power to invite Members from the smaller parties to attend its meetings and take part in its deliberations.

There was an initial reluctance on the part of the minority parties to exercise this right. It was argued that they were not prepared to accept a second-class status on the Committee (see Backbench Business Committee 2015, 11; Procedure Committee 2014, 2). However, representatives of the minority parties have since taken up the Committee's invitation to participate, following a review into the issue by the Procedure Committee in March 2015. The Chair of the Procedure Committee wrote to the Leader of the House 'to ask him to ensure that he or his successor as Leader in the new Parliament address the need to ensure appropriate minority party membership representation on the Backbench Business Committee and across all select committees in the discussions which will take place at the start of the Parliament' (Backbench Business Committee 2015, para 37).

Smaller parties may not have been appointed as members of the Backbench Business Committee, but any MP is eligible to apply for a backbench debate (see Case Study 18). Whether the potential influence of smaller parties really was enhanced through reforms to backbenchers' rights might be judged by the success of applications made. Evidence suggests that it has been a useful place for MPs from smaller parties to request time in the Chamber. In the 2015–16 session, for example, 15 applications were made by MPs from outside the two main parties, accounting for 17 per cent of the total applications made (Backbench Business Committee 2015, Annex 5). Several of these were successful. Liberal Democrat MP Stephen Gilbert, for instance, held a two-hour Westminster Hall debate on NHS specialized services (HC Debates, 15 January 2015, cc. 335–67WH). There is no evidence that debates have been proposed to further party agendas; rather the Members proposing debates have been encouraged to work across parties to demonstrate interest in topics before the Committee selects them (Backbench Business Committee 2015, Annex 1). For instance, Liberal Democrat MP Greg Mulholland worked with MPs from the larger parties to request a backbench debate on pubs and planning legislation.

Conclusion

The presence of smaller parties in the Commons remains limited except where a party's regional electoral support can overcome, and may disproportionately benefit from, the 'winner takes all' nature of the electoral system for the Westminster Parliament. Parliament today offers more opportunities for smaller political parties to influence debate and policy, but this is still quite limited. While the multilevel party system in the UK helps to shape the political environment that parties are working in, such as coalition or minority governing arrangements in Parliament, the influence of smaller parties on parliamentary business is shaped by the extent of formal and informal rights in the functions and roles of Parliament. But if smaller parties have more opportunities since 2015, they also face challenges such as their ability to retain or improve their representation in Parliament. This has been particularly the case for the SNP, as Case Study 13 illustrates.

Further Reading

CLARK, A. (2012) *Political Parties in the UK*, Basingstoke: Palgrave.

COPUS, C., CLARK, A., REYNAERT, H., and STEYVERS, K. (2009) 'Minor Party and Independent Politics Beyond the Mainstream: Fluctuating Fortunes but a Permanent Presence', *Parliamentary Affairs*, Vol. 62 (1), pp. 4–18.

JUDGE, D. (1993) *The Parliamentary State*, London: Sage.

LINDSAY, I. (2007) 'The SNP and Westminster' in G. Hassan (ed.), *The Modern SNP: From Protest to Power*, Edinburgh: Edinburgh University Press, pp. 93–104.

Case Study 13: The SNP in the House of Commons 2015–17

The result of the UK general election in May 2015 brought renewed public and academic interest in the role and functions of smaller parties in Parliament. A party which stood only in constituencies in Scotland (the SNP) had achieved third party status in the Commons. With its new status, the SNP could draw on more rights and privileges in parliamentary business, and have more opportunities to hold the executive to account. However, this status presented a challenge for the SNP Westminster Group on how to respond. This case study discusses the roles adopted by the party in Westminster.

Since the election of its first MP at Westminster in 1945, the SNP has been a minority party in the Commons. In the post-war period until 1999, support for the party had fluctuated and its electoral representation in UK general elections remained low. Before the May 2015 general election the best performance electorally for the party was October 1974 when it secured 11 seats on 30.4 per cent of the vote in Scotland. In May 2015, the SNP won 56 of 59 constituencies in Scotland. It secured 50 per cent of the votes in Scotland, compared to 24.3 per cent for the Labour Party, 14.9 per cent for the Conservative Party, and 7.5 per cent for the Liberal Democrat Party.

Of the 56 SNP MPs elected, only seven had previous experience as an MP, including the former party leader Alex Salmond. Following the party's stance on the upper House there are no SNP peers. The new SNP MPs included some who had joined the party following the 2014 Scottish independence referendum result, alongside those who had been in the party for a number of years (Keen 2015). The vast majority of newly elected SNP MPs therefore had no direct experience of the Westminster Parliament as elected representatives. Mhairi Black, the SNP MP for Paisley and Renfrewshire South, became the youngest MP in Westminster since 1667.

As third largest party in the Commons, the SNP secured additional resources and formal rights to participate in parliamentary business. Enhanced Short money funds enabled the party to expand the support for its parliamentary group such as appointing staff to support specific policy remits. Following the 2015 election, the SNP was due to receive approximately £1.2m in that parliamentary term compared to £187,000 it received in the previous parliamentary term (BBC News 2015).

The party's strategy in relation to its representation at Westminster evolved in light of a shifting electoral and political environment. This included the repercussions of electoral divergence between Scotland and England particularly since the late 1980s, the introduction of legislative devolution in 1999, and also the 2014 Scottish independence referendum. In the 2015 campaign the party had sought to present itself as 'Scotland's voice in Westminster' (SNP 2015). Holding the executive to account on issues identified in the 2015 manifesto shaped the group's involvement in the House of Commons.

Contribution to ongoing constitutional debates was part of the SNP group's activity in the Commons but the interplay between constitutional concerns and 'reserved' legislative matters shaped the tone of their contributions. The constitutional debate in the Commons on the 2016 Scotland Act, on English votes for English laws (EVEL), on the Brexit result of the EU referendum in June 2016, and on reforms to the practices and processes in the UK Parliament, including relations with the Scottish Parliament, were key issues for the SNP, but this was carried out alongside its stance on 'austerity' politics. As third party, the SNP contributed to every Prime Minister's Questions, acquiring in this way considerably more visibility than they had had before 2015. Its MPs also chaired the Scottish Affairs Select Committee and the Energy and Climate Change Select Committee, which gave them a bigger say on matters of particular importance for the party.

The SNP group at Westminster has considered its role as one of contributing directly to legislative debates and to scrutiny of the UK Conservative government. Its stance on non-devolved matters has evolved with its approach to UK politics more broadly. Interventions on fox hunting and shop opening hours were early examples of this approach in the 2015 Parliament, where the party's very public intentions to vote against the government on issues not explicitly relating to Scotland caused the government to shelve the policies rather than risk defeat in the Commons Chamber. Changes to pension arrangements for women born in the 1950s was another issue the group campaigned on in the Commons. On Syria and on extending UK 'air strikes', the SNP opposed the Conservative Party and, in a vote in the Commons in December 2015, voted not to approve further UK air military action (Wintour and Perraudin 2015). The SNP group has acted under the discipline of the party whip—for instance on Syria and military action the SNP parliamentary group voted as a bloc. The party's strong cohesion and discipline, and interventionist attitude towards legislation on issues which are devolved in Scotland, have thus enabled it to have a visible impact on legislation and government policy.

The party highlighted concerns where it argued that, due to the electoral divergence between Scotland and England, there are tensions regarding several major issues such as welfare reform and the renewal of Trident. The SNP used opportunities in the Commons and in its committees to raise these concerns. For example, the parliamentary consequences of EVEL for devolved matters has been an area where the SNP has highlighted concerns following the changes to the Standing Orders in October 2015 (see for example HC Debates, 22 October 2015, cc. 1119–258).

The SNP's transition to third largest political party in the 2015 Parliament was the result of a huge increase in the number of its elected representatives in Scotland. But it brought much more than greater numbers in the Commons. As its 2017 election manifesto demonstrated (SNP 2017, 4), the additional privileges granted to the second opposition party in terms of speaking rights and committee appointments enabled it to have a much greater impact in its opposition to government legislation and in pushing for new policy measures.

Primary sources

- House of Commons (2016) *Standing Orders of the House of Commons—Public Business*, 2016, February, London: The Stationery Office, HC 2. Online at: https://www.publications.parliament.uk/pa/cm201516/cmstords/0002/so-2.pdf [accessed 27 June 2017].

- Procedure Committee (2014) *Letters from Charles Walker, Chair of the Procedure Committee to Pete Wishart and Natascha Engel regarding minority party participation in the Backbench Business Committee*, London: House of Commons, 23 June. Online at: http://www.parliament.uk/documents/commons-committees/procedure/EngelWishartBBComminorityrep.pdf [accessed 27 June 2017].

- Procedure Committee (2014) *Oral Evidence: Minority party participation in the Backbench Business Committee*, London: House of Commons, 14 May. Online at: http://data.parliament.uk/writtenevidence/committeeevidence.svc/evidencedocument/procedure-committee/minority-party-participation-in-the-backbench-business-committee/oral/9677.pdf [accessed 27 June 2017].

- House of Commons Reform Committee (2009) *Rebuilding the House: First Report of Session 2008-09*, London: The Stationery Office, HC 1117. Online at: https://www.publications.parliament.uk/pa/cm200809/cmselect/cmrefhoc/1117/1117.pdf [accessed 27 June 2017].

- SNP (2017) *Stronger for Scotland: SNP Manifesto*, Edinburgh: Scottish National Party. Online at: https://d3n8a8pro7vhmx.cloudfront.net/thesnp/pages/9544/attachments/original/1496320559/Manifesto_06_01_17.pdf?1496320559 [accessed 27 June 2017].

➡ FURTHER CASE STUDIES

- The Liberal Democrats in the 2010 or 2015 Parliaments.
- The Green Party in the House of Commons.
- DUP in the 2017 Parliament.

References

ARNOTT, M. A. (2015) 'The Coalition's Impact on Scotland: Policy, Governance and Expectations' in M. Beech and S. Lee (eds.), *Coalition Politics Evaluated: Examining the Cameron-Clegg Government*, Basingstoke: Palgrave Macmillan, pp. 162–77.

BACKBENCH BUSINESS COMMITTEE (2015) *Work of the Committee in the 2010–15 Parliament: First Special Report of Session 2014–15*, London: The Stationery Office, HC 1106. Online at: https://www.publications.parliament.uk/pa/cm201415/cmselect/cmbackben/1106/1106.pdf [accessed 26 June 2017].

BBC NEWS (2015) 'Q&A: How much Short money do parties get?', *BBC News*, 13 May. Online at: http://www.bbc.co.uk/news/uk-politics-32719087 [accessed 1 June 2017].

DENVER, D. (2014) 'Elections and Voting', in Bill Jones and Philip Norton (eds.), *Politics UK*, 8th edition, Abingdon: Routledge, pp. 118–35.

HAWKINS, O., KEEN, R., and NAKATUDDE, N. (2015) *General Election 2015*, House of Commons Library Briefing Paper Number CBP 7186, 28 July.

HAZELL, R. and RAWLING, R. (2015) *Devolution, Law Making and the Constitution*, London: Imprint.

HAZELL, R. and YONG, B. (2012) *The Politics of Coalition: How Conservative and Liberal Democrat Government Works*, London: Hart Publishing.

HOUSE OF COMMONS (2016) *Standing Orders of the House of Commons—Public Business, 2016*, London: The Stationery Office, HC 2. Online at: https://www.publications.parliament.uk/pa/cm201516/cmstords/0002/so-2.pdf [accessed 27 June 2017].

HOUSE OF COMMONS REFORM COMMITTEE (2009) *Rebuilding the House: First Report of Session 2008–09*, London: The Stationery Office, HC 1117. Online at: https://www.publications.parliament.uk/pa/cm200809/cmselect/cmrefhoc/1117/1117.pdf [accessed 27 June 2017].

KEEN, R. (2015) *England, Scotland, Wales: MPs and voting in the House of Commons*, House of Commons Briefing Paper Number SN07048, 26 June.

LUCAS, C. (2015) *Honourable Friends? Parliament and the Fight for Change*, London: Portobello Books.

MCKAY, W. et al. (eds.) (2004) *Erskine May: Parliamentary Practice*, 23rd edition, London: Butterworths Law.

MARTIN, R. and KELLY, R. (2015) *The Backbench Business Committee*, House of Commons Library Briefing Paper Number 7225, 10 June. Online at: http://researchbriefings.files.parliament.uk/documents/CBP-7225/CBP-7225.pdf [accessed 23 August 2017].

MODERNISATION COMMITTEE (2002) *Modernisation of the House of Commons: A Reform Programme: Second Report of Session*, London: The Stationery Office, HC 1168-I.

PLAID CYMRU (2017) *Plaid Cymru to Vote against Tory hard-Brexit*, 1 February. Online at: http://www2.partyof.wales/brexit-secondreading [accessed 26 June 2017].

PROCEDURE COMMITTEE (2014) *Oral Evidence: Minority party participation in the Back-bench Business Committee*, London: House of Commons, 14 May. Online at: http://data.parliament.uk/writtenevidence/committeeevidence.svc/evidencedocument/procedure-committee/minority-party-participation-in-the-backbench-business-committee/oral/9677.pdf [accessed 27 June 2017].

ROGERS, R. and WALTERS, R. (2015) *How Parliament Works*, 7th edition, London: Routledge.

RUSSELL, M. and COWLEY, P. (2016) 'The Policy Power of the Westminster Parliament: The "Parliamentary State" and the Empirical Evidence', *Governance*, Vol. 29 (1), pp. 121–37.

SNP (2015) *Stronger for Scotland: SNP Manifesto*, Edinburgh: Scottish National Party.

SNP (2017) *Stronger for Scotland: SNP Manifesto*, Edinburgh: Scottish National Party.

WINTOUR, P. and PERRAUDIN, F. (2015) 'Alex Salmond insists on UN mandate for military action in Syria', *The Guardian*, 15 November. Online at: https://www.theguardian.com/politics/2015/nov/19/alex-salmond-insists-on-un-mandate-for-military-strikes-in-syria [accessed 26 June 2017].

PART IV

Scrutiny and Accountability

14

Accountability in Parliament

Mark Bennister and Phil Larkin

INTRODUCTION

The accountability of the government to Parliament is a 'fundamental principle' of the British Constitution (Woodhouse 1994, 3). Yet, in spite of the ubiquity of the term, there is no single definition of accountability nor general agreement on what it means to be accountable (Bovens 2010, 946–7). What the characteristic definitions do share is the emphasis on the requirement to give an explanation or 'account': the government is formally required to explain itself to Parliament. A popular way of conceptualizing Parliament's place in the accountability process is as part of a 'chain of delegation' (Strøm 2000). In this formulation, democratic authority lies in the hands of the citizens. But, lacking the time and expertise to actively participate in the day-to-day process of running the country, these citizens delegate much of this responsibility to a subset of their number who become parliamentarians. Parliamentarians then delegate a significant proportion of this role to a further subset of their number who become the government. There exists a variety of mechanisms to allow Parliament a degree of control over how government uses the authority delegated to it. These can either be prior (or *ex ante*) authorization—for instance, through the requirement that a government's spending or legislation must be approved by Parliament—or after the event (*ex post*) accountability measures (Strøm 2000).

Though accountability and scrutiny are often conflated, they are not the same (White 2015, 3). Accountability is best thought of as a formal bond, while scrutiny is more of a distinct activity. The government is routinely scrutinized by the media, think tanks, academics, NGOs, and a host of other bodies with a direct interest in what government is or is not doing. Yet, in few of these cases could we say the government is accountable to them. Accountability implies a formal relationship through which government is responsible to Parliament. To make this accountability relationship between government and Parliament a reality—for government to be *held to account*—Parliament must have the means to cross-examine and scrutinize government. Without adequate scrutiny measures, accountability becomes an empty concept.

Accountability in the Westminster model

The main elements attributed to the 'Westminster model' combine to create a strong executive. The electoral system has magnified the votes cast to create disproportionately large majorities in the Commons, making single-party government the norm, and coalitions and minority government rare. Allied with strong party discipline, this has limited the capacity of non-government parties to exercise control of government in Parliament. Non-governing parties have little bargaining power if their votes are not needed to authorize spending or pass legislation. Government does of course require the consent of Parliament—or at least the House of Commons—to survive (with bargaining power amplified under the 2017 minority government). That consent is usually tacitly given to the leader of the largest party; it could be withdrawn, providing Parliament's ultimate sanction. However, it is rarely used: since 1900, only three governments have suffered defeats on confidence motions (January 1924, October 1924, and March 1979) and on each occasion, the governing party lacked an overall majority of seats.

As governments can dominate Parliament, they face limited institutional constraints on their ability to govern. Consequently, the Westminster model has usually been characterized by a greater emphasis on *ex post* accountability than *ex ante* authorization. The onus has been on getting government to explain itself after the fact: in the much-used phrase attributed to former Prime Minister Arthur Balfour, 'democracy is government by explanation' (Rogers and Walters 2015, 79). Parliament carries out this function by interrogating government—either in writing or orally. While government is created by the Commons, the Lords can also play a significant role in holding government to account. Although the focus is often on the Lords' role in revising legislation, much of its time is dedicated to the accountability function, such as questions or committee inquiries.

Ministers are accountable to Parliament both collectively and as individuals. Collectively, they are bound to the government through the principle of cabinet responsibility which holds that decisions arrived at by cabinet are binding on its members. Although this is occasionally relaxed, as it was during the EU referendum, those who cannot stand by cabinet decisions are usually expected to resign. Ministers are also accountable as individual members of the government for the conduct of policy within their area of responsibility. The *Ministerial Code* makes clear that 'ministers have a duty to Parliament to account, and be held to account, for the policies, decisions and actions of their departments and agencies' (Cabinet Office 2016, 1).

Yet, the nature of government accountability to Parliament is slightly vague in practice. Executive accountability to Parliament is not something that is set out in statute: there is no law that states when a minister should apologize or resign. Instead, the area is governed by convention; non-legal shared understandings of how the constitution works. The difficulty is that the understanding of the rules is not always shared and, in the absence of agreement, convention amounts to little more than what government thinks it can get away with in any given circumstance (Bogdanor 2009). This does not mean that governments are able to do whatever they like, but that the constraints they do face are largely political, such as the need to keep their party unified or the desire to be re-elected, rather than institutional.

The duty to account for the actions of a department involves providing information about its activities to Parliament: for example, answering oral questions, fielding written questions, making statements, or leading debates. Nevertheless, how ministers are 'held to account' is more contingent. In carrying out their ministerial duties, the *Ministerial Code* states that ministers should be truthful and as open as possible in their dealings with Parliament, and that any minister found to have knowingly misled Parliament should resign. They are expected to conduct themselves with propriety, and conflicts of interest are noted (Cabinet Office 2016, 1). This relates to standards of personal conduct in office, but says little about what ministers are actually accountable for in practice. The convention of ministerial responsibility is sometimes interpreted to mean that a minister is responsible for anything done by the civil service staff of their department, regardless of whether the minister played any part in it. The 1954 Crichel Down case, when Agriculture Minister Sir Thomas Dugdale took responsibility for the failings of his department over compulsory purchase of land by the Crown and resigned, is taken to illustrate this. A more common interpretation distinguishes between policy and operational issues, with the minister responsible for policy failure and the civil service for failures of implementation (the so called 'Maxwell Fyffe doctrine', named after the Home Secretary at the time of the Crichel

Down case). Ministers are *accountable* to Parliament in terms of being required to explain what has happened, but not necessarily *responsible* for it.

This distinction between operational and policy matters provides an opportunity for ministers to try to evade responsibility by portraying failure of policy as failure of implementation. Just as opposition parties might wish to push a minister into admitting a serious failing of policy or administration and an embarrassing climbdown or even resignation, so the government will be anxious to defend the minister from such accusations, pass blame to the civil service, and make any remedial action seem planned. This highlights the extent to which accountability is an inherently political process: the government tries to deny short-comings or deflect responsibility for them, while the opposition and other non-governing parties try to expose shortcomings and attribute them to the government.

Holding to account suggests an ability to impose some sanction for poor performance (Bovens 2010, 952; Mulgan 2003, 9). Yet, while Parliament can require explanation from and cross-examination of a minister, there is little power to apply sanction. The power to appoint or remove ministers lies with the prime minister. Parliament's main means of sanction involves ensuring public exposure and hence public embarrassment for both the individual minister and the government. Again, governments are reluctant to concede that a policy has failed or that the minister is responsible, so calls for resignations are usually resisted. Significantly, most ministerial resignations are the result of matters of personal integrity or disagreements with government policy, rather than because they have overseen a significant failure of policy (Dowding and Kang 1998).

Recent reforms of accountability mechanisms

At a minimum, accountability implies that the government must be required to give an account of its actions and this is largely achieved through answering questions, either on the Floor of the House, in writing, or in committees. Contrary to the decline of parliament thesis and much popular opinion, recent reforms have enhanced Parliament's capacity to question government—to hold it to account (Flinders and Kelso 2011).

There is a paradox when considering government accountability to Parliament: while Parliament itself is dismissed as unaccountable and untrustworthy, it is also the most significant mechanism for promoting accountability, and increasing public accountability involves increasing Parliament's role. Following the MPs' expenses scandal in 2009, the time when Parliament's reputation reached its nadir, reforms were made to the select committee appointment procedure and the way in which non-government time was managed with the introduction of the Backbench Business Committee (see Chapter 28). These reforms aimed to enhance Parliament's role of holding government to account. In a political context, where faith in the competence and integrity of those we charge with governing us is low, Parliament has the necessary tools to challenge, question, and cajole the government of the day into explaining its actions.

 Parliamentary terms Backbench Business Committee

A committee of MPs responsible for selecting topics for debate in the House of Commons which are put forward by backbench MPs. These debates are often very topical and highly important.

The most famous (or infamous) mechanism through which government is questioned is Prime Minister's Questions (PMQs), held weekly when Parliament is sitting. However, under intense media spotlight, it is more an opportunity for partisan point scoring and as a 'release valve' for tribal conflict, than a means of extracting information from the executive. MPs from the non-governing parties attempt to land hefty and very public blows to the prime minister's credibility, while government backbenchers ask helpful questions (often given to them by the party leadership) designed to allow the prime minister to be seen in the most positive light. As a result, PMQs is usually regarded as of limited use as a proper accountability mechanism (see Chapter 17). The secretaries of state each face their own regular Question Time on their policy area, led by the opposition's shadow minister. Ordinarily, these have a much lower media profile and consequently avoid some of the worst excesses of PMQs. They also allow a more in depth cross-examination of government policy as enacted by ministers.

 Parliamentary terms Prime Minister's Questions (PMQs)

A weekly 30-minute session in the House of Commons Chamber where MPs can put questions to the prime minister, typically without notice of the topic.

The accountability of ministers to the legislature in terms of answering questions, giving statements, leading debates, and piloting legislation is supplemented by a formal relationship with the departmental select committee (see Chapter 17). Select committee sessions typically allow more relevant and sustained scrutiny of the minister and their department. Furthermore, they usually work with cross-party consensus which means that the extreme partisanship of PMQs is avoided and scrutiny of government can take place in a more dispassionate and evidence-based context. This has given select committees a greater perceived legitimacy.

When Parliament's reputation was at its lowest following the expenses scandal, one of the measures it took to restore its reputation was to enhance select committee independence by changing the way chairs were appointed, with elections replacing selection by the party whips. Direct elections for select committee chairs has evidently instilled greater legitimacy and authority in the position, which flows into holding the executive to account (Fisher 2015, 421). This has increased the pressure on ministers to account for actions in front of the relevant committee, both increasing the profile of many of these hearings and publicly testing the credentials of a minister. A more activist and assertive select committee system has seen inquiries and witness sessions extend beyond holding the executive to account, raising the question of Parliament as a tool in wider public accountability. For instance, the Parliamentary Commission on Banking Standards, set up in 2012 in the wake of the financial crisis to examine professional standards and culture of the UK banking sector, was a joint committee of both Houses looking beyond government policy into areas of corporate governance (see Case Study 15). More recently, the select committee inquiry into the sale of BHS brought the Work and Pensions and Business, Innovation and Skills Committees together in June 2016. The inquiry included high-profile evidence sessions with those responsible for the collapse of BHS, including a memorable performance by Sir Philip Green. As with the appearance of Mike Ashley in front of the BIS Committee's investigation into the practices of Sports Direct, the reach of this parliamentary activity has moved into the public accountability arena, beyond the narrower executive lines of delegation. Ashley and Green both initially refused to attend hearings, but realized that non-attendance would have been publicly more damaging.

There has been one significant exception to the select committee scrutiny that has only relatively recently been addressed: prime ministers (with no formal departmental responsibility) have not been subject to the more detailed scrutiny that select committees conduct. Since 2002, the Liaison Committee (the select committee comprising the chairs of the other select committees) has conducted regular hearings with the prime minister, scrutinizing the role as head of government. As we discuss in Case Study 14, these do not entirely replicate the more systematic scrutiny performed by the departmental select committees, but are perhaps a small step towards making the prime minister more accountable to Parliament.

One development, the granting of Urgent Questions, has increased the ability of MPs to make swift challenges to the executive. Speaker John Bercow made a habit of granting requests for urgent questions to force ministers to come before the House to: respond, report, and explain a high-profile issue of the day. Speaker Bercow granted 385 questions between 2009 and 2017, compared to just 42 granted in the final five years of his predecessor. An Urgent Question may not just put the government on the spot, but tease out a statement on the issue that may not have otherwise been forthcoming. This is not strictly speaking a structural reform, but more of a behavioural reform associated with Speaker Bercow. Other reforms have increased the structural scope of accountability. For instance, the Backbench Business Committee has developed (albeit limited) control over parts of the parliamentary agenda, and now sessions in Westminster Hall present an additional arena in which the executive is held to account (see Case Study 18). Such developments exist alongside the long-standing tools for MPs to elicit information via the tabling of written questions which require a formal government response, and which have shown a year-on-year increase in both the Commons and the Lords.

Most discussion of accountability is focused on the relationship between the executive and the legislature, on the strengthening of the link in the chain of accountability from Parliament to government. However, the link between the citizen and Parliament has been under at least as much scrutiny. MPs are accountable to voters in their constituencies, but also to local and national party organizations. While accountability through the electoral process has traditionally been seen as the means for ensuring this (and remains so), it has been supplemented by other institutional measures. These have typically been introduced following a scandal, highlighting how accountability mechanisms are often strengthened in response to declining trust (Mulgan 2003, 1). In the 1990s, links between MPs and lobbyists became headline news with revelations about 'cash for questions'. In response, the post of Parliamentary Commissioner for Standards was introduced to oversee the Register of Members' Interests. Significantly, as an external appointment, this marked a partial break with the established tradition of parliamentary self-regulation. However, it was only partial as the Commissioner worked through a select committee, the Committee on Standards and Privileges. In a further break with the principle of self-regulation, since 2013 the role has been performed by the Committee on Standards, which includes MPs and lay members. The expenses crisis of 2009 prompted further reform with the introduction of the Independent Parliamentary Standards Authority (IPSA). In addition to regulating MPs' pay, IPSA oversees and makes public MPs expenses claims. A legacy of public distrust certainly continues, but MPs are now operating with an unprecedented degree of transparency.

Conclusion

In spite of the characterization of Westminster as executive-dominated, Parliament has numerous mechanisms through which it can force government to account for its actions and scrutinize that account which it has shown willing to use. Recent reforms have increased Parliament's capacity to scrutinize government. Stronger select committees, the use of urgent questions, and Liaison Committee sessions with the prime minister are some examples of the strengthening of the accountability function. Forcing the government to explain its policy on Syria or conducting 25-plus inquiries into Brexit suggests that parliamentarians take this aspect of their work seriously.

Further Reading

BENNISTER, M., KELSO, A., and LARKIN, P. (2016) *Questioning the Prime Minister: How Effective Is The Liaison Committee?* Online at: https://canterburypolitics.files.wordpress.com/2016/11/questioning-the-prime-minister-final-project-report.pdf [accessed 27 June 2017].

KELSO, A., BENNISTER, M., and LARKIN, P. (2016) 'The Shifting Landscape of Prime Ministerial Accountability to Parliament', *British Journal of Politics and International Relations*, Vol. 18 (3), pp. 740–54.

MULGAN, R. (2003) *Holding Power to Account: Accountability in Modern Democracies*, Basingstoke: Palgrave MacMillan.

WHITE, H. (2015) *Parliamentary Scrutiny of Government*, London: Institute for Government. Online at: https://www.instituteforgovernment.org.uk/sites/default/files/publications/Parliamentary%20scrutiny%20briefing%20note%20final.pdf [accessed 22 August 2017].

WOODHOUSE, D. (1994) *Ministers and Parliament: Accountability in Theory and Practice*, Oxford: Clarendon Press.

Case Study 14: Prime ministerial accountability and the Liaison Committee

The prime minister stands outside much of the conventional means by which Parliament holds the government to account. Much of that is structured around government departments and their budgets, but the prime minister has no department. Parliament does not ratify the prime minister, as in some jurisdictions. Instead, prime ministers remain in post as long as they retain the confidence of the House of Commons. By convention, the prime minister regularly appears in the House (answering questions at PMQs, making statements and speeches, or participating in debates). However, the prime minister can decide when to appear, and how often. This creates a complex and inherently fluid accountability relationship between the prime minister and Parliament.

LIAISON COMMITTEE EVIDENCE SESSIONS

With contemporary, media-conscious prime ministers generally spending less time in Parliament as power has become more centralized in Downing Street, one accountability reform has bucked the trend (Bennister and Heffernan 2014). In 2002, after initial resistance, Tony Blair agreed to appear twice a year before the Liaison Committee, the select committee comprising the chairs of the House of Commons select committees, to answer questions on policy matters. This has now covered four prime ministers on 32 occasions up to 2017 (11 with Tony Blair, five with Gordon Brown, 15 with David Cameron, and, prior to the 2017 general election, one with Theresa May). Yet, the focus of the media and public has remained on PMQs and, to date, these appearances before the Liaison Committee have gained limited popular attention.

The sessions allow MPs to challenge the prime minister on the government's record in a calmer, less partisan, and more deliberative environment than the weekly PMQs (Kelso, Bennister, and Larkin 2016). The sessions have no established remit: the Standing Orders merely state that 'The committee may also hear evidence from the Prime Minister on matters of public policy'. A small group within the committee chooses questions, focusing on matters where the prime minister 'makes a difference'. The topics have tended to concentrate on foreign affairs and defence matters, but have ranged widely across machinery of government, social policy, and constitutional issues. Generally each session is split between two topics, though there have been single sessions on the Scottish independence referendum and the EU referendum.

LIAISON COMMITTEE: UP TO THE JOB OF SCRUTINIZING THE PM?

These sessions go some way towards putting prime ministerial accountability on a more systematic footing. Located in a committee room away from the partisan cut and thrust of the Floor of the House, the Liaison Committee sessions have been characterized by far greater in-depth questioning and, crucially, more extensive cross-examination of prime ministerial answers. Although the sessions were initially mocked as 'bore-a-thons' that failed to deliver the headline-generating political theatre journalists may have hoped for, that is in fact the key point: the sessions can involve exchanges on broad government strategy and contemporary issues, providing a far more detailed prime ministerial justification of policy decision-making (Kelso, Bennister, and Larkin 2016, 748). When canvassed, the public found these sessions positive, but knew little about them (Hansard Society 2014).

The Liaison Committee is in many respects well suited to conduct scrutiny of the prime minister. Although the Committee discharges other administrative tasks, it does contain the most senior committee chairs and performs a leadership role in the Commons. Since 2010, the chairs of the departmental select committees have been elected by the whole House of Commons, giving them an enhanced legitimacy. The Committee can draw on the accumulated knowledge of the chair of any of the relevant select committees and their staff, which helps redress the resource asymmetry between Parliament and the executive. The conduct of the sessions has evolved to become more focused, with a reduction in the number of committee members participating in each session, fewer topics covered, and an increase in the number of sessions in a year.

The first session in July 2002 with Tony Blair contained 123 questions, asked by 23 different MPs over two and half hours, ranging across four broad themes. By comparison, David Cameron's final session as prime minister had 80 questions over 90 minutes, with only 14 MPs attending. The sessions may not be as demanding as the weekly PMQs for prime ministers, but they need to be across the detail. Tony Blair, having agreed to appear, was confident and comfortable with the format; questioning, in particular on foreign policy and public sector reform, challenged him to set out policy goals. Gordon Brown proved less comfortable with the format, and the Committee had detailed exchanges on the global financial crisis and Brown's constitutional reform proposals. David Cameron agreed in 2010 to shorter, but more frequent sessions with fewer committee members involved. He found himself quizzed more directly about his own specific role in government policy and decision-making. For example, the first session included questions about Cameron's role during the comprehensive spending review, his involvement in ministerial conflict resolution in the Coalition, and his agenda-setting capacity (Liaison Committee 2010, Q.1–7), prompting illuminating answers from the prime minister about his position at the heart of government. The Committee also spent an entire session exploring what the prime minister meant by the 'Big Society' (Liaison Committee 2011), a theme chosen because Cameron said he was so passionate about it. Conservative Andrew Tyrie MP, who became Chair of the Committee in 2015, proved a more interventionist Chair than his predecessor Liberal Democrat Alan (now Lord) Beith. Under Tyrie's tenure, not only did the sessions include sharper exchanges with the prime minister (see in particular the session prior to the EU Referendum with David Cameron in May 2016), but the Committee also widened its remit to take evidence from Sir John Chilcot (in November 2016).

The dynamic changed again with Theresa May's only appearance before the 2017 general election, when she faced noticeably sharp questioning from Yvette Cooper and Hilary Benn on immigration numbers and Brexit plans in a session dominated by attempts to tease out more detail from a cautious prime minister. Though occasionally the sessions are illuminating in the way they expose how much control of policy detail prime ministers possess, they are still political theatre in which MPs wish to make overlong statements or, in the words of one Chair, 'give the PM a bloody nose' (Bennister, Kelso, and Larkin 2016, 24).

When David Cameron appeared before the Committee in November 2010 and was informed by the Chair that 'the purpose of these sessions ... is quite different from Wednesday's Question Time', the prime minister's succinct response was, 'That's a relief' (Liaison Committee 2010, Q1). The format does make it easier for the prime minister to have a series of exchanges with each MP. Each session stands on its own, and apart from the occasional exchange of follow-up letters from the Chair, there is no link from one session to the next, and no report is produced. However, the Liaison Committee is a different type of committee from other select committees. It is the only one to question the prime minister and contains MPs with authority and expertise. The questioning has become sharper and the Chair more interventionist, making the sessions much less comfortable for the prime minister than in 2002. The sessions provide a forum whereby the prime minister, as head of the executive, has to account for policy decisions taken and be pressed on their likely impact in a less partisan, but more incisive, parliamentary arena. This is an important accountability function. The sessions have the potential to be more effective in holding the prime minister to account, but at least they are now an accepted and valuable part of the scrutiny process. This case study illustrates how accountability works through a specific tool, focusing on a key government actor, the prime minister. It also demonstrates that scrutiny is not just about political theatre, but also about incisive, detailed, and focused questioning.

Primary sources

- Liaison Committee (n.d.) Homepage. Online at: http://www.parliament.uk/business/committees/committees-a-z/commons-select/liaison-committee/ [accessed 27 June 2017].

- Liaison Committee (2002) *Minutes of Evidence: Tony Blair*, 23 July. Online at: https://www.publications.parliament.uk/pa/cm200102/cmselect/cmliaisn/1095/2071601.htm [accessed 27 June 2017].

- Liaison Committee (2015) *Legacy Report: First Report of Session 2014–15*, London: Stationery Office, HC 954. Online at: https://www.publications.parliament.uk/pa/cm201415/cmselect/cmliaisn/954/954.pdf [accessed 27 June 2017].

- Liaison Committee (2016) Oral evidence session with Prime Minister Theresa May, 20 December, Parliament.tv. Online at: http://www.parliamentlive.tv/Event/Index/373e8648-fe36-4d16-9949-6c4372491793 [accessed 27 June 2017].

→ FURTHER CASE STUDIES

- Public Accounts Committee oral evidence sessions.
- Questioning of Philip Green by the Joint Select Committee inquiry, between the Select Committee on Work and Pensions and the one on Business, Innovation and Skills, into the sale of BHS (June 2016).
- Robin Cook's speech in the House of Commons following his resignation from government on 17 March 2003 over the decision to commit British troops to Iraq.

References

BENNISTER, M. and HEFFERNAN, R. (2014) 'The Limits to Prime Ministerial Autonomy: Cameron and the Constraints of Coalition', *Parliamentary Affairs*, Vol. 68 (1), pp. 25–41.

BENNISTER, M., KELSO, A., and LARKIN, P. (2016) *Questioning the Prime Minister: How Effective Is The Liaison Committee?* Online at: https://canterburypolitics.files.wordpress.com/2016/11/questioning-the-prime-minister-final-project-report.pdf [accessed 23 June 2017].

BOGDANOR, V. (2009) *The Changing British Constitution*, London: Hart.

BOVENS, M. (2010) 'Two Concepts of Accountability: Accountability as a Virtue and as a Mechanism', *West European Politics*, Vol. 33 (5), pp. 946–67.

CABINET OFFICE (2016) *Ministerial Code*, London: Cabinet Office. Online at: https://www.gov.uk/government/uploads/system/uploads/attachment_data/file/579752/ministerial_code_december_2016.pdf [accessed 23 June 2017].

DOWDING, K. and KANG, W.-T. (1998) 'Ministerial Resignations 1945–97', *Public Administration*, Vol. 76 (3), pp. 411–29.

FISHER, L. (2015) 'The Growing Power and Autonomy of House of Commons Select Committees: Causes and Effects', *Political Quarterly*, Vol. 86 (3), pp. 419–26.

FLINDERS, M. and KELSO, A. (2011) 'Mind the Gap: Political Analysis, Public Expectations and the Parliamentary Decline Thesis', *British Journal of Politics and International Relations*, Vol. 13 (2), pp. 249–68.

HANSARD SOCIETY (2014) *Tuned in or Turned off? Public Attitudes to Prime Minister's Questions*, London: Hansard Society.

KELSO, A., BENNISTER, M., and LARKIN, P. (2016) 'The Shifting Landscape of Prime Ministerial Accountability to Parliament', *British Journal of Politics and International Relations*, Vol. 18 (3), pp. 740–54.

LIAISON COMMITTEE (2010) *The Prime Minister: Oral evidence taken before the Liaison Committee*, 18 November, London: The Stationery Office, HC HC608-i. Online at: https://www.publications.parliament.uk/pa/cm201011/cmselect/cmliaisn/uc608-i/60801.htm [accessed 23 June 2017].

LIAISON COMMITTEE (2011) *The Prime Minister: Oral evidence taken before the Liaison Committee*, 8 November, London: The Stationery Office, HC 608-iv. Online at: https://www.publications.parliament.uk/pa/cm201012/cmselect/cmliaisn/608/11110801.htm [accessed 23 June 2017].

MULGAN, R. (2003) *Holding Power to Account: Accountability in Modern Democracies*, Basingstoke: Palgrave MacMillan.

ROGERS, R. and WALTERS, R. (2015) *How Parliament Works*, 7th edition, London: Routledge.

STRØM, K. (2000) 'Delegation and Accountability in Parliamentary Democracies', *European Journal of Political Research*, Vol. 37 (3), pp. 261–89.

WHITE, H. (2015) *Parliamentary Scrutiny of Government*, London: Institute for Government. Online at: https://www.instituteforgovernment.org.uk/sites/default/files/publications/Parliamentary%20scrutiny%20briefing%20note%20final.pdf [accessed 23 June 2017].

WOODHOUSE, D. (1994) *Ministers and Parliament: Accountability in Theory and Practice*, Oxford: Clarendon Press.

15

Evidence from Outside

Andrew Defty and Hannah White

INTRODUCTION

Parliament does not have a long tradition of drawing on external evidence in the scrutiny of policy and legislation. While government ministers have long relied on the civil service to provide the necessary expertise to support policy, until recently most backbench MPs relied overwhelmingly on their own experience and expertise when seeking to hold the government to account. Throughout the nineteenth and most of the twentieth century, being a Member of Parliament was a part-time occupation, and Members drew on their professional experience outside of Parliament to provide informed scrutiny of government policy and legislation (Judge 1981; Rush 2001). To some extent, this tradition continues, most notably in the House of Lords, where many Members retain external occupations and bring that expertise to bear within the Chamber. However, since the latter part of the twentieth century, opportunities for Parliament to draw on external evidence have expanded considerably, and external evidence is now a central feature of Parliament's scrutiny and legislative functions.

In drawing on evidence from outside Parliament, a distinction may be made between the use of external evidence in the scrutiny of government policy and administration, and its use in the scrutiny of legislation. The creation of the departmental select committee system in 1979 significantly enhanced Parliament's capacity to draw on external evidence in the scrutiny of government policy and administration. However, formal mechanisms for applying external evidence to the legislative process have been somewhat slower to develop. In recent years, the greater use of draft bills has enhanced opportunities for pre-legislative scrutiny, including by external actors, while the introduction of public bill committees in 2006 has allowed for select committee-style external evidence-taking as part of the legislative process. In addition to these formal mechanisms for drawing in external evidence, a number of other factors have served to enhance Parliament's and parliamentarians' ability to draw on external evidence, including the work of all-party parliamentary groups, and developments in communications technology. While there are significant benefits to these mechanisms, each also has its limitations some of which are cross-cutting.

 Parliamentary terms Pre-legislative scrutiny

Scrutiny of draft bills by committees of either House, or by a joint committee.

The scrutiny of policy and administration: select committees

The creation of the modern select committee system in 1979 was perhaps the most significant development in terms of drawing external evidence into Parliament. Select committees examine the expenditure, administration, and policy of government departments and associated public bodies (see Chapter 16). They do this by undertaking detailed inquiries and publishing reports into the work of departments and aspects of public policy. Select committees choose their own topics for inquiry and, in carrying out their work, make extensive use of evidence from outside Parliament, inviting written submissions and hearing from witnesses, including those responsible for delivering policy, service users, and independent experts. Select committees have become a prominent feature on the parliamentary landscape, their reports receive a formal response from the government, may be debated in Parliament, and increasingly attract media attention.

A typical select committee inquiry will begin with a call for submissions of written evidence. In addition to a general call, a committee may request submissions from key stakeholders such as professional associations, think tanks, trade unions, charities, and user groups. Written evidence will be collated and is usually published on the committee's website (Rogers and Walters 2015, 321). This will be followed by several oral evidence sessions. Some of those invited to give oral evidence may have already submitted written evidence, while others may have been invited as interested parties or recognized experts.

 Parliamentary terms   Written evidence

Evidence from MPs, peers, outside experts, organizations, and the general public which is submitted in written form to a select committee or a bill committee.

 Parliamentary terms   Oral evidence

When key stakeholders and interested parties (e.g. government ministers, civil servants, businesses, charities, academics) are invited before a committee of MPs to answer questions on a specific issue or on a proposed bill.

Oral evidence takes place over several days and the nature of the sessions may vary. Early sessions usually involve panels comprised of several expert witnesses. These are primarily information gathering sessions, designed to maximize the range of expertise available to the committee, and tend to be non-confrontational. There may also be sessions in which evidence is taken from those with direct experience of a particular policy. For example, a recent Work and Pensions Committee inquiry on employment opportunities for young people took evidence from several young people who had used government employment services (Work and Pensions Committee 2016). Significant witnesses, including government ministers, tend to be interviewed towards the end of the evidence-gathering process, and may be interviewed on their own, in order to allow for more sustained and forensic examination. The Work and Pensions Committee inquiry referred to above, for example, concluded with evidence from the Minister for Employment, Damian Hinds, in which he was asked to respond to the comments of the young people who had earlier given evidence (Work and Pensions Committee 2016). These later sessions may be more adversarial, particularly if the committee feels that witnesses are not being entirely open. The inquiry into the demise of the retailer BHS (see Chapter 14), for example, began with a number of information-gathering sessions with panels comprising representatives of the pensions regulator and the financial and legal services sector. In later sessions, Philip Green, the former owner of BHS, and Dominic Chappell, who bought the failing store shortly before liquidation, were interviewed individually and at length, in order to determine how the store collapsed and what plans were in place to rectify the shortfall in its pensions fund (Work and Pensions and Business, Innovation and Skills committees 2016).

Although the select committees have allowed for parliamentary scrutiny to be informed by an extraordinary range of external evidence, a number of studies have raised questions about the nature and range of witnesses called to give evidence (Berry and Kippin 2014; Geddes 2017). While government departments provide a large proportion of witnesses, among non-governmental witnesses some groups, such as charities and think tanks, are well represented, while others, such as trade unions, are relatively under-represented (Geddes 2017). There is also a clear geographical bias among those called to give evidence, with more than half of select committee witnesses coming from London and the south of England. Similarly, although select committees make extensive use of expert witnesses from universities, there is a clear preference for witnesses from Russell Group institutions, Oxford and Cambridge in particular, and more than half of academic witnesses come from universities in London and the south-east. Perhaps most alarmingly, one study found that more than three-quarters of all select committee witnesses were men (Berry and Kippin 2014). This may, in part, be explained by a lack of diversity in those institutions from which witnesses are drawn, but some committees have begun to monitor the diversity of witnesses. The relatively short time frame involved in most inquiries may also encourage a reliance on more readily accessible and experienced witnesses. Nevertheless, by relying on the 'usual suspects' committees are unlikely to ensure a broad evidence-base.

There are also questions about the capacity of select committees to make effective use of external evidence (see White 2015a). Some inquiries are, by their nature, incredibly complex. Committees are supported by a small team of clerks, and may also employ specialist advisers, such as lawyers or academics, who may be engaged on a temporary basis to advise the committee on particular issues. Nevertheless, committees are heavily reliant on the capacity of committee members to understand and engage with the evidence and, in particular, to scrutinize witnesses. The Parliamentary Commission on Banking Standards, an ad hoc committee which examined the complex issue of corporate governance in the UK banking sector, experimented with a much wider use of specialist advisers, including a QC, to examine witnesses on behalf of the Commission (see Case Study 15).

The legislative process: draft bills and public bill committees

Parliament's use of external evidence in the scrutiny of government policy and administration is now well-established. However, such evidence-taking was not, until recently, a significant feature of the legislative process. The movement towards the publication of more bills in draft form has enhanced opportunities for external input into legislation. Pre-legislative scrutiny usually provides for a much longer process of external scrutiny than is available once a bill is introduced. The government aims to publish draft bills at least three months before bringing them forward. Draft bills are usually subject to scrutiny by the relevant departmental select committee, although in some cases, if a draft bill is particularly large and complex, a joint committee of both Houses may be established to examine it. Draft bills may also attract scrutiny from more than one select committee. In 2016, for example, the draft Investigatory Powers Bill, was subject to scrutiny by a joint committee, by the House of Commons Science and Technology Committee and the Parliamentary Intelligence and Security Committee (see Case Study 7).

Committees undertaking scrutiny of draft bills will usually collect a substantial volume of written submissions and undertake a longer and more in-depth period of oral evidence-taking than is afforded elsewhere in the legislative process. Evidence-taking at this stage provides an opportunity for input by those likely to be affected by a piece of legislation, as well as expert scrutiny from professional bodies and academics. Although the complexity of the legislation and time taken to appoint a committee may limit the time available for evidence taking, pre-legislative scrutiny is widely assumed to improve the quality of bills (see Chapter 7). There is evidence that governments are prepared to accept the recommendations made on the basis of evidence provided during pre-legislative scrutiny, and that evidence taken at this formative stage may also be used in debates during the passage of a bill (Oliver et al. 2005; Norton 2013).

There are further opportunities for outside evidence to have an impact once a bill has been introduced, although this is a relatively recent development. It is possible for bills to be sent to select committees for detailed examination after second reading, although this is rare (Rogers and Walters 2015, 181). Similarly, while a special standing committee procedure was established in 1980 to enable evidence-taking during the committee stage of a bill, this was only used nine times (Thompson 2014, 385). External evidence-taking only became a standard feature of the legislative process in 2006, following a recommendation from the Modernisation of the House of Commons Select Committee. The Modernisation Committee identified several benefits of embedding external evidence-taking in the legislative process:

> It is first and foremost a mechanism for ensuring that Members are informed about the subject of the bill and that there is some evidential basis for the debate on the bill. Evidence-gathering is also, by its nature, a more consensual and collective activity than debate, and there is evidence that those outside Parliament have a more positive view of select committee proceedings than of debate. So there is a reputational benefit to Parliament in being seen to engage in a more open, questioning and consensual style of law-making, before moving on to the necessary partisan debate. (Modernisation of the House of Commons Select Committee 2006).

Following the Committee's recommendations, standing committees were reformulated as public bill committees and given the power to take evidence from external witnesses as part of the committee stage of a bill (see Chapter 9). Not all public bill committees take evidence, and some will accept written evidence without holding formal evidence sessions. Bills which start in the House of Lords do not have an oral evidence-taking stage, although this is the result of practice rather than procedure. In the 2015–16 parliamentary session, 22 bills were considered by public bill committees (see Table 15.1). Eight bill committees held oral evidence sessions, and a further seven took written evidence only. In total there were 21 oral evidence sessions and 788 written submissions were made. The number of written submissions received by individual bill committees varied considerably, from five for the Bank of England and Financial Services Bill, to 154 for the Housing and Planning Bill. Written submissions will usually be taken for as long as the committee is sitting and will be posted on the Parliament website. Oral evidence sessions take place at the beginning of a public bill committee's work and, in contrast to the lengthy period of pre-legislative scrutiny, only last for a few days. Bill committees will usually hold between two and four oral evidence sessions before moving on to their established role of line-by-line scrutiny of bills, where this evidence can then be integrated.

As with select committees, those asked to give evidence include interested groups, experts in the field and, in most cases, departmental officials and the relevant government minister. However, as with select committees there have been criticisms of the selection of witnesses. These have focused on the role of whips in selecting witnesses, and the limited role for committee members, particularly opposition Members, to add witnesses. It has also been argued that access to the public bill committees is limited, with a relatively small circle of well-connected organizations or individuals being called to give evidence (Levy 2010; Thompson 2014). It is also apparent that rather than providing an opportunity for new evidence to emerge, in some cases public bill committees merely provide a further opportunity to review evidence which may already have been provided to Parliament in other forms. This is particularly the case if a bill has been published in draft form and/or subject to pre-legislative scrutiny by a select committee. For example, of the 17 organizations or individuals who gave oral evidence to the Investigatory Powers Bill Committee in 2016, 12 had previously given oral evidence to the joint select committee which had examined the draft bill. Moreover, given that bill committees do not have the same level of clerical support as select committees and usually sit for only a few days, it is not clear how, or whether they have the capacity, to absorb what may be a substantial volume of written evidence.

Nevertheless, research on public bill committees has shown that the introduction of external evidence-taking has had an impact on the legislative process. Louise Thompson found broad acceptance on the part of MPs that the introduction of evidence-taking had enhanced the policy knowledge of MPs when considering legislation; this is particularly the case among opposition MPs who do not benefit from civil service support. Thompson (2014, 390) observes that external evidence taking has 'helped to level the playing field' between government and opposition MPs. She also found that MPs often make use of oral evidence to strengthen their arguments in the line-by-line scrutiny of bills, and may use proposals made by witnesses when drafting amendments to bills. Moreover, there is some evidence that evidence-taking has a direct impact on legislative outcomes. Committees which take oral evidence propose a greater number of amendments. Although the number of amendments accepted by governments at committee stage remains low, there has been an increase in ministerial undertakings to reconsider aspects of bills which have arisen from oral evidence sessions (see Chapter 9).

Informal mechanisms

In addition to the formal mechanisms already outlined, there are a number of other means by which evidence and expertise is drawn into Parliament, some of which are well established, while others reflect more recent developments.

In addition to formal committee work, parliamentarians may gain access to information and expertise from outside Parliament through all-party parliamentary groups (APPGs). As shown in Chapter 11, there are many hundreds of APPGs covering a diverse

Table 15.1 Evidence-taking by public bill committees (PBCs) in the 2015–16 session

Total number of bills considered by the House of Commons PBCs	22
Bills which took oral and written evidence	7
Bills which took oral evidence only	1
Written evidence only	7
Bills taking oral or written evidence	15
Total oral evidence sessions held	21
Total number of written submissions received	788

Source: House of Commons, *Sessional Return, session 2015–16*, HC1

range of issues and activities. In addition to allowing like-minded parliamentarians to meet and discuss particular issues of mutual interest, APPGs also provide a forum in which parliamentarians can meet with interested parties and experts from outside Parliament, including charities, professional bodies, learned societies, and trade associations. APPGs may invite external speakers, organize seminars, produce reports, and lobby on behalf of particular issues or policies. The Parliamentary and Scientific Committee is the oldest such group and has well-established links with scientific bodies in academia and industry. Its activities include monthly seminars in Parliament, attended by some of the country's leading scientists, and external visits to scientific and industrial establishments. One of the most recently established APPGs, the All-Party Parliamentary Cycling Group, actively promotes cycling and sustainable transport policies, and has conducted a number of high-profile inquiries. Its *Get Britain Cycling* inquiry took evidence from over 100 witnesses, including representatives of road transport user groups, cycling charities and professional bodies, the police, local authorities, and government ministers. The subsequent report, which included 18 recommendations, was the subject of a Westminster Hall debate, received a lengthy response from the government and was followed by the announcement of an additional £214 million investment in cycling (All-Party Parliamentary Cycling Group 2013).

While the submission of written evidence, coupled with invitations for carefully selected individuals to speak to parliamentarians, have been the primary, formal, and informal mechanisms by which Parliament has sought to draw in evidence from outside, advances in technology have provided parliamentarians with new opportunities to seek external evidence and, in some cases, to access it directly from within Parliament. In 2015 the Speaker's Commission on Digital Democracy recommended that 'the House of Commons should experiment with new ways to enable the public to contribute to different stages of the law-making process, primarily by digital means' (Digital Democracy Commission 2015, 44). The Commission made a number of suggestions for using digital technology to draw in evidence from outside, including exploring alternative means for enabling the public to put questions to ministers and the establishment of a digital discussion forum to operate in parallel to parliamentary debates (Digital Democracy Commission 2015).

The select committees have, perhaps not surprisingly, been particularly active in using new technology to engage with those outside Parliament. While most now use social media to announce inquiries and call for evidence, the Education Committee and the Communities and Local Government Committee have used social media to solicit questions for ministers under the hashtags #AskGove and #AskPickles. These initiatives, which generated several thousand questions from the public, clearly posed a challenge to the committees. In both cases, a selection of questions were put directly to the minister during a 'quick-fire' oral evidence session, with their responses posted on YouTube. Although this only allowed for a small number of questions to be put directly to the minister, the committees also claimed that the public responses informed their own questioning. Such methods provide a potentially powerful source of evidence and, moreover, one which ministers may be more reluctant to dismiss than questions posed by a panel of fellow MPs. However, they also produce a highly selective and partial representation of public opinion, and unless systematically applied may appear as little more than eye-catching supplements to the traditional work of select committees.

Technological developments have also created opportunities for parliamentarians to access information from outside directly from within the parliamentary Chambers. The use of electronic devices within the Chambers of both Houses has been the subject of considerable debate. In 2011, the House of Lords trialled the use of handheld electronic devices, although not laptops, in the Chamber, but peers were not permitted to use them to search for material which might be used in proceedings. When the House of Commons Procedure Committee looked at the issue it found that not only would such a ban be difficult to enforce in the House of Commons, it was also suggested that the use of electronic devices for consulting material and checking facts might lead to better informed debate. The Committee concluded that 'Members should be allowed to use electronic handheld devices for any purpose when in the Chamber whilst not speaking' and that they should also be permitted to use them as 'an aide memoire, whilst speaking in a debate' (Procedure Committee 2011, 9). Both Chambers now permit the use of handheld devices, and in 2015 all MPs were provided with an electronic tablet. While the use of such devices occasionally prompts concerns that Members may not be focused on their primary role, they are perhaps just the latest manifestation of a gradual opening up of Parliament to external evidence, experience, and expertise.

Conclusion

The opportunities for Parliament to draw in evidence from outside have increased considerably in recent years. The use of external evidence is now an established feature of the scrutiny of government policy, administration, and legislation. There are also a growing number of less formal mechanisms through which various parliamentary bodies and individual parliamentarians access external evidence. While some of these are well established, others, such as the use of social media, are new and somewhat experimental. The capacity of Parliament and its Members to access external evidence has, to some extent, served to balance the government's monopoly on information in relation to policy and legislation (see White 2015b). There remain, however, limitations to Parliament's use of external evidence. The process of selecting evidence and finding an appropriate balance between witnesses is clearly challenging. Parliament, and particularly its committees, are often criticized for drawing on a limited pool of expertise; there are, however, significant challenges involved in identifying and engaging with a wider range of external evidence, not least in terms of resources. While there are further opportunities for exploiting new mechanisms for getting evidence into Parliament, considerable responsibility continues to rest on parliamentary committees and individual parliamentarians both to seek out the best evidence, and to make best use of the evidence that is available.

Further Reading

Brazier, A., Kalitowski, S., Rosenblatt, G., and Korris, M. (2008) *Law in the Making: Influence and Change in the Legislative Process*, London: The Hansard Society.

Coleman, S. (2004) 'Connecting Parliament to the Public via the Internet', *Information, Communication and Society*, Vol. 7 (1), pp. 1–22.

Liaison Committee (2015) *Building Public Engagement: Options for Developing Select Committee Outreach*, London: The Stationery Office, HC470. Online at: https://www.publications. parliament.uk/pa/cm201516/cmselect/cmliaisn/470/47002.htm [accessed 23 June 2017].

Thompson, L. (2015) *Making British Law: Committees in Action*, Basingstoke: Palgrave.

White, H. (2015) *Select Committees Under Scrutiny: The Impact of Parliamentary Committee Inquiries on Government*, London: Institute of Government. Online at: https://www. instituteforgovernment.org.uk/publications/select-committees-under-scrutiny [accessed 2 February 2017].

Case Study 15: Use of external evidence by the Parliamentary Commission on Banking Standards

The Parliamentary Commission on Banking Standards ('the Commission') was a temporary joint committee with Commons and Lords membership. It was established by Parliament in July 2012 in the wake of the financial crisis and the LIBOR scandal about the fixing of the London Inter-Bank Offered Rate. The Commission offers an interesting case study of the use of external evidence by parliamentary committees because, in addition to using normal evidence-gathering methods, it enjoyed two unusual powers. These were the right to create an unlimited number of subcommittees, and the power to invite specialist advisers to examine witnesses on its behalf.

ROLE AND MEMBERSHIP OF THE COMMISSION

Rather than being a permanent select committee with an ongoing remit to scrutinize a government department or particular policy area, the Commission was an ad hoc joint committee established to look into standards in the banking industry. It also undertook pre-legislative scrutiny of the Financial Services (Banking Reform) Bill during its existence of just less than a year.

The ten members of the Commission included: the then Chair and several members of the Commons Treasury Committee, a former Chancellor of the Exchequer, a former Cabinet Secretary, and Bishop Justin Welby, who became Archbishop of Canterbury during the course of the Commission's work. The previous experience and expertise that the members brought to their work significantly enhanced the credibility of the Commission's recommendations in the eyes of the banking industry towards whom many of these were directed.

Although in many ways the Commission operated like any conventional parliamentary committee, it was conceived by its members and Chair, Andrew Tyrie MP, as an opportunity to trial new committee working methods, particularly in relation to its use of external evidence.

WORKING METHODS

Like a typical select committee the Commission made use of evidence from outside Parliament, in the form of written and oral evidence. However, unlike a typical committee, the Commission had an unlimited budget underwritten by a 'blank cheque' from the government, which enabled it to undertake more activity and draw on more sources of external advice and support than would be normal for a joint committee of this type.

The Commission received numerous pieces of written evidence and made significant use of the power normally afforded to Committees to 'send for persons, papers and records'. It used this power to access corporate records from financial institutions, including HBOS, which shed light on the processes that led to the financial crisis. And it heard oral evidence from a total of 252 witnesses. The Commission appointed more than 20 specialist advisers to support its evidence gathering and analysis and, in addition to its core parliamentary staff, drew on the expertise of staff appointed on secondment from external organizations including commercial banks, the Treasury, and the Bank of England. This enabled the Commission to ensure its evidence gathering, conclusions, and recommendations were well informed.

Unusually, the Commission was given the power to establish an unlimited number of subcommittees (described as 'panels') with a quorum of just one member. Commons committees are normally allowed to establish only a single subcommittee with a quorum of three. The Commission established 11 panels on subjects as diverse as HBOS, Scotland, and corporate governance. This power significantly expanded the Commission's capacity to gather external evidence because each panel was able to conduct its own evidence sessions and fact-finding visits. By the end of its inquiry, the Commission had published nearly 5,000 pages of evidence and reports online. While the volume of evidence the Commission gathered added to the credibility of its conclusions, it is doubtful that its staff and members could have genuinely assimilated this quantity of material in the time available. This was not least because some of the evidence gathered by panels was heard by only one or two members, and panels were not given the power formally to report to the main Commission.

The Commission was also given the power to invite specialist advisers to examine witnesses on its behalf. It is very unusual for anyone other than parliamentarians to be allowed to get involved in parliamentary proceedings because of the risk that this might invalidate the 'parliamentary privilege' that protects parliamentarians from prosecution for what they say in the course of their parliamentary work. The Commission used this novel power to appoint barristers as specialist advisers. They were used to research and develop lines of questioning and to ask questions during oral evidence sessions. The Commission found that barrister-led questioning was very useful in certain circumstances, particularly to establish on the record facts that had already been identified through background research in relation to its inquiries into HBOS. It was felt to be less useful for exploring issues in general and encouraging witnesses to identify matters of which the Commission had been unaware.

IMPACT OF THE COMMISSION

The Commission's evidence gathering seems to have enabled it to achieve significant impact. The government accepted a very high proportion of the recommendations and, because of the credibility of the work they had undertaken, Commissioners were able to secure some significant amendments to the Financial Services (Banking Reform) Bill during its passage through the Lords. However, the most significant factors contributing to the Commission's impact were not novel, and could in theory be enjoyed by any parliamentary committee. These were: political backing (the impetus and legitimacy the Commission derived from cross-party support); resources (the government's 'blank cheque'); and relationships (the contacts, status, and expertise of its members).

This case study demonstrates therefore the importance of outside evidence in enabling MPs to draw sensible conclusions in relation to complex issues. The Commission's efforts to gather a substantial body of evidence—using both normal select committee tools and two more unusual powers—enabled it to develop recommendations that were seen as credible by both government and the financial services industry, and which therefore were implemented.

Primary sources

- Parliamentary Commission on Banking Standards (2013) *Changing Banking for Good: First Report of Session 2013–14*, London: The Stationery Office, Vols. 1 and 2, HL Paper 27-I and II, HC 175-I and II. Online at: https://www.publications.parliament.uk/pa/jt201314/jtselect/jtpcbs/27/27.pdf [accessed 27 June 2017].

- Financial Services (Banking Reform) Act 2013. Online at: http://www.legislation.gov.uk/ukpga/2013/33/pdfs/ukpga_20130033_en.pdf [accessed 27 June 2017].

FURTHER CASE STUDIES

- Evidence taking by the Work and Pensions and Business, Energy and Industrial Strategy Committees as part of their joint inquiry into the collapse of BHS (2016).

- Inquiry by the Women and Equalities Committee into sexual harassment and sexual violence in schools, focusing in particular on its collaboration with the young people's charity, Fixers (2016).

- Evidence session with Secretary of State Eric Pickles, Communities and Local Government Committee, for which the Twitter hashtag #AskPickles was used to collate questions, 22 January 2014.

References

ALL-PARTY PARLIAMENTARY CYCLING GROUP (2013) *Get Britain Cycling: Report from the Inquiry.* Online at: https://allpartycycling.files.wordpress.com/2013/04/get-britain-cycling_goodwin-report.pdf [accessed 2 February 2017].

BERRY, R. and KIPPIN, S. (2014) *Parliamentary Select Committees: Who Gives Evidence?*, London: Democratic Audit.

DIGITAL DEMOCRACY COMMISSION (2015) *Open Up! Report of the Speaker's Commission on Digital Democracy*, London: House of Commons. Online at: http://www.digitaldemocracy.parliament.uk/documents/Open-Up-Digital-Democracy-Report.pdf [accessed 2 February 2017].

GEDDES, M. (2017) 'Committee Hearing of the UK Parliament: who gives evidence and does this matter' *Parliamentary Affairs*, advanced access.

JUDGE, D. (1981) *Backbench Specialisation in the House of Commons*, London: Heinemann.

LEVY, J. (2010) 'Public Bill Committees: An Assessment Scrutiny Sought; Scrutiny Gained', *Parliamentary Affairs*, Vol. 63 (3), pp. 534–44.

MODERNISATION OF THE HOUSE OF COMMONS SELECT COMMITTEE (2006) *The Legislative Process: First Report of Session 2005–06*, London: The Stationery Office, HC 1097. Online at: https://www.publications.parliament.uk/pa/cm200506/cmselect/cmmodern/1097/1097.pdf [accessed 23 June 2017].

NORTON, P. (2013) *Parliament in British Politics*, 2nd edition, Basingstoke: Palgrave Macmillan.

OLIVER, D., EVANS, P., NORTON, P., and LEE, C. (2005) 'Modes of Scrutiny' in P. Giddings (ed.), *The Future of Parliament: Issues for a New Century*, Basingstoke: Palgrave Macmillan, pp. 125–44.

PROCEDURE COMMITTEE (2011) *Use of Hand-held Electronic Devices in the Chamber and Committees: Third Report of Session 2010–11*, London: The Stationery Office, HC889. Online at: https://www.publications.parliament.uk/pa/cm201011/cmselect/cmproc/889/889.pdf [accessed 23 June 2017].

ROGERS, R. and WALTERS, R. (2015) *How Parliament Works*, 7th edition, Abingdon: Routledge.

RUSH, M. (2001) *The Role of the Member of Parliament Since 1868: From Gentlemen to Players*, Oxford: Oxford University Press.

THOMPSON, L. (2014) 'Evidence Taking Under The Microscope: How has oral evidence affected the scrutiny of legislation in House of Commons committees?', *British Politics*, Vol. 9 (4), pp. 385–400.

WHITE, H. (2015a) *Select Committees Under Scrutiny: The Impact of Parliamentary Committee Inquiries on Government*, London: Institute for Government.

WHITE, H. (2015b) *Select Committees Under Scrutiny: Case Studies from the 2010–15 Parliament*, London: Institute for Government.

WORK AND PENSIONS COMMITTEE (2016) *Oral Evidence: Employment Opportunities for Young People*, London: The Stationery Office, HC586. Online at: http://data.parliament.uk/writtenevidence/committeeevidence.svc/evidencedocument/work-and-pensions-committee/employment-opportunities-for-young-people/oral/44215.pdf [accessed 2 February 2017].

WORK AND PENSIONS AND BUSINESS, INNOVATION AND SKILLS COMMITTEES (2016) *BHS: First Report of the Work and Pensions Committee and Fourth Report of the Business, Innovation and Skills Committee of Session 2016–17*, London: The Stationery Office, HC 54. Online at: https://www.publications.parliament.uk/pa/cm201617/cmselect/cmworpen/54/54.pdf [accessed 23 June 2017].

16

Select Committees

Alexandra Kelso

INTRODUCTION

In the UK's asymmetrical political system, which traditionally provides for strong, single-party executives, the power and resources of government are acknowledged as routinely outstripping those of Parliament. Oversight work conducted on the Floor of the House of Commons by individual MPs is disadvantaged by the government's superior access to information and civil service support. Scrutiny procedures in the Chamber are based largely on questioning and debates. While valuable, such procedures are not widely acknowledged as being best placed to deliver the kind of in-depth and forensic scrutiny required to hold the government to account. This chapter demonstrates how House of Commons select committees provide a valuable mechanism through which MPs can pool their scrutiny efforts by working together as a formally constituted team. In doing so they address some of the resource disadvantages that they face inside the Chamber, and offer a more robust system of oversight.

The role of select committees

Although the House of Commons had previously utilized committees of MPs to carry out scrutiny tasks, a comprehensive system of select committees 'to examine the expenditure, administration and policy of the principal government departments' was only established in 1979. For the first time, government departments would be effectively shadowed by a committee of MPs who would examine their 'expenditure, administration and policy' (HC Debates, 25 June 1979, cc. 33–251). Originally, 12 departmental select committees were introduced, though their names and number have changed as a result of changes in government departments, as each select committee usually scrutinizes a specific department. In addition to the departmental-shadowing committees there are others which pursue more wide-ranging agendas across the breadth of government activities, such as the Public Accounts Committee (PAC), the European Scrutiny Committee, and the Science and Technology Committee. The Lords also includes committees similar to these (see Chapter 19).

Select committees are cross-party, with membership restricted to backbench MPs and reflecting the party balance in the House, typically containing about 11 members. Each committee is led by a chair, an MP who, since the 2010 Parliament, has been elected by their parliamentary colleagues; committee members are now also elected. As such they differ from Lords committees (see Chapter 19). Chairs also reflect party balance, though in the case of specific committees, such as the Public Accounts Committee, the chair must come from the official opposition. Select committees determine their own work agendas and decide for themselves which topics to investigate. There are inevitably far more issues to be explored than there is committee time available, and committee members must therefore work together to agree which subjects are most deserving of their attention. Committee work is structured around running focused inquiries into specific issues, and the range of topics being investigated at any given time is quite remarkable. For example, in 2016 there were inquiries into antisemitism (Home Affairs), the foster care system (Education Committee), and winter pressures on A&E departments (Health Committee). Committee chairs are responsible for managing the committee and giving direction to these inquiries.

 Parliamentary terms Cross-party lines

Where MPs from different parties work together rather than operating in the adversarial format which is more typical of the House of Commons Chamber.

The inquiry process typically follows a set pattern (in both chambers). A committee will announce its intention to examine a particular topic, outline the scope of the inquiry and the key questions or problems that it wants to explore, and then invite evidence to be submitted for consideration and to help the committee with its work. A substantial portion of committee time is taken up conducting oral evidence sessions with witnesses that the committee believes can offer useful information and insight into inquiry topics. These evidence sessions are held in public, and can include very high-profile figures; see, for example, the Culture, Media and Sport Committee's questioning of Rupert Murdoch and Rebekah Brooks in July 2011 as part of its inquiry into phone hacking at News International, which attracted considerable news coverage. Committees regularly call government ministers, the leaders and staff of non-departmental public bodies, and policy stakeholders ranging from policy experts to consumers of public services as witnesses. The Health Committee, for example, heard evidence from Minister of State Philip Dunne MP, as well as the Director of NHS England's Urgent and Emergency Care, as part of its inquiry into winter pressures in accident and emergency departments (Health Committee 2016a). At the conclusion of an inquiry, the select committee publishes a report on its findings, which typically: outlines the nature of the inquiry and the problem or issue underpinning it; provides a description of what was discovered; voices criticisms about decisions, policy design, and service delivery where these are merited; and offers a list of recommendations targeted at those with responsibilities for the policy issue examined.

Inquiry recommendations serve several purposes. For example, criticisms from a select committee might place the public spotlight on government ministers, civil servants, and other public figures, and force them to answer publicly for mistakes. The Public Accounts Committee's inquiry into the government's funding of Kids Company, for example, was highly critical of the government's lack of scrutiny of how this funding was being used (Public Accounts Committee 2015b). In addition, recommendations are often designed to highlight where improvements in public services or policymaking are required to stop mistakes being made in future, and to improve policy delivery and ensure better use of public resources. The saliency of inquiry topics naturally determines whether committee reports will receive any media attention, and those reports which criticize government actions are undoubtedly more newsworthy than those that do not. The Culture, Media and Sport Committee's report into phone hacking in 2012 was very critical of Rupert Murdoch as Chairman of News Corp. Their conclusion that Murdoch was 'not fit' to lead a major international company was heavily reported in the press (e.g. Cusick et al. 2012; Deans and Plunkett 2012).

However, the value of select committee work cannot be boiled down simply to whether or not reports receive media attention. Select committees are responsible for a large number of reports each year, with 226 being published in the 2015–16 session alone (House of Commons 2016). It is unreasonable to expect all of these to get media attention. Government departments are expected to respond to select committee reports and their recommendations. Although the quality of these responses is certainly patchy, requiring departments to respond ensures that reports get at least some attention from key decision makers while those responses are being prepared. Some key reports are also presented and debated in the House of Commons, such as the debates on the NHS in England in the 2015–16 session (HC Debates, 2 February 2017, cc. 1233–7). This enables MPs to further reinforce their arguments and recommendations, but in a way which demonstrates the cross-party nature of the report. Doing this with a departmental minister at the despatch box, listening to the debate and responding directly to the various points raised, can be very effective.

The effectiveness of select committees

Committee-based scrutiny infrastructure has long been heralded as integral to the effectiveness of parliamentary accountability procedures, and the departmental select committee system is routinely described as a 'good thing' which has enabled MPs to deliver increasingly incisive and critical analyses of government decisions and policies (e.g. Modernisation Committee 2002; Liaison Committee 2000; Rogers and Walters 2015, 330–4). Thus, select committees are typically viewed largely as oversight institutions, which engage in worthy investigative work designed to delve into the detail of departmental policy, spending, and administration, and thus keep government on its toes.

Yet, while this work might be worthy, and keep backbench MPs busy and occupied, there have for some time been mixed views about whether it has any tangible impact on government. While detailed investigations and focused evidence sessions might be illuminating, that does not mean that these oversight activities actually change departmental behaviour or policy. Government is not compelled to do anything that a select committee recommends, and for some critics select committees do not significantly alter the balance of power between the executive and the legislature (Barclay 2013; Liaison Committee 2012). While this criticism may have had a lot of merit in the first few decades following the establishment of the departmental select committee system, more recent research does suggest that the picture is far more nuanced. An exhaustive analysis of the work of seven select committees between 1997 and 2010 indicated that, while it is incredibly difficult to measure policy impact, it appeared that around 40 per cent of select committee recommendations were accepted by government, and around the same proportion were eventually implemented (Russell and Benton 2011). These included prohibiting the sale of imitation firearms to those under 18 years old, a recommendation made by the Home Affairs Select Committee in 2000 and accepted by the government, as well as protections for whistle-blowers in the NHS, a recommendation made by the Health Select Committee and also accepted by the government (see Russell and Benton 2011, 58). Thus, select committees not only play a crucial role in shining a spotlight onto government activities, but they also contribute to substantive policy change and improvement.

Although select committees operate as crucial scrutiny and oversight workhorses, and ones which can result in policy impact, they can also be analysed from other perspectives. For example, as committees invite the public to submit evidence to their inquiries, and as they meet with many different policy stakeholders during oral hearings, they also constitute a site of deliberative democratic exchange inside Parliament, a point which is easily overlooked. Select committees provide a forum where MPs can meet with different sectors of the public to hear about their experiences of public policy and the consequences of policy decision-making, and thus commit to the parliamentary record a vast wealth of information that might not be obtained otherwise. This not only helps committee Members to better understand the impact of government policies and decisions, it also enables the views and experiences of the public to feed directly into the construction of inquiry conclusions and recommendations. Most select committee reports specify where evidence gathered during the inquiry process has contributed to and underpinned the report itself, in order to demonstrate the evidence base on which the committee is drawing.

Thus, the select committee inquiry format enables the public to contribute to parliamentary work in a way that is not as easily facilitated by other procedural mechanisms inside the House of Commons. Therefore, while select committees are traditionally viewed from the perspective of their contribution to the effectiveness of parliamentary scrutiny, they should also be assessed and understood in terms of their capacity to facilitate democratic dialogue between parliamentarians and the public, in a way that not only enriches the quality of public life but also feeds into the policymaking process.

Key recent developments

The departmental select committee system has undergone significant developments over the last 40 years. One of the most important developments concerns how the process of selecting committee members has changed, and how the role of the committee chair has evolved, as a result of the Wright reforms of 2010 (see Chapter 28). Other changes, such as the consideration of more controversial topics, are perhaps the result of this more visible and cross-party appointments process.

Elected committee chairs and membership

Rogers and Walters (2015, 333) note that the effectiveness of a select committee depends 'above all, on its chair and its members'. When committees were first established, the party whips largely controlled select committee appointments. Although the Commons had to approve the final membership lists, these would be decided behind closed doors. Committee chairs would be decided by committees themselves, though here once again the party whips exerted influence. Perceived troublemakers would therefore be unlikely to be appointed to committees, yet alone chair them. This sometimes led to backbench rebellions, such as when the former Chair of the Transport Committee Gwyneth Dunwoody was not reappointed, having presided over critical reports on the government's transport policy (Kelso 2003). The Wright reforms implemented during the 2010 Parliament included the direct election of select committee chairs and members by the House of Commons as a whole. Each party is assigned a proportion of committee chairs (and of members per committee), and those seeking election must demonstrate cross-party support to make it onto the ballot. Some of those selected in the first elections, such as Margaret Hodge (PAC) and Andrew Tyrie (Treasury Committee), would go on to play pivotal roles in high-profile inquiries. Elected membership has been particularly important in some instances, such as the new Committee on Exiting the European Union in the 2015–17 Parliament, where the balance between 'Leave' and 'Remain' MPs was seen as crucial. Such is the electoral legitimacy and authority now enjoyed by select committee chairs that it has been key to developing a new grouping of parliamentary political leaders (Kelso 2016). When quizzing government ministers, or any other important witnesses, chairs clearly now ask far more difficult and challenging questions than was typical in the past, as any comparison of transcripts will demonstrate, and they can do this because they are now elected to these chair roles on the grounds that this is exactly what they will do. The role of committee chairs can be particularly important during oral evidence sessions, where they play an integral role in setting the direction and tone of questioning. Their assertiveness during such sessions is undoubtedly aided by their electoral mandate from the House.

Increased committee activity

Select committees are now extraordinarily active parts of the parliamentary machine. They conduct more inquiries than ever before, hold more evidence sessions than ever before, and publish a remarkable number of inquiry reports, accompanied by what is often a staggering volume of supporting evidence submitted to the committee in both oral and written formats. In 2015–16 alone select committees held 872 oral evidence sessions (House of Commons 2016, 60). While the rate and volume of work varies between committees, and reflects different committee preferences and styles of operation, any comparison between the current activities and outputs of select committees and those from a few years ago easily demonstrates the significantly increased workloads with which they now engage. For example, in the 2013–14 parliamentary session, the Home Affairs Committee published 18 inquiry reports, compared to just five in the 1998–9 session. Committees also receive far more evidence than ever before as part of their inquiries, and this helps MPs to gain understanding about what is going on outside in the 'real world' beyond Westminster.

This increased workload naturally brings new challenges. MPs who seek select committee membership must be prepared for the extensive time commitments involved in attending private committee meetings and oral evidence sessions, and for the additional reading loads required in order to be prepared to contribute to inquiry work—although MPs certainly vary in how much work they do for their committees, and are likely to contribute more to some inquiries than others, depending on their level of interest. Because of the workloads involved, committee staff play a significant role in helping MPs to manage the inquiry process; that support ranges from sifting through submitted evidence and drawing the attention of MPs to salient points, to drafting inquiry reports for committee Members to read and revise as they see fit. It is therefore important to understand that while select committees are driven by MPs, a lot of the important work that underpins their successful operation is conducted by parliamentary staff working in partnership with Members in order to fulfil committee goals (see Chapter 4).

Exploring highly controversial topics

Early select committees were often criticized for avoiding issues that might make cross-party working difficult, or which might annoy the government and ruin MPs' chances of promotion. However, they have now become crucial arenas in which important and often highly controversial topics are explored in detail, and it is the oral evidence session format which has contributed to their development in this area. For example, the Public Accounts Committee's inquiries into tax avoidance during the 2013–14 session used the public oral evidence session as a forum in which the leaders of large corporations such as Google could be interrogated about their taxation practices (PAC 2013a)—and in a way which ensured public and media outrage at how the corporations explained and defended those practices, while also quizzing the accountancy firms which assisted corporations with their taxation practices (PAC 2013b) and grilling HMRC representatives on how they go about ensuring that the proper levels of tax are paid by such large corporate actors (PAC 2015a). In this example, the Committee returned repeatedly to the same issue in order to hear evidence from a range of stakeholders about exactly what was going on and therefore how taxation policy could be made to work better. At a time when the effects of public sector austerity were a central aspect of political discussion, these investigations into whether giant corporations were 'paying their way' touched a raw nerve, and the oral evidence sessions featured prominently in the media as a result.

The Culture, Media and Sport Committee's lengthy (2012) inquiry into phone hacking also enjoyed extensive media coverage. While the Committee's final report on this issue was not unanimous (demonstrating that there are occasions when select committees cannot agree on cross-party lines), the chief value of that inquiry lay in the Committee's ability to bring before it a public figure like Rupert Murdoch, and to compel him to answer for the activities of the staff he employed.

In addition to focused topical inquiries, select committees also regularly hold standalone evidence sessions with government ministers, during which MPs ask questions about how ministers are running their departments and how they are dealing with key policy issues. See, for example, the session with then Secretary of State for Education Michael Gove in January 2012, when MPs used over two hours to ask questions on a very wide range of subjects, including a selection from 5,000 questions suggested by the public through a Twitter hashtag #AskGove (Education Select Committee 2012). These sessions in particular offer MPs a unique opportunity to interrogate government ministers in a focused way that is not always possible through ministerial Question Time in the House.

Developing policy expertise

A key success of the contemporary select committee system is that it has helped MPs to specialize and develop policy expertise. Most MPs naturally have extensive policy knowledge and understanding, not least because they draw on the experiences of their constituents in order to contribute to parliamentary debate and legislative work. But the committee environment greatly facilitates the deepening of that expertise, given the breadth and depth of information to which MPs are exposed during inquiry work. This has increasingly led to select committee members, and especially committee chairs, being acknowledged in the Chamber when relevant topics are being debated, and the Speaker frequently prioritizes contributions from committee chairs so that their expertise can feed directly into proceedings. This demonstrates the strengthened scrutiny role for backbench MPs. Indeed, the development of the committees in the last few years has helped to develop among backbenchers exactly those sorts of skills and attributes which many observers have long argued are integral to ensuring the House of Commons is better able to scrutinize government and hold it to account for its actions. However, Hannah White shows that there is still considerable leeway in strengthening MPs' questioning skills (White 2015). While some committees have undertaken training in this area, this is still very patchy.

Conclusion

Although still relatively young in parliamentary terms, the modern comprehensive system of select committees is a significant and valuable component of Parliament's scrutiny and oversight role. There is still much that remains to be improved, of course. Perennial complaints about committees being under-resourced are unlikely to disappear. Similarly, although select committees demonstrate a remarkable degree of cross-party collaboration, any observation of them at work during committee hearings also illustrates that, while there may be instances of impressive team working, there is also often a sense that they appear to be less of a team and more a series of individuals who 'get their turn' to ask questions, and this 'turn taking' can sometimes impede the effectiveness of evidence sessions and the interrogatory depth they can generate. Of course, all institutions have flaws and weaknesses, but it is clear that the select committee system has developed significantly in recent years, has become more professional, and has made huge strides towards developing the backbench specialism that is essential if the House of Commons is to succeed in holding to account the vast machine of central government.

Further Reading

Drewry, G., ed. (1985) *The New Select Committees: A Case Study of the 1979 Reforms*, Oxford: Clarendon Press.

Kelso, A. (2016) 'Political leadership in parliament: The role of select committee chairs in the UK House of Commons', *Politics and Governance*, Vol. 4 (2), pp. 115–26.

Russell, M. and Benton, M. (2011) *Selective Influence: The Policy Impact of House of Commons Select Committees*, London: The Constitution Unit.

White, H. (2015) *Select Committees under Scrutiny: The impact of parliamentary committee inquiries on government*, London: Institute for Government.

Case Study 16: The Public Accounts Committee's 2017 inquiry into the financial sustainability of the NHS

NHS funding has been the focus of many inquiries by Commons and Lords select committees over the course of the 2010 and 2015 Parliaments (see PAC 2016a; Health Committee 2016b; Long Term Sustainability of the NHS Committee 2017). These inquiries have most notably involved the Commons Public Accounts Committee (PAC), which held 16 inquiries relating to NHS funding over the course of a single year (see PAC 2017, Q1). The PAC is a long-standing Commons Committee (established by William Gladstone in 1861) whose purpose is to examine 'the value for money ... of public spending' and to hold government and civil servants 'to account for the delivery of public services' (UK Parliament 2017). The Committee is always chaired by a Member of the official opposition party and has a formidable reputation, being described as 'the queen of the select committees' (UK Parliament 2007). In November 2016 the PAC announced a further inquiry into the financial sustainability of the NHS (PAC 2016b), led by its Chair, Labour MP Meg Hillier. It is a good example of how a select committee can continue to gain momentum on a topic by working with other select committees and how the work of committees and their chairs can raise the profile of particular policy issues through the media.

WHAT HAPPENED?

The PAC took oral evidence from a number of high-profile figures in January 2017. They included the Chief Executive of NHS England, Simon Stevens, as well as Chris Hopson, the Chief Executive of NHS Providers. Chris Wormald, the Department of Health's top civil servant, was also called to give evidence. The hashtag #NHSfinance was used by those following the inquiry's proceedings. Although the questions asked at the session were divided among committee members, the Chair played a key role in pressing witnesses through follow-up questions and in guiding the direction of the discussions.

In the evidence session Simon Stevens contradicted the prime minister's NHS funding figures, stating that the health service had received less funding than it had asked for in the last funding round (PAC 2017, Q54); this was naturally picked up by the media as a big story. His decision to hold up a copy of the *Daily Mail* newspaper during the evidence session to confirm that 'the NHS trails the rest of Europe in what we spend on doctors, beds and scanners' (ibid., Q123) also attracted considerable media attention (Mason and Walker 2017; Dathan 2017). Over the next few days Simon Stevens' comments to the PAC were corroborated by the Chair of the Health Select Committee, Conservative MP Sarah Wollaston, who thanked him for using his 'duty of candour' when speaking to MPs (Mason 2017; Davies 2017).

This scrutiny of key individuals involved in NHS management and operations by the PAC was not the only parliamentary activity in this policy area at the time. In fact, the issue was dominating the agenda of both Parliament and the press that day. Just that morning the press had reported that Number 10 were losing faith in NHS boss Simon Stevens (Mason and Walker 2017; BBC News 2017). It was the focus of Prime Minister's Questions, with Leader of the Opposition Jeremy Corbyn using all of his questions to press Theresa May on NHS funding (see HC Debates, 11 January 2017, cc. 305–8). It was also the subject of an opposition day debate in the Commons on the same afternoon (HC Debates, 11 January 2017, cc. 335–427). This added to the very heated atmosphere between key parliamentary, government, and NHS figures on the issue.

The Committee's report was published the following month and did not pull any punches in its conclusions about NHS funding. It stated prominently that the 'bickering' of key players 'does little to inspire confidence', and that a 'united effort' was needed to solve the problems ahead (PAC 2017, 3). It made a number of recommendations, setting deadlines for NHS England and the Department of Health to set out 'a clear and transparent recovery plan' (ibid., 5). As would be expected, it attracted much attention from those both inside and outside Parliament (BBC News 2017). By the time Parliament was dissolved in May 2017, the government had not responded to the Committee's report

INSIGHTS INTO THE FUTURE OF SELECT COMMITTEE WORK

The PAC inquiry uncovered new information regarding NHS funding and provided useful questioning of the key figures involved. But this case in particular shows that select committee work is much stronger when it is not carried out in isolation. The evidence session itself seemed to be the arena in which a 'war of words' between Number 10 and the NHS Chief Executive was being played out (Dathan 2017). But this was only made possible by the emphasis placed on the issue through other parliamentary mechanisms (oral questions and an opposition day debate) at the same time. Sarah Wollaston's role in supporting one of the Committee's key witnesses added further pressure on the government. Although overlap with departmental select committees has been said to be 'unhelpful' (Rogers and Walters 2015, 249), this type of cooperation between committee chairs can help to add momentum to issues. Indeed, D'Arcy (2017) cites this type of cooperation between chairs as an 'emerging trend' in committee work. But this case study also shows some of the challenges facing select committees in their quest to scrutinize the actions and policies of government and public bodies. Rogers and Walters write that the PAC in particular has fallen victim to 'the temptations of confrontational questioning and media headlines', and that this has had an impact on its effectiveness (Rogers and Walters 2015, 249). This is perhaps linked with the election of committee chairs and the associated increases in legitimacy and authority, and therefore also visibility. But even without a published government response to its report, the PAC was successful in drawing attention to key issues of NHS sustainability and in increasing the transparency of NHS funding. Given the dominance of the NHS across a number of select committees, the momentum created by the PAC inquiry is likely to build further during the 2017 Parliament.

Primary sources

- Liaison Committee (2012) *Select Committee Effectiveness, Resources and Powers: Second Report of Session 2012-13*, London: Stationery Office, HC 697. Online at: https://www.publications.parliament.uk/pa/cm201213/cmselect/cmliaisn/697/697.pdf [accessed 27 June 2017].

- Public Accounts Committee (2013) *Tax Avoidance—Google: Ninth Report of Session 2013-14*, London: The Stationery Office, HC 112. Online at: https://www.publications.parliament.uk/pa/cm201314/cmselect/cmpubacc/112/112.pdf [accessed 27 June 2017].

- UK Parliament (2007) *Holding Government to Account: 150 Years of the Committee of Public Accounts*, London: UK Parliament. Online at: https://www.parliament.uk/documents/commons-committees/public-accounts/pac-history-booklet-pdf-version-p1.pdf [accessed 27 June 2017].

- *House of Commons Sessional Returns.* Online at: https://www.parliament.uk/business/publications/commons/sessional-returns/ [accessed 27 June 2017].

 FURTHER CASE STUDIES

- The election of Sarah Wollaston as Chair of the Health Select Committee in June 2014.
- The Public Accounts Committee's inquiry into HSBC and tax avoidance.
- The questioning of UK Athletics and UK Sport representatives by the Culture, Media and Sport Committee as part of its Doping in Sport inquiry (2016–17).

References

BARCLAY, S. (2013) 'Are Parliament's Select Committees Working? I Say No', *The Spectator*, 5 November.

BBC NEWS (2017) 'MPs criticise Theresa May and NHS over "bickering"', *BBC News*, 27 February. Online at: http://www.bbc.co.uk/news/health-39096430 [accessed 16 June 2017].

CULTURE, MEDIA AND SPORT COMMITTEE (2012) *News International and Phone-hacking: Eleventh Report of Session 2010–12*, London: The Stationery Office, HC903. Online at: https://www.publications.parliament.uk/pa/cm201012/cmselect/cmcumeds/903/903i.pdf [accessed 24 June 2017].

CUSICK, J., MILMO, C., FOLEY, S., MORRIS, N., and BURRELL, I. (2012) 'Murdoch: The damning verdict', *The Independent*, 1 May. Online at: http://www.independent.co.uk/news/uk/politics/murdoch-the-damning-verdict-7704392.html [accessed 15 June 2017].

D'ARCY, M. (2017) 'How will History Remember the 2015–17 Parliament?', *BBC News*, 9 May. Online at: http://www.bbc.co.uk/news/election-2017-39848296 [accessed 16 June 2017].

DATHAN, M. (2017) 'The PM's wrong! NHS chief blasts Theresa May for claiming the Government has given the NHS more money than it asked for', *Daily Mail*, 11 January. Online at: http://www.dailymail.co.uk/news/article-4108728/Theresa-NHS-chief-Simon-Stevens-said-daggers-drawn-amid-growing-crisis-health-service.html [accessed 23 August 2017].

DAVIES, C. (2017) 'Tory Health Committee Chair Defends NHS Chief in Funding Row with PM', *The Guardian*, 15 January. Online at: https://www.theguardian.com/politics/2017/jan/15/nhs-funding-row-sarah-wollaston-defends-simon-stevens-theresa-may [accessed 17 June 2017].

DEANS, J. and PLUNKETT, J. (2012) 'Phone Hacking: Select committee report unveiled', *The Guardian*, 1 May. Online at: https://www.theguardian.com/media/blog/2012/may/01/select-committee-report-james-rupert-murdoch [accessed 15 June 2017].

EDUCATION SELECT COMMITTEE (2012), *Michael Gove answers #AskGove twitter questions*. Online at: http://www.parliament.uk/education-committee-askgove-twitter-questions [accessed 24 June 2017].

HEALTH COMMITTEE (2016a) *Oral Evidence: Winter Planning*, London: House of Commons, HC 277. Online at: http://data.parliament.uk/writtenevidence/committeeevidence.svc/evidencedocument/health-committee/winter-planning/oral/38279.pdf [accessed 24 June 2017].

HEALTH COMMITTEE (2016b) Letter from the Chair to the Chancellor of the Exchequer, 26 October. Online at: http://www.parliament.uk/documents/commons-committees/Health/Correspondence/2016-17/chair-to-chancellor-NHS-funding-26-10-2016.pdf [accessed 16 June 2017].

HOUSE OF COMMONS (2016) *Sessional Returns: Session 2015–16*, London: The Stationery Office, HC1.

KELSO, A. (2003) 'Where were the massed ranks of parliamentary reformers? Attitudinal and contextual approaches to parliamentary reform', *The Journal of Legislative Studies*, Vol. 9 (1), pp. 57–76.

KELSO, A. (2016) 'Political leadership in parliament: The role of select committee chairs in the UK House of Commons', *Politics and Governance*, Vol. 4 (2), pp. 115–26.

LIAISON COMMITTEE (2000) *Shifting the Balance: Select Committees and the Executive: First Report of Session 1999–2000*, London: The Stationery Office, HC 300. Online at: https://www.publications.parliament.uk/pa/cm199900/cmselect/cmliaisn/300/30003.htm [accessed 24 June 2017].

LIAISON COMMITTEE (2012) *Select Committee Effectiveness, Resources and Powers: Second Report of Session 2012–13*, London: Stationery Office, HC 697. Online at: https://www.publications.parliament.uk/pa/cm201213/cmselect/cmliaisn/697/697.pdf [accessed 24 June 2017].

LONG-TERM SUSTAINABILITY OF THE NHS COMMITTEE (2017) *The Long-term Sustainability of the NHS and Adult Social Care: Report of Session 2016–17*, London: The Stationery Office, HL Paper 151. Online at: https://www.publications.parliament.uk/pa/ld201617/ldselect/ldnhssus/151/151.pdf [accessed 24 June 2017].

MASON, R. (2017) 'NHS's Simon Stevens Defended by MPs in Health Funding Row', *The Guardian*, 11 January. Online at: https://www.theguardian.com/society/2017/jan/11/nhs-boss-simon-stevens-defended-by-mps-health-funding-row [accessed 27 June 2017].

MASON, R. and WALKER, P. (2017) 'NHS England Chief Hits Back at Theresa May on Health Service Funding', *The Guardian*, 11 January. Online at: https://www.theguardian.com/society/2017/jan/11/nhs-england-chief-executive-simon-stevens-funding-theresa-may-public-accounts-committee [accessed 16 June 2017].

MODERNISATION COMMITTEE (2002) *Select Committees: First Report of Session 2001–02*, London: The Stationery Office, HC 224-I. Online at: https://www.publications.parliament.uk/pa/cm200102/cmselect/cmmodern/224/22402.htm [accessed 24 June 2017].

PUBLIC ACCOUNTS COMMITTEE (PAC) (2013a) *Tax Avoidance—Google: Ninth Report of Session 2013–14*, London: The Stationery Office, HC112. Online at: https://www.publications.parliament.uk/pa/cm201314/cmselect/cmpubacc/112/112.pdf [accessed 24 June 2017].

PUBLIC ACCOUNTS COMMITTEE (PAC) (2013b) *Tax Avoidance: The Role of Large Accountancy Firms: Forty-fourth Report of Session 2012–13*, London: The Stationery Office, HC870. Online at: https://www.publications.parliament.uk/pa/cm201213/cmselect/cmpubacc/870/870.pdf [accessed 24 June 2017].

PUBLIC ACCOUNTS COMMITTEE (PAC) (2015a) *Improving Tax Collection: Fiftieth Report of Session 2014–15*, London: The Stationery Office, HC974. Online at: https://www.publications.parliament.uk/pa/cm201415/cmselect/cmpubacc/974/974.pdf [accessed 24 June 2017].

PUBLIC ACCOUNTS COMMITTEE (PAC) (2015b) *The Government's Funding of Kids Company*, London: The Stationery Office, HC504. Online at: https://www.publications.parliament.uk/pa/cm201516/cmselect/cmpubacc/504/50402.htm [accessed 24 June 2017].

PUBLIC ACCOUNTS COMMITTEE (PAC) (2016a) *Sustainability and Financial Performance of Acute Hospital Trusts: Thirtieth Report of Session 2015–16*, London: The Stationery Office, HC 709. Online at: https://www.publications.parliament.uk/pa/cm201516/cmselect/cmpubacc/709/709.pdf [accessed 27 June 2017].

PUBLIC ACCOUNTS COMMITTEE (PAC) (2016b) 'Committee confirms inquiries for early 2017 programme', *Public Accounts Committee News*, 9 November. Online at: http://www.parliament.uk/business/committees/committees-a-z/commons-select/public-accounts-committee/news-parliament-2015/2017-future-programme-16-17/ [accessed 16 June 2017].

PUBLIC ACCOUNTS COMMITTEE (PAC) (2017) *Financial Sustainability of the NHS: Forty-third Report of Session 2016–17*, London: The Stationery Office, HC 887. Online at: https://www.publications.parliament.uk/pa/cm201617/cmselect/cmpubacc/887/887.pdf [accessed 24 June 2017].

ROGERS, R. and WALTERS, R. (2015) *How Parliament Works*, London: Routledge.

RUSSELL, M. and BENTON, M. (2011) *Selective Influence: The Policy Impact of House of Commons Select Committees*, London: The Constitution Unit.

UK PARLIAMENT (2007) *Holding Government to Account: 150 Years of the Committee of Public Accounts*, London: UK Parliament. Online at: https://www.parliament.uk/documents/commons-committees/public-accounts/pac-history-booklet-pdf-version-p1.pdf [accessed 24 June 2017].

UK Parliament (2017) *Our Role—Public Accounts Committee*. Online at: http://www.parliament.uk/business/committees/committees-a-z/commons-select/public-accounts-committee/role/ [accessed 24 June 2017].

WHITE, H. (2015) *Select Committees Under Scrutiny: The Impact of Parliamentary Committee Inquiries on Government*, London: Institute for Government. Online at: https://www.instituteforgovernment.org.uk/sites/default/files/publications/Under%20scrutiny%20final.pdf [accessed 24 June 2017].

17

Questioning the Government

Stephen Bates, Peter Kerr, and Ruxandra Serban

INTRODUCTION

Parliamentary democracy is underpinned by the delegation of power and by accountability: citizens vote for MPs to represent them in Parliament; Parliament then delegates power to ministers, and, in turn, ministers must answer to Parliament for their actions. This relationship between government ministers and Parliament is based on the doctrine of individual ministerial responsibility, according to which ministers must explain the policies, actions, and decisions of their departments in Parliament (Woodhouse 1994; Gay 2012; Cabinet Office 2016). Beyond the ultimate manifestation of responsibility—a ministerial resignation or sacking—accountability is routinely carried out in Parliament through various questioning procedures which present ministers and the government with the opportunity to explain and defend their decisions.

Types of parliamentary questions

Parliamentary questions, then, are a key way in which MPs and peers can hold the government, the prime minister, ministers, and departments to account. According to Erskine May, parliamentary questions are used ostensibly to 'obtain information or to press for action' from the government (Jack, Hutton, and Johnson 2011, 344) but they may also allow parliamentarians to pursue other goals. They can also be used in a highly partisan way, especially in the case of supplementary questions, to attack alleged shortcomings of the government, the prime minister, and/or individual ministers, or the purported merits of an alternative policy. As such, questioning procedures may also contribute to a wider range of functions beyond scrutiny and accountability that Parliament performs in the UK political system.

There are two main types of parliamentary questions. Oral questions are both asked and answered on the Floor of the House of Commons or the House of Lords and comprise five subtypes—departmental, questions to the prime minister, urgent, business, and House of Lords. Written questions are submitted by MPs and peers in order to receive a written reply from ministers or the government and are 'often used to obtain detailed information about policies and statistics on the activities of government departments' (UK Parliament 2017b). Written questions comprise four subtypes—ordinary, named day, oral questions not answered during Question Time, and House of Lords. Thus, parliamentarians have a range of various questioning procedures available to them which, as described in the following sections, may suit different purposes. Table 17.1 shows how frequently the different types of question have been used since 1997.

Oral questions

Departmental questions are posed during Commons Question Time, which is the first business item in the House of Commons from Monday to Thursday, and can take two forms: those which have been tabled in advance and which allow ministers to prepare responses; and topical or spontaneous ones of which ministers do not have advance notice. Supplementary questions on the same topic can be posed in response to advance notice questions, both by the MP who tabled the original question, and any other MP in the Chamber who is called by the Speaker of the House of Commons.

 Parliamentary terms Departmental Question Time

Time scheduled in the Commons Chamber for MPs to ask questions to ministers responsible for government departments.

Unlike questions posed to ministers, MPs do not have to provide advance notice for any *questions to the prime minister* during Wednesday's Prime Minister's Questions (PMQs), although some may choose to do so. Most MPs choose to ask an open, non-transferable question about the prime minister's engagements for the day, allowing them to then pose a supplementary question on any topic within the government's responsibility (although only the first MP called actually asks the tabled engagement question). The Leader of the Opposition is allowed to pose up to six questions during each session of PMQs, and the leader of the third largest parliamentary party is allowed to pose two (unless they are in government, as was the case with the Liberal Democrats between 2010 and 2015, during which time no party leader other than the Leader of the Opposition was allowed to pose more than one question). Supplementary questions to the prime minister can also be posed after a prime ministerial statement or speech in much the same manner as happens during Departmental Question Time.

Urgent questions can potentially be posed by any MP on any sitting day. They are not printed on the day's Order Paper but are, in the opinion of the Speaker (whose decision is final in such matters), of an urgent nature and on a matter of public importance. In the debate following the urgent question, the MP who tabled the question can pose a supplementary question to the minister responding, as well as any MP in the Chamber, if called by the Speaker. In the House of Lords, these kinds of questions are known as private notice questions. *Business questions* are those posed to the Leader of the House after they have announced the forthcoming business in the House, each week on a Thursday. They are often used to request time for a debate on a particular topic, but can also be used to make partisan points about the performance of the government and the behaviour and opinions of particular ministers.

 Parliamentary terms Urgent questions

Questions for immediate answer by a government minister in the House of Commons. If a request to the Speaker for an urgent question is granted, the relevant minister must come to the Commons to answer it, immediately after Question Time. The equivalent procedure in the Lords is a private notice question.

Oral questions in the House of Lords are posed to the government as a whole, rather than to individual departments as in the House of Commons, and are asked in two main forums: Question Time and Questions for Short Debate. Due to the fact that most ministers reside in the House of Commons, Question Time in the House of Lords, which takes place at the beginning of the day's business from Monday to Thursday, is shared in practice between ministers and spokespersons from various departments. Questions for Short Debate are usually taken at the end of the day's business and entail a debate, finishing with a government reply.

Written questions

The main difference between the different kinds of written questions relates to when the questioner can expect a response. *Ordinary questions* do not have to be answered by a specific date (although convention dictates that the MP can normally expect a response within seven days), whereas *named day questions*, which only occur in the House of Commons, involve MPs specifying the date by which they should receive an answer. With regard to named day questions, MPs must give a minimum of two days' notice and must not table more than five of these types of question on any given day. *Oral questions not answered during Question Time* are, as the name implies, oral questions tabled but not answered during oral Question Time. They are passed on to the relevant government department as 'named day' questions. House of Lords written questions are similar to *ordinary written questions*, although these questions are posed to the government as a whole, rather than to ministers. Peers can table up to six questions each day and can expect an answer within 14 days.

The purposes of parliamentary questions

Over the past three decades, media, public and, indeed, academic scrutiny of parliamentary questions has tended to focus on possibly the most visible parliamentary institution and almost certainly the most criticized: Prime Minister's Questions (PMQs). Since the 1980s, this spectacle has increasingly become the subject of widespread criticism, on the basis that its formal function of holding the prime minister and government to account has gradually become eroded and replaced with attempts on both sides of the House to use the occasion for partisan point-scoring and adversarial, often childlike, verbal jousting (see Bates et al. 2014; Hansard Society 2014). As Jackie Ashley (2012) contends:

> [PMQs] has become a staggering and useless bore-athon, in which pink-faced men hurl dodgy statistics, act out synthetic and hyperbolic displays of anger and trudge their way through the lamest jokes a scriptwriter ever penned. Around them the rest of the house behave exactly like the Muppets, bouncing around with revolving eyeballs and funny hair, making wa-wa noises. Except, to be fair, that I've already made it sound much more interesting than it actually is.

Moreover, prime ministers have increasingly received questions on a wider range of topics (Bates et al. 2014, 270–1), despite not formally being responsible for a government department (Hennessy 2000; Blick and Jones 2010), and consequently not directly responsible for specific policy areas. These trends, and the theatrical behaviour often on show during PMQs, can certainly be seen as detrimental to adequate scrutiny which, in turn, may suggest that Parliament is ineffective at holding the government accountable, and may reinforce the widespread idea that Parliament is a weak institution, dominated by the executive.

However, it must be recognized that questioning procedures—of which PMQs is the most prominent—enable parliamentarians to pursue multiple goals. Beyond the formal scrutiny purposes of requesting information and explanations about the government's activity and decisions, and demanding remedial action where necessary (see Bull 2013), questioning procedures contribute to the wider range of functions that Parliament performs in the UK political system. Recognizing these broader purposes of questions during

Table 17.1 Number of questions which appeared on the Order Paper in the House of Commons

Session	Sitting Days	Written questions				Oral questions				Urgent questions	
		Named Day	Ordinary	Total	No. per Sitting Day	Oral	No. per Sitting Day	No. reached for answer	% reached for answer	Total	No. per Sitting Day
2015–16	158	13,283	22,673	35,956	227.6	4742	33.7	3603	76.0%	77	0.49
2014–15	133	11,638	18,548	30,186	227.0	4240	33.6	3044	71.8%	45	0.34
2013–14	162	13,010	30,227	43,227	266.8	5037	33.8	3822	75.9%	35	0.22
2012–13	143	12,123	30,172	42,295	295.8	4607	33.5	3381	73.4%	38	0.27
2010–12	295	30,498	77,255	97,753	331.4	9484	32.5	4710	49.7%	74	0.25
2009–10	69	4307	21,160	25,467	369.1	1924	25.4	962	50.0%	12	0.17
2008–09	139	8907	47,285	56,192	404.3	4113	23.5	1314	31.9%	11	0.08
2007–08	165	12,351	61,006	73,357	444.6	5151	22.1	2690*	52.2%	4	0.02
2006–07	146	10,590	47,235	57,825	396.1	3736	25.7	1775	47.5%	9	0.06
2005–06	208	15,374	79,667	95,041	456.9	5353	25.6	2712	50.7%	14	0.07
2004–05	65	3974	18,318	22,292	343.0	1438	31.2	848	59.0%	4	0.06
2003–04	157	8712	46,163	54,875	349.5	3687	29.6	2079*	56.4%	12	0.08
2002–03	162	9486	45,950	55,436	342.2	4118	27.9	2270*	55.1%	10	0.06
2001–02^	201	23,688	49,217	72,905	362.7	6528	32.1	2203	33.7%	10	0.05
2000–01	83	8062	8654	16,716	201.4	2780	32.2	906	32.6%	7	0.08
1999–2000	170	16,212	20,569	36,781	216.4	5747	31.1	2106	36.6%	9	0.05
1998–99	149	13,199	18,950	32,149	215.8	5008	31.9	1943	38.8%	12	0.08
1997–98	241	23,532	29,120	52,652	218.5	8113	30.0	3382	41.7%	28	0.12

* Urgent questions were called private notice questions during and before this session

^ Includes questions answered in Westminster Hall

Source: House of Commons Sessional Returns (2017) and Sandford (2015)

PMQs, as well as the less conspicuous questioning procedures outlined previously, allows the reconsideration of both often maligned parliamentary institutions, and the effectiveness of Parliament itself to scrutinize the government and hold it to account.

PMQs is, officially, an occasion that 'gives MPs the chance to question the Prime Minister' (UK Parliament 2017a) but, of course, PMQs is not simply about this. As both the highest profile parliamentary event bar none (Riddell 1998, 166–7) and the absolutely dominant form of prime ministerial activity in Parliament (Dunleavy, Jones, and O'Leary 1990, 123), PMQs is also about party morale, making a name for oneself, media exposure, party standing, public image, policy agendas, good government, and institutional authority. Questions posed during PMQs provide a high-profile means for MPs to maintain Parliament's representational link between government and citizens, by placing issues before the government which concern their constituents, as well as advocating various causes. Furthermore, given their rhetorical, interactional, and often confrontational nature, questions during PMQs facilitate inter-party conflict, clashes between government and opposition, and contribute to the socialization of parliamentarians into their institutional roles.

It is this multi-purpose nature of PMQs that, in part at least, gives rise to its adversarial nature and what is often criticized as 'scrutiny by screech' (Bercow 2010b). It also leads to different types of questions and answers, as displayed in Table 17.2. In their traditional

Table 17.2 Types of questions and answers at PMQs

Category		Definition
Standard question		A question which is straightforward to answer.
Unanswerable question		A question which either appears to be designed deliberately to provoke discomfort and/or evasion, or contains and/or is premised on incorrect information.
Helpful question		A question which acts as a prompt to allow the PM to set out the government position/policy and/or attack the opposition.
Full reply		An answer in which requested information is provided, and/or the PM's views are made clear on the issue in hand.
Non-reply		An answer in which the specific question is evaded, and/or a completely different question is answered, and/or the requested information is not provided, and/or the PM's views on the topic in hand are withheld.
Intermediate reply	partial	An answer in which the requested information is incomplete, and/or the PM responds on their own terms, and/or the PM responds to a closely related issue, and/or the PM's views on the topic in hand are ambivalent.
	deferred	An answer in which it is claimed that a full reply in terms of information and/or views can only be given at some point in the future.
	referred	An answer which is referred to the relevant minister.

Source: Bates et al. 2014

supportive role, government backbench MPs may ask 'helpful' questions prepared before-hand, which give ministers the opportunity to present government actions in a favourable light, and to attack the opposition. As the main role of the opposition in the UK system is to be the 'government-in-waiting', opposition MPs can use questions to criticize individual ministers and government policy, and Leaders of the Opposition have the opportunity to present themselves as viable potential prime ministers and to display leadership, both of which are helpful in maintaining party cohesion and morale. Thus, it is perhaps the case that questions posed during PMQs should not be judged solely, or mainly, on whether they have fulfilled a formal scrutiny function. These different kinds of questions also help to explain both why prime ministers may not always choose to answer a question as fully as might be the case, as well as the language used in providing that response. There is often a lot of com-ment about talk during PMQs and prime ministerial discourse—whoever the incumbent—is often self-referential (Sealey and Bates 2016). This self-referentiality—prime minister's explicitly representing themselves, their thoughts, and their actions—can arguably be seen as a defence mechanism in the face of questions which are always potentially hostile and face-threatening and, therefore, as a means of maintaining or enhancing authority.

The broader purposes of questions can also be seen during Departmental Question Time, but it is significantly more measured in tone and more focused on specific issues, contrary to the highly charged political exchange of PMQs. As a consequence, questions at PMQs may make media headlines, but they are less likely to extract information to the same level of detail as questions addressed to the department responsible for a particular policy area. This is the case both for oral questions posed during Departmental Question Time and, particularly perhaps, written questions. There are thus significant differences between the ways in which scrutiny of a particular area of policy can be carried out through oral and written questions posed beyond PMQs in less visible forums. Although less regular than PMQs, each department is assigned a full hour for Question Time, during which the minister must answer around 25 questions and potential supplementary and topical ques-tions; during a typical parliamentary session, each department tends to receive thousands of questions for written answer (Procedure Committee 2016, 11; see also Table 17.1), dem-onstrating its scrutiny capacity.

Moreover, the significant procedural and cultural differences between the Commons and the Lords make it difficult to offer qualitative comparisons between the ways in which questions operate. The overall less partisan and measured tone of Question Time in the Lords—highlighted by the fact that no more than four questions are taken during Question Time—indicates that the upper chamber complements the House of Commons by offering an additional venue for the scrutiny of government policy in Parliament in which topics can be addressed in more detail and with more Members intervening (Russell 2013).

Reforming parliamentary questions

Questions about whether, and how best to, reform parliamentary questions, and more spe-cifically PMQs, have been aired in both parliamentary and public debates for a number of years. In 1995, a Procedure Committee report into PMQs recommended wholesale reform of the then twice weekly event, on the basis that PMQs 'could no longer be held to pass the test that the purpose of a question is to obtain information or press for action' (Procedure Committee 1995; see also Procedure Committee 2002). Yet, beyond the Labour govern-ment making PMQs weekly for 30 minutes, rather than twice weekly for 15 minutes, in 1997, little substantive reform was forthcoming.

The question of reform received fresh impetus in 2009 in the wake of the parliamen-tary expenses scandal, the establishment of the Wright Committee (see Chapter 28), and the election of John Bercow to the role of Speaker of the House of Commons. On taking over the role, Bercow highlighted the reform of parliamentary questions as one potential route towards both increasing backbench scrutiny of the work of ministers, and improving public perceptions of the House (Bercow 2010a). In terms of the former, the Speaker has consistently attempted to provide more opportunities for backbench MPs to put questions to ministers. As Figures 17.1 and 17.2 demonstrate, Bercow has granted more urgent

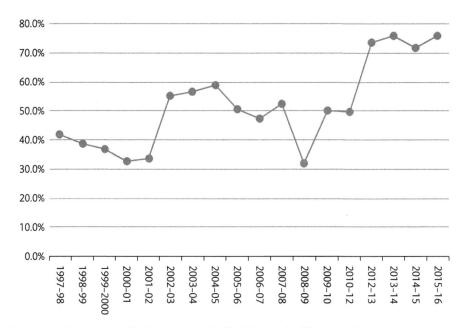

Figure 17.1 Percentage of oral questions tabled by MPs reached for answer by session, 1997–2016

Source: House of Commons Sessional Returns (2017) and Sandford (2015)

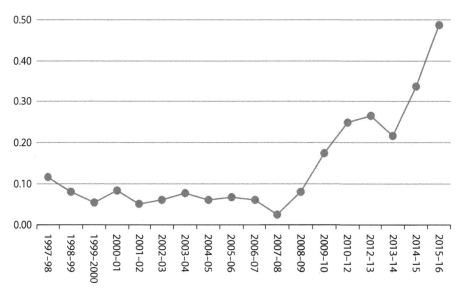

Figure 17.2 Number of urgent questions in the House of Commons per sitting day by session, 1997–2016

Source: House of Commons Sessional Returns (2017) and Sandford (2015)

questions in an attempt to make Parliament more responsive to important topical developments—such as the cover-up of a failed test of the Trident nuclear missile system in 2017 (Walker 2017)—and to increase the accountability of ministers. Bercow (2010a) has also highlighted his desire to 'make rapid progress down the order paper so that as many as possible of those in the House who want to pose an inquiry to a minister have that opportunity'; using different means for the same end, he has also unofficially extended PMQs—quite considerably in some cases—in order to allow more questions to be posed, and thus increasing scrutiny of the executive.

Bercow (2010b) has also put forward a number of suggestions for reforming PMQs and changing its overall culture. He has argued that the balance of allocated time for asking questions should be shifted away from the Leader of the Opposition towards backbenchers, either by lengthening the time of PMQs to a 45- or 60-minute session, or by reducing the opposition leader's questions from six to three or four. Moreover, after writing to the leaders of all three main parties to appeal for an end to the 'orchestrated barracking' which creates a 'wall of noise' (Watt 2014), Bercow urged all-party talks on reforming PMQs (May 2015). These proposals have, so far, come to nothing. Nevertheless, through the increased use of urgent questions and his attempts to raise the numbers of questions asked, the Speaker has received a degree of praise from some quarters for his reforms to questioning procedure, although his interventionist style has also led to him being accused of not being impartial enough for the role that the Speaker plays in the scrutiny of government (Kettle 2017). Writing in *The Spectator*, James Forsyth (2013) remarked that:

> This approach, the Bercow doctrine, has made it far easier for Parliament to challenge the executive ... [B]y granting so many urgent questions, he has ensured that ministers who have something to announce—or account for—come to the Commons to do so. They know that the choice they face is between making a statement or Bercow granting the opposition an urgent question and them being summoned to the Chamber to answer it. Given that situation, most ministers choose to make a statement.

Conclusion

The lack of reform of PMQs, despite widespread criticism, highlights some of the basic conundrums which the issue of parliamentary questions throws up. While it is generally noted that PMQs has come to dominate public perceptions of Parliament, and that it contributes to a generally negative view of both MPs and UK democracy, it has nevertheless been difficult for MPs to move beyond the essentially adversarial character of British party politics and the sometimes feverish style of debates on show. For some, this is not a problem in need of a solution, given that PMQs remains the most watched part of parliamentary business, largely due to its adversarial character, and the broader purposes of parliamentary questions discussed previously. For such commentators, the more serious business of scrutiny and accountability happens through other types of parliamentary business, such as in the work of select committees, or through Departmental Question Times and formal written questions.

Further Reading

BATES, S. R., KERR, P., BYRNE, C., and STANLEY, L. (2014) 'Questions to the Prime Minister: A Comparative Study of PMQs from Thatcher to Cameron', *Parliamentary Affairs*, Vol. 67 (2), pp. 253–80.

CHESTER, D. N. and BOWRING, N. (1962) *Questions in Parliament*, Oxford: Clarendon Press.

FRANKLIN, M. and NORTON, P., eds. (1993) *Parliamentary Questions*, Oxford: Clarendon Press.

HOUSE OF COMMONS (2013) *Parliamentary Questions: Brief Guide*, London: House of Commons Information Office.

SANDFORD, M. (2015) *Parliamentary Questions: Recent Issues*, House of Commons Library Briefing Paper Number 04148, 6 May.

Case Study 17: Theresa May's inaugural session of PMQs

Occurring as normal at midday on a Wednesday, and scheduled to last half an hour, Theresa May's first session of PMQs took place on 20 July 2016, a week after she assumed the office of prime minister (HC Debates, 20 July 2016, cc. 816–26). Despite the novelty of the new prime minister, this session displays the different purposes of parliamentary questions outlined earlier, as well as both the different types of questions and responses, and the self-referentiality of prime ministerial discourse.

The very first question posed to May by a fellow Conservative MP can be seen as a good example of a *helpful question*:

> *John Glen:* Given her unwavering commitment to delivering economic stability and national security in our United Kingdom's interest, does she welcome Monday's emphatic vote in this House for the Trident Successor programme, and will she ensure that economic stability and national security remain the guiding principles of her premiership?
>
> *The Prime Minister:* I thank my hon. Friend for his kind remarks. I join him in enthusiastically welcoming the vote taken in this House on Monday evening to renew our nuclear deterrent. I think that vote showed the commitment of this House: it showed that we have not only committed to our own national security, but considered the security of European and NATO allies. We can now get on with the essential job of renewing our nuclear deterrent. May I thank the 140 Labour Members of Parliament who put the national interest first and voted to renew the nuclear deterrent? (HC Debates, 20 July 2016, cc. 816–17)

The purpose of this question is clear (beyond, of course, allowing the questioner to curry favour with the whips' office and possibly increase his chances of promotion). It allows the prime minister to provide information through setting out the government's position—an official purpose of parliamentary questions—but it also allows her to assert her authority, to contrast (implicitly) her position with that of the Labour leadership, and to highlight divisions within the opposition. The self-referentiality of prime ministerial discourse can also be seen in May's response ('I thank ...', 'I join him ...', 'I think ...', 'May I thank ...'). The use of 'I think ...', in particular, acts not as a marker of uncertainty but, instead, allows May to turn attention to herself in order both to introduce her judgement about the vote and its importance for security issues and, in doing so, to adopt an authoritative stance.

Other *helpful questions* were asked during the session, for example by Daniel Kawczynski:

> We all stand with the people of France, and particularly Nice, following the appalling terrorist act there last week. Will the Prime Minister update the House on how the security collaboration between our two countries can help to prevent such attacks in future, and will she reassure the French people that although we are leaving the European Union, the close links between our two countries will remain steadfast? (HC Debates, 20 July 2016, c. 821)

However, while helpful to the prime minister, this question should not be viewed as toadying. Rather, it acts as a prompt to allow the prime minister to set out the government's position regarding security collaboration and, perhaps more importantly, send condolences to and express solidarity with the people of France.

In some ways, this session was not a normal session of PMQs. In addition to the usual *helpful questions* discussed above, it also included a number of compliments to the prime minister with MPs often congratulating her on her achievement of becoming only the second female prime minister. However, despite this congratulatory air, May was still asked a number of *unanswerable questions*, including this one from the Leader of the Opposition:

> Jeremy Corbyn: The Prime Minister is rightly concerned that:
>   'If you're black, you're treated more harshly ... than if you're white.'
>   Before appointing her new Foreign Secretary, did she discuss with him his description of black people as 'piccaninnies' and ask why he had questioned the motives of US President Obama on the basis of his 'part-Kenyan' heritage? (HC Debates, 20 July 2016, c. 818)

Perhaps unsurprisingly, May did not answer Corbyn's question, instead choosing to speak about her actions in relation to stop and search policies while Home Secretary. Indeed, the question—and others like it such as those from Angus Robertson (cc. 820–1) and Tim Farron (c. 826)—is not really being asked to seek information and, therefore, a direct answer. Rather, it is being posed to criticize, to cause discomfort, to send a message about the values of the questioner and their party, and to highlight perceived hypocrisy.

These exchanges—in response to both *helpful* and *unanswerable* questions—should perhaps, then, not be viewed and appraised solely, or even mainly, in terms of scrutiny and accountability, but rather in terms of some of the other goals of questions. However, there were other questions posed during this session which fit more squarely with the formal purpose of obtaining information or pressing for action and, in this sense, can be considered *standard questions* which often received *full replies*. For example, in response to Nusrat Ghani's question about the different forms of extremism in which she called for the government to end the use of the term 'honour' in the description of 'self-styled honour crimes', May responded by setting out the government's broad approach to tackling extremism and clearly asserting her position: 'I absolutely agree with her that there is absolutely no honour in so-called honour-based violence. It is violence and a criminal act, pure and simple' (HC Debates, 20 July 2016, c. 822).

Despite not always answering questions as fully as she might have, May's first performance at PMQs was widely praised for her command of the House; her comment directed at Jeremy Corbyn—'Remind him of anybody?' (HC Debates, 20 July 2016, c. 819)—being seen as particularly effective. However, May's strong start was not maintained, with journalists such as Iain Martin stating that the prime minister had yet to find her footing (Martin 2016) and highlighting the difficulty of doing PMQs.

The difficulty of PMQs—both for questioner and prime minister—lies in it not being simply about asking and answering questions. As May's inaugural session highlights, questioning the prime minister and the government more broadly is more than seeking information and pressing for action; it is also about, among other things, representing constituents, advocating causes, facilitating inter-party conflict, displaying leadership and authority, and maintaining party cohesion and morale.

Primary sources

- House of Commons (2016) *Sessional Returns: Session 2015–16*, London: The Stationery Office, HC 1. Online at: https://www.publications.parliament.uk/pa/cm201617/csession/1/1.pdf [accessed 29 June 2017].

- Procedure Committee (2002) *Parliamentary Questions: Third Report of Session 2001–02*, London: The Stationery Office, HC 622. Online at: https://www.publications.parliament.uk/pa/cm200102/cmselect/cmproced/622/622.pdf [accessed 27 June 2017].

- Procedure Committee (2009) *Written Parliamentary Questions: Third Report of Session 2008–09*, London: The Stationery Office, HC 859. Online at: https://www.publications.parliament.uk/pa/cm200809/cmselect/cmproced/859/859.pdf [accessed 27 June 2017].

- Procedure Committee (2016) *Monitoring of Written Parliamentary Questions: Progress Report for Session 2015–16*, London: The Stationery Office, HC 191. Online at: https://www.publications.parliament.uk/pa/cm201617/cmselect/cmproced/191/19102.htm [accessed 27 June 2017].

- Prime Minister's Questions (HC Debates, 20 July 2016, cc. 816–26), on Parliament.tv. Online at: http://parliamentlive.tv/event/index/eab066a6-b66d-48a5-ab48-21aeeb7400db?in=12:01:50 [accessed 27 June 2017].

 FURTHER CASE STUDIES

- Questions to the prime minister on the British phone hacking scandal (Ed Miliband, HC Debates, 6 July 2011, c. 1501).

- Urgent question on Tata Steel in the UK (HC Debates, 16 October 2014, c. 445).

- Oral questions in the House of Lords (HL Debates, 26 April 2017).

References

ASHLEY, J. (2012) 'John Bercow is changing the House of Commons. Credit to him', *The Guardian*, 26 February. Online at: https://www.theguardian.com/commentisfree/2012/feb/26/bercow-changing-commons-thuggish-tendencies [accessed 2 May 2017].

BATES, S. R., KERR, P., BYRNE, C., and STANLEY, L. (2014) 'Questions to the Prime Minister: A Comparative Study of PMQs from Thatcher to Cameron', *Parliamentary Affairs*, Vol. 67 (2), pp. 253–80.

BERCOW, J. (2010a) 'Reform in a New Parliament—Reviving the Chamber', Speech to the Hansard Society, 9 June. Online at: http://www.johnbercow.co.uk [accessed 3 May 2017].

BERCOW, J. (2010b) 'Speech to the Centre for Parliamentary Studies', 6 July. Online at: http://www.johnbercow.co.uk [accessed 3 May 2017].

BLICK, A. and JONES, G. W. (2010) *Premiership: The Development, Nature and Power of the British Prime Minister*, Exeter: Imprint Academic.

BULL, P. (2013) 'The role of adversarial discourse in political opposition: Prime Minister's Questions and the British phone-hacking scandal', *Language and Dialogue*, Vol. 3 (2), pp. 254–72.

CABINET OFFICE (2016) *Ministerial Code*, London: Cabinet Office. Online at: https://www.gov.uk/government/uploads/system/uploads/attachment_data/file/579752/ministerial_code_december_2016.pdf [accessed 24 June 2016].

DUNLEAVY, P., JONES, G. W., and O'LEARY, B. (1990) 'Prime Ministers and the Commons: Patterns of Behaviour, 1868 to 1987', *Public Administration*, Vol. 68 (1), pp. 123–40.

FORSYTH, J. (2013) 'John Bercow must rein it in—Parliament can't afford to depose two Speakers in a row', *The Spectator*, 16 November. Online at: https://www.spectator.co.uk/2013/11/the-speaker-could-soon-be-silenced/ [accessed 3 May 2017].

GAY, O. (2012) *Individual Ministerial Accountability*, House of Commons Library Standard Note SN/PC/06467, 8 November. Online at: http://researchbriefings.files.parliament.uk/documents/SN06467/SN06467.pdf [accessed 24 June 2017].

HANSARD SOCIETY (2014) *Tuned In or Turned Off? Public Attitudes to Prime Minister's Questions*, London: Hansard Society. Online at: http://www.hansardsociety.org.uk/ [accessed 12 January 2016].

HENNESSY, P. (2000) *The Prime Minister: The Office and its Holders Since 1945*, London: Allen Lane.

HOUSE OF COMMONS (2017) *Sessional Returns*. Online at: http://www.parliament.uk/business/publications/commons/sessional-returns/ [accessed 29 June 2017].

JACK, M., HUTTON, M., and JOHNSON, M. (2011) *Erskine May: Parliamentary Practice*, 24th edition, London: Lexis Nexis.

KETTLE, M. (2017) 'Reformist Speaker John Bercow places himself in eye of another storm', *The Guardian*, 10 February. Online at: https://www.theguardian.com/politics/2017/feb/10/reformist-speaker-john-bercow-places-himself-in-eye-of-another-storm [accessed 3 May 2017].

MARTIN, I. (2016) 'Clear Win for Corbyn. Bad PMQs for May', *Reaction*, 16 November. Online at: https://reaction.life/clear-win-corbyn-bad-pmqs-may/ [accessed 6 June 2017].

MAY, J. (2015) 'John Bercow urges party leaders to reform PMQs', *PoliticsHome*, 9 June. Online at: https://www.politicshome.com/news/uk/social-affairs/politics/news/62787/john-bercow-urges-party-leaders-reform-pmqs [accessed 23 August 2017].

PROCEDURE COMMITTEE (1995) *Prime Minister's Questions: Seventh Report of Session 1994–95*, London: The Stationery Office, HC 555.

PROCEDURE COMMITTEE (2002) *Parliamentary Questions: Third Report of Session 2001–02*, London: The Stationery Office, HC 622. Online at: https://www.publications.parliament.uk/pa/cm200102/cmselect/cmproced/622/622.pdf [accessed 24 June 2017].

PROCEDURE COMMITTEE (2016) *Monitoring of Written Parliamentary Questions: Progress Report for Session 2015–16*, London: The Stationery Office, HC 191. Online at: https://www.publications.parliament.uk/pa/cm201617/cmselect/cmproced/191/19102.htm [accessed 24 June 2017].

RIDDELL, P. (1998) *Parliament under Pressure*, London: Victor Gollancz.

RUSSELL, M. (2013) *The Contemporary House of Lords: Westminster Bicameralism Revived*, Oxford: Oxford University Press.

SANDFORD, M. (2015) *Parliamentary Questions: Recent Issues*, House of Commons Library Briefing Paper Number 04148, 6 May. Online at: http://researchbriefings.files.parliament.uk/documents/SN04148/SN04148.pdf [accessed 24 June 2017].

SEALEY, A. J. and BATES, S. (2016) 'Prime Ministerial self-reported actions in Prime Minister's Questions 1979–2010: a corpus-assisted analysis', *Journal of Pragmatics*, Vol. 104, pp. 18–31.

UK PARLIAMENT (2017a) *Prime Minister's Questions News*. Online at: http://www.parliament.uk/business/news/parliament-government-and-politics/parliament/prime-ministers-questions/ [accessed 23 August 2017].

UK Parliament (2017b) *Written Questions and Answers*. Online at http://www.parliament.uk/about/how/business/written-answers/ [accessed 3 May 2017].

Walker, P. (2017) 'Sack the person who covered up Trident failure, says senior Tory', *The Guardian*, 23 January. Online at: https://www.theguardian.com/uk-news/2017/jan/23/labour-pushes-for-answers-on-failed-trident-nuclear-test [accessed 3 May 2017].

Watt, N. (2014) 'John Bercow calls for an end to "orchestrated barracking" at PMQs', *The Guardian*, 18 February. Online at: https://www.theguardian.com/politics/2014/feb/18/john-bercow-pmqs-letter-party-leaders [accessed 3 May 2017].

Woodhouse, D. (1994) *Ministers and Parliament: Accountability in Theory and Practice*, Oxford and New York: Clarendon Press/Oxford University Press.

18

The Role of a Backbench MP

Mark Shephard and Jack Simson Caird

INTRODUCTION

In this chapter we examine the nature and roles of backbench MPs as well as considering their impact and influence, with emphasis placed on the Backbench Business Committee. Quantifying the political influence of any particular parliamentary group is notoriously difficult. Further, the nature of the role of the backbencher in the House of Commons is subject to contextual factors which change fairly frequently, particularly as a result of changes to the political context—most obviously the size of the government of the day's majority, but also parliamentary reform such as the creation of the Backbench Business Committee, which is the focus of Case Study 18. Our analysis starts with an exploration of what the role of an MP entails, before considering recent developments.

The role of the backbench MP

A backbench MP is a Member of Parliament who holds no governmental office and no opposition shadow frontbench position. The term 'backbench' refers to where the MPs sit in the House of Commons—behind those with either ministerial frontbench or shadow ministerial frontbench positions. The definition of a backbencher holds in many other parliamentary systems where the executive is drawn from the legislative branch (for example, Australia, Canada, and New Zealand). However, emphasis on backbench roles might vary in different parliamentary systems. For example, MPs in parliamentary systems like the UK and Canada that use single-member districts give a higher priority to constituency work (Heitshusen, Young, and Wood 2005). In systems where there is a separation of powers (for example, the USA), the distinction between frontbench and backbench does not hold as the executive and legislative branches are distinct entities. Instead, other distinctions are made such as seniority and being in the minority or majority party.

 Parliamentary terms Backbenchers

MPs or peers who are not members of the government and who do not have frontbench roles in opposition parties. Backbench MPs sit behind the front benches on either side of the Commons Chamber.

The level of political influence of backbenchers is contested. Parts of the media and academia champion and celebrate their influence. Others are much more dismissive of their significance. Ultimately, significance and impact will depend on the lens applied to the study of backbench MPs, as well as the specific time period and the length of time under investigation. To get at this we need to explore the myriad roles that exist and set this alongside an appreciation of political context and institutional opportunities at any one time.

Roles can, and have been, perceived through many different lenses. Formal roles can include those that come with the job of being an MP, for example the scrutiny of legislation and representation of constituents. In contrast, informal roles may comprise those that the MP chooses to focus on, such as being a policy advocate for a particular issue or cause.

Considering the difficulties in pinning down the roles of backbench MPs, the House of Commons Modernisation Committee recognized that there was 'no neat description', but rather 'interconnected roles' that were 'sometimes mutually reinforcing and sometimes conflicting' (Modernisation Committee 2007, 3). Common roles of MPs identified by the Modernisation Committee (ibid., 9) included: supporting their party; representing and furthering the interests of their constituency and constituents; scrutinizing government (holding to account, monitoring, stimulating, challenging …); initiating, reviewing, and amending legislation; contributing to policy development; and promotion of public understanding (for example, of Parliament, parties …).

Even if it appears that MPs might be prioritizing one role over another, and that there is a perceived hierarchy to these roles—such as policy advocacy having a higher status than constituency 'social work' (Searing 1995)—we should be careful not to compartmentalize roles as distinct from and/or preferable to one another. The standing of a backbench MP in their constituency, for instance, may rely in part on the effectiveness of their activities in the House, while their capacity to scrutinize the government may rely on how well they know an industry in their constituency, and so on. MPs may choose not to limit themselves to the fulfilment of one role, when it may be possible to fulfil multiple roles at the same time. For instance, in asking a question at Prime Minister's Questions, an MP might ask about a policy issue, framed through the party, or even constitutional, lens, but also ask it in a way that connects it to a constituent or their constituency. In April 2017, for example, then backbencher Labour MP Rachael Maskell asked Prime Minister Theresa May about job losses at a multinational company in her constituency post-Brexit and whether the prime minister could intervene to avert the losses (HC Debates, 26 April 2017, c. 1106). Indeed, this multiple role fulfilment is now pretty standard practice, and for good electoral reasons. As Vivyan and Wagner (2016) find, voters prefer MPs who do both national policy work as well as paying strong attention to their constituency. But while in some instances the two roles may well be complementary, the sheer scale of the work generated by modern constituency offices does nonetheless reduce the resources and time available for other work (see Chapter 25).

Donald Searing's (1995) study of MPs makes an entirely different distinction between formal and informal roles. Whereas formal roles are associated with non-backbench leadership positions (parliamentary private secretary, whip, junior minister, and minister), informal roles are largely the preserve of the backbencher and are categorized according to four categories: constituency Member; policy advocate; ministerial aspirant; and parliamentarian. Drawing on interviews with MPs, Searing noted how even if MPs tended to fulfil multiple roles, most would concentrate on one particular role, although this role could change over time as context (for example, in government versus in opposition) and institutional arrangements (for example, introduction of select committees) varied.

Searing subdivides 'constituency Member' into 'welfare officers' (who try and help individual constituents) and 'local promoters' (who focus on collective constituency issues such as unemployment). In a study of new MPs, Rosenblatt (2006, 75) found that the vast majority cited constituency representation (advocate and social worker) as their main role when they first entered Parliament, and stressed this even more when they were one year into the job. Similarly, Campbell and Lovenduski (2015) find that younger MPs are more constituency-orientated. They also find that both MPs and the public rank the constituency role the highest, and that female MPs tend to rate the constituency role higher than their male colleagues on average.

Policy advocates are classified by Searing into three types: 'ideologues' (a small group who prioritize abstract political ideas over policy success); 'generalists' (about a third, who appreciate the interconnectedness of policy domains and who prioritize executive oversight on latest issues); and 'specialists' (the majority, who see that effective influence is derived from focus on narrow policy fields). Measuring influence on policy, for example, is not easy. First, the biggest influence may be immeasurable because it is about what governments do not do (due to feared opposition), rather than what they actually do (Bachrach and Baratz 1962). Second, ministerial amendments to legislation are often the product of prior concerns from backbench MPs and/or amendments that were withdrawn on the proviso that the government would take action to address the issue(s) raised (Shephard and Cairney 2005). Third, some actions that look like attempts at policy influence might actually be about something else, such as attempts to gain information, or to make partisan points (Shephard and Cairney 2005). In short, when we measure the impact of backbench MPs we need to be careful not to miss indirect impacts and ulterior behavioural motives.

Both Searing (1995) and Wright (2010) make a distinction between those backbench MPs that seek to influence power (Wright's 'why' MPs) and those that seek power (Wright's 'when' MPs). Wright points out that Parliament needs both types of MP to function effectively and that MPs may change from one type to another during their careers. A classic example of a switch in roles happens when an MP's party, which was in power, then loses an election. When your party is in government you might be less willing to scrutinize the government (the 'why') than when you are in opposition. Typically, those that seek power were traditionally ministerial aspirants, of which Searing (1995) distinguishes between two main types: 'high flyers' who aim for higher ministerial office and 'subalterns' who aim for junior ministerial office. However, institutional changes at Westminster—most notably additional remuneration for select committee chairs (from 2003) and the removal of whips' patronage powers by introducing the election of select committee chairs by secret cross-party ballot (from 2010)—have provided MPs with alternative positions of power at the backbench level. This is an important development, because traditionally power-seekers typically had to be deferential to party leaders to gain positions of power. One consequence of this is that it has altered the dynamics between backbenchers and frontbenchers in the House of Commons, granting the former more freedom for independent scrutiny and dissent. White (2015) finds that electing select committee chairs has also meant not only that more experts have been elected as chairs, but that the greater legitimacy provided by cross-party selection has empowered chairs, particularly previously weaker opposition backbench chairs (see Chapter 16). The net result has been an increase in the campaigning roles of chairs; for example, Graham Allen MP used his chairing of the Political and Constitutional Reform Committee to campaign for a written constitution (White 2015, 7).

Wright (2010) also identifies key types of backbench MPs based on their prime behaviours: 'lickspittles' (slaves to the party line); 'loyalists' (can be critical but are mainly loyal to the party); 'localists' (constituency is the focus); 'legislators' (oversight, committees); 'loners' (independents and 'mavericks'); and finally 'loose cannons' (weird and unhinged). Wright makes an important contribution to the discussion of roles, as he points out that many lists of roles fail to take into consideration the importance of campaigning and keeping an eye on all the things MPs need to do to get re-elected, interests advanced, and promotion within the party. The importance of campaigning is noticeable through MPs' Twitter accounts. This then raises the question about which sources should be used to analyse MPs' roles. If we limit ourselves to formal institutional channels and procedures such as those depicted in Hansard, we miss other less formal channels such as social media and face-to-face interactions, which are often more revealing of MP behaviour.

While research on dissent indicates that backbench MPs have become more independently minded in the last ten years (Cowley 2015), there is often a perception that opportunities to act on their own initiative have declined due to both increased party control and increased executive control over parliamentary business (Modernisation Committee 2007, 5). However, talk of decline is relative to the time period under consideration. Roles will reflect and be affected by institutional developments. The introduction of departmental select committees in 1979, for example, granted the backbencher greater opportunity for government departmental scrutiny—albeit in large part contingent on the willingness of ministers and civil servants to comply with committee requests. Compliance is also a product of subject area—for instance, defence and foreign affairs are notoriously difficult areas for MPs to illustrate impact (Shephard 2010; White 2015). The introduction of a parallel debating chamber (Westminster Hall) in 1999 provided backbenchers with an additional debating space that gives more time for backbench MPs to raise and debate topical issues, often of a less partisan nature, such as tumble dryer safety, grandparents' rights of access to grandchildren, and dog attacks on dogs. Although oral questions rarely take place, this forum does provide a potential agenda-setting venue for backbenchers to promote and advance issues that may need urgent attention and/or government action. In addition, the establishment of a Scrutiny Unit to assist committee work in 2002 (see Chapter 4), the introduction of evidence-taking public bill committees in 2006, the election of members and chairs of select committees by secret ballot from 2010, and the establishment of the Backbench Business Committee in 2010 (see Case Study 18) have injected new opportunities and avenues for the fulfilment of roles. Of course, you can improve the institutional opportunities and resources for backbench MPs, but if time is not infinite and if pressures from other sources such as the constituency increase, then they may not be able to capitalize on the new possibilities for role enhancement.

Conclusion

A lack of definitiveness and prescription on how to be a backbench MP is a defining feature of the role. The roles of backbench MPs are diverse and will vary over time as an MP's circumstances change (Searing 1995; Rush 2001). The role of an MP isn't limited to their activity within Parliament. Their activities on social media, for instance, are also an important means for connecting with constituents. Of course, the types of roles being fulfilled are very much down to the individual backbench MP, something which Crewe (2015) notes is a product of not just the present, but also past experiences and future expectations. Beyond personality types, the role of a backbencher will be shaped by external factors such as seniority and marginality of seat, and internal factors such as procedure type and institutional developments including the election of select committee members and chairs. But, as Searing (1995) concludes, it is how politicians adapt to their circumstances that explains which roles come to the fore, and how they are fulfilled. The Commons has tried to prescribe these more clearly, both by investigating roles and by educating and inducting new recruits into the roles of backbench MPs. It has also created new institutions and procedures like the Backbench Business Committee to try to encourage more backbench input and influence. However, fundamentally, internal conflicts in terms of the role of the Commons, especially governing versus scrutiny, push MPs towards their parties and constituents (and committees). Ultimately, the Commons is a Member-led place which is trying to be more institutionally focused, but it is very difficult to be prescriptive of role, given the conflicting pressures MPs face. Still, overall, there has clearly been an empowerment of backbench MPs, who now have more opportunities to raise their constituents' concerns and to scrutinize government.

Further Reading

CREWE, E. (2015) *House of Commons: An Anthropology of MPs at Work*, London: Bloomsbury.

RUSH, M. (2001) *The Role of the Member of Parliament Since 1868*, Oxford: Oxford University Press.

RUSH, M. and GIDDINGS, P. (2011) *Parliamentary Socialisation: Learning the Ropes or Determining Behaviour?*, Basingstoke: Palgrave MacMillan.

SEARING, D. (1995) 'Backbench and Leadership Roles in the House of Commons', *Parliamentary Affairs*, Vol. 48 (3), pp. 418–37.

WRIGHT, T. (2010) 'What are MPs For?', *Political Quarterly*, Vol. 81 (3), pp. 298–308.

Case Study 18: Backbench Business Committee

The Backbench Business Committee is rightly cited as an example of the empowerment of backbench MPs. The Committee was created in 2010 as a result of the recommendations of the Wright Committee. It enables backbench Members of Parliament, rather than the government, to select topics for debate on the Floor of the House and in Westminster Hall. The Standing Orders provide that 35 days are allocated in each session for backbench business. This alone is sufficient to demonstrate a change in the extent of the influence of backbench MPs. They now have their distinctive and autonomous identity reflected in their own control of a portion of the House of Commons' timetable. Since it began work in the 2010 Parliament the Committee's debates have highlighted Members' desire, post-expenses scandal, to connect with the public. The ability to select subjects for debate, and most importantly to enable votes on motions on the Floor of the House, free from government control, has served to secure greater autonomy for backbench MPs.

The procedure for applying for a debate is refreshingly transparent. The relevant form can be downloaded from the Committee's home page on Parliament's website. The application highlights some important features of the Committee's work. A Member can apply for either a 90-minute, three-hour, or six-hour debate. The latter is a full day's debate in the Chamber on a Thursday, whereas the 90-minute debate is normally held in Westminster Hall on a Tuesday morning. The sponsoring Member, or Members (up to three can apply), can request a general debate on a particular issue, or for a debate to be held on a substantive motion (which expresses an opinion). Only the latter can lead to a division (a vote). A general debate on a subject, for example Welsh affairs or epilepsy, can enable a range of Members from different parties to discuss matters that are important to their constituents and to raise particular political priorities. A debate and a positive vote on a motion, which states a clear view—for example that the House is in favour of increasing the penalties for animal cruelty—can enable Members to send a powerful political message.

The sponsoring Member(s) must attend a hearing before the Committee and pitch the case for their particular topic. The Committee is composed of eight members including the Chair. In the 2015 Parliament, it was chaired by an opposition Member Ian Mears MP (Labour), who sat alongside two other Labour MPs, five Conservative MPs, and one from the Scottish National Party. This public pitching before the Committee emphasizes the shift away from the usual channels and backroom negotiations.

In the 2010 Parliament there were 384 backbench business debates. The range of subjects reflects the diversity of interests of Members. What is striking is that, freed from the constraints of scrutinizing government business, the House of Commons chooses subjects that are topical and high on the news agenda, as well as subjects that have a direct bearing on the lives of constituents. An example of such a topical debate was the request for a debate on mental health sponsored by Paul Burstow MP (Liberal Democrat), Madeleine Moon MP (Labour), and Charles Walker MP (Conservative). The cross-party pitch emphasized the need to build on the momentum generated by a previous backbench business debate on the issue held in June 2012. The pitch succeeded and the debate, on 16 May 2013, was memorable as many Members openly shared their own experience of mental health conditions (HC Debates, 16 May 2013, cc. 813–72). The debate generated much positive media comment, just as the earlier debate had done, with reports praising Members' bravery in sharing their own struggles. This shows the capacity of these types of debates to enable Members to connect with the public in a meaningful way.

A surprising feature of the subjects chosen is the number of debates on foreign affairs. For example, the 2014–15 session included debates on: UK foreign policy towards Iran, ending the conflict in Palestine, Ukraine and UK relations with Russia, Yemen, and the destruction and looting of historic sites in Syria and Iraq. This belies the parochial focus which is often said to characterize the concerns of modern Members.

Arguably the most significant Backbench Business Committee debate held in the 2010 Parliament occurred on 24 October 2011, on a motion calling on the government to introduce a bill to provide for holding a national referendum on whether the United Kingdom should remain in or leave the European Union. The motion was defeated, with 111 Members voting for and 483 against. The Conservative Party's manifesto for the 2010 general election did not include a pledge for a referendum on the UK's membership of the European Union. The government whipped against the vote, but despite this, 81 Conservative backbench Members voted for the motion. According to Lord Norton of Louth, this rebellion, on a motion that would never have happened without the control of scheduling afforded to backbenchers, played a significant role in the Conservative Party's subsequent decision to include a pledge to hold a referendum in their manifesto in the 2015 general election (see Norton 2016).

The critical point is that the Backbench Business Committee has enabled backbenchers to harness the institutional weight of the Commons to communicate political messages in a way that was not previously possible. One can imagine that if the Committee had existed in the early 2000s backbenchers could have made life uncomfortable for the then government on foreign policy and immigration. Future governments will not welcome the inevitable debates on subjects they would rather avoid, and that is a sign of the Committee's success in empowering backbenchers.

Another prominent debate held in the 2010 Parliament was that on prisoner voting on 10 February 2011. The 2006 judgment of the European Court of Human Rights (ECHR) held that the UK's statutory ban on prisoners voting was a breach of convention rights. This proved highly controversial. One of the reasons was that the Court's judgment stated that a factor relevant to finding the breach was that Parliament had not explicitly debated the rights implications of the ban. The government was reluctant to bring forward any response. However, the Backbench Business Committee enabled this to be debated for the first time. The debate was on a motion which responded to the ECHR's comment, and sought to communicate to the Court that the ban was supported by a majority in the Commons. The motion was agreed by 234 to 22. The debate has been criticized by legal scholars for the quality of its engagement with the rights engaged by the Court (Fredman 2013, 292). However, the vote and direct involvement by the Commons was noted by the Court in its judgment on the *Scoppola* case in 2012. The result of the vote has been repeatedly cited by the government when making the case to the Council of Europe as to why it has not implemented the ECHR's judgment. In this case a Backbench Business Committee debate has served a useful purpose for the government, enabling them to show that Parliament had not only addressed, but explicitly endorsed the human rights implications of the blanket ban on prisoner voting.

Not all of the debates are on headline-grabbing subjects. On 24 March 2016, a Backbench Business Committee debate was held on court closures. This was sponsored by Helen Hayes MP (Labour) following the government's announcement the previous month that, after holding a consultation, 86 courts and tribunals would close. Closing courts in this way is not covered by statute, so does not require legislation, and therefore no debate in the Commons would ordinarily have been held on the subject. However, within local communities, and therefore constituencies, the closure of a local court can be keenly felt. Many Members were understandably keen to draw attention to this policy when a court or tribunal was being closed in their own constituency. The debate was held on a motion, which was agreed without a division. The debate might not have generated much comment beyond local press, but it enabled a number of Members to show their commitment to an issue of importance to their constituents, which may not otherwise have been subject to significant debate in a national forum.

CONCLUSION

The introduction of the Backbench Business Committee was an attempt to encourage greater backbench input and influence over parliamentary debates. It has brought some notable successes, arguably helping provide the spark for the referendum on the UK's membership of the European Union. It is also an example of how parliamentary procedures can enable MPs to fulfil multiple roles. The topics selected for debate in Parliament fit well with constituency-roles such as Searing's 'local promoter' or Wright's 'localists', but we can also easily identify the role of policy advocate in areas ranging from domestic policy to foreign affairs. In doing so it has clearly empowered backbenchers, providing a means through which they can fulfil the roles which they deem to be the most important.

Primary sources

- Backbench Business Committee (n.d.) *Backbench Business Committee home page.* Online at: http://www.parliament.uk/business/committees/committees-a-z/commons-select/backbench-business-committee/ [accessed 22 August 2017].

- House of Commons Debate on Voting by Prisoners (HC Debates, 10 February 2011, cc. 523–86). Online at: https://hansard.parliament.uk/commons/2011-02-10/debates/11021059000001/VotingByPrisoners [accessed 22 August 2017].

- House of Commons Debate on Mental Health (HC Debates, 16 May 2013, cc. 563–872). Online at: https://hansard.parliament.uk/commons/2013-05-16/debates/13051646000001/MentalHealth [accessed 22 August 2017].

- Modernisation Committee (2007) *Revitalising the Chamber: The Role of the Back Bench Member: First Report of Session 2006–07*, London: The Stationery Office, HC 337. Online at: https://www.publications.parliament.uk/pa/cm200607/cmselect/cmmodern/337/337.pdf [accessed 22 August 2017].

FURTHER CASE STUDIES

- Select a handful of backbench MPs from different parties and analyse their Twitter activity for a period of a week.
- Select a PMQ session and analyse how backbench MPs utilize this opportunity.
- Select a specific select committee and watch two of their evidence sessions, one pre- and one post-Wright reforms, to compare MPs' behaviour.

References

BACHRACH, P. and BARATZ, M. S. (1962) 'Two Faces of Power', *American Political Science Review*, Vol. 56 (4), pp. 947–52.

CAMPBELL, R. and LOVENDUSKI, J. (2015) 'What should MPs do? Public and parliamentarians' views compared', *Parliamentary Affairs*, Vol. 68 (4), pp. 690–708.

COWLEY, P. (2015) 'The Most Rebellious Parliament of the Post-War Era', *Political Studies Association Blog*, 28 March. Online at: https://www.psa.ac.uk/insight-plus/blog/most-rebellious-parliament-post-war-era [accessed 20 September 2016].

CREWE, E. (2015) *The House of Commons: An Anthropology of MPs at Work*, London: Bloomsbury.

FREDMAN, S. (2013) 'From Dialogue to Deliberation: Human Rights Adjudication and Prisoners' Rights to Vote', *Public Law*, June, pp. 292–311.

HEITSHUSEN, V., YOUNG, G., and WOOD, D. M. (2005) 'Electoral Context and MP Constituency Focus in Australia, Canada, Ireland, New Zealand, and the United Kingdom', *American Journal of Political Science*, Vol. 49 (1), pp. 32–45.

MODERNISATION COMMITTEE (2007) *Revitalising the Chamber: The Role of the Back Bench Member: First Report of Session 2006–07*, London: The Stationery Office, HC 337. Online at: https://www.publications.parliament.uk/pa/cm200607/cmselect/cmmodern/337/337.pdf [accessed 24 June 2017].

NORTON, P. (2016) 'Why was there a referendum?', *The Norton View*, 24 June. Online at: https://nortonview.wordpress.com/2016/06/24/why-was-there-a-referendum/ [accessed 2 June 2017].

ROSENBLATT, G. (2006) *A Year in the Life: From Member of Public to Member of Parliament*, London: Hansard Society. Online at: https://assets.contentful.com/u1rlvvbs33ri/6N22oTpQ cgKowCEuMoI4wo/9cda4f09fef2ae1e7f4f416f386f4506/Publication__A-Year-in-the-Life-From-member-of-public-to-Member-of-Parliament-2006.pdf [accessed 23 August 2017].

RUSH, M. (2001) *The Role of the Member of Parliament Since 1868*, Oxford: Oxford University Press.

SEARING, D. (1995) 'Backbench and Leadership Roles in the House of Commons', *Parliamentary Affairs*, Vol. 48 (3), pp. 418–37.

SHEPHARD, M. (2010) 'Parliamentary Scrutiny and Oversight of the British "War on Terror": Surrendering Power to Parliament or *Plus ça Change*?' in J. E. Owens and R. Pelizzo, *The 'War on Terror' and the Growth of Executive Power?*, New York: Routledge, pp. 87–116.

SHEPHARD, M. and CAIRNEY, P. (2005) 'The Impact of the Scottish Parliament in Amending Executive Legislation', *Political Studies*, Vol. 53 (2), pp. 303–19.

VIVYAN, N. and WAGNER, M. (2016) 'House or home? Constituent preferences over legislator effort allocation', *European Journal of Political Research*, Vol. 55 (1), pp. 81–99.

WHITE, H. (2015) *Select Committees Under Scrutiny: The Impact of Parliamentary Committee Inquiries on Government*, London: Institute for Government. Online at: https://www.instituteforgovernment.org.uk/sites/default/files/publications/Under%20scrutiny%20final.pdf [accessed 24 June 2017].

WRIGHT, T. (2010) 'What are MPs For?', *Political Quarterly*, Vol. 81 (3), pp. 298–308.

19

Scrutiny by the House of Lords

Patrick Milner

INTRODUCTION

The House of Lords is the second chamber of the UK Parliament. It legislates, considers matters of public policy, and holds the government of the day to account. In recent times, the House has assumed a strengthened role by scrutinizing the policies and actions of the executive in great detail. Legislating is still the primary function of the House, but the increasing focus on scrutiny has given it a very distinct character which contrasts that of the House of Commons. As this chapter shows, the House of Lords fulfils its scrutiny function in different ways. It scrutinizes draft primary legislation as part of the legislative process, as well as secondary legislation in committees. It conducts in-depth inquiries, investigates matters of public policy in committees, and questions the government through oral and written questions. Peers debate current issues and the findings of committees, and scrutinize the government's actions in the Council of the European Union, commenting on policy positions through a committee process and by corresponding directly with ministers.

 Parliamentary terms   Secondary legislation

Legislation made by ministers which makes very specific or detailed changes to the law in line with powers set out in an existing Act of Parliament. It may also be referred to as delegated legislation. Most secondary legislation takes the form of individual statutory instruments.

Conventions informing the scrutiny role of the House of Lords

Understanding the main functions of the House of Lords is key to understanding the constitutional settlement of the UK. The work of the House of Lords complements that of the House of Commons, but Parliament does not enjoy 'perfect bicameralism'—two chambers with indistinguishable and equal powers. Instead, the two chambers have different powers, particularly on bills relating to finance, as explained in Chapter 7. The interactions between the two Houses have at times been fraught, and they still disagree on a regular basis as part of the ordinary legislative process. The seemingly contradictory terms 'upper House' and 'second Chamber' shed more light on this relationship.

 Parliamentary terms   Convention

A way of working which is not written down in formal parliamentary documents.

Historically, the membership of the House constituted representatives from the nobility and the clergy, hence the elevated term 'upper House'. However, the primacy of the House of Commons as the democratically elected Chamber is now acknowledged by all. There are a number of conventions and statutes which, together, enshrine the primacy of the Commons over the second Chamber. The main conventions, as highlighted by the Joint Committee on Conventions (2006), are as follows:

- The Salisbury Convention which means that bills implementing manifesto commitments are not opposed by the House of Lords at second reading and are not subject to 'fatal' amendments which, in effect, kill a bill.
- The House of Lords does not usually object to secondary legislation.
- The financial privilege of the House of Commons which concerns its special right to decide levels of public taxation and public spending.
- Governments should get their business 'in reasonable time'.

The nature of conventions, however, means that they are not necessarily closely defined and they change over time. This makes for an organic relationship between the two Houses which is always evolving, with the balance of power shifting over time. Although the House of Lords has limited powers in theory, in practice, its real powers can be significant and are often political. Ministers in the House may be confronted with piercing lines of inquiry by peers with unparalleled expertise in a given area, and the merits of government policy are often questioned by peers sitting on their own benches.

The main scrutiny functions of the Lords

The scrutiny functions exercised by the House are diverse and provide peers with the opportunity to question the government on the same issue in a variety of ways.

Scrutinizing draft primary legislation

The House of Lords plays an essential role in amending the content of bills, highlighting problems and suggesting improvements. In the 2015–16 session, for example, the Lords spent 578 hours examining government bills in the Chamber and in grand committee (House of Lords 2016, 1). The stages through which a bill must pass in both Houses to become law were explained in Chapter 7. However, there are a number of important differences between the consideration of bills in the Commons and the Lords. First, amendments can, in certain cases, be made at the third reading of the bill. Peers often propose 'probing amendments', a similar practice to that in the Commons, where they do not necessarily seek to 'test the opinion of the House' by triggering a vote, but instead to debate a point of detail in the hope that the government will reconsider and make amendments to the bill in a particular way before the next formal stage of consideration. Probing amendments often appear at committee stage and report stage in the Lords and may finally be put to a vote at third reading. Second, amendments are selected differently. This means that if a Member of the House of Lords wishes to debate their amendment or push it to a vote, they are always able to do so providing that the government have allocated enough time for the bill as a whole to be debated. All amendments therefore have at least the chance of being debated. Third, the Lords do not agree programme motions in advance of the main stages of a bill (see Chapter 7). In the Commons, programme motions can limit the time for backbenchers and opposition parties to debate and amend government bills.

In the Lords, there are therefore fewer limitations on peers being able to amend a bill or debate a point of detail, and there are fewer time constraints. Of course, amendments agreed in the Lords then have to be agreed to in the Commons and so it is not necessarily easier to secure a lasting legislative change. The political reality, however, is different and the government often have to explain matters of policy detail in the Lords which they have not had to do in the Commons.

The House of Lords also carries out pre-legislative scrutiny jointly with the House of Commons. This detailed examination of an early draft of a government bill is carried out by a joint committee made up of Members from both Houses. The committee produces a report before the final version of the bill is presented to Parliament for formal consideration. Recent examples of draft bills examined by joint committees include the Draft Deregulation Bill, the Draft Modern Slavery Bill, the Draft Voting Eligibility (Prisoners) Bill, the Draft Investigatory Powers Bill, and the Draft Protection of Charities Bill. Although membership of pre-legislative committees is determined by the whips (government, opposition, and other parties) in both Houses, the recommendations they make often demonstrate a willingness to criticize the contents of draft bills (see Case Study 7).

Scrutinizing secondary legislation in committees

The Lords has a reputation for examining the detail, not only of bills, but also of secondary legislation. This takes place in three main committees: the Joint Committee on Statutory Instruments (JCSI); the Secondary Legislation Scrutiny Committee (SLSC); and the Delegated Powers and Regulatory Reform Committee. Should one or more of these committees draw attention to a specific piece of secondary legislation or delegated power, the relevant report is drawn to the attention of the House at the appropriate moment, such as when a statutory instrument (SI) is about to be approved, or when a clause in a bill containing powers for a minister to create an SI is being debated. In certain circumstances draft secondary legislation must be explicitly approved by the House (Case Study 19).

The JCSI is appointed to consider SIs which are put before Parliament because of provisions in a piece of primary legislation. It does not assess the merits of these SIs, or the underlying policy; that is the responsibility of other parliamentary committees. In most cases, before SIs can become law, they have to be presented to Parliament in draft, or 'laid before Parliament' for approval or for a Member to object. The Standing Orders state that the Committee is able to refer an SI to both Houses if:

- it is poorly drafted;
- it appears to have retrospective effect without the express authority of the parent legislation;
- there appears to have been unjustifiable delay in publishing an instrument or laying it before Parliament; or
- there are any other reasons which do not impinge upon the merits of the SI or the policy behind it.

It is the SLSC which examines the policy merits of Regulations and other types of secondary legislation that are subject to parliamentary procedure. It normally considers SIs within 12 to 16 days of them having been laid before Parliament. This leaves enough time for Members of the House to pursue any issues raised in the report by asking a question or tabling a motion for debate within the 40-day period in which a Member may lay a motion to reject negative instruments (which is known somewhat confusingly as a 'prayer'). Through its reports, the Committee draws to the 'special attention of the House' any SI laid in the previous week which it considers may be interesting, flawed, or inadequately explained by the government. The Committee also scrutinizes Public Bodies Orders to consider whether they meet the conditions set out in section eight of the Public Bodies Act 2011; these require the minister to demonstrate that the Order improves the efficiency, effectiveness, economy, and accountability of public functions.

The Delegated Powers and Regulatory Reform Committee is different to the JCSI and the SLSC in that its focus is the delegated powers contained in *draft* primary legislation which relate to secondary legislation. The remit of the Committee is 'to report whether the provisions of any bill inappropriately delegate legislative power, or whether they subject the exercise of legislative power to an inappropriate degree of parliamentary scrutiny' (UK Parliament 2017). Delegated powers are frequently included in government bills. These powers allow ministers to use 'delegated legislation' (usually in the form of SIs) to do things which would otherwise require primary legislation. The powers are often practical and sensible: for example, a bill may set out all the key elements of a policy, but allow a minister to make minor modifications to the policy as circumstances change over time, by making a set of regulations.

The Committee considers bills when they are introduced into the Lords. The government provide a memorandum for each bill, identifying each of the delegations, their purpose, the justification for leaving the matter to delegated legislation, and explaining why they consider the proposed level of parliamentary oversight to be appropriate. The Committee examines whether the delegations in each bill are appropriate, being careful to restrict its consideration to the delegation in question, and not the merits of the overall policy. The Committee's recommendations are made in reports to the House, usually before the start of the Committee stage of the bill.

Investigative committees

Unlike in the Commons, select committees in the House of Lords do not shadow the work of government departments. Their inquiries are generally longer and focus on specialist subjects in detail, making the most of members' expertise. They are generally made up of between 12 and 19 members who are appointed by the Committee of Selection. This committee is made up of the leaders of the main parliamentary groups, the Convenor of the cross-bench peers, the Senior Deputy Speaker, and a number of backbenchers.

There are currently six main select committees in the House of Lords:

- the European Union Committee (with six thematic subcommittees);
- the Science and Technology Committee;
- the Communications Committee;
- the Constitution Committee;
- the Economic Affairs Committee (with an annual Finance Bill Sub-Committee); and
- the International Relations Committee.

These are known as 'sessional' committees as they are reappointed at the start of each parliamentary session. They carry out multiple inquiries and have a reputation for revisiting issues on a regular basis. The committees comprise Members with relevant expertise in a particular area (see Chapter 23), and each one conducts inquiries on issues within their terms of reference. The inquiries operate in a similar fashion to Commons committees, with a public call for evidence, written submissions, oral witnesses, and a final report. The government will normally respond to a report, either in the form of a Command Paper, a document which is laid before Parliament, or by sending the response directly to a committee. The government have undertaken to reply within two months of the publication of reports wherever possible, but they may ask a committee to agree to an extension. In specific cases, where reports' recommendations affect bodies outside government—such as the European Commission—a committee will receive responses from more than one source.

 Parliamentary terms   Command paper

Government documents, such as White Papers, which are presented to Parliament.

In recent years, the House has appointed ad hoc committees, such as the Committee on Sexual Violence in Conflict and the Committee on the Long-term Sustainability of the NHS, to look at issues outside the subject areas covered by the sessional committees. Members of the House can propose topics for these ad hoc committees by drafting submissions for consideration by the Liaison Committee. This Committee has a similar membership to that of the Committee of Selection. The advent of ad hoc committees has allowed the House to instigate timely inquiries into topical issues as they arise.

Questions

Members can ask questions orally or in writing. Ministers may also be asked to respond to debates on topical issues. In the 2015–16 session, peers asked 8,842 oral and written questions (House of Lords 2016, 2). A 30-minute Question Time takes place at the start of business in the Chamber from Monday to Thursday. A maximum of four questions on different topics are directed at the government, and the relevant minister in the House will answer the question from the despatch box. Following the initial question there is a chance for a short exchange of related, or 'supplementary', questions. The government minister must answer each one. Peers can also submit written questions pertaining to areas of government responsibility, which are expected to be answered within two weeks. All questions and responses are published in Hansard. Occasionally, government ministers may make important policy announcements or deliver updates on national and international issues in the Lords Chamber. This is done through a ministerial statement, such as the details of a recent European Council meeting or a substantial change in domestic policy (see, for instance, HL Debates, 26 June 2017, c. 175). Statements made in the Commons are often repeated in the Lords, and there will be time for short questions or comments by peers afterwards.

Debates

Given the considerable experience and expertise of many Members of the Lords, debates in the Chamber can be particularly valuable and informative. In the 2015–16 session, 345 hours of debates were held in the Chamber (House of Lords 2016, 1).
Debates fall into three main categories:

- General debates: Usually held on Thursdays, this may be one long debate or a number of shorter debates lasting around five hours in total. Each party receives opportunities to initiate general debates, and backbench peers may also propose subjects for debate.

- Short debates: Usually taking place at the end of business or during meal times, short debates are around 60 to 90 minutes long. Since October 2013, peers have the opportunity to debate a topical question in a short, one-hour debate every Thursday. Frontbench and backbench peers can propose subjects for these debates by submitting a form of words to the Table Office. Provided a number of criteria are met, such as topicality, recent coverage in the press, and government responsibility, the entries are included in a blind ballot.

- Debates on committee reports or general issues which can take place on any sitting day.

Members from all sides of the House can take part in debates, and a government minister responds to the points peers have made at the end of the discussion.

EU scrutiny

The House of Lords has a well-known reputation for in-depth scrutiny of EU policy and draft legislative proposals, as explained in Chapter 10. The sheer volume of reports and correspondence to UK ministers on draft EU legislative proposals is greater than in any other parliamentary Chamber in the EU. The main work of EU scrutiny in the House of Lords takes place in the EU Select Committee. The EU Committee is made up of seven committees: a large select committee made up of 19 members, and six subcommittees appointed by the main select committee, each dealing with different policy areas.

The EU Select Committee is responsible for overseeing the work of six subcommittees. In addition, it may carry out cross-cutting inquiries, such as Brexit and parliamentary scrutiny (European Union Committee 2016d). The Committee takes oral evidence from government ministers and others, including European Commissioners and MEPs.

The six subcommittees conduct inquiries into more specific policy areas, carrying out detailed scrutiny of EU proposals and raising any concerns they may have directly with government ministers. This ensures that decision-making is transparent, something which is particularly important if the committees believe that there are any pressing legal or political issues involved. For example, the Energy and Environment Sub-Committee engages with the government on an annual basis on the subject of fishing quotas and the political agreement at EU-level which dictates how much of each stock can be landed by UK fisheries. The six subcommittees are:

- EU Financial Affairs Sub-Committee;
- EU Internal Market Sub-Committee;
- EU External Affairs Sub-Committee;
- EU Energy and Environment Sub-Committee;
- EU Justice Sub-Committee;
- EU Home Affairs Sub-Committee.

The result of the EU referendum in June 2016 provided an opportunity for the subcommittees to conduct short, topical investigations into the key issues that are involved in the negotiations on Brexit, such as fisheries (European Union Committee 2016a), UK–Irish relations (European Union Committee 2016b), and the future trade relationship between the UK and the EU (European Union Committee 2016c).

The committees' scrutiny work is underpinned by a 'Scrutiny Reserve Resolution' which has been agreed by the House. This resolution means that the Committee must finish its scrutiny before the government can formally agree to it.

The 2009 Treaty on European Union requires national parliaments to monitor proposed EU laws for compliance with the principle of 'subsidiarity'. This principle means that action should only be taken at EU level if it cannot be taken effectively at a lower level, whether this be national, regional, or local. It thus ensures that decisions are taken as closely as possible to citizens. If the EU Committee believes that a proposal breaches the principle of subsidiarity, it invites the House of Lords to agree to what is known as a Reasoned Opinion. This is, in effect, a 'yellow card'; if other national parliaments offer similar opinions, the European Commission will review the proposal and publish an official response (see Chapter 10). Since the procedure was established in 2009, three proposals have gathered the requisite number of Reasoned Opinions from parliamentary chambers to solicit a response from the European Commission. These concerned collective action rights for workers (May 2012), regulation on the establishment of the European Public Prosecutor's Office (October 2013), and revisions to the Posted Workers Directive concerning workers sent to another country by their employer (May 2016).

Conclusion

Members of the House of Lords spend a considerable amount of their time scrutinizing policy, whether this be primary legislation from the government, secondary legislation, or EU proposals. Scrutiny in the Lords also takes place through questions to the government and debates. It has some very prominent differences to the House of Commons, and this makes its work very distinctive to observe. Of particular note here are its practices of self-regulation and the greater freedom for the consideration of amendments. This means that, as Case Study 19 demonstrates in detail (see also Case Study 8), the Lords very often plays a key role in holding the government to account and in forcing the government to make concessions on measures of public policy.

Further Reading

EVENNETT, H. (2016) *Delegated Legislation in the House of Lords since 1997*, House of Lords Library Note LLN 2016/001, 5 January. Online at: http://researchbriefings.files.parliament. uk/documents/LLN-2016-0001/LLN-2016-0001.pdf [accessed 27 June 2017].

LIAISON COMMITTEE (2016) *Investigative Select Committee Activity in Session 2015–16: 1st Report of Session 2016–17*, London: The Stationery Office, HL Paper 26. Online at: https://www. publications.parliament.uk/pa/ld201617/ldselect/ldliaisn/26/26.pdf [accessed 27 June 2017].

RUSSELL, M. (2013) *The Contemporary House of Lords: Westminster Bicameralism Revived*, Oxford: Oxford University Press.

TORRENCE, M. (2015) *Select Committees in the House of Lords*, House of Lords Library Note LLN 2015/057, 3 November. Online at: http://researchbriefings.files.parliament.uk/documents/ LLN-2016-0057/LLN-2016-0057.pdf [accessed 27 June 2017].

Case Study 19: The House of Lords and Tax Credits

Tax Credits are a form of benefit introduced by the 1997 Labour government to help low-paid families. The present system dates from 2003 and includes: Working Tax Credit (WTC) for those in work, and Child Tax Credit (CTC) for those with children. The government's draft Tax Credits (Income Thresholds and Determination of Rates) (Amendment) Regulations 2015 sought to change the income threshold for WTCs from £6,420 to £3,850, and the income threshold for those only claiming CTCs from £16,105 to £12,125. Politically this change was very controversial and it attracted widespread attention both inside and outside Parliament (see Ross 2015). As a draft statutory instrument (SI), the approval of both Houses was required before it could pass into law. The House of Lords does not normally object to SIs passage to the statute book and, in fact, until October 2015, it had rejected only five SIs since the Second World War. This case study examines how the Lords reacted to this controversial SI and its consequences.

THE LORDS' DEBATE ON TAX CREDIT REGULATIONS

The draft Tax Credits (Income Thresholds and Determination of Rates) (Amendment) Regulations 2015 were debated in the House of Lords on Monday 26 October 2015. Unusually for this type of SI, the main debate took place in the Chamber, and four amendments were tabled to the government's motion to approve it.

The first amendment, in the name of Liberal Democrat peer Baroness Manzoor, was clearly a 'fatal' amendment. This is where the wording of an amendment is specifically designed to prevent the SI from becoming law. In this case, the amendment would have amended the motion to read: 'this House declines to approve the draft regulations laid before the House on 7 September'. This was defeated: 99 contents to 310 not contents (see HL Debates, 26 October 2015, Division 1).

The second amendment, in the name of cross-bench peer Baroness Meacher, stated that 'this House declines to consider the draft regulations laid before the House on 7 September until the government lay a report before the House, detailing their response to the analysis of the draft regulations by the Institute for Fiscal Studies, and considering possible mitigating action'. This amendment was passed: 307 contents to 277 not contents (HL Debates, 26 October 2015, Division 2). Consequently the SI could not pass into law immediately, and it led to disagreement about whether this had killed the SI or simply delayed it.

The third amendment, in the name of Labour peer Baroness Hollis of Heigham, was identical to that of Baroness Meacher, with an additional proposal that transitional arrangements be introduced for those affected by the change in policy. This amendment was also passed: 289 contents to 272 not contents (see HL Debates, 26 October 2015, Division 3). As half of the Hollis amendment had the same effect as the Meacher amendment, it was in effect substituted for Baroness Meacher's. The debate then focused on whether this combined amendment was 'fatal' or 'non-fatal'.

There was widespread disagreement about the appropriateness and effect of the actions the House took. The debate centred on three areas:

Whether it was appropriate for the House not to pass the SI

The Parliament Acts do not apply to SIs. This means that the Lords has the same power as the Commons over SIs which are laid before it. If the Lords agrees a fatal amendment to an SI, it does not become law (or ceases to be law), regardless of the Commons' view. This is confirmed by the *Companion to the Standing Orders*, the procedural handbook of the House (House of Lords 2017), and the Joint Committee on Conventions (2006) report on SIs. There is no formal mechanism for resolving differences between the Houses on SIs.

Whether it was appropriate for the House not to pass a measure that deals solely with taxation or public spending

The House of Lords' power over bills which concern only taxation or expenditure (and certain related matters) is limited by section 1 of the Parliament Act 1911. Any bill certified as a Money Bill by the Commons Speaker must be passed unamended by the House of Lords within one month. Its power over other bills dealing with money is limited by convention rather than statute. While the financial privilege of the Commons rests on clear resolutions, there are fewer sources of authority governing how the Lords deals with SIs which concern only taxation or expenditure. This may in part be because at the time the key measures about Commons financial primacy were passed (1670s and 1911), SIs did not exist in the form they do today.

Whether the amendments agreed to were fatal or non-fatal

Baroness Manzoor's amendment was clearly fatal, but there was debate about the effect of the two amendments that were agreed. Some argued that they did not kill the SI but merely temporarily prevented it becoming law. Those making this case argued that it could pass in future if certain conditions were met. Others argued that the House had a choice of whether or not to approve the draft SI, and the effect of the amendments was not to approve it.

The government was clearly unhappy about the way the House had dealt with the SI in question, and the Chancellor of the Exchequer made public statements about how the episode had raised 'constitutional issues' (BBC News 2015). The next day (Tuesday 27 October 2015), the government announced a review into the powers of the House of Lords in relation to secondary legislation. The review was led by a former leader of the House, Lord Strathclyde, with a remit to examine how the government might 'secure their business in Parliament' and 'how to secure the decisive role of the elected Commons in relation to its primacy on financial matters and secondary legislation' (see HM Government 2015, 25). The findings were published on Thursday 17 December 2015 and recommended that the government enshrine in statute a procedure for the House of Commons to insist on the safe passage of secondary legislation, in effect overriding the House of Lords. The government announced the following year that they would not bring forward legislation to this effect (HL Debates, 17 November 2016, cc. 1538–40).

The House of Lords has not dealt with an SI in a similar manner since, but there is widespread speculation about how a Chamber with much more confidence will interact with future controversial proposals in secondary legislation, particularly on measures relating to Brexit. Parliamentary procedure is seldom straightforward, but the Tax Credits controversy of 2015 demonstrated that where there is a will, procedure can be used inventively to almost any end.

Primary Sources

- House of Lords Order Paper for Monday 26 October 2015. Online at: https://www.publications.parliament.uk/pa/ld201516/minutes/151026/ldordpap.htm [accessed 27 June 2017].

- House of Lords Debate on Tax Credits (Income Thresholds and Determination of Rates) (Amendment) Regulations 2015 (HL Debates, 26 October 2015, cc. 976–1042). Online at: https://www.publications.parliament.uk/pa/ld201516/ldhansrd/text/151026-0001.htm#1510269000354 [accessed 27 June 2017].

- House of Lords (2016) *The Standing Orders of the House of Lords Relating to Public Business*, London: House of Lords, HL Paper 3. Online at: https://www.parliament.uk/documents/publications-records/House-of-Lords-Publications/Rules-guides-for-business/Standing-order-public-business/Standing-Orders-Public.pdf [accessed 27 June 2017].

- Tax Credits (Income Thresholds and Determination of Rates) (Amendment) Regulations 2015. Online at: http://www.legislation.gov.uk/ukdsi/2015/9780111138946 [accessed 27 June 2017].

- UK Government (2016) *Government Response to the Strathclyde Review: Secondary Legislation and the Primacy of the House of Commons and the Related Select Committee Reports*, London: The Stationery Office, Cm 9363. Online at: http://qna.files.parliament.uk/ws-attachments/649308/original/Strathclyde%20response%20(1).pdf [accessed 27 June 2017].

FURTHER CASE STUDIES

- The Strathclyde Review into secondary legislation and the primacy of the House of Commons (2015).
- The Great Repeal Bill and delegated legislation.
- The government's use of an SI to permit fracking under English National Parks and World Heritage Sites through the Onshore Hydraulic Fracturing (Protected Areas) Regulations 2015.

References

BBC News (2015) 'Osborne: "House of Lords vote raises constitutional issues"', *BBC News*, 27 October. Online at: http://www.bbc.co.uk/news/av/uk-politics-34650659/osborne-house-of-lords-vote-raises-constitutional-issues [accessed 27 June 2017].

European Union Committee (2016a) *Brexit: Fisheries: 8th Report of Session 2016–17*, London: The Stationery Office, HL 78. Online at: https://www.publications.parliament.uk/pa/ld201617/ldselect/ldeucom/78/78.pdf [accessed 27 June 2017].

European Union Committee (2016b) *Brexit: UK–Irish Relations: 6th Report of Session 2016–17*, London: The Stationery Office, HL 76. Online at: https://www.publications.parliament.uk/pa/ld201617/ldselect/ldeucom/76/76.pdf [accessed 27 June 2017].

European Union Committee (2016c) *Brexit: The Options for Trade: 5th Report of Session 2016–17*, London: The Stationery Office, HL 72. Online at: https://www.publications.parliament.uk/pa/ld201617/ldselect/ldeucom/72/72.pdf [accessed 27 June 2017].

European Union Committee (2016d) *Brexit: Parliamentary Scrutiny: 4th Report of Session 2016–17*, London: The Stationery Office, HL 50. Online at: https://publications.parliament.uk/pa/ld201617/ldselect/ldeucom/50/50.pdf [accessed 18 July 2017].

HM Government (2015) *Strathclyde Review: Secondary Legislation and the Primacy of the House of Commons*, London: The Stationery Office, Cm 9177. Online at: https://www.gov.uk/government/uploads/system/uploads/attachment_data/file/486790/53088_Cm_9177_Web_Accessible.pdf [accessed 18 July 2017].

House of Lords (2016) *Statistics on Business and Membership: Session 2015–16*, London: House of Lords. Online at: http://www.parliament.uk/documents/publications-records/House-of-Lords-Publications/Records-activities-and-membership/Business-membership-statistics/HL-Sessional-Statistics-on-Business-and-Membership-2015-16.pdf [accessed 27 June 2017].

House of Lords (2017) *Companion to the Standing Orders and Guide to the Proceedings of the House of Lords*, London: House of Lords. Online at: https://publications.parliament.uk/pa/ld/ldcomp/compso2017/compso02.htm [accessed 23 August 2017].

Joint Committee on Conventions (2006) *Conventions of the UK Parliament: Report of Session 2005–06*, London: The Stationery Office, HC 1212-I, HL Paper 265-I. Online at: https://www.publications.parliament.uk/pa/jt200506/jtselect/jtconv/265/265.pdf [accessed 27 June 2017].

Ross, T. (2015) 'Cabinet in crisis as ministers turn on George Osborne and his tax credit letter timed to ruin Christmas', *The Telegraph*, 24 October. Online at: http://www.telegraph.
co.uk/news/politics/georgeosborne/11953344/Cabinet-in-crisis-as-ministers-turn-on-
George-Osborne-and-his-tax-credit-letter-timed-to-ruin-Christmas.html [accessed 27
June 2017].

UK Parliament (2017) *Delegated Powers and Regulatory Reform Committee—Role of the
Committee*. Online at: http://www.parliament.uk/business/committees/committees-a-z/lords-
select/delegated-powers-and-regulatory-reform-committee/role/ [accessed 28 October 2016].

20

Media Scrutiny of Parliament

Mark D'Arcy

INTRODUCTION

It is a familiar lament that the reporting of Parliament has declined and continues to decline. This chapter argues that although coverage of law-making and scrutiny in Parliament may be sporadic even in the heavyweight newspapers, that complaint is over-focused on traditional media. Look elsewhere, and it becomes possible to argue that, quite unexpectedly, we live in a new golden age of public access to Parliament.

The changing coverage of Parliament

The days when all major newspapers routinely featured Hansard-style reports of debates are long gone. Writing in the1970s, Sir Gerald Kaufman noted that he expected ministers to 'do quite well' out of the gallery reporters who report parliamentary debates, but by 1997 much less of their material was printed, 'objective reporting of parliamentary proceedings now being regarded as a bore' (Kaufman 1997, 152). Mainstream coverage of Parliament now tends to focus on points of contention. In recent Budgets, for example, interest has tended to focus on such issues as the proposal to cut Tax Credits (the 2015 Budget and the constitutional aftershocks when the Lords asked MPs to think again—see Case Study 19), the proposal to impose higher probate fees (the 2017 Budget), or the proposed 'pasty tax' on hot food (the 2012 'Omnishambles Budget'), precisely because these were issues where rebellion was threatened.

 Parliamentary terms Hansard

The Official Report: the official record of debates in each House.

There was a telling example of this when the Treasury Committee (2012) quizzed the Chancellor, George Osborne, on the 2012 Budget. He was asked probing questions on his economic strategy, but what caught the media attention was Labour MP John Mann asking when he last ate a Greggs pasty. His answer led to him being denounced as 'out of touch' by commentators (e.g. Chorley and Merrick 2012). The incident demonstrated not just that rebellion is inherently more interesting than serene agreement, but also that the whole brew is best served with a dash of populism.

The mainstream media also seeks parliamentary stories which relate to its particular agendas: Brexit, gay marriage, and internet surveillance powers, for example. And then there is the quirky, the emotionally charged, or the entertaining—Lords Question Time is a reliable source of quirkiness, and more recent intakes of MPs have given emotional speeches discussing their experience of mental illness, the suicide of a family member, the loss of a child, and similar highly charged issues in ways which would have been unimaginable a few years ago. These speeches have attracted considerable attention. There are also occasions where events in Parliament dramatize an existing narrative about politics. The classic example is expenses abuse, such as the expenses scandal in 2009, which fed the perception that 'they're only in it for what they can get', and had an enormous impact on the institution and its MPs (see Case Study 31). Finally, there are moments when a leader fails to attract support in the Chamber, or there is visible hostility between cabinet colleagues, which are now much easier to report, because the footage can be replayed at length.

Readers will note that what is not in this list is systematic scrutiny of legislation during its passage through Parliament. For example, the press bench is normally deserted in Commons public bill committees, which scrutinize the detail of bills. As long ago as 1983, the then Employment Minister Alan Clark recorded of a standing committee: 'for a start (good) there are never any press there, so gaffes and cock-ups go unreported. The Official Report is printed late, and by the time it's out, nobody bothers' (Clark 1993). Although legislative committees are today very different (see Chapter 9), they still lack media attention.

On the other hand, for those who do want to follow Parliament, there is now more public access than at any time in history. Live coverage (mostly of the Commons Chamber) is now available on BBC Parliament, while the full panoply of Commons, Lords, Westminster Hall, and Moses Room sittings, plus committee hearings can be viewed on the much-expanded Parliament TV online video service (www.parliamentlive.tv), both live and as archived recordings. This has implications for media reporting of proceedings and for the media's role in the way the public receives information about Parliament.

Journalistic scrutiny

But does greater access to parliamentary proceedings amount to effective scrutiny? The key issue is interpretation. The procedures are often impenetrable, counter-intuitive, and laden with jargon. A more subtle cultural point is that parliamentarians work inside a very particular subculture within which it is perfectly normal for MPs to switch from finger-jabbing confrontation to blokey friendship without missing a beat. It is entirely understandable to those who grasp that politicians have to both demonstrate tribal fealty and build alliances across party lines, but it can be incomprehensible to outsiders.

So how do journalists who are, up to a point, insiders, go about reporting Parliament? The first task for any parliamentary reporter is to study the Order Papers—or agendas—of the two Houses and identify what is of interest. And because they are rather barebones documents, this has to be 'intelligence-led'—informed by briefings from MPs involved in particular events. What will be the crucial amendment in a bill committee or in a report stage debate? When will it be debated? Might someone break party ranks? Is a select committee witness going to be given a hard time? These conversations (which are increasingly supplemented by watching what parliamentarians post on social media) are the lifeblood of parliamentary reporting, but they require the background knowledge to spot potential stories and ask the right questions of the right people.

The increasing audience

One measure of public interest is the viewing figures for live broadcasts of the Commons on BBC Parliament, and the listening figures for Radio 4's venerable round-up, *Today in*

Parliament. Before the Iraq invasion, in 2003, BBC figures showed that BBC Parliament attracted about 700,000 viewers a year. Interest in the Iraq debates tripled that figure, and although viewing subsided a little in the years after the invasion, it remains well above pre-Iraq levels and is creeping upwards. Today the viewing figures are around 2.1 million people per year. This also reflects increased accessibility, with more people able to watch on Freeview and satellite, but a tripling of audience in the modern broadcasting environment is unique.

It is reasonable to assume that viewers want unmediated coverage of great events, perhaps driven by distrust of the way they are reported. But the fact that the figures did not slump back to their pre–Iraq levels is harder to interpret. Tony Grew, a veteran of the Westminster Press Gallery and founder of @ParlyApp (a Twitter account that follows parliamentary proceedings), suggests public interest in Parliament at least partly reflects the government majority in the Commons. Interest flagged when the first two Blair governments enjoyed vast majorities, but revived when Labour lost ground in the 2005 election and MPs became increasingly rebellious. The novel circumstances of the Coalition years sustained interest—and the narrow Conservative majority of 2015 created a third successive government vulnerable to Commons uprisings, then followed by the 2017 hung parliament with an even more vulnerable government. It is certainly not over-speculative to suggest that Brexit will keep interest high. When actions in Parliament matter so much, viewing of its proceedings is likely to increase.

Parliamentlive.tv offers a new route for public access. Relaunched in the spring of 2015, it offers up to 20 streams of live coverage from the Commons and Lords Chambers and, crucially, from their committees. It also provides on-demand video or audio of all proceedings going back to 2007—an enormous resource. This has given select committees a far greater audience, as Figure 20.1 shows. In 2016, the number of people watching commons select committees on parliamentlive.tv passed the 1 million mark for the first time. The most watched event was the Treasury Select Committee (2016) hearing when Boris Johnson was questioned about the economic case for Brexit on 23 March 2016. This attracted 35,605 viewers (Parliament TV 2016).

An important technical point is that the relaunch allowed users to access the service on tablets and mobile phones. This is significant, because 30 per cent of smartphone owners

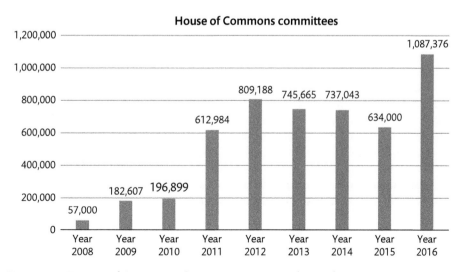

Figure 20.1 Viewing of Commons Select Committees on Parliamentlive.tv
Source: UK Parliament (2016)

use their device as their primary news source (Wakefield 2016) and the figure rises to 42 per cent when considering the age group 18 to 34. Interestingly, Westminster Hall debates attract a high proportion of mobile and tablet users. Westminster Hall is the Commons parallel debating chamber, where issues are discussed and ministers respond, but no votes are held. These debates can be on subjects selected by the Backbench Business Committee on the basis of cross-party interest and topicality or adjournment debates, chosen by the Speaker, or they can be debates on e-petitions, scheduled by the new Petitions Committee.

The increasing role of new media

The Hansard Society's 14th *Audit of Political Engagement*—an annual opinion poll tracing attitudes towards Parliament found that e-petitions are now the second most popular mode of public engagement with Parliament (after watching proceedings on TV or the internet), with 22 per cent of respondents claiming to have created or signed an e-petition on the Parliamentary petition website. A further 40 per cent were prepared to sign a petition if they were motivated by a particular concern (Hansard Society 2017, 32).

As Chapter 30 shows in more detail, there is increasing evidence that e-petitions have become a particularly important route for channelling new media interest in specific issues into engagement with Parliament. In its report on its first year in operation, the Commons Petitions Select Committee (2016) noted that 48 per cent of signatories reached the e-petitions website via social media (30 per cent typed the address into a browser, 10 per cent reached it via a search engine, and 12 per cent via links from other websites). And viewers of petition debates have been attracted by hashtag-based social media campaigns. The #WASPI petition (Women Against State Pension Inequality), debated on 1 February 2016, is a very good example of a campaign successfully raised through Twitter. Not all petition debates attract the same level of attention on social media, but in some cases this has clearly contributed to wider engagement with Parliament (Asher, Leston-Bandeira, and Spaiser 2017).

Anecdotally, the effect of this seems to be both to bring issues before MPs that might not have been debated in previous eras, and to attract far more MPs to take part—and perhaps attempt a more emotional speech, because they are increasingly aware that significant numbers will be watching. This is turn piques media interest and perhaps shifts attention onto issues not driven by the internal Westminster agenda.

E-petition debates have become an important driver of views of parliamentlive.tv, because Westminster Hall proceedings are not normally broadcast live elsewhere. The debate on a petition calling for a second EU referendum in September 2016 saw 111,000 unique viewers. The e-petition on legalizing cannabis generated 110,523 (Parliament TV 2016). By disseminating a link to the video stream, just as the debate started, online users were encouraged to watch and share, and, unusually, they watched the live feed of the Second Referendum Petition debate for an average 45 minutes. The fact that petitioners are prepared to spend time following up the issue suggests their engagement was more than mere 'clicktivism'.

There are limitations to the parliamentlive.tv service—there is no captioning of speakers and no attempt to explain procedure. The principal value of petitions debates is that they air a concern and that the government has to respond; but it is often not appreciated that the debate will not culminate in a vote, still less a change in government policy. At most it might encourage a rethink, but it is not clear that those who watch the proceedings always understand this point. Asher, Leston-Bandeira, and Spaiser (2017) show that, for instance, supporters of the grouse shooting petition became very disillusioned with Parliament as they were observing the debate of this petition in Parliament.

Similarly, since 2010, the Backbench Business Committee has given ordinary MPs debating time for issues of cross-party concern, as Case Study 18 explains. Again this mechanism allows an airing for subjects that would not otherwise be debated. It is frequently used by all-party parliamentary groups to publicize their causes and, equally importantly, extract a response from ministers. These endeavours are increasingly promoted on social media—which pushes them onto the radar of the mainstream media.

A third area attracting increasing social media attention is private members' bills. In the 2016–17 session there was intense social media interest in the bill from the SNP MP John Nicolson, to pardon gay men for historic sexual offences that would no longer be considered a crime (see Case Study 20). The government developed concerns that it could, unintentionally, pardon historic child sex offenders, and it was 'talked out' by Conservative MPs who kept speaking to prevent it being voted on. This rather arcane tactic baffled many viewers—and it highlights the need to explain the intricate framework within which MPs and peers operate. Again, high levels of social media comment have pushed this kind of incident higher up the mainstream media agenda.

A mission to explain?

A key role for the parliamentary media is to explain what is happening. Is a particular vote the last word on a question? Can the Lords override the Commons? Why are MPs suddenly making interminable speeches in a debate on some innocuous private members' bill? The upper House is probably the area where explanation is most necessary. Given the increasingly independent-minded behaviour of peers, which translated into 98 defeats for the government during the two years of the 2015 Parliament, their activities deserve far more attention than they actually get. The biggest understanding gap is over what happens after the government has lost a vote on some extremely detailed point of legislation. That is far from the end of the story. Not only must parliamentary reporters describe the public part of the process, with votes to insist on amendments or offer amendments in lieu, they must also attempt to detect and explain the behind the scenes events, and the peculiar in-house psychology of the Lords, where many peers have deep inhibitions about pushing challenges to the Commons too far. The presentation of these battles in the media is important to the peers challenging the government, because it can influence wavering MPs, and perhaps pressurize ministers into a compromise to avoid embarrassment in the Commons. Labour peers are active in pushing their views via a blog (www.labourlords.org.uk/blog) which frequently sets out their views on legislation which is in play, and via the @LabourLordsUK Twitter feed.

And the issues involved can be very significant. When peers voted to, in effect, refer back £4.4 billion in Tax Credit cuts to the Commons, they blew a huge hole in the then Chancellor George Osborne's budget strategy, provoking a threat from the government to curtail their powers—but had the government attempted to reject their decision, they may have faced a serious Commons rebellion, because of the considerable publicity given to the effects of the cuts. Since the EU referendum, some commentators have suggested that the overwhelmingly Europhile Lords might find some way to block Brexit (e.g. Bush 2017). That probably underestimates peers' inhibitions around their status as an appointed, not elected, House—but it is certainly a sincerely held concern.

Procedural issues can baffle the vast online commentariat operating around Parliament. Much of the comment is highly partisan, but it does influence mainstream journalists, who seek outside comment as an antidote to their own presence in the 'Westminster bubble'. Some of the online coverage is accurate, but some is uninformed or just plain wrong. Some is even malicious—for example, the *Spectator*'s Isabel Hardman

(2014) debunked the Twitter meme of pictures of a packed Commons 'debating MPs' pay' and an empty House 'debating welfare cuts'. She demonstrated that this was 'fake news' and that the pictures were not actually of the debates claimed. So there is a clear 'mission to explain' and sometimes even a 'mission to debunk' for those Westminster journalists who understand parliamentary procedure. Sites like the BBC's Parliament Live and @ParlyApp, among others, perform this service, both with instant commentary and also longer analysis pieces.

New media, new comment

BBC figures reveal considerable interest in the working of Parliament, and, since the EU referendum, about the process of Brexit—a story entitled 'Commons vote to ratify Brexit very likely, says No 10' (BBC News 2016a) attracted 1,077,856 hits from unique users. Another, 'Sturgeon tells May she's not bluffing over referendum', attracted 1,014,736 (BBC News 2016b). More frivolously, a story from PMQs, entitled 'PM's innuendo in response to MP Peter Bone prompts laughter', attracted 485,616 hits (BBC News 2016c). An article on the BBC website by this author on the procedural manoeuvres which cornered the Conservative leadership into committing to the EU referendum, dealing with such arcana as the Backbench Business Committee and the Speaker's ruling allowing an additional amendment in the 2013 Queen's Speech debate, attracted 339,000 views in just over a week (D'Arcy 2016). The impression from this data is that there can be considerable interest in the most high-profile policy and process issues, but that people also enjoy stories about personalities and comedic moments.

New media like *BuzzFeed*, the *Huffington Post*, and *Politico*, which tend to be less reverent about Parliament than the 'Dead Tree Press', have joined the press lobby and all of them are seeking more than one press pass—a sign their readers are interested in Parliament and politics. *BuzzFeed*, for example, offers a blend of fairly standard straight political reporting and comment, and items like 'We Used That Viral Face App On 13 Politicians And It Will Make You Say "Nope"' (Le Conte 2017). The key difference between their activities and the traditional media is that they are extremely sensitive to the number of page views they attract—giving them a hard populist edge and a determination to be eye-catching at all times. The 'damburst moment' for the new media probably came when a reporter from the *Guido Fawkes* website was admitted to lobby briefings— the inner sanctum of the parliamentary press system, where the prime minister's official spokesperson briefs journalists and takes questions—giving them the same access as the traditional players.

 Parliamentary terms Lobby briefings

Briefings from 10 Downing Street press officials to journalists accredited to work in, and report from, the Parliamentary Estate. Includes a mixture of non-attributable briefings and on the record quotes from the Prime Minister's Spokesman.

The 2009 expenses scandal may have been broken by a traditional newspaper, the *Daily Telegraph*, but it also provided a feast for bloggers. They led a tidal wave of criticism which swept several MPs from Parliament and led to a complete change in the culture around expenses, and above all a sharp fall in public respect for Parliament and parliamentarians. It would not have happened without a massive leak of confidential data—and it led to individual politicians being skewered for their expenses claims, often with extensive and embarrassing quotes from their correspondence with the then Commons Fees Office. The bloggers piled in to elaborate on individual cases, pursue the MPs involved, and speculate on their possible imprisonment or deselection.

However, thanks to the internet, Parliament is also able to provide more neutral online sources of information and to present these directly to the public, rather than through the mediation of the press. For instance, its website (www.parliament.uk) offers a wealth of documentation—including *Hansard* reports of debates and committee hearings, and select committee reports and evidence. Impressively, there has been a 459.3 per cent increase in the viewing of *Hansard* online. From April to July 2016, there were 1,751,260 page views of Hansard on the Parliament.uk website, compared to 381,293 in the same period in 2015 (UK Parliament 2016). This probably reflects a high-temperature period in politics, particularly the EU referendum campaign, and the impact of a systems upgrade which made the site 'device neutral' and its content easier to share, as well as the Petitions Committee's practice of sending links to relevant Commons proceedings to people who have signed petitions.

Independent websites like TheyWorkForYou.com and The Public Whip crunch data about MPs (including expenses returns) to allow voters an overview of their activities. A survey of TheyWorkForYou users found that 75.2 per cent were 'just browsing' with no particular questions in mind; 10.9 per cent wanted to contact their MP, via its WriteToThem service, 6.6 per cent visited for work purposes, and 3.1 per cent wanted to share the content via social media (MySociety 2015). The results suggested current events drove the subjects visitors searched for; the survey was conducted in the aftermath of the 2015 general election, when the pages most viewed were on the new Culture Secretary, John Whittingdale's voting record, and (then Labour Leadership candidate) Jeremy Corbyn's profile page. So, where once only those with the resources to conduct extensive paper-based research could profile the voting and speaking behaviour of parliamentarians, this information is now accessible to anyone—for the traditional parliamentary media it is now easy and routine, but it is just as available to the outside commentariat.

Conclusion

There is plenty of raw data available to inform the Greek chorus of online commentary which now surrounds the work of Parliament. Although some mourn the loss of parliamentary pages in the broadsheet newspapers, perhaps they're bemoaning the demise of the candle industry in the era of electric light—with real-time viewing and instant comment and analysis, parliamentary journalism may be entering a new golden age, with new strengths but also serious new weaknesses. For journalists, social media has altered the news cycle. As noted earlier, reporters now draw on online commentary on issues as they unfold, making the news itself interactive. For Parliament, the consequences of this mass commentary are less clear; Edmund Burke famously told the electors of Bristol (in 1774) that their representative owed them 'not his industry only, but his judgment; and he betrays, instead of serving you, if he sacrifices it to your opinion'. But Burke did not have voters who could read every word he uttered in the Commons, still less study and even replay his expression and body language in the Chamber, and comment in real time. When the Houses of Parliament burned down in 1834, the Prime Minister, Lord Melbourne, resisted the idea of taking over Buckingham Palace as its new home, on the argument that it would allow a vast public gallery for the Commons. He recalled the way raucous spectators intimidated the revolutionary French National Assembly; perhaps a twenty-first-century cyber-version of that issue is now surfacing. How effectively today's MPs and the media can cope, amidst the new cacophony of comment around Parliament, will determine the fate of the institution.

Further Reading

CREWE, E. (2005) *Lords of Parliament: Manners, Ritual and Politics*, Manchester: Manchester University Press.

McBRIDE, D. (2013) *Power Trip*, London: Biteback.

MARR, A. (2005) *My Trade: A Short History of British Journalism*, London: Macmillan.

MULLIN, C. (2010) *Decline and Fall: Diaries 2005–2010*, London: Profile Books.

SHIPMAN, S. (2016) *All Out War: The Full Story of how Brexit sank Britain's Political Class*, London: William Collins.

Case Study 20: John Nicolson's Sexual Offences (Pardons Etc.) PMB

When social media and Parliament collide, the result is often confusion and anger. This is frequently demonstrated when the public observe the private members' bill process in action. The mannered manoeuvrings and tactical game-playing are now watched by a wider audience than ever before, and they often baffle those who tune in for what they expect to be a serious debate on a cause dear to their hearts.

A classic example of this came with the battle over the SNP MP John Nicolson's private members' bill to pardon gay men with historic convictions for offences that would not be crimes now (it would cover an estimated 16,000 men). Mr Nicolson topped the Commons annual private members' bill ballot, giving him guaranteed debating time for the bill of his choice.

Mr Nicolson, an experienced journalist before entering Parliament, orchestrated an effective media campaign, with plenty of newspaper and TV coverage. He chose the first available debating slot for his Sexual Offences (Pardons Etc.) Bill on Friday 21 October 2016, and a social media campaign around the hashtag #TuringBill (a reference to the computer pioneer and wartime codebreaker Alan Turing, who committed suicide following a gross indecency conviction) drummed up interest.

There were 731,376 hits for a BBC politics website story explaining his bill (BBC News 2016d), and later 289,056 for a story on its failure to reach its second reading (BBC News 2016e). Behind the scenes, Nicolson was negotiating with ministers on the precise content of the bill, and found himself caught between the demands of pressure groups like Stonewall and the limits of what the government was prepared to do.

The government had originally supported his bill, but became concerned that a blanket pardon could, unintentionally, cover child sex offences. Mr Nicolson believed the bill already dealt with this point, and when agreement was not reached, the government whips organized a filibuster—a deliberate spinning out of debate—to kill this bill. Quite deliberately, private members' bills are vulnerable to these tactics. The normal time-limiting of Commons speeches does not apply, so if three or four MPs drone on long enough, they can use up the available debating time, without the bill being put to the vote. In that event it disappears into a parliamentary limbo from which few re-emerge (see Chapter 12 for more detail on private members' bill procedure).

The way to break through a filibuster is a 'closure motion'—a procedural motion that 'The Question Be Now Put'. But this requires the support of 100 MPs and, even if 'won' by 99 to 30, will fail without that level of support. So the promoter of a private members' bill must organize a minimum of 100 supporters to beat a filibuster.

Mr Nicolson didn't quite manage it. His closure motion was 'won' by 57 votes to nil, but fewer than 100 MPs having voted for it, it was not carried. And when debating time ran out the Justice Minister Sam Gyimah had been speaking for 25 minutes.

One notable feature of the final moments was the loud countdown provided by Mr Nicolson—aimed at the audience outside. Having monitored the growing outrage of his supporters he fuelled it by highlighting that time was running out. The SNP are adept at creating social media theatre in the Chamber—a more recent example was their rendition of the EU anthem, Beethoven's 'Ode to Joy', during a vote of the European Union (Notification of Withdrawal) Bill.

At first Twitter commentators were baffled, then (aided by some users explaining the concept of filibuster) outrage began to grow. Some commentators speculated about the government's reasoning. One Twitter commentator suggested:

> @foshtown There can be no doubt after #TuringBill and #chilcot that Lab&Con will literally vote to be gelded with a hot spoon rather than vote with SNP

Mr Nicolson took the opportunity to point Twitter users at an after the match interview he had recorded:

> @MrJohnNicolson I'm on 'Today in Parliament' tonight @BBCRadio4 explaining what happened to my #TuringBill. Tory MPs supported it. Minister talked it out.

A handful of people took to Twitter to defend the government and repeat the minister's argument that the Nicolson Bill risked extending pardons to child sex offenders:

> @Romford_stu #TuringBill let's cut the crap & left wing lies. The pardons are going ahead but the SNP paedo bill isn't.

There were retweets of the Commons Procedure Committee's (2016, 5) report on what it called the 'broken and discredited' private members' bill system. Much of the anger from Scottish observers was directed at Ruth Davidson, the gay leader of the Scottish Conservatives, and bitter condemnation was directed against Sam Gyimah, both on social media and in much of the extensive mainstream coverage—which frequently drew on tweets describing the debate. *The Sun*, for example, quoted tweets by MPs, the Labour whips' office account, and the Scottish First Minister Nicola Sturgeon, as well as from members of the public who had been watching (Fisk and Morris 2016). This is an example of the growing trend for social media to both drive and inform mainstream coverage of Parliament. In a report on private members' bills, the Commons Procedure Committee noted that the system was damaging the reputation of Parliament and that this had been exacerbated by increased coverage of events online. It concluded that the system 'reflects very badly on the House's image: it is, in the words of one Member, "a problem which it is in everybody's interest to solve"' (Procedure Committee 2016: 3).

Primary sources

- D'Arcy, M. (2016) 'Redundant Bill?', *BBC News*, 20 October. Online at: http://www.bbc.co.uk/news/uk-politics-parliaments-37717694 [accessed 27 June 2017].
- Nicolson, J. (2016) 'Today in Parliament', *BBC Radio 4*, 21 October.
- Commons debate on the Sexual Offences (Pardons Etc.) Bill (HC Debates, 21 October 2016, cc. 615–1145). Online at: https://hansard.parliament.uk/commons/2016-10-21/debates/82F53633-3EFC-4BFF-BCA1-BF97B4A2F37B/SexualOffences(PardonsEtc)Bill [accessed 27 June 2017].
- Procedure Select Committee (2016) *Private Members' Bills: Third Report of Session 2015–16*, London: The Stationery Office, HC 684. Online at: https://www.publications.parliament.uk/pa/cm201516/cmselect/cmproced/684/684.pdf [accessed 27 June 2017].

FURTHER CASE STUDIES

- Reporting of the parliamentary tactics of the #WASPI campaign (2015 Parliament).
- Select a private members' bill likely to be debated, watch its debate, and analyse the reactions on social media commentary of private members' bills.
- Compare press reporting and social media commentary on any Prime Minister's Questions.

References

ASHER, M., LESTON-BANDEIRA, C., AND SPAISER, V. (2017), 'Assessing the effectiveness of e-petitioning through Twitter conversations', paper given at Political Studies Association annual conference, Glasgow, April 2017. Online at: https://www.psa.ac.uk/sites/default/files/conference/papers/2017/Twitter_discussions_on_e-petitions_MA_CLB_VS_PSA_April2007.pdf [accessed 22 August 2017].

BBC NEWS (2016a) 'Commons vote to ratify Brexit deal likely, says No 10', *BBC News*, 18 October. Online at: http://www.bbc.co.uk/news/uk-politics-37691270 [accessed 6 June 2017].

BBC NEWS (2016b) 'Sturgeon tells May she's "not bluffing" over referendum', *BBC News*, 24 October. Online at: http://www.bbc.co.uk/news/uk-politics-37747995 [accessed 6 June 2017].

BBC NEWS (2016c) 'PM's innuendo in response to MP Peter Bone prompts laughter', *BBC News*, 19 October. Online at: http://www.bbc.co.uk/news/uk-politics-37706274 [accessed 6 June 2017].

BBC NEWS (2016d) '"Alan Turing law": Thousands of gay men to be pardoned', *BBC News*, 20 October. Online at: http://www.bbc.co.uk/news/uk-37711518 [accessed 24 June 2017].

BBC NEWS (2016e) '"Turing Bill" for gay pardons fails in Parliament', *BBC News*, 21 October. Online at: http://www.bbc.co.uk/news/uk-politics-37707030 [accessed 6 June 2017].

BUSH, S. (2017) 'Will the House of Lords block Brexit?', *The New Statesman*, 20 February. Online at: http://www.newstatesman.com/politics/staggers/2017/02/will-house-lords-block-brexit [accessed 6 June 2017].

CHORLEY, M. AND MERRICK, J. (2012) 'Out of Touch. Out of Control: The Tories in Turmoil', *The Independent*, 31 March. Online at: http://www.independent.co.uk/news/uk/politics/out-of-touch-out-of-control-the-tories-in-turmoil-7606224.html [accessed 6 June 2017].

CLARK, A. (1993) *Diaries: In Power 1983–1992*, London: Orien Books.

D'ARCY, M. (2016) 'Brexit: How rebel MPs outfoxed Cameron to get an EU referendum', *BBC News*, 29 December. Online at: http://www.bbc.co.uk/news/uk-politics-parliaments-38402140 [accessed 6 June 2017].

FISK, R. AND Morris, A. (2016) 'We Can Do Better Than This: MPs shout 'shame' as Government talks out Turing Bill to pardon gay men convicted of now abolished sexual offences', *The Sun*, 21 October. Online at: https://www.thesun.co.uk/news/2023493/government-accused-of-trying-to-hijack-plans-for-turings-law-and-not-wanting-to-go-far-enough-with-pardons/ [accessed 6 June 2017].

HANSARD SOCIETY (2017) *Audit of Political Engagement 14*, London: Hansard Society.

HARDMAN, I. (2014) 'The menace of memes: How pictures can paint a thousand lies', *The Spectator Coffee House* blog. Online at: https://blogs.spectator.co.uk/2014/11/the-menace-of-memes-how-pictures-can-paint-a-thousand-lies/ [accessed 6 June 2017].

KAUFMAN, G. (1997) *How to be a Minister*, London: Faber & Faber.

LE CONTE, M. (2017) 'We Used That Viral Face App On 13 Politicians And It Will Make You Say "Nope"', *BuzzFeed*, 25 April. Online at: https://www.buzzfeed.com/marieleconte/we-used-that-viral-faceapp-on-13-politicians-and-it-will?utm_term=.ckxb8K7v9#.jbBEZ7pVr [accessed 6 June 2017].

MYSOCIETY (2015) 'Understanding TheyWorkForYou's Users ... Without the Power of Mind Reading', 14 November. Online at: https://www.mysociety.org/2015/11/04/understanding-theyworkforyous-users-without-the-power-of-mind-reading/ [accessed 22 August 2017].

PARLIAMENT TV (2016) Viewing figures, data provided by email to author, December 2017.

PETITIONS SELECT COMMITTEE (2016) *Your Petitions: A Year of Action*, London: Petitions Committee. Online at: http://www.parliament.uk/documents/commons-committees/petitions/Your-Petitions-A-Year-of-Action.pdf [accessed 22 August 2017].

PROCEDURE SELECT COMMITTEE (2016) *Private Members' Bills: Third Report of Session 2015–16*, London: The Stationery Office, HC 684. Online at: https://www.publications.parliament.uk/pa/cm201516/cmselect/cmproced/684/684.pdf [accessed 24 June 2017].

TREASURY COMMITTEE (2012) *Budget 2012: Thirtieth Report of Session 2010–12*, London: The Stationery Office, HC 1910-II. Online at: https://www.publications.parliament.uk/pa/cm201012/cmselect/cmtreasy/1910/191002.htm [accessed 24 June 2017].

TREASURY SELECT COMMITTEE (2016) *Oral Evidence: The Economic and Financial Costs and Benefits of UK's EU Membership Inquiry*, London: The Stationery Office, HC 499. Online at: http://data.parliament.uk/writtenevidence/committeeevidence.svc/evidencedocument/treasury-committee/the-economic-and-financial-costs-and-benefits-of-uks-eu-membership/oral/31014.pdf [accessed 24 June 2017].

UK PARLIAMENT (2016) Webpage views for Parliament.tv, figures supplied by email to author, December 2016.

WAKEFIELD, J. (2016) 'Social media "outstrips TV" as news source for young people', *BBC News*, 15 June. Online at: http://www.bbc.co.uk/news/uk-36528256 [accessed 6 June 2017].

PART V

Representation

21

The Rise of the Professional Politician?

Peter Allen and Philip Cowley

INTRODUCTION

One of the standard arguments about Parliament relates to its composition. Who's there? And are they the right sort of people? This debate is partly about gender (as discussed in Chapter 22), but it also encompasses other variables such as ethnicity and class—and in recent years has included discussion of whether we have too many 'professional' or 'career' politicians. As Nigel Farage, sometime UKIP leader, has put it:

> You know the people I'm talking about. They all go to the same schools. They all go to Oxford. They all study PPE. They leave at 22 and get a job as a researcher for one of the parties and then become MPs at age 27 or 28 ... we are run by a bunch of college kids who've never done a day of work in their lives! (Goodwin and Milazzo 2015, 7)

Such complaints are not confined to the political right. Andy Burnham, former Labour Secretary of State for Health and party leadership contender, said, 'All the current generation of politicians, myself included, typically came up through the back offices. We're the professional politician generation, aren't we?' (Aitkenhead 2013). These sort of observations are then often wrapped up in a wider narrative about the 'triumph of the political class', the core of which is said to be made up of professional politicians (Oborne 2007).

Unfortunately, this debate has been bedevilled by a lack of clarity about what these phrases mean. People often conflate three interconnected ideas: i) the professional politician, ii) the career politician, and iii) the political class. These terms are often used as if they are synonyms, but they can usefully be applied to refer to three different phenomena. This chapter therefore begins by explaining the different meanings that these phrases have, before discussing why the presence of such politicians in Parliament is often seen as a problem. It then shows that, however defined, there are in fact fewer professional politicians than is frequently assumed—but goes on to explain why they appear to be so prevalent.

Career politicians, professional politicians, and the political class

We start, then, with some definitions. A *career politician* is one who is seeking to sustain a consistent and long-standing income from political life through a lengthy stint in office. Career politicians live for, but also off, politics. A *professional politician*, by contrast, can be defined as one who has entered the legislature via a route that saw them work primarily in or around politics before standing for election. In this category we would include those who work for MPs, or as ministers' special advisers (SpAds), as well as those who work for political parties or in the growing cottage industry of political think tanks. And third, the *political class* is a more collective phrase that refers to a group of elected politicians who are in some sense seen to be unrepresentative of the population at large—because they consist of too many career or professional politicians, or are out of touch in some other way. This encapsulates the idea that politicians are somehow a class apart, have never had 'real jobs', do not understand the concerns of 'normal people', and are distant and cut off from voters.

Although the sense of a distinct political class no doubt intensified after the expenses scandal of 2009, such complaints are not new (King 1981). Career politicians have long been part of politics—Winston Churchill, for example, was by almost any definition a career politician—and there have always been criticisms of politicians for being detached or distant. Where there has been a change more recently is in terms of the routes MPs take into politics. Research always used to note that career politicians came disproportionately from a relatively small group of occupations—known as 'brokerage' or 'politics-facilitating' occupations—such as law, lecturing, or journalism, which provide skills useful in politics, as well as other advantages such as flexible work patterns or easy access to Westminster. More recently, however, there has been a rise of more directly instrumental occupations, those with closer links to the political elite, as the professional politician has become a more important figure at Westminster.

Key assumptions

The common interpretation of this issue generally proceeds in two stages. First, we are told that 'all' or 'most' MPs are professional politicians, they are 'all the same', and so on. The second stage involves a more normative claim: that is, one about what *should be* the case, with the rise of the career or professional politician generally being held to be a bad thing, and something which we should condemn. We will discuss later the extent to which this is an accurate portrayal of the contemporary House of Commons. But first it is worth considering why the professional politician is widely considered to be such a negative development. After all, in many other areas of life being professional—as opposed to being an amateur—is usually seen to be positive, and to correlate with higher standards of performance and quality.

Broadly speaking, there are two arguments made against the professional politician. The first is a functionalist argument: that the optimal way to manage national affairs is to draw on a wide range of occupational experience from different spheres of society and the economy. In other words, when looking to determine economic policy or health policy, say, it might be a good idea to have economists, business owners, doctors, or nurses in the room when doing so—not just professional politicians, who are assumed to lack expertise in any areas beyond Westminster politicking.

This leads to the second type of criticism, which draws on a broader argument in favour of political equality and representation. Although ending up at the same position as the functionalist case, the force of this argument comes from a different source. Instead of arguing that it would produce 'better' outcomes in specific policy areas, the argument focuses on questions of justice and fairness, and brings into question the right or qualification of any one group of people to dominate positions of political power. It effectively flips the functionalist argument, making it not about who *isn't* present in the Commons, but rather who is. As Anne Phillips famously wrote about the disproportionate presence of men in parliaments, we should ask 'by what "natural" superiority of talent or experience men could claim a right to dominate assemblies?' (Phillips 1995, 65); the same argument could apply to those who went into politics early.

One potential defence of professional politicians hinges on the idea that domain-specific knowledge is not as important as once might have been thought. This decline in importance can be argued to be the result of depoliticization, the process by which decisions that were once made by politicians as part of a process of political debate are increasingly left to be decided by markets and other purportedly non-political mechanisms. Moreover, when in government, politicians are supported by a permanent administrative body that is supposed to have the expertise and policy knowledge needed to govern. Given this fact, individuals who excel at the practice of politics itself might prove to be the best option for the administration of public resources, rather than a more representative group who may lack the relevant experience.

Ultimately, one's response to this normative question can be informed by empirical evidence but will also depend on your conception of what politics is, what constitutes 'enough' political equality in terms of participation, and where the trade-off between any apparent benefits of professionalization and greater inclusiveness may lie.

Contemporary developments

Perhaps unsurprisingly, when we examine the composition of the House of Commons (or the Lords), we discover that both Farage and Burnham are wrong to believe that 'they all study PPE' or that 'all the current generation of politicians' fit the descriptions we have outlined. Figure 21.1, for example, gives the percentage of MPs with a professional background in politics. It shows that nearly 17 per cent of the MPs elected in 2015 had an occupational and political background that might lead us to describe them as professional politicians. Seventeen per cent is a number languishing some way behind 'all' of them. That said, there has been a clear and steady increase in the proportion of MPs who we could so classify, with their number increasing from around 3 per cent of the

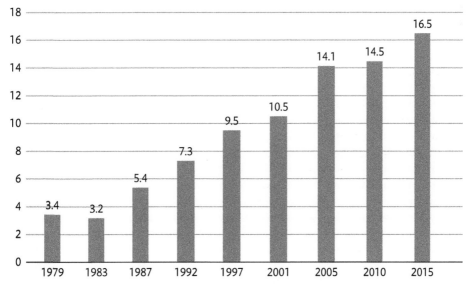

Figure 21.1 Percentage of MPs with occupational backgrounds as politicians or political workers, 1979–2015

Source: Data taken from Criddle (1987–2015), *British General Election of ...* series

Commons in the late 1970s and early 1980s. From 1987 onwards, the increase has been parliament-on-parliament.

It is also not true to say that all—or even most—MPs have studied PPE at Oxford, although it is certainly the case that the educational profile of MPs differs significantly from the British population as a whole. Following the 2015 election, 32 per cent of MPs were privately educated (compared to 7 per cent of the population), and 89 per cent had degrees. Of this group, 25 per cent were awarded their degrees by either Oxford or Cambridge universities, around 22 per cent of all MPs. This compares to around 40 per cent of the UK adult population who are estimated to have a degree (Sutton Trust 2015).

As with other similar exercises, the precise figure one is left with when trying to assess the number of professional politicians in Parliament is dependent on how the researcher classified the pre-parliamentary experience of MPs. These data are arguably a conservative measure of the extent of professionalization given the relatively strict parameters implied by the term 'political worker'—this does not include journalists or lobbyists, for example. But however you measure the phenomenon, you reach two conclusions: a) the number of professional politicians is on the rise, but b) they still constitute a minority of MPs.

One reason why more MPs have previously had careers in and around Westminster now than in the past is simply because there are more pre-Westminster careers now than there were before. In the 1970s, parliamentary allowances were minimal, so few MPs employed researchers, and SpAds were much less numerous. The think tank world was similarly embryonic. It is not all that surprising that with the rise in the number of people working in and around Westminster has come a greater number of MPs with a background from those areas.

More surprising, perhaps, is the persistent belief in the all-conquering nature of the professional politician. One explanation, discussed in greater detail in Case Study 21, which follows this chapter, is that professional politicians have different kinds of careers compared to their colleagues, receiving preferential promotions and career advancement (Cowley 2012; Allen 2013). Such treatment results in them holding frontbench positions in greater numbers than MPs without the experience that they have, and thus perhaps creates an optical illusion in which professional politicians *seem* to be more dominant than they actually are. In particular, SpAds, perhaps the absolute embodiment of the professional politician, appear to have advantages over candidates and MPs with other backgrounds at every stage of their political careers (Goplerud 2015): they progress on to the frontbenches extremely quickly—indeed, far quicker even than other MPs who might fit a broader description of professional politician. There is something particular to being a SpAd that aids political careers, making them the ultimate professional politicians in both theory and practice. In other words, backbench MPs may still be overwhelmingly non-professional, but those who reach ministerial office are much more likely to be professionals. As is the case with cyclists in the *Tour de France*, two types of MPs now exist at Westminster: the elite and the *domestiques*. The former may still be a minority, but they experience a much faster career trajectory.

Other research suggests that professional politicians are elected to the Commons at a younger age than their colleagues, which may be the result of a conscious decision on their part, with ambitious young candidates seeking out professionalized political experience as part of mounting their candidacy (Durose et al. 2013). The relative youth of professional politicians can also be seen among political elites, with many recent leaders of the main political parties matching this description—being elected at a young age, progressing quickly, and reaching the top jobs much faster than non-professionals (Cowley 2012).

The three main UK party leaders who fought the 2015 election—Nick Clegg, Ed Miliband, and David Cameron—all had the backgrounds of archetypal professional politicians as well as reaching the leadership of their parties after very short careers at

Westminster (Cowley 2016). In the emergence of Jeremy Corbyn, Vince Cable, and Theresa May, we may perhaps see a backlash of sorts against the desire for youth, although all three are hardly outsiders. Corbyn, in particular, who has been an MP since 1983 and whose pre-parliamentary career consisted almost entirely of work for trade unions and as a councillor, is the very epitome of a career politician.

The public, however, are much less charitable to professional politicians. In 2014, opinion pollsters YouGov asked people what they felt were unsuitable characteristics in a politician. Out of a list of 14 characteristics, respondents had to choose the three or four they thought were 'most unsuitable in a leading politician'. The single most unsuitable characteristic was: that they have never had a 'real' job outside the world of national politics/think tanks/ journalism/local government before becoming an MP, which was chosen by a massive 55 per cent of respondents. This was far more unpopular with the public than things that were actually illegal—such as taking cocaine or heroin when younger (14 per cent) or being caught shoplifting (5 per cent) (Kellner 2014).

Similarly, survey experiments testing voters' preferences about election candidates have shown that experience in politics is not rewarded by voters. While the public recognize that professional politicians may have more experience of Westminster, it does not make them any more positive about such people overall (Campbell and Cowley 2014). Voters value traits such as being local to an area and demonstrating independence of mind—traits that can be taken as the polar opposite of those held by the archetypal professional politician (Campbell et al. 2016).

One reason why the rise of the professional politician is often considered to have negative consequences is because such politicians are assumed to have pushed people with other occupational backgrounds out of Parliament. In particular, the rise of the professional politician has coincided with a sharp decline in the proportion of MPs from working-class backgrounds (Evans and Tilley 2017). This decline is much sharper than the fall in the size of the working-class population in the country as a whole, to the point where just 3 per cent of MPs elected in 2015 had a background in manual work, and professional politicians have tended to be more middle-class and better educated than traditional working-class candidates (see Goplerud 2015). This in turn has been heralded as a potential cause of the decline in working-class voter turnout over the last two decades, a development that has hit the Labour Party particularly hard. It may even have played a role in facilitating the rise of UKIP as an electoral force in British politics, as there is evidence that working-class voters have been put off turning out to vote for Labour when these kinds of professionalized middle-class candidates are put forward in working-class constituencies (Heath 2016).

There is something in this argument—and it is certainly true that the changing class composition of Parliament has been downplayed or ignored for far too long—but it is also easy to stereotype. For one thing, the occupational background of MPs has long been unrepresentative of the wider population: it was only in the final third of the twentieth century that the landed gentry on the Conservative benches gave way to a more solidly middle-class group of MPs. Moreover, the debate is not helped by the tendency among some observers to talk about the working-class like something out of an episode of *Steptoe and Son*, rather than the more complicated reality of modern-day life. It is common, for example, to see figures cited on the decline in the number of MPs with a background in mining. Given the destruction of the British mining industry, this is hardly surprising. A more sober assessment might instead reflect that, while traditional working-class jobs seemed to have a link to politics through trade unions and left-wing political parties, the kinds of jobs that have developed in their wake, mostly in the service industry, do not boast the same connections. Lastly, given that, as already demonstrated, professional politicians still remain a minority in the Commons, it is not likely that the sole, or even main, reason there are fewer working-class MPs is because under 20 per cent of the House can be defined as professional.

Conclusion

Although the precise numbers will depend on your definition of choice, there are more professional politicians now than 30 years ago—and their number is increasing steadily. Despite this, they remain a minority, and are much less widespread than is commonly asserted, although they are promoted faster and further than their colleagues without such experience. The normative debate around whether or not this increase is a good or bad thing is largely unresolved, and depends heavily on your perception of political decision-making and representation, although all the evidence from opinion polls and survey experiments is that voters are not fans of professional politicians and do not especially want professional politicians to represent them.

Senior politicians always claim to take this issue very seriously, and to want a wider pool of candidates for Westminster, but remedial action here—unlike with, say, gender or ethnicity—remains largely exhortatory. The Coalition's plans to introduce 200 all-postal primaries, part of a plan to open up politics to non-standard candidates, was one of its very first reform proposals to be discarded after 2010, both on grounds of cost and because it had begun to dawn on those involved that candidates selected in this way might be worryingly independent-minded (Cowley 2015). There is anyway an irony in very senior politicians, who themselves are almost always career politicians down to their fingertips, calling for there to be fewer people like them involved in politics. It is a political version of St Augustine: Lord, elect fewer people like me, but not just yet.

Further Reading

ALLEN, P. (2018) *The Political Class: Why It Matters Who Our Politicians Are*, Oxford: Oxford University Press.

CAIRNEY, P. (2007) 'The Professionalisation of MPs: Refining the "Politics-Facilitating" Explanation', *Parliamentary Affairs*, Vol. 60 (2), pp. 212–33.

COWLEY, P. (2016) 'Political Recruitment and the Political Class' in R. Heffernan et al. (eds.), *Developments in British Politics 10*, London: Palgrave, pp. 122–42.

GOPLERUD, M. (2015) 'The First Time is (Mostly) the Charm: Special Advisers as Parliamentary Candidates and Members of Parliament', *Parliamentary Affairs*, Vol. 68 (2), pp. 332–51.

Case Study 21: The class of 1997

Labour's landslide election victory in 1997 led to the largest turnover in the composition of the House of Commons since the war. The election was also memorable for a doubling in the number of women MPs, most of them Labour. Less visibly, but still importantly, it also saw a notable increase in the number of MPs who had entered the Commons from political occupations. To use the terminology of this chapter, these were 'professional' politicians, who had cut their teeth in national politics, working in and around Westminster before standing for election themselves. Given that government and opposition frontbenchers are mostly drawn from the Commons, this meant that the recruitment pool following the 1997 election was more professionalized than ever before.

Table 21.1 Five-point scale of frontbench and other leadership positions

5—Cabinet minister/shadow cabinet/Lib Dem shadow cabinet/chief whips/party leaders

4—Ministers of state/shadow ministers/Lib Dem shadow ministers/whips

3—Under-secretaries of state/opposition spokespeople/Lib Dem spokespeople/junior whips/Advocate General

2—Parliamentary private secretaries (PPS)

1—Backbenchers

Labour won the two elections that followed, giving the party an unprecedented three consecutive terms in government. The subsequent 2010 election also saw a very large turnover in Members of the Commons, partly because of Labour's electoral defeat but also because of a high number of retirements following the expenses scandal of 2009. One or two exceptions aside, anyone elected to the Commons for the first time in 1997 would almost certainly have reached the highest political office they would ever achieve before the end of this 13-year period. The New Labour era thus offers a self-enclosed period of time in which we can study the careers of a sizeable number of MPs. This is what is known as a 'cohort study' and is often used in medicine to track the life cycles of individuals with certain illnesses or from various social or ethnic groups. The key aim of a cohort study is to draw out patterns across these groups over time. In this case study, we use the 1997 intake as a cohort study of political careers—showing the impact that being a professional politician makes on career progression.

Because political careers are so varied and complicated, we need to construct a scale to simplify the differing levels of seniority that an MP can reach, and to do so in a way that allows comparison across opposition and government. This is detailed in Table 21.1, which outlines a simple five-point scale of political positions.

As Table 21.2 shows, 36 per cent of MPs who entered the Commons for the first time in 1997 did not leave the backbenches in the 13 years that followed. Around 13 per cent of MPs were promoted to the position of PPS, 17 per cent to level 3 positions, and 23 per cent to the level of minister of state and equivalent positions. Twelve per cent made it all the way to level 5 positions, which include cabinet roles and equivalents.

However, those MPs with professionalized experience—by which we mean those who had worked in or around politics before becoming MPs—did noticeably better. Fewer of this group remained on the backbenches, few of them held level 2 or 3 positions, and far more of them held the most prestigious and influential ministerial roles at the top of the parliamentary career ladder. Professional politicians were about twice as likely as MPs overall to make it to level 4 or 5, and about three times as likely to make it to the highest level of all.

Table 21.2 Comparison of promotions of complete cohort and MPs with professionalized pre-parliamentary political experience

Highest office of promotion	Overall cohort (%) (n=242)	'Professionalized' MPs (%) (n=50)	Women in cohort (%) (n=72)
Level 5—Cabinet	12.0	30.0	9.7
Level 4—Minister	22.7	34.0	20.8
Level 3—Junior minister	16.5	4.0	15.3
Level 2—PPS	13.2	8.0	13.9
Level 1—Backbencher	35.5	24.0	40.3

In addition, professional politicians were also more likely to be promoted quickly: over 90 per cent of those who ended up in level 5 positions gained their initial promotion in their first term in Parliament. This compares to just 24 per cent of those MPs whose careers peaked at the level of PPS. They were also promoted into higher positions in these first promotions, with 28 per cent of MPs with professionalized political experience first promoted into level 4 positions compared to just 14 per cent of all MPs who made it off the backbenches.

There is therefore clear evidence of what we can term a preferential career path for MPs with professionalized political experience: having entered the Commons, they are promoted more quickly, into better jobs, and ultimately reach the top of the pile in greater numbers than other MPs.

Given the large and sudden increase in the number of women MPs in 1997, it is also worth noting that the career trajectories of women MPs—detailed in the final column of Table 21.2—were indistinguishable from those of men in the same cohort (Allen 2016). Proportionally, men and women reached levels of the frontbench hierarchy at the same rate and were given similar kinds of ministerial portfolios to work on.

One of the functions of the House of Commons—indeed, historically, one of its key functions—was as a recruitment pool and training ground for would-be ministers and party leaders (Norton 2013). While the only route to the top in British politics continues to be through the House of Commons (and thus it still retains its monopoly status on ministerial ambition), 'its value as a place where would-be leaders are tested and tried out appears to be on the wane' (Cowley 2012, 36). Even if the public are not great fans of professional politicians, as discussed in this chapter, Parliament is clearly a more hospitable environment for such MPs, with professional politicians achieving much faster progression. There is a lot of talk—often misguided and historically inaccurate—about parliamentary decline (Cowley 2006), but when it comes to the selection of political elites the Commons does appear to be losing one of its roles.

Primary sources

- Parliamentary Candidates UK. Online at: http://parliamentarycandidates.org/ [accessed 27 June 2017].

- Audickas, L. (2016) *Social Background of MPs 1979–2015*, House of Commons Library Research Briefing Paper CBP 7483, 25 January. Online at: http://researchbriefings.files.parliament.uk/documents/CBP-7483/CBP-7483.pdf [accessed 27 June 2017].

 FURTHER CASE STUDIES

Cohort studies like this can be undertaken with any parliamentary cohort, of any party. But ideally you want relatively large numbers of MPs and to study them over a reasonably long time period. The former makes it more likely that any differences identified are genuine rather than random variation. The latter allows for MPs to have had a full career. Examples might be the 1979 or 1983 Conservative cohorts or Labour's from 1945 or 1964/1966. Anyone reading this volume in 2030 might like to look at the Conservative intake in 2010; the SNP intake in 2015 might be worth studying in 2035.

References

AITKENHEAD, D. (2013) 'Andy Burnham interview: "We've lost the art of thinking bigger"', *The Guardian*, 9 August. Online at: https://www.theguardian.com/theguardian/2013/aug/09/andy-burnham-interview-thinking-bigger [accessed 18 October 2016]

ALLEN, P. (2013) 'Linking the pre-parliamentary political experience and political careers of the 1997 General Election cohort', *Parliamentary Affairs*, Vol. 66 (4), pp. 685–70.

ALLEN, P. (2016) 'Achieving Sex Equality in Executive Appointments', *Party Politics*, Vol. 22 (5), pp. 609–19.

CAMPBELL, R. and COWLEY, P. (2014) 'What Voters Want: Reactions to Candidate Characteristics in a Survey Experiment', *Political Studies*, Vol. 62 (4), pp. 745–65.

CAMPBELL, R., COWLEY, P., VIVYAN, N., and WAGNER, M. (2016) 'Legislator Dissent as a Valence Signal', *British Journal of Political Science*, Early view. Online at: http://dx.doi.org/10.1017/S0007123416000223 [accessed 22 August 2017].

COWLEY, P. (2006) 'Making Parliament Matter?' in P. Dunleavy et al. (eds.), *Developments in British Politics 8*, London: Palgrave, pp. 36–55.

COWLEY, P. (2012) 'Arise, Novice Leader! The Continuing Rise of the Career Politician in Britain', *Politics*, Vol. 32 (1), pp. 31–8.

COWLEY, P. (2015) 'Parliament' in Anthony Seldon and Mike Finn (eds.), *The Coalition Effect*, Cambridge: Cambridge University Press, pp. 136–56.

COWLEY, P. (2016) 'Political Recruitment and the Political Class' in R. Heffernan et al. (eds.), *Developments in British Politics 10*, London: Palgrave, pp. 122–42.

CRIDDLE, B. (1987) 'MPs and Candidates' in D. Butler and D. Kavanagh (eds.), *The British General Election of 1987*, New York: St Martin's Press, pp. 191–210.

CRIDDLE, B. (1992) 'MPs and Candidates' in D. Butler and D. Kavanagh (eds.), *The British General Election of 1992*, Basingstoke: Palgrave Macmillan, pp. 211–30.

CRIDDLE, B. (1997) 'MPs and Candidates' in D. Butler and D. Kavanagh (eds.), *The British General Election of 1997*, Basingstoke: Palgrave Macmillan, pp. 186–209.

CRIDDLE, B. (2001) 'MPs and Candidates' in D. Butler and D. Kavanagh (eds.), *The British General Election of 2001*, Basingstoke: Palgrave Macmillan, pp. 182–207.

CRIDDLE, B. (2005) 'MPs and Candidates' in D. Butler and D. Kavanagh (eds.), *The British General Election of 2005*, Basingstoke: Palgrave Macmillan, pp. 146–67.

CRIDDLE, B. (2010) 'More Diverse Yet More Uniform: MPs and Candidates' in D. Kavanagh and P. Cowley (eds.), *The British General Election of 2010*, Basingstoke: Palgrave Macmillan, pp. 306–29.

CRIDDLE, B. (2015) 'Variable Diversity: MPs and Candidates' in P. Cowley and D. Kavanagh (eds.), *The British General Election of 2015*, Basingstoke: Palgrave Macmillan, pp. 336–60.

DUROSE, C., RICHARDSON, L., COMBS, C. E., and GAINS, F. (2013), '"Acceptable Difference": Diversity, Representation and Pathways to UK Politics', *Parliamentary Affairs*, Vol. 66 (2), pp. 246–67.

EVANS, G. and TILLEY, J. (2017) *The New Politics of Class: The Political Exclusion of the British Working Class*, Oxford: Oxford University Press.

GOODWIN, M. and MILAZZO, C. (2015) *UKIP*, Oxford: Oxford University Press.

GOPLERUD, M. (2015) 'The First Time is (Mostly) the Charm: Special Advisers as Parliamentary Candidates and Members of Parliament', *Parliamentary Affairs*, Vol. 68 (2), pp. 332–51.

HEATH, O. (2016) 'Policy Alienation, Social Alienation and Working-class Abstention in Britain, 1964–2010', *British Journal of Political Science*, Early view, http://dx.doi.org/10.1017/S0007123416000272 [accessed 22 August 2017].

KELLNER, P. (2014) 'Sex, drugs, money and old school ties', *YouGov*, 10 March. Online at: https://yougov.co.uk/news/2014/03/10/sex-drugs-money-and-old-school-ties-which-bits-mps/ [accessed 24 June 2017].

KING, A. (1981) 'The Rise of the Career Politician in Britain—And Its Consequences', *British Journal of Political Science*, Vol. 11 (3), pp. 249–85.

NORTON, P. (2013) *Parliament in British Politics*, 2nd edition, Basingstoke: Palgrave Macmillan.

OBORNE, P. (2007) *The Triumph of the Political Class*, London: Pocket Books.

PHILLIPS, A. (1995) *The Politics of Presence*, Oxford: Oxford University Press.

SUTTON TRUST (2015) *Parliamentary Privilege: The MPs*, Research Brief no. 4, May. Online at: http://www.suttontrust.com/wp-content/uploads/2015/05/Parliamentary-Privilege-The-MPs-2015-2.pdf [accessed 17 November 2016].

22

Women in the House of Commons

Rosie Campbell, Sarah Childs, and Elizabeth Hunt

INTRODUCTION

It is an opportune moment to review the progress of women's participation and repre-sentation in the House of Commons: 2018 marks the centenary of the Representation of the People Act and the Parliament (Qualification of Women) Act. The former gave the vote to women aged over 30 with property, while the latter permitted women to stand as candidates and be elected as MPs. The history of women in the UK House of Commons is one of ongoing numerical under-representation, relative to their percentage in the population. At the beginning of the 2015 Parliament 191 women MPs were elected out of a total of 650 MPs; by its end in May 2017 another five women MPs had been elected, bringing the total to 196. The snap general election called by Theresa May for June 2017 saw the total number of women rise to 208, but this gave rise to very little change in the overall percentage—up 2 per cent to 32 per cent of all MPs.

This chapter opens with a review of the progress in women's descriptive representa-tion over the last century, drawing particular attention to the differences in the pro-portion of women MPs elected by the main political parties. The improvements in the numbers of women MPs in the last decade or so, together with the party asymmetry, are explained by reference to the supply and demand model of political recruitment (Norris and Lovenduski 1995). While we advocate a 'quota-plus strategy' to address both sides of this model, we very much identify political parties as key gatekeepers. We then revisit arguments for women's equal participation in politics, suggesting that women's descriptive representation is linked to symbolic and substantive representation. We furthermore question resistance to the claim that women's representation matters. The chapter closes by considering the masculinized nature of the political institution that women MPs inhabit, and discussing the recommendations made in 2016 in *The Good Parliament* report (Childs 2016), which outlines a blueprint for a diversity-sensitive House of Commons.

Women's descriptive representation

The first woman MP to win election to the Commons was Constance Markievicz in 1918, although as a Sinn Féin MP she did not take up her seat. The first to take her seat was Nancy Astor. She represented Plymouth Sutton from 1919 to 1945, taking over from her husband, who on the death of his father had ascended to the House of Lords. Figure 22.1 documents men's and women's representation between 1918 and 2017. Significant progress has been achieved in the last 20 years, although the upward trajectory is not always linear, with some

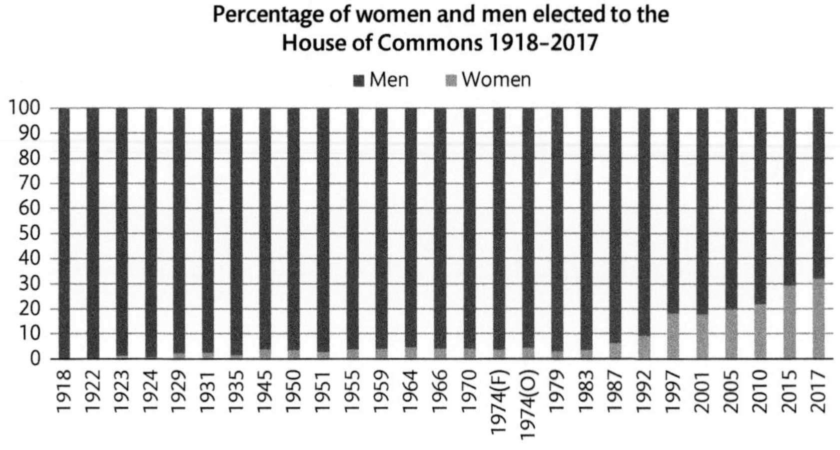

Percentage of women and men elected to the House of Commons 1918–2017

■ Men   ■ Women

Figure 22.1 Percentage of women and men elected to the House of Commons 1918–2017

Source: Rallings and Thrasher (2007); Cracknell, McGuinness, and Rhodes (2010); Hawkins, Keen, and Nakatudde (2015)

elections seeing fewer women MPs returned than previously (e.g. 2001). The step change was 1997; the doubling in the number of women MPs resulted in large part from Labour's use of a quota—all-women shortlists (AWS). Of the 120 women MPs elected in 1997, 101 were Labour, 35 of these from AWS.

The UK Parliament ranks 46th in the Inter-Parliamentary Union's (IPU) global league table (IPU 2017). Within the UK it fares unfavourably compared to the new devolved institutions, other than the Northern Ireland Assembly which is 28 per cent female. Elsewhere women represent 42 per cent in the National Assembly for Wales, 40 per cent in the Greater London Authority, 40 per cent of UK MEPs, and 35 per cent in the Scottish Parliament.

A key feature of women's representation at Westminster is asymmetry by party, as shown in Figure 22.2. In Labour's favour since the 1980s, and most notably in 1997, this pattern remains significant today. In the 2015–17 Parliament, Labour and the SNP had significantly higher proportions of women MPs. The Liberal Democrats lost all their women MPs in 2015; the Conservatives increased the percentage of women on their benches from 9 to 16, and then to 21 over the last three elections, but their proportion of women MPs was half that of Labour's, as a percentage of their respective parliamentary parties. The SNP's huge success in 2015 saw it jump from one to 20 women MPs. Among MPs from other parties three were women. After the election of 2017, despite being widely heralded in the media as record-breaking, the House remains less than one-third female. There are now more than 200 women MPs, but the parity threshold to cross is 325.

In addition to the under-representation of women in the Commons, relative to their presence in the population, mothers are particularly absent. In terms of the diversity of women MPs, survey data from 2012 revealed a further dimension for discussions of women's descriptive representation—a motherhood gap. Some 45 per cent of women MPs compared to 28 per cent of male MPs had no children (Campbell and Childs 2014). Regarding ethnicity, the total number of Black and Minority Ethnic (BME) MPs would need to double to over 80 to reflect BME presence in the population: in 2015 there were 41 BME MPs, of whom 20 were women. The numbers rose at the 2017 general election to 52, 8 per cent of the House. One 2017 'first' included the election of the Sikh woman MP, Preet Gill.

The number of women who are elected at Westminster is determined by political parties who select candidates; voters in the UK are usually indifferent to the sex of a party's

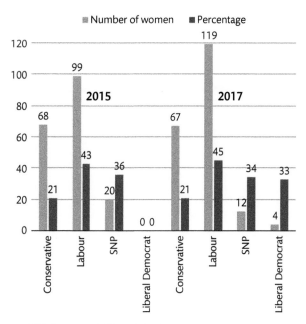

Figure 22.2 Women MPs by party, 2015 and 2017

Source: www.parliamentarycandidates.org

candidate. All of the main parties are rhetorically committed to increasing the number of women MPs; all engage in activities to encourage and enable women to stand, providing training and mentoring for example. These strategies address the supply of women seeking selection as a candidate, but do not target party demand for women candidates. Labour's quota policy—AWS—is a demand-side intervention, designed to override any prejudice among party selectorates. Research from the 1990s and 2000s demonstrated that female prospective candidates had faced both explicit and implicit discrimination when seeking selection; examples included women candidates being asked what their husbands would do for sex if they were to be elected, what colour their knickers were, and who would look after the children (Shepherd-Robinson and Lovenduski 2002). Such overt discrimination is less common today, although MPs and candidates 'off the record' may talk about not wearing the 'right clothes' or hearing responses such as 'our constituency isn't ready for a woman' (Childs 2008; Childs and Webb 2012). If demand-side strategies attempt to reset the terms of candidate selection—to level the playing field and provide equal opportunities—research also shows that the supply of women may increase when parties signal a clear demand for women candidates through a party quota. The recent election in the Republic of Ireland, in which a new quota law was in place, witnessed a 90 per cent increase in the number of women candidates (Buckley 2016).

Table 22.1 shows the placement of women candidates by seat safety at the 2015 general election. This captures the likelihood of each party translating women candidates into MPs on polling day. The difference in the percentage of women candidates Labour selected in their targets compared to the total proportion illustrates how AWS work: increasing the proportion of women who are likely to be elected. There may always be resistance to the idea of quotas in principle, but the evidence in respect of sex/gender quotas in the UK (Campbell and Childs 2015a) and globally is in the same direction: quotas (when well designed) deliver increased numbers of women into legislatures (www.quotaproject.org). There is a 10 percentage point

Table 22.1 Women candidates by party and seat type 2015

	All seats		Target seats	
	Women candidates %	Men candidates %	Women candidates %	Men candidates %
Total	27	73	-	-
Conservative	26	74	28	72
Labour	34	66	52	47
SNP	36	64	-	-
Liberal Democrat	26	74	35	65
UKIP	13	87	20	80

Source: www.parliamentarycandidates.org

difference between countries using sex/gender quotas and those that do not. And of those countries with more than 30 per cent women MPs, over 80 per cent use some kind of quota (Norris and Krook 2011).

The numbers and percentages of women MPs elected by the main parties in 2017 once again reveal party asymmetry in women's representation at Westminster: Labour has 119 women MPs, constituting 45 per cent of all Labour MPs; the Tories saw a decline in their number from 70 to 67, with the percentage remaining stagnant at 21 per cent; the SNP also experienced a decline leaving them with only 12 women MPs; while the Liberal Democrats stopped being all male and are now 33 per cent female, albeit on small numbers—four women MPs (Childs, Kenny, and Smith 2017).

Does women's representation matter?

Objectively women are under-represented relative to the population; whether this 'matters' depends on your politics. The feminist case for women's political presence is multidimensional (Phillips 1995; Mansbridge 1999). There are claims that women representatives will give voice to and act for women; others that women representatives symbolize women's ability to 'do' politics, and act as role models. Justice arguments emphasize fairness: how can it be that in the twenty-first century women are marginal in parliamentary politics and effectively governed by men? These arguments have had considerable traction in the last decade or so, with political elites, the parties, and to some extent the public (see Case Study 22).

However, confidence about the acceptance of such arguments into mainstream culture may have been premature and overly optimistic. They are increasingly subject to what might be called the 'PC' critique. The first element of this critique—the 'merit' argument—questions women's political ambition, suitability, and qualifications. Defenders of the merit argument often claim that women selected by party quotas and equality promotion measures will be substandard tokens. Such an argument is laughable: Parliament only needs 300 'good' women out of millions. Furthermore, research on New Labour women MPs who were elected through AWS found them to be equally well qualified (Allen, Cutts, and Campbell 2016) and as successful as other candidates (Cutts and Widdop 2012). The second element—the class argument—charges that women's representation has been prioritized over working-class men's, and that the women who have been elected to Parliament are *all* middle-class. This argument is seemingly resonating loudly. It is also deeply flawed: it is middle-class men's over-representation which squeezes out the spaces in Parliament. In any case, representation is not a zero sum game—middle-class women 'versus' working-class men. Women are members of the working-class, and working-class women are under-represented too. Critically, quota strategies for women are not incompatible with increasing the wider diversity of candidates and MPs (Nugent and Krook 2016); in fact if they are well designed, quotas should foster heterogeneity of representation by overthrowing white, male, middle-class political privilege.

Women's symbolic representation: role models

Theresa May's succession as the UK's second Conservative woman prime minister in July 2016 is another example of women breaking into the male political elite. The longest serving Home Secretary, she was best placed to take over the Conservative party when its leading men stabbed each other in the back in July 2016. Few doubted that she was qualified for the job, bar the other Conservative female candidate, who questioned May's commitment to—'stake in'—the future of the UK on the basis of May's non-motherhood (Coates and Sylvester 2016). From a perspective of gender equality, the public and the commentariat's reaction was reassuringly dismissive if not hostile to such a claim. May's very presence in the top job is symbolic. On the death of Margaret Thatcher, the UK's first woman PM, popular discussion (mostly) agreed that Thatcher had proven that women could be effective prime ministers (Childs 2013). Qualitative research has also shown that Conservative women MPs of today talk about how growing up with a woman PM inspired them to get involved in politics—the role model effect (Childs and Webb 2012). The outcome of the 2017 general election—an election in which May and the Conservative Party had been widely expected to do well—and the associated critical media representation of May's leadership, raises important questions for future research regarding representation, gender, and political leadership.

Acting for women

For many women activists and feminists the promise of women's presence in Parliament is greater attention to women's issues, interests, and perspectives (Phillips 1995). However, it is mistaken to confuse women's bodies with feminist minds—simply increasing the number of women in Parliament will not necessarily deliver 'better' policies for women. There is no universally agreed set of women's issues (Celis et al. 2014); women differ in what they consider to be in the 'interests of women', by party and other identities; and what role do men play in 'acting for' women? To what extent do political institutions—Parliament and parties—constrain the articulation of, and responsiveness to, women (Lovenduski 2005)? At the very minimum, there is agreement among feminists that the political interest of women is to have a seat at the political table (Jónasdóttir 1990).

Whether women representatives make (enough of) a substantive difference has become the subject of substantial academic research, as well as much conjecture. Arguments for the representation of women do not require that women do 'make a difference' in terms of substantive representation, but it remains an important empirical question. Researchers have, *inter alia*, found sex differences in political attitudes between women and men candidates and MPs on what are commonly understood as women's issues. There is evidence too of attitudinal congruency between women MPs and the women they represent. Turning to behaviour, we can see differences in the types of parliamentary questions asked, with women more likely to ask gendered questions and signing more women's and feminist Early Day Motions. Women's and men's membership of select committees is also gendered, and women's presence on committees can affect the nature of inquiries. For example, Fiona MacTaggart MP speaks of her time on the Defence Committee, and of it addressing issues to do with service families as well as bombs (Childs 2008). Reviewing the UK Parliament since 1997, Joni Lovenduski (2005) concluded that while it was not always possible to prove conclusively that a particular outcome resulted from the actions of (only) women, there was rather a lot of circumstantial evidence. A decade on, her conclusion has considerably greater force. What constitutes a mainstream political issue, indisputably, has been revolutionized by feminists over the last 20 to 30 years. Such conclusions can also be found in global evidence (for example Swers 2002 on the US Congress), and closer to home, studies of the Scottish Parliament and the National Assembly for Wales (Mackay and McAllister 2012).

In our recent review of what the 2010 Coalition government did for women (Campbell and Childs 2015b) we explored how the government addressed the issues of violence against women (VAW) and childcare. The issue of VAW rose up the parliamentary agenda in the 1990s despite having been hitherto regarded as marginal, and indeed a radical issue. It is now a central and agreed part of the 'women's issue agenda', as evidenced by parties' pledges in successive general election manifestos. VAW is also the focus of sustained legislative and policy interventions. A key legacy of the 1997–2010 New Labour years, under the Coalition Theresa May was joined by William Hague and then Prime Minister David Cameron in championing the issue. Moving to childcare, the issue was also a key concern for many incoming New Labour women MPs in 1997. It was very much part of the government's economic strategy under Blair and Brown, and a major concern among Treasury ministers, many of whom were women. As with VAW, childcare is an issue over which the main parties now compete at election time. Childcare policy reveals inter-party differences: between market-based and state solutions, and in respect of the contexts in which women's choices about paid employment are made. Such inter-party differences illustrate that representatives' gender and party identities influence how MPs, female and male, act for women in the UK Parliament.

A gender-sensitive House of Commons

The institutions in which MPs act mediate much, if not all, of what they do, how they experience Parliament, and how their presence and action is received. The feminist institutionalist turn in contemporary gender and politics research (Mackay, Armitage, and Malley 2014) acknowledges—at the outset—that women enter political institutions not of their own making. The job of the feminist institutionalist is to map and interrogate how the 'formal architecture and informal networks, connections, conventions, rules and norms of institutions' differentially impact women and men, and differently raced women and men (Lovenduski 2010, 1998). Research has revealed the masculinized nature of UK parliamentary politics and that women MPs experience Parliament as gendered actors (Crewe 2015; Lovenduski 2012; Benger 2015). To take one example, in parliamentary debates women MPs are much more likely to be interrupted (Shaw 2000).

According to the IPU a gender-sensitive parliament (GSP) is one that responds to the 'needs and interests' of both women and men in terms of its 'structures, operations, methods and work' (IPU 2011). The UK Parliament falls a long way short of achieving this standard. Table 22.2 documents the 'diversity insensitivities' of the current UK House of Commons. It uses traffic light colours to signal whether the Commons is doing badly (red)

Table 22.2 'RAG' analysis of the UK House of Commons: representation and inclusion

Dimension	Measure	Red	Amber	Green
Equality of participation	Diversity of MPs (sex, ethnicity, class, sexuality, disability)	X		
	Women's House leadership positions	X		
	Women's participation (internal structures, committees)		X	
Infrastructure	Standing Orders		X	
	Calendar and sitting hours	X		
	Equalities and diversity body (policy)			X
	Equalities and diversity body (institutional)	X		
	Parliamentary buildings and spaces		X	
	Childcare and child-friendly provisions		X	
	Maternity and parental leave	X		
Culture	House commitment and action plan	X		
	Chamber culture (PMQs and debates)	X		

or well (green). Amber signals that there has been some improvement but that considerably more needs to be done. Only in a single instance does the Commons unambiguously score green: the Women and Equalities Committee, which was set up after the 2015 general election, temporary then, and made permanent in 2017.

The Good Parliament report published in 2016 identifies 43 recommendations that have the potential to make the membership of the House more representative; enable Members to be more effective in their parliamentary work, both individually and collectively; and to enhance the representational relationship between the British public, Members, and the House of Commons as an institution (Childs 2016). The recommendations address (i) equality and participation in the House; (ii) parliamentary infrastructure; and (iii) Commons culture. The first dimension identifies the barriers to women's equal selection and election to the House (as discussed in the first part of this chapter) but also examines whether women MPs are able to participate as equals once they are present in the House. The second dimension takes a critical look at how Parliament facilitates the work of Members and whether this privileges a particular type of MP—explicitly or implicitly. As such it includes 'everything from the buildings and furniture of Parliament to the official rules and working practices that underpin the array of Members' parliamentary activities' (Childs 2016, 7). The third dimension acknowledges 'that the official, written-down rules never tell the whole story about how institutions function on the ground—this is what might be thought of as the "normal way of doing things"' (ibid., 8).

Each recommendation in the report is attached to a responsible actor within Parliament—a minister, a committee, or an MP, for example. By making this link, individual actors, and the House as an institution, can be held to account for their (in)action. This is critical to changing the Commons, because historically it has lacked the institutional will to address issues of representation and inclusion. MPs are often regarded as individual office holders, which can obscure a wider *institutional* responsibility. Despite the efforts of key individuals in bringing about change (see Case Study 22 and Ruddock 2016), this is no longer a satisfactory state. Informed directly by the IPU's GSP framework, a new body of MPs—the Commons Reference Group on Representation and Inclusion—has been established by the Speaker. Its creation meets the IPU's criteria of an institutional equalities and diversity body, and, by generating a 'programme of action' for the next Parliament, it will take the lead on transforming the House of Commons from the masculinized institution that it currently is, to one that is sensitive to gender, and indeed other diversities.

Conclusion

The outcome of the 2017 general election for women's representation should remind students of politics that the descriptive under-representation of women is ongoing. Everyday notions of an ever upwards trajectory is mistaken; the numbers of Conservative women MPs declined; in Scotland the percentage of women declined from 34 per cent to 29 per cent, and overall Westminster is still two-thirds male. The one hundredth anniversary of women's gaining the right to vote and sit in the House (2018) should serve as a salutary reminder that political equality is far from achieved in the UK. Indeed, as this chapter has shown, the outcomes of elections for women's representation reflect party decisions; permissive legislation allows for quotas. To date only Labour has chosen to use quotas at Westminster, and this legacy remains a significant reason for the different levels between parties and the low levels of representation overall. This is why advocates of gender equality in politics call for legislative quotas. There is also plenty to do in transforming the gender sensitivity of the UK Parliament (and for that matter the political parties), both to increase the supply of women seeking selection as candidates, and to promote the individual and collective effectiveness of women MPs once they are present at Westminster. Then there are questions of women's substantive representation—of what it means for representatives to act for women. Here, as this chapter has demonstrated, what is in the interests of women is likely to be strongly influenced by party ideology.

Further Reading

- CAMPBELL, R. and CHILDS, S. (2014) *Deeds and Words: Gendering Politics After Joni Lovenduski*, Colchester, Essex: ECPR Press.
- CHILDS, S. (2008) *Women and British Party Politics*, London: Routledge.
- LOVENDUSKI, J. (2005) *Feminizing Politics*, Cambridge: Polity.
- PHILLIPS, A. (1995) *The Politics of Presence*, Oxford: Oxford University Press.

Case Study 22: Parliamentary efforts to address under-representation: the Speaker's Conference 2008

A Speaker's Conference is a mechanism to bring representatives of the political parties together, under the chairmanship of the (politically impartial) Speaker, to consider an issue of constitutional importance. The first Speaker's Conference (1916–17) was significant for reaching a consensus on the right of women to vote. This agreement paved the way for the Representation of the People Act 1918. The remit of the 2008 Speaker's Conference (on parliamentary representation), as agreed by the House of Commons, was to:

Consider the disparity between the representation of women, ethnic minorities and disabled people in the House of Commons and their representation in the UK population at large (Speaker's Conference 2010a).

The Conference was established as a committee of Members of the House of Commons, and was given until the dissolution of Parliament in March 2010 to complete its work and report with recommendations to address under-representation. In view of the significant additional demands which the Conference would place on the Speaker, Anne Begg MP (now Dame Anne Begg) was appointed to act as the Vice-Chair. The other MPs who were appointed to the Conference were chosen to ensure the group would be as widely representative of the Commons as possible. The Conference approached its work in the manner of a select committee inquiry: it invited written submissions, conducted seminars, took formal oral evidence from witnesses, and held a number of informal meetings (including in Manchester, Leeds, Cheltenham, Cardiff, and East London) to ask how the barriers to election for people from under-represented communities, including the LGBT+ community, could be addressed.

THE ROLE OF POLITICAL PARTIES

The Conference found that political parties are the 'gatekeepers' to elected office, because local party support is a 'virtual necessity' for candidates to succeed at elections to the UK Parliament (Speaker's Conference 2010a). The Conference also identified 'supply-side barriers' which may deter people from putting themselves forward as candidates, and 'demand-side barriers' which may stop people from being selected once they have put themselves forward.

Supply-side barriers included: the costs of candidacy (loss of earnings, transport, accommodation, care costs), cultural and social pressures, access to networks and training, and the culture of Parliament (e.g. the confrontational style of debate; late sittings). Demand-side barriers included direct discrimination—e.g. women being challenged about their family lives—and indirect discrimination. The latter may lead a constituency selection panel to choose a candidate who 'looks like' other MPs—white, male, and middle class.

While political parties are not directly accountable to Parliament, the cross-party support for the Speaker's Conference encouraged them to participate fully in the inquiry. Early in its work the Conference conducted cross-party talks with senior officials from the three main political parties in the House of Commons (then Labour, Conservative, and Liberal Democrat). Having seen that the inquiry was being conducted impartially, the parties agreed to monitoring of candidate selection from 2009. The main parties voluntarily (albeit after reminders) submitted returns detailing candidate sex and ethnicity, how they had been selected (e.g. open primary, all-women shortlist), and whether or not they identified as disabled (Speaker's Conference 2010b). The Conference believed that greater transparency about candidate selection would ensure that parties were held to account for their selections.

The leaders of the three main parties (Gordon Brown, David Cameron, and Nick Clegg) were persuaded to attend a public evidence session held by the Conference and to make public commitments to address under-representation in their parties (Speaker's Conference 2010c).

EFFECTING CHANGE

It is important to be realistic about what the Speaker's Conference might have hoped to achieve. Previous Conferences had considered questions which were sometimes complex or potentially divisive but where there was a clear decision that could be taken and implemented. (For example, should women be allowed to vote? Or, how should elections be paid for?) The issues for the

2008 Conference were always unlikely to be resolved swiftly and decisively. Determinants of political representation are multiple—while some can be redressed immediately, others reflect wider societal attitudes and structural issues which may take longer to change.

Some improvements in the diversity of MPs are evident, as this chapter has documented. The Conference may also have helped to raise awareness of the importance of diverse representation on the grounds of justice, legitimacy, and effectiveness. The Conference secured legislation which would make candidate diversity monitoring mandatory, in s106 of the Equality Act 2010, although this provision is yet to be brought into effect. An 'access to elected office' fund to help meet additional campaigning costs incurred by disabled candidates was established in 2010 but was closed after the 2015 election (Government Equalities Office 2017). A nursery has been established on the Parliamentary Estate and an access to elected office fund for Scotland was established in 2016.

The Conference was required to report by the end of the 2005 Parliament. As it was not reconstituted in the 2010 Parliament, it could not continue to hold meetings or request information, to hold the government to account. However, Dame Anne Begg and other Conference members continued to press for action while they remained in the House, for example by arranging backbench debates which ministers had to answer, such as the debate on parliamentary representation on 12 January 2012. The All-Party Parliamentary Group on Women in Parliament took up the issue of women's under-representation (APPG on Women in Parliament 2014) and successfully pressured for the creation of a Women and Equalities Select Committee, which was created in 2015. Furthermore, the 2016 *The Good Parliament* report was centrally informed by the lessons of the 2008 Speaker's Conference. While one cannot point to a direct effect, the 2008 Speaker's Conference was undoubtedly an important step towards recent actions to enhance representation—specifically the support from Mr Speaker from that first report to subsequent ones, as well as the input from Sarah Childs.

This case study shows the importance of cross-party support to effect change in women's representation. It also demonstrates that change often occurs over a period of time and as a result of a series of actions, reports, and policy, rather than thanks to a single act.

Primary sources

- Childs, S. (2016) *The Good Parliament*, Bristol: Bristol University. Online at: http://www.bris.ac.uk/media-library/sites/news/2016/july/20%20Jul%20Prof%20Sarah%20Childs%20The%20Good%20Parliament%20report.pdf [accessed 24 June 2017].

- Speaker's Conference (on Parliamentary Representation) (2010a) *Final Report*, HC 239-I, London: The Stationery Office. Online at: https://www.publications.parliament.uk/pa/spconf/239/239i.pdf [accessed 14 April 2017].

- Speaker's Conference (on Parliamentary Representation) (2010c) *Minutes of Evidence 20 October 2009*, HC 239-III, London: The Stationery Office. Online at: https://www.publications.parliament.uk/pa/spconf/239/9102001.htm [accessed 14 April 2017].

- Women in Parliament APPG (2014) *Improving Parliament: Creating a Better and More Representative House*, London: House of Commons. Online at: http://www.appgimprovingparliamentreport.co.uk/ [accessed 24 June 2017].

- Women and Equalities Committee (2016) *Women in the House of Commons, after the 2020 General Election: Fifth Report of Session 2016–17*, London: The Stationery Office, HC 630. Online at: https://www.publications.parliament.uk/pa/cm201617/cmselect/cmwomeq/630/630.pdf [accessed 24 August 2017].

FURTHER CASE STUDIES

- The Women and Equalities Select Committee's (2016) inquiry and report into women in Parliament.
- Debate on *The Good Parliament* report (HC Debates, 2 November 2016, cc. 391–416WH).
- The case for a Speaker's Conference (see HC Debates, 12 November 2008, cc. 896–912).

References

ALLEN, P., CUTTS, D., and CAMPBELL, R. (2016) 'Measuring the Quality of Politicians Elected by Gender Quotas—Are They Any Different?', *Political Studies*, Vol. 64 (1), pp. 143–63.

ALL-PARTY PARLIAMENTARY GROUP ON WOMEN IN PARLIAMENT (2014) *Improving Parliament: Creating a better and more representative House*, London: House of Commons. Online at: http://appgimprovingparliamentreport.co.uk/download/APPG-Women-In-Parliament-Report-2014.pdf [accessed 14 April 2017].

BENGER, J. (2015) *Report for the House of Commons Administration Committee on the findings of the interview study with Members on women's experience in Parliament*, London: House of Commons, Administration Committee, 21 August 2015. Online at: http://www.parliament.uk/documents/commons-committees/admin-committee/Memoranda.pdf [accessed 8 June 2017].

BUCKLEY, F. (2016) 'The 2016 Irish election demonstrated how gender quotas can shift the balance on female representation', *LSE European Politics and Policy Blog*, 16 March. Online at: http://blogs.lse.ac.uk/europpblog/2016/03/16/the-2016-irish-election-demonstrated-how-gender-quotas-can-shift-the-balance-on-female-representation/ [accessed 8 June 2017].

CAMPBELL, R. and CHILDS, S. (2014) 'Parents in Parliament: "Where's Mum?"', *Political Quarterly*, Vol. 85 (4), pp. 487–92.

CAMPBELL, R. and CHILDS, S. (2015a) 'All aboard the pink battle bus? Women Voters, Candidates and Party Leaders, and Women's Issues at the 2015 General Election', *Parliamentary Affairs*, Vol. 68 (1), pp. 206–23.

CAMPBELL, R. and CHILDS, S. (2015b) 'What the Coalition Did for Women: A New Gender Consensus, Coalition Division and Gendered Austerity' in A. Seldon and M. Finn (eds.), *The Coalition Effect, 2010–2015*, Cambridge: Cambridge University Press, pp. 397–429.

CELIS, K., CHILDS, S., KANTOLA, J., and KROOK, M. L. (2014) 'Constituting women's interests through representative claims', *Politics & Gender*, Vol. 10 (2), 149–74.

CHILDS, S. (2008) *Women and British Party Politics: Descriptive, Substantive and Symbolic Representation*. London: Routledge.

CHILDS, S. (2013) 'Thatcher's Gender Trouble: Ambivalence and the Thatcher Legacy', *Political Studies Association Blog*, 17 April. Online at: https://www.psa.ac.uk/political-insight/blog/thatcher%e2%80%99s-gender-trouble-ambivalence-and-thatcher-legacy [accessed 8 June 2017].

CHILDS, S. (2016) *The Good Parliament*, Bristol: University of Bristol. Online at: http://www.bristol.ac.uk/media-library/sites/news/2016/july/20%20Jul%20Prof%20Sarah%20Childs%20The%20Good%20Parliament%20report.pdf [accessed 8 June 2016].

CHILDS, S., KENNY, M., and SMITH, J. (2017) 'Let's Put the Champagne on Ice: The Commons' Missing Women', *Political Studies Association Blog*, 13 June. Online at: https://www.psa.ac.uk/insight-plus/blog/let%E2%80%99s-put-champagne-ice-commons%E2%80%99-missing-women [accessed 24 June 2017].

CHILDS, S. and WEBB, P. (2012) *Sex, Gender and the Conservative Party*, London: Palgrave Macmillan.

COATES, S. and SYLVESTER, R. (2016) 'Being a Mother Gives me Edge on May—Leadsom', *The Times*, 9 July. Online at: https://www.thetimes.co.uk/edition/news/being-a-mother-gives-me-edge-on-may-leadsom-0t7bbm29x [accessed 8 June 2017].

CRACKNELL, R., McGUINNESS, F., and RHODES, C. (2010) *General Election 2010*, House of Commons Library Research Paper 10/36, 2 February. Online at: http://researchbriefings.files.parliament.uk/documents/RP10-36/RP10-36.pdf [accessed 24 June 2017].

CREWE, E. (2015) *The House of Commons*, London: Bloomsbury.

CUTTS, D. and WIDDOP, P. (2012) 'Was Labour penalised where it stood all women shortlist candidates? An analysis of the 2010 UK General Election', *British Journal of Politics and International Relations*, Vol. 15 (3), pp. 435–55.

GOVERNMENT EQUALITIES OFFICE (2017) *Access to Elected Office Fund*. Online at: https://www.gov.uk/access-to-elected-office-fund/overview [accessed 14 April 2017].

Hawkins, O., Keen, R., and Nakatudde, N. (2015) *General Election 2015*, House of Commons Library Research Paper CBP7186, 28 July. Online at: http://researchbriefings.parliament.uk/ResearchBriefing/Summary/CBP-7186 [accessed 24 June 2017].

IPU (2011) *Gender Sensitive Parliaments: Towards parliaments that respond to the needs and interests of both men and women in their structures, operations, methods and work*, Geneva: Inter-Parliamentary Union.

IPU (2017) *Women in National Parliaments—situation by 1st June 2017*, Geneva: Inter-Parliamentary Union. Online at: www.ipu.org/wmn-e/classif.htm [accessed 24 June 2017].

JÓNASDÓTTIR, A. (1990) 'On the Concept of Interest, Women's Interests, and the Limitations of Interest Theory' in K. Jones and A. Jónasdóttir (eds.), *The Political Interests of Gender, Developing Theory and Research with a Feminist Face*, London: Sage, pp. 33–65.

LOVENDUSKI, J. (1998) 'Gendering research in political science', *Annual Review of Political Science*, Vol. 1 (1), pp. 333–56.

LOVENDUSKI, J. (2005) *Feminizing Politics*, Cambridge: Polity Press.

LOVENDUSKI, J. (2010) 'A long way to go: The final report of the Speaker's Conference on Parliamentary Representation', *Political Quarterly*, Vol. 81 (3), pp. 438–42.

LOVENDUSKI, J. (2012) 'Prime Minister's questions as political ritual', *British Politics*, Vol. 7 (4), pp. 314–40.

MACKAY, F., ARMITAGE, F., and MALLEY, R. (2014) 'Gender and political institutions' in R. Campbell and S. Childs (eds.), *Deeds and Words: Gendering Politics after Joni Lovenduski*, Colchester: ECPR Press, pp. 93–112.

MACKAY, F. and McALLISTER, L. (2012) 'Feminising British politics: six lessions from devolution in Scotland and Wales', *Political Quarterly*, Vol. 83 (4), pp 730–4.

MANSBRIDGE, J. (1999) 'Should Blacks Represent Blacks and Women Represent Women: A Contingent "Yes"', *Journal of Politics*, Vol. 61 (3), pp 628–57.

NORRIS, P. and KROOK, M. L. (2011) *Gender Equality in Elected Office: A Six Step Action Plan*, OSCE Draft Report, Vienna: OSCE. Online at: https://www.hks.harvard.edu/fs/pnorris/Acrobat/OSCEReport_Gender_equality_Norris-Krook.pdf [accessed 8 June 2017].

NORRIS, P. and LOVENDUSKI, J. (1995) *Political Recruitment: Gender, Race, and Class in the British Parliament*, New York: Cambridge University Press.

NUGENT, M. and KROOK, M. L. (2016) 'Gender quotas do not pose a threat to "merit" at any stage of the political process', *Democratic Audit blog*, 19 February. Online at: http://www.democraticaudit.com/2016/02/19/gender-quotas-do-not-pose-a-threat-to-merit-at-any-stage-of-the-political-process/ [accessed 8 June 2017].

PHILLIPS, A. (1995) *The Politics of Presence*, Oxford: Oxford University Press.

RALLINGS, C. and THRASHER, M. (2007) *British Electoral Facts 1832–2006*, London: Routledge.

RUDDOCK, J. (2016) *Going Nowhere*, London: Biteback.

SHAW, S. (2000) 'Language, Gender and Floor Apportionment in Political Debates', *Discourse & Society*, Vol. 11 (3), pp. 401–18.

SHEPHERD-ROBINSON, L. and LOVENDUSKI, J. (2002) *Women and Candidate Selection in British Political Parties*, London: Fawcett.

SPEAKER'S CONFERENCE (2010a) *Speaker's Conference (on Parliamentary Representation): Final Report*, HC 239-I. London: The Stationery Office. Online at: https://www.publications.parliament.uk/pa/spconf/239/239i.pdf [accessed 14 April 2017].

SPEAKER'S CONFERENCE (2010b) *Speaker's Conference (on Parliamentary Representation): Monitoring Report and candidate selection data*. London: The Stationery Office. Online at: http://www.publications.parliament.uk/pa/spconf/spconf.htm [accessed 14 April 2017].

SPEAKER'S CONFERENCE (2010c) *Speaker's Conference (on Parliamentary Representation): Minutes of Evidence 20 October 2009*, HC 239-III. London: The Stationery Office. Online at: https://www.publications.parliament.uk/pa/spconf/239/9102001.htm [accessed 14 April 2017].

SWERS, M. (2002) *The Difference Women Make: The Policy Impact of Women in Congress*, Chicago: Chicago University Press.

23

Representation in the Lords

Peter Dorey and Matthew Purvis

INTRODUCTION

As Britain has long considered itself to be an excellent example of a 'representative democracy', the existence of the unelected House of Lords as one of the two Houses of Parliament has long been subject to criticism, especially (but not solely) from the Left. This is because the House of Lords today—one of the largest second chambers in the world—is still an almost wholly nominated, unelected, parliamentary institution, with most peers formally appointed by the Queen, albeit nominated by the prime minister of the day. However, some peers are also appointed by a House of Lords Appointments Commission, mainly those of a non-political nature. Such appointments, combined with the 26 places reserved for Church of England bishops and 92 seats for hereditary peers, has led to sustained complaints that the House of Lords cannot be considered representative, and is incompatible with Britain's status as a parliamentary democracy. However, such criticism strongly implies that representation can only be genuine or worthwhile if the 'representative' institution is elected, rather than having its membership determined by some other means. This, though, is a rather narrow and prescriptive criterion of representation, for there are several others. Indeed, like many key words in politics (such as 'democracy' and 'power'), 'representation' itself is an essentially contested concept: its very definition is subject to different interpretations and perspectives, to the extent that books have been written on the various meanings of representation, one of the most notable being Hanna Pitkin's (1967) *The Concept of Representation*. Moreover, two academics have relatively recently applied Pitkin's categories of representation specifically to the House of Lords, albeit linked to peers' own views of their roles and representativeness (Bochel and Defty 2012).

 Parliamentary terms Appointments Commission

An independent seven-member public body which vets the appointment of life peers from political parties and recommends individual nominations for non-party political life peerages.

However, rather than seeking to emulate Pitkin's rather esoteric and discursive philosophical study of forms of representation, this chapter will consider four discrete modes of representation and representativeness vis-à-vis the House of Lords: political representativeness; social representativeness; individual representation; sectional representation.

Political representativeness

Prior to the House of Lords Act 1999, which removed all but 92 of the hereditary peers (as Case Study 23 explains), the Conservative Party enjoyed a significant advantage in the House of Lords, because the overwhelming majority of hereditary peers were Conservatives, reflecting the fact that many of them emanated from aristocratic backgrounds, and often owned (or inherited) considerable land, property, and/or wealth. They were hardly likely to be in favour of radical redistribution or egalitarianism. However, when most of the hereditary peers were removed in 1999, the size of the House fell from around 1,200 peers eligible to sit and vote, to around 786 today. Following this reform, political representation in the House of Lords changed significantly, whereupon no party has since enjoyed an overall majority, as shown in Table 23.1 which provides a snapshot of the relative party strengths today.

Indeed, in this key respect, the 2016 political composition of the House of Lords actually represented the share of the vote attracted by the main parties in the 2015 general election rather more closely than the actual number of seats won in the House of Commons. This is because Britain's first-past-the-post electoral system often awards a share of seats in the House of Commons to the two largest parties which greatly exceeds their actual share of the vote in the general election.

Such over-representation is not replicated in the (appointed) House of Lords, meaning that the political composition of the second chamber is actually somewhat closer to the main parties' share of votes in the general election. For example, having won virtually 37 per cent of votes in the 2015 general election, the Conservatives currently occupy 32 per cent of seats in the House of Lords. Meanwhile, Labour's peers constitute 26 per cent of the second chamber's membership, while the party won 30 per cent of votes cast in the 2015 general election. The 2017 general election resulted in a much higher proportion of vote share between the two main parties, and one would suspect that if this trend continues it will reflect itself eventually in the House of Lords' party composition. Obviously, membership of the two Houses is determined totally differently—election versus appointment—but our point is that seats in the post-1999 House of Lords have, overall, more closely corresponded to the share of the votes won by the main parties in general elections. Indeed, it could be argued that although this has not been a conscious or explicit objective when appointing new life peers, the House of Lords is actually more politically representative of the British electorate, not in spite of being unelected, but precisely because it is not elected.

Table 23.1 Party representation in the House of Lords, October 2016 (excluding 26 *ex officio* Bishops)

Party	Life peers	Hereditaries	Total peers	% of total
Conservative	207	49	256	33
Labour	203	4	207	26
Liberal Democrat	100	4	104	13
Cross-benchers	149	32	181	23
Others (minor parties)	14	1	15	2
Non-affiliated	22	1	23	3
Total	**695**	**91**	**786**	**100**

Source: Kelly and Taylor (2016)

Parliamentary terms Life peers

Members of the House of Lords appointed by the monarch following nomination by a political party or by the House of Lords Appointments Commission and whose title is not hereditary.

However, because peers are appointed for life, the party balance is somewhat slower and harder to change, especially for smaller parties. For example, between 2010 and 2015, 51 Liberal Democrat peers were appointed to make its strength more representative of the 2010 general election vote, where the party polled 23 per cent of votes cast and returned 57 MPs. Following the 2015 general election, the party's Lords strength was disproportionate compared to its 8 per cent of the vote and eight MPs, because their peers were not reduced to reflect this dramatic loss of support. Meanwhile, although UKIP polled 4 million votes in the 2015 election, representing a 12.6 per cent share, it only had three peers in the House of Lords—barely 0.5 per cent of party-affiliated Members.

Social representativeness

To its critics, the House of Lords has traditionally been a bastion of elitism and privilege, due to its overwhelmingly upper-class membership: many peers symbolized the old aristocracy—wealthy landowners and mansion-dwellers who inherited their titles, property, riches, and seats in the House of Lords upon the death of their fathers. Yet this portrayal has been inaccurate and unfair for a long time, certainly since 1958, when the Life Peerages Act was passed. Hitherto, the vast majority of the House of Lords' membership comprised hereditary peers—men who inherited their titles when their fathers died. However, from 1958 onwards, an increasing number of peers were women, whose representation has since grown to just over a quarter of the House today. However, as women constitute 51 per cent of the British population, this clearly still falls far short of offering true social representativeness, reflecting to some extent the challenges of gender representation inherent in UK political parties and the House of Commons itself (see Chapter 22).

The Life Peerages Act 1958 created a new category of peer, namely individuals who were appointed to the House for their lifetime, usually as a reward for distinguished public service, or outstanding success in their previous career. Their title would not be passed on to their offspring when they died. True, most of these life peers were from a relatively narrow range of professions, and hence did not mirror the British population overall, but they still made the House of Lords somewhat more socially representative than it had ever been previously, while also increasing the ratio of (appointed) life peers compared to hereditary peers. So although the second chamber certainly did not witness an influx of traffic wardens or train drivers, there was a steady increase in the numbers and range of peers from other careers and occupations. Baldwin has emphasized the extent to which, since the 1958 Act, 'the House of Lords has acquired newly ennobled bankers, engineers, diplomats, lawyers, businessmen, economists, trade unionists, military commanders, politicians, academics, educationalists, scientists, administrators, and senior civil servants', and that their specialist expertise has greatly enhanced the breadth and depth of knowledge in the House, such that 'its role in representing important "interests" in society has been reinforced' (Baldwin 1990, 156). Indeed, the former Chancellor of the Exchequer, Lord (Geoffrey) Howe, suggested that as a consequence of the influx of post-1958 life peers, 'the diversity of real expertise now available must far exceed that in any other legislative chamber in the world' (Howe 2005, 136).

Table 23.2 Main occupational backgrounds of peers compared to MPs (%), excluding former MPs and ministers

Peers (2012)		MPs (2015)	
Business/commerce	8.6	Business	30.7
Academia (HE)	7.7	Political (party worker, SpAd, etc.)	17.1
Banking/finance	7.3	Lawyer	14.2
Lawyer	7.0	White collar*	11.3
Voluntary sector/NGOs	4.3	Author/publisher/journalist	5.4
Journalism/media/publishing	3.8	School teacher	2.6
Politics (not MPs or ministers)	3.2	Civil service/local government	2.6
Trade unionism	3.2	College/university lecturer	2.6
Local govt/public sector	2.9	Doctor	1.6
Medicine	2.3	Farmer	1.1
Culture/arts/sport	2.3	Miner	1.1

* This category includes the voluntary sector, and trade union officials
Sources: Lords Appointments Commission (2012); Audickas (2016)

Certainly, some occupations and professions have enjoyed a higher representation in the House of Lords than in the House of Commons, as illustrated in Table 23.2.

Even when there is a parity between the number (or proportion) of MPs and peers emanating from similar occupational backgrounds, there is often a subtle qualitative difference, for the latter will often have reached a higher or more senior stage in their careers by the time they enter the House of Lords. For example, Shell has noted that although 'the number of doctors may be roughly similar in the two Houses … those in the Lords as life peers tend to be very senior figures at the peak of the profession, while those in the Commons are generally younger and more junior'; and the same is true, he adds, of trade unionists (Shell 2007, 81). This reflects the fact that it is only later in a career that a person will have acquired considerable expertise, or maybe achieved public recognition, and thus be deemed worthy of a peerage.

Furthermore, the average age of peers on appointment is 58, compared to 50 for MPs elected at the 2015 general election. It is noteworthy that appointments—both those nominated by parties and those nominated by the Appointments Commission to be independent cross-bench peers—have also increasingly reflected the diversity of the people of the United Kingdom. For example, the last Parliament saw the largest proportion of women appointed, and by 2013, 22 per cent of those nominated by the Appointments Commission were from a minority ethnic background (Purvis 2014). However, in both instances this falls short of the number of appointments that would be required were this to proportionately reflect these parts of society.

 Parliamentary terms Cross-benchers

Peers in the House of Lords who do not sit according to party groups, being therefore independent.

These factors have imbued some of the House of Lords' debates and scrutiny (of government legislation) with greater expertise, and thereby enabled some peers to speak more knowledgeably or authoritatively on particular topics. In this respect, the social background of many life peers has significantly enhanced the House of Lords' representative function, and ensured that some sections of British society will, indirectly at least, have a voice which might not be heard as much, or as clearly, in the House of Commons, particularly as the latter is characterized by a higher degree of partisanship.

For example, at second reading on the Housing and Planning Bill in 2016, peers from a range of professional and community backgrounds contributed, including those with experience serving as local councillors, a former Chair of English Heritage, a retired head civil servant who now chairs the Peabody Trust, a housing charity, a number of chartered surveyors, the chief executive of a health and community care charity, and the former chief executive of the National Housing Federation. Such was the expertise the House brought to the Bill that the government compromised on several amendments concerning starter homes and accepted a number of amendments from peers, one of which required property agents to be a member of a client money protection scheme, to protect landlords' and tenants' money if an agency went into administration.

Meanwhile, the House of Lords' select committees are renowned for the calibre of their membership, due to the previous occupational backgrounds and consequent expertise of their members. For example, expertise is evident among the peers serving (in 2017) on the highly respected Select Committee on Science and Technology, which includes a former professor of fluid mechanics who subsequently became a chief executive of the Met Office, a professor of civil engineering, a former chief scientific adviser to the Ministry of Defence, an author/journalist on popular science, a President of the Royal Geographic Society/ Chair of Trustees at the Royal Botanic Gardens, Kew, and the Chair of the Woodland Trust.

Consequently, although the House of Lords is obviously devoid of the democratic legitimacy that MPs enjoy, it can boast other strengths and modes of representativeness, most notably 'a diversity and depth of experience within its ranks that is not found in the House of Commons' (Shell 2007, 113).

Individual representation

As peers are not elected by the people, they do not have constituency responsibilities to fulfil, and as a consequence will not normally be sent the type of correspondence that MPs routinely receive, and which usually reflects local issues or problems which constituents may experience with regard to matters of public policy, such as housing allocation and social security claims (see Chapter 25). Nor do peers need to make themselves available, via weekly local surgeries, in the same manner as MPs. However, peers do still receive correspondence from individuals, but it is generally less voluminous than that sent to MPs (about 25 per cent of correspondence sent to Parliament is for the House of Lords/peers), and usually of a different character.

There are three main ways or reasons whereby peers are approached by individuals seeking representation or redress of grievances. First, some citizens might perceive peers to be a potentially more amenable, responsive, or prestigious target than an MP. Second, a peer might be contacted by an individual whose attempt at seeking redress of a grievance or problem via their MP has been unsuccessful or unsatisfactory. In such instances, contacting a peer will probably be viewed as the next stage in pursuing the matter further. Even if a constituent is likely to be mistaken in expecting a peer to solve a problem which the local MP has been unable to remedy, writing to a peer might fulfil Parliament's indirect 'safety valve' function on behalf of citizens who are (or feel) aggrieved; the citizen might feel satisfied that they have pursued their complaint or grievance as far as they can, even if they have failed to elicit the solution they were hoping for.

Third, and most commonly, peers will receive correspondence from individuals who are either linked to a sectional interest, or who have specialist professional expertise, albeit acting independently. In the case of the former, a senior official of a sectional interest might write to peers, or the organization might encourage its members themselves to write to peers on a specific issue relevant to that body. For example, in 2016, a campaign group opposing the proposed HS2 rail project urged its supporters to write to peers, in lieu of an imminent House of Lords debate and vote on the issue. The group, 'Stop HS2', provided supporters with a list of specific arguments (against the project) to convey to peers, and also provided a link which listed all the peers in the House of Lords: this link then provided a 'send an email' facility for each peer (Stop HS2 2016).

With regard to 'independent' individuals with specialist expertise writing to peers, they will usually do so either in connection with some aspect of public policy or legislation which the House of Lords is currently debating, or in response to a call by a select committee for evidence (see Chapter 19). For example, when the House of Lords Select Committee on Social Mobility conducted an inquiry in 2016 into the transition from school to work for 14 to 24 year-olds, its call for written evidence from 'interested individuals and organizations' yielded submissions from more than 20 individuals, most of whom were academics with expertise in aspects of economics, education, employment, social/gender inequalities, or youth cultures (Social Mobility Committee 2016). Many of these respondents were subsequently invited to present oral evidence to the Select Committee.

Sectional representation

Just like individuals, sectional interests (pressure groups, professional associations, etc.) will also lobby peers to table amendments to legislation, particularly at committee stage (Grant 2000, 158; Norton 2013, 254). Indeed, the House of Lords 'has increasingly become a focus for lobbying' by sectional interests since the 1980s (Baldwin 1990, 158). Sometimes, such lobbying will reflect a failure to secure success at the corresponding legislative stage in the House of Commons, often due to somewhat stronger party discipline. However, it might also reflect an assumption by a sectional interest that the greater expertise of some peers will elicit a more sympathetic hearing or response.

Sectional interests are also a major source of evidence to House of Lords select committees. For example, in the aforementioned Social Mobility Select Committee inquiry into the transition from school to work, among the bodies which submitted written evidence were: the Association of Teachers and Lecturers; Barnardo's; British Chambers of Commerce; Careers South West; Centrepoint (a charity for homeless young people); Joseph Rowntree Foundation; Nacro (a charity for young offenders); the Prince's Trust; the Royal College of Speech and Language Therapists. This list indicates the wide range of types of organizations who submit evidence to inquiries, therefore ensuring the representation of different perspectives of sectional representation. Representatives were subsequently invited to give oral evidence to the peers on the Select Committee.

Conclusion

We have seen that the unelected House of Lords fulfils two vital modes of representation. First, the appointed peers can provide the second chamber with a greater degree of party political balance and representativeness than found in the House of Commons (where governing parties are often over-represented, in the sense that they can win a majority of seats/MPs on as little as 36 per cent of vote share). These unelected peers also mean that the House of Lords is somewhat more socially representative than the elected House of Commons, because many peers emanate from a slightly wider range of careers and professions than

MPs. This is certainly not to claim that the House of Lords is in any way a microcosm of British society, but it does mean that the second chamber includes many peers drawn from somewhat different occupations than MPs: more engineers and scientists, for example.

As a consequence of its *relative* political and social representativeness, the House of Lords fulfils a second mode of representation, namely the articulation and expression of views which might not be heard in the House of Commons. Lower levels of partisanship, less political point-scoring, lack of constituency responsibilities, and greater expertise derived from recent (and invariably highly distinguished) careers, all mean that peers can generally devote more time, speak more freely, and offer more authoritative or nuanced insights into debates and scrutiny.

The House of Lords fulfils these vital modes of representation not in spite of its unelected membership, but precisely because it is not elected. Indeed, its unelected character means that the Lords can represent British society as a whole in one other crucial way—namely by taking a longer term or holistic view of policies and legislation, and thus in a manner which contrasts favourably with the often partisan and/or short-term outlook of MPs and parties in the Commons. By representing different interests to MPs, or perhaps doing so in different ways, and adopting a broader, wider or longer term perspective on important policy issues, the House of Lords simultaneously plays a vital role in complementing the work of the House of Commons, and in providing sundry modes of representation, as a direct consequence of *not* being elected.

Further Reading

BOCHEL, H. and DEFTY, A. (2012) 'A more representative chamber: representation and the House of Lords', *Journal of Legislative Studies*, Vol. 18 (1), pp. 82–97.

DOREY, P. and KELSO, A. (2011) *House of Lords Reform Since 1911: Must the Lords Go?*, Basingstoke: Palgrave Macmillan.

NORTON, P. (2017) *Reform of the House of Lords*, Pocket Politics, Manchester: Manchester University Press.

RUSSELL, M. (2013) *The Contemporary House of Lords: Westminster Bicameralism Revived*, Oxford: Oxford University Press.

SHELL, D. (2007) *The House of Lords*, Manchester: Manchester University Press.

Case Study 23: The 1999 House of Lords Act and consequent reform

In 1999, the Labour government passed a House of Lords Act which removed most of the hereditary peers from the second chamber, although 92 were allowed to remain in lieu of further reform. According to Labour's 1997 election manifesto, this was intended to be 'the first step in a process of reform to make the House of Lords more democratic and representative' (Labour Party 1997). However, the implied second step failed to be completed, due partly to lack of agreement among Labour MPs and ministers over precisely how—or how far—the second chamber should be made 'democratic' or 'representative'. This case study shows how the Labour Party strongly condemned the undemocratic and unrepresentative membership of the House of Lords, yet remained unsure about how to reform it, something which has stifled reform attempts since 1997.

There has long been a lack of agreement among Labour MPs about the merits of an elected or appointed House. Supporters of an appointed House fear that an elected second chamber would possess sufficient democratic legitimacy to challenge the Commons. They have also seemed uncertain about how to define 'representativeness'; as political representativeness (and thus about party composition and balance), or as the Chamber being representative of British society, in terms of, for example, ethnicity, gender, and occupation.

To compound the lack of agreement, some Labour MPs have favoured a combination of these two options—namely a partly elected, partly appointed second chamber—yet even this has yielded disagreements over the precise balance to be aimed for, such as: 80:20, 60:40, 50:50, 40:60, or 20:80. These disagreements were clear during the 1997–2007 Blair governments' attempts to reform the Lords, such that when Labour lost the 2010 election after 13 years in power, it remained 'unfinished business'. Nor was this the first time a Labour government had failed to complete its professed commitment to establishing a more representative House of Lords; the 1969 Parliament (No. 2) Bill had been abandoned as a consequence of disagreements within the Labour Party over how—or even whether—to alter the membership of the second chamber (Dorey and Kelso 2011, ch. 5).

As if to avoid such a fate, the 1999 House of Lords Act was immediately followed by the establishment of a Royal Commission, whose remit was:

- To consider and make recommendations on the role and functions of a second chamber.
- To make recommendations on the method or combination of methods of composition required to constitute a second chamber fit for that role and those functions.

Yet it was immediately notable that the latter task did not allude to democracy or elections, and some Labour politicians were immediately sceptical about their government's commitment to a genuinely democratic and more representative House of Lords. They strongly suspected that once most of the hereditary peers had been removed, and the Conservative Party's hitherto prevalence in the second chamber terminated, the cabinet—and particularly Tony Blair himself—would consider the Lords to be sufficiently representative (politically at least), in which case there would be little, if any, further reform. As the veteran Labour left-winger Tony Benn remarked, it was quite likely that what was intended to be 'stage one' of a two-stage process of House of Lords reform would actually 'become the permanent solution' (HC Debates, 2 February 1999, c. 746).

Indeed, the Royal Commission's January 2000 report endorsed a predominantly appointed House of Lords which comprised 550 peers, although three options for a minority of these to be elected were offered: 65, 87, or 195 (Cabinet Office 2000). The non-elected peers would be appointed by an independent commission (thereby limiting prime ministerial patronage) which should seek to ensure greater representation for women and ethnic minorities.

Thereafter, the Blair government's proposals for proceeding to 'stage two' were mired in confusion, not least because of lack of enthusiasm among most cabinet ministers (Robin Cook being a notable exception). A November 2001 White Paper proposed a 600-Member House of Lords in which 20 per cent of Members were elected (Department for Constitutional Affairs 2001), 20 per cent appointed by an independent commission, and the remaining 60 per cent appointed by the party leaders in accordance with their party's strength in the House of Commons. This proposal was widely condemned by MPs and peers from all parties, and duly abandoned in July 2002, when the government announced the creation of an all-party joint (MPs and peers) committee to examine options for determining membership of the upper House, whereupon any proposals would be subject to a free vote.

In fact, the all-party committee offered seven proposals, ranging from an all-elected to an all-appointed House of Lords, and five combinations of part-elected and part-appointed peers. Yet when MPs voted on these options in February 2003, none of them enjoyed majority support, and Labour MPs themselves were deeply divided. For example, 175 Labour MPs voted for a wholly appointed House of Lords, and 181 voted against (HC Debates, 4 February 2003, cc. 225–43).

However, when MPs voted on a similar range of options in March 2007 (reflecting the lack of urgency ascribed to completing 'stage two'), there were clear majorities for a wholly elected House of Lords (HC Debates, 7 March 2007, cc. 1602–28). However, Blair was replaced by Gordon Brown three months later, and although the new prime minister indicated his commitment to establishing a mostly elected second chamber, the cabinet minister with responsibility for this issue, Jack Straw, announced that 'stage two' would not be completed until after the next (2010) general election. Labour lost that election, and 'stage two' has still not been completed because few senior Conservative or Labour MPs genuinely want an elected House of Lords, not least because it would almost inevitably claim to have a mandate from the voters, and thereby challenge the Commons, and thus the government therein.

CONCLUSION

In spite of Labour's often radical rhetoric, its leaders have often been constitutional conservatives when in government. The failure of the Blair government to complete 'stage two' of House of Lords reform reflected a lack of enthusiasm among many Labour MPs and ministers for an elected second chamber, primarily because of the likelihood that this would imbue it with democratic legitimacy, and thus challenge the House of Commons.

This means the House of Lords remains overwhelmingly appointed, so that concerns about its limited 'representativeness' remain. The 1999 removal of most hereditary peers ensured that the House of Lords was much more politically representative; no party has a majority in the second chamber, just as no party wins a majority of votes in British general elections. However, this relative *political* representativeness has not really been accompanied by greater *social* representativeness, in terms of the gender, ethnicity, or occupational backgrounds. The post-1999 House of Lords remains overwhelmingly white, male, and dominated by peers emanating from a relatively narrow group of elite professions. The slow and sporadic nature of House of Lords reform means that there is still a long way to go before Britain can boast of a second chamber which is truly socially representative of the population over which it presides.

Primary sources

- Brown, T. (2017) *House of Lords: Statistical Profile of Membership—January 2017*, House of Lords Library Note 008, 6 February. Online at: http://researchbriefings.files.parliament.uk/documents/LLN-2017-0008/LLN-2017-0008.pdf [accessed 27 June 2017].

- Coleman, C. (2017) *House of Lords: Party and Group Strengths and Voting*, House of Lords Library Note 16, 15 March. Online at: http://researchbriefings.files.parliament.uk/documents/LLN-2017-0016/LLN-2017-0016.pdf [accessed 27 June 2017].

- Department for Constitutional Affairs (2001) *The House of Lords—Completing the Reform*, London: Department for Constitutional Affairs, Cm5291. Online at: http://webarchive.nationalarchives.gov.uk/+/http:/www.dca.gov.uk/constitution/holref/holreform.htm [accessed 27 June 2017].

- Winetrobe, B. K. (1999) *The House of Lords Bill: 'Stage One' Issues*, House of Commons Library Research Paper 99/5, 28 January. Online at: http://researchbriefings.files.parliament.uk/documents/RP99-5/RP99-5.pdf [accessed 27 June 2017].

- Winetrobe, B. K. and Gay, O. (1999) *The House of Lords Bill: Options for 'Stage Two'*, House of Commons Library Research Paper 99/6, 28 January. Online at: http://researchbriefings.files.parliament.uk/documents/RP99-6/RP99-6.pdf [accessed 27 June 2017].

➜ FURTHER CASE STUDIES

- The level of representation from small/minor party peers in the Lords since 1999.
- House of Lords reform during the Coalition government.
- The range of evidence submitted to the NHS Sustainability Committee (2016–17 session).

References

AUDICKAS, L. (2016) *Social Background of MPs 1979–2015*, House of Commons Library Briefing Paper CBP 7483, 25 January. Online at: http://researchbriefings.files.parliament.uk/documents/CBP-7483/CBP-7483.pdf [accessed 25 June 2017].

BALDWIN, N. (1990) 'The House of Lords' in M. Rush (ed.), *Parliament and Pressure Politics*, Oxford: Clarendon Press, pp. 152–77.

BOCHEL, H. and DEFTY, A. (2012) 'A more representative chamber: representation and the House of Lords', *Journal of Legislative Studies*, Vol. 18 (1), pp. 82–97.

CABINET OFFICE (2000) *Independent Report: A House for the Future: Royal Commission on the Reform of the House of Lords*, London: Cabinet Office.

DEPARTMENT FOR CONSTITUTIONAL AFFAIRS (2001) *The House of Lords Completing the Reform*, London: Department for Constitutional Affairs, Cm5291. Online at: http://webarchive.nationalarchives.gov.uk/+/http:/www.dca.gov.uk/constitution/holref/holreform.htm [accessed 25 June 2017].

DOREY, P. and KELSO, A. (2011) *House of Lords Reform Since 1911: Must the Lords Go?*, Basingstoke: Palgrave Macmillan.

GRANT, W. (2000) *Pressure Groups and British Politics*, Basingstoke: Macmillan.

HOWE, G. (2005) 'Membership of the House of Commons and the House of Lords: A Comparison and a Discussion' in N. D. J. Baldwin (ed.), *Parliament in the 21st Century*, London: Politico's, pp. 138–9.

KELLY, R. and TAYLOR, R. (2016) *Peerage Creations since 1997*, House of Commons Library Standard Note SN05867, 8 February. Online at: http://researchbriefings.files.parliament.uk/documents/SN05867/SN05867.pdf [accessed 25 June 2017].

LABOUR PARTY (1997) *New Labour Because Britain deserves better—party manifesto*. Online at: http://labourmanifesto.com/1997/1997-labour-manifesto.shtml [accessed 25 June 2017].

LORDS APPOINTMENTS COMMISSION (2012) *Note on the updated data on the breadth of expertise and experience in the House of Lords*, Commission Secretariat, June. Online at: http://lordsappointments.independent.gov.uk/media/25803/membership%20research%20june%202012.pdf [accessed 24 June 2017].

NORTON, P. (2013) *Parliament in British Politics*, 2nd edition, Basingstoke: Palgrave Macmillan.

PITKIN, H. (1967) *The Concept of Representation*, Berkeley: University of California Press.

PURVIS, M. (2014) *Membership of the House of Lords: Ethnicity, Religion and Disability*, House of Lords Library Note 017, 12 June. Online at: http://researchbriefings.files.parliament.uk/documents/LLN-2014–017/LLN-2014-017.pdf [accessed 25 June 2017].

SHELL, D. (2007) *The House of Lords*, Manchester: Manchester University Press.

SOCIAL MOBILITY COMMITTEE (2016) *List of written evidence, House of Lords*. Online at: http://www.parliament.uk/business/committees/committees-a-z/lords-select/social-mobility/ publications/?type=Written#pnlPublicationFilter [accessed 25 June 2017].

STOP HS2 (2016) *Write to the House of Lords before Thursday's Vote*, 11 April. Online at: http://stophs2.org/news/15385-write-house-lords-thursdays-vote [accessed 25 June 2017].

24

Whips and Rebels

Mark Stuart

INTRODUCTION

In many respects, British government is *party* government. MPs are normally elected under a party label and their job is to deliver a majority on legislation in the House of Commons as ministers or loyal backbenchers. In order to get its legislation passed, the government needs its MPs to be disciplined, and that job belongs to the whips. The title of 'whip' is derived from a hunting term, dating from the days when the hunting party needed to keep the hounds in check.

The roles of both parliamentary whips and backbench MPs is shrouded in myth and mystery. While the whips are widely seen as bullies and cajolers, MPs are regarded as spineless and overly loyal. As this chapter shows, neither of these caricatures is reflected in reality. In more recent times, the role of the whips has become much harder because of growing rebelliousness on the part of MPs—a rebellion occurs when an MP votes against their party line in the division (voting) lobbies. This was especially true in the Coalition government of 2010–15, where the government whips had to try to satisfy the demands of two parties— Liberal Democrat and Conservative, as Case Study 24 demonstrates.

Whips: myths and reality

The three main functions of the whips are management, communication, and persuasion. Without the management function of the whips, most busy MPs would struggle to know which way to vote in the division lobbies. Therefore, a weekly whip is announced by each party, indicating to backbenchers when their attendance is required on a scale of importance from a one-line whip (attendance optional) to a three-line whip, when they are expected to turn up to vote. When MPs vote, the process takes about 15 minutes. MPs pass through one of two lobbies—'aye' and 'no'—and a helpful couple of whips, usually from the government and one of the opposition parties, stand outside the lobbies acting as tellers, ticking off the names of the MPs as they pass through. Unlike many other systems, there is no electronic voting in the House of Commons, nor is there any immediate prospect of such an innovation occurring. During voting, MPs may be able to chat briefly with a minister or a frontbencher, and sometimes last-minute concessions on legislation are granted as a result. The second main function of the whips is communication. The best whips are those who see their role both as communicating the views of the leadership down to MPs but also gathering intelligence on the troops, and passing that information back up to the leadership.

Parliamentary terms Whips

MPs or peers who are responsible for managing the Members of their party, and in particular for ensuring that party Members vote in line with their party's policy. They are also responsible for organizing much of the business of Parliament (e.g. appointments to public bill committees) and will often do this through informal conversations with whips in other parties—'the usual channels'. Each party has a chief whip and several other whips.

The most important function which concerns us in this chapter is the persuasive role of the whips. Normally, whips begin by intelligence gathering—compiling a list of potential rebels—and try to pick rebels off one by one, dangling certain 'carrots' such as the lure of promotion, office space, and free trips abroad as incentives to ensure loyalty. They may also deploy 'sticks', warning MPs that their path to promotion may be blocked, or that disciplinary proceedings may be taken against them following a rebellious vote. These persuasive techniques do not usually extend to MPs being bullied by the whips. Back in the 1970s, physical threats were often used by the whips to persuade MPs to vote with the government in the division lobbies. Such tactics are now extremely rare, and yet the myth of the whip as a kind of parliamentary bouncer persists.

Similarly, the idea of MPs as lickspittle loyalists became especially prevalent in the early Blair years. The media variously characterized MPs as 'sheep', 'daleks', and 'robots'. The new intake of Labour women MPs who entered the House of Commons in 1997 were singled out for particular abuse, being unfairly labelled 'Blair's babes' (Childs 2004). In reality, MPs are not powerless automatons. Rather, they negotiate with ministers and whips, gaining concessions.

 Parliamentary terms Usual channels

Discussions and informal arrangements concerning parliamentary business which take place between party whips, usually behind the scenes.

Growing rebelliousness

The myths surrounding the bovine loyalty of MPs date from the early 1950s, when parliamentary rebellions were very rare. Research by Philip Norton (1975, 1980), however, began to identify an increase in the *rate* of rebellion in the late 1960s and early 1970s. This rate is calculated by tallying up all the occasions when at least one MP votes against the party line in a parliamentary session, divided by the total number of votes (divisions) in that session. More recently, Philip Cowley (2002, 2005) undertook two detailed studies of Blair's first two Labour governments, from 1997 to 2001 and from 2001 to 2005, which identified a marked growth in rebelliousness on the part of backbench MPs. Cowley engaged in a great deal of number crunching of socio-economic and other data to uncover why MPs were becoming more rebellious, coding an MP's age, gender, year of election, size of majority, and so on. None of these produced statistically significant results. Rather, MPs were rebelling for two main reasons. Firstly, if their ideology or beliefs differed from the leadership, they were more likely to rebel against the party line (Cowley 2002, 101–5 and 116–18). Secondly, because having done so once, they developed a *habit* of rebellion. Voting against the party line became like an addiction, and the job of the whips was to try to stop MPs from developing that addiction in the first place.

Table 24.1 Percentage rate of rebellion among government
backbench MPs 2001–15

Parliament	Percentage rate of rebellion
2001–5	21%
2005–10	28%
2010–15	35%

Further research by Benedetto and Hix (2007) identified disgruntled ex-ministers as another reason for growing rebelliousness. During Blair's decade in power, over 90 ministers were sacked or resigned from office, thereby increasing the numbers of malcontents on the backbenches. Not all of these ministers rebelled regularly, often preferring to express their dissent by voice rather than vote (Cowley 2005, 206–13). Nevertheless, the overall result was that Gordon Brown, who succeeded Tony Blair as prime minister in June 2007, inherited a rebellious party from his predecessor. Far from enjoying a honeymoon period with his backbenchers, Brown experienced his first rebellion within 45 minutes of kissing hands with the Queen at Buckingham Palace (Cowley and Stuart 2014b, 5–6). The pattern was set. As Table 24.1 shows, each of the last three Parliaments have become more rebellious than the previous one. In terms of the rate of rebellion, the 2001–5 Parliament had been the most rebellious since records began in 1945. That was surpassed when the 2005–10 Parliament won that accolade. And almost inevitably, the 2010–15 Coalition government notched up the most rebellious Parliament in post-war history with a rate of rebellion of 35 per cent.

Factors causing Coalition rebellions 2010–15

However, a whole series of new factors made the role of the party whips much harder in the new Coalition government. For a start, there was an organizational problem. Instead of managing a single party, the new Coalition whips' office had to contain rebellion in two parties, Conservative and Liberal Democrat. During this period, there were 17 Coalition whips—14 Conservatives and three Liberal Democrats. The chief whip was always a Conservative and the deputy was always a Liberal Democrat (Cabinet Office 2010, para 5.3). Each set of party whips was required to sort out their own MPs, but inevitably some collaboration was required.

The new political reality also required a fresh set of rules in relation to whipping. The interim Coalition Agreement specifically allowed the Liberal Democrats to abstain on nuclear power and tuition fees (Conservative Party 2010, 5 and 11). But as the Coalition progressed, sometimes the two partners just made it up as they went along. On 29 January 2013, in retaliation for Conservatives voting down Lords reforms (see later in this section), the Liberal Democrats voted against the government's proposed boundary changes. Conservatives and Liberal Democrats whipped their sides in opposite directions, in clear contravention of the Coalition Agreement. Had such an outcome occurred in a coalition in continental Europe, it would almost certainly have led to the collapse of the government, and yet despite much bad temper, the UK's first peacetime coalition since the 1930s carried on as if nothing had happened.

Throughout its life, the Coalition enjoyed an overall majority (calculated by the total number of government MPs—Conservative plus Liberal Democrat—minus the other parties combined) of roughly 80. There were a total of 57 Liberal Democrats, 22 of whom had government jobs and 35 who remained on the backbenches. Even if all these Liberal Democrats had voted against the Coalition, the government could not have been defeated. Conscious of the fact that voters hate divided parties, the government wanted to avoid the appearance of disunity. Therefore, purely winning a vote was not sufficient in a coalition comprising two parties. Each side of the Coalition needed to be satisfied with the drafting of legislation. And yet, here lay the rub. Any concession to one wing of the Coalition (principally the right of the Conservative Party) had the potential to cause upset with the other wing (mainly the Liberal Democrat left). A good example of this occurred during the passage of the Health and Social Care Bill in the 2010–12 session, when Liberal Democrat pressure secured a rare pause in the legislation, but any further concessions had to be squared with Conservative MPs keen to proceed with greater private sector involvement in the National Health Service (Timmins 2012).

Early on in the Coalition's life, this author coined the term 'wobbly wings' to describe the large ideological spread in the Coalition between the Conservative right and the Liberal Democrat left (Cowley and Stuart 2012a). Right-wing Conservative MPs tended to oppose the Coalition's constitutional reforms, including fixed-term parliaments and further European integration. On 10 July 2012, 91 Conservative MPs voted against the second reading of the House of Lords Reform Bill, the largest rebellion by government MPs on the second reading of any bill in the post-war period, and the largest rebellion of the 2010–15 Parliament.

Meanwhile, left-leaning Liberal Democrat MPs tended to object to the Coalition's social policies, particularly those relating to cuts in public expenditure. Only very rarely did these two wings combine together to challenge government policy. The second largest Liberal Democrat rebellion of the Parliament occurred on 9 December 2010, when 21 Liberal Democrats combined with only six Conservative MPs, the Labour Party, and other minor parties, to vote against the raising of university tuition fees from £3,000 to £9,000, reducing the government's majority to 21. The largest Liberal Democrat rebellion of the Parliament, however, occurred on 18 November 2014 when 25 Liberal Democrat MPs voted in favour of an amendment in the name of Greg Mulholland MP requiring pub companies to allow their tenants a market rent option, instead of being contractually 'tied' or obliged to buy beer from their parent company. The rebellion resulted in a defeat for the Coalition.

However, because the two 'wobbly wings' of the Coalition were ideological opposites, such defeats were rare. The first of these defeats happened only two years into the Coalition, on 31 October 2012, when 53 Conservatives combined with the official opposition to support a cut in the European Union budget. Then, on 29 August 2013, 30 Conservatives and nine Liberal Democrat MPs combined with the Labour Party to defeat the government on military intervention in Syria, losing by 13 votes (see Case Study 24).

What made the task of the whips even harder in the Coalition was that they no longer enjoyed the powers of patronage that they had in the previous Parliament. As a result of the implementation of the Wright reforms after the 2010 general election (see Chapter 16), neither the chairs nor the members of select committees were chosen by the whips, but instead elected by secret ballot. The whips therefore lacked the usual carrots which they could dangle in front of backbench MPs to ensure they remained loyal to the government.

Compounding the lack of patronage was the fact that there were insufficient government jobs to go round. In the run-up to the 2010 general election, two dozen Conservative MPs with junior opposition frontbench roles assumed that their side would win the general election. Instead, post-election, around half of these Conservatives were forced to sit on the sidelines as Liberal Democrat MPs took the jobs they had been expecting to occupy in government. This became known as the 'Norman Baker factor', after the somewhat maverick Liberal Democrat MP for Lewes, who was unexpectedly appointed Parliamentary Under-Secretary of State for Transport in May 2010. Unsurprisingly, it was not long before these disgruntled MPs began to rebel.

Normally, at the beginning of a Parliament, the whips can draw on the fact that their leader has won an election based on a manifesto as a kind of glue to hold the parliamentary party together. But in May 2010, David Cameron failed to win the general election outright, so he did not enjoy the kind of personal loyalty among his MPs which had been afforded to Tony Blair following his landslide victories in 1997, and to a lesser extent in 2001. It was therefore no use saying to a Conservative MP that Cameron had won the election and therefore he deserved the loyalty of his MPs, because he had not won. Worse still, Conservative MPs were not being asked to be loyal to their party's manifesto, but rather to a Coalition Agreement, a post-election deal which no member of the public had voted on. So, if a Conservative MP contemplating rebellion was approached by a whip asking them to be loyal to the government, they could claim that they were being asked to support a measure which had not appeared in the manifesto. A good example of this was the Fixed-Term Parliaments Bill in the 2010–12 session, where 16 Conservative MPs voted against the legislation during its passage (Cowley and Stuart 2012c, 97), rightly pointing out that it could not be found in their manifesto. Would-be Conservative rebels were therefore bolstered by a type of rival legitimacy—they were remaining loyal to the manifesto on which they had fought the election.

The most challenging aspect of the whips' role in the 2010–15 Parliament was the influx of new MPs into the House of Commons. Not only did they comprise an unusually high percentage of the total number of MPs—36 per cent—but new Conservative MPs constituted 48 per cent of the parliamentary party. Normally, new MPs are relatively loyal at the beginning of a Parliament, and only become more rebellious as preferment is denied to them. But in 2010, many new Conservative MPs knew in advance that there were not enough jobs to go round, so they were more ready to rebel from the outset. Over 90 of these new Conservatives held marginal seats and were keen to show their constituents that they were standing up for their concerns, as opposed to toeing the party line. The result was that even by the end of the first session of the 2010–15 Parliament, around half of the new intake of MPs had rebelled. So, in contrast to previous Parliaments, growing rebellion was not only driven by MPs who had a track record of previous rebelliousness (and therefore had developed the habit of rebellion), but also by a new, more forthright generation of Conservative backbenchers.

The biggest concern for the 2010 intake of Conservative MPs (as for other intakes) was the issue of Europe. Whereas non-European issues attracted an average size of rebellion of just five Conservative MPs, on the issue of Europe there was a median average of 23 rebel Tory backbenchers. The largest Europe-related rebellion in the 2010–15 Parliament occurred on 24 October 2011 when 81 Conservative MPs (and one Liberal Democrat) voted in favour of a backbench business motion urging the government to hold a referendum on Britain's continued membership of the European Union (Cowley and Stuart 2012b). There is little doubt that such backbench pressure, combined with the rise in support for the United Kingdom Independence Party (UKIP), played a part in David Cameron's decision in his Bloomberg Speech in January 2013 to commit to an in–out referendum on Britain's membership of the EU. But what is most interesting is that even with this promise, backbench Conservative MPs were not content to let the issue rest. In May 2013, they did something which was without precedent in the post-war era—challenging government policy in the Queen's Speech. Such was the pressure on David Cameron that he agreed to support a private member's bill which hoped to pass legislation paving the way for an in–out referendum. The bill would later fail, due to opposition from Labour and the Liberal Democrats, but not content with this concession, some 110 Conservative backbenchers voted in favour of an amendment regretting the absence of a referendum bill from the Queen's Speech. The vote was not technically a rebellion, since the Conservatives allowed their backbenchers (but not ministers) a free vote, but it illustrated the sheer power of MPs in the 2010–15 Parliament to shape government policy, conclusively killing the myth that MPs were powerless automatons.

Conclusion

At a book launch in 2012, Philip Cowley claimed the public were 'frankly mad' if they believed that MPs were weak actors in the Westminster system. He was right. The 2010–15 Parliament had demonstrated that government backbench MPs had increased their power to amend government policy. Such powers did not go away in the 2015 Parliament either, not least because the government's majority was so wafer-thin that it only took half a dozen Conservative MPs to object to a policy for the prime minister to have to reconsider it. This would then become particularly problematic in the 2017 Parliament when the government lost its majority.

Further Reading

COWLEY, P. (2002) *Revolts and Rebellions: Parliamentary Voting Under Blair*, London: Politico's.

COWLEY, P. (2005) *The Rebels: How Blair Mislaid His Majority*, London: Politico's.

COWLEY, P. (2015) 'The Coalition and Parliament' in A. Seldon and M. Finn (eds.), *The Coalition Effect, 2010–2015*, Cambridge: Cambridge University Press, pp. 136–56.

COWLEY, P. and STUART, M. (2014) 'In the Brown Stuff?: Labour Backbench Dissent Under Gordon Brown, 2007–10', *Contemporary British History*, Vol. 28 (1), pp. 1–23.

NORTON, P. (1975) *Dissension in the House of Commons, 1945–1974*, London: Macmillan.

Case Study 24: The government defeat on Syria military intervention, August 2013

On 29 August 2013, following the recall of Parliament, the Coalition government was defeated by 283 votes to 270 on the issue of whether Britain should consider military intervention in Syria. The government lost by 13 votes. Although the number of Coalition rebels was relatively modest—30 Conservatives joined just nine Liberal Democrats in voting against the motion (Cowley and Stuart 2014a)—the impact of the vote was huge. Speaking immediately afterwards, Prime Minister David Cameron indicated that he would respect the will of the House of Commons and the British people that they did not wish to see military action, adding, 'I get that, and the government will act accordingly' (HC Debates, 29 August 2013, cc.1555–6).

What made this vote extremely unusual was the fact that normally the official opposition supports the government in matters of this kind, but for the first time since the Suez Crisis of 1956, the Labour Party's frontbench voted against the government. Several members of Labour's shadow cabinet threatened to resign, meaning that Labour leader Ed Miliband shifted quite suddenly from guarded support for military action to outright opposition (Eaton 2013; Nelson 2013). The long shadow cast by the Blair government's decision to press ahead with military action against Iraq in 2003 seemed to have scarred large sections of the Parliamentary Labour Party, making them hostile to almost any form of military intervention. Even though the government motion promised a further House of Commons vote before military action actually took place, such assurances proved insufficient to bring Labour MPs on board.

However, the shifting stance of the official opposition masks another important feature of this type of vote, namely that matters relating to war and peace are far harder to whip than normal legislation. The role of the whips during a controversial government bill is to ensure that the rebels do not vote against it all at the same time. To do so would be to risk defeat. Therefore, the whips seek to *spread* the rebels across the bill's various stages (e.g. the second reading and third reading votes). But votes on matters of war and peace are not subject to government legislation. There was no government bill in 2003, for instance, proposing to invade Iraq, merely a government motion and an opposition amendment, both of which were defeated. The Coalition whips therefore lacked the ability to spread the rebels across various stages. Yes, they could encourage rebel MPs to switch their support from the opposition amendment to the government motion, but their room for manoeuvre was extremely limited.

Compounding the problem for the whips is that matters of war and peace tend to involve moral issues, where the granting of concessions is highly problematic. The whips cannot promise that the government will 'half invade' a country. There is therefore an 'either/or' element attached to votes on foreign and defence policy, their binary nature making them very hard to whip (Cowley 2005, 111).

Nevertheless, the Coalition could have avoided defeat had the Conservative whips' office been functioning effectively. As this chapter explains, one of the key functions of the whips is intelligence gathering. In this case, the whips should have picked up on two crucial pieces of intelligence. First, on 6 June 2013, 81 Conservative MPs signed a letter penned by Andrew Bridgen, the Conservative MP for Leicestershire North West, demanding a House of Commons vote before the UK sent any arms to the Syrian rebels (BBC News 2013). Then, in July 2013, John Baron MP, a member of the Foreign Affairs Select Committee, asked the Backbench Business Committee for a debate calling on the House of Commons not to arm the Syrian rebels. After much discussion, Natascha Engel MP, the Chair of the Backbench Business Committee, granted a debate on 11 July 2013, in which the House of Commons agreed by 114 votes to one that 'lethal support should not be provided to anti-government forces in Syria without the explicit prior consent of Parliament' (HC Debates, 11 July 2013, cc. 627–8). Although the motion was not formally binding, the fact it was passed put pressure on the government to recall Parliament (Backbench Business Committee 2015, 9).

Such open displays of discontent should have acted as an early warning signal to the government. At this point, the whips should have begun compiling lists of potential Conservative rebels based on the 11 July vote and the Bridgen letter, and starting conversations with a view to changing their minds. Instead, complacency set in. It was only at the last minute that whips and ministers, including the prime minister, were brought on board to try to bring the rebels back into line (Hardman 2013), but by then it was too late.

Further analysis of the division lists shows that of the 30 Conservative MPs who rebelled over Syria, 16 belonged to the 2010 intake. As this chapter shows, the 2010–15 Parliament was characterized by a new breed of MPs who were more concerned with listening to the concerns of their constituents than voting with the government. In this case, the public mood was overwhelmingly against military intervention. One example will suffice. Andrew Percy, the Conservative MP for Brigg and Goole, and one of the 2010 intake who voted against the government, sent out 2,000 emails to his constituents to ask their views on possible military intervention in Syria, received over 800 responses, and commented on his website shortly after the vote: 'The feedback from residents really influenced the way I voted' (Percy 2013).

More broadly, the Coalition defeat over Syria provides yet another example of the growing power of MPs. Ever since the Iraq War of 2003, MPs have increasingly insisted on a debate and a vote in the House of Commons before British military action takes place (Kaarbo and Kenealy 2015; Strong 2015). Such evidence further smashes the persistent myth that MPs are somehow spineless loyalists incapable of changing the policies of an over-mighty executive.

Primary sources

- Arms to Syria debate (HC Debates, 11 July 2013, cc. 587–628). Online at: https://hansard.parliament.uk/commons/2013-07-11/debates/13071159000002/ArmsToSyria [accessed 27 June 2017].
- Syria and the Use of Chemical Weapons (HC Debates, 29 August 2013, cc. 1425–556). Online at: https://hansard.parliament.uk/commons/2013-08-29/debates/1308298000001/SyriaAndTheUseOfChemicalWeapons [accessed 27 June 2017].
- Backbench Business Committee (2015) *Work of the Committee in the 2010-2015 Parliament: First Special Report of 2014-15*, London: The Stationery Office, HC 1106. Online at: https://www.publications.parliament.uk/pa/cm201415/cmselect/cmbackben/1106/1106.pdf [accessed 27 June 2017].

 FURTHER CASE STUDIES

- Liberal Democrat influence on Coalition health policy during the Health and Social Care Bill (2010–12 session).
- Conservative pressure on the Coalition to hold a referendum on membership of the EU, and the Backbench Business Committee motion on an EU referendum, 24 October 2011.
- Party splits on the European Union (Notification of Withdrawal) Bill (2016–17 session).

References

Backbench Business Committee (2015) *Work of the Committee in the 2010–2015 Parliament: First Special Report of 2014–2015*, London: The Stationery Office, HC 1106. Online at: https://www.publications.parliament.uk/pa/cm201415/cmselect/cmbackben/1106/1106.pdf [accessed 24 June 2017].

BBC News (2013) 'Tory MPs demand vote on Syrian arms', *BBC News Online*, 6 June. Online at: http://www.bbc.co.uk/news/uk-politics-22802438 [accessed 18 September 2016].

Benedetto, G. and Hix, S. (2007) 'The Rejected, the Ejected, and the Dejected: Explaining Government Rebels in the 2001–2005 British House of Commons', *Comparative Political Studies*, Vol. 40 (7), pp. 755–81.

Cabinet Office (2010) *Coalition Agreement for Stability and Reform*, London: Cabinet Office. Online at: https://www.gov.uk/government/uploads/system/uploads/attachment_data/file/78978/coalition-agreement-may-2010_0.pdf [accessed 25 June 2017].

Childs, S. (2004) *New Labour Women MPs: Women Representing Women*, London: Routledge.

Conservative Party (2010) *Conservative Liberal Democrat coalition negotiations: Agreements reached, 11 May 2010*. Online at: http://conservativehome.blogs.com/files/conlib-agreement-1.pdf [accessed 24 June 2017].

Cowley, P. (2002) *Revolts and Rebellions: Parliamentary Voting Under Blair*, London: Politico's.

Cowley, P. (2005) *The Rebels: How Blair Mislaid his Majority*, London: Politico's.

Cowley, P. and Stuart, M. (2012a) 'A Coalition with Two Wobbly Wings: Backbench Dissent in the House of Commons', *Political Insight*, Vol. 3 (1), pp. 8–11.

Cowley, P. and Stuart, M. (2012b) 'The Cambusters: The Conservative European Union Rebellion of October 2011', *The Political Quarterly*, Vol. 83 (2), pp. 402–6.

Cowley, P. and Stuart, M. (2012c) *The Bumper Book of Coalition Rebellions. Or: Dissension amongst the Coalition's Parliamentary Parties, 2010–2012: A Data Handbook*, Nottingham: University of Nottingham.

Cowley, P. and Stuart, M. (2014a) *The Four-Year Itch. Or: Dissension amongst the Coalition's Parliamentary Parties, 2013–2014: A Data Handbook*, Nottingham: University of Nottingham. Online at: http://revolts.co.uk/wp-content/uploads/2014/06/Four-year-itch_cover_full.pdf [accessed 18 September 2016].

Cowley, P. and Stuart, M. (2014b) 'In the Brown Stuff? Labour Backbench Dissent Under Gordon Brown, 2007–2010', *Contemporary British History*, Vol. 28 (1), pp. 1–23.

Eaton, G. (2013) 'Labour set to whip MPs over Syria as Diane Abbott warns she could resign', *The New Statesman*, 28 August. Online at: http://www.newstatesman.com/politics/2013/08/labour-set-whip-mps-over-syria-diane-abbott-warns-she-could-resign [accessed 18 September 2016].

Hardman, I. (2013) 'Syria Defeat: What happened to the whips?', *The Spectator*, 29 August. Online at: http://blogs.spectator.co.uk/coffeehouse/2013/08/syria-defeat-what-happened-to-the-whips/ [accessed 18 September 2016].

Kaarbo, J. and Kenealy, D. (2015) 'No, Prime Minister. Explaining the House of Commons Vote on Intervention in Syria', *European Security*, Vol. 25 (1), pp. 28–48.

Nelson, F. (2013) 'Syria defeat: What next for David Cameron?', *The Spectator*, 30 August. Online at: http://blogs.spectator.co.uk/coffeehouse/2013/08/syria-defeat-what-next-for-david-cameron/ [accessed 18 September 2016].

Norton, P. (1975) *Dissension in the House of Commons, 1945–1974*, London: Macmillan.

Norton, P. (1980) *Dissension in the House of Commons, 1974–1979*, Oxford: Clarendon.

Percy, A. (2013) 'Syria', *Andrew Percy: News*, 2 September. Online at: http://www.andrewpercy.org/news/675-syria [accessed 18 September 2016].

Strong, J. (2015) 'Why Parliament Now Decides on War: Tracing the Growth of the Parliamentary Prerogative Through Syria, Libya and Iraq', *British Journal of Politics and International Relations*, Vol. 17 (4), pp. 604–22.

Timmins, N. (2012) *Never Again? The Story of the Health and Social Care Act 2012: A Study in Coalition Government and Policy Making*, London: King's Fund/Institute for Government. Online at: http://www.kingsfund.org.uk/sites/files/kf/field/field_publication_file/never-again-story-health-social-care-nicholas-timmins-jul12.pdf [accessed 16 September 2016].

25

MPs and their Constituencies

David Judge and Rebecca Partos

INTRODUCTION

MPs are often accused—especially by the popular press, populist parties and politicians, and by the Twitterati—of living in a 'Westminster bubble'. MPs themselves occasionally casually invoke the term to portray their colleagues at Westminster as insulated and isolated from the daily concerns of the rest of the UK's populace. Yet this clichéd and caricatured picture fails to capture the routine, indeed institutionalized, representational pinpricks that perpetually puncture this bubble. Every day, MPs in acting as the representatives of their respective geographical areas inject the opinions, concerns, and tribulations of their constituents into the workings of Parliament. Such representational work is often overlooked or ignored by outside observers and commentators, but in the words of one ex-MP, Paul Burstow (2016), it provides a necessary 'reality check' for all MPs that links them to the lives of those they are elected to represent. Tragically it took the murder of Jo Cox, MP for Batley and Spen, while performing her constituency representative role in June 2016, to remind populists and the wider public, all too briefly, that MPs don't inhabit a Westminster-centric bubble but are in fact rooted in localities throughout the UK. This chapter examines, therefore, the dimensions of this constituency representative role: of what 'constituency' means for MPs and their local electorates; and how perceptions of locality affect the work of MPs and the expectations of constituents alike.

MPs are representatives of territorially defined constituencies

There are two things that all MPs have in common, despite the multiple differences associated with their gender, ethnicity, class, partisan allegiances, or with their parliamentary or executive roles. First, they are all elected representatives. Second, they are representatives of territorially defined constituencies. Historically, territorial foundations underpinned the development of the key principles of representative government in Britain—of consent, legitimation, and the authorization of decision-making. Indeed, medieval English parliaments were rooted in territorial representation where, at that time, constituencies effectively constituted geographically defined 'communities of interest', and representatives were drawn from local communities simply 'because that is where and how people defined themselves' (Rehfeld 2005, 71). Since those times an 'implicit theory of representation' has continued to underpin UK parliamentarism. This holds that each MP represents:

> not only a certain proportion of the national electorate but also an area of the national territory which is more than an aggregation of those individuals' homes. Part of the MP's role ... is to

represent a place, a spatially bounded territorial unit whose residents have common interests; the place is thus more than a sum of its component parts—and is often equated with the elusive concept of a community. (Rossiter, Johnston, and Pattie 2013, 856–7)

The contemporary significance of this 'implicit theory' is to be found in the fact that the name of the constituencies that MPs represent is still used as the formal mode by which Members refer to each other in the Chamber of the House of Commons. Attempts to remove this ancient form of address—what *The Independent* newspaper listed among the 'absurd rules' of Parliament (Stone 2015)—have been countered on the principled grounds that: 'Members do not sit in the House as individual citizens, they are there as representatives of their constituencies: and it is in that capacity that they should be addressed' (Modernisation Committee 1998, paras 38–9). Certainly, the changes to constituency boundaries scheduled to be effected after 2018—to reduce the number of constituencies from 650 to 600 and to ensure that nearly all constituencies will have an electorate within the range 71,031 to 78,507—will complicate this mode of address; as new constituencies are given different and often longer names (to reflect the incorporation of two or more separate geographical areas). Equally, as Rossiter, Johnston, and Pattie (2013, 884) note, 'increasingly such names will have less relevance' for 'organic' notions of community, and an 'implicit theory of representation', which embed geographically based communities of interest at the heart of UK parliamentary representation.

MPs represent 'communities of interest'

In a very real sense, however, the notion of representing local 'communities of interest', even before the proposed 2018 boundary changes, has posed complicated practical problems for MPs. If communities of interest are defined, as they were historically in the pre-industrial and industrial eras, primarily in terms of geographically proximate economic interests—of agrarian, manufacturing, extraction industries, or commercial interests—then it was plausible to claim, as Edmund Burke did in the eighteenth century (Burke [1780] 1801), that there were specific, objective, locally rooted interests capable of representation by constituency MPs. In the 'post-industrial', 'post-material' world of the twenty-first century, however, territorial representation conceived in terms of a dominant constituency 'community economic interest' is harder, if not impossible, to justify and effect. Alternatively, communities of interest may now be conceived in terms of concentrations of people from the same ethnic, religious, cultural or racial groups, or social class, or other demographic aggregates. Where these groups are spatially concentrated then territory might be taken to serve as a 'reasonably good proxy for communities of interest that happen to be territorially segregated' (Rehfeld 2005, 158). The difficulty with such an argument is, as Rehfeld (2005,158) goes on to point out, that 'when territory becomes a proxy for some other community of interest, the "communities of interest" justification no longer justifies the use of territory per se. Rather, territory is justified as a means to represent the other interests for which it serves as a proxy'.

'Constituencies' within constituencies

One way to attempt to resolve this problem is to move the analytical focus away from notions of pre-existing local communities of interests and to argue that, in many ways, MPs have to construct an image of the constituency they seek to represent. This entails examining how MPs conceive of their constituency and the heuristics (cognitive shortcuts) that they use to construct an image of who their constituents are, and what they think needs to be represented. Equally it entails examining how the represented themselves conceive of constituency (or how the claims made by the representative about this image are received), and the congruence between voters and their MPs of what the constituency is and what needs to be represented.

In clarifying what 'constituency' means to most MPs, the work of Richard Fenno (1978) on 'homestyle', although published some four decades ago and focused on the USA, still proves to be of considerable value. Of particular note is Fenno's (1978, 1–29) identification of constituency as a series of concentric circles which embrace successively smaller subsets of the population in a geographical electoral area. Indeed, detailed studies of constituency representation in Britain have drawn upon Fenno's four-fold distinction between geographical, re-election, primary, and personal constituencies (see Cain, Ferejohn, and Fiorina 1979, 520–2; Norton and Wood 1993, 27–8; Judge 1999, 152–3). The innermost, and smallest, circle is the 'personal constituency', which can be identified as an MP's closest constituency party colleagues, caseworkers and researchers, spouse or partner, and close personal friends. The 'primary constituency' can be identified as the representative's strongest supporters and approximates, in the UK context, to party activists—party members, and, increasingly, registered supporters—and local party opinion leaders, who might include local councillors, and respectively, for Labour MPs, local trade unionists or, for Conservative MPs, officers of local business associations or chambers of commerce. The third circle is the 're-election constituency', which consists of voters who voted for the MP; and the fourth, and widest, circle is the territorial entity of the constituency itself.

The size of each concentric circle diminishes rapidly in size, from 'geographical constituencies' with an average size of just over 72,000 electors in 2017, to 're-election constituencies' with less than half that number—with only 23 constituencies in 2017 returning MPs with the support of more than 50 per cent of registered voters, and with 69 constituencies returning MPs with the support of less than 30 per cent of the local electorate. The size of 'primary constituencies' varies across the main political parties. In mid-2016, the national membership of the Conservative Party was estimated at around 140,000, but only two local Associations recorded over 1,000 members, and only 50 more had over 500 members. In the Labour Party, in March 2017, national party membership stood at 517,000 (down from a peak of over 550,000 in July 2016). Nonetheless, many local constituency parties had doubled, trebled, quadrupled or even, in some cases, quintupled their membership since 2015. The SNP had earlier witnessed dramatic increases in constituency party membership after the Scottish independence referendum of 2014, and averaged more than 2,000 members per constituency just after the 2016 EU referendum. With increased membership came increased attention to policy congruence between the views of party members and the voting patterns of MPs in Westminster. At the extremes in the Labour Party, the spectre of deselection of MPs, which had haunted Labour MPs in the 1970s and 1980s, re-emerged.

Finally, the fourth and most central of the concentric circles is the 'personal constituency'. Here MPs may seek, from friends, family, and their constituency caseworkers, alternative and informal information about the constituency, other than from electoral and partisan circles; or may even seek psychological respite from the unremitting demands of their wider constituencies.

If MPs make sense of their constituencies by reimagining them as concentric nested constituencies, how do constituents make sense of parliamentary constituencies and their connection to their representatives? One way is by invoking notions of 'locality'.

'Locality' is important for constituents, parties, and MPs

The notion of descriptive representation, as Chapter 22 makes clear, is central to debates about parliamentary representation in the twenty-first century. In essence, descriptive representation, as Mansbridge (1999, 629) points out, has at its core some notion of 'shared experiences' between representatives and the represented, which allow the latter to be 'in some sense typical of the larger class of persons whom they represent'. Historically, the 'shared experience' of most significance in most representative democracies has been 'locality'.

Whereas contemporary discussion of descriptive representation has focused primarily upon gender, ethnicity, and sexual orientation, Childs and Cowley (2011, 16) have made a case for a re-examination of the claims for the descriptive representation of locality. Certainly, survey evidence has consistently pointed to the fact that voters have a preference for local candidates that are 'of' a geographical constituency (Cowley 2013, 22; Childs and Cowley 2011, 5; Evans et al. 2017). Equally, survey experiments have revealed the impact of local residency upon voters' positive perceptions of parliamentary candidates (Campbell and Cowley 2014, 754–7), and of constituents' preferences for MPs to work hard on local constituency issues (Vivyan and Wagner 2016, 96). Yet how exactly 'locality' or 'local issues' are conceived by constituents remains undetermined (see Campbell and Lovenduski 2014, 693; Judge 2014, 81).

Nonetheless, political parties have recognized the potential electoral advantages to be gained from selecting local candidates; and candidates themselves have increasingly stressed in their election materials their local connections—of variously being born, educated, worked, or resided in the constituency (and, in some cases, all of these). In turn, once elected, MPs are aware of potential electoral gains to be made by close attention to constituency matters. While the capacity of MPs to build a 'personal vote', through building a reputation as diligent promoters and defenders of local interests and opinions, is restricted in the UK by the primacy of the national focus of party voting, nonetheless, a local 'incumbency bonus' has been identified (see Smith 2013; Cutts and Russell 2015, 74–6). However, such a 'bonus' is subject to the vagaries of the nature of electoral competition in the UK. As the 2015 general election illustrated, Liberal Democrat MPs lost out to Conservative candidates in England largely irrespective of their constituency profile, reputation, and standing; and, in Scotland, Labour and Liberal Democrat MPs were swept aside by an SNP landslide—irrespective of their past performance in relation to their constituencies.

Constituency work and parliamentary work are often counterposed

It is commonplace to counterpose the 'parliamentary' work of MPs against their 'constituency' work. In essence, there is a perceived split between legislative roles (focused upon policy advocacy, legislation, and oversight/scrutiny) and representative roles (focused upon linkage between citizens, civil society associations, party organizations, and decision makers). Indeed, MPs themselves often juxtapose their legislative and representative roles (Procedure Committee 2012, 7). Thus, for example, in 2015, experienced MPs reflecting on their work in the House of Commons revealed that for many a choice had had to be made between 'politics [in Westminster] and local issues' and, in choosing the latter, one MP ruefully commented that 'he felt less of a parliamentarian' (Tinkler and Mehta 2016, 10–11).

This choice appears to have become even starker, as more MPs have come to spend a greater proportion of their time dealing with constituency concerns than was the case in earlier decades. At the end of the 1990s, Norris (1997, 30) noted that constituency work had more than doubled since the 1970s, to the extent that MPs were spending about 30 per cent of their time dealing with constituency matters. More recently, in 2012, a survey of 151 MPs found a further increase—insofar as 79 per cent of respondents believed that the proportion of time spent 'dealing with constituency correspondence or casework' had increased since they first entered Parliament (Procedure Committee 2012, Ev. w105); and 61 per cent stated that the proportion of time spent with constituents had also increased. In the light of this increase, perhaps not surprisingly, 76 per cent recorded that the actual number of hours spent on constituency correspondence and casework had grown, and 59 per cent stated that the hours spent with constituents had increased. In the same survey, 'representing constituency interests' was ranked by 78 per cent of respondents among their top three role priorities, which was higher than the 69 per cent who listed 'holding government to account', and the 60 per cent who listed 'scrutinizing legislation'. In addition, 54 per cent of respondents also listed 'dealing with individual constituents' as being among their top three priorities. Overall, half of MPs claimed to spend more than 40 per cent of their time in their constituency. Fully half of MPs also stated that they worked, in total, 70 hours or more a week during parliamentary sessions (with only 5 per cent working fewer than 50 hours per week).

 Parliamentary terms Casework

Matters (mainly personal, local, or individualized) raised with MPs by their constituents.

Not surprisingly, given this increase, the belief that MPs are spending too much of their time on constituency service has strengthened. These fears, however, are long-standing. Over a decade ago, Philip Cowley warned that 'there must now be a real concern that MPs are so focused on the parochial they have no time for the national, let alone the international, picture' (Modernisation Committee 2007, Ev.14). More recently, Conservative MP James Gray (2015) asked, what for him, were the rhetorical questions: 'Is it really our job to deal with immigration appeals, benefits disputes, Child Support Agency arguments, planning applications, school placements and the like? Is there not a risk that it diverts us from our true purpose of running the country and holding the government to account?' Indeed, there have long been suggestions that MPs should be restricted, by convention or proscription, from intervening in local matters that are the primary responsibility of local authorities, devolved parliaments, or other local agencies (see for example Riddell 1997, 18; Procedure Committee 2012, Ev. w6). Yet the response by many MPs to this suggestion is essentially fatalistic: 'Whatever the reasons [for increased constituency workload] it is clear that these pressures, once raised, are very unlikely to diminish' (Procedure Committee 2012, 9).

These pressures point to at least two, often discrete, roles nested within the 'constituency service' role. One is commonly referred to as the welfare officer role, with MPs carrying out casework on behalf of aggrieved constituents. In this role MPs act as intermediaries, literally to 're-present' the grievances of individual constituents to, and to seek redress from a host of service providers—local authorities, central government departments and agencies, private utilities, and private welfare service organizations—and, in reverse, to inform the complainant of the response. The other role is concerned with territorial advocacy—the promotion or protection of constituency interests, such as local industrial and economic development, local businesses or services, environmental improvement, or some other community project. A recurring paradox of this advocacy role, especially for MPs in the governing party, is that party representatives who are mandated to a national electoral programme might also seek simultaneously to promote dissonant local policies in the process of representing constituency interests. For example, the UK press were quick to point out that even David Cameron, as prime minister and as a key advocate of austerity budgeting, was willing to write to Oxfordshire County Council, in September 2015, to record his disappointment with its proposals to make 'significant cuts to frontline services—from elderly day centres, to libraries, to museums ... [and] to close children's centres' in his and other parliamentary constituencies in Oxfordshire. As the Leader of Oxfordshire Council noted pointedly in his reply: 'Central to the [2015 Conservative] Manifesto was removing the deficit. This does mean reductions in public expenditure' (see Hudspeth 2015).

Conclusion

Survey evidence reveals that constituents are, generally, largely ignorant of the work done on their behalf by their MPs; with successive Hansard Society *Audits* (2011, 32; 2013, 51) recording that many constituents were unaware that most MPs held advice surgeries and meetings to discuss local interests and concerns, and that only a minority knew the name of their local MP. Yet, survey evidence also reveals that voters express a preference for MPs to split their time 60:40 between national and constituency work, which corresponds closely to the prioritization of most MPs (Vivyan and Wagner 2016, 96). In other words, there is not a zero-sum relationship between 'constituency' and 'parliamentary' work, but rather— when conceived as a representational relationship—the former links and informs the latter. This applies to all MPs, including ministers who—unlike many executive members in other parliamentary systems—still involve themselves in 'constituency service' roles. This linkage is increasingly apparent in the enhanced flows of communication (increasingly digital) in both directions between constituents, either as individuals or as groups, and their representatives in Parliament. This linkage is the essence of parliamentary representation, and serves to puncture notions of a 'Westminster bubble'.

Further Reading

CHILDS, S. and COWLEY, P. (2011) 'The Politics of Local Presence: Is there a Case for Descriptive Representation?', *Political Studies*, Vol. 59 (1), pp. 1–19.

CREWE, E. (2015) *The House of Commons: An Anthropology of MPs at Work*, London: Bloomsbury.

NORTON, P. and WOOD, D. M. (1993) *Back from Westminster: British Members of Parliament and Their Constituents*, Lexington: University Press of Kentucky.

Case Study 25: Constituency casework

Constituency service features prominently in MPs' perceptions of their role, as well as in their daily activities. A key dimension of such service is 'casework', where MPs take on the 'cases' of constituents by assisting them in their interactions—often tetchy and dispiriting—with central or local government bodies and agencies, or private companies and commercial organizations. MPs and their constituency staff, some of whom are known as caseworkers, are confronted with an ever-changing kaleidoscope of grievances, problems, and issues brought to them by their constituents. Caseworkers take on the heavy lifting for MPs by building up a picture of constituents' problems and seeking to resolve the myriad issues. To capture the essence of casework, what follows is an indicative aggregated case study, based upon the reflections of two experienced constituency caseworkers—'Caseworker A', supporting a Labour MP in the north-east of England, and 'Caseworker B', who worked for a Conservative MP in eastern England.

SURGERIES

Surgeries provide the opportunity for constituents to meet face-to-face with their local MP and the MP's caseworkers. The location of surgeries varies from the traditional (constituency offices; community centres; libraries; village halls), through more innovative settings (supermarkets; farmers' markets; farms; pubs, McDonalds; hospitals); to the mobile (including an ice cream van, camper van, and a converted bus). Caseworker B noted that her MP held surgeries around a kitchen table within the MP's office in the town centre, on the grounds that the informal space would be less stressful for constituents. These surgeries were held at variable times, alternating between afternoons and evenings, so as to allow people with different commitments to attend. In the constituency in the north-east of England, the MP, assisted by the senior caseworker, held 'themed' surgeries—with four 'immigration surgeries' scheduled each month in addition to general surgeries. Surgeries may be open access, with constituents free to 'drop in' or, increasingly, after the death of Jo Cox in 2016, by appointment, as MPs became more security conscious.

CONSTITUENCY CASES

Constituency cases are many and varied. In terms of numbers, Ronnie Cowan (2017), SNP MP for Inverclyde, for example, recorded 2,248 constituent contacts and dealt with 3,423 constituency cases in the 2015–17 session; Phillip Lee (2017), Conservative MP for Bracknell, dealt with 1,000 individual constituent cases and an estimated 40,000 casework emails in 2016–17; and in the same period, Jo Stevens (2017), Labour MP for Cardiff Central, held 139 surgeries and provided casework assistance to 2,147 constituents. In terms of variety, our sample caseworkers noted that the practice of 'assisting anyone living in the constituency', and that 'no matter is too big or too small', led to them dealing with cases from the almost comic through to the truly tragic. As one of them observed: 'You deal with many weird and wonderful issues as a caseworker. One that sticks in the mind is the man who came to see us in a surgery who wanted a new toilet as his "deposits were too large" and kept blocking the plumbing! We contacted the Housing Association to request the adaptation. Sadly, they refused.' At the other end of the spectrum, testimony was provided of the daily tragic personal consequences of, for example, homelessness and inadequate accommodation, ill health, refusal of asylum applications or UK citizenship, the ravages of addiction, or of abuse—in its variegated racial, sexual, domestic, or workplace guises; all of which are issues recurrently raised by constituents to MPs.

PROCESSING CASES

Attending a surgery is often the last resort for constituents. Many may be frustrated and distressed. Many may have difficulty in articulating the exact nature of their problem, given the cross-cutting difficulties confronting them. In addition, MPs and caseworkers frequently have to manage the expectations of their constituents.

In seeking to assist constituents, MPs and their caseworkers engage with a vast range of organizations and institutions—local or national, government or non-government, public or private. Given most casework typically involves liaising with local organizations, over time, caseworkers tend to develop networks of contacts within the constituency which may help to expedite the resolution of problems. Caseworker A provided two examples: first, in seeking to resolve the issue of a disabled person who had not received their benefits for over eight weeks, she made phone calls—on the constituent's behalf—to the Department of Work and Pensions and to a contact at the local Jobcentre; second, when dealing with a complaint about 'fly-tipping', direct contact with the local council, and reporting the offence to the police, rapidly cleared the case. In each of these cases, the issue was swiftly resolved with minimal effort, and although it could be said that the constituents could have directed their concerns elsewhere, these examples show the ease with which matters can be settled—and the extent to which organizations become more amenable—when an MP becomes involved. While some cases may be resolved speedily with a phone call from the MP's office, many may take months or even years, and prolonged contact with multiple organizations, to try to reach a solution (not always successfully). Caseworker B provided an example of a fairly typical case:

> Originally from Thailand, Mrs Z married an English man before moving to the UK with him and their son. [When] her husband became abusive and forced her to work in a brothel, [Mrs Z] managed eventually to escape and made an application for Indefinite Leave to Remain on the basis of domestic violence. We contacted the then UK Border Agency to ensure her case was dealt with swiftly and it was processed within six weeks.

After Mrs Z's immigration status was updated, the MP's staff were then able to arrange for Mrs Z and her son to move from temporary accommodation to more permanent housing by lobbying the local council's housing team on her behalf.

Only a small proportion of constituents require the services and interventions of their MPs, but for those who do—particularly those who find it difficult to articulate their problems, or to identify who is responsible for their difficulties, or who is capable of resolving their predicament—MPs not only listen but also transmit the grievances of the powerless to the powerful. This is representative linkage in operation. This is the historic role of the 'redress of individual grievance' performed in the twenty-first century.

Primary sources

- Ben Gummer MP (Minister for the Cabinet Office and Paymaster General), *Handling Members' Correspondence in 2015: Written Statement*, HCWS118, 21 July 2016. Online at: https://www.parliament.uk/business/publications/written-questions-answers-statements/written-statement/Commons/2016-07-21/HCWS118/ [accessed 27 June 2017].

- MPs' personal websites, which usually include very rich information and data about their activities. See for example Chi Onwurah MP (Labour–http://chionwurahmp.com) and Andrew Jones MP (Conservative–http://www.andrewjonesmp.co.uk/wp-content/uploads/2012/04/Andrew-Jones-MP-Annual-Report-20141.pdf) [accessed 27 June 2017].

- Procedure Committee (2012) *Sitting Hours and the Parliamentary Calendar: First Report of Session 2012–13*, London: The Stationery Office, HC 330. Online at: http://www.publications.parliament.uk/pa/cm201213/cmselect/cmproced/330/33002.htm [accessed 27 June 2017].

- *W4MP Casework Guide*. Online at: http://www.w4mp.org/library/guides/2010-guide-to-working-for-an-mp-for-new-staff/casework/ [accessed 27 June 2017].

- Woodhouse, J. (2017) *Data Protection: Constituency Casework*, House of Commons Library Briefing Paper Number 1936, 27 February. Online at: http://researchbriefings.parliament.uk/ResearchBriefing/Summary/SN01936 [accessed 27 June 2017].

➡ FURTHER CASE STUDIES

- Identify a selection of MPs (from different parties, different parts of the UK, different stages of their parliamentary career, etc.) and examine the relative prominence of news and information about their constituency and constituency issues on their websites.

- Identify, as a constituent, the various means by which you can contact your MP, what issues they can help you with, and how they can pursue these issues. (Clue: start with www.parliament.uk)
- Using the search term 'constituency casework' on *Hansard Online* (at https://hansard.parliament.uk) identify, for a given period, how often and what types of constituency issues are raised in debates in the House of Commons.

References

BURKE, E. ([1780] 1801) 'Speech at Bristol at the Conclusion of the Polls', in *Works*, Vol. 4, London: Rivington.

BURSTOW, P. (2016) 'As any MP knows, constituency surgeries are a vital part of democracy', *The Conversation*, 17 June. Online at: https://theconversation.com/paul-burstow-as-any-mp-knows-constituency-surgeries-are-such-a-vital-part-of-democracy-61240 [accessed 24 June 2017].

CAIN, B. E., FEREJOHN, J. A., and FIORINA, M. P. (1979) 'The House is Not a Home: British MPs in Their Constituencies', *Legislative Studies Quarterly*, Vol. 4 (4), pp. 501–23.

CAMPBELL, R. and COWLEY, P. (2014) 'What Voters Want: Reactions to Candidate Characteristics in a Survey Experiment', *Political Studies*, Vol. 62 (4), pp. 745–65.

CAMPBELL, R. and LOVENDUSKI, J. (2014) 'What Should MPs Do? Public and Parliamentarians' Views Compared', *Parliamentary Affairs*, Vol. 68 (4), pp. 690–708.

CHILDS, S. and COWLEY, P. (2011) 'The Politics of Local Presence: Is there a Case for Descriptive Representation?', *Political Studies*, Vol. 59 (1), pp. 1–19.

COWAN, R. (2017) *Annual Review 2016–17*. Online at: https://ronniecowanmp.files.wordpress.com/2017/05/ronnie-cowan-mp-2016-2017-annual-review1.pdf [accessed 22 June 2017].

COWLEY, P. (2013) 'Why Not Ask the Audience? Understanding the Public's Representational Priorities', *British Politics*, Vol. 8 (2), pp. 138–63.

CUTTS, D. and RUSSELL, A. (2015) 'From Coalition to Catastrophe: The Electoral Meltdown of the Liberal Democrats', *Parliamentary Affairs*, Vol. 68 (1), pp. 70–87.

EVANS, J., ARZHEIMER, K., CAMPBELL, R., and COWLEY, P. (2017) 'Candidate Localness and Voter Choice in the 2015 General Election in England', *Political Geography*, Vol. 59 (1), pp. 61–71.

FENNO, R. E. (1978) *Home Style: House Members in Their Districts*, Boston: Little Brown.

GRAY, J. (2015) 'What is an MP for?', *PoliticsHome*, 3 November. Online at: https://www.politicshome.com/news/uk/social-affairs/politics/house/60356/james-gray-what-mp [accessed 9 April 2017].

HANSARD SOCIETY (2011) *Audit of Political Engagement 8*, London: Hansard Society.

HANSARD SOCIETY (2013) *Audit of Political Engagement 10*, London: Hansard Society.

HUDSPETH, I. (2015) Letter to David Cameron from Leader of Oxfordshire County Council. Online at: http://www.oxfordmail.co.uk/resources/files/35654 [accessed 22 June 2017].

JUDGE, D. (1999) *Representation: Theory and Practice in Britain*, London: Routledge.

JUDGE, D. (2014) *Democratic Incongruities: Representative Democracy in Britain*, Houndmills: Palgrave Macmillan.

LEE, P. (2017) *Annual Report 2016–17*. Online at: http://www.phillip-lee.com/wp-content/uploads/ANNUAL-REPORT-2017-FINAL.pdf [accessed 22 June 2017].

Mansbridge, J. (1999) 'Should Blacks Represent Blacks and Women Represent Women? A Contingent "Yes"', *Journal of Politics*, Vol. 61 (3), pp. 628–57.

Modernisation Committee (1998) *Modernisation of the House of Commons: Fourth Report of Session 1997–98*, London: Stationery Office, HC 600.

Modernisation Committee (2007) *Revitalising the Chamber: The Role of the Backbench Member: First Report of Session 2006–07*, London: Stationery Office, HC 337. Online at: https://www.publications.parliament.uk/pa/cm200607/cmselect/cmmodern/337/337.pdf [accessed 24 June 2017].

Norris, P. (1997) 'The Puzzle of Constituency Service', *Journal of Legislative Studies*, Vol. 3 (2), pp. 29–49.

Norton, P. and Wood, D. M. (1993) *Back from Westminster: British Members of Parliament and Their Constituents*, Lexington: University Press of Kentucky.

Procedure Committee (2012) *Sitting Hours and the Parliamentary Calendar: First Report of Session 2012–13*, London: Stationery Office, HC 330. Online at: https://www.publications. parliament.uk/pa/cm201213/cmselect/cmproced/330/33002.htm [accessed 25 June 2017].

Rehfeld, A. (2005) *The Concept of Constituency: Political Representation, Democratic Legitimacy, and Institutional Design*, Cambridge: Cambridge University Press.

Riddell, P. (1997) 'Out of Kilter with the Commons', *The Times*, 25 August.

Rossiter, D., Johnston, R., and Pattie, C. (2013) 'Representing People and Representing Places: Community, Continuity and the Current Redistribution of Parliamentary Constituencies in the UK', *Parliamentary Affairs*, Vol. 66 (4), pp. 856–86.

Smith, T. H. (2013) 'Are You Sitting Comfortably? Estimating Incumbency Advantage in the UK: 1983–2010—A Research Note', *Electoral Studies*, Vol. 32 (1), pp. 167–73.

Stevens, J. (2017) *Annual Report 2016–17*. Online at: https://issuu.com/jostevensmp/docs/ annual_report_2017_booklet_v2_sprea [accessed 22 June 2017].

Stone, J. (2015) '9 absurd rules about what you can't do in Parliament', *The Independent*, 14 May. Online at: http://www.independent.co.uk/news/uk/politics/9-absurd-things-youre-not-allowed- to-do-in-parliament-10250704.html [accessed 23 August 2017].

Tinkler, J. and Mehta, N. (2016) *Report to the House of Commons Administration Committee on the Findings of the Interview Study with Members on Leaving Parliament*, Administration Committee, London: House of Commons. Online at: https://www.parliament.uk/documents/ commons-committees/admin-committee/Interview-study-Members-leaving-Parliament- report-April-2016.pdf [accessed 25 June 2017].

Vivyan, N. and Wagner, M. (2016) 'House or Home? Constituent Preferences over Legislator Effort Allocation', *European Journal of Political Research*, Vol. 55 (1), pp. 81–99.

26

MPs Campaigning for their Constituencies

Oonagh Gay

INTRODUCTION

The last four decades have seen an increase in the time devoted by MPs' offices to individual constituents, which has grown into a general advice service, as we saw in Chapter 25. This casework tends to overlay the more traditional role of speaking for the constituency as a whole. Both this holistic and individual casework are on the increase, and tend to support each other. For example, when a constituent with industrial injuries reveals a more general problem with associated benefits, research by the MP's office can highlight the extent of the failure across the constituency and this can often develop into a campaign the MP will lead on. MPs from mining areas were at the forefront of campaigns to have pneumoconiosis recognized as an industrial disease in the 1970s, for example. Many MPs consider campaigning for their constituency to be their most important job. This chapter explores the mechanisms they use to promote and resolve local issues, which may start as individual constituency cases, but develop into broader campaigns. MPs can use Parliament and their local standing to influence policy agendas and become national figures.

Why do MPs undertake constituency projects?

A seminal article, 'The Puzzle of Constituency Service' (Norris 1997), showed that constituency work seemed to have only minimal electoral benefit, since party loyalties appeared to govern re-election. In the past couple of decades, however, the focus on constituency work has intensified. New MPs elected in 2010 reported spending 28 per cent of their time on casework and 21 per cent on constituency meetings and events (Korris 2011). There are both push and pull factors at work. The electorate is more highly educated, more demanding, and less deferential. Lobbying groups manipulate social media to promote local communication with MPs. Local authorities have lost powers to outsource services, and council leaders are overshadowed by the area's parliamentary representative.

MPs have become full time and professional, understanding the value of a high profile locally, as highlighting local ties leads to popularity for candidates (Campbell and Cowley 2014). Indeed, electoral studies indicate that MPs seen as active in their constituencies generate an incumbency effect and that parties are converging in constituency campaigning techniques (Fisher et al. 2014). In dealing with local issues, MPs have learned to conciliate these with wider national issues and compartmentalize party and constituency loyalties, so that they may accept a national policy of closing small A&E departments, for instance, but still head a campaign to save the facility locally. This is unsurprising in the British norm of service to a geographic area.

Crewe found also that constituency work gives MPs autonomy in contrast to a per-ceived 'lobby fodder' role in the formal Westminster environment (Crewe 2015). MPs highlight the personal satisfaction gained from individual and project casework. Ex-MPs have described the fulfilment they found in building a local profile, particularly when a government career was not feasible. In exit interviews by parliamentary staff in 2015, ex-MPs considered that they were leaving their local area in a better state than when they had been elected, and highlighted benefits such as attracting new investment or a greater sense of community to the area. Some who had focused more on campaigning felt that building public awareness of a particular issue was their greatest achievement (Tinkler and Mehta 2016). There are therefore clear personal and career factors making constituency campaigning worthwhile to MPs. In terms of themes adopted for campaigns, although transport and infrastructure have become important, unemployment has long been at the heart of constituency projects.

Ellen Wilkinson and the Jarrow Crusade

The first modern example of how constituency unemployment could be used to win national publicity was the Jarrow Crusade. The Labour MP Ellen Wilkinson's constituency had been thrown into deep distress by the closure of shipbuilding in the Great Depression of the 1930s, compounded by the refusal of steel owners to open a plant in the area. Dismissive comments by the minister Walter Runciman that Jarrow should find its own salvation led the local council to decide to march to London to present a petition to the new parliamentary session in October 1936. As its parliamentary representative, Wilkinson led the march of 200 people, taking 22 days to reach Parliament.

The campaign achieved tremendous publicity, despite the Labour Party's concerns that the march would be hijacked by the Communist-led National Unemployed Workers Movement, which was organizing a series of hunger marches. However, the government refused to meet the marchers, resulting in Wilkinson's famous speech at Hyde Park: 'Jarrow as a town has been murdered' (Wilkinson 1939).

As MP, Wilkinson was able to present the petition in the Commons and so force a government response. She had power to initiate a short debate where the lack of government action was noted, assembling a cross-party meeting of MPs. Among them was Clement Attlee, Leader of the Labour Party, who did not speak. However, on 8 November, Attlee and a dozen other Labour MPs broke with the party's established policy and gave full support to the Hyde Park rally that ended the National Hunger March. So one immediate result was a change in Labour Party policy.

In the short term, the Jarrow Crusade did not alleviate distress, but in the long term it highlighted the necessity of external intervention. The town would go on to recover gov-ernment shipbuilding contracts during the Second World War and Wilkinson became the second female Labour cabinet minister in 1945. Jarrow remains a potent example of how constituency concerns can shape a parliamentary career.

Raising constituency issues in Parliament

As Wilkinson found, MPs have a unique advantage over council, community, and business leaders when engaging in project work, since membership of the Commons allows them to exert direct pressure on the government. In the Commons they can use a wide range of parliamentary tools to pursue their campaign.

One such tool is the petition, as shown in Wilkinson's case in the 1930s, and previously in the nineteenth century with anti-slavery and Chartist petitions, which had demonstrated the force of constituency influence on the legislature. Although this public petitions system, submitted through MPs rather than directly to Parliament, is much less used today, it still exists in practice and can be used quite effectively. See, for example, the WASPI (Women Against State Pension Inequality) campaign which culminated in October 2016 with 198 MPs presenting in the Commons Chamber petitions that had been signed by thousands of their constituents (HC Debates, 11 October 2016, cc. 261–74).

MPs also post ministerial responses to their parliamentary questions on their blogs, or in local media, even when there is an inadequate departmental response. Adjournment debates also offer opportunities. Conservative backbencher Richard Drax used his debate on ambulance waiting times to focus on his constituency, and the minister responding had been briefed on the specific challenges of South Western Ambulance Service (HC Debates, 17 October 2016, c. 743). Transcending party boundaries, MPs tend to work together in highlighting constituency issues, as demonstrated in a debate on shipbuilding policy on the Clyde, initiated by the SNP, but receiving support from DUP and Labour (HC Debates, 18 October 2016, c. 340WH).

A debate on the future of cooperatives in July 2016 enabled Co-op Party members to join forces with Conservative and SNP MPs to press for more government support (HC Debates, 14 July 2016, c. 190WH). The long-standing MP for Grimsby, Austin Mitchell, instigated a group for MPs from fishing constituencies, which was granted a general debate by the Backbench Business Committee (HC Debates, 11 December 2014, cc. 1003–55). The speeches made were then publicized in each individual constituency, reminding the government of the collective force of the industry.

MPs involved in constituency campaigns are adept at tabling amendments or presenting private members' bills (PMBs) even when there is no chance of success. The action can be reported locally and feature on websites or social media, as well as signalling views to colleagues in Parliament. And some MPs do succeed in changing the law. For example, the Sunbeds (Regulation) Act 2010 originated from a PMB presented by Labour MP Julie Morgan and bans the use of commercial tanning equipment by under-18s. She used constituency examples to make her case (HC Debates, 29 January 2010, cc. 1054). There is some evidence that initiating PMBs increases the local popularity of the MP (Bowler 2010).

The collaborative working involved in all-party parliamentary groups (APPG) can be very effective in raising constituency profiles. For example, the London–Stansted–Cambridge Corridor APPG, chaired by Labour MP David Lammy, promotes the economic development of the area, and its secretariat is provided by the LSC consortium of public and private businesses; MPs with neighbouring constituencies are members. Lammy initiated a Westminster Hall debate in 2014 to highlight the importance of upgrading rail links to Stansted airport (HC Debates, 12 February 2014, c. 320WH).

Party mechanisms and lobbying ministers

Government backbenchers may also use their party machinery to good effect. The diaries of Labour MP Chris Mullin relate his ability to raise issues directly with Prime Minister Tony Blair, for example, using his presence on party committees (Mullin 2009). Similarly, Andy Burnham, as Secretary of State for Culture, Media and Sport, secured direct cabinet agreement from Prime Minister Gordon Brown to a second inquiry into the Hillsborough football disaster of 1989, a cause he had championed for two decades.

These mechanisms are unlikely on their own to build a successful constituency campaign. It is crucial for the MP to mobilize wider support. For example, Ian Liddell-Grainger's constituency of Bridgwater contains the nuclear power station Hinckley Point, and he has been a strong proponent of the economic benefits of nuclear power. He used his blog to publicize support beyond his constituency and build a group of 19 MPs to promote nuclear power (e.g. Liddell-Grainger 2017).

MPs need to be sophisticated in their approach to lobbying ministers. They must not entrench hostility to the local project by ridiculing government arguments. Initially the MP begins with quiet conversations. Only when these are rebuffed are they likely to generate local protest as a way of pressuring government (Norton and Wood 1993). Conversely, ministers are likely to be susceptible to personal approaches from MPs because they share a common role as constituency representatives, and understand the pressures. Dropping notes into the pockets of ministers when all are together in the voting lobby has been a successful approach (Crewe 2015).

Ministers and constituencies: dilemmas of constituency projects

The key principle of the *Ministerial Code* is that government facilities and funds should not be used for constituency campaigning. Where ministers have to take decisions within their departments which might have an impact on their own constituencies, they are required to consult their Permanent Secretary, and in some cases will rearrange departmental responsibilities. However, ministers may contact government on constituency issues provided they make clear they are acting as constituency representatives and not as a minister (Cabinet Office 2015).

Where constituency interests clash with government policy and the MP is a minister, tensions can be acute. Recently this has surfaced in a number of constituencies in regard to transport policy. The choice between expansion at Heathrow and Gatwick airports led the Conservative MP Zac Goldsmith to promise in 2008 to stand down and fight a by-election if the government decided on a third runway at Heathrow. His constituency, Richmond Park, would be directly affected by the consequent increase in air traffic and pollution. He resigned in October 2016, but lost the subsequent by-election to the Liberal Democrats on 1 December 2016, on a wave of anti-Brexit sentiment. His constituents had decided that the EU was a more pressing matter than Heathrow. Resignation can be a high-risk strategy. He would later regain his seat (by a very small margin of 45 votes) at the 2017 general election.

Likewise, Boris Johnson made opposition to Heathrow expansion central to his London Mayor manifesto. His continued opposition as Foreign Secretary, and that of Education Secretary Justine Greening, appeared to be behind the decision of the new prime minister, Theresa May, to suspend cabinet collective responsibility during a year-long consultation on the choices involved (Parker 2016).

Conclusion

MPs have unique advantages through Parliament to publicize constituency campaigns and many tools which they can utilize to good effect. If they are to be successful, they must make sure that they build alliances locally. They must also cooperate beyond party loyalties if they are to achieve a national profile, something which will increase the likelihood of their constituency campaign being successful.

Further Reading

CREWE, E. (2015) *The House of Commons: An Anthropology of MPs at Work*, London: Bloomsbury Academic.

GAY, O. (2005) 'MPs go back to their constituencies', *Political Quarterly*, Vol. 76 (1), pp. 57–66.

KORRIS, M. (2011) *A Year in the Life: From Member of Public to Member of Parliament*, London: Hansard Society.

NORTON, P. (2013) 'Parliament and Citizens in the United Kingdom' in C. Leston-Bandeira, (ed.), *Parliaments and Citizens*, London: Routledge, pp. 139–54.

Case Study 26: Cheryl Gillan and HS2

This case study analyses actions by Conservative MP Cheryl Gillan to represent her constituency's opposition to the high-speed railway HS2. Proposals to build a high-speed rail line from London to Manchester and Leeds, via Birmingham, won Labour government backing after 2009, and has had the support of the Conservatives since May 2010. Gillan's constituency of Chesham and Amersham is directly affected by the proposed line, and falls within part of the Chilterns Area of Outstanding Natural Beauty (AONB).

Proponents argue that the line is urgently needed to meet projected future demand, to tackle the capacity constraints on the West Coast Main Line, and to deliver wider economic and regional benefits. Opponents claim that the case is overstated and that future capacity requirements can be met through other, cheaper means. Phase 1 of the HS2 project would take the line from London to the West Midlands by 2026, while Phase 2 would run from the West Midlands to the north of England by 2032–3.

The route for Phase 1 was published for consultation in February 2011 (McLoughlin 2013), eliciting strong responses from those concerned about the effects on the Chilterns and other AONBs and on the borough of Camden, particularly around Euston Station. The government announced changes to mitigate some of these concerns, but was more willing to adapt the proposals for Euston, since this would involve a cost reduction, than it was to help AONBs with extra tunnelling.

A new railway throws up many challenges to those MPs whose constituencies are to be cut through. Constituents will be very concerned about the resulting economic and visual damage, and their opposition is strengthened by controversy over the economic benefits of a high-speed line. Government ministers with seats in affected areas have particular difficulties in juggling collective responsibility with the need to retain sufficient local support. This makes the position of Cheryl Gillan of particular interest.

Cheryl Gillan was first elected to Parliament in 1992 for the constituency of Chesham and Amersham. She became Welsh Secretary in the Coalition government of 2010. Her opposition to HS2 had been long term. A strong local campaign to ensure that the route would be fully tunnelled underneath the Chilterns has so far been unsuccessful, although a partial extension of the tunnelled area was announced in September 2015. However, this did not offer full protection for the AONB.

In 2010, Gillan made clear that she would be prepared to defy any whipped vote on HS2 (Bucks Free Press 2010) and she submitted a full response to the government HS2 consultation in 2011, expressing her opposition despite her cabinet position (Gillan 2011).

However, she did not resign when Transport Minister Justine Greening announced that HS2 would proceed in January 2012. In the event, Ms Gillan was sacked as Welsh Secretary as part of a wider reshuffle in September 2012. Returning to the backbenches offered a chance to step up her opposition to HS2 within days and, using her high profile, Gillan was able to criticize the project in a series of media appearances. In the *Daily Telegraph* she wrote:

> For any Government to function effectively, it is vital and right that Cabinet members remain loyal and maintain collective responsibility. HS2 has not made doing so easy for me. I saw the anxiety HS2 is creating across my constituency week after week. My departure from the Cabinet has changed matters. Now I am liberated and free to say what I think about HS2—and I certainly will. I have written to Patrick McLoughlin, the new Transport Secretary, urging him to axe HS2. (Gillan 2012)

As a Conservative, Gillan was aware that she faced competition from UKIP, which also took an anti-HS2 position. She used parliamentary mechanisms available to her such as the All-Party Parliamentary Group for Integrated Transport Policy; Cavendish Communications (a consultancy) is paid to act as the group's secretariat by its clients Heathrow Hub Ltd and Conserve the Chilterns and Countryside. Opposing her was an APPG for High Speed Rail which had industry backing.

Legislation was introduced to Parliament in 2013 for HS2 to proceed. It was a hybrid bill, which has elements of both a public and private bill—the key additional scrutiny stage here is a special select committee to consider petitions against the bill from directly and specially affected individuals, organizations, or groups. This adds significant time to the parliamentary process and allows more concerted lobbying. Cheryl Gillan moved a cross-party amendment to oppose the passage of the HS2 Phase One hybrid bill on 28 April 2014; of her 50 supporters, most were Conservatives whose constituencies were affected. The Speaker, John Bercow, with a Chilterns constituency, could not vote, but expressed his opposition on his website and in oral evidence to the High Speed Rail Committee (Bercow 2017). Gillan was ruled ineligible under procedural rules to join the bill committee, as an MP with a clear interest.

In the 2015 general election, Gillan's safe seat was hardly dented by a UKIP surge against her; the UKIP candidate gained 13.7 per cent vote share, compared with her 59.1 per cent. Local dissatisfaction is tempered by Gillan's clear opposition to HS2 and her ability to articulate this. As a backbencher, she continued to campaign through parliamentary questions and debates, and with other affected MPs attempted unsuccessfully to petition the Lords Committee. Parliamentary rules forbid MPs in general from petitioning the other House.

There was a setback for anti-HS2 campaigners when the new Transport Secretary Chris Grayling confirmed the project, offering extra funds for environmental improvements in affected areas, including the Chilterns, on 12 October 2016. The hybrid bill passed in February 2017, despite Gillan's efforts, as there was cross-party support from both frontbenches. She continues to argue for effective compensation and oversight.

Gillan successfully mobilized constituency concern about the disruptive impact of major infrastructure work represented by HS2, and fought off UKIP as a result, which lacked her access to parliamentary mechanisms. Gillan's return to the backbenches gave her more opportunities to use her parliamentary position to highlight the arguments against HS2, even if ultimately she was unable to cancel the project. This shows how effective MPs can find constituency campaigning in terms of building their national profile, and as an outlet for their capabilities, once ministerial office is over.

Primary sources

- Butcher, L. (2017) *High Speed 2 (HS2) Phase 1*, House of Commons Library Briefing Paper Number SN316, 16 February. Online at: http://researchbriefings.parliament.uk/ResearchBriefing/Summary/SN00316 [accessed 27 June 2017].

- *High Speed Rail (London—West Midlands) Act 2017*. Online at: http://services.parliament.uk/bills/2013-14/highspeedraillondonwestmidlands.html [accessed 27 June 2017].

- UK Parliament Outreach Service (n.d.) *Get Your Voice Heard: A Guide to Campaigning at Westminster*, London: UK Parliament. Online at: http://www.parliament.uk/documents/commons-information-office/Brief-Guides/Outreach-Publications/Campaigning-at-Westminster.pdf [accessed 27 June 2017].

 FURTHER CASE STUDIES

- Stella Creasy MP and the campaign against payday loans.
- Andrew Miller MP's campaign for better ferry services on the Isle of Wight.
- Steve Rotheram MP's campaign for a public inquiry into the Hillsborough disaster.

References

BERCOW, J. (2017) *High Speed 2*. Online at: http://www.johnbercow.co.uk/content/high-speed-2 [accessed 20 June 2017].

BOWLER, S. (2010) 'Private Members' Bills in the UK Parliament: Is There an "Electoral Connection"?', *Journal of Legislative Studies*, Vol. 16 (4), pp. 476–94.

BUCKS FREE PRESS (2010) 'MP to "defy party" over high speed trains', *Bucks Free Press*, 30 March. Online at: http://www.bucksfreepress.co.uk/chalfonts/5517421.display/ [accessed 6 September 2012].

CABINET OFFICE (2015) *Ministerial Code*, London: Cabinet Office.

CAMPBELL, R. and COWLEY, P. (2014) 'What Voters Want: Reactions to Candidate Characteristics in a Survey Experiment', *Political Studies*, Vol. 62 (4), pp. 745–65.

CREWE, E. (2015) *The House of Commons: An Anthropology of MPs at Work*, London: Bloomsbury.

FISHER, J., JOHNSTON, R., CUTTS, D., PATTIE, C., and FIELDHOUSE, E. (2014) 'You get what you (don't) pay for: The impact of volunteer labour and candidate spending at the 2010 British General Election', *Parliamentary Affairs*, Vol. 67 (4), pp. 804–24.

GILLAN, C. (2011) 'Submission to the Consultation on HS2 on behalf of the Constituency of Chesham and Amersham', 29 July. Online at: https://www.cherylgillan.co.uk/sites/www.cherylgillan.co.uk/files/hs2_-_chesham_and_amersham_submission.pdf [accessed 25 June 2017].

GILLAN, C. (2012) 'HS2 flies in the face of Conservative values', *The Telegraph*, 8 September. Online at: http://www.telegraph.co.uk/comment/9530357/Cheryl-Gillan-HS2-flies-in-the-face-of-Conservative-values.html [accessed 20 June 2017].

KORRIS, M. (2011) *A Year in the Life: From Member of Public to Member of Parliament: Interim Briefing Paper*, London: Hansard Society. Online at: https://assets.contentful.com/u1rlvvbs33ri/2o4NYUjBty6CaaI4imQm6M/44e515d5737a18bcf52d02146edecb78/Publication__A-Year-In-the-Life-From-Member-of-Public-to-Member-of-Parliament.pdf [accessed 23 August 2017].

LIDDELL-GRAINGER, I. (2017) '180 days makes all the difference!', *Peregrine's Blog*, 31 March. Online at: http://liddellgrainger.org.uk/180-days-makes-all-the-difference/ [accessed 20 June 2017].

MCLOUGHLIN, P. (2013) *HS2 Phase One Consultations*, Written Statement to Parliament, London: Department for Transport. Online at: https://www.gov.uk/government/speeches/hs2-phase-one-consultations [accessed 25 June 2017].

MULLIN, C. (2009) *Diaries: A View from the Foothills*, London: Profile Books.

NORRIS, P. (1997) 'The Puzzle of Constituency Service', *Journal of Legislative Studies*, Vol. 3 (2), pp. 29–49.

NORTON, P. and WOOD, P. M. (1993) *Back from Westminster*, Kentucky: Kentucky University Press.

PARKER, G. (2016) 'Theresa May signals favouring Heathrow expansion', *Financial Times*, 18 October.

TINKLER, J. and MEHTA, N. (2016) *Report to the House of Commons Administration Committee on the findings of the interview study with Members on leaving Parliament*, London: House of Commons. Online at: https://www.parliament.uk/documents/commons-committees/admin-committee/Interview-study-Members-leaving-Parliament-report-April-2016.pdf [accessed 25 June 2017].

WILKINSON, E. (1939) *The Town That Was Murdered: The Life Story of Jarrow*, London: Victor Gollancz.

PART VI

Challenges and Reform

27

Parliament and Devolution

Cathy Gormley-Heenan and Mark Sandford

INTRODUCTION

The decision to devolve power to Scotland, Wales, and Northern Ireland in the final years of the twentieth century triggered debate about the territorial composition of the UK, and the relationships between its constituent parts. It also raised fundamental questions about the impact of devolution on issues of national identity, sovereignty, economy, power, and effective governance. Most academic studies and textbooks covering devolution and Parliament have concentrated on inter-*governmental* relations, not inter-*parliamentary* relations. This is because the relationships between the UK and the devolved regions are dominated by inter-governmental relations between the Westminster government and the Scottish government, Welsh government, and Northern Ireland Executive, with Parliament's role marginal at best. And so this chapter explores that lesser-known relationship between the UK Parliament and the devolved legislatures established in Scotland, Wales, and Northern Ireland. It sets out the key features of those institutions, and tracks the way in which Parliament's relationships with them have developed since their inception. It shows that Parliament's influence on devolution in the UK has been marginal to date, making only low-key and minimal adjustments to its own practices to reflect the influence of devolution (Norton 2013). That said, it is argued that these subtle changes in practices at Westminster suggest that Parliament increasingly reflects wider shifts in public attitudes about the relationships between the territories of the United Kingdom, particularly in the aftermath of the Brexit referendum.

Devolution and parliamentary sovereignty

The initial decision in 1997 to devolve has been followed by successive waves of devolution of power to Scotland, Wales, and Northern Ireland. This, plus the conventions and ways of working that have surrounded them, has given constitutional personality to the devolved legislatures; something that has been acknowledged by sections in both the Scotland Act 2016 and the Wales Act 2017 which state that the devolved bodies 'are a permanent part of the United Kingdom's constitutional arrangements' and that they 'are not to be abolished except on the basis of a decision of the people of [Scotland/Wales] voting in a referendum' (Scotland Act 2016; Wales Act 2017). This wording seems to be at odds with the most fundamental principle of the UK's constitution, that of parliamentary sovereignty. The principle of parliamentary sovereignty means that the UK Parliament can, at least in theory, choose to abolish these devolved legislatures if it so wishes, and the sections of the Scotland and Wales Acts mentioned are merely 'declaratory', which means that they do not have binding force. Therein lies the tension between Parliament, parliamentary sovereignty, and devolution, a tension which may be severely tested (repeatedly) as the UK prepares to leave the European Union, particularly given that the devolved territories of Scotland and Northern Ireland voted to remain in the EU. As Case Study 27 demonstrates, Brexit may yet serve as an illustrative example of what can happen when the unstoppable force of devolution of power meets the immovable object of parliamentary sovereignty.

 Parliamentary terms Devolved powers

Legislative powers which have been moved from the UK Parliament to the Scottish Parliament, the Welsh Assembly, or the Northern Ireland Assembly, under devolution.

The establishment and development of the devolved legislatures

The Scottish Parliament, National Assembly for Wales,[1] and Northern Ireland Assembly are similar in that they are parliamentary systems of government, comprising single-chamber legislatures, cabinet executives (Scottish government; Welsh government; Northern Ireland Executive), oppositions, and a number of subject committees. The Northern Ireland Assembly and Executive are slightly different in that both the Assembly and Executive operate on the basis of consociationalism, or 'power-sharing', between the two main political traditions of unionism and nationalism, and before 2016 it did not have the legislative framework in place for the establishment of an official opposition.

Each devolved legislature exercises a broad range of domestic policy competences and is responsible for substantial budgets. Each uses a proportional electoral system, originally designed to guard against single-party dominance. The key features of the legislatures are set out in Table 27.1.

The former Secretary of State for Wales, Ron Davies, famously said 'devolution is a process, not an event' (Davies 1999). This has been borne out since 1999. Each of the devolved legislatures has gradually added to its powers since its inception. For example, Wales took on a complex system of Assembly Measures from 2007. The Assembly was able to pass laws on a range of defined matters, with the permission of the Secretary of State for Wales in the UK Parliament. It then assumed primary legislative powers in 2011, allowing it to legislate freely in matters for which it had responsibility. And under the Wales Act 2017, it will assume some tax-raising powers (and it is expected to become a Parliament, rather than an Assembly). Scotland took on control of a number of taxes from the UK government as of 2015, and will obtain more under the Scotland Act 2016. And after several periods of suspension between 2001 and 2007 due to political disagreements, the Northern Ireland Assembly has resumed sitting since 2007 and assumed full powers over policing and justice in 2011 (although at the time of writing, it has not resumed sitting following the 2017 election).

Interactions with devolved parliaments

Inter-governmental relations in the UK have been ad hoc and overwhelmingly bilateral, between the UK government and the separate devolved governments. Despite repeated recommendations by various parliamentary committees (Justice Committee 2009;

---

[1] In June 2017 the Welsh Assembly Commission announced that, following the Wales Act 2017, legislation would be issued to rename the National Assembly for Wales as the Welsh Parliament/Senedd Cymru.

Table 27.1 The UK's devolved bodies

	Scottish Parliament	Northern Ireland Assembly	National Assembly for Wales
Referendums	Devolution 1997 Tax-raising powers 1997 Independence 2014	Devolution 1998	Devolution 1997 Devolution 2011
Key Acts of Parliament	Scotland Act 1998 Scotland Act 2012 Scotland Act 2016	Northern Ireland Act 1998 Northern Ireland (St Andrews Agreement) Act 2006*	Government of Wales Act 1998 Government of Wales Act 2006 Wales Act 2014 Wales Act 2017
Model of powers	Reserved powers model	Reserved and excepted powers	Transferred powers model
Electoral system used	Additional Member System	Single Transferable Vote	Additional Member System
Number of members	129 MSPs: 73 constituencies, 56 top-up members	90 MLAs: 18 constituencies, 5 MLAs per constituency	60 AMs: 40 constituencies, 20 top-up members
Elections	1999; 2003; 2007; 2011; 2016	1998; 2003; 2007; 2011; 2016; 2017	1999; 2003; 2007; 2011; 2016
Political representation (most recent)	SNP: 63 Conservative: 31 Labour: 24 Green: 6 Liberal Democrat: 5	DUP: 28 Sinn Féin: 27 UUP: 10 SDLP: 12 Alliance: 8 TUV: 1 Green: 2 People Before Profit: 1 Independent: 1	Labour: 29 Plaid Cymru: 12 Conservative: 11 UKIP: 7 Liberal Democrat: 1
Government (most recent)	SNP minority	DUP/Sinn Féin coalition (to 2017)	Labour/Liberal Democrat coalition
Budget (2015/16)	£37.3 bn	£20.6 bn	£15.9 bn

Note: *Plus many more, containing provisions for elections, justice/peace

Constitution Committee 2016; Scottish Affairs Committee 2010), the UK government has avoided establishing a broader framework through which issues of common interest can be discussed and disputes aired.

In addition, the UK's inter-governmental relations have also been almost entirely informal, 'regulated by convention, concordat, memorandums of understanding and

guidance notes' (Bingham Centre 2015, 9). A formal structure of joint ministerial committees (JMCs) was established at the outset of devolution, but these have met very
rarely. Between 1999 and 2007, when Labour was in power in the UK, Scotland, and
Wales, the JMCs were barely used. Their use increased after 2007, when Labour Party
dominance gave way to an SNP minority in Scotland and a Labour–Plaid Cymru
coalition in Wales: annual reports and other information have since been published.
However, the JMCs remain far from a systematic framework. This reduces their status
and thus their effectiveness as a forum for securing effective relationships.

Division of powers

This informal mode of relationship has been facilitated by the perceived sharp distinction between devolved and reserved matters. There are relatively few areas where the
UK and devolved governments share responsibilities ('concurrent powers'). In the terms
used in inter-governmental relations literature, the UK's structures are strongly 'dualist'
in character. This means that each tier of government is expected to operate separately,
with distinct responsibilities. 'Dualism' signifies that there *is* a line dividing the two tiers'
spheres of responsibility, although it can be complex to work out exactly where this line is
drawn. An 'interlocking' approach to inter-governmental relations would feature greater
and more regular joint working between the two tiers of government. This is a common feature of central-regional relations in other developed states, sometimes leading
to inter-governmental disputes. There is some evidence of such 'interlocking' in the UK
arrangements, with overlapping, shared, and interdependent powers—fuel poverty is one
such example, with the UK government responsible for energy tariffs and energy efficiency, and the devolved administrations responsible for insulation, heating assistance,
and cold weather payments (Birrell and Gormley-Heenan 2015)—but this is the exception rather than the rule.

 Parliamentary terms   Reserved powers

Legislative power over issues such as foreign affairs and security which are expressly held by
the UK Parliament and not devolved to other institutions. Northern Ireland has an additional
category of 'excepted powers' which can never be devolved.

The Westminster approach

Parliament has been slow to adapt to devolution (Norton 2013) and has not sought to
exploit the bilateral and informal approach to inter-governmental relations to stamp its
own authority on devolved relationships. Instead, it has largely limited itself to adjusting
its procedures where necessary to take account of devolution. For instance, a critical issue
at the outset of devolution was whether Parliament would still wish to pass legislation
on devolved matters. Parliamentary sovereignty would dictate that it could, but doing so
would be seen to breach the spirit of devolution. This question has been governed by the
'Sewel Convention': a convention which states that the UK Parliament 'will not normally
legislate with regard to devolved matters without the consent of the [devolved legislature]'
(Scotland Act 2016, s2; Wales Act 2017, s2)

Parliamentary terms Sewel Convention

A convention under which the UK Parliament does not pass legislation on matters which have been devolved to Scotland under the devolution settlement without the consent of the Scottish Parliament, given in a legislative consent motion. Similar conventions exist in respect of the Welsh Assembly and Northern Ireland Assembly.

When the UK Parliament does seek to legislate on devolved matters, the relevant devolved legislatures indicate their consent for it to do so via legislative consent motions (LCMs). In practice, LCMs cover relatively uncontentious matters. However, the giving of consent is managed via inter-governmental negotiations behind the scenes, marginalizing the role of the legislatures. There are no inter-parliamentary coordination mechanisms to address Sewel Convention matters, and when a devolved legislature refuses to pass an LCM it cannot enforce its decision. The Scottish Parliament and Northern Ireland Assembly have refused to pass an LCM on one occasion each, and the National Assembly for Wales on seven occasions. The Scottish Parliament's rejection related to Universal Credit's impact on devolved services, and the Northern Ireland Assembly's rejection related to caps on redundancy payments in the public sector (Miller 2016). On each occasion, the UK government has pushed the legislation through the UK Parliament. This signals that in cases of such disagreement the UK government has the final say—maintaining the doctrine of parliamentary sovereignty.

In procedural adjustments since devolution, the House of Commons has tended to shy away from using procedural changes to seek to enhance its role. For instance, devolved matters can no longer be discussed in the Chamber of the House of Commons or be the subject of Parliamentary Questions, following a Speaker's ruling in July 1999. The Commons has retained select committees for Scottish Affairs, Northern Ireland Affairs, and Welsh Affairs, reflecting the retention of government departments with those titles. This is despite recommendations that the three government departments be combined into a single Department for the Union (e.g. Constitution Committee 2002).

Joint working between legislatures has been conspicuous by its absence. Though Commons select committees are permitted to share evidence with their devolved counterparts, they may not (with the exception of the Welsh Affairs Committee) hold formal joint meetings with them. The paucity of formal relationships can lead to overlapping inquiries and a confusion of focus. One such example relates to the Northern Ireland peace process and the issue of an 'administrative scheme' purported to deal with the so called 'On the Runs'—a category of people wanted in connection with paramilitary offences in the period before the Good Friday Agreement of 1998. Lady Justice Hallett was appointed by the UK government to conduct a judge-led independent inquiry; the Northern Ireland Affairs Select Committee began its own separate inquiry; and the Northern Ireland Assembly's Justice Committee also held its own hearings. This was unhelpful in two respects: firstly, because suggestions were made that one inquiry should take priority over another inquiry, and secondly because the findings of the various inquiries did not sit easily together. Hallett's private inquiry concluded that the scheme may have been flawed but was *not* 'unlawful', while the select committee inquiry concluded that the legality of the scheme was questionable.

Thus until devolution, Parliament's approach to territorial questions was one of a unified approach acknowledging territorial distinctiveness. This relationship is embodied within the Palace of Westminster itself: stained-glass designs on the four sides of Central Lobby represent England, Scotland, Wales, and Ireland. Following devolution, the House of Commons began quietly to step back from this approach: many of the procedures have begun to fall into disuse. In its place is a more explicitly quasi-federal approach, where Parliament has ceded its active authority to the devolved legislatures. In turn, it has acknowledged the territorial character of the UK via special procedures which, for the first time, link voting rights in the House of Commons to territorial representation—'English votes for English laws' (Gover and Kenny 2016). These small changes in procedure in the House of Commons reflect—but also solidify and legitimize—changes in the wider attitudinal undercurrents regarding the territories of the UK (Jeffery et al. 2014).

Procedural shifts

Prior to devolution, the UK Parliament acted occasionally as a legislature for Scotland or Northern Ireland alone, passing laws that extended solely to those territories. Since devolution, it has passed far fewer Scotland-only Acts: only five in 17 years, compared with between three and nine per year in the preceding years of the 1990s. The numbers of UK Acts applying only to Wales or to Northern Ireland have remained steady both before and after devolution; but their content has altered notably. Most Acts concerning Northern Ireland have related to police, justice, or the peace process both before and after devolution. There have been no Wales-only Acts since the advent of legislative devolution in 2011.

The House of Commons has also stepped back from detailed scrutiny of government in Scotland, Wales, and Northern Ireland. For example, in 1993–4, written parliamentary questions (with answers given) to the territorial Secretaries of State ran at 2,286 (Scottish Office), 2,100 (Welsh Office), and 1,277 (Northern Ireland Office). By 2013–14, the equivalent figures were 274, 288 and 468 respectively (UK Parliament 2017). Grand Committees for Scotland, Wales, and Northern Ireland, consisting of all MPs from each territory, met regularly up to 1997 to debate matters of contemporary interest and to provide a parliamentary voice for each area. But the Scottish Grand Committee has not met since 12 November 2003; the Northern Ireland Grand Committee last met on 9 September 2013, and has met only five times since 2008. The latter last used its powers to consider secondary legislation in 2006.

In recent Parliaments, the composition of the Scotland and the Northern Ireland Affairs Committees have departed from the norm for select committees—reflecting the balance of parties in the House as a whole. In the 2017 Parliament the Scottish Affairs Committee consisted of three SNP, four Conservative, one Liberal Democrat, and three Labour MPs; and the Northern Ireland Affairs Committee, four Conservative, three Labour, and four MPs from Northern Ireland parties. Devolution (and the recent lower representation of UK parties among Scottish and Northern Irish MPs) has eroded the territorial select committees' adherence to the convention of representation reflecting the political balance of the Commons.

At a broader level, the issue of the number of voters living in each parliamentary seat has become politically charged in recent years. Scotland, Wales, and Ireland have all had periods of being over-represented in the House of Commons compared to their population. Scotland and Wales were over-represented from 1965 onwards, reflecting the fact that electoral quotas for constituency size are calculated separately for each territory. Scotland's over-representation ceased at the 2005 general election, and Wales' will cease if the 2016–18 boundary review comes into effect. Northern Ireland was under-represented during the existence of the Stormont Parliament (1921–72), but it has been represented proportionately since 1983. On the other hand, England has always been numerically dominant: even when it held the fewest seats by percentage between 1885 and 1918, 461 of 670 seats (68.8 per cent) were English (Rallings and Thrasher 2012).

These gradual changes in procedure suggest that the House of Commons, tentatively and gradually, has been helping to redefine the role of territory in the UK's constitution.

This effect is likely to be sharply intensified by the introduction of English votes for English laws (now known as EVEL) in 2015. This followed the report of the McKay Commission in 2013, which recommended that some form of EVEL be adopted, on the principle that 'decisions with a separate and distinct effect for England (or England-and-Wales) should normally be taken only with the consent of a majority of MPs from England (or England-and-Wales)' (McKay Commission 2013, 40).

New Standing Orders for the House of Commons (83J to 83O), introduced in 2015, define in considerable detail what constitutes an 'English law' (and an 'England-and-Wales law'), and restrict voting rights on bill clauses, as well as paragraphs in secondary legislation, to MPs for English constituencies. The 'EVEL procedure' requires matters defined as 'English laws' to be subject to a 'dual lock', approved by a majority *both* of English MPs *and* UK MPs. It does not allow English MPs to initiate, or to amend, 'English laws'. Sir William McKay called the form of EVEL introduced 'a forest in which I lose myself' (Public Administration and Constitutional Affairs Committee 2015, Q65); but despite discord and warnings accompanying its introduction, EVEL has proved relatively uncontroversial in its first year of operation (Gover and Kenny 2016).

Conclusion

In the last ten years, Parliament has seen a decline in procedures specific to the devolved territories, balanced by a more explicit acknowledgement of the multi-territorial nature of the United Kingdom in small-scale procedural shifts. This has not resulted from a series of conscious, strategic decisions, and likewise, the changes within Parliament cannot be portrayed as a strategic response. But they suggest that Parliament is affected by, and participating in, broader changes in the understanding of territory in the UK. As the UK comes to be regarded as a union of four distinct territories (Gover and Kenny 2016), Parliament is tacitly acknowledging this change—most forcefully by the introduction of the unique system of English votes for English laws.

If Parliament is affected by, and participating in, a wider, subtle drift towards a United Kingdom that is more explicitly a union of four distinct territories, will the informal style of inter-governmental relations adopted so far remain robust? So far, inter-'parliamentary' relations have been characterized by occasional devolution of additional powers in response to political pressures, on the back of the Calman (Scottish Government 2009), Holtham (Holtham Commission 2010), Silk (Commission on Devolution in Wales 2012), and Smith (Smith Commission 2014) reports. This ad hoc approach will face severe challenges from the complexities of exiting the European Union.

Further Reading

BINGHAM CENTRE FOR THE RULE OF LAW (2015) *A Constitutional Crossroads: Ways Forward for the United Kingdom*, London: British Institute of International and Comparative Law.

BIRRELL, D. and GORMLEY-HEENAN, C. (2015) *Multi-level Governance in Northern Ireland*, Basingstoke: Palgrave Macmillan.

GOVER, D. and KENNY, M. (2016) *Finding the Good in EVEL*, London: QMUL. Online at: http://www.ucl.ac.uk/constitution-unit/news/EVEL_Report_A4_FINAL.pdf [accessed 27 June 2017].

PAUN, A. and MILLER, G. (2016) *Four-nation Brexit: How the UK and Devolved Governments should Work Together on Leaving the EU*, London: Institute for Government.

PUBLIC ADMINISTRATION AND CONSTITUTIONAL AFFAIRS COMMITTEE (2016) *The Future of the Union, Part Two: Inter-institutional Relations in the UK: Sixth Report of Session 2016–17*, London: The Stationery Office, HC 839. Online at: https://www.publications.parliament.uk/pa/cm201617/cmselect/cmpubadm/839/839.pdf [accessed 27 June 2017].

Case Study 27: Brexit and devolution

In June 2016, 52 per cent of voters in the UK opted to leave the EU in a referendum. This majority result at the UK level was complicated by the fact that not all territories within the UK voted in the same way. So while the UK, as a whole, voted to leave, there was a 50/50 split between the four UK regions. In Scotland, 62 per cent of the electorate voted to remain in the EU; 56 per cent of the electorate in Northern Ireland also voted to remain. But 53 per cent in Wales and in England voted to leave (Uberoi 2016). These different voting patterns of the devolved regions on Brexit have provoked a territorial dilemma. The possible implications of Brexit on territorial governance (known as the 'Brexit consequentials'), as well as the illustration of different centres of political gravity across the UK on EU membership, suggests the likelihood of long-running disagreement.

This is because Brexit challenges the assumption that the division of powers between the centre and the devolved regions is distinct in nature. There is clear evidence of overlapping, shared, and interdependent powers relating to the exit plans from the EU. This has been highlighted by the People's Challenge Group, a group of people who crowdfunded £175,000 to bring about a High Court case to test whether parliamentary approval was needed to trigger Article 50 of the Treaty of Lisbon, beginning the UK's two-year exit process; and also the cross-political party group challenge in Northern Ireland's High Court on the same issue. The High Court ruled that Parliament must approve the triggering of Article 50. A government appeal was dismissed by the UK Supreme Court in January 2017, confirming the original High Court ruling. However, the Supreme Court took a different view when it came to consider the role of the devolved institutions and unanimously ruled that the Scotland, Wales, and Northern Ireland legislatures did not have a right of veto over the Article 50 process.

The challenge of overlapping, shared, and interdependent powers will be most evident when the UK Parliament repeals the 1972 European Communities Act. This is because it must also seek to amend the devolution legislation for Scotland and Northern Ireland, since EU law has been incorporated into the legislation establishing the devolved institutions. But under the Sewel Convention, as discussed in this chapter, the UK Parliament does not normally legislate on something which falls within the legislative competence of the devolved legislatures. Until the Supreme Court ruling, the assumption was that the Sewel Convention would oblige the UK government to seek the consent of the Scottish and Northern Irish legislatures via the use of a legislative consent motion (LCM). The Supreme Court ruled, however, that the Sewel Convention did not give rise to a legally enforceable obligation, and therefore no LCM would be needed to trigger Article 50. By extension, the same logic may apply to any further bills related to Brexit. If the Sewel Convention were to be respected in the context of such bills, and should Scotland and/or Northern Ireland refuse to legislate—and that is possible since both have done so in the past—then Westminster could legislate anyway, maintaining the doctrine of parliamentary sovereignty. In asserting that doctrine, however, Parliament risks escalating a territorial disagreement over Brexit into a constitutional crisis for the United Kingdom.

Despite such high constitutional stakes, coordinated inter-parliamentary activity between the Westminster Parliament and the devolved legislatures has remained limited post-referendum. The British–Irish Parliamentary Assembly did meet in July 2016 to launch an inquiry into the possible effects on British–Irish relations of the UK leaving the EU, and met again in November 2016. However, there has been no attempt yet to develop joint or complementary inquiries involving all UK legislatures, notwithstanding their overlapping, shared, and interdependent remits on European matters. That the Northern Ireland Assembly currently exists in something of a political vacuum and, at the time of writing, has been in suspension since the Assembly election of March 2017, is a further complicating factor.

There is also a difference of response between the devolved legislatures themselves. Though Northern Ireland voted to stay in the EU, its Assembly failed to respond immediately by establishing a Brexit-related inquiry or issuing calls for evidence. By contrast, even though Wales voted to leave the EU, the Welsh Assembly convened a new committee—the External Affairs and Additional Legislation Committee—in July 2016, with a remit to examine: 'the implications for Wales of the United Kingdom's withdrawal from the European Union and to ensure Welsh interests are safeguarded during the withdrawal process, in any new relationship with the European Union and in the intra-UK post-withdrawal arrangements for relevant policy, finance and legislation' (External Affairs and Additional Legislation Committee 2016). The Scottish Parliament also established a specific inquiry into 'The EU referendum and its implications for Scotland' through its Culture, Tourism, Europe and External Relations Committee (2016). Almost every select committee at Westminster was taking evidence for their concurrent and coordinated inquiries, and yet inter-parliamentary activity on a key matter of territorial governance has, thus far, been negligible.

This case study demonstrates the difficulties for Parliament in handling territorial governance disagreements. Acknowledging these difficulties led to the launch of a Public Administration and Constitutional Affairs Committee (2017) inquiry into Brexit and devolution with a focus, among other things, on 'the importance of effective relationships between different administrations and institutions in facilitating a successful Brexit'. The current lack of structures for institutional coordination mean that the UK's inter-governmental and inter-parliamentary system can appear incoherent in a crisis. In attempting to address this perception of incoherence the Committee is concerned with the mechanisms that *could* be put in place to ensure that the devolved interests are represented, not only in the Brexit negotiation process, but also in terms of the ratification of an exit agreement; the repatriation of EU competences and shared competencies. Parliament may have been slow to adapt to devolution overall, but the Brexit effect may yet hasten things.

Primary sources

- British–Irish Parliamentary Assembly (2016) Impact of Brexit on British-Irish Relations, inquiry page. Online at: http://www.britishirish.org/bipa-european-affairs-committee-to-look-at-impact-of-brexit-on-british-irish-relations/ [accessed 27 June 2017].

- *EU Exit: Devolved Governments* (HC Debates, 21 July 2016, cc. 427–54WH). Online at: https://hansard.parliament.uk/commons/2016-07-21/debates/92AFA638-0EBE-4963-A15F-CF6F1401C366/EUExitDevolvedGovernments [accessed 27 June 2017].

- Northern Ireland Affairs Committee (2016) *Future of the Land Border with the Republic of Ireland*, inquiry page. Online at: http://www.parliament.uk/business/committees/committees-a-z/commons-select/northern-ireland-affairs-committee/inquiries/parliament-2015/inquiry3/ [accessed 27 June 2017].

- Scottish Affairs Committee (2016) Scotland's Place in Europe, inquiry page. Online at: http://www.parliament.uk/business/committees/committees-a-z/commons-select/scottish-affairs-committee/inquiries/parliament-2015/scotland-place-europe-16-17/ [accessed 27 June 2017].

- UCL Constitution Unit, UCL European Institute, and UCL School of Public Policy (2016) 'Brexit: Its Consequences for Devolution & the Union', online video, 19 May. Online at: https://vimeo.com/168454709 [accessed 27 June 2017].

FURTHER CASE STUDIES

- The West Lothian Question and 'English votes for English laws' (EVEL).
- The establishment of the Brexit Cabinet Committee in October 2016.
- The Political and Constitutional Affairs Committee inquiry into The Future of the Union and Inter-Institutional Relations in the UK (2016).

References

BINGHAM CENTRE FOR THE RULE OF LAW (2015) *A Constitutional Crossroads: Ways Forward for the United Kingdom*, London: British Institute of International and Comparative Law.

BIRRELL, D. and GORMLEY-HEENAN, C. (2015) *Multi-level Governance in Northern Ireland*, Basingstoke: Palgrave Macmillan.

COMMISSION ON DEVOLUTION IN WALES (2012) *Empowerment and Responsibility: Financial Powers to Strengthen Wales*, Cardiff: The Stationery Office.

CONSTITUTION COMMITTEE (2002) *Devolution: Inter-Institutional Relationships in the United Kingdom*, London: The Stationery Office, HL 28. Online at: https://www.publications.parliament.uk/pa/ld200203/ldselect/ldconst/28/28.pdf [accessed 25 June 2017].

CONSTITUTION COMMITTEE (2016) *The Union and Devolution: 10th Report of Session 2015–16*, London: The Stationery Office, HL 149. Online at: https://www.publications.parliament.uk/pa/ld201516/ldselect/ldconst/149/149.pdf [accessed 25 June 2017].

CULTURE, TOURISM, EUROPE AND EXTERNAL RELATIONS COMMITTEE (2016) *The EU referendum and its implications for Scotland*. Online at: http://www.parliament.scot/parliamentarybusiness/CurrentCommittees/100259.aspx [accessed 23 August 2017].

DAVIES, R. (1999) *Devolution: A Process Not an Event*, The Gregynog Papers, Vol. 2 (2), Cardiff: Institute of Welsh Affairs.

EXTERNAL AFFAIRS AND ADDITIONAL LEGISLATION COMMITTEE (2016) Committee Profile. Online at: http://www.assembly.wales/en/bus-home/committees/Pages/Committee-Profile.aspx?cid=449 [accessed 19 June 2017].

GOVER, D. and KENNY, M. (2016) *Finding the Good in EVEL*, London: QMUL. Online at: http://www.ucl.ac.uk/constitution-unit/news/EVEL_Report_A4_FINAL.pdf [accessed 27 June 2017].

HOLTHAM COMMISSION (2010) *Fairness and Accountability: A New Funding Settlement for Wales*, Cardiff: The Stationery Office.

JEFFERY, C. et al. (2014) Taking England Seriously: The New English Politics, Edinburgh: Centre for Constitutional Change. Online at: http://sites.cardiff.ac.uk/wgc/files/2014/10/Taking-England-Seriously_The-New-English-Politics.pdf [accessed 22 August 2017].

JUSTICE COMMITTEE (2009) *Devolution: A Decade On: Fifth Report of Session 2008–09*, London: The Stationery Office, HC 529. Online at: https://www.publications.parliament.uk/pa/cm200809/cmselect/cmjust/529/529i.pdf [accessed 25 June 2017].

McKAY COMMISSION (2013) *Report of the Commission on the Consequences of Devolution for the House of Commons*, London: HM Government. Online at: http://webarchive.nationalarchives. gov.uk/20130403030652/http://tmc.independent.gov.uk/wp-content/uploads/2013/03/The-McKay-Commission_Main-Report_25-March-20131.pdf [accessed 26 June 2017].

MILLER, G. (2016) 'Presumed consent? The role of Scotland, Wales and Northern Ireland in the Brexit process', *Institute for Government*, 11 August. Online at: https://www.instituteforgovernment.org.uk/blog/presumed-consent-role-scotland-wales-and-northern-ireland-brexit-process [accessed 25 June 2017].

NORTON, P. (2013) *Parliament in British Politics*, 2nd edition, Basingstoke: Palgrave Macmillan.

PUBLIC ADMINISTRATION AND CONSTITUTIONAL AFFAIRS COMMITTEE (2015) *English Votes for English Laws and the Future of the Union*, Oral evidence, 27 October, HC523. Online at: http://data.parliament.uk/writtenevidence/committeeevidence.svc/evidencedocument/public-administration-and-constitutional-affairs-committee/english-votes-for-english-laws-and-the-future-of-the-union/oral/23805.pdf [accessed 25 June 2017].

PUBLIC ADMINISTRATION AND CONSTITUTIONAL AFFAIRS COMMITTEE (2017) 'Brexit and devolution inquiry launched', *PACAC News*, 8 March. Online at: http://www.parliament.uk/business/committees/committees-a-z/commons-select/public-administration-and-constitutional-affairs-committee/news-parliament-2015/brexit-and-devolution-16-17/ [accessed 25 June 2017].

RALLINGS, C. and THRASHER, M. (2012) *British Electoral Facts 1832–2012*, London: Biteback.

Scotland Act 2016, chapter 11. Online at: http://www.legislation.gov.uk/ukpga/2016/11/pdfs/ukpga_20160011_en.pdf [accessed 25 June 2017].

SCOTTISH AFFAIRS COMMITTEE (2010) *Scotland and the UK: Cooperation and Communication between Governments: Fourth Report of Session 2009–10*, London: The Stationery Office, HC 256. Online at: https://www.publications.parliament.uk/pa/cm200910/cmselect/cmscotaf/256/256.pdf [accessed 25 June 2017].

SCOTTISH GOVERNMENT (2009) *Report of the Commission on Scottish Devolution [the Calman Commission]*, Edinburgh: The Stationery Office.

SMITH COMMISSION (2014) *Report of the Smith Commission for Further Devolution of Powers to the Scottish Parliament*, London: The Stationery Office.

UBEROI, E. (2016) *European Union Referendum 2016*, House of Commons Library Briefing Paper Number 7639, 29 June. Online at: http://researchbriefings.files.parliament.uk/documents/CBP-7639/CBP-7639.pdf [accessed 25 June 2017].

UK PARLIAMENT (2017) Parliamentary search data supplied personally to author.

Wales Act 2017, chapter 4. Online at: http://www.legislation.gov.uk/ukpga/2017/4/pdfs/ukpga_20170004_en.pdf [accessed 25 June 2017].

28

Parliament and Modernization

Mark Goodwin and Martyn Atkins

INTRODUCTION

To many observers, Parliament seems deeply attached to, or even defined by, the main-tenance of the trappings of a bygone era. New laws must be affirmed in Norman French. New MPs arriving at Westminster have no immediate entitlement to an office from which to work, but are provided with a silk sash from which to hang their swords in a cloakroom before entering the Chamber. In the Lords, 92 hereditary peers still enjoy the right to make legislation. Until recently, it was compulsory to wear a collapsible top hat to make a point of order in a division.

Modernization, then, might not be a term one would immediately associate with the institution. Keeping pace with changes in the wider society has proved to be a serious challenge for an institution that is in many ways still wedded to the past. One common account of the British state during the middle decades of the twentieth century was that it remained fundamentally an *ancien régime* in terms of its structures, institutions, and cultures, but with representative democracy grafted on. Parliament, as the key rep-resentative institution in the UK, demonstrates this tension perhaps better than any other, retaining many elements of the pre-democratic era. This chapter illustrates these tensions and demonstrates the difficult path to modernization taken in Parliament since 1997.

The meaning of modernization

Despite its antiquated image, Parliament has regularly considered issues of modernization. The House of Commons appointed a select committee dedicated to its own modernization (the Modernisation Committee) for 13 years from 1997. Yet the reforms undertaken in the name of modernization can bear little relation to a common understanding of that term. Modernization is both a ubiquitous and a nebulous concept. While the content of Parliament's modernization process is sometimes difficult to define, one common element is the belief that political institutions ought not to exist outside of, and apart from, the wider society, but that they ought to reflect that society, its values, and norms. In this sense of modernization, it is clear that progress has been sluggish.

Alix Kelso's *Parliamentary Reform at Westminster* (2009) is a key text on the phase of parliamentary modernization following the election of the Blair government in 1997. Kelso argues that the focus of modernization has been turned inwards towards the legis-lative process and the Parliament–government relationship rather than outwards in an attempt to respond to changing external environments and cultures. For Kelso, the modernization process pursued by MPs, with the House of Commons Modernisation

Committee as its main vehicle, restricted itself largely to two principal classes of reform—those aimed at ensuring the expeditious handling of the government's legislative programme (efficiency reforms), and those aimed at enhancing the scrutiny and accountability functions of Parliament (effectiveness reforms). These two classes of reform both address one of the fundamental relationships defining the nature of Parliament: its relationship with the executive branch. Efficiency reforms can be understood as assertions of executive power over the legislature, while effectiveness reforms usually involve claims for greater agency and influence for Parliament over government.

The second defining relationship, between Parliament and citizens, has historically received less attention in the formal process of modernization. It has become more prominent very recently though, with the Modernisation Committee's (2004) report and the work of the Speaker's Digital Democracy Commission (2015). When Parliament engages in its own version of modernization, it tends to concern itself mainly with contestation over the respective powers of government and Parliament—and, crucially, with how far each is able to control the key parliamentary resource of time.

Controlling parliamentary time

The manifesto on which the Labour government was elected in 1997 committed it to procedural modernization (Labour Party 1997). The emphasis of the Modernisation Committee in the early years was clearly on efficiency reforms that sought to enable the new government's legislative agenda. This is perhaps unsurprising given that the Leader of the House was appointed to the Committee and invariably chosen as its Chair. The Committee also routinely included among its members those close to government (such as parliamentary private secretaries)—a fact that remained a bone of contention for parliamentary reformers throughout its life.

This period, covering the first five to six years after the establishment of the Committee, is characterized by 'modernization' being largely a euphemism for smoothing the legislative pathway of the new government, rather than addressing Parliament's long-standing grievance regarding its subordinate role with respect to government. The main order of business for the Committee was the establishment of a system of legislative programming led by whips (see Chapter 7), signalling the new government's intention to stake its claim over the key resource of parliamentary time and to eliminate opportunities for the opposition and backbenchers to use that time as a weapon in the legislative process. The principal recommendation in its first report on the legislative process (Modernisation Committee 1997) was to introduce procedures whereby governments could propose a motion for an order (known as a 'programme motion') setting out a timetable for subsequent stages of any new legislation, usually voted on immediately after a new bill's second reading. This system of legislative timetabling through the use of programme motions has since become well established on almost all government bills (except for Finance Bills), much to the chagrin of many backbenchers. It is often regarded as a means of unduly restricting the time available for the scrutiny and debate of important aspects of proposed legislation. Exemplary of the way these motions have been regarded is the apparent greater willingness of MPs to register dissent by opposing the government on programme motions rather than on the substance of bills. For example, in the 2012 House of Lords Reform Bill, the planned programme motion was not moved by the government once it became apparent that the opposition, together with government backbenchers, would vote against it. The failure to establish a schedule for the Bill's passage through the Commons ultimately resulted in the withdrawal of the Bill.

It is striking how many of the reforms considered by the Modernisation Committee concerned ownership and control of time. In a system where the checks on government initiative are comparatively weak, one of the main obstacles is simply the lack of time for processing government business: hence the Committee's focus on freeing up space in the timetable. This has included recommendations to 'carry over' the consideration of public bills from one session of Parliament to the next (Modernisation Committee 2006), and the designation of the Grand Committee Room, off Westminster Hall, into a parallel chamber for the debate of issues that would otherwise have been squeezed out from the main Chamber due to lack of time (Modernisation Committee 1999). Changes to Commons sitting hours also made up a large proportion of the work of the Modernisation Committee in these early years: revisions to sitting hours were recommended, and implemented in 1998, 1999, 2003, and 2005. These changes have often been presented as a 'family-friendly' move to reduce antisocial working hours, and there has certainly been some progress in this direction. For example, the number of weekdays on which the House sits until 10 p.m. or later has been reduced from four to one since 1997. But as debates on the proposals illustrate (see, for example, Kelso 2009, 63–8), the net effect was simply to further reduce the time available to scrutinize the work of government or to challenge the government to make concessions, thereby serving only to tilt the scales further towards the executive. Dissatisfaction with the new sitting hours led to further reviews of the parliamentary timetable in 2005 and 2012 (Modernisation Committee 2005; Procedure Committee 2012).

Increasing the effectiveness of parliamentary scrutiny

Over time, the Modernisation Committee shifted attention more to Parliament's roles in scrutinizing government and in representing citizens. Reappointed after the 2001 election, the Committee developed proposals that leaned more towards effectiveness and, to a lesser extent, representation, rather than efficiency alone, reflecting the Labour Party's manifesto commitment to 'modernise the procedures of the House of Commons so it can effectively fulfil its functions of representation and scrutiny' (Labour Party 2001). With Robin Cook as Chair, the Committee undertook an inquiry into the functioning of select committees. Departmental select committees in the Commons have developed as the key parliamentary organs for oversight of government departments, so a focus on strengthening select committees in itself indicated a shift of emphasis away from speeding up legislation, towards Parliament's capacity for scrutiny of the government.

In 2002, the Committee recommended that select committees ought to pursue a set of defined core tasks, employ more dedicated support staff, and provide additional payment for select committee chairs (Modernisation Committee 2002). A revamped Liaison Committee, with new responsibilities and a membership comprising the chairs of existing select committees, was also recommended. The Committee's recommendations to reduce the influence of the whips over the appointment of select committee chairs and members were, however, blocked. These proposals on committee recruitment, which presented perhaps the clearest threat to the government's means to controlling and influencing the work of committees, were revisited by the Wright Committee with greater success in 2009 and 2010, as Case Study 28 shows. The Modernisation Committee made further progress on scrutiny and effectiveness through a second inquiry on the legislative process in the 2005–06 session. In its (2006) report the Committee recommended the introduction of the new public bill committee system (see Chapter 9). The Committee also recommended greater parliamentary involvement in pre- and post-legislative scrutiny. Implementation of these recommendations has been limited and unsystematic in the years since, perhaps reflecting the reluctance of the executive to cede additional scrutiny powers over legislation to Parliament.

Representing the public

The representative function of Parliament tended not to be a priority for the Modernisation Committee. The closest the Committee came to addressing this aspect came with an inquiry on 'Connecting Parliament with the Public' during the 2003–04 session. While the title of the report might suggest some movement in the direction of greater public involvement in the work of Parliament, its recommendations focused on informing the public about the role and work of Parliament through changes to the Parliamentary Education Service, better citizenship education, improved facilities for visitors, and a more professional press operation. The emphasis was on telling the public what Parliament does, rather than changing its processes. Over a decade on from that report, the Speaker's Commission on Digital Democracy found that the public regarded Parliament as distant, opaque, antiquated, and exclusive. The fact that it was still necessary in 2015 for the Commission to recommend that 'by 2020, the House of Commons should ensure that everyone can understand what it does' tends to illustrate further the relatively low priority given to changes in Parliament's relationship with citizens in the modernization process (Digital Democracy Commission 2015, 7); though we should note the recent introduction of an e-petitions system. Efficiency often takes priority over effectiveness, which in turn often takes priority over representation and participation.

Passing the baton to the Wright Committee

Towards the end of the Gordon Brown administration, the Modernisation Committee ceased to be the main vehicle for parliamentary modernization. The Committee's last report was issued in July 2008 and it failed to meet in subsequent sessions. Impetus for parliamentary reform was carried forward by a new Select Committee on Reform of the House of Commons, often referred to as the 'Wright Committee' after its Chair, the Labour MP and long-time supporter of parliamentary reform, Dr Tony Wright. The new committee was convened in the wake of the MPs' expenses scandal, which opened a window of opportunity for reform.

One key difference between the Wright Committee and the Modernisation Committee was that the membership of the former was restricted to backbenchers, many of whom had standing interests in the reform of Parliament. From the outset, the new committee's agenda reflected this by more assertively promoting the rights of Parliament—and in particular the House of Commons—as a body outside the control of government. The Committee's main areas of activity were in reducing government control over membership of select committees (see Chapter 16), enhancing Parliament's ownership and control of the Commons timetable, and involving the public with legislation—a clear break with the outlook of its predecessor. However, the limited degree to which the Wright recommendations have been implemented to date demonstrates that this was only a partially successful counter-strike by Parliament against the perceived dominance of the executive.

Technological modernization

Besides the persistence of the archaic language patterns and a tendency towards nostalgic traditionalism, Parliament has repeatedly demonstrated itself to be slow and conservative in adapting to changes in technology and working practices. The Commons refused to allow television cameras into the Chamber for a full 25 years before reluctantly ceding this privilege at the end of 1989. Parliament's online presence, although improving, has also been slow to develop: the main website (parliament.uk), for example, has struggled to keep pace with changes in web design, although it is being redesigned at the time of writing. While the House of Commons Commission has adopted a 'digital first' strategy and both Houses have slashed their printing bills, the paper document (in printed or PDF form) remains a default for parliamentary data, slowing the progress of the data.parliament project (www.data.parliament.uk/) which seeks to bring the institution into the age of open data and freedom of information. In this area, Parliament has lagged far behind sources such as The Public Whip and TheyWorkForYou in putting parliamentary data into the public domain, both for transparency and for reuse. Reflecting this technological conservatism, Parliament retains head-count in-person voting for divisions despite the availability of electronic systems that could not only render the process more efficient, but also allow voting by Members not physically present in the Chamber. MPs are still required to assemble in the Chamber to engage in debate and argument during plenary sessions, and witnesses are still generally required to appear in person before MPs for questioning during committee hearings, despite the development of technologies that would permit a variety of means of accomplishing the same ends. There have been a number of interesting experiments in online public engagement, for example, an online public consultation undertaken, appropriately, by the Commons Science and Technology Committee (2005) during its inquiry into Human Reproductive Technologies and the Law; a public reading stage for the 2013 Children and Families Bill (see Leston-Bandeira and Thompson 2017), and in the facility for social media engagement with select committee work. While committees have experimented with new forms of public engagement, these have not been embedded into House of Commons processes, and the House's default pattern of working remains decidedly analogue.

Nevertheless there are signs that Parliament is finally adjusting to the realities of modern communications technologies. The Speaker's Commission on Digital Democracy has performed a useful agenda-setting function in attempting to bring Parliament into the twenty-first century in this area. The report of the Commission represents perhaps the clearest attempt yet to frame parliamentary modernization as a means to improve the quality of democracy, representation, and public engagement (Digital Democracy Commission 2015). It is perhaps significant that the Commission enjoyed a high degree of independence from the administrative and political structures of both Houses and drew principally on the expertise of non-parliamentarians.

Modernization of working practices

In the broad area of working practices, Parliament has similarly made halting progress in adapting to the changing nature of professional work in the wider society. The buildings are in many places decrepit and unfit for purpose, requiring a major renovation (Deloitte 2014). The main chambers of the Commons and Lords are not large enough to house all Members at one time and can struggle to accommodate divisions efficiently. Though some progress has been made on the issue of estates, with the opening of the Portcullis House building in 2001 providing much needed office and meeting room space for the Commons, and the acquisition of 1 Millbank providing an increase in capacity for the Lords, provision in this area arguably remains inadequate for a modern, professional workplace.

Induction programmes have been introduced for new MPs since the 2005 cohort, though the earlier iterations were criticized for focusing too much on financial probity and administration rather than the nature of parliamentary scrutiny, process, and government work (Fox and Korris 2012). Parliamentarians receive little support in the fields of training, professional development, and human resources. Indeed, the Commons and Lords have no HR department for their Members, who are self-employed workers without contracts. The laxity of governance arrangements around allowances which MPs were entitled to claim was brought starkly to light by the 2009 expenses scandal, since when the payment of salaries and allowances to MPs has been put on an independent and statutory footing. The establishment of the Independent Parliamentary Standards Authority (IPSA) has gone some considerable way to professionalizing this aspect of parliamentary work, providing more standardized guidance to MPs on issues such as hiring staff and claiming allowances for accommodation and office costs. These issues are perhaps indicative of the ongoing tension between an amateurish gentlemanly tradition that once dominated in the conduct of parliamentary business and the greater openness, transparency, and accountability that modernization requires.

Parliament's wider working culture also contains elements that many would consider less than modern. Changes to sitting hours may have been presented as at least partly a nod to more family-friendly working, but the rhythms of parliamentary work still impose demands on parliamentarians that might be considered incompatible with a reasonable work–life balance in many other fields. Further evidence of the resistance of the House of Commons to adapt to generally accepted standards of contemporary professional work can be seen in the fact that no on-site provision for childcare was made until 2010, and that was introduced in the teeth of some opposition: it was dismissed by one MP as 'gesture politics of the worst kind' (Goslett 2012).

Conclusion

In assessing the theme of parliamentary modernization, it is tempting to invert Tony Wright's claim that the past two decades have seen plenty of modernization but little parliamentary reform (HC Debates, 9 November 2000, c. 510). Arguably the endeavours of the Modernisation Committee, and subsequently the Wright Committee, have produced a fair amount of parliamentary reform, albeit with a limited scope, but only slow, reluctant, and incremental modernization as that term would usually be understood outside the House: that is to say, a reflection of the norms of the society which Parliament is meant to serve. The processes that politicians and Parliament alike have described as modernization, such as those undertaken by the Commons Modernisation Committee, have generally been internal reforms, directed at the relationship between Parliament and government much more than towards the external environment, whether in terms of adapting to societal change or in terms of sharing power more widely among citizens.

These 'modernization' reforms have highlighted in particular the importance of control and ownership of time within that executive–legislative relationship. Time is arguably the key resource in Parliament. For a government with a legislative programme, control of time in Parliament is critical and is jealously guarded. As the Wright report argued, government wants decisions, while Parliament seeks explanation, accountability, and debate (House of Commons Reform Committee 2009, 13). Modernization-as-efficiency, from a government perspective, often means increasing control over parliamentary time, and speeding up the legislative process. By contrast, Parliament has tended to focus on effective scrutiny, which seems to require a slower, more deliberative, and extended process. The contest over speed of the process is critical.

Yet it also reveals a deeper conflict regarding the status, function, and purpose of Parliament. If Parliament's primary function is understood by would-be reformers as the efficient processing and approval of government business, it is likely that they will prioritize efficiency reforms. If the main purpose is understood as checking, scrutinizing, challenging, and holding government to account, effectiveness reforms will be pursued. If Parliament is understood as first and foremost a body charged with representing the will and the interests of citizens in the process of government, representative reforms will be prioritized. Some progress of reform has occurred in all these dimensions, but it is clear that the dominance of the first narrative has often limited the opportunities for reform in the second or third categories.

Further Reading

DIGITAL DEMOCRACY COMMISSION (2015) *Open Up! Report of the Speaker's Commission on Digital Democracy*, London: House of Commons. Online at: http://www.digitaldemocracy. parliament.uk/documents/Open-Up-Digital-Democracy-Report.pdf [accessed 27 June 2017].

HOUSE OF COMMONS REFORM COMMITTEE (2009) *Rebuilding the House: First Report of Session 2008–09*, London: The Stationery Office, HC 1117. Online at: https://www.publications. parliament.uk/pa/cm200809/cmselect/cmrefhoc/1117/1117.pdf [accessed 23 June 2017].

KELSO, A. (2009) *Parliamentary Reform at Westminster*, Manchester: Manchester University Press.

MODERNISATION COMMITTEE (1997) *The Legislative Process: First Report of Session 2005–06*, London: The Stationery Office, HC 1097. Online at: https://www.publications.parliament.uk/ pa/cm200506/cmselect/cmmodern/1097/1097.pdf [accessed 23 June 2017].

MODERNISATION COMMITTEE (2002) *Modernisation of the House of Commons: A Reform Programme: Second Report of Session 2001–02*, London: The Stationery Office, HC 1168-I. Online at: https://www.publications.parliament.uk/pa/cm200102/cmselect/cmmodern/1168/1168.pdf [accessed 23 June 2017].

Case Study 28: The impact of the Wright Committee

This case study addresses the establishment, work, and impact of the Committee on Reform of the House of Commons, a select committee of the House chaired by Dr Tony Wright MP. The Committee was established in July 2009 to consider and report back on four specific matters by 13 November that year: the appointment of members and Chairs of select committees; the appointment of the Chair and Deputy Chair of Ways and Means; scheduling business in the House; and enabling the public to initiate Commons debates and proceedings.

CONTEXT

Speaking in the House of Commons in June 2009, Prime Minister Gordon Brown gave his support to the creation of a new select committee to continue the modernization process:

> We must also take forward urgent modernisation of the procedures of the House of Commons, so I am happy to give the government's support to a proposal from my hon. Friend the Chairman of the Public Administration Committee [Tony Wright] that we will work with a special parliamentary commission comprising Members from both sides of this House, convened for a defined period to advise on necessary reforms. (HC Debates, 10 June 2009, c. 796)

This announcement was important because, first, it was clear that the parliamentary body to be established would advise the government, and not the House. The initiative on implementation would therefore lie with the government. The 'special parliamentary commission' in fact took the form of a select committee with no additional powers. It made its reports to the House, but no provision was made for its recommendations to be considered for implementation, despite the Committee's expectations to the contrary (see House of Commons Reform Committee 2009, 15).

Second, the term 'modernization' of House procedures was used without any explanation. The Wright Committee would not use the term at all in its reports, and summarized its remit with one clear principle: that 'the government should get its business, the House should get its scrutiny and the public should get listened to' (House of Commons Reform Committee 2009, 20). Eschewing the problematic concept of 'modernization', it set out its own reform agenda, based on six principles elaborated in its first report (House of Commons Reform Committee 2009, 18–35).

These included general aims for reform such as enhancing the control of the Commons over its agenda and procedures, promoting cross-party working, and enhancing the transparency of House activity to both MPs and the public. They also acknowledged constraints on reform proposals, such as not impeding the ability of parties to debate issues of their choosing and recognizing that the government is entitled to having its own business considered—and concluded—at times of its own choosing.

THE WRIGHT COMMITTEE'S RECOMMENDATIONS

The Committee reported its findings in November 2009, making recommendations under all but one of the four key areas it had been commissioned to examine—the Commons Procedure Committee reported separately on proposals to elect the Chair and Deputy Chair of Ways and Means (Procedure Committee 2010). Among its recommendations was the suggestion that select committee chairs be elected by the whole House and that committee members should be chosen by more 'transparent and democratic means' (House of Commons Reform Committee 2010, 24). The Committee also recommended that a House Business Committee be established, to propose a weekly programme of business for debate and decision in government time. A Backbench Business Committee, with a Chair and members elected by the House, should schedule the business for debate and decision in backbench time. Finally, it stressed that the focus of House activities in public engagement must move beyond information provision to actively assisting public participation in the legislative process.

The Committee was generally consensual in its approach, but there were disagreements. An alternative draft report, seeking to postpone detailed consideration of the matters under discussion into the next Parliament, was voted down (House of Commons Reform Committee 2010, 86), as was a proposal to leave out detailed recommendations on the operation of a House Business Committee (ibid., 97).

IMPLEMENTATION OF THE WRIGHT REFORMS

Although the prime minister gave his support to many of the Committee's recommendations (20 January 2010), the process whereby the House decided on the recommendations for implementation was complicated. The report itself was debated in February 2010, not on the motion drafted by the Committee but on an alternative proposition from the government (HC Debates, 22 February 2010, cc. 37–127). Only some of the recommendations were agreed to. Time was found the following month for further consideration of recommendations which the House had previously opposed. These were agreed to, with amendments, on a free vote. Among these amendments were provisions to ensure the Chair of the Public Accounts

Committee should be an opposition Member, to establish a Backbench Business Committee, and to give agreement in principle to the establishment of a House Business Committee (HC Debates, 4 March 2010, cc. 1052–101). In order to consolidate the gains made, and to insure against the risk of inertia after the forthcoming general election, the Committee published a further report on implementation issues, setting out in detail proposals for the establishment of a Backbench Business Committee, just before the dissolution of Parliament in March 2010 (House of Commons Reform Committee 2010).

THE IMPACT AND PROGRESS OF THE WRIGHT REFORMS

Some reforms, such as elections for select committees and setting up the Backbench Business Committee, took effect from the start of the 2010 Parliament. But the impact of these reforms has been mixed. Some select committee elections, such as the Conservative Party elections for members of the Exiting the European Union Committee in September 2016, have generated substantial media interest (e.g. Syal 2016), but not all elections are contested. The election of chairs and members of committees has increased the independence of committees, but several issues remain (Political and Constitutional Reform Committee 2013), including inquorate meetings and difficulties filling vacancies. Committee chairs may now make short statements in the Chamber to launch reports, but amendments to bills and motions may not be tabled in the name of a committee (Procedure Committee 2011). Some committees have engaged more with legislative business, but the formal role of committees in legislative scrutiny remains limited (Political and Constitutional Reform Committee 2013). The Backbench Business Committee was welcomed as 'a successful and effective innovation' (Procedure Committee 2012, 8), yet modest improvements to the system's operation to strengthen its independence were resisted by the government (Procedure Committee 2013).

Some of the recommendations have not been acted upon. For example, the government did not fulfil a commitment to establish a House Business Committee by the third year of the 2010 Parliament (Political and Constitutional Reform Committee 2013), because no consensus had been found within government on how to implement it.

WHAT DOES THIS TELL US ABOUT PARLIAMENT AND MODERNIZATION?

Modernization, in the parliamentary context, remains a nebulous concept. The Wright Committee avoided the term 'modernization' entirely and instead sought to define its own reform agenda. Its work was made more difficult by the limited autonomy of the House to actually decide on reforms. The government envisaged that the Committee would merely advise on necessary reforms—it declined to put the Committee's own motion to the House for decision. The final acceptance of its recommendations was tightly controlled by the government, although free votes were eventually allowed. Government proposals to defer consideration of a Backbench Business Committee were successfully countered only by an exceptionally strong political response from the Wright Committee and the House as a whole (House of Commons Reform Committee 2010).

Parliamentary reform is challenging. The changes to the way select committees are composed has had a positive effect on the independence of parliamentary scrutiny, but cannot be described as transformative. The election of chairs and members has increased the perception of independence, and has given the appearance of a system more prepared to challenge government, but the evidence for increased MP engagement with committees since the Wright reforms, and for greater impact on government policy, remains thin. Gains made in securing support for a proposition in the House can easily be thwarted by opponents in government. Progress against the six principles set out by the Wright Committee has been inconsistent.

Primary sources

- House of Commons Reform Committee (2010) *Rebuilding the House: Implementation: First Report of Session 2009–10*, London: The Stationery Office, HC 372. Online at: https://www. publications.parliament.uk/pa/cm200910/cmselect/cmrefhoc/372/372.pdf [accessed 27 June 2017].

- The debate on the Wright report (HC Debates, 22 February 2010, cc. 37–132). Online at: https://www.publications.parliament.uk/pa/cm200910/cmhansrd/cm100222/debtext/100222-0006. htm#1002228000004 [accessed 27 June 2017]. Also the subsequent debate and decisions on contested recommendations (HC Debates, 4 March 2010, cc. 1062–100). Online at: https://www.publications.parliament.uk/pa/cm200910/cmhansrd/cm100304/debtext/100304-0011. htm#10030456000003 [accessed 27 June 2017].

- The debate and decisions of the House on the establishment of a Backbench Business Committee (HC Debates, 15 June 2010, 778–845). Online at: https://www.publications.parliament. uk/pa/cm201011/cmhansrd/cm100615/debtext/100615-0020.htm#1006163000004 [accessed 27 June 2017].

- Procedure Committee (2012) *Review of the Backbench Business Committee: Second Report of Session 2012–13*, London: The Stationery Office, HC 168. Online at: https://www.publications. parliament.uk/pa/cm201213/cmselect/cmproced/168/168.pdf [accessed 27 June 2017].

- Political and Constitutional Reform Committee (2013) *Revisiting Rebuilding the House: The Impact of the Wright Reforms: Third Report of Session 2013–14*, London: The Stationery Office, HC 82. Online at: https://www.publications.parliament.uk/pa/cm201314/cmselect/cmpol-con/82/82.pdf [accessed 27 June 2017].

 FURTHER CASE STUDIES

- Political and Constitutional Reform Committee (2010 Parliament).
- The Speaker's Commission on Digital Democracy (2015).
- *The Good Parliament* report (2016).

References

DELOITTE (2014) *Palace of Westminster Restoration and Renewal Programme: Independent Options Appraisal*, 8 September. Online at: http://www.parliament.uk/documents/lords-information-office/2015/Independent-Options-Appraisal-final-report-A3.pdf [accessed 22 June 2017].

DIGITAL DEMOCRACY COMMISSION (2015) *Open Up! Report of the Speaker's Commission on Digital Democracy* , London: House of Commons. Online at: http://www.digitaldemocracy. parliament.uk/documents/Open-Up-Digital-Democracy-Report.pdf [accessed 23 June 2017].

FOX, R. and KORRIS, M. (2012) 'A Fresh Start? The Orientation and Induction of New MPs at Westminster Following the 2010 General Election', *Parliamentary Affairs*, Vol. 65 (3), pp. 559–75.

GOSLETT, M. (2012) 'Parliamentary creche costing £34000 a child branded a waste of money as it's nearly two-thirds empty', *Daily Mail*, 8 February. Online at: http://www.dailymail.co.uk/news/article-2098024/Parliamentary-creche-costing-34-000-child-branded-waste-money-nearly-thirds-empty.html [accessed 23 June 2017].

HOUSE OF COMMONS REFORM COMMITTEE (2009) *Rebuilding the House: First Report of Session 2008–09*, London: The Stationery Office, HC 1117. Online at: https://www.publications. parliament.uk/pa/cm200809/cmselect/cmrefhoc/1117/1117.pdf [accessed 23 June 2017].

HOUSE OF COMMONS REFORM COMMITTEE (2010) *Rebuilding the House: Implementation: First Report of Session 2009–10*, London: The Stationery Office, HC 372. Online at: https://www.publications. parliament.uk/pa/cm200910/cmselect/cmrefhoc/372/372.pdf [accessed 23 June 2017].

KELSO, A. (2009) *Parliamentary Reform at Westminster*, Manchester: Manchester University Press.

LABOUR PARTY (1997) *New Labour: Because Britain Deserves Better*, London: Labour Party.

LABOUR PARTY (2001) *Ambitions for Britain: Labour's Manifesto 2001*, London: Labour Party.

LESTON-BANDEIRA, C., and THOMPSON, L. (2017) 'Integrating the View of the Public into the Formal Legislative Process: Public Reading Stage in the UK House of Commons', *Journal of Legislative Studies*, DOI: 10.1080/13572334.2017.1394736

LIAISON COMMITTEE (2015) *Building Public Engagement: Options for Developing Select Committee Outreach: First Special Report*, London: The Stationery Office, HC 470. Online at: https://www.publications.parliament.uk/pa/cm201516/cmselect/cmliaisn/470/47002.htm [accessed 23 June 2017].

MODERNISATION COMMITTEE (1997) *The Legislative Process: First Report of Session 1997–98*, London: The Stationery Office, HC 190. Online at: https://www.publications.parliament.uk/ pa/cm199798/cmselect/cmmodern/190i/md0102.htm [accessed 23 June 2017].

MODERNISATION COMMITTEE (1999) *Sittings of the House in Westminster Hall: Second Report of Session 2008-09*, London: The Stationery Office, HC 194. Online at https://publications. parliament.uk/pa/cm199899/cmselect/cmmodern/194/19402.htm [accessed 18 October 2017].

MODERNISATION COMMITTEE (2002) *Select Committees: First Report of Session 2001–02*, London: The Stationery Office, HC 224. Online at https://publications.parliament.uk/pa/ cm200102/cmselect/cmmodern/224/22402.htm [accessed 18 October 2017].

MODERNISATION COMMITTEE (2004) *Connecting Parliament with the Public: First Report of Session 2003–04*, London: The Stationery Office, HC 368. Online at: https://www.publications. parliament.uk/pa/cm200304/cmselect/cmmodern/368/368.pdf [accessed 23 June 2017].

MODERNISATION COMMITTEE (2005) *Sitting Hours: First Report of Session 2004–05*, London: The Stationery Office, HC 88. Online at: https://publications.parliament.uk/pa/cm200405/ cmselect/cmmodern/88/88.pdf [accesseed 24 August 2017].

MODERNISATION COMMITTEE (2006) *The Legislative Process: First Report of Session 2005–06*, London: The Stationery Office, HC 1097. Online at: https://publications.parliament.uk/pa/ cm200506/cmselect/cmmodern/1097/1097.pdf [accessed 24 August 2017].

POLITICAL AND CONSTITUTIONAL REFORM COMMITTEE (2013) *Revisiting Rebuilding the House: The Impact of the Wright Reforms: Third Report of Session 2013–14*, London: The Stationery Office, HC 82. Online at: https://www.publications.parliament.uk/pa/cm201314/cmselect/ cmpolcon/82/82.pdf [accessed 23 June 2017].

Procedure Committee (2010) *Election of the Speaker and of the Deputy Speakers: First Report of Session 2009–10*, London: The Stationery Office, HC 341. Online at: https://www.publications. parliament.uk/pa/cm200910/cmselect/cmproced/341/34102.htm [accessed 23 June 2017].

PROCEDURE COMMITTEE (2011) *Improving the Effectiveness of Parliamentary Scrutiny: (a) Select committee amendments (b) Explanatory statements on amendments (c) Written parliamentary questions: Government Response to the Committee's Second Report of Session 2010–11*, London: The Stationery Office, HC 1063. Online at: https://www.publications.parliament.uk/pa/ cm201012/cmselect/cmproced/1063/1063.pdf [accessed 23 June 2017].

PROCEDURE COMMITTEE (2012) *Review of the Backbench Business Committee: Second Report of Session 2012–13*, London: The Stationery Office, HC 168. Online at https://www.publications.parliament.uk/pa/cm201213/cmselect/cmproced/168/168.pdf [accessed 23 June 2017].

PROCEDURE COMMITTEE (2013) *Review of the Backbench Business Committee: Government Response to the Committee's Second Report of Session 2012–13*, London: The Stationery Office, HC 978. Online at http://www.publications.parliament.uk/pa/cm201213/cmselect/cmproced/978/978.pdf [accessed 18 October 2017].

SCIENCE AND TECHNOLOGY COMMITTEE (2005) *Human Reproductive Technologies and the Law: Fifth Report of Session 2004–05*, London: The Stationery Office, HC 7-1. Online at: https://www.publications.parliament.uk/pa/cm200405/cmselect/cmsctech/7/7i.pdf [accessed 23 June 2017].

SYAL, R. (2016) 'MPs criticise "ridiculously large" Brexit select committee', *The Guardian*, 11 October. Online at: https://www.theguardian.com/politics/2016/oct/11/mps-criticise-ridiculously-large-brexit-select-committee [accessed 23 June 2017].

29

Parliament and Public Engagement

Cristina Leston-Bandeira and Aileen Walker

INTRODUCTION

Today's UK Parliament is a far more open institution than the one of the 1990s, let alone the 1960s, facilitating public engagement through a very wide range of means. It is also, however, an institution which is far more vulnerable and criticized by the public and media alike. This chapter identifies what public engagement entails and why the UK Parliament has invested so heavily in this over the last decade. It then analyses how this role developed and the increase in activity, before reflecting on whether this has led to changes in public attitudes towards Parliament.

Defining public engagement

Public engagement is a buzzword of the twenty-first century. At one time taken for granted as a passive recipient of services, the public has now become a key priority for many organizations and institutions, particularly in the public sector. This is markedly so with political institutions such as Parliament. However, public engagement is a very broad concept and it is not always clear what it actually entails.

Overall it refers to any action that is specifically targeted at the public. But this can include a wide range of types of activity: from simply providing information, to facilitating ways for the public to have a say in decision-making. Put simply, it can refer to anything from a leaflet explaining how laws are made in Parliament, through to the possibility of submitting an e-petition or having some form of input into bills as they are being scrutinized. It refers, therefore, to different types of actions. This is why the idea of a spectrum of engagement is often used to describe different forms of public engagement, which ultimately correspond to different types of outcome.

Arnstein was the first author to identify different steps in the process of engagement. She outlined eight rungs of a ladder of participation, which identified different levels of involvement from the public, from 'manipulation from the state' to 'citizen control' (Arnstein 1969). This idea of a process of engagement and of different gradients of involvement has been developed more recently to better understand the activity of parliamentary public engagement (Kelso 2007; Carman 2009; Fox 2009; Clark and Wilford 2012; IPU 2012; Walker 2012; Leston-Bandeira 2014). In short, parliamentary public engagement includes four key elements: informing, educating, consulting, and participating. The idea of a ladder identifies therefore very different forms of engagement; it also raises questions about how these relate to each other—for example, whether people need to be informed and educated about Parliament first, in order to actually participate in specific activities. Or indeed, whether having an understanding of Parliament leads to higher levels of trust in the institution.

Explaining the importance of parliamentary public engagement today

Four key inter-related factors explain the rise in the importance of public engagement for parliaments: the steady trend of increasing scepticism towards politics, the expansion in access to education and information, the rise in opportunities created by digital media, and the rising appeal of participatory democracy (Leston-Bandeira 2016). Public support for political institutions has undergone a general trend of decline for some decades (Dalton 2004; Stoker 2006; Hay 2007; Norris 2011; Mair 2013; Lee and Young 2013). In his oft-quoted book, Dalton (2004) demonstrated a steady erosion of support for political institutions across well-established democracies since the 1960s. A few years later, Norris (2011, 107) explored fluctuations in this support across continents and institutions, but ultimately concluded that confidence in legislatures, specifically, had suffered the strongest decline. This trend was also confirmed by studies specifically focusing on trust in Parliament (Magalhães 2006; Van der Meer 2010).

As Figure 29.1 shows, this trend is apparent in the UK, with an overall decline in the proportion of the public saying they tend to trust Parliament: from an average of 45 per cent of the population in 1995, to 36 per cent in 2016, with a particularly low point in 2009, largely attributed to the expenses scandal that year (Hansard Society 2010; Lee and Young 2013). This trend is not out of line with a similar decline across Europe though; and, as Figure 29.1 shows, values for 2016 indicate higher levels of trust in the UK than the average across all European Union countries. After declining to an all-time low in 2009, trust in Parliament has since been rising in the UK.

A rise in distrust, combined with a drop in voter turnout at the turn of the twenty-first century, led to an expansion of parliamentary public engagement over the last decade, in an attempt to reverse these trends. As indicators of public disengagement mounted up, the institution came under increasing pressure to redress the trend (Leston-Bandeira 2016). But the expansion of parliamentary public engagement is also due to changing public expectations.

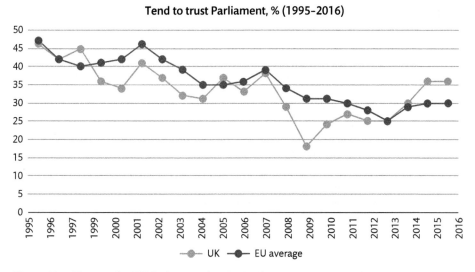

Figure 29.1 Trust in the UK Parliament (1995–2016)

Source: Eurobarometer (2016)

Note: The question was not asked in the 1998 Eurobarometer.

When, at one time, the public would delegate all things political to those elected, today the reality is more complex. Much higher levels of access to education and information have led to the development of the 'critical citizen' (Norris 1999). This implies a new form of citizen politics (Dalton 2007), where citizens are empowered to interpret reality by themselves, rather than delegating it to others. A highly mediatized society and effortless access to information have empowered the public to develop their own interpretation of different matters. They are more likely to disagree with politicians' decisions as a result. Politics is also far more fluid and multidimensional (Dalton 2004, 195), meaning that the public is moved by more specific issues, rather than general overarching principles—e.g. access to education, which characterized politics until the end of the 1960s. As Webb puts it, we have moved from an era of aggregation of interests to one of the articulation of specific interests (Webb 2013).

At the same time, expectations of political performance are much higher, and there is less tolerance for the non-delivery of political promises, services, and goods (Dalton 2004; Norris 2011). There is also an expectation of increasing transparency and accessibility to political institutions. The rise of the internet since the mid-1990s is a key factor in this development, facilitating and bolstering this process further (Coleman and Blumler 2009). Access to, and sharing of, information is part of the fabric of our modern society, providing the means for the public to search and interpret information without the need of mediators—and, indeed, to report on issues directly.

Simultaneously, the public increasingly expects to have a say in between elections. If at one time the expectation was to only express political preferences every five years, today's reality is very different. From the rise, since the 1970s, of participatory democracy approaches such as participatory budgets (Fung and Wright 2003; Smith 2009), to the ever-expanding consultation processes, to the incessant 24/7 commentary on political events facilitated through social media, there is an expectation that the public should be involved in ongoing political considerations, rather than only being called upon at the time of election; and again, digital tools enable this to happen more easily (Coleman and Blumler 2009). This has clear implications for Parliament, which is expected to be far more open to the public than it would have been, say, in the 1960s. This expectation of public involvement is therefore another factor that has pushed the UK Parliament to develop its public engagement activity.

The development of public engagement in the UK Parliament

The UK Parliament has had education and public information services since the late 1970s, but the most significant development of its public engagement role can be dated to 2005. It is from this point onwards that an expansion of services specifically dedicated to the role of parliamentary public engagement occurs.

This came after the approval of the Modernisation Committee's (2004) report on *Connecting Parliament with the Public* by 375 to 14 votes in the Commons in January 2005. The very clear endorsement of the report by the House marked a key turning point for investment in new activities, and for the development of a more outward-facing approach (Leston-Bandeira 2016). The report focused specifically on the relationship between the House of Commons and the public, making recommendations particularly on strengthening public accessibility to Parliament, with a strong emphasis on education and visitor services, but also touching on media, petitions, the website, and online consultations. As it outlined:

> It is the purpose of this Report to make recommendations which will better reconcile the necessary purpose of Parliament with the reasonable expectation of the people to have access to the processes by which we govern ourselves. (Modernisation Committee 2004, 9)

Since then, the old Department of the Library expanded considerably in the number of staff and in its functions, to become the Department of Information Services, then becoming two separate teams in a 2016 restructure, one of which, the Participation Team, now focuses solely on connecting with the public. This expansion and restructuring demonstrate Parliament's investment in the area of public engagement. The introduction of the Parliamentary Outreach service in 2008 (initially a pilot project, but now a permanent feature) was a key milestone in the development of this new approach to public engagement. Its key principle was that Parliament should go to where the people are, and it therefore established outreach representation outside Westminster. It signifies a change from a passive assumption that the public engages with Parliament if they are interested in its parliamentary business, to an approach that actively disseminates the role and value of Parliament to the public. Likewise, the inauguration of the new Education Centre in 2015 marked another milestone, considerably expanding Parliament's capacity to cater for visiting school parties (see Case Study 29).

Initially, Parliament's public engagement strategy focused mainly on promoting understanding and awareness of the role of Parliament. In fact, one of its key objectives has been to promote the differentiation between Parliament and government; officials regularly state that this is the main common misunderstanding of Parliament. Hansard Society research confirms that 51 per cent of the public thinks that Parliament and government are the same (Kalitowski 2009, 352). More recently, the public engagement strategy has also embraced the promotion of a sense of value—that Parliament matters and is relevant to individuals' lives (Judge and Leston-Bandeira 2017).

As Parliament's public engagement role has expanded, it has also become more complex and embedded into parliamentary business. For a long time, engagement simply signified better education and information services. But now it is listed, for instance, as part of select committees' core tasks (Kelly and Suchenia 2013, 6). The use of social media to engage the public in ongoing inquiries is now also part of routine work by committees: from the use of the Twitter hashtag #AskGove back in 2012, for the public to ask questions to then Secretary of State for Education Michael Gove, to the now regular use of bespoke hashtags for most inquiries and partnership with outside groups, such as WeNurses, to collate evidence for specific inquiries, to the new e-petitions system introduced in 2015 (see Chapter 30).

Has public engagement delivered?

The UK Parliament's public engagement has undoubtedly become more complex and pervasive over the last decade. But has it delivered? And what does this mean? Evaluation of public engagement activity is, in fact, one of the key challenges in understanding this area. As the data below show, there is a clear rise in activity; what remains unclear though are the effects of this activity. Whether this activity has reached a public who would not normally engage with Parliament, for instance, and whether this has led to a change in the public's awareness and perceptions of the institution.

As the Hansard Society's yearly *Audits of Political Engagement* have regularly shown, most of the population does not engage with Parliament, and many would not wish to. Its 2016 *Audit* showed that 56 per cent of the public had not engaged with Parliament through any of eight diverse possibilities listed, from contacting an MP through following Parliament's social media accounts (Hansard Society 2016, 27). Of these, 28 per cent said they would never engage, even if they felt strongly about an issue. The 2017 *Audit* showed a rise in engagement with Parliament, namely in signing e-petitions (23 per cent), though overall, 31 per cent of the population said they have had no contact with Parliament, including voting (Hansard Society 2017, 42). Yet Parliament has seen an exponential rise in public engagement activity.

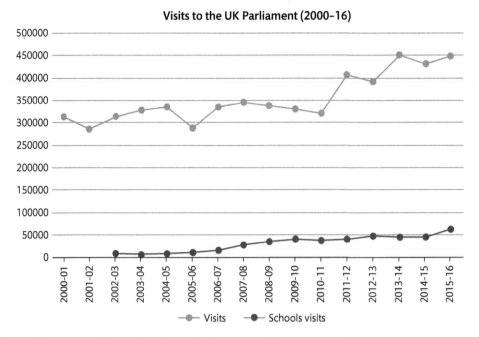

Figure 29.2 Visits and schools visits to the UK Parliament (2000–16)

Sources: House of Commons Commission (2005; 2007, 98; 2011, 37; 2016, 52); and for data on school visits from 2002/2003 to 2004/2005: Parliamentary Education Service (2015)

Note: 'Visits' includes totals for: Visitors to the Chamber Galleries (House of Commons only), Members' tours (both Houses), Summer Opening, and Saturday Openings.

Services for visitors, for instance, have seen a clear rise in use and complexity. A range of different types of tours are now offered. Figure 29.2 shows that the number of people visiting Parliament on tours has risen, particularly since 2010, and stands at just under half a million people per year. However, the demographics of who is visiting remain unclear, particularly whether it includes people beyond those who are already engaged. The *Audit of Political Engagement* repeatedly shows that those engaging with Parliament tend to be among the oldest, most affluent generations, with higher levels of education (see Hansard Society 2017, 44). Still, school visits have also seen a boost, helped by a transport subsidy scheme for those schools far away from London; this has led to a rise in visits from state schools and from outside London/the south-east. This is particularly clear since 2015, following the opening of the Education Centre.

Parliament has also developed its online educational resources considerably, from award-winning games (such as 'MP for a Week'), to online resources and lesson plans targeting teachers. There is evidence of increasing use of these resources, such as a rise in views of its YouTube learning videos from a monthly average of 34,909 in 2014/15, to 69,083 in 2016 (Parliament Education Service 2016). This is mirrored by the expanding role of outreach activities, now labelled as community-focused activity. Table 29.1 shows an overall increase in activity and participants. The UK Parliament now also holds ad hoc events with more intense programmes of activities, such as the annual Parliament Week in November, which in 2016 included the participation of 25,406 people in this one-week long programme of events across the country (Parliament Participation Team 2017).

Most of this activity takes place separately to parliamentary business though, mainly at the lower level of the engagement ladder (information). Recently it has become somewhat more integrated with ongoing parliamentary business. As observed above, public engagement is now explicitly part of select committees' core tasks, with social media regularly used

Table 29.1 Outreach and engagement activity (2011–17)**

	2011/12	2012/13	2013/14	2014/15	2015/16	2016/17
Community workshops	362	363	355	293	306	334
Other activity*	86	98	372	583	555	534
Total activity	**448**	**461**	**727**	**876**	**861**	**868**
Total participants	**17,048**	**15,960**	**20,356**	**24,157**	**23,822**	**20,415**

Source: Parliament Participation Team (2017)

Notes: * Other activity includes: Select committee engagement activities, Universities Programme, Adults with Learning Disabilities Programme, Mr Speaker and Lord Speaker outreach programmes, Train the Trainer, Women in Parliament Programme. ** Financial years—e.g. from beginning of April to end of March.

to inform and consult the public about inquiries, including live tweeting of evidence sessions. The online public reading forum on the Children and Families Bill (2013) is another example, which enabled the public to comment directly on a bill's clauses and schedules, prior to its scrutiny in committee. The forum was open for two weeks, during which 1,099 comments were posted. However, the actual scrutiny of the bill by parliamentarians hardly mentioned the public reading, denoting poor integration of this initiative into parliamentary business (Leston-Bandeira and Thompson 2017).

Digital debates were introduced in 2015 to try to improve integration with parliamentary business, following a recommendation in the Digital Democracy Commission's report (2015). Digital debates take place on specific topics due to be debated in Parliament and, importantly, are sponsored by those MPs leading the parliamentary debates (often Westminster Hall debates). They take place typically on Twitter through a bespoke hashtag a few days before the actual parliamentary debate, with the respective MPs leading the debate interacting live with posts for a couple hours; MPs then refer to the online contributions in the actual parliamentary debate. Table 29.2 shows that 20 digital debates took place in the first year following their introduction in June 2015. The figures show that debates, such as the one on UK Aid, led by MPs Steve Double and Stephen Twigg, involved the participation of 3,363 people, through 7,844 tweets. It is unclear, though, what this participation entails, and there is considerable variation in participant numbers; but they illustrate the integration of public engagement with ongoing parliamentary business, and feature elements of consultation and participation. The new e-petitions system is another example of this type of activity (see Chapter 30).

There is therefore plenty of evidence to demonstrate the expanding and increasingly complex public engagement activity by Parliament. Research now needs to focus on the effects of this activity. We know that a question asked through the hashtag #AskPickles in 2014 led the Secretary of State for Communities and Local Government to change the law to enable council meeting agendas to be circulated electronically (Communities and Local Government Committee 2015, 11), and that the Women and Equalities Committee (2016, 13) was able to engage with a hard-to-reach public, the transgender community, thanks to public engagement work linked to an e-petition on the topic. But our understanding of the effects of public engagement is still poor—in particular, whether it changes the public's attitudes towards Parliament. The *Audit of Political Engagement* gives us an indication of which means of engagement are most used by the public, with traditional

Table 29.2 Digital debates (June 2015–June 2016)

Topic of debate	Date*	Number of tweets/ posts**	Number of contributors	Platform used
Early years development and school readiness	12/06/2016	232	n.a.	Mumsnet forum
#EBACCdebate	28/06/2016	5,696	2,254	Twitter
Carers	06/06/2016	193	n.a.	Facebook
#UKAidDebate	13/06/2016	7,844	3,363	Twitter
#VotingWomen	08/06/2016	1,376	806	Twitter
#Alzdebate	11/04/2016	2,998	1,268	Twitter
International Women's Day #IWD2016	07/03/2016	n.a.***	n.a.***	Twitter
#StopYouthViolence	22/02/2016	6,315	1,725	Twitter
Crohn's and Colitis	17/02/2016	1,068	n.a.	Facebook
#funding4cycling	02/02/2016	3,084	1,546	Twitter
Diversity in STEM #WomenInSTEM	18/01/2016	4,217	2,019	Twitter
#Access2Jobs	11/01/2016	1,718	679	Twitter
#CFDebate	07/12/2015	1,121	265	Twitter
Fuel poverty	23/11/2015	88	31	MoneySavingExpert forum
Women and Low Pay #DoDemocracy	17/11/2015	687	313	Twitter
Maternity Discrimination #MothersWork	02/11/2015	1,196	412	Twitter
YMCA England #YoungJobseekers	26/10/2015	572	157	Twitter
#WeNurses (NHS contracts and conditions)	11/09/2015	860	214	Twitter
#artsfunding	15/07/2015	1,004	558	Twitter
#rddebate	16/06/2015	2,678	354	Twitter

Notes: * Date corresponds to the first day of digital debate. ** Number of tweets/posts corresponds to total, prior and after debate in Parliament. *** Statistics could not be calculated due to high level of usage of #IWD2016 internationally by unrelated organizations.

broadcasting media (TV, radio) being the main way through which the public engages with Parliament, and the new e-petitions system offering Parliament's clearest inroad to boosting public engagement numbers (Hansard Society 2016, 28). Usage does not reflect effect on attitudes though.

The 2016 *Audit of Political Engagement* gave a somewhat positive response, showing that 52 per cent of the public felt they had a good knowledge of the UK Parliament

(Hansard Society 2016, 24). Likewise, 73 per cent of the public thought that Parliament was essential to democracy, and 58 per cent thought that Parliament debates and makes decisions on issues that matter to them (ibid., 25); in all cases, these were the highest values ever recorded for these questions. Although positive, this was a survey done in an election year (2015), when interest in politics tends to be higher. Indeed, the 2017 *Audit* shows a decline in those values—e.g., a drop to 45 per cent for knowledge about Parliament (Hansard Society 2017, 26), and only 30 per cent being fairly satisfied with the way Parliament works (ibid., 27). Still, previous Audits do show a steady increase in the proportion of the public feeling more knowledgeable about Parliament, from a mere 33 per cent in 2004, to 47 per cent in 2015 (Hansard Society 2016, 24). One could argue that this is the result of a much more active effort from Parliament to inform the public about its role; but so far there is no direct evidence of causal effect. Importantly also, despite some fluctuations, satisfaction with democracy, Parliament, MPs in general, and own MP, continue to remain stubbornly low, at around 30 per cent. Data from Ipsos MORI (2011, 2014) confirm these trends, showing in fact that while knowledge about Parliament has increased, satisfaction has declined. The Audits also show that those with more knowledge about Parliament are not necessarily those more satisfied with the institution, which is why more research is needed on specific public engagement activities to develop a better understanding of their effect.

Conclusion

Public engagement entails a wide range of types of activity, from simple information to active participation in political processes. This chapter shows that the UK Parliament has developed its public engagement function quite considerably over the last decade. This encompasses an expansion and a diversification of the type of activities offered, from visits to public consultation via social media. While public engagement tends to take place separately from parliamentary business, it has recently become more integrated. Four factors explain the investment in public engagement, such as an attempt to reverse a steady trend of decline in trust. However, while there is evidence of increased usage of parliamentary public engagement and a higher proportion of the public knowledgeable about Parliament, there is little evidence of this resulting in improved rates of political satisfaction. Importantly, we still know little about how parliamentary public engagement affects public attitudes, and whether it impacts on actual parliamentary business.

Further Reading

HANSARD SOCIETY (2004–2016) *Audits of Political Engagement*. All online at: http://www.auditofpoliticalengagement.org/ [accessed 22 August 2017].

KELSO, A. (2007) 'Parliament and political disengagement: Neither waving nor drowning', *The Political Quarterly*, Vol. 78 (3), pp. 364–73.

LESTON-BANDEIRA, C. (2016) 'Why Symbolic Representation Frames Parliamentary Public Engagement', *British Journal of Politics and International Relations*, Vol. 18 (2), pp. 498–516.

MODERNISATION COMMITTEE (2004) *Connecting Parliament with the Public: First Report of Session 2003–04*, London: Stationery Office, HC 368. Online at: http://www.publications.parliament.uk/pa/cm200304/cmselect/cmmodern/368/368.pdf [accessed 22 August 2017].

WALKER, A. (2012) 'A People's Parliament?', *Parliamentary Affairs*, Vol. 65 (1), pp. 270–80.

Case Study 29: Parliament's Education Centre

This case study examines the provision of an education centre at the UK Parliament, the difficulties encountered in delivering it, and the role it performs in terms of Parliament's public engagement activity.

School visits form a central part of Parliament's public engagement activity as they target a hard-to-reach audience: young people. They focus on two key steps in the ladder of engagement—information and education—while developing in young people a sense of value of the institution. Demand from schools has been very high, with school visit numbers increasing from just under 10,900 in 2006/07 (House of Commons Commission 2007, 16), to over 46,000 in 2013/14 (House of Commons Commission 2014, 6), while still remaining hugely oversubscribed. Feedback on the value of undertaking a school visit to Westminster has also been apparent for some time, as this teacher feedback shows:

> the location gives first-hand experience of the work of Parliament—there is no substitute for the reality of Westminster ... it is actually being in the very place where work takes place that is for most people very exciting–this involvement is the key to effective impact. (Parliament Education Service 2008)

However, finding space for school visits has always been a major challenge at Westminster. Accommodation on the Parliamentary Estate is notoriously limited and, until the opening of Parliament's Education Centre, the school visits programme had operated out of committee and meeting rooms. This was less than ideal in terms of capacity, the nature of the space, and the need to share entrances and facilities with Members, staff, and other visitors. While the need to engage with young people was identified as a key priority, Parliament lacked the space to do this effectively. Several plans were developed and discounted before a dedicated education centre was finally delivered in July 2015.

THE REQUIREMENT FOR AN EDUCATION CENTRE

In 2007, both Houses of Parliament gave an explicit mandate to prioritize young visitors and provide a dedicated centre for visiting school pupils, as noted by the House of Commons Administration Committee:

> the focus of visitor services should be on educational visitors as the most productive way to improve Parliament's engagement with the public ... If we are to develop our education and visitor facilities to enable Parliament to reach out to schools and provide greater support for learners of all ages, we should invest in a dedicated space and provide the support to do so. (Administration Committee 2007, 34)

This recommendation was endorsed by the House of Lords Information Committee (2007), and later in 2007 both Houses agreed to the recommendation in a motion on the Floor of each House (HC Debates, 12 June 2007, c. 720; HL Debates, 16 Oct 2007, c. 675).

A plan to deliver an education centre within the Palace of Westminster was developed, but foundered in 2009 on significant structural grounds. The Administration and Information Committees continued to support the provision of a dedicated education centre, restating their commitment and growing frustration. The Information Committee (2009, 10) noted, for instance, that 'the Committee is looking forward to the opening of the Parliamentary Education Centre, which is crucial to enable larger numbers of children to visit Parliament'. While the Administration Committee (2012, 24) noted that 'it is deeply frustrating that nearly five years have passed without substantive action to provide [education] facilities or to put in place alternative means of meeting the clearly expressed aspirations of both Houses to invite up to 100,000 schoolchildren a year to visit the estate'.

A new feasibility study in 2012 again reviewed options to meet the design brief within a reasonable timescale. The study identified viable locations for a short-term solution, including the emergence of a new idea around a demountable, modular building. This was the breakthrough that was needed. This, and support at the highest level from the Speaker and the House of Commons Commission.

Planning permission was subsequently granted for ten years for a demountable building on Victoria Tower Gardens. This demonstrates the difficulties in integrating extra provision to support public engagement within the Parliamentary Estate. Although the Education Centre now exists, it is still only a temporary structure.

WHAT THE EDUCATION CENTRE OFFERS

School visits to the Education Centre consist of a tour of the Palace of Westminster, an educational workshop, and a Q&A session with the school's MP.

Four themed learning spaces—Commons, Lords, Monarchy, and 'Your Parliament'—help explain the composition and role of Parliament. Creative use of technology is incorporated into the centre, including augmented reality through which elements of the heritage and history of the Palace of Westminster are brought to life—for example, by transposing iPads over paintings of past monarchs, these become cartoons talking directly to pupils. While the centre is located next to the Palace of Westminster, the building's glass walls and high-level windows maintain a constant visual connection with the Palace (see Figure 29.3). The mix of old and new is an important narrative as students are encouraged to think about the evolution of Parliament and the role they can play shaping the future of democracy in the UK.

The visits therefore aim to educate pupils about Parliament's history and role, to suggest a sense of value to young people visiting, while also linking to ongoing politics through a meeting with their MP.

Figure 29.3 The Education Centre
Source: Roger Harris Photography

IMPACT OF THE EDUCATION CENTRE

The effects of the Education Centre on young people are still unclear, but it has undoubtedly enabled a significant increase in capacity, with 63,383 visits in 2015/16 alone (House of Commons Commission 2016, 52), its first year of opening, and capacity for up to 100,000 students a year (20 schools a day). Its dedicated facilities have also provided important practical facilities, improving the students' experience of Parliament. And finally, through its purpose-designed, genuine learning environment, the space itself has been brought to life to help tell the story of Parliament.

The reaction from pupils, teachers, MPs, and staff has been overwhelmingly positive, as some of the early teacher feedback attests (Parliament Education Service 2017):

> The new Education Centre made the trip easier on a practical level, it was far quicker going through security and we were able to store bags. (November 2015)
>
> This was my second visit. I thought the first time was good but the Education Centre has clearly made a huge difference to the way school trips are run and I shall now look forward to bringing another group of children next year. (November 2015)
>
> This trip was perhaps the best one I have experienced in over 20 years of bringing students to Parliament. I thought that the new Education Centre is superb. (December 2015)

With a reach of 100,000 young people each year, Parliament's Education Centre has the potential to directly engage with a million young people over a ten-year period. This provides a unique opportunity for studies on the effect of parliamentary public engagement on young people.

This case study demonstrates that public engagement is a very recent activity for the UK Parliament, and not always a very straightforward one to implement. It also illustrates different elements of parliamentary public engagement, such as informing and educating, and Parliament's focus on young people, as a key target audience for engagement.

Primary sources

- Administration Committee (2007) *Improving Facilities for Educational Visitors to Parliament: First Report of Session 2006–07*, London: The Stationery Office, HC 434. Online at: http://www.publications.parliament.uk/pa/cm200607/cmselect/cmadmin/434/43402.htm [accessed 27 June 2017].

- Administration Committee (2012) *Visitor Access and Facilities: First Report of Session 2012–13*, London: The Stationery Office, HC 13. Online at: http://www.publications.parliament.uk/pa/cm201213/cmselect/cmadmin/13/1302.htm [accessed 27 June 2017].

- Information Committee (2009) *Are the Lords Listening? Creating Connections between People and Parliament: First Report of Session 2008–09*, London: The Stationery Office, HL 138. Online at: http://www.publications.parliament.uk/pa/ld200809/ldselect/ldinformation/138/13802.htm [accessed 27 June 2017].

- Parliament's Education Centre. Online at: http://www.parliament.uk/education/visit-parliament-with-your-school/faqs-and-subsidy/the-education-centre/ [accessed 27 June 2017].

➡ FURTHER CASE STUDIES

- UK Parliament Week, which takes place every year in November (see https://www.ukparliamentweek.org/).

- Digital debate about Baby Loss, 10–13 October 2016 (http://www.parliament.uk/get-in-volved/have-your-say-on-laws/digital-debates/baby-loss/).

- Tours of Parliament as engagement opportunities (see http://www.parliament.uk/visiting/visiting-and-tours/tours-of-parliament/).

References

ADMINISTRATION COMMITTEE (2007) *Improving Facilities for Educational Visitors to Parliament: First Report of Session 2006–07*, London: The Stationery Office, HC 434. Online at: https://publications.parliament.uk/pa/cm200607/cmselect/cmadmin/434/434.pdf [accessed 25 August 2017].

ADMINISTRATION COMMITTEE (2012) *Visitor Access and Facilities: First Report 2012–13*, London: The Stationery Office, HC 13. Online at: http://www.parliament.uk/documents/TSO-PDF/committee-reports/13.pdf [accessed 25 August 2017].

ARNSTEIN, S. (1969) 'A Ladder of Citizen Participation', *Journal of the American Institute of Planners*, Vol. 35 (4), pp. 216–24.

CARMAN, C. (2009) *Engaging the Public in the Scottish Parliament's Petitions Process*, Edinburgh: Ipsos MORI. Undertaken on behalf of the Scottish Parliament's Public Petitions Committee. Online at: http://archive.scottish.parliament.uk/s3/committees/petitions/inquiries/petition-sProcess/Engagingthepublicinthepetitionsprocess.pdf [accessed 25 June 2017].

CLARK, A. and WILFORD, R. (2012) 'Political Institutions, Engagement and Outreach: The Case of the Northern Ireland Assembly', *Parliamentary Affairs*, Vol. 65 (2), pp. 380–403.

COLEMAN, S. and BLUMLER, J. (2009) *The Internet and Democratic Citizenship*, Cambridge: Cambridge University Press.

COMMUNITIES AND LOCAL GOVERNMENT COMMITTEE (2015) *The Work of the Communities and Local Government Committee since 2010: Tenth Report of Session 2014–15*, London: The Stationery Office, HC 821. Online at: http://www.publications.parliament.uk/pa/cm201415/cmselect/cmcomloc/821/821.pdf [accessed 25 June 2017].

DALTON, R. (2004) *Democratic Challenges, Democratic Choices: The Erosion of Political Support in Advanced Industrial Democracies*, Oxford: Oxford University Press.

DALTON, R. (2007) *Citizen Politics*, Washington, DC: CQ Press.

DIGITAL DEMOCRACY COMMISSION (2015) *Open Up! Report of the Speaker's Commission on Digital Democracy*, London: House of Commons. Online at: http://www.digitalde-mocracy.parliament.uk/documents/Open-Up-Digital-Democracy-Report.pdf [accessed 25 June 2017].

EUROBAROMETER (2016) *Standard EB 1995–2016*. Online at: http://ec.europa.eu/COMMFront-Office/publicopinion/index.cfm/General/index [accessed 25 June 2017].

FOX, R. (2009) 'Engagement and Participation: What the Public Want and How our Politicians Need to Respond', *Parliamentary Affairs*, Vol. 62 (4), pp. 673–85.

FUNG, A. and WRIGHT, E., eds. (2003) *Deepening Democracy—Institutional Innovations in Empowered Participatory Democracy*, London: Verso.

HANSARD SOCIETY (2010) *Audit of Political Engagement 7*, London: Hansard Society. Online at: https://assets.contentful.com/xkbace0jm9pp/4utWyL6rVuIgIMmkYgeEMI/7e5c5ad0a 94a293b16127107728e4089/Audit_of_Political_Engagement_7__2010_.pdf [accessed 25 June 2017].

HANSARD SOCIETY (2016) *Audit of Political Engagement 13*, London: Hansard Society. Online at: https://assets.contentful.com/u1rlvvbs33ri/24aY1mkabGU0uEsoUOekGW/06380afa29a63008e97fb41cdb8dcad0/Publication__Audit-of-Political-Engagement-13.pdf [accessed 25 June 2017].

HANSARD SOCIETY (2017) *Audit of Political Engagement 14*, London: Hansard Society. Online at: https://www.hansardsociety.org.uk/research/audit-of-political-engagement [accessed 25 June 2017].

HAY, C. (2007) *Why We Hate Politics*, Cambridge: Polity.

HOUSE OF COMMONS COMMISSION (2005) *Twenty-Seventh Annual Report of the House of Commons Commission—Financial Year 2004/05*. Online at: http://www.publications.parliament.uk/pa/cm200405/cmselect/cmcomm/65/6501.htm [accessed 25 June 2017].

HOUSE OF COMMONS COMMISSION (2007) *Twenty-Ninth Report of the House of Commons Commission: Financial Year 2006/07*, London: The Stationery Office, HC 708. Online at: https://www.publications.parliament.uk/pa/cm200607/cmselect/cmcomm/708/708.pdf [accessed 25 June 2017].

HOUSE OF COMMONS COMMISSION (2011) *Thirty-Third Report of the Commission, and Annual Report of the Administration Estimate Audit Committee: Financial Year 2010/11*, London: The Stationery Office, HC 1439. Online at: https://www.publications.parliament.uk/pa/cm201012/cmselect/cmcomm/1439/1439.pdf [accessed 25 June 2017].

HOUSE OF COMMONS COMMISSION (2014) *Thirty-sixth Report of the Commission, and Annual Report of the Administration Estimate Audit Committee: Financial Year 2013/14*, London: The Stationery Office, HC 596. Online at: http://www.parliament.uk/documents/commons-commission/36-report-HC-596.pdf [accessed 25 June 2017].

HOUSE OF COMMONS COMMISSION (2016) *Thirty-Eighth Report of the Commission, and Report of the Administration Estimate Audit Committee: Financial Year 2015/16*, London: The Stationery Office, HC 788. Online at: http://www.parliament.uk/documents/commons-commission/CommissionAnnualReport_2015-16.pdf [accessed 25 June 2017].

HOUSE OF LORDS INFORMATION COMMITTEE (2007) *Improving Facilities for Educational Visitors to Parliament: 1st Report of Session 2006–07*, London: The Stationery Office, HL 117. Online at: https://publications.parliament.uk/pa/ld200607/ldselect/ldinformation/117/117.pdf [accessed 25 August 2017].

HOUSE OF LORDS INFORMATION COMMITTEE (2009) *Are the Lords Listening? Creating Connections between People and Parliament: 1st Report of Session 2008–09*, London: The Stationery Office, HL 138. Online at: https://publications.parliament.uk/pa/ld200809/ldselect/ldinformation/138/138i.pdf [accessed 25 August 2017].

IPSOS MORI (2011) *Knowledge of Parliament 1991–2010*, 30 March. Online at: https://www.ipsos.com/ipsos-mori/en-uk/knowledge-parliament-1991-2010 [accessed 25 August 2017].

IPSOS MORI (2014) *Views of Westminster*, 11 November. Online at: https://www.ipsos.com/ipsos-mori/en-uk/views-westminster [accessed 25 August 2017].

IPU (2012) *Global Parliamentary Report: The Changing Nature of Parliamentary Representation*. Geneva: Inter-Parliamentary Union.

JUDGE, D. and LESTON-BANDEIRA, C. (2017) 'The Institutional Representation of Parliament', *Political Studies*, forthcoming.

KALITOWSKI, S. (2009) 'Parliament for the People? Public Knowledge, Interest and Public Perceptions of the Westminster Parliament', *Parliamentary Affairs*, Vol. 62 (2), pp. 350–63.

KELLY, R. and SUCHENIA, A. (2013) *Select Committees Core Tasks*, House of Commons Library Standard Note SN/PC/03161, 29 January. Online at: http://researchbriefings.files.parliament.uk/documents/SN03161/SN03161.pdf [accessed 25 June 2017].

Kelso, A. (2007) 'Parliament and Political Disengagement: Neither Waving nor Drowning', *Political Quarterly*, Vol. 78 (3), pp. 364–73.

Lee, L. and Young, P. (2013) 'Politics: A Disengaged Britain? Political interest and participation over 30 years' in A. Park, C. Bryson, E. Clery, J. Curtice, and M. Philips (eds.), *British Social Attitudes 30*, London: NatCen Social Research, pp. 62–86. Online at: http://www.bsa.natcen.ac.uk/media/38723/bsa30_full_report_final.pdf [accessed 25 June 2017].

Leston-Bandeira, C. (2014) 'The Pursuit of Legitimacy as a Key Driver for Public Engagement: The European Parliament Case', *Parliamentary Affairs*, Vol. 67 (2), pp. 415–36.

Leston-Bandeira, C. (2016) 'Why Symbolic Representation Frames Parliamentary Public Engagement', *British Journal of Politics and International Relations*, Vol. 18 (2), pp. 498–516.

Leston-Bandeira, C. and Thompson, L. (2017) 'Integrating the view of the public into the formal legislative process: public reading stage in the UK House of Commons', *The Journal of Legislative Studies*, DOI: 10.1080/13572334.2017.1394736.

Magalhães, P. (2006) 'Confidence in Parliaments: Performance, Representation and Accountability' in M. Torcal and J. P. Montero (eds.), *Political Disaffection in Contemporary Democracies: Social Capital, Institutions and Politics*, London: Routledge, pp. 190–214.

Mair, P. (2013) *Ruling the Void: The Hollowing of Western Democracy*, London: Verso.

Modernisation Committee (2004) *Connecting Parliament with the Public: First Report of Session 2003–04*, London: The Stationery Office, HC 368. Online at: http://www.publications.parliament.uk/pa/cm200304/cmselect/cmmodern/368/368.pdf [accessed 25 June 2017].

Norris, P., ed. (1999) *Critical Citizens: Global Support for Democratic Governance*, Oxford: Oxford University Press.

Norris, P. (2011) *Democratic Deficit: Critical Citizens Revisited*, Cambridge: Cambridge University Press.

Parliamentary Education Service (2008) 'Business case for a Parliamentary Education Centre', internal documentation provided to authors.

Parliamentary Education Service (2015) Data on visits, email message to authors (2 February 2015).

Parliamentary Education Service (2016) Data on YouTube views, email message to authors (25 October 2016).

Parliamentary Education Service (2017) Teacher feedback, email message to authors (13 April 2017).

Parliament Participation Team (2017) Data on outreach activities, email message to authors (28 April 2017).

Smith, G. (2009) *Democratic Innovations: Designing Institutions for Citizen Participation*, Cambridge: Cambridge University Press.

Stoker, G. (2006) *Why Politics Matters*, Basingstoke: Palgrave.

Van der Meer, T. (2010) 'In What We Trust? A Multi-level Study into Trust in Parliament as an Evaluation of State Characteristics', *International Review of Administrative Sciences*, Vol. 76 (3), pp. 517–36.

Walker, A. (2012) 'A People's Parliament?', *Parliamentary Affairs*, Vol. 65 (1), pp. 270–80.

Webb, P. (2013) 'Who is willing to participate? Dissatisfied democrats, stealth democrats and populists in the UK', *European Journal of Political Research*, Vol. 52 (6), pp. 747–72.

Women and Equalities Committee (2016) *Transgender Equality: First Report of Session 2015–16*, London: The Stationery Office, HC 390. Online at: http://www.publications.parliament.uk/pa/cm201516/cmselect/cmwomeq/390/390.pdf [accessed 25 June 2017].

30

Parliament and Petitions

Thomas Caygill and Anne-Marie Griffiths

INTRODUCTION

Petitioning is an established way for the general public to communicate their views to those who hold public office. The right to petition has been exercised since Saxon times and was recognized in Magna Carta, and in the Bill of Rights of 1689 (House of Commons Information Office 2010, 2). Petitioning is often mistakenly seen as a form of direct democracy, when in fact it is a form of advocacy democracy. Advocacy democracy involves citizens participating in policy deliberation and policy formation by influencing the decisions of policymakers (Dalton, Scarrow, and Cain 2004, 126). There are two main ways for citizens to petition Parliament and the government. Both the House of Commons and House of Lords have a long-established paper petitions system (although it is rarely used in the Lords) and in 2015 it became possible for the public to petition the House of Commons and government electronically. This chapter outlines the two different systems, discussing in particular how the new e-petitions system has tried to address some of the common criticisms about the relationship between the UK Parliament and the public.

The changing nature of participation

This chapter rests against a backdrop of declining formal participation with Parliament—the most conventional form being voting in elections. Elections lie at the very heart of representative democracy; they are the source from which democracies and parliaments draw their legitimacy. Although turnout in the 2017 general election was 69 per cent (BBC News 2017), this is down 2 per cent on the 20-year high in 1997 and down 15 per cent from a post-war high in 1950 (Audickas, Hawkins, and Cracknell 2017). Using such an indicator, it would appear that conventional participation and engagement with the formal institutions of the state has declined. However, it may be that there has been a change in the mode of participation, from conventional to less conventional modes (Hay 2007, 23) as well as citizens supplementing conventional modes with less conventional modes.

Petitioning is one of these less conventional modes, and has become one of the more popular ways for the general public to participate in the political process (Bochel 2013, 798; Stoker 2006, 35). Stoker (2006, 92) argues that petitioning is an example of a low-key and low-commitment type of participation.

Parliamentary terms Petition

A formal request for a specific action or to raise an issue of importance, sent by the public to Parliament. It can be sent through MPs in the form of public (paper) petitions, or directly to Parliament through the online e-petitions system.

The decline in conventional participation could be down to critical citizens who 'adhere strongly to democratic values but who find the existing structures of representative government ... to be wanting' (Norris 1999, 3). They are therefore more realistic in their expectations of government, better educated, and less deferential than their parents and grandparents (Hay 2007, 41), as discussed in Chapter 29. Using this theory, the decline in conventional participation could be attributed to citizens being more critical in their judgements on the performance of institutions, such as parliaments, which were established centuries ago and which may be in need of reform. While conventional methods of participation have declined, Parliament itself has begun to adapt and reform its structures to encourage different forms of participation. The creation of the e-petitions system is a key example of this.

There are a number of key assumptions which members of the public make about Parliament. The first is that Parliament does not debate or make decisions on issues that people care about. The Hansard Society's *Audit of Public Engagement* for 2016 showed that 42 per cent of respondents did not believe that Parliament did so, or were not sure (Hansard Society 2016, 25). There is an assumption among the public that they are unable to make a difference and effect change within the political system. In 2015 only 17 per cent of people surveyed believed that they had some influence over national decision-making (Hansard Society 2015, 36). We will return to these key assumptions throughout this chapter.

Contemporary developments in petitioning the UK Parliament

Public (paper) petitions

Both the House of Commons and the House of Lords have long-standing procedures for their Members to present petitions to the House. However, in the House of Lords this procedure is very rarely used. We thus concentrate here on the use of public petitions in the House of Commons.

Public petitions must comply with a fairly strict set of rules. They must be addressed to the House of Commons, state who the petitioners are, explain what the petition is about, and request a clear action that is within the power of the House of Commons (UK Parliament 2016). Only MPs can present public petitions to the House of Commons, but they are under no obligation to do so.

MPs can present public petitions in two ways. Most commonly, they can choose to present the petition formally in person on the Floor of the House. This opportunity takes place towards the end of a day's sitting, just before the adjournment debate. MPs can make a brief statement about the petition, but cannot make a speech, and there can be no debate. This can be a good way to raise awareness of a cause, but the fact that the whole process usually takes only a minute or two can be disappointing for petitioners. Petitions can also be presented informally by MPs placing the petition directly into a bag at the back of the Speaker's Chair. For critical citizens, and citizens who want high-impact and low-commitment ways of participating, this mechanism leaves a lot to be desired.

Almost all public petitions receive a response, called an observation, from the government within two months, which is then printed in Hansard (see Figure 30.1). This is

House of Commons **Hansard**

Contents / Petitions / Petitions / Wales

Welsh Assembly Oath or Affirmation

Share this debate

10 October 2016
Volume 615

The petition of Gruffydd Meredith,

Declares that there should be an option for new Welsh Assembly members to swear an oath or make an affirmation to the people of Wales instead of to a monarchy and/or crown; further that there should still be an option for new Welsh Assembly members to swear an oath or to make an affirmation to a monarchy if they so wished; further that this would provide a fairer choice for new elected representative which would be a better reflection of the broad scope of view in society; further that there is no requirement for members of the Northern Ireland Assembly to take any oath or affirmation but instead requires that members take a Pledge of Office; further that this proposed similar choice for Wales is important for Welsh political plurality and fairness; and further that an online petition on a similar matter has been signed by over 1,000 individuals.

The petitioner therefore requests that the House of Commons makes the necessary amendments to any present or draft legislation which governs the taking of oaths and the making of the affirmation to ensure that new Welsh Assembly members have the option to swear an oath or make an affirmation to the people of Wales rather than to a monarchy and/or crown.

And the petitioner remains, etc.—*[Presented by Kevin Brennan, Official Report, 20 July 2016; Vol. 613, c. 927.]*

[P001701]

Observations from The Secretary of State for Wales (Alun Cairns):

The Oath of Allegiance sworn by Members of the National Assembly for Wales is a promise to be loyal to the British monarch, and their heirs and successors. Members of the Northern Ireland Assembly have the option to take a Pledge of Office instead of an oath to the monarch. This is as a result of the specific historic and political circumstances in Northern Ireland. There are no plans to change the requirement for members of the National Assembly for Wales.

Figure 30.1 Example of a petition being presented in the Commons
Source: HC Debates, 10 October 2016, P001701

one of the advantages of this system, as the government is required to respond regardless of the number of signatures the petition has. However, these responses are usually brief, and do not offer much indication that public petitions influence the government's decision-making.

This is not a system that challenges the key assumptions about Parliament. The public petitions system is not one which could satisfy critical citizens, especially if citizens are looking for high-impact, low-cost options for participation. Indeed, Norton (2005, 193) goes so far as to suggest that the exercise of petitioning under this system 'is largely a wasted one'.

The e-petitions system

In May 2014, the House of Commons agreed to establish a 'collaborative' e-petitions system which would enable members of the public to petition the House of Commons and to press for action from the government. In December 2014, the House of Commons Procedure Committee published a report, *E-petitions: A Collaborative System* (Procedure Committee 2014), which made detailed recommendations for the establishment of a new e-petitions system. This report was endorsed by the House of Commons in February 2015. The Committee's (2014, 39–40) recommendations amounted to a significant improvement on the public petitions system, with an accessible website that all members of the public can use to sign petitions, a committee to provide political and administrative oversight of the system, and finally a dedicated team of staff to improve interactions between the system and the public. The new Petitions Committee was established on 20 July 2015, and the new e-petitions site launched the following day.

Once a petition has been started and has received five supporting signatures, Committee staff check to see whether the petition meets the established rules. Petitions which comply with the rules are accepted and published, and remain open for signature for six months. Petitions which do not meet the rules are rejected. Committee staff, in an online response which is made public (unless the petition contains content that is illegal, offensive, or confidential), explain the reason why the petition has been rejected, and if possible suggest what other action the petitioner could take. This provides further engagement with, and support for, petitioners.

Between the establishment of the Committee in July 2015 and the closure of the website at the dissolution of Parliament on 3 May 2017:

- over 30,000 petitions were submitted;
- 10,950 petitions were accepted and opened for signature;
- over 31 million signatures were added to e-petitions;
- over 14 million unique email addresses were used to sign e-petitions.

The Petitions Committee

The Committee's role is to oversee the petitions systems. It has 11 members, with a party balance reflecting the composition of the House of Commons (in the 2015 Parliament this meant six Conservative members, four Labour members, and one SNP member). As with other select committees, the Committee Chair is elected by the whole House by secret ballot, and the members are elected by their parties. The Committee is responsible for considering petitions and deciding what action to take. It meets each week when the House is sitting to consider all petitions which have received over 100,000 signatures, and petitions with more than 10,000 signatures which have received a response from the government. The Committee has the power to:

- ask for more information about a petition in writing or in person—from petitioners, the government, or other relevant people or organizations;
- write to the government or another public body to press for action on a petition;
- ask another parliamentary committee to look into the topic raised by a petition;
- conduct its own inquiry into a petition, and make recommendations to the government;
- put forward petitions for debate in the House of Commons.

The introduction of a dedicated committee has led to the creation of new avenues for action on petitions. This new system introduces a degree of flexibility and allows for action to be tailored to the needs of different petitions, rather than a one-size-fits-all approach. Every petition signed by at least 10,000 people receives a written response from the government, which is published on the website and sent by email to everyone who has signed the petition. The Petitions Committee reviews all of the government's responses. If the Committee considers that a government response does not adequately and clearly address the request made by the petition, it writes to the government to ask for an improved response.

For example, the Committee decided that the government's response to a petition calling for the law to be changed to make offering 'gay conversion therapy' a criminal offence didn't give a clear answer to the request made by the petition. In particular, the Committee was concerned that the response did not address the petition's request for legislation. In answer to a letter from the Committee Chair, the government provided a more detailed response which explained why it believed that legislation was 'a blunt instrument and not suited to this issue' (Petitions Committee 2017). This systematic review of petition responses by a cross-party committee introduces a level of scrutiny and accountability to the process which is not present in the public petitions system, and it shows petitioners that there is a parliamentary body which is willing to act on their behalf.

What effects do e-petitions have?

With levels of traditional public participation with Parliament seemingly in decline and citizens feeling as though they are unable to effect any change in areas which concern them, it is important to assess the impact of the e-petitions system on Parliament and public participation.

Debating issues of relevance to the public

As we have seen, one common criticism of Parliament is that it does not debate issues that are relevant to the public. The e-petitions system somewhat addresses this criticism through its power to schedule debates and its dedicated slot in Westminster Hall (the second debating chamber of the House of Commons) for petition debates on a Monday at 4.30 p.m., for up to three hours. This enables relevant issues, raised by the public, to be properly debated in the Chamber.

 Parliamentary terms　Westminster Hall

A debating chamber (the Grand Committee Room) just off Westminster Hall, in which some Commons business takes place (e.g. debates on e-petitions, backbench debates).

Petitions with 100,000 signatures or more will usually be debated, unless: the subject has recently been debated or is likely to be debated in the near future; the Petitions Committee (or another parliamentary or government body) has decided to pursue the issue in another way; or the subject is unsuitable for debate in Parliament. For example, the Committee did not schedule a debate on a petition calling for Benjamin Netanyahu to be arrested on a visit to the UK, because this was something that the UK government said it was not able to do under UK and international law.

Other petitions, with fewer signatures, may be debated if they are topical and there is widespread support for a debate. This introduces a level of flexibility, in ensuring that petitions which do not achieve the 100,000-signature threshold, but are worthy of debate, can be debated. The Petitions Committee is also able to apply to the Backbench Business Committee for time for debate in the main Chamber. However, this mechanism was not used in the 2015–17 Parliament. The e-petitions system therefore provides an avenue through which the public can influence what debates take place in Parliament.

The e-petitions system also allows committee staff to send emails to everyone who has signed a petition, to give them updates informing them when the petition has been scheduled for debate, and including details of how to watch online. This has led to a large increase (some 300 per cent) in the number of people watching parliamentary debates and reading Hansard. Committee staff can also alert petitioners to other parliamentary activity relevant to their petition, such as related select committee inquiries. The system therefore gives the public the opportunity to have an input into issues which are debated by Parliament, and facilitates regular communication between the institution and interested citizens.

Giving the public a voice

The Petitions Committee has made a commitment to maximize the potential for petitioners and other members of the public to be involved with debates on petitions. This includes creating opportunities for petitioners and others to engage with MPs so that their views inform debate.

The Committee has used a variety of approaches to allow the public to share their views with MPs before debates take place, including:

- inviting petitioners and campaigners to Parliament (for example, inviting students of nursing and allied health professions to share their views with MPs before a debate on a petition about the NHS Bursary);

- inviting the public to share their views on social media, sometimes with the MP leading the debate (for example, a Twitter debate about international development with the MP leading the debate and the Chair of the International Development Committee);

- working in partnership with online communities such as Mumsnet to create opportunities for people to share their views and discuss the issues being debated (for example, a thread on Moneysavingexpert.com about the cost of car insurance for young people).

Debates in Westminster Hall allow MPs the opportunity to discuss the case for and against the action requested by the petition, as well as to press the government for action or ask the relevant minister to respond to specific questions. They can be a vital tool in influencing ministerial decisions. For example, after a petition debate about the protection of police dogs and horses, the government changed its response to the petition. As a result, it asked the Sentencing Council, as part of a review on guidelines for sentencing in the Magistrates' Courts, including sentencing for animal cruelty offences, to consider assaults on police animals as an aggravating factor.

In addition, the Petitions Committee, like other select committees, can undertake inquiries and produce reports with recommendations for the government. The Committee has chosen to start inquiries into petitions which raise matters of significant public interest which are not already being debated or looked into in Parliament, and where the government's response to the petition hasn't given the Committee confidence that the government is taking steps to address the issue. The ability to launch an inquiry means there is a greater chance of applying pressure and achieving change than under the public petitions system (see Case Study 30).

Allowing petitioners to participate in debates in this way thus enables the public to have greater interaction with MPs and to help guide or influence what happens in Parliament. It can also enable the public to effect policy change by the government.

Challenges

Public understanding of the detail of the petitions system remains low. The e-petitions website has been used by millions of people—but few fully understand the process for deciding which petitions are debated, the opportunities for engaging further with Parliament, or that the Petitions Committee can conduct detailed inquiries into petitions. This makes it more difficult to challenge widespread assumptions that the system is ineffective.

The sheer number of e-petitions also presents a challenge. Between July 2015 and the dissolution of Parliament in May 2017, over 30,000 petitions were started on the site, and nearly 11,000 were accepted. It is obviously impossible for the Petitions Committee to take action on more than a small percentage of these petitions. This means that the majority of people who start a petition will not see action from Parliament as a result.

It can also be hard to identify clearly what impact a petition has had on policy. Successful petitions usually form part of a wider campaign, and it can often be months or years before change happens (Leston-Bandeira 2017). That makes it very hard to demonstrate to petitioners that their action has had a direct effect on government or Parliament.

Conclusion

The petitioning system provides an avenue for increasing public participation with institutions. The public petitions system is just one way for citizens to petition Parliament, but it does not challenge the key assumptions often held about the institution. In some cases, it could reinforce them—albeit unintentionally. The e-petitions system, on the other hand, gives the public the opportunity to put issues onto the parliamentary agenda. Case Study 30 shows that, when using petitions as part of a broader campaign, the public can make a difference and change policy. On an individual level, the e-petitions system helps to connect people more closely with Parliament by allowing members of the public to access advice and information about petitioning. However, while progress has been made, challenges remain—in particular: a lack of public understanding of how the e-petitions system works; the sheer number of petitions and the relatively small number that see action taken; and the difficulty in identifying the impact a petition has had on the policy process. It will be for the Petitions Committee, its secretariat, and Parliament to decide how to move forward in addressing these challenges.

Further Reading

BOCHEL, C. (2013) 'Petitions Systems: Contributing to Representative Democracy?', *Parliamentary Affairs*, Vol. 66 (4), pp. 798–815.

CARMAN, C. (2010) 'The Process is the Reality: Perceptions of Procedural Fairness and Participatory Democracy', *Political Studies*, Vol. 58 (4), pp. 731–51.

PETITIONS COMMITTEE (2016) *Funding for Research into Brain Tumours: First Report of Session 2015–16*, London: The Stationery Office, HC 554. Online at: http://www.publications.parliament.uk/pa/cm201516/cmselect/cmpetitions/554/554.pdf [accessed 27 June 2017].

PROCEDURE COMMITTEE (2009) *E-petitions: Call for Government Action: Second Report of Session 2008–09*, London: The Stationery Office, HC 493. Online at: http://www.publications.parliament.uk/pa/cm200809/cmselect/cmproced/493/493.pdf [accessed 27 June 2017].

PROCEDURE COMMITTEE (2014) *E-petitions: A Collaborative System: Third Report of Session 2014–15*, London: The Stationery Office, HC 235. Online at: http://www.publications.parliament.uk/pa/cm201415/cmselect/cmproced/235/235.pdf [accessed 27 June 2017].

Case Study 30: The petition calling for more funding for brain tumour research

It can be difficult to work out what role a petition has played in a wider campaign to influence public policy—not least because changing policy can be a lengthy and complicated process. But that's not always the case. A petition started in early August 2015—less than a month after the parliamentary petitions website opened—was able to have a clear and direct effect on policy within a year.

The petition was started by Maria Lester on the anniversary of the death of her brother, Stephen Realf, from a brain tumour. Stephen had been diagnosed when he was just 19, and died when he was 26. Maria's petition called for more funding for brain tumour research, highlighting both the relatively low levels of spending (compared to research into other cancers) and the fact that brain tumours are the biggest cancer killer of people under 40.

When the Petitions Committee first looked at the petition, it had around 20,000 signatures and had received a response from the government (UK government and Parliament 2017). The Committee would not usually take action on a petition at this stage, other than taking note of the government's response. In this case, however, the response did not give the Committee confidence that the government had grasped the seriousness of the concerns highlighted by the petition. The Committee therefore decided that the subject deserved detailed examination.

The Committee was keen that this should be a public-led, as well as public-initiated inquiry. It opened a web thread on the parliamentary website on which people could share their views and experiences. There were 1,100 contributions in just five days (Petitions Committee 2015). Some of those who responded were invited to a private event, where they could talk with Committee members in small groups. The Committee also held two oral evidence sessions, including taking evidence from the petition's creator, Maria Lester, and her parents.

In March 2016 the Committee published a report (Petitions Committee 2016). To some extent, it looks like a traditional select committee report. But it is also very different: there are photographs of sons and daughters lost to brain tumours far too young, and the personal experiences of patients and their families are recounted in depth, often in their own words.

A month later, it was standing room only in Westminster Hall for MPs and the public when the petition was debated. The then Minister for Life Sciences, George Freeman, announced that the government now accepted that it needed to do more to increase the amount of funding for brain tumour research, saying:

> I want to announce today that the government accept that we need to do more in this space, committing to a number of specific actions that reflect the concerns that have been raised, both [in the petition debate] and in the Petitions Committee and the all-party group report. (HC Debates, 18 April 2016, cc. 258–9WH)

This was a huge change from the government's initial response. The minister explained that he would be convening a working group of clinicians, charities, and officials to discuss how to address the need for more brain tumour research. Campaigners, including the Realf family, now had a chance to work at the heart of government to change policy.

Maria Lester, who started the petition with the support of the charity Brain Tumour Research, said:

> This isn't the end of my quest [...] A petition alone is not going to change the world. But perhaps—just perhaps—it might catch the attention of the politicians who can. (Petitions Committee 2016, 9)

This example shows how a petition can put an important, but neglected, issue on the political agenda. It also shows that just getting MPs talking about an issue can lead directly to positive action for a campaign. So why was this petition so successful? First, the petition made a clear call for action from the government, supported not only by Maria's tragic personal experience, but also by facts and figures provided by Brain Tumour Research.

Second, it was on a subject that isn't party political. All of the witnesses who gave evidence to the Committee agreed that the problems had been going on for decades, under successive governments. That made it easier for the Committee to reach a consensus about the recommendations to make—which made for a powerful, unanimous report. In the debate on the petition, MPs from all sides of the House spoke up for their constituents.

Thirdly, and perhaps most importantly, the campaigners behind the petition understood that there is more to petitioning than simply starting a petition and getting signatures. Brain tumour patients and their families across the country engaged with their MPs and asked them to take action. This not only led to a huge turnout for the petition debate, but also encouraged MPs to put pressure on the government in other ways—including asking questions to the prime minister.

CONCLUSION

We can see that a petition can play a central role in channelling support for a campaign and in raising awareness of an issue among MPs. The petition alone did not lead to a change in government policy—but it's clear that the change in policy would not have happened without the petition.

It's also important to note that, although the petition was judged to be successful, it hasn't yet achieved its aim of increasing funding. By the time the 2015 Parliament was dissolved, the work of the Task and Finish Group set up by the government had not been completed, and implementing any recommendations made will take longer still. Like many successful petition campaigns, it will have taken months or even years before the petition results in concrete action.

The role of the Petitions Committee itself was crucial in this case. Having a cross-party group of MPs reviewing government responses, with the power to conduct detailed investigations, meant that an important issue was not neglected—even though it didn't have as many signatures as more high-profile petitions. A system based purely on the number of signatures obtained by a petition would not have produced the same effect.

Primary sources

- Debate on the petition: *Brain Tumours* (HC Debates, 18 April 2016, c. 213WH). Online at: https://hansard.parliament.uk/Commons/2016-04-18/debates/16041811000001/BrainTumours [accessed 27 June 2017].

- Petitions Committee (2015) *Funding for brain tumour research web forum*, 30 October. Online at: http://www.parliament.uk/business/committees/committees-a-z/commons-select/petitions-committee/inquiries/parliament-2015/funding-for-research-into-brain-tumours/web-forum/ [accessed 21 June 2017].

- Petitions Committee (2016) *Funding for Research into Brain Tumours: First Report of Session 2015–16*, London: The Stationery Office, HC 554. Online at: https://www.publications.parliament.uk/pa/cm201516/cmselect/cmpetitions/554/554.pdf [accessed 27 June 2017].

- Petitions Committee (2016) *Funding for Research into Brain Tumours: Government Response to the Petitions Committee's First Report of Session 2015–16: First Special Report of Session 2016–17*, London: The Stationery Office, HC 292. Online at: https://www.publications.parliament.uk/pa/cm201617/cmselect/cmpetitions/292/292.pdf [accessed 27 June 2017].

- Petitions Committee (2016) *Your Petitions: A Year of Action*, London: House of Commons. Online at: http://www.parliament.uk/documents/commons-committees/petitions/Your-Petitions-A-Year-of-Action.pdf [accessed 27 June 2017].

FURTHER CASE STUDIES

- Oral and written evidence on the Meningitis B petition and respective debate (March and April 2016).
- Web forum on the petition about high heels and workplace dress codes (June 2016) and respective inquiry report (January 2017).
- Oral evidence and debate on the petition about grouse shooting (October 2016).

References

AUDICKAS, L., HAWKINS, O., and CRACKNELL, R. (2017) *UK Election Statistics: 1918–2017*, House of Commons Library Briefing Paper Number 16/17, 27 April. Online at: http://researchbriefings. files.parliament.uk/documents/CBP-7529/CBP-7529.pdf [accessed 25 June 2017].

BBC NEWS (2017) 'Election 2017: The result in maps and charts', *BBC News*, 10 June. Online at: http://www.bbc.co.uk/news/election-2017-40176349 [accessed 11 June 2017].

BOCHEL, C. (2013) 'Petitions Systems: Contributing to Representative Democracy?', *Parliamentary Affairs*, Vol. 66 (4), pp. 798–815.

DALTON, R. J., SCARROW, S. E., and CAIN, B. E. (2004) 'Advanced Democracies and the New Politics', *Journal of Democracy*, Vol. 15 (1), pp. 124–38.

HANSARD SOCIETY (2015) *Audit of Political Engagement 12*, London: Hansard Society. Online at: https://assets.contentful.com/xkbace0jm9pp/3Rh8DJ77x6QGOG6Ei020kS/ dc15490944711a83936ce24107230242/Audit_of_Political_Engagement_12__2015_.PDF [accessed 25 June 2017].

HANSARD SOCIETY (2016). *Audit of Political Engagement 13*, London: Hansard Society. Online at: https://assets.contentful.com/u1rlvvbs33ri/24aY1mkabGU0uEsoUOekGW/ 06380afa29a63008e97fb41cdb8dcad0/Publication__Audit-of-Political-Engagement-13. pdf [accessed 25 June 2017].

HAY, C. (2007) *Why we Hate Politics*, Cambridge: Polity Press.

HOUSE OF COMMONS INFORMATION OFFICE (2010) *Public Petitions*, House of Commons Information Office Factsheet P7, London: House of Commons. Online at: https://www.parliament. uk/documents/commons-information-office/P07.pdf [accessed 25 June 2017].

HOUSE OF COMMONS PROCEDURE COMMITTEE (2014) *E-petitions: A Collaborative System: Third Report of Session 2014–15*, London: The Stationery Office, HC 235. Online at: http://www. publications.parliament.uk/pa/cm201415/cmselect/cmproced/235/235.pdf [accessed 25 June 2017].

LESTON-BANDEIRA, C. (2017) 'What is the point of petitions in British Politics?', *LSE British Politics and Policy Blog*, 7 February. Online at: http://blogs.lse.ac.uk/politicsandpolicy/what- is-the-point-of-petitions/ [accessed 25 June 2017].

NORRIS, P. (1999) 'Introduction: The Growth of Critical Citizens?' in P. Norris (ed.), *Critical Citizens: Global Support for Democratic Governance*, Oxford: Oxford University Press, pp. 1–28.

NORTON, P. (2005) *Parliament in British Politics*, Basingstoke: Palgrave Macmillan.

PETITIONS COMMITTEE (2015) *Funding for brain tumour research web forum*, 30 October. Online at: http://www.parliament.uk/business/committees/committees-a-z/commons-select/ petitions-committee/inquiries/parliament-2015/funding-for-research-into-brain-tumours/ web-forum/ [accessed 21 June 2017].

PETITIONS COMMITTEE (2016) *Funding for Research into Brain Tumours: First Report of Session 2015–16*, London: The Stationery Office, HC 554. Online at: https://www.publications.parliament.uk/pa/cm201516/cmselect/cmpetitions/554/554.pdf [accessed 25 June 2017].

PETITIONS COMMITTEE (2017) *Letter from the Chair to the Secretary of State for Health and reply*, 28 March. Online at: https://www.parliament.uk/documents/commons-committees/petitions/Letter-from-Chair-to-Secretary-of-State-for-Health-and-reply-March17.pdf?utm_source=Petition&utm_medium=email&utm_campaign=174988&utm_content=chair_leter_DOH [accessed 25 June 2017].

STOKER, G. (2006) *Why Politics Matters: Making Democracy Work*, Basingstoke: Palgrave Macmillan.

UK GOVERNMENT AND PARLIAMENT (2017) *Fund more research into brain tumours, the biggest cancer killer of under-40s*, Government response to petition, 3 February. Online at: https://petition.parliament.uk/petitions/105560 [accessed 25 June 2017].

UK PARLIAMENT (2016) *Ask your MP to present a petition*. Online at: http://www.parliament.uk/get-involved/sign-a-petition/paper-petitions/ [accessed 6 September 2016].

31

Parliament and Freedom of Information

Ben Worthy

INTRODUCTION

This chapter examines the impact of the UK's Freedom of Information (FOI) Act 2000 on Parliament. Since 2005, the law has, as many hoped, helped make both Houses of Parliament more open and accountable. The most high-profile effect of the law came in 2009 when FOI played a part in exposing the abuse of the expense allowance system. This led to the resignation of a number of MPs and the Speaker of the House of Commons, as well as a series of knock-on reforms, including the creation of an independent body, IPSA (Independent Parliamentary Standards Authority), to oversee MPs' expenses, and a new Recall Act introducing a process in which a sitting MP can be removed by public petition. Whether FOI has transformed the culture of the two institutions is less clear, despite the scandal. But what it has done is indirectly kick-started a series of other reforms, so that FOI now sits alongside a whole range of instruments, from e-petitions to Open Data, intended to make Parliament more open and accessible. This chapter reviews what FOIs consist of, their application to legislatures and Westminster specifically, before discussing the extent of the impact of the FOI Act on the UK Parliament.

 Parliamentary terms IPSA (Independent Parliamentary Standards Authority)

An independent body which determines MPs' pay and pension arrangements and regulates MPs' allowances.

FOI and legislatures

At their heart, Freedom of Information (FOI) laws are about opening up institutions to make them more transparent and accountable. It is hoped that these laws can also increase public trust, by making institutions less secretive, and help to create more open and participative cultures.

FOI laws, also known as Access to Information or Right to Information, give citizens (and often anyone) a legal right to get information held by a public body within a certain time frame, subject to certain exclusions around national security, personal information, and policymaking. Most laws have an independent appeal system, as in the UK where there is a commissioner (Independent Commission on Freedom of Information) and then a tribunal with the possibility of further appeal through the courts. Although there are now 100 countries with some form of access to information legislation, not all of them cover legislatures—this means that not all legislatures have a statutory duty to disclose information. The United States Congress is famously not covered by the US Freedom of Information Act (US Department of Justice 2016), whereas the Indian Parliament is covered under its 2005 Right to Information Act (Indian Government 2005).

There is some wariness over making legislatures subject to FOI (Snell and Upcher 2002). This stems from fears that it could hinder their work and open up a number of sensitive areas, from constituent–Member correspondence to select committee confidentiality; or that it could breach long held legal privileges. Snell and Upcher (2002) spoke of the 'manifold problems' that placing FOI atop a Westminster parliamentary system can create. It is often 'depicted as a threat or hindrance' to the smooth and confidential running of legislatures with the potential to undermine 'important constitutional and other conventions of traditional governance'(Snell and Upcher 2002, 35).

FOI and Westminster 2005–16

The UK FOI Act came into force in 2005 and covers more than 100,000 public bodies, including the House of Commons and House of Lords for their administrative work. FOI covers both Houses separately, but MPs or peers are not covered as individuals; only the information that the institutions of Parliament hold comes under the law (Worthy 2013). Originally, the draft law was not intended to cover Parliament, but both Houses were added at a later stage without, it seems, much discussion or thought (Hazell, Worthy, and Bourke 2012). As well as the general protections in the law, both Houses of Parliament also have a special exclusion power. Under section 34 of the Act, the Speaker of the House of Commons or the Clerk of the Parliaments in the House of Lords can issue an exemption if the request infringes parliamentary privilege. The exemption, called a certificate, is designed to protect parliamentary privilege, or to avoid 'prejudice to the effective conduct of public affairs'.

 Parliamentary terms Parliamentary privilege

Legal immunity granted to MPs and peers—such as freedom of speech—to enable them to do their jobs.

Patterns of use

Use of FOI laws generally increases over time. Requests to both Houses have grown since the Act came into force, and numbers almost quadrupled in the first five years—from 259 requests in 2005, to 910 in 2009 (Worthy and Bourke 2011, 8). For the last few years, levels have stayed mostly somewhere above 800 a year, meaning a rate of just over two requests per day, as Table 31.1 shows. They have also become more complex as requesters become more experienced and learn to ask more detailed and lengthier questions.

On the issue of whether Westminster is more open as a result, a 2011 study found that 'the most common result of requests to Parliament has been full disclosure (where all the information is released), in contrast to the accusations made about Parliament's inherent

Table 31.1 FOI requests to Parliament 2010–16

Year	House of Commons	House of Lords	Total
2010	634	n.a.	n.a.
2011	475	179	654
2012	514	205	719
2013	646	213	859
2014	621	232	853
2015	604	250	854
2016	573	203	776

Source: House of Commons and House of Lords Disclosure Logs (2016)

secretiveness or derision of the Act' (Worthy and Bourke 2011, 9). Somewhere around 30–40 per cent of requests result in full disclosure, with another 10–20 per cent partially answered (Worthy and Bourke 2011, 9). A significant proportion appear to be sent incorrectly to Parliament (Worthy and Bourke 2011). On the whole, around a third or more of FOIs are fully answered, with Parliament being fully transparent.

In terms of where the requests go, the House of Commons receives far more than the Lords, with a roughly 80 to 20 per cent split. The actual centre of interest lies with MPs and their activities, and nearly 50 per cent of all requests relate to these. Likewise, for the House of Lords, peers and what they do are the main focus. Catering is also a popular area for requests for both Houses, especially around money owed by Members, public subsidies of food, drink, or alcohol sold. As Table 31.2 shows, aside from these broad patterns, request topics are highly variable, covering all sorts of topics, from freemasonry membership to fracking and fist fights. They go from large issues or stories in the media, to focused questions on a particular Member or topic.

As Snell (2001) points out, any FOI regime is 'unpredictable in terms of requestor, type of request, timing and outcome' and 'government information management techniques are apt to be portrayed as excessive secrecy or cover-ups': so any denial (even if legal under the Act) is often met with complaints that something is being covered up or kept secret (Snell 2001, 188). FOI is often used by a mixture of members of the public, NGOs, businesses, and journalists, all with very different motives and aims (Worthy and Hazell 2017). A 2010 estimate of requests to Westminster suggested that 17 per cent came from the media, 12 per cent were made through an online FOI-portal WhatDoTheyKnow. com (which allows people to publish their requests and responses), and 71 per cent were from an unidentifiable source, probably members of the public and NGOs (Hazell, Worthy, and Bourke 2012). For Parliament, it is likely that there is a greater proportion of NGOs and journalists, and that some requests represent 'fishing' expeditions to see what can be found. It is such use by journalists that frequently attracts attention and causes controversy.

In other countries members of the legislature make frequent use of access laws (Mendel 2005). Interestingly, in the UK, a small band of MPs and peers have themselves become regular users of the law (Worthy 2014b). Although small in number, parliamentarians' requests can generate waves and publicity. The Libor banking scandal, tax status of peers, and lists of visitors to the prime minister's country residence (Chequers), have all been unearthed by MPs (Worthy 2014a).

Table 31.2 A sample of FOI requests to the House of Commons and House of Lords, 2016

House of Commons

Ethnicity of House staff

Serjeant's expenses for the last five years

Speaker's expenses for last five years

Reports of flooded toilets on the Parliamentary Estate

Consumption of alcohol in Members' bars and restaurants

Business case for restoration of encaustic tiles

Businesses with a fracking license and MPs with an interest

Filming by specified member on the Parliamentary Estate

MPs with a disability

MPs who have had the most warnings since 2010 (formal or informal) for misconduct

List of passes MP has sponsored during parliamentary career

Correspondence between the Speaker and MP

House of Lords

Percentage of staff from ethnic minorities—of those, how many of Muslim faith

Expense claims and costs incurred by Black Rod in each of the last five years

Charles I death warrant

Copies of menus and details of catering subsidy

Access to closed security files in the archives

Spending on pest control in the House of Lords in each of last six years

Contributions towards pensions of senior staff

Vellum printing costs

Top 500 website visits October 2015 to January 2016

Development of nuclear energy projects in the UK, meetings, documents, and correspondence January 2013

Source: House of Commons and House of Lords Disclosure Logs (2016)

What impact has FOI had?

One of the common questions about FOI is whether it has helped to cultivate a more open culture in Parliament. Undoubtedly it has led to more information being disclosed. Information released has covered everything from the restaurant tabs of MPs, CO_2 emissions of its buildings, costs of construction of the Visitors Centre, details of peers with criminal convictions, and the use of parliamentary facilities by outside organizations (Hazell, Worthy, and Bourke 2012). The Act mandates proactive disclosure (without requests) of certain categories of information, and both Houses have also published material on decision-making, administrative background documents, and spending data.

The key question though is whether MPs and officials have embraced the idea of openness or been 'dragged' or forced towards it. Parliament was already a relatively open institution with a public written record, televised proceedings, and public access: the number of questions asked informally to the information office each year far outstrips the number of FOIs made (Hazell, Worthy, and Bourke 2012).

Assessments of whether Parliament has a more 'open' culture because of FOI are divided: in the Hazell, Worthy, and Bourke (2012) study some officials and MPs felt Parliament had a much more transparent way of doing things, while others felt the institution was just going through the motions. One major study concluded that 'FOI has had an impact on "house-keeping" arrangements, but culturally the Commons and Lords have changed less' (Worthy and Bourke 2011, 12). An examination by the Ministry of Justice of FOI in 2011 concluded:

> Parliament has become more transparent; whereas it has always published the proceedings of debates and committee hearings, it now makes available details of parliamentarians' expenses and 'inner workings' of parliamentary facilities that were not previously released. (Ministry of Justice 2011, 85)

Perhaps Westminster can be contrasted with the approach of the newer devolved legislatures. The Scottish Parliament dealt with expenses requests by publishing all the details of its MSPs' expenses when a request was made (Winetrobe 2008). It adopted, therefore, very early on, a more active approach to information, by making it available without the need for requests. Westminster has developed towards the same approach, though not to the same extent.

FOI has also produced accountability in both Houses, from passes for lobbyists to restoration costs and pest infestation. *The Daily Telegraph* claimed that the leakers of expenses information felt MPs were abusing the system and 'no one could hold them to account' (Winnett and Rayner 2009, 359). For a few Members, the expenses scandal meant the ultimate accountability before the law. There is also a continual lower hum of questions and accountability over everything from cost of MPs' portraits to bar bills. FOI requests also reopened an old type of scandal in July 2007, over lobbying access. Both Germany and Hungary have seen similar scandals exposed by their own FOI laws.

However, because requests focus on MPs and peers, some have argued it leads to a focus on small issues, or trivia. MPs and peers have claimed that FOI provides a 'patchy' sort of accountability that is mainly media driven and depended on what was being asked for (Hazell, Worthy, and Bourke 2012). However, there was no 'expenses election' in 2010, partly because so many MPs stepped down and in part because the voting system and electorate didn't work that way (Pattie and Johnston 2012; Vivyan, Wagner, and Tarlov 2014—see Case Study 31).

As it exposes by its nature, FOI raises uncomfortable headlines. Use by journalists attracts attention because of the headlines it generates, sometimes with a focus on small or controversial issues, as Table 31.3 shows. As the Justice Committee (2012, 18) pointed out, such friction is inevitable in an environment such as the UK:

> Evidence of irregularities, deficiencies and errors is always likely to prove more newsworthy than evidence that everything is being done by the book and the public authority is operating well. Greater release of data is invariably going to lead to greater openness ... which may sometimes be unfair or partial.

Despite the concerns of FOI damaging delicate areas, there is no evidence of any negative impact on the sensitive areas of what Parliament does. Parliamentary Privilege exemption (s.34) was used (partially) in 5 per cent of cases in the first four years by the Commons, on only 11 occasions by the Lords, and roughly around 2 per cent of the time by the House of Commons since then (Hazell, Worthy, and Bourke 2012).

Nevertheless, the media exposure and questions raised by FOI led to some resistance. In 2007, David Maclean MP proposed a private member's bill designed to exempt both Houses from the FOI Act in a process that involved some collusion between the government and opposition frontbenches. There were also a series of minor attempts to alter the

Table 31.3 Selected FOI-based newspaper headlines, 2016

'Taxpayers fund more than £3.7m of subsidised food and drink in Parliament's bars and restaurants' (*MailOnline*, 4 August 2016)
'MPs' security under review despite being beefed up this year over fears about lack of protection from gun and knife-wielding attackers' (*MailOnline*)
'£6K SUITS' (*The Sun*, 16 June 2016)
'MPs freeze booze prices in their subsidised bars—as they pocket another inflation-busting pay rise' (*MailOnline* 6 April 2016)
'MPs order, order, order £1.2m worth of alcohol' (*Daily Mirror*, 15 March 2016)
'SNP Party Members among the 14 MPs who had official House of Commons credit cards suspended after racking up £58,000 worth of expenses debts' (*Daily Record*, 5 March 2016)
'Ian Paisley has his credit card blocked after running up parliamentary expenses debts of £27,000' (*Belfast Telegraph*, 4 March 2016)

Sources: Hayes 2009; Burgess 2015

application of FOI in 2008 and 2009, and there has been continual low-intensity warfare with the Independent Parliamentary Standards Authority (IPSA)—the independent body established to oversee MPs use of their expenses (see Case Study 31)—often fought across the media, as MPs resent the intrusion but also feel mistakes are made (for which they are blamed) (Gay 2014).

Overall, the arrival of FOI has changed the UK Parliament and how it works. Many of the indirect effects came through the MPs' expenses scandal of 2009 that exposed abuse of the expenses system. The reforms that followed in its wake included the 'Wright reforms' to select committees (see Chapter 28), and the Recall Act of 2015 that allows constituents, in certain circumstances, to trigger a recall election against a sitting MP (Russell 2011; Wright 2015). The ongoing plans to reduce the size of the House of Commons to 600 MPs may be another distinct unintended legacy.

FOI has also altered a number of regulations and arrangements in both Houses. An FOI request by MP Gordon Prentice highlighted irregularities in tax status, focusing on peer (and Conservative Party donor) Lord Ashcroft. As a result of this, the Constitutional Reform and Governance Act of 2010 altered the law so that Members of the House of Lords must be tax domiciled in the UK. MPs' use of credit card and payment systems also changed as a result of requests (Worthy and Bourke 2011).

The FOI law was part of a long line of reforms designed to open up Parliament, from the battle over the publication of Hansard in the early 1800s, to the televising of debates in 1989. FOI laws do not exist in isolation. Examining the law a decade after it was passed, it now fits within a wider set of changes designed to open up and engage the public—stretching from e-participation, to Open Data, and the recent Speaker's Commission on digital democracy. There are also a range of online innovations, some from Parliament itself, such as the Lords Digital Chamber, a new mobile device app to more easily see how MPs voted, to third-party innovations such as mySociety's TheyWorkForYou.com and the voting website PublicWhip. The push towards legislative openness is now worldwide, being championed by the Open Government Partnership. New developments, such as the metric Open Parliament Data, that crowdsources a comparable metric of how open various legislatures around the world are, offer new ways to push for more transparent legislatures (Open Parliament 2016).

Conclusion

The FOI Act has now been in force for over a decade and it has had a wide-ranging impact. Some of this lies in the revelation of parts which remained hidden until recently; some lies in a change of practice towards a disclosure-first approach. Although the use of FOIs may often seem to focus on trivia, they do also address serious issues and remain an important tool for the public, parliamentarians, NGOs, and journalists alike. At a time when Westminster may now come under considerably more pressure as it paves the way for Brexit, the actions of parliamentarians and public scrutiny will become stronger. On the other hand, MPs and peers may be more inclined to use FOIs if the government is, in their view, too secretive about what's happening. Whatever the future holds, FOI will play a role.

Further Reading

HAZELL, R., WORTHY, B., and BOURKE, G. (2012) 'Open House: Freedom of Information and its Impact on the UK Parliament', *Public Administration*, Vol. 90 (4), pp. 901–21.

SNELL, R. and UPCHER, J. (2002) 'Freedom of information and Parliament: A limited accountability tool for a key constituency?', *Freedom of Information Review*, Vol. 100, pp. 35–41.

WORTHY, B. (2014) 'Freedom of Information and the MPs' Expenses Crisis' in J. vanHeerde-Hudson (ed.), *The Political Costs of the 2009 British MPs' Expenses Scandal*, London: Palgrave, pp. 27–43.

WORTHY, B. and BOURKE, G. (2011) *The Sword and the Shield: The use of FOI by Parliamentarians and the Impact of FOI on Parliament*, London: Constitution Unit.

Case Study 31: The MPs' expenses scandal of 2009

In 2005, a group of journalists and an MP made a series of FOI requests relating to how MPs used their expenses under the Additional Cost Allowance scheme. Following a series of appeal rulings and a long-running court case, the details of all MPs' expenses claims were leaked to *The Daily Telegraph* in May 2009. The resulting scandal led to a number of resignations, prosecutions, and a series of reform attempts, though it ultimately led to less far-reaching change than many hoped or expected. This case study explores the factors which led to the MPs' expenses scandal and the impact that this had on Parliament.

CONTEXT

In 2009, David Cameron, the then Leader of the Opposition, managed to utterly misunderstand or misrepresent the expenses crisis:

> What *The Daily Telegraph* did –the simple act of providing information to the public –has triggered the biggest shake-up of our political system. It is information –not a new law, not some regulation –just the provision of information that has enabled people to take on the political class, demand answers and gets those answers. (David Cameron, quoted in Winnett and Rayner 2009, 348)

In this brief statement Cameron managed to view the facts and draw all the wrong conclusions: it was a new law, it wasn't citizens, and there was not quite a 'radical shake-up' afterwards. The MPs' expenses crisis happened as a result of a law (passed by a Labour government), a legal process (from appeal to High Court), and an old-fashioned (and paid for) leak. The fierce reaction of the authorities once FOI requests were submitted, and the structure of the Commons—that left the process of dealing with the FOIs leaderless—did the rest.

THE TRIGGERING OF THE SCANDAL

The roots of the crisis lie further in the past in the obscure and self-serving expenses system, called the Additional Cost Allowance, and an agreement concocted informally by Michael Foot and Margaret Thatcher in the 1980s to allow MPs to quietly 'top up' salaries from their expenses (though a group of MPs already published details of their expenses voluntarily—see Allington and Peele 2010; Little and Stopforth 2013). A series of FOI requests over expenses in 2005 by a group of journalists for 14 selected MPs' expenses from various years were initially refused. These gradually worked their way through the appeals system, triggering hostility and denial.

Following some embarrassing revelations in the Upper Tribunal, and growing suspicion in the media that there was something to hide, a Supreme Court ruling ordered publication. Before the redacted data could be released, unhappy ex-servicemen working on the documents leaked the information to *The Daily Telegraph* who published the full details in May 2009.

For a few Members of the Commons, the consequences were severe. Five MPs faced prison as a result of the revelations, and the Speaker of the House of Commons, Michael Martin, had to resign. Perhaps more importantly, the damage done to the institution's reputation was considerable, and nearly a quarter of MPs decided to step down at the next election, creating a significant turnover in MPs. Since 2009, FOI revelations have highlighted other issues, including MPs renting houses from other MPs, the cost of Member's portraits, and the Commons' and Lords' bar bills. The details of expenses use has also continued to claim careers past and present and led to several high-profile resignations since 2009, including one serving minister, David Laws, in 2010, and one former minister, Denis MacShane, in 2012.

IMPACT OF THE EXPENSES SCANDAL ON PARLIAMENT

The initial media and public attention focused on high-profile and unusual uses of parliamentary expenses, such as attempted claims for a duck house or moat cleaning. This meant a wide variety of claims—from the trivial, to very serious allegations of tax avoidance—were mixed together and not fully understood (Kelso 2009). Although the leak was given on the promise of treating all politicians equally, *The Daily Telegraph* focused on the government, giving the Conservative opposition time to defend itself, and emphasizing less, for example, David Cameron's use of £80,000 of his Commons Additional Costs Allowance to pay his mortgage for five years.

The expenses scandal changed Parliament in several ways. Perhaps the lasting institutional legacy for Parliament was the creation of the Independent Parliamentary Standards Authority (IPSA), an independent body that oversees MPs use of their expenses. The body has proved controversial, with constant conflict and complaints over its operation and work, including threats by then Prime Minister David Cameron to abolish it (Gay 2014). MPs have continued to criticize IPSA for what it claims is excessive, heavy-handed regulation and bureaucracy, but with little public sympathy.

The scandal also triggered broader constitutional change and discussion, leading to an offer of alternative voting (AV) reform from the Labour government, and David Cameron's promise to cut the number of MPs from 653 to 600 (Renwick, Lamb, and Numan 2011). It also led to a series of reforms, as identified in this chapter, such as the Wright reforms to select committees and the 2015 Recall Act, with the new law (as yet unused) allowing the public, in certain circumstances, to trigger a recall election for misbehaving Members (Russell 2011; Wright 2015).

However, in two areas the scandal made no difference: voting and trust. The scandal took place a year before the May 2010 general election, but, despite media hype, voters were unwilling or unable to turn the vote into an 'expenses' election. This was in part because so much else, from 13 years of Labour in power, to the 2007 banking crisis, dominated the campaign. One study concluded that voters lacked the information and the tools: they were unaware if their MP had abused their expenses, and the first-past-the-post system was not designed for such direct accountability (Vivyan, Wagner, and Tarlov 2014). There were small signs that, for example, female MPs suffered more than their male counterparts, and that Labour voters were less forgiving than Conservative (Larcinese and Sircar 2012).

The lasting impact on trust is also unclear. Trust levels straight after the scandal dropped considerably, but have since been moving back upwards (see Chapter 29)—though it may be argued that this is as a result of reform initiatives undertaken exactly to address the damage caused by the scandal. The Hansard Society (2010) found that the expenses scandal, to many, acted as a confirmation of public suspicion, rather than a revelation. Though the public were undoubtedly angered, the media frenzy may have desensitized already cynical citizens (Allen and Birch 2014). In this sense, the expenses scandal 'lit up the sky but did not change the underlying terrain' (Allen and Birch 2014, 148).

CONCLUSION

Westminster is undoubtedly more open and accountable due to FOI, though exactly how much more is a matter of debate. The Act, and especially the MPs' expenses scandal, has also helped trigger changes to a wide range of areas, from select committee powers to tax residency rules. However, FOI only highlights some areas and activities, and may not create a more 'open' culture. The law also works best with other tools: and it took journalists, long court cases, and a paid-for leak to really see the whole picture of expenses. Nor does openness and exposure always bring reform. For all the hopes of a radical shake-up, the change has been, on the whole, limited and incremental.

Primary sources

- Freedom of Information Act (2000) c. 36. Online at: http://www.legislation.gov.uk/ukpga/2000/36/contents [accessed 27 June 2017].

- House of Commons (2016) *Freedom of Information Request Logs*. Online at: https://www.parliament.uk/site-information/foi/foi-and-eir/commons-request-disclosure-logs/ [accessed 27 June 2017].

- House of Lords (2016) *Freedom of Information Disclosure Logs*. Online at: http://www.parliament.uk/mps-lords-and-offices/offices/lords/freedom-of-information-in-the-house-of-lords/log/ [accessed 27 June 2017].

→ FURTHER CASE STUDIES

- 'After the duck house … where MPs' expenses went next', *The Guardian*, 17 May 2016: https://www.theguardian.com/politics/2016/may/17/mps-expenses-martin-williams-parliament-ltd

- 'MPs spend £250,000 of public money on vanity portraits', *Evening Standard*, 13 January 2014: https://www.standard.co.uk/news/politics/mps-spend-250000-of-public-money-on-vanity-portraits-9056130.html

- The work undertaken by the IPSA.

References

ALLEN, N. and BIRCH, S. (2014) 'Tempests and Teacups: Politicians' Reputations in the Wake of the Expenses Scandal' in J. vanHeerde-Hudson (ed.), *The Political Costs of the 2009 British MPs' Expenses Scandal*, Basingstoke: Palgrave Macmillan, pp. 132–52.

ALLINGTON, N. F. B. and PEELE, G. (2010) 'Moats, Duckhouses and Bath Plugs: Members of Parliament, the Expenses Scandal and Use of Web Sites', *Parliamentary Affairs*, Vol. 63 (3), pp. 385–406.

BURGESS, M. (2015) *Freedom of Information: A Practical Guide for UK Journalists*, London: Routledge.

GAY, O. (2014) 'The New Regime: The Role of IPSA' in J. vanHeerde-Hudson (ed.), *The Political Costs of the 2009 British MPs' Expenses Scandal*, Basingstoke: Palgrave Macmillan, pp. 175–95.

HANSARD SOCIETY (2010) *Audit of Political Engagement 7: The 2010 Report with a Focus on MPs and Parliament*, London: Hansard Society.

HAYES, J. (2009) *A Shock To The System: Journalism, Government and the Freedom of Information Act 2000*. Online at: http://reutersinstitute.politics.ox.ac.uk/publication/shock-system [accessed 12 November 2015].

HAZELL, R., WORTHY, B., and BOURKE, G. (2012) 'Open House: Freedom of Information and its Impact on the UK Parliament', *Public Administration*, Vol. 90 (4), pp. 901–21.

HOUSE OF COMMONS (2016) *Freedom of Information Request Logs*. Online at: https://www.parliament.uk/site-information/foi/foi-and-eir/commons-request-disclosure-logs/ [accessed 27 June 2017].

HOUSE OF LORDS (2016) *Freedom of Information Disclosure Logs*. Online at: http://www.parliament.uk/mps-lords-and-offices/offices/lords/freedom-of-information-in-the-house-of-lords/log/ [accessed 27 June 2017].

INDIAN GOVERNMENT (2005) *Right to Information Act*, Ministry of Law and Justice, Act no. 22 of 2005. Online at: http://righttoinformation.gov.in/rti-act.pdf [accessed 27 June 2017].

JUSTICE COMMITTEE (2012) *Post-legislative Scrutiny of the Freedom of Information Act 2000: First Report of Session 2012–13*, London: The Stationery Office, HC 96-I. Online at: https://publications.parliament.uk/pa/cm201213/cmselect/cmjust/96/96.pdf [accessed 24 August 2017].

KELSO, A. (2009) 'Parliament on its knees: MPs' expenses and the Crisis of Transparency at Westminster', *Political Quarterly*, Vol. 80 (3), pp. 329–38.

LARCINESE, V. and SIRCAR, I. (2012) *Crime and Punishment the British Way: Accountability Channels Following the MPs' Expenses Scandal*, Political Science and Political Economy Working Paper (09/12), London School of Economics.

LITTLE, G. and STOPFORTH, D. (2013) 'The Legislative Origins of the MPs' Expenses Scandal', *The Modern Law Review*, Vol. 76 (1), pp. 83–108.

MENDEL, T. (2005) *Parliament and Access to Information: Working for Transparent Governance*, Washington, DC: World Bank/ Commonwealth Parliamentary Association. Online at: http://siteresources.worldbank.org/WBI/Resources/Parliament_and_Access_to_Information_with_cover.pdf [accessed 24 August 2017].

MINISTRY OF JUSTICE (2011) *Memorandum to the Justice Select Committee*, London: The Stationery Office.

OPEN PARLIAMENT (2016) Data. Online at: beta.openparldata.org/explore/ [accessed 27 June 2017].

PATTIE, C. and JOHNSTON, R. (2012) 'The electoral impact of the UK 2009 MPs' expenses scandal', *Political Studies*, Vol. 60 (4), pp. 730–50.

RENWICK, A., LAMB, M., and NUMAN, B. (2011) 'The expenses scandal and the politics of electoral reform', *The Political Quarterly*, Vol. 82 (1), pp. 32–41.

RUSSELL, M. (2011) 'Never Allow a Crisis Go To Waste: The Wright Committee Reforms to Strengthen the House of Commons', *Parliamentary Affairs*, Vol. 64 (4), pp. 612–33.

SNELL, R. (2001) 'Administrative compliance—evaluating the effectiveness of freedom of information', *Freedom of Information Review*, Vol. 93, pp. 26–37. Online at: http://papers.ssrn.com/abstract=2540700 [accessed 24 August 2017].

SNELL, R. and UPCHER, J. (2002) 'Freedom of information and parliament: A limited accountability tool for a key constituency?', *Freedom of Information Review*, Vol. 100, pp. 35–41.

US DEPARTMENT OF JUSTICE (2016) *The Freedom of Information Act (FOIA), 5 U.S.C. § 552*. Online at: https://www.justice.gov/oip/freedom-information-act-5-usc-552 [accessed 27 June 2017].

VIVYAN, N., WAGNER, M., and TARLOV, J. (2014) 'Where did electoral accountability fail? MP misconduct, constituent perceptions and vote choice' in J. vanHeerde-Hudson (ed.), *The Political Costs of the 2009 British MPs' Expenses Scandal*, Basingstoke: Palgrave Macmillan, pp. 111–31.

WINETROBE, B. K. (2008) 'Precedent vs Principle: the Convergence of the UK and the Scottish Parliaments', draft paper, Wroxton Workshop, July 2008.

WINNETT, R. and RAYNER, G. (2009) *No Expenses Spared*, London: Bantam Press.

WORTHY, B. (2013) 'Freedom of Information and Parliament' in D. Oliver (ed.), *Parliament and the Law*, Oxford: Hart Press, pp. 139–60.

WORTHY, B. (2014a) 'A Powerful Weapon in the Right Hands? How Members of Parliament have used Freedom of Information in the UK', *Parliamentary Affairs*, Vol. 67 (4), pp. 783–803.

WORTHY, B. (2014b) 'Freedom of Information and the MPs' Expenses Crisis' in J. VanHeerde-Hudson (ed.), *The Political Costs of the 2009 British MPs' Expenses Scandal*, Basingstoke: Palgrave Macmillan, pp. 27–43.

WORTHY, B. and BOURKE, G. (2011) *The Sword and the Shield: The use of FOI by Parliamentarians and the Impact of FOI on Parliament*, London: Constitution Unit.

WORTHY, B. and HAZELL, R. (2017) 'Disruptive, Dynamic and Democratic? Ten Years of Freedom of Information in the UK', *Parliamentary Affairs*, Vol. 70 (1), pp. 22–42.

WRIGHT, T. (2015) 'Recalling MPs: Accountable to Whom?', *The Political Quarterly*, Vol. 86 (2), pp. 289–96.

PART VII

Concluding Thoughts

32

Conclusion: The Future of Parliamentary Politics

David Judge, Cristina Leston-Bandeira,
and Louise Thompson

Political scientists have a mixed record in predicting the political future; and so, as political scientists, we won't engage in expansive 'futurology' and 'guestimates' about the future of Parliament in this chapter. Instead, in exploring the future of parliamentary politics, we will invoke the words often attributed to Albert Einstein: 'The future is an unknown, but a somewhat predictable unknown. To look to the future we must first look back upon the past.' If we can identify what Parliament was and is, and what it did and still does—which has been the central connecting thread interwoven through the preceding chapters—then we can provide a basis for exploring what we might expect Parliament to be and do in the future. Individually, the previous 31 chapters of this book have explored what Parliament does and why it does what it does. Collectively, these chapters provide an overarching assessment of the contemporary significance of Parliament in the UK's political system by revealing what it 'is' as an institution. While it is not our intention to reprise the analyses of earlier chapters, it is our intention, however, to identify key puzzles implicit in these analyses which raise fundamental questions about what Parliament is and why it exists. In turn, this will help us to identify the 'predictable unknowns' as starting points for exploring the future.

'Predictable unknowns': puzzles and functions

Gerhard Loewenberg, one of the pre-eminent analysts of parliaments in modern times, has argued that 'legislatures are puzzling institutions' inasmuch as they 'are unlike other political institutions' (2011, 1). In making this case he maintains that there are three principal puzzles that need 'hard thinking' in order to understand legislatures: representation; collective decision-making (in terms of internal organization and procedure); and their role in the political system (as connectors between government and the public). In identifying these three primary puzzles, Loewenberg echoes a set of three key functions ascribed earlier, by Copeland and Patterson (1994), to legislatures—linkage, decision-making, and legitimation. The importance of these interlinked functions is elemental 'because a parliament's very reason for existence is found in them', and changes in claims surrounding these institutional functions 'go to the heart of [their] role in a political system' (Copeland and Patterson 1994, 154). To understand the possible futures of Parliament we need, therefore, to understand the past puzzles and associated functions that have defined Parliament as an institution (what it is) and its roles within the wider political system (what it does), and to use these to structure our discussion of the 'predictable unknowns' facing the UK Parliament.

Thinking hard about representation and linkage

The 'who', 'what', and 'how' questions

The chapters in Part V outlined the contemporary significance of representation in Parliament and the changing emphases and tensions observable in answering the 'who', 'what', and how' questions of representation. The 'who' question focuses attention on the similarity (or otherwise) of social characteristics between those represented and their representatives, and has increasingly found an answer in calls to enhance descriptive representation. At the heart of a definition of descriptive representation is the idea of shared experiences whereby representatives are 'in some sense typical of the larger class of persons whom they represent' (Mansbridge 1999, 644).

Historically the shared experience of greatest significance in most representative democracies, and certainly in the UK, has been locality. The contemporary significance of geographic location has been visible in voters' preferences for local candidates, as well as in constituency activity by their MPs and in the work patterns of MPs in Westminster. The impact of geographical differences, and voters' shared experiences associated with those differences, was clearly evident in the responses of MPs to Brexit in Westminster. The 2016 EU referendum exposed deep geographical divisions between Leave and Remain supporters in disparate parliamentary constituencies. These geographical differences, and voters' shared experiences associated with those differences, will undoubtedly continue to drive debate in Westminster, and determine the votes of MPs, during the course of the implementation of Brexit. The importance of these shared interests, whether conceived in terms of 'forgotten' geographical areas or of 'left behind' social groups, is that demands for Parliament to reflect more closely those interests and opinions will be amplified more forcefully in the Brexit and post-Brexit context. In the immediate future, the cross-cutting pressures on representatives whose personal referendum voting preferences are diametrically opposed to those of the vast majority of their constituents (most notably for Labour MPs) will reveal, dramatically, the complexities of the linkage relationship between the represented and their representatives.

If Brexit has reinserted the claims of the 'left behind' into the normative case for descriptive representation, the claims of women and ethnic minorities—the most forceful claims of the recent past—will continue to dominate demands for Parliament to be more like the society from which its Members are drawn. Despite the 2017 general election returning perhaps the most diverse Parliament yet (Apostolova et al. 2017), campaigners for a more socially representative Parliament continued to argue that much still remained to be done in the future. This argument had been amplified by the House of Commons' Women and Equalities Committee, which recommended that the government set a domestic target of 45 per cent representation of women in Parliament by 2030 (Women and Equalities Committee 2017, 11). The Committee was in 'no doubt that a representative and diverse House of Commons is beneficial to the effective functioning of parliamentary democracy' (ibid., 34). Equally, it was in no doubt that parliamentary effectiveness would be enhanced by 'fair representation of many different groups of people, including women, ethnic and religious minorities, lesbian, gay, bisexual and transgender people, people from diverse socioeconomic backgrounds, disabled people and more' (ibid., 34). But advocacy of 'fair representation' for multiple diverse groups brings with it future problems of intersectionality, and how to deal, both conceptually and practically, with the multidimensionality of social group identities (see Severs, Celis, and Erzeel 2016; Evans 2016).

On the specific issue of ensuring more social diversity in Westminster, political parties have had the primary responsibility in the past and have been charged with bearing 'the lion's share of responsibility' in the future (Women and Equalities Committee 2017, 34).

On the more general issue of 'what' is being represented, political parties will also be expected to perform a key future role in the 'representation of ideas'. Indeed, the primary representational focus of political parties in Westminster, in the past as well as in the present, has been the 'politics of ideas', which assumes a 'shared ideology' or 'same political viewpoint' between represented and representative. However, the simplicities of electoral competition between two dominant class-based parties, and of the internal cohesion within those parties in the Commons, are a thing of the past. Internal ideological cohesion within parliamentary parties—and between MPs and wider party members and supporters—has been stress-tested to its furthest limits by significant and reinforcing ideological fissures, all the more amplified in the post-Brexit referendum era.

These splits, in turn, have impacted on the 'how' of representation. How a representative in Parliament should act has typically been conceived in terms of a continuum defined by the polar positions of trustee and delegate. Whereas representatives and represented alike recognize the logic of delegation implicit in party support when MPs make their voting decisions in Westminster, this logic may be cross-cut in practice by alternative delegation demands emanating from an MP's constituency, or a counterposed logic of trusteeship where MPs privilege their personal consciences, or their own interpretations of a wider national interest, above the sectional interests of their party or locality. These cross-cutting representational forces were manifest in many MPs' speeches in the debate on the European Union (Notification of Withdrawal) Bill in January 2017 (see for example HC Debates, 31 January 2017, cc. 830–2, 890, 928, 981). These cross-pressures will undoubtedly continue to manifest themselves in future debates about Brexit (both as process and as policy).

Amplifying the voice of the people in the representative process

If representational linkage is likely to be more descriptive and inclusive in the future, it is also more likely to be less, or un-, mediated. While they clearly play an instrumental part in representative democracy, parties and representatives' key role as mediators between people and governance has increasingly been questioned. This has happened simultaneously through declining levels of trust in political institutions and the rise of new forms of democracy, namely direct advocacy and participatory democracy, which often sit uneasily alongside representative democracy. Whereas a standard model of representative democracy largely assigns a passive role to voters between elections, increasingly this model has been modified by participatory expectations on the part of the public, whereby citizens seek to be consulted between elections, contribute to setting the political agenda, make their own representations and inputs in the decision-making process, and monitor closely the activities of parliamentarians. These expectations have been recognized in the Westminster Parliament's prioritization of enabling the public 'to engage constructively and to have an input into parliamentary processes' (House of Commons Service 2015, 35). The chapters in Part VI have examined the extent to which this commitment has guided contemporary practice, but here we extrapolate recent trends into the near future.

The difficulties in reconciling ideas about popular sovereignty and direct public participation with notions of parliamentary sovereignty and indirect public participation in decision-making were made apparent, starkly, by the 2016 EU referendum and its aftermath. As a result, parliamentarians have become more risk-averse towards future UK-wide referendums (see Ipsos MORI 2017). Less dramatically, the tension between the inclusion of the people and their exclusion—inherent within the very concept of representative democracy (see Judge 2014)—has been manifest in the development of the UK Parliament's e-petitions system. The creation of the Petitions Committee in 2015 led to innovative and creative public engagement initiatives and resulted in immediate and notable impacts on the public policy agenda (most notably in the brain tumour and the dress code petitions). The 'inclusionary' success of the new e-petitions system, measured by the submission of 31,731 e-petitions within only 20 months of the e-petitions website going live, was, however, offset by the practical organizational 'exclusionary' restrictions, measured by the small proportion obtaining a government response (471) or the number of petition debates in Parliament (39) (Leston-Bandeira 2017, 5). More tellingly, fully 65 per cent of e-petitions were rejected in this period. The current challenges in dealing with such high volumes of petitions are clear. In the immediate future, Parliament will be required to address the questions already posed by these challenges: How to accommodate such high demand? How to distinguish between what is prudent and what is popular? How to manage public expectations? Future answers to these questions will require serious thought about how the UK Parliament can fulfil its (inclusionary) commitment to openness, engagement, and accessibility while addressing the practical (exclusionary) considerations of internal organizational efficacy, efficiency of in-house decision processes, and fulfilment of a broader civic responsibility for decision-making (in the sense of occupying an institutional space shielded from populist demands).

The tension posed by the inclusion–exclusion paradox of parliamentary democracy has also been a feature of other e-participatory initiatives at Westminster. Inclusionary intent has been apparent in: the crowdsourcing of questions for select committee scrutiny sessions, the experiment with crowdsourcing of questions to be asked at PMQs, more structured e-consultation exercises undertaken by parliamentary committees, alongside e-consultation exercises trialled by individual MPs with their constituents, and e-monitoring platforms. Yet current concerns about the capture of such initiatives—by organized publics (for example professional lobby groups) at the expense of unorganized publics and technologically voiceless publics (expressed in the term 'digital divide'); by unmediated clicktivism; by hacktivists; by unaccountable, often secretive, corporations; and by the pedlars of 'fake news'—hold the potential to be magnified in the future as the scope and penetration of digital technologies expand exponentially.

Parliament has, of course, sought to respond to the challenges of the ever-changing digital world. In 2015, the Digital Democracy Commission set a target that 'by 2020 Parliament should be fully active and digital', which had clear inclusionary intents of enabling the public to contribute to the law-making process, 'to have their say' in House of Commons debates, and of engaging people through 'an issue-based approach'. But the Commission's report was seen as 'the start of a conversation, not the end' (Digital Democracy Commission 2015, 75). A key part of this future conversation will reflect the tensions between inclusion and exclusion, between participation (input) and decision-making (output), and between the articulation and promotion of specific, often sectional interests, and the filtering and assessment of those interests against wider collective ideas about *the* public interest and *the* national interest. To date, Parliament has claimed an exclusive ability to determine and weigh the latter against the former. But this distinctive ability may yet come to be challenged in the future by emerging technologies and algorithms which enable large volumes of citizen-generated text and speech patterns to be summarized, and, on this basis, for the strength of public opinion on key issues to be estimated.

Thinking hard about collective decision-making

One of the key puzzles of parliaments identified by Loewenberg (2011, 49) is that the 'equal status of each member of a legislature presents a fundamental challenge to its capacity to reach collective decisions'. According to him, the only way to resolve this puzzle is for legislatures to accept 'an implicit hierarchy, which entails delegating authority to committees, party groups and to leaders' (ibid., 59). The chapters in Parts III and IV have examined how this delegation works in the contemporary practice of Westminster. What we aim to do here, however, is to project some of the key recent organizational and procedural developments into the future and so identify some of the 'predictable unknowns'.

What is predictable is that, just as with the puzzle of representation, technologically-assisted engagement and inclusion programmes will be a predominant feature of future thinking about law-making, scrutiny, and accountability processes in Westminster. What is predictable, equally, is that parliamentary decision-making processes will continue to be dominated by leadership hierarchies built upon interlocked government and party positions. What is less predictable, however, after the 2017 general election, is the extent to which pre-existing parliamentary norms associated with executive dominance—based on resilient parliamentary majorities—and procedural devices which, despite reforms such as the Backbench Business Committee, have privileged the executive, will be modulated in the near future as a minority government (underpinned by a small party) tests its capacity to secure the passage of its legislative programme through Parliament. In these circumstances the Commons and the Lords will remain, to use Mezey's (1979, 47) categorization, 'reactive'. In this reactive position, they will set the parameters of government action through a capacity to modify, delay, and deliberate on such action, but will normally be unable to veto it (although a hung parliament makes party management more precarious and ordinary government majorities less certain). Nonetheless, even in the prevalent circumstances of executive majorities of recent decades, the capacity to modify and exert influence over government policies should not be underestimated. Indeed, even before 2017, there was growing research evidence that Parliament's specific impact on legislative outputs and, more generally, its scrutiny of government activity through the select committee system had increased in recent decades (see Russell and Cowley 2016; Russell and Gover 2017).

Parliament's increased influence reflects both attitudinal change and procedural and organizational change (as examined in the chapters in Parts III and IV). The essence of these changes has been to challenge what Thompson (2015, 66) has called the 'culture of resistance' embedded in government to parliamentary amendment of its legislation, or what others have called an 'executive mentality' which privileges power hoarding in the hands of ministers in decision-making more generally (see Judge 1993, 143; Flinders 2002, 30; Kelso 2009, 19). This challenge to executive dominance has also been evident in some of the public engagement strategies outlined in the chapters.

Modern legislation may be complex and increasing in volume, but notable steps have been taken to make it more comprehensible to those beyond Parliament. In recent years, Parliament has modernized its online provision of legislative documents. A recognition of the need for user-friendly language and for the provision of explanatory statements alongside amendments to bills has provided a partial antidote to the almost impenetrable procedural and linguistic obscurities of the past. The House of Commons has piloted a public reading stage, building on previous government consultations on legislation, to encourage citizens to add comments and suggestions to a legislative text (see Leston-Bandeira and Thompson 2017). Select committees have been empowered to conduct pre-legislative scrutiny, on the premise that governments are more likely to make concessions to Parliament before the formal introduction of a bill at Westminster. The Liaison Committee (2015, 25) has identified the merits of this system, and has argued that, in the future, 'there is scope to go further', stressing 'the benefits of pre-legislative scrutiny in terms of improving the quality of legislation which reaches the statute book and in easing the passage of controversial, technical and complex bills'. Yet there are limits to expanding this scope. Thus, for example, in March 2017 David Davis (Brexit Secretary) made it absolutely clear that the vastly politically contentious European Union (Withdrawal) Bill would not be subject to pre-legislative scrutiny (HC Debates, 30 March 2017, c. 435), a position confirmed after the general election of 2017.

Indeed, the enormity of the legislative task of disentangling UK law from EU law in the wake of Brexit threatens to overwhelm Parliament's recent strengthened scrutiny capacity. The immediate future will be dominated not only by fundamental political debates about the meaning of Brexit and its economic, social, and constitutional consequences, but also by parallel procedural debates about the what and how of legislative scrutiny. In particular, future generations of students of Parliament will be obliged to pay far more attention to the procedures for the scrutiny of what is variously called 'delegated legislation', 'statutory instruments', or 'subordinate legislation', or what are often referred to as 'Henry VIII clauses'. In so doing, the historic problems associated with the parliamentary scrutiny of secondary legislation will be highlighted; and the significant constitutional risks arising from the wide discretionary powers afforded to governments by the use of such legislation will have to be mitigated (Constitution Committee 2017).

Simultaneously, the repatriation of legislative powers by Westminster will also re-energize territorial pressures for regional or national solutions to the problems of collective decision-making in the UK. Since late 2015 there has been provision—through the operation of English votes for English laws (EVEL)—for English, or sometimes English and Welsh, or even English and Welsh and Northern Irish MPs only to consider certain bills (or parts of bills) that apply in their part of the UK. The complexities and opacity of the procedure have generated much criticism. Indeed, just before the 2017 general election, Gover and Kenny (2017) in 'looking to the future' (of a then expected Conservative majority government) voiced 'serious concerns' that the additional legislative burden that Brexit will place on Parliament might call into question key features of EVEL. One of these was the possibility that Brexit 'could well bring to the surface new tensions and disagreements within the Conservative Party, and the EVEL procedures may become an additional site where such conflicts are played out'. These concerns were only magnified after the 2017 election when the reduction in the number of Conservative MPs in England and Wales simultaneously increased the need for even more judicious internal party management within designated EVEL procedures, as well as increasing the dependence of the government on non-English MPs to secure successful passage of 'English only' bills at the later stages of the legislative process (where a majority of UK MPs is required). In a post-Article 50 world (stretching far into the long term) and one of hung parliaments (potentially short-term), the exact future of collective decision-making at Westminster is a realm of 'unknowns'.

Thinking hard about legitimation

Historically, the UK Parliament has fused the core principles of representation, consent, and authorization into the legitimation of state policy-making processes and their outputs. The notion of parliamentary legitimation has been central to the exercise of public power by the UK state. Over time the foundational legitimation claims of the modern state have come to be associated with democratic authorization and accountability afforded by election. Moreover, Westminster, as seen in Part II, has served symbolically, through its rituals and architecture, as the epicentre of the state and the collective embodiment of its constituent nations. This centrality has been ossified in 'the fundamental principle of the UK constitution' of parliamentary sovereignty (DExEU 2017, 13). This is a principle that has been at the heart of historic constitutional battles between Parliament, political executives, and the judiciary, and which continues to drive constitutional contestation over the issues of the UK state's relationship with the EU, with its own subnations, with the popular will of its people as articulated through referendums, and with the use of the judiciary's interpretive powers.

Just as the unfettered scope of parliamentary sovereignty has been a continuing feature of official discourse, so too have the practical constraints on that convention been routinely revealed in the practice of UK governance. These constraints were apparent in the decision of February 2017 to trigger Article 50 of the Treaty on the European Union and so serve notice of the UK's intention to withdraw from the EU. For all that the principle of the legal supremacy of Parliament was reasserted by the Supreme Court in 2017, in its majority judgment that an Act of Parliament was required to authorize ministers to trigger Article 50, the practical supremacy of the government (exercised through its control of conjoined party and executive hierarchies in Westminster) was evident throughout the passage of the Brexit legislation. In practice, therefore, the theoretical sovereignty of Parliament rapidly transmogrifies into the daily routines of what Griffith (1982, 14) revealingly called 'executive sovereignty'. Indeed, Dicey, the nineteenth-century academic jurist widely credited with popularizing the notion of parliamentary sovereignty, was well aware that, even by the beginning of the twentieth century, the 'power of passing any bill whatever' had passed to the 'House of Commons, or, in plain language, *to the majority thereof*' (Dicey [1915] 1982, xli; emphasis added). In which case, he maintained that parliamentary government in the UK 'means a very vicious form of government by party' ([1894] cited in Cosgrove 1980, 107).

In the twenty-first century, the prescriptions of a legislature-centred mode of decision-making intrinsic in the notion of parliamentary sovereignty continue to be used by governments to justify the practices of executive-centred decision-making. In looking to the past, this incongruity has been one of the fundamental 'predictabilities' of parliamentary politics. In looking to the future, the predictabilities of the past help us to formulate 'predictable unknowns'. Hence, predictably, governments will continue to legitimize their actions through specific claims to parliamentary authorization and consent, and through general claims to permissive consent stemming from electoral processes and mandates. The 'unknowns' arise, however, in the short term, at least after June 2017, from the uncertain durability of a minority government (dependent on a confidence and supply agreement with a small party) and the extent to which adversarial and partisan norms in the Commons are permeated, in the absence of clear electoral mandates, by more consensual and more porous policy accommodations in the face of domestic (UK) political fluidity and external (EU) negotiating rigidity.

In the longer term, 'unknowns' may be more predictable and arise from:

- the potential restitution of executive ascendency—asserted by a dominant governing party or parties in Parliament (memorably termed 'elective dictatorship' by Lord Hailsham (1978))—and the extent to which such a return to 'normality' would undermine the very legitimation rooted in the historic principles of consequential parliamentary authorization and consent;
- the sustaining of parliamentary opposition to such ascendency in an era of party reconstitution (with multiparty and intra-party dimensions);
- the degree of erosion to the unifying ideology of Westminster sovereignty powered by nationalist aspirations of substate parliaments and governments and their responses to Brexit;
- the challenges posed by the amplification of populist claims of 'popular sovereignty';
- the advancement of 'non-electoral' representative claims; and
- the expansion of 'democratic innovations' beyond Parliament driven by ideas of direct, unmediated democratic participation and sustained by exponential technological development.

While we make no pretence of knowing the future, we are convinced, along with all the authors of the chapters in this book, that an understanding of Parliament—of its functions, roles, puzzles, and limitations—is vital to the vibrancy of democracy in the UK. *Exploring*

Parliament has provided a guide through what, for many readers, has been unfamiliar political terrain. Future exploration, to return to the words attributed to Einstein, will prospect the unknown; but, with an understanding of Parliament's past and present, this should be an exploration of 'the somewhat predictable unknown'. We wish you an enlightened journey into the parliamentary future.

References

APOSTOLOVA, V., AUDICKAS, L., BAKER, C., BATE, A., CRACKNELL, R., DEMPSEY, N., McINNES, R., RUTHERFORD, T., and UBEROI, E. (2017) *General Election 2017: Results and Analysis*, House of Commons Library Briefing Paper Number CBP 7979, 11 July. Online at: http://researchbriefings.files.parliament.uk/documents/CBP-7979/CBP-7979.pdf [accessed 25 June 2017].

CONSTITUTION COMMITTEE (2017) *The Great Repeal Bill and Delegated Powers: Ninth Report of Session 2016–17*, London: The Stationery Office, HL Paper 123. Online at: https://www.publications.parliament.uk/pa/ld201617/ldselect/ldconst/123/123.pdf [accessed 27 June 2017].

COPELAND, G. W. and PATTERSON, S. C. (1994) 'Changing an Institutionalized System' in G. W. Copeland and S. C. Patterson (eds.), *Parliaments in the Modern World: Changing Institutions*, Ann Arbor: Michigan University Press, pp. 151–160.

COSGROVE, R. A. (1980) *The Rule of Law: Albert Venn Dicey, Victorian Jurist*, Houndmills: Macmillan.

DExEU (Department for Exiting the European Union) (2017) *The United Kingdom's Exit from and New Partnership with the European Union*, London: Stationery Office, Cm 941. Online at: https://www.gov.uk/government/uploads/system/uploads/attachment_data/file/589191/The_United_Kingdoms_exit_from_and_partnership_with_the_EU_Web.pdf [accessed 27 June 2017].

DICEY, A. V. ([1915] 1982) *An Introduction to the Law of the Constitution*, 8th edition, Indianapolis: Liberty Fund.

DIGITAL DEMOCRACY COMMISSION (2015) *Open Up! Report of the Speaker's Commission on Digital Democracy*, London: House of Commons. Online at: http://www.digitaldemocracy.parliament.uk/documents/Open-Up-Digital-Democracy-Report.pdf [accessed 27 June 2017].

EVANS, E. (2016) 'Diversity Matters: Intersectionality and Women's Representation in the USA and UK', *Parliamentary Affairs*, Vol. 69 (3), pp. 569–85.

FLINDERS, M. (2002) 'Shifting the Balance? Parliament, the Executive and the British Constitution', *Political Studies*, Vol. 50 (1), pp. 23–42.

GOVER, D. and KENNY, M. (2017) 'The Government's "English Votes for English Laws" Review: An Assessment', *Constitution Unit Blog*, 5 April. Online at: https://constitution-unit.com/2017/04/05/the-governments-english-votes-for-english-laws-review-an-assessment/ [accessed 25 June 2017].

GRIFFITH, J. A. G. (1982) 'The Constitution and the Commons' in *Parliament and the Executive*, London: Royal Institute of Public Administration.

HAILSHAM, LORD (1978) *The Dilemma of Democracy*, Glasgow: Collins.

HOUSE OF COMMONS SERVICE (2015) *Corporate Business Plan 2015/16 to 2017/18*, London: House of Commons. Online at: https://www.parliament.uk/documents/commons-commission/Commons-Management-Board/CBP-2015-16-2017-18.pdf [accessed 27 June 2017].

IPSOS MORI (2017) *MPs—Winter Survey 2016*. Online at: http://www.qmul.ac.uk/media/downloads/hss/191811.pdf [accessed 22 August 2017].

JUDGE, D. (1993) *The Parliamentary State*, London: Sage.

JUDGE, D. (2014) *Democratic Incongruities: Representative Democracy in Britain*, Houndmills: Palgrave Macmillan.

KELSO, A. (2009) *Parliamentary Reform at Westminster*, Manchester: Manchester University Press.

LESTON-BANDEIRA, C. (2017) 'An Evaluation of the e-Petitions System—report for the Petitions Committee', July 2017, unpublished.

LESTON-BANDEIRA, C. and THOMPSON, L. (2017) 'Integrating the View of the Public into the Formal Legislative Process: Public Reading Stage in the UK House of Commons', *Journal of Legislative Studies*, Vol. 23 (4), pp. 508–528.

LIAISON COMMITTEE (2015) *Legacy Report: First Report of Session 2014–15*, London: The Stationery Office, HC 954. Online at: https://publications.parliament.uk/pa/cm201415/cmselect/cmliaisn/954/954.pdf [accessed 24 August 2017].

LOEWENBERG, G. (2011) *On Legislatures: The Puzzle of Representation*, Boulder, CO: Paradigm.

MANSBRIDGE, J. (1999) 'Should Blacks Represent Blacks and Women Represent Women? A Contingent "Yes"', *Journal of Politics*, Vol. 61 (3), pp. 628–57.

MEZEY, M. (1979) *Comparative Legislatures*, Durham, NC: Duke University Press.

RUSSELL, M. and COWLEY, P. (2016) 'The Policy Power of the Westminster Parliament: The "Parliamentary State" and the Empirical Evidence', *Governance*, Vol. 29 (1), pp. 121–37.

RUSSELL, M. and GOVER, D. (2017) *Legislation at Westminster: Parliamentary Actors and Influence in the Making of British Law*, Oxford: Oxford University Press.

SEVERS, E., CELIS, K., and ERZEEL, S. (2016) 'Power, Privilege and Disadvantage: Intersectionality theory and political representation', *Politics*, Vol. 36 (4), pp. 346–54.

THOMPSON, L. (2015) *Making British Law*, Houndmills: Palgrave Macmillan.

WOMEN AND EQUALITIES COMMITTEE (2017) *Women in the House of Commons after the 2020 Election: Fifth Report of Session 2016–17*, London: The Stationery Office, HC 630. Online at: https://www.publications.parliament.uk/pa/cm201617/cmselect/cmwomeq/630/630.pdf [accessed 27 June 2017].

Glossary of Parliamentary Terms

Note: This glossary was put together using the definitions included in the book's chapters and the online Glossary of the UK Parliament (http://www.parliament.uk/site-information/glossary/).

ACT OF PARLIAMENT Legislation passed by both Houses of Parliament and given royal assent by the monarch; in simple terms it refers to our laws. Also referred to as 'primary legislation' or 'statute'.

ADJOURNMENT DEBATE The half-hour debate held in the Commons Chamber at the end of each parliamentary day.

ALL-PARTY PARLIAMENTARY GROUPS (APPGs) Cross-party and non-partisan groups of MPs and peers who seek to further the interests of a particular policy concern, country, or region.

AMENDMENT A proposed addition, removal, or change to a motion or to the wording of a clause or schedule in a bill.

APPOINTMENTS COMMISSION An independent seven-member public body which vets the appointment of life peers from political parties and recommends individual nominations for non-party political life peerages.

BACKBENCH BUSINESS COMMITTEE A committee of MPs responsible for selecting topics for debate in the House of Commons which are put forward by backbench MPs. These debates are often very topical and highly important.

BACKBENCH BUSINESS COMMITTEE DEBATE A debate requested by one or more backbench MPs and scheduled by the Backbench Business Committee. It can take place in the Commons Chamber or in Westminster Hall.

BACKBENCHERS MPs or peers who are not members of the government and who do not have frontbench roles in opposition parties. Backbench MPs sit behind the front benches on either side of the Commons Chamber.

BAR (OF THE HOUSE) The point beyond which guests and visitors are not allowed when the House of Commons is sitting. This takes the form of a (retractable) bar and a white line in the carpet across the entrance to the House of Commons Chamber and a railing in the House of Lords Chamber.

BICAMERAL Refers to both Houses of Parliament: the House of Commons (lower chamber) and the House of Lords (upper chamber).

BILL A proposal for primary legislation which will be scrutinized by Parliament. If the bill is approved by both Houses and receives royal assent from the monarch it becomes law and is then known as an Act.

BLACK ROD The official responsible for order and security in the House of Lords.

BUSINESS Refers to what is in the parliamentary schedule (e.g. 'the day's business'). In the Commons such business may take place in the Chamber, in Westminster Hall, or in the committee rooms.

CARRY-OVER A procedure which allows a bill to move from one parliamentary session to the next if its scrutiny has not been completed. This procedure prevents a bill from failing if it has not been approved by Parliament at the end of a session.

CASEWORK Matters (mainly personal, local, or individualized) raised with MPs by their constituents.

CHIEF WHIP Responsible for managing the whips in each parliamentary group; has overall responsibility for whip matters.

CLAUSE A subsection of a bill. Clauses are debated at committee and report stage in each House, and can be amended or removed.

CLERK OF THE PARLIAMENTS The most senior official in the House of Lords.

CLERK OF THE HOUSE The most senior official in the House of Commons.

CLOSURE MOTION In the Commons, a motion made without notice during a debate, which, if accepted and passed with over 100 MPs voting in favour, leads to the end of the debate and a vote on the matter being discussed.

COMMAND PAPER Government documents, such as White Papers, which are presented to Parliament.

COMMITEE OF SELECTION A Commons committee, usually comprised of whips, which is responsible for nominating MPs for general committees and select committees. The Lords have an equivalent committee.

COMMITTEE ON STANDARDS AND PRIVILEGES A Commons select committee which oversaw the work of the Parliamentary Commissioner for Standards. It dealt with complaints regarding the Code of Conduct for Members and MPs' standards and matters of privilege. In 2013 the Committee was split into a Committee on Standards and a separate Committee of Privileges.

COMMITTEE STAGE The first point at which a bill can be amended. A bill is considered on a 'line-by-line' basis on the Floor of either House or in a committee room. Amendments may add, remove, or amend words, sentences, clauses of, or schedules to the bill.

CONVENTION A way of working which is not written down in formal parliamentary documents.

CRANBORNE MONEY Similar to Short money in the Commons, Cranborne money is assistance given to the two largest opposition parties in the House of Lords, as well as to the Convenor of the cross-bench peers.

CROSS-BENCHERS Peers in the House of Lords who do not sit according to party groups, being therefore independent.

CROSS-PARTY LINES Where MPs from different parties work together rather than operating in the adversarial format which is more typical of the House of Commons chamber.

CROSSING THE FLOOR When an MP or a peer changes his or her parliamentary group (political party).

DELEGATED LEGISLATION See *Secondary legislation*

DEPARTMENTAL QUESTION TIME Time scheduled in the Commons Chamber for MPs to ask questions to ministers responsible for government departments.

DESPATCH BOX One of a pair of wooden boxes located on the government and opposition sides of the Table of the House in the Commons Chamber. Ministers and shadow ministers stand at these boxes to give their speeches, and ask or respond to questions and statements. The Lords have an equivalent pair of boxes.

DEVOLVED POWERS Legislative powers which have been moved from the UK Parliament to the Scottish Parliament, the Welsh Assembly, or the Northern Ireland Assembly, under devolution.

DIVISION A formal vote where numbers are counted. To vote, MPs or peers walk through one of two voting lobbies ('Aye' or 'No' in the Commons, 'Content' or 'Not content' in the Lords). They are counted, and their names are taken, as they walk through.

DRAFT BILL A bill which is published in draft form to allow for pre-legislative scrutiny by Parliament and/or external consultation before it is formally introduced as a legislative proposal.

EDM (EARLY DAY MOTION) A mechanism in the Commons whereby MPs may add their names to a motion in order to show their support for, or draw attention to, an issue or concern.

ERSKINE MAY Guide to parliamentary practice, outlining interpretations of parliamentary rules. Originally written by Thomas Erskine May (1815–86), Clerk of the House of Commons from 1871 to 1886. Widely considered the most authoritative statement of parliamentary practice.

EVEL (ENGLISH VOTES FOR ENGLISH LAWS) A procedure introduced in the Commons in 2015 for any government bill (or part of a bill) which affects England, or England and Wales, only, to ensure that it has the consent of MPs from constituencies in England (or England and Wales).

EXPLANATORY MEMORANDUM A government document sent to Parliament explaining aspects of secondary legislation. In the EU context, it sets out the government's position in relation to a specific EU legislative proposal, outlining its main financial, legal, and policy implications.

FATAL AMENDMENT In the Lords, an amendment to a motion to approve secondary legislation that, if passed, means that the legislation cannot enter into law.

FILIBUSTER Techniques used to 'talk out' a motion or bill—e.g. long speeches, making excessive points of order—until the time allocated for debate runs out.

FIRST READING The first introduction of a bill to the House of Commons or House of Lords. The long and short title of the bill are read and a date is given for the second reading debate.

FLOOR OF THE HOUSE The House of Commons Chamber.

FRONTBENCHERS Government ministers, and opposition spokespersons from the largest opposition parties, in the Commons and Lords. They sit on the front benches nearest the Table on either side of the Chamber.

GOVERNMENT BUSINESS Legislation, debates, or statements initiated by the government. This accounts for the majority of the work of both Chambers.

GRAND COMMITTEES Large debating forums of MPs or peers. In the Commons they are generally composed of MPs related to a specific nation or region of the UK to discuss and debate matters. Under the EVEL procedures, MPs from constituencies in England or England and Wales form a Legislative Grand Committee to give their consent to specific legislative proposals. In the Lords this term is used to describe the committee stage of a bill taken away from the Chamber itself, which all peers may attend.

GREEN PAPER Government consultation paper on a draft policy where it wishes to legislate or develop policy.

HAND-OUT BILL A bill drafted by the government and given to a backbench MP to introduce as a private members' bill. Hand-out bills are usually supported by the government, which means that they have a higher chance of becoming law.

HANSARD The Official Report: the official record of debates in each House.

HOUSE OF COMMONS COMMISSION The statutory body responsible for overseeing the administration of the House of Commons.

HYBRID BILL A government bill which affects the general public but which may also have a significant impact for specific individuals or groups. Examples include the Channel Tunnel Rail Link Bill (1994), the Crossrail Bill (2005), and the High Speed Rail (London–West Midlands) Bill (2013–14). The procedure for considering these bills is complex, as individuals and companies specifically affected are able to submit petitions which are considered by committees in either House. Passing a hybrid bill is typically a much longer process than passing a public bill.

INDEPENDENT PARLIAMENTARY STANDARDS AUTHORITY (IPSA) An independent body which determines MPs' pay and pension arrangements and regulates MPs' allowances.

JOURNAL OFFICE The office responsible for the House of Commons Journal, the formal record of proceedings in the House, and for advice on Commons procedure and privilege. The House of Lords has an equivalent office.

KNIVES In committee and report stages in the Commons, deadlines by which the scrutiny of certain parts of a bill must be completed. When 'the knife falls' (i.e. when the deadline is reached), scrutiny must move on to the next part of the bill.

LEADER OF THE HOUSE OF COMMONS A government minister with responsibility for organizing the government's business. The Commons and the Lords each have their own Leader.

LEGISLATIVE PROGRAMME The bills which the government wishes to introduce (and pass) in a given parliamentary session. Most of these will be listed in the Queen's Speech at the start of the session.

LIAISON COMMITTEE (COMMONS) A large committee comprised of the chair of every select committee. It has a number of roles relating to select committee work, but is perhaps most well known for its regular questioning of the prime minister.

LIAISON COMMITTEE (LORDS) A committee comprising the leaders of the main parliamentary groups, the Convenor of the cross-bench peers, the Senior Deputy Speaker, and a number of backbenchers. It also acts as the Committee of Selection, determining proposals for select committee membership. Responsible for reviewing all committee activity in the Lords and considering proposals from peers for new committee inquiries. It approves any new Lords committees and facilitates coordination with the Commons.

LIFE PEERS Members of the House of Lords appointed by the monarch following nomination by a political party or by the House of Lords Appointments Commission. A life peer's title is not hereditary.

LINE-BY-LINE SCRUTINY Where MPs or peers go through a bill in great detail, with

the ability to discuss any line or clause of the bill.

LOBBY BRIEFINGS Briefings from 10 Downing Street press officials to journalists accredited to work in, and report from, the Parliamentary Estate. Includes a mixture of non-attributable briefings and on the record quotes from the prime minister's official spokesman.

LOBBY Journalists accredited to work on the Parliamentary Estate.

LOBBYISTS Individuals and/or organizations working outside Parliament who seek to influence MPs and peers.

LORD SPEAKER Oversees proceedings in the House of Lords Chamber and, as Chair of the House of Lords Commission, has responsibility for the administration of the Lords.

LORDS REPORT See *Report stage*

MACE Symbolizes the authority of the monarch and is placed in the Commons and Lords Chambers whenever they meet.

MARSHALLED LIST OF AMENDMENTS Lists of amendments which are published before a bill's committee or report stages. The amendments are arranged in the order in which they will be considered.

MINISTERIAL CODE A document approved by the prime minister, setting out the rules which government ministers must adhere to in the course of their ministerial duties.

MINISTERIAL RESPONSIBILITY The responsibility of ministers for the actions of their government department.

MINISTERIAL STATEMENTS Oral or written statements from a government minister to the House of Commons or House of Lords, responding to important events or setting out government policy or actions. MPs are allowed to put questions to the minister following a statement. Oral statements are often used for ministers to deliver urgent information.

MONEY BILL A bill which focuses on changes to taxation or involves public money or loans. If a bill is certified as such by the Speaker of the House of

Commons under the Parliament Act 1911, and has not been passed unamended by the Lords within one month of passing the Commons, it may be become law, regardless of whether the House of Lords has agreed to it.

MOTION A proposal for debate or decision which can be voted on.

MOVING AN AMENDMENT Presenting an amendment formally for consideration. Amendments are usually moved by the MP or peer who authored them.

OFFICIAL OPPOSITION The largest opposition party in the House of Commons.

OPPOSITION DAYS In the Commons, 20 days in each session during which the topic of debate is selected by one of the two largest opposition parties; smaller opposition parties can only get these through negotiation with the government or with larger parties.

OPPOSITION DEBATE Debates on issues which have been chosen by the opposition parties on one of the 20 opposition days allotted in each parliamentary session.

ORAL EVIDENCE When key stakeholders and interested parties (e.g. government ministers, civil servants, businesses, charities, academics) are invited before a committee of MPs to answer questions on a specific issue, or on a proposed bill.

ORDER PAPER A document published every day the Commons is sitting, setting out the business for the day. This will include a list of questions and legislative stages, and motions for debate and approval before the House. The House of Lords also uses an Order Paper.

(A) PARLIAMENT The period of time between one general election and the next (usually five years).

PARLIAMENT ACT The Acts passed regarding the legislative powers of the House of Lords in 1911 and 1949. Mostly used to discuss changes in the power of the Lords and Commons. The 1911 Act replaced the Lords' power to reject a bill with the power to delay a bill for up to two years. The 1949 Act reduced this delaying power to one year before a bill can be reintroduced and passed by the Commons. This Act also changed the rules on Money Bills so that they would become law no later than one month after leaving the Commons.

PARLIAMENTARY COMMISSIONER FOR STANDARDS The person responsible for regulating the conduct of MPs.

PARLIAMENTARY COUNSEL A group of experienced legislative drafters who are familiar with the technical and legal wording of legislation and who draft bills for ministers.

PARLIAMENTARY ESTATE The group of buildings which houses MPs, peers, and parliamentary staff.

PARLIAMENTARY GROUP A group of MPs from the same political party.

PARLIAMENTARY PRIVATE SECRETARY (PPS) A backbench MP appointed to assist a government minister in parliamentary duties, and who receives no government salary.

PARLIAMENTARY PRIVILEGE Legal immunity granted to MPs and peers, such as freedom of speech, to enable them to do their jobs.

PEERS Members of the House of Lords.

PETITION A formal request for a specific action or to raise an issue of importance sent by the public to Parliament. It can be sent through MPs in the form of public (paper) petitions, or directly to Parliament through the online e-petitions system. A different type of petition (with its own separate set of procedures) can also be presented by groups or individuals who are affected by a specific private (or hybrid) bill to register their position in relation to the bill (see *private bill* and *hybrid bill*).

PLENARY When business is taken on the Floor of the House of Commons or House of Lords Chamber.

PRE-LEGISLATIVE SCRUTINY Scrutiny of draft bills by committees of either House, or by a joint committee.

PRIMARY LEGISLATION See *Act of Parliament*

PRIME MINISTER'S QUESTIONS (PMQs) A weekly 30-minute session in the House of Commons Chamber where MPs can put questions to the prime minister, typically without notice of the topic.

PRIVATE BILL A bill put forward by those outside Parliament, typically companies or local authorities. These types of bills affect only a specific group of people or a particular area, e.g. Faversham Oyster Fishery Company Act 2017. Procedures for scrutinizing private bills are different from those for public bills. Those affected can present petitions to express their views and request amendment of the bill. These petitions are different from public petitions and are governed by their own set of Standing Orders.

PRIVATE MEMBER Members of either House who are not Ministers of the Crown, and so are not part of the government (no matter which party they belong to). Opposition frontbenchers are considered to be private Members.

PRIVATE MEMBERS' BILL Bills which are introduced not by government ministers, but by individual MPs or peers, usually backbenchers.

PROBING AMENDMENT Amendments to bills put forward by MPs or peers to provoke debate or seek clarification about a proposal. The proposers of these amendments typically do not intend them to be approved; once the required information has been received in debate, they will withdraw them from consideration rather than pressing them to a vote.

PROCEDURE COMMITTEE The Commons committee that considers Commons public business rules and procedures, and makes recommendations for change. A similar committee exists in the Lords.

PROGRAMME MOTION A proposed timetable for the progress of a bill's scrutiny in the Commons Chamber and/or in a public bill committee. The programme motion sets out the date and/or time by which each stage of scrutiny should be completed, or the schedule for scrutiny of certain parts of the bill. The programme motion is typically agreed following the second reading vote on the bill. Programme motions in committee include information on how many sessions and how many oral evidence sessions will be held, as well as the order in which items will be scrutinized and the 'outdate'—the date by which the committee's scrutiny is completed.

PUBLIC AND PRIVATE BILL OFFICES Administer all business relating to legislation and provide advice to MPs and others on public and private legislation. The House of Lords has equivalent offices.

PUBLIC BILL These are general bills which affect the whole population. They comprise the majority of primary legislation considered by Parliament in each session. They can be government bills or private members' bills.

PUBLIC BILL COMMITTEE A group of MPs, typically numbering between 16 and 50, who consider a bill in detail on a 'line-by-line' basis following its second reading in the Commons. Although any MP can table an amendment to the bill, only members of the committee are able to speak in committee or formally move amendments.

QUEEN'S SPEECH A speech read by the monarch to both Houses at the start of each parliamentary session. It is delivered in the House of Lords. It is drafted by the government and outlines bills which the government plans to introduce during the session.

QUESTION TIME See *Departmental Question Time* and *Prime Minister's Questions*

QUORUM The minimum number of MPs or peers needed to participate in a vote in order for the decision to be valid; or the minimum number of members required for a committee to function.

REASONED AMENDMENT An amendment which is moved at the start of a second reading debate on a bill in order to curtail the bill's passage. A reasoned amendment will list a series of reasons why the bill should not proceed.

REASONED OPINION An objection expressed by a national parliament in relation to EU draft legislation that seems to breach the principle of *subsidiarity* (e.g. proposals for which the objectives could be sufficiently achieved by the member states individually).

REPORT STAGE Consideration in the Commons Chamber of amendments made to a bill at committee stage. Debate typically focuses on the most controversial aspects of the bill. Any MP may participate.

RESERVED POWERS Legislative power over issues such as foreign affairs and security, which are expressly held by the UK Parliament and not devolved to other institutions.

SCHEDULE A part of a bill which appears after all of the bill's clauses. Usually contains detailed, technical information about the implementation of the bill. Schedules can be debated and can be amended or removed in either House.

SCRUTINY The detailed examination of government action, policy, proposals, and spending.

SECOND READING A debate on the general principles of a bill in which any MP or peer is eligible to speak. No amendments can be made at this stage. There is a vote at the end of the debate on whether the bill should receive a second reading. If agreed, the bill moves to committee stage.

SECONDARY LEGISLATION Legislation made by ministers which makes very specific or detailed changes to the law in line with powers set out in an existing Act of Parliament. It may also be referred to as *delegated legislation*. Most secondary legislation takes the form of individual statutory instruments.

SELECT COMMITTEES Groups of MPs or peers who work on a cross-party basis to provide oversight and scrutiny of government, policies, and public bodies through inquiries. Committees publish reports with recommendations, to which the government must then respond.

SERJEANT-AT-ARMS Responsible for keeping order in the House of Commons and the Commons part of the Parliamentary Estate, at the Speaker's direction. The Serjeant-at-Arms has the ceremonial role of carrying the Mace during the Speaker's Procession at the start of each sitting day.

SESSION Used to describe the parliamentary year. The State Opening of Parliament marks the beginning of a parliamentary session. Most sessions last a calendar year, but some may be longer—e.g. 2010–12. In June 2017 the government announced that it expected the first session of the 2017 Parliament to last until 2019.

SEWEL CONVENTION A convention under which the UK Parliament does not pass legislation on matters which have been devolved to Scotland under the devolution settlement without the consent of the Scottish Parliament, given in a legislative consent motion. Similar conventions exist in respect of the Welsh Assembly and Northern Ireland Assembly.

SHADOW MINISTER A member of the largest opposition party who is designated as the party's official spokesperson on a policy area, and 'shadows' the work of the relevant government minister. The shadow minister will face the government minister across the despatch box at Departmental Question Time and during statements and debates on legislation.

SHORT MONEY Financial assistance allocated to opposition parties on the basis of a formula based on the number of MPs returned and votes received at the last election. The equivalent in the House of Lords is referred to as *Cranborne money*.

SITTING Used to describe a parliamentary day: i.e. the period between prayers at the opening of the sitting and the time when the House adjourns for the day.

SPEAKER An MP who is responsible for chairing debates in the House of Commons and for maintaining order. The Speaker is elected by MPs and is required to be politically impartial once elected. The Speaker makes important decisions about the work of the House, including calling MPs to speak, selecting amendments, and arbitrating disputes between MPs.

STANDING ORDERS Rules, made by either House, which set out the way certain aspects of House procedures operate. They establish procedures for important matters such as the election of the Speaker and Lord Speaker, the operation of programming on bills, and nominations to select committees.

STATE OPENING The beginning of the parliamentary session, which is opened by the monarch. Often referred to as 'the Queen's Speech'.

STATUTE An Act of Parliament.

STATUTE BOOK A term used to describe all of the bills which have successfully passed through Parliament and are currently in force. Once a bill has received royal assent it is considered to be 'on the statute book' until repealed.

STATUTORY INSTRUMENTS See *Secondary legislation*

STATUTORY DUTY A duty placed on organizations, companies, or professions which is set out in an Act of Parliament.

SUBSIDIARITY A principle enshrined in the Treaty on European Union, intended to indicate the respective responsibilities of legislatures at EU, national, and subnational level. Its stated aim is to ensure that decisions are taken as closely to the citizen as possible. Under this principle, EU legislation should only refer to matters that cannot be dealt with at national level. If one or both chambers of a national parliament considers that draft legislation at EU level breaches this principle, they may object to it.

SUNSET CLAUSE A clause in a bill stating that the bill itself will cease to have effect after a certain date. Further legislation, or an express decision by one or both Houses, is usually required to prolong the effect of the legislation.

(TO) TABLE To put forward an amendment, a motion, or a question for consideration.

TABLE (OF THE HOUSE) The table or desk in the House of Commons Chamber between the two front benches and in front of the Speaker's Chair. House of Commons clerks sit here when the House is sitting. There is a similar table in the Lords.

TABLE OFFICE The Commons office in which parliamentary questions, motions for the Order Paper, and EDMs may be tabled.

TEN-MINUTE RULE BILL A form of private members' bill which can be introduced by backbenchers in the House of Commons under the 'ten-minute rule'. An MP is allocated ten minutes to make a speech about a proposed new bill and why it should be introduced. If the bill is introduced and granted a first reading, it is printed and published, but typically has very little chance of becoming law.

THIRD READING A very short stage in the consideration of a bill. This takes place after a bill's report stage and may involve a final speech from the government minister, opposition spokespersons, and other MPs who have been involved in the bill's passage.

TIME LIMITS IN DEBATES Some speeches by backbench MPs in the Commons are governed by time limits, imposed by the Speaker or Deputy Speaker, to allow all MPs who wish to speak to do so. Often an announced time limit will decrease as a debate progresses.

TRILOGUE DISCUSSIONS Informal discussions between the EU Council and the European Parliament, with the support of the European Commission, often to find agreement on draft legislation.

URGENT QUESTIONS Questions for immediate answer by a government minister in the House of Commons. If a request to the Speaker for an urgent question is granted, the relevant minister must come to the Commons to answer it, immediately after Question Time. The equivalent procedure in the Lords is a private notice question.

USUAL CHANNELS Discussions and informal arrangements concerning parliamentary business which take place between party whips, usually behind the scenes.

WESTMINSTER HALL A debating chamber (the Grand Committee Room) just off Westminster Hall in which some Commons business takes place (e.g. debates on e-petitions, backbench debates).

WESTMINSTER HALL DEBATES Debates which are held in the Grand Committee Room, a parallel debating chamber adjacent to Westminster Hall, rather than in the main Commons Chamber. These debates are typically on issues raised by backbenchers, on e-petitions, or on select committee reports.

WHIPS MPs or peers who are responsible for managing the Members of their party and, in particular, for ensuring that party Members vote in line with their party's policy. They are also responsible for organizing much of the business of Parliament (e.g. appointments to public bill committees) and will often do this through informal conversations with whips in other parties—'the *usual channels*'. Each party has a chief whip and several other whips.

WHITEHALL A collective term referring to civil servants who support the work of government departments. Many of these departments line Whitehall, the road between Trafalgar Square and Parliament Square.

WHITE PAPER A published government proposal for future legislation.

WITHDRAWING AN AMENDMENT To remove an amendment from further consideration, usually following a reply from a government minister.

WRITTEN EVIDENCE Evidence from MPs, peers, outside experts, organizations, and the general public, which is submitted in written form to a select committee or a bill committee.

Index